PLAYS BY RENAISSANCE AND RESTORATION DRAMATISTS
General Editor: Graham Storey

MARSTON

VOLUMES IN THIS SERIES

PUBLISHED

The plays of Cyril Tourneur, edited by George Parfitt: *The Revenger's Tragedy*; *The Atheist's Tragedy*

The selected plays of Philip Massinger, edited by Colin Gibson: *The Duke of Milan*; *The Roman Actor*; *A New Way to Pay Old Debts*; *The City Madam*

The selected plays of Thomas Middleton, edited by David L. Frost: *A Mad World, My Masters*; *A Chaste Maid in Cheapside*; *Women Beware Women*; *The Changeling* (with William Rowley)

The plays of William Wycherley, edited by Peter Holland: *Love in a Wood*; *The Gentleman Dancing Master*; *The Country Wife*; *The Plain Dealer*

The comedies of William Congreve, edited by Anthony Henderson: *The Old Batchelour*; *The Double-Dealer*; *Love for Love*; *The Way of the World*

The plays of Sir George Etherege edited by Michael Cordner: *The Comical Revenge*; or *Love in a Tub*; *She Would If She Could*; *The Man of Mode*; or *Sir Fopling Flutter*

The selected plays of John Webster, edited by Jonathan Dollimore and Alan Sinfield: *The White Devil*; *The Devil's Law Case*; *The Duchess of Malfi*

The selected plays of John Ford, edited by Colin Gibson: *'Tis Pity She's a Whore*; *The Broken Heart*; *Perkin Warbeck*

FORTHCOMING

The selected plays of Ben Jonson, edited by Johanna Procter: *Sejanus*; *Epicoene*, or *The Silent Woman*; *Volpone*

The selected plays of Ben Jonson, edited by Martin Butler: *The Alchemist*; *Bartholomew Fair*; *The New Inn*; *A Tale of a Tub*

THE SELECTED PLAYS OF

JOHN MARSTON

Antonio and Mellida

Antonio's Revenge

The Malcontent

The Dutch Courtesan

Sophonisba

EDITED BY

MACDONALD P. JACKSON

Associate Professor of English,
University of Auckland, New Zealand

AND

MICHAEL NEILL

Associate Professor of English,
University of Auckland, New Zealand

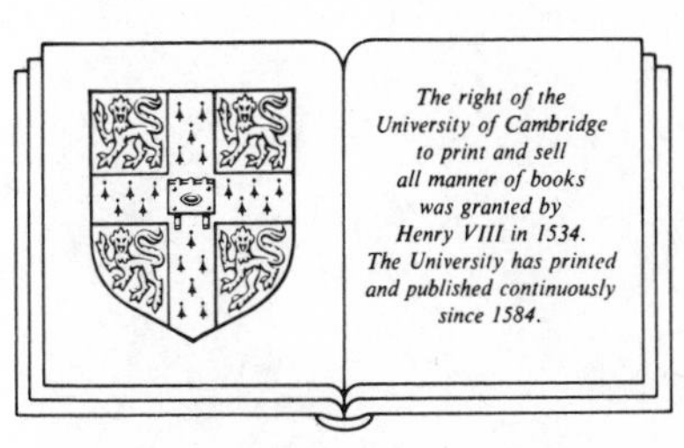

CAMBRIDGE UNIVERSITY PRESS

CAMBRIDGE
LONDON NEW YORK NEW ROCHELLE
MELBOURNE SYDNEY

Published by the Press Syndicate of the University of Cambridge
The Pitt Building, Trumpington Street, Cambridge CB2 1RP
32 East 57th Street, New York, NY 10022, USA
10 Stamford Road, Oakleigh, Melbourne 3166, Australia

First published 1986

Printed in Great Britain at
the University Press, Cambridge

British Library cataloguing in publication data

Marston, John
The selected plays of John Marston. – (Plays by
Renaissance and Restoration dramatists)
I. Title II. Jackson, MacDonald P. III. Neill,
Michael IV. Series
822′.3 PR2691.5

Library of Congress cataloguing in publication data

Marston, John, 1575?–1634.
The selected plays of John Marston.
(Plays by Renaissance and Restoration dramatists)
Bibliography: p.
Contents: Introduction – Antonio and Mellida –
Antonio's revenge – The malcontent – [etc.]
I. Jackson, MacDonald Pairman. II. Neill,
Michael. III. Title. IV. Series.
PR2692.J33 1986 822′.3 85–18966

ISBN 0 521 21746 6 hard covers
ISBN 0 521 29247 6 paperback

PREFACE TO THE SERIES

This series provides the best plays (in some cases, the complete plays) of the major English Renaissance and Restoration dramatists, in fully-annotated, modern-spelling texts, soundly edited by scholars in the field.

The introductory matter in each volume is factual and historical rather than critical: it includes, where appropriate, a brief biography of the playwright, a list of his works with dates of plays' first performances, the reasons for the volume editor's choice of plays, a short critical biography and a note on the texts used. An introductory note to each play then gives the source material, a short stage-history, and details of the individual editions of that play. Facsimiles of the original or early title-pages are given.

Annotation is of three types. Short notes at the foot of the page are designed to gloss the text or enlarge on its literary, historical or social allusions. At the end of the volume, in two separate appendices, editors have added more substantial explanatory notes and have commented on textual variants.

The volumes are intended for anyone interested in English drama in two of its richest periods, but they will prove especially useful to students at all levels who want to enjoy and explore the best work of these dramatists.

Graham Storey

CONTENTS

INTRODUCTION

Life and works

John Marston was born in 1576 and baptised in the parish church of Wardington, Oxfordshire, on 7 October. His father, after whom he was christened, came from a family of Shropshire gentry but was settled in Oxfordshire. In addition to substantial landholdings in that county, the elder Marston had established a prosperous career for himself in the law, practising in both Coventry and London; he was a bencher of the Middle Temple and was elected Reader at that Inn in 1592 – a measure of wealth as well as professional distinction since it involved the incumbent in heavy financial outlays. His wife was Mary Guarsi, daughter of an Italian physician resident in England; and it was no doubt from his mother that the dramatist acquired that fluency in Italian which he could not resist exhibiting in his plays.

At the age of fifteen Marston entered Brasenose College, Oxford, where he was awarded his B.A. two years later on 5 February 1593/4. It was Marston senior's intention that his son should follow him into the law. Marston had already been admitted to membership of his father's Inn, the Middle Temple, in 1592; he was in residence there by 1595, and from 1597 shared his father's chambers in London. He was to remain a member of the Middle Temple (apart from a brief expulsion for failure to pay his fees in 1601) until he left London permanently in 1608/9. Filial piety, however, does not appear to have figured prominently amongst his motives for this attachment: what Marston gained at the Middle Temple was an entrée to the smartest of London literary circles.

Though organised primarily as institutions for legal training, the Inns of Court had in effect become, by the end of the sixteenth century, 'the third university of England' and the preferred finishing school for the sons of the nobility and gentry, many of whom had no intention of pursuing a career in the law. The members of what Jonson called 'the noblest nurseries of humanity and liberty' together made up the largest and most cohesive educated group in London: as a succession of grateful dedications testify, they were an important source of literary patronage; and these 'witty young masters of the Inns of Court' made up (after the court) perhaps the most powerful and certainly the best-informed section of the theatre-going public. The Inns themselves encouraged an interest in drama as an adjunct to the study of rhetoric, while their annual revels made them significant centres of amateur theatrical activity. At the same time, amongst those young gentlemen whose interest in the polite accomplishments of a liberal education was greater than their dedication to the law, there formed lively and influential literary coteries. Caputi and Finkelpearl have traced the outlines of such a group – well-established by the time of Marston's admission – at the Middle Temple in the 1590s; prominent in its distinguished membership was the poet Sir John Davies, and it maintained loose links with the Donne and Jonson circles. Among Marston's younger Middle Temple contemporaries was the dramatist John Ford (admitted 1602), while Francis Beaumont joined the nearby Inner Temple in 1600.

Marston was quickly drawn into this literary world, to the confusion of his father's ambitions, and by 1599 had already achieved a certain notoriety. In that year Marston *père* drew up a will in which he bequeathed 'to my said son John my furniture etc. in my chambers in the Middle Temple, my law books etc. to my said son, whom I hoped would have profited by them in the study of the law, but man proposeth and God disposeth etc.' In an earlier draft he had been even franker about his disappointment, consigning his books to 'him that deserveth them not, that is my wilful disobedient son, who I think will sell them rather than use them, although I took pains and had delight therein; God bless him and give him true knowledge of himself, and to forgo his delight in plays and vain studies and fooleries'. Marston was no doubt wryly recalling such paternal tirades when he had Rodolfo in *What You Will* reflect on the perversity of children:

> the son of a divine
> Seldom proves preacher, or a lawyer's son
> Rarely a pleader, for they strive to run
> A various fortune from their ancestors.
>
> (Wood, II, 242)

Among the 'fooleries' he so despised, the elder Marston would presumably have included his son's first published work *The Metamorphosis of Pygmalion's Image* (1598), an erotic poem in the Ovidian style made fashionable by Marlowe and Shakespeare, to which the young poet attached (with an equally alert eye for the modish) *Certain Satires* in the harsh and obscure Juvenalian manner cultivated by late Elizabethan satirists such as Hall and Guilpin. The enterprise was successful enough to be followed in the same year by a second volume of satire, *The Scourge of Villainy*; and it was controversial enough to necessitate a retraction, in which Marston claimed that *Pygmalion's Image* had been misunderstood by an ignorant public and that it was actually designed as a parody of the lubricious genre to which their concupiscent imaginations had assigned it. Modern critics remain divided on the sincerity of this claim, which raises problems of tone and context very much like those that have perplexed readers of the *Antonio* plays, with their characteristically unstable mixtures of satire, burlesque, melodrama and highly-coloured emotionalism. In any case no apologetics, however sincerely meant, would have been enough to save Marston's writing from the indignation of the authorities; and in 1599 the young poet was one of the principal objects of a ban on satiric writing announced by the Archbishop of Canterbury and the Bishop of London. *Pygmalion's Image* and *The Scourge* were among those works singled out for burning by the public hangman, and Marston's fledgling career as a verse satirist was checked by the command that 'no satires or epigrams be printed hereafter'. However, it is likely that his interests were already shifting towards that more public literary arena where his real fame was to be won.

The 'delight in plays' of which Marston senior complained had probably already borne fruit in *Histriomastix*, an elaborate moral interlude, frequently satirical in tone, which was perhaps written for the Middle Temple's Christmas revels in 1598/9. Although the play was published anonymously there is strong internal evidence to connect it with Marston. While it was once supposed that Marston was revising an old play, recent opinion is divided between those who believe him to be the sole author and those who are persuaded by David Lake's powerful linguistic arguments for its being a collaborative work. Whatever the truth, Marston's dramatic talent seems to have been sufficiently well known by 1599 to find an outlet in the professional theatre; for in September of that year Henslowe paid 'Mr Maxton the new poet' two pounds for some unspecified contributions, and at about the same time Marston began to establish himself as a playwright for one of the newly revived companies of boy actors, the Children of Paul's. For them he wrote a series of plays that revealed a lively and original talent: the broad farce *Jack Drum's Entertainment* (1600), the experimental tragicomedy *Antonio and Mellida* (1599/1600), the revenge tragedy *Antonio's Revenge* (1600/1601), and the comedy *What You Will* (1601). (Some of the suggested dates of composition for these plays, as for those named below, are, of course, approximate or uncertain.) By 1601 Marston's reputation was sufficient to find him a place, with Shakespeare, Jonson and Chapman, in the pages of *Love's Martyr*, as one of 'the best and chiefest of our modern writers'.

The Children of Paul's, like the rival boy company at the Blackfriars to which Marston transferred his talents in the new reign, maintained a protective and comforting fiction of amateur status. Nominally choirboys, rehearsing plays before a casually assembled audience as part of their educational programme, they were in fact organised as fully professional companies. But the supposedly 'private' nature of their performances both helped to defend them from the hostility of the city authorities and supplied an additional, rather flattering inducement to the more exclusive audience which these smaller and more expensive theatres necessarily sought to cultivate. For a rising gentleman-poet like Marston, moreover, such work offered an outlet for theatrical ambition untainted by the vulgar professionalism of the 'public' playhouses on the Bankside or in Shoreditch. But, while preserving his gentleman-amateur status, the work must have been profitable enough once Marston had secured his position by buying a share in the Blackfriars troupe (*c.* 1603/4). He continued in the capacity of shareholder-dramatist for four years, beginning the new relationship with his tragicomic masterpiece *The Malcontent* (1603), followed by his best comedy, *The Dutch Courtesan* (1604/5), a second essay in satiric tragicomedy, *The Fawn* (1605), and his attempt to match Jonson in the elevated genre of 'Roman' tragedy, *Sophonisba* (1606). A third tragedy, *The Insatiate Countess*, seems to have been left unfinished when Marston quitted the stage and to have been completed by William Barkstead, and perhaps Lewis Machin, for production in about 1610.

The open challenge to Ben Jonson issued in the prefatory note to *Sophonisba* marked the final phase of a prolonged and complicated relationship. With the prickly Jonson, as conscious of his professional dignity as Marston of his amateur detachment, any friendship was likely to be turbulent. But the surviving biographical evidence reveals in Marston a temperament almost as combative as Jonson's own. Manningham's anecdote of the poet's brush with a city heiress suggests a young man cultivating the art of insult:

> John Marston, the last Christmas he danced with Alderman More's wife's daughter, a Spaniard born, fell into a strange commendation of her wit and beauty. When he had done, she thought to pay him home, and told him she thought he was a poet. ''Tis true', said he, 'for poets feign and lie, and so did I when I commended your beauty, for you are exceeding foul.'

It is the style of brutal repartee in which his best comic characters excel – of a piece with the hectoring behaviour of the braggart Furor Poeticus, satirised by a university wit in *The Second Part of the Return from Parnassus* (1599–1601), who 'Cuts, thrusts, and foins at whomsoever he meets'. Even more characteristic are his mock dedications, expressing Marston's disdain for the literary public – half-serious anticipations of the angry contempt that consumed Jonson's later years: *Pygmalion's Image* is offered 'To the world's mighty monarch, Good Opinion', *The Scourge of Villainy* 'To his most esteemed and best beloved self', and *Antonio and Mellida* 'To the only rewarder and most just poiser of virtuous merits, the most honourably renowned

Nobody, bounteous Maecenas of Poetry and Lord Protector of oppressed innocence'.

Ironically his first clash with Jonson seems to have been provoked by Marston's attempt to create a flattering portrait of the emergent dramatist in the character of Chrisoganus in *Histriomastix*. Jonson hit out at Marston in *Every Man Out of His Humour* and Marston seems to have responded by caricaturing Jonson as Brabant Senior in *Jack Drum's Entertainment* (where Brabant is wickedly made the victim of a cuckolding which Jonson himself claimed to have achieved) and again as Lampatho Doria in *What You Will*. Jonson retaliated in *Cynthia's Revels* (1600), the play that established his own claim to write for the sophisticated private theatres, and even more effectively through the character of Crispinus in *Poetaster* (1601). How seriously we should take this quarrel remains a matter for debate. If Jonson's boast to Drummond that 'He had many quarrels with Marston, beat him, and took his pistol from him' has any substance in fact, then it must reveal – especially coming from a former bricklayer to a gentleman – an episode of genuine bitterness. But it seems likely that much of their literary sparring was conducted for the amusement of the coterie of wits at Paul's and the Blackfriars, whose sense of belonging to an exclusive in-group it would undoubtedly have flattered; and the fact that Lampatho Doria is at one point dubbed with Marston's own satiric pseudonym, Kinsayder, seems to convert the caricature into a teasing anamorphic double-portrait of the two rivals. Whatever the case, they must have been thoroughly reconciled by 1604/5 when they combined with Chapman to produce the exuberant city comedy, *Eastward Ho*; and in 1605 Jonson's tragedy *Sejanus* appeared in print with commendatory verses by Marston attached to it. The furore provoked by the staging of *Eastward Ho*, however, may have meant the end of their friendship: the play's broad satire of the Scots party at court brought down the king's rage upon the authors; Chapman was imprisoned and Jonson, by his own account, voluntarily joined him; Marston, on the other hand, who is likely enough (on the evidence of his other plays) to have contributed to the anti-Scottish satire, apparently fled London and contrived to avoid arrest until the uproar was over. Jonson is unlikely to have forgiven such a betrayal; and the open contempt for Jonson's pedantic method of composition expressed in the note 'To the Reader' of *Sophonisba* suggests that by 1606 a final breach had occurred.

Marston may have remained tactfully out of sight until the completion of his Roman tragedy; but by July 1606 he was sufficiently restored to official favour to be invited to devise the city pageant to welcome the King of Denmark to London; and in the following year he was commissioned to write the *Ashby Entertainment* for the Dowager Countess of Derby. Then, in 1608, he seems to have been involved in the writing of a Blackfriars play that again satirised the Scottish faction at court and rather too plausibly represented the king himself as a drunken, bad-tempered sot. In March all the theatres in London were closed in reprisal, and in his rage James swore that the children would 'never play more, but should first beg their bread'. Marston was summoned before the Privy Council in June on unspecified charges and sentenced to a brief term of imprisonment.

Whatever its cause, this event apparently turned Marston away from the theatre, for he now sold his share in the Blackfriars to one Robert Keysar for a hundred pounds. But it is more than likely that the dramatist was already looking towards a new career. At some time about 1605 he had married Mary Wilkes, daughter of one of James's favourite chaplains, William Wilkes, with whom the Marston household were to live for eleven years, and whose curate, in his living at Barford, Wiltshire, Marston was to become. In the tragedy, *The Insatiate Countess*, left unfinished at about this time, Guido is made to mock Roberto's retreat to a monastery in terms which seem to anticipate the dramatist's own decision to take orders in 1609:

> This is conversion, is't not? as good as might have been; he turns religious upon his wife's turning courtesan. This is just like some of our gallant prodigals: when they have consumed their patrimonies wrongfully, they turn capuchins for devotion. (Wood, III, 35)

It is possible, of course, that these lines are the work

of Barkstead; but like the later hit put into the mouth of Abigail ('They say [my husband] has compiled an ungodly volume of satires against women, and calls his book *The Snarl*', Wood, III, 46), they have exactly the air of wry self-mockery that characterises those passages with which Marston typically 'signed' his plays. He did in any case enter St Mary's College, Oxford, to study for the priesthood on 24 September 1609 and was ordained priest in the church of Stanton Harcourt, Oxfordshire, two months later. He appears to have acted as curate to his father-in-law until he was preferred to the living of Christchurch, Hampshire, in October 1616. Little else is known of him. In August 1616 he had been the victim of a highway robbery near Knightsbridge at the hands of Sir George Sandys; in 1621 he inherited a Coventry property from his mother; in 1624 his only son died in infancy; in 1631 he resigned his living and returned to London, where in 1633 he intervened to have his name removed from the title-page of William Sheares's collected edition of his plays.

The publication of his works was a measure of Marston's fame, for it implicitly claimed him as the equal of Lyly, Jonson and Shakespeare, the only other dramatists to have been so honoured; but Marston's intervention was a measure of his indifference to what might once have delighted him. When he died in the following year (24 June 1634), to be buried beside his father in the Middle Temple Church, he had cut upon his tomb the enigmatic motto, *Oblivioni Sacrum*. A memorial dedicated to oblivion – it was a paradox that the young Marston, who included in *The Scourge of Villainy* a poem 'To Everlasting Oblivion', would have enjoyed, but one that the older man seems to have meant. The distance he had travelled from his sometime friend and rival, Ben Jonson, that furious custodian of his own immortality, could hardly have been more eloquently displayed.

The text of this edition

The plays have been re-edited from the early Quartos. Details of textual sources are given in the introductions to individual plays. Textual notes at the back of this volume record substantive departures from the dialogue of the foundation text, changes to its assignment of speeches, and a selection of variants from subsequent editions. We have relied on modern editors for information about press-variants among extant copies of a Quarto. Trivial typographical errors, where the right reading is obvious, have been silently corrected. The stage directions derive from the foundation text: additions or alterations are set within square brackets. Slight changes to the position of stage directions have not been noted.

Spelling, punctuation and presentation of the text have been modernised. Modifications of the originals include the regularisation of speech prefixes, the expansion of abbreviations and of the ampersand and tilde, the alteration of faulty or archaic word division (including the introduction or suppression of hyphens), the spelling out of numerals, the reduction of capitals according to present-day practice, the standardisation of act and scene headings and the addition of line-numbering, changes to the style of type (italics, roman, small capitals), and adjustments to the lineation. In modernising the text we have profited from a discussion of the attendant problems by Stanley Wells in *Modernizing Shakespeare's Spelling* (Oxford: Clarendon Press, 1979). Wells's recommendations are mostly in accord with our own instincts: their tendency is towards a more thorough-going modernisation than has been customary in modern-spelling editions. So in the present edition *belkt* appears as *belched*, *cruddles* as *curdles*, *lanthorne* as *lantern, bankrout* as *bankrupt, corse* as *corpse*, *enow* as *enough*, *soddered* as *soldered*, and so on. We have, however, preserved the Quarto forms of certain expletives – *Paugh*, *Fut*, *Phew*, and the like. Syllabic past-participial and preterite endings that occur within verse have been represented by *èd*, non-syllabic endings by *ed* (or occasionally *t*, as in *burnt*). We have respected the elisions and contractions of the Quartos, but standardised their forms (to *thou'rt*, *you're, they're*, for example). The punctuation, though modern and our own, takes account of the pointing of the Quartos (which is sometimes rather subtle, sometimes silly) and the practices of other editors. Marston's is a highly original dramatic language, incorporating the ellipses, interruptions, sidetrackings, stutterings and syntactical ambiguities of real speech. Dashes may serve to indicate the hiatuses or the shifts of address, which are erratically and variously marked in the Quartos, but most features of Marston's style seem best served by a full range of conventional stops, with commas predominant, and slightly fewer colons, semi-colons and exclamation marks than editorial tradition has favoured.

Each play of Marston's undoubted sole authorship seems to have been first printed from a manuscript in his own hand. Most of the Quartos have several of the following features: inverted commas marking *sententiae*, marginal directions and annotations, prologue, dedication, epilogue, and list of dramatis personae in which names are linked by braces, a classical tag as epigraph, speech prefixes punctuated with colons, act divisions, and elaborate stage directions with some use of Latin; and certain unusual spellings recur from play to play. Common defects in the Quartos are minor mislineation and the misattribution of speeches.

In 1633 William Sheares published an Octavo collecting the two *Antonio* plays, *Sophonisba, What You Will, The Fawn* and *The Dutch Courtesan*. This publication, which reprinted the Quartos, with some editorial tinkering, was not approved by Marston, and its new readings lack authority, but it has interest as a source of conjectural emendations. In preparing our edition we have collated the 1633 Octavo with the appropriate Quartos, and have consulted also the collections of Bullen and Wood, and the separate editions mentioned in the introductions to individual plays.

A select bibliography

A comprehensive critical bibliography will be found in Terence P. Logan and Denzell S. Smith (eds.), *The New Intellectuals: A Survey and Bibliography of Recent Studies in English Renaissance Drama* (Lincoln, Nebraska, and London: University of Nebraska Press, 1977), pp. 171–247 ('John Marston', compiled by Cecil M. McCulley). R. W. Ingram, *John Marston* (Boston: Twayne, 1978), attaches a select critical bibliography;

and a useful brief account of the main lines of Marston criticism is included in the first chapter of George L. Geckle, *John Marston's Drama: Themes, Images, Sources* (Rutherford, Madison, Teaneck: Fairleigh Dickinson University Press, 1980).

Books

The first book-length account of Marston was Morse S. Allen's rather limited study, *The Satire of John Marston* (Columbus, Ohio: F. J. Heer Printing Co., 1920); A. J. Axelrad's *Un Malcontent Élizabéthain: John Marston* (Paris: Didier,1955) is a much fuller treatment but marred by a psychological bias that tends to see the ruling themes of sex and hypocrisy as expressing the author's neurotic obsessions, through too straightforwardly accepting the malcontents of the plays as Marston's own spokesmen. More important are two monographs which appeared in the 1960s: Anthony Caputi's intelligent and scholarly *John Marston, Satirist* (New York: Cornell University Press, 1961) is perhaps too much of a thesis-work, determined to force all the writing into its chosen neo-Stoic framework; but the balance is redressed by Philip J. Finkelpearl's equally sober, but more flexible examination of Marston's moral and philosophical preoccupations in *John Marston of the Middle Temple* (Cambridge, Mass.: Harvard University Press, 1969). If Finkelpearl is especially valuable for placing the plays in their social and intellectual milieu, two recent books are to be welcomed for their attempt to restore the plays' specifically theatrical dimensions: John Scott Colley's *John Marston's Theatrical Drama* (Salzburg: Universität Salzburg, 1974) follows the now familiar line of stressing the elements of burlesque and self-conscious theatricality in Marston's writing but is weakened by some rather naïve speculation on production possibilities; Michael Scott's *John Marston's Plays: Theme, Structure, and Performance* (London: Macmillan, 1978), although benefiting from a study of stage-history and some first-hand acquaintance with Marston's plays in the theatre, is over-determined to stress Marston's 'modernity', with the promiscuous aid of Stanislavsky, Artaud, Gide, Brecht, Sartre, Peter

Brook, Dudley Moore and John Cleese – it is an approach which leads to the virtual exclusion of *Sophonisba*, often thought to be Marston's finest play. More balanced is R. W. Ingram's engagingly written, if somewhat superficial, introductory study, *John Marston* (Boston: Twayne, 1978); but confidence in Ingram's judicious middle course is shaken by a number of careless inaccuracies. The two most recent books both set out to approach Marston through the well-worn paths of themes and imagery; unfortunately, while each finds much to say about themes, neither really succeeds in substantiating Una Ellis-Fermor's original claims about the dramatic importance of Marston's imagery. Ejner J. Jensen in *John Marston, Dramatist: Themes and Imagery in the Plays* (Salzburg: Universität Salzburg, 1979) repudiates the currently fashionable emphasis on burlesque and parody in favour of laborious exposition of the plays' didactic designs. George L. Geckle's *John Marston's Drama: Themes, Images, Sources* (Rutherford, Madison, Teaneck: Fairleigh Dickinson University Press, 1980), though more scholarly than Jensen's book, is confessedly more fragmentary, being composed of a series of specialised essays on previously unexplored aspects of individual plays; Geckle's readings, uneven in quality, share some of Jensen's remorseless moralising.

Essays and articles
General

The earliest attempt at a general critical account of Marston's achievement is in Lecture III of Hazlitt's *Lectures on the Literature of the Age of Elizabeth* (London: 1820); Hazlitt is responsive to Marston's satiric vigour and sceptical independence of mind; he is also characteristically alert to 'an air of burlesque' in *Antonio and Mellida*. Equally interesting, despite its rhetorical excesses (*Histriomastix* is dismissed from the canon as an 'abortion of letters . . . a very mooncalf begotten by malice upon idiocy'), is Swinburne's essay in *The Age of Shakespeare* (London: Chatto and Windus, 1908). Swinburne is particularly sensitive to Marston's occasional lyric grace and to his talent for comic invention; even his complaints about the dramatist's uneven composition partially anticipate the insights of later critics into the plays' deliberate Mannerist disjunctiveness. T. S. Eliot's 1934 essay on Marston, reprinted in *Selected Essays* (London: Faber, 1941), shows his brand of neo-classicism at its most limiting; he responds with generosity to the 'austere and economical' *Sophonisba* but (while finding things to praise in *The Malcontent*, *The Dutch Courtesan* and *The Fawn*) considers the rest of the work generally 'lifeless' and marred by lapses in taste. In contrast to recent work stressing Marston's intense theatricality, Eliot uncovered a playwright disabled by his instinctive contempt for the coarse medium in which he was compelled to work. Eliot's interest in the plays primarily as expressions of a 'positive, powerful, and unique personality' echoed Theodore Spencer's fascination with Marston's 'apparently repellent' but 'original' personality (*Criterion*, 13 (1933–4), 581–99), and began a psychologising tradition which includes Samuel Schoenbaum's influential 'The precarious balance of John Marston' (*PMLA*, 67 (1952), 1069–78). Even more hostile are the criticisms of T. B. Tomlinson in *A Study of Elizabethan and Jacobean Drama* (Cambridge: Cambridge University Press, 1964) and David Frost in *The School of Shakespeare* (Cambridge: Cambridge University Press, 1968). Both see Marston as a herald of later Jacobean decadence, and for Frost he leads the *totentanz* of Shakespeare's slavish imitators, pandering to 'depraved tastes' with a 'scissors and paste method of composition' enlivened only by occasional revelations of his own ambiguous personality.

Una Ellis-Fermor's *The Jacobean Drama* (London: Methuen, 1936), while sharing Eliot's belief that Marston's 'genius . . . was not primarily dramatic', was nevertheless among the first studies to point up Marston's formal inventiveness and to recognise the 'theatrical brilliance' of those sleights by which he often conceals his dramatic weakness; Ellis-Fermor also makes out an unusually strong case for Marston's qualities as a poet, finding in his linguistic richness the true successor to Marlowe and the early Shakespeare and in his occasional mastery of a 'sweet stillness' of lyric tone the precursor of Ford. The essays of Robert Ornstein in

The Moral Vision of Jacobean Tragedy (Madison and Milwaukee: University of Wisconsin Press, 1965) and Arthur C. Kirsch in *Jacobean Tragic Perspectives* (Charlottesville: University of Virginia Press, 1972) lay a similar stress on Marston's conscious artfulness, though Ornstein finds it tainted by indiscipline and theatrical opportunism.

Some thematic and formal approaches

In addition to Caputi's book, a number of essays have argued the importance of Stoicism in Marston's drama. Michael Higgins discusses 'The conventions of the Stoic hero as handled by Marston' in *MLR*, 39 (1944), 338–46; Paul M. Zall, in 'John Marston, moralist', *ELH*, 20 (1953), 186–93, sees the plays as exploring the tension between Renaissance psychological determinism and the Stoic/Calvinist insistence on the need to extirpate the passions; Geoffrey D. Aggeler's 'Stoicism and revenge in Marston', *ES*, 51 (1970), 507–17, treats *Antonio's Revenge* and *The Malcontent* as Stoic anti-revenge dramas; while Gustav Cross in 'The retrograde genius of John Marston', *Review of English Literature*, 2:4 (1961), 19–27, argues that the Stoic hagiography of *Sophonisba* represents a sudden repudiation of Marston's earlier sceptically disillusioned stance. Roger Stilling's *Love and Death in Renaissance Tragedy* (Baton Rouge: Louisiana State University Press, 1976) and Leonora Leet Brodwin's *Elizabethan Love Tragedy* (London and New York: London and New York University Presses, 1972) have a common interest in Marston's use of the conventions of love tragedy. Of the two, Stilling is the less thesis-bound, but each is as determined as Cross and the Stoic school to insist that 'Marston was first and foremost a moralist.' G. K. Hunter's 'English folly and Italian vice', in John Russell Brown and Bernard Harris (eds.), *Jacobean Theatre*, Stratford-upon-Avon Studies 1 (London: Arnold, 1960), though alert to morality patterns in the plays, explores the intellectual background of Marston's political ideas with a graceful avoidance of didactic strain.

A number of critics have investigated the relation between Marston's plays and his inheritance as a writer of verse satire. These include John Peter in *Complaint and Satire in Early English Literature* (Oxford: O.U.P., 1956) which develops the derogatory opinions of his earlier essay in *Scrutiny*, 17 (1950–1), 132–53, to conclude that 'Marston might have been a much better dramatist had he never heard of satire.' O. J. Campbell, by contrast, in *Comicall Satyre and Shakespeare's Troilus and Cressida* (San Marino, California: Huntington Library, 1938), sees Marston's satiric intentions as constantly deflected or distorted by the inappropriate dramatic genres in which he had to work. Alvin Kernan's *The Cankered Muse* (New Haven: Yale University Press, 1959) offers a more balanced assessment; but the liveliest and most sympathetic account of Marston as a theatre satirist is in R. A. Foakes, *Shakespeare: The Dark Comedies to the Last Plays: From Satire to Celebration* (London: Routledge and Kegan Paul, 1971) – a consolidation of Foakes's earlier criticism, emphasising the playfully self-conscious, parodic aspect of the writing. Marston's development of the Malcontent character as a satiric spokesman has been traced by E. E. Stoll in 'Shakespeare, Marston and the Malcontent type', *MP*, 3 (1906), 281–303, and Bridget Gellert Lyons in *Voices of Melancholy* (London: Routledge and Kegan Paul, 1971).

Finally, there exist a variety of studies which enhance the sense of Marston's plays as pieces for performance. Michael Shapiro's *Children of the Revels* (New York: Columbia University Press, 1977) offers an important reconstruction of the style (or styles) cultivated by the boy players; he argues that Marston's work is best understood in terms of a 'mosaic' technique designed to produce startling juxtapositions of 'natural', 'declamatory' and 'parodic' acting styles. Reavley Gair's *The Children of Paul's: The Story of a Theatre Company, 1553–1608* (Cambridge: Cambridge University Press, 1982) is an essential complement to Shapiro's work; Gair is particularly alert to the spectacular dimension of Marston's writing, and sees the variety of his style as reflecting the attempt to create 'a musical rhetorical score' for his 'chorister–actors'. The use of music in the plays has been examined by Christian Kiefer ('Music and Marston's *The Malcontent*', *SP*, 51 (1954), 163–71) and by David G. O'Neill in a three-part article ('The influence of music in the works of John Marston', *Music and Letters*, 53 (1972), 122–33, 293–308, 400–10); where Kiefer is concerned with actual musical episodes, O'Neill is principally interested in Marston's musical metaphors and his moral and psychological applications of Renaissance musical theory. Dieter Mehl's *The Elizabethan Dumb Show* (London: Methuen, 1965) casts valuable light not only on Marston's formal dumb-shows, but on his expressive use of various forms of pantomime and 'silent action' – an area which is also explored in Brownell Salomon's semiological 'Visual and aural signs in the performed English Renaissance play', *Renaissance Drama*, n.s. 5 (1972), 143–69.

Essays on individual plays

Much of the best writing on Marston is to be found in the introductions to excellent individual editions in the Revels, Regents, New Mermaid and Fountainwell series. Outstanding are G. K. Hunter's editions of the *Antonio* plays for Regents (1965, 1966). Hunter's account of the deliberate discontinuities of Marston's designs, of his 'grotesque conjunction of comic and tragic attitudes', and 'Pirandello-like awareness of the play-world deliberately made unreal', established what has become the predominant modern view of this comical–tragical diptych. Reavley Gair's Revels edition of *Antonio's Revenge* (1978) is a useful supplement to Hunter; its substantial and scholarly introduction is particularly enlightening about the theatre for which the *Antonio* plays were written. Hunter's *The Malcontent* for Revels (1975) is also a distinguished piece of work: the introduction develops Hunter's emphasis on the 'Mannerist' qualities of Marston's writing – his asymmetrical composition, stylistic and psychological disjunctions, his 'restless dissatisfaction with received dramatic forms' and his continuing fascination with the theatrical nature of identity. Hunter shows how the mixed form of *The Malcontent* depends on Renaissance ideas of tragicomedy as combining satiric and pastoral conventions (see also his earlier article 'Italian tragicomedy on the English stage', *Renaissance Drama*, n.s. 6 (1973), 123–48). Bernard Harris, on the other hand, in his New Mermaid introduction (1967) intelligently examines Marston's specific dependence on Guarini's pioneering tragicomedy, *Il Pastor Fido*, as well as his use of classical sources to create a framework of didactic analogy.

The Dutch Courtesan has been edited for Regents by Martin Wine (1965); in contrast to his admirable *Malcontent* in the same series (1965), this edition is rather solemn in its approach to a comedy whose professed aim is 'not to instruct but to delight'; it does, however, usefully analyse Marston's handling of his source-material as a key to the moral attitudes of the play. Peter Davison's Fountainwell text (1968) offers a genuinely critical introduction, responsive to the play's theatrical strengths without glossing over its dramatic weaknesses; Davison sees the whole ethos of the play as shaped by Montaigne's *Essays*. Also deserving of mention is David Blostein's introductory essay for *The Fawn* in the Revels series (1978); it includes an excellent discussion of Marston's plays in their intellectual context which contrives to make the final withdrawal into the church seem a natural conclusion to the dramatist's career.

Few would claim the *Antonio* plays as Marston's best work, but because they show his experimental, disjunctive style at its most extreme they have become a kind of touchstone in the assessment of his *oeuvre*, provoking much of the most thoughtful and imaginative criticism. Earlier critics tended to approach them through the revenge-play tradition; essays in this vein include Ashley H. Thorndike's 'The relations of *Hamlet* to contemporary revenge drama', *PMLA*, 17 (1902), 125–220, Fredson Bowers's section on *Antonio's Revenge* in his *Elizabethan Revenge Tragedy* (Princeton: Princeton University Press, 1940), and J. H. Smith *et al.*, '*Hamlet, Antonio's Revenge* and the *Ur-Hamlet*', *SQ*, 9 (1958), 493–8. More sophisticated recent approaches to revenge convention include J. W. Lever's *The Tragedy of State* (London: Methuen, 1971), which emphasises the political dimensions of *Antonio's Revenge*, and Charles and Elaine Hallet, *The Revenger's Madness: A Study of Revenge Tragedy Motifs* (Lincoln, Nebraska, and London: University of Nebraska Press, 1980). Lever and the Hallets concur in opposing the current vogue for reading the *Antonio* plays in terms of varying degrees of self-conscious parody. The pioneer of this approach was R. A. Foakes in 'John Marston's fantastical plays', *PQ*, 41 (1962), 229–39; Foakes's view of these plays as 'primarily parodistic or grotesque' was qualified by Hunter (who found his view of parody 'intolerably coarse-grained') and variously developed by a succession of critics, including Elaine Berland, 'The function of irony in Marston's *Antonio and Mellida*, *SP*, 66 (1969), 739–55; and Allan Bergson, 'The ironic tragedies of Marston and Chapman', *JEGP*, 69 (1970), 613–30, and 'Dramatic style as parody in Marston's *Antonio and Mellida*', *SEL*, 11 (1971), 307–25. Philip J. Ayres in 'Marston's *Antonio's Revenge*: the morality of the revenging hero', *SEL*, 12 (1972), 359–74, attempts a reconciliation of two main lines of approach, arguing that Marston intended 'a parodistic exposure of the Kydian revenger' while continuing to treat the dilemma of revenge with complete moral seriousness; this line of argument is further developed in '*Antonio's Revenge*: Marston's play on revenge plays', *SEL*, 23 (1983), 277–94, by Barbara J. Baines, who argues that the play is a metadramatic reflection on 'the theatrical merits and the moral limitations of the [revenge tragedy] genre'. But perhaps the finest recent essay is Jonathan Dollimore's urbane and suggestive 'Marston's *Antonio* plays and Shakespeare's *Troilus and Cressida*: the birth of a radical drama', *Essays and Studies* (1980), 48–69 (now chap. 2 of his *Radical Tragedy* (Brighton: Harvester Press, 1984)). Dollimore sees Marston and Shakespeare as working towards a new kind of drama whose disjunctive shape would reflect the condition of a world which no longer seemed answerable to those providential certainties implicit in earlier dramatic forms. Dollimore's essay extends and refines the ironic readings of Marston developed by Foakes and Hunter; but an effective attack on this approach was opened by Richard Levin in '*The New Inn* and the proliferation of good bad drama', *EIC*, 22 (1972), 41–7, and carried on by T. F. Wharton, 'Old Marston or new Marston: the *Antonio* plays', *EIC*, 25 (1975), 357–69; they argue that ironic readings are in principle irrefutable and can be used to explain away the grossest carelessness and incompetence. Foakes's reply to Levin appeared in *EIC*, 22 (1972), 327–9; and Levin returned to the attack in

EIC, 24 (1974), 312–17.

Wharton's critique of Marston actually began with '*The Malcontent* and "dreams, visions, fantasies" ', *EIC*, 24 (1974), 261–74, a lively essay, concentrating on the ambiguous role of Malevole, and the play's consequent moral incoherence, which paradoxically has the effect of making it seem a much more interesting piece than do many of the essays designed to buttress the traditional view of *The Malcontent* as Marston's masterpiece. Among these, D. J. Houser's 'Purging the commonwealth: Marston's disguised dukes and *A Knack to Know a Knave*', *PMLA*, 89 (1974), 993–1006, places it within a highly didactic sub-genre of Disguised Duke tragicomedies; while William W. E. Slights's ' "Elder in a deform'd church": the function of Marston's Malcontent', *SEL*, 13 (1973), 360–73, in seeking to rebut Finkelpearl's view of Malevole as a 'virtuous machiavel', replaces ingenious paradoxicality with ingenuous orthodoxy. Brownell Salomon, 'The theological basis of imagery and structure in *The Malcontent*', *SEL*, 14 (1974), 271–84, seems equally in thrall to Jonson's gibe that Marston's clerical father-in-law might have written his plays, and Marston his father-in-law's sermons. More rewarding though equally solemn is Donald K. Hendrick's attempt to explore the character of Malevole/Altofront through 'The masquing principle in Marston's *Malcontent*', *ELR*, 8 (1978), 24–42. In *Elizabethan Theatre 6* (1978) William Babula examines Marston's unique tragicomic mixture of revenge tragedy and satire in 'The avenger and the satirist: John Marston's Malevole' (pp. 48–58), while R. A. Foakes discounts any attempt to find ethical coherence in *The Malcontent* in favour of celebration of its bizarre 'atmosphere of "tragic slapstick" ' in 'On Marston, *The Malcontent*, and *The Revenger's Tragedy*' (pp. 59–75).

Despite (or perhaps because of) the fact that it is generally recognised as Marston's most entertaining and accessible play, *The Dutch Courtesan* has not been particularly well served by its critics. J. J. O'Connor's thesis in 'The chief source of Marston's *Dutch Courtezan*', *SP*, 64 (1957), 509–15, is that the play replaces an original interest in the ethics of love and friendship by a moralistic preoccupation with sin and redemption; Gustav Cross's 'Marston, Montaigne and morality: *The Dutch Courtezan* reconsidered', *ELH*, 27 (1960), 30–43, by contrast, argues that the play embodies the liberal naturalism of Montaigne; while for Sylvia Feldman in *The Morality Patterned Comedy of the Renaissance* (The Hague: Mouton, 1970) it is little more than an updated Morality drama, illustrating the difference between Love and Lust, with Malheureux cast in the role of mankind. A useful corrective to such didactic simplifications is Harry Keyishian's 'Dekker's *Whore* and Marston's *Courtesan*', *ELN*, 4 (1966–7), 261–6, which advances the idea that Marston's comedy is designed as a deliberate satiric retort to the simple-minded moralisation of Dekker's *1 Honest Whore*. Donna B. Hamilton's 'Language as theme in *The Dutch Courtesan*', *Renaissance Drama*, n.s. 5 (1972), 75–87, interestingly extends Finkelpearl's perceptions about the use of different styles as Jonsonian moral indicators. Finally, two books place *The Dutch Courtesan* in the tradition of City Comedy: Brian Gibbons's *Jacobean City Comedy* (London: Hart-Davis, 1968) – which also comments on *Antonio and Mellida, The Malcontent* and *The Fawn* – perceptively analyses the play as exposing a city world where 'prostitution [is] a model for all forms of . . . enterprise'; Alexander Leggatt's *Citizen Comedy in the Age of Shakespeare* (Toronto: University of Toronto Press, 1973) sees it as a work of complicated irony anatomising the contradictions (endemic to the citizen comedy convention) between jocular presentation of sexuality and sermonising commentary upon it.

Of all Marston's major plays, *Sophonisba*, despite the esteem in which it was held by Swinburne and Eliot, has received least attention. By far the best discussion is Peter Ure's '*Sophonisba*: a reconsideration' in his *Elizabethan and Jacobean Drama* (Liverpool: Liverpool University Press, 1974); Ure's careful consideration of the sources precedes an analysis which stresses the play's conscious classicism, its historically-minded attempt to evoke a 'Roman' world, and the 'solemn and marmoreal splendours' that link it to Ford's 'classical' tragedy, *The Broken Heart*; Ure discovers in *Sophonisba* a genuinely 'tragic rationale' and a resolution of the moral inconsistency and morbidity which he sees as marring the earlier plays. A much less flattering account of Marston's classicism is given in C. O. Macdonald's *The Rhetoric of Tragedy* (Amherst: University of Massachusetts Press, 1966); while William Kemp's edition of the play (New York and London: Garland Publishing, 1979) contains a brief critical introduction, emphasising its modification of Marston's earlier attitudes to Stoicism, and the symmetry and balance of its 'pseudo-classical' design. Finally, Eldred Jones's lacklustre *Othello's Countrymen* (London: Oxford University Press, 1965) considers the play in the light of Elizabethan attitudes towards Africans, concentrating particularly on the type-figures of Vangue and Zanthia.

Editions

J. O. Halliwell's three-volume *The Works of John Marston* (London: J. R. Smith, 1856) was little more than a lightly corrected reprint of Sheares's Octavo. It was soon superseded by A. H. Bullen's *The Works of John Marston* (London: J. C. Nimmo, 1887), three volumes in modernised spelling. Bullen demonstrates his shrewd literary intelligence and wide reading in the Elizabethan–Jacobean period, but he handles the text with a nineteenth-century insouciance over those questions of authority and relationship which occupy twentieth-century editors; his textual and interpretative notes are sporadic. H. Harvey Wood's *The Plays of John Marston* (Edinburgh: Oliver and Boyd, 1934–9), also in three volumes, has an unsystematic collation of variants, some helpful explanatory notes, and several good editorial conjectures, which Wood is too timid about introducing into his old-spelling text; the whole edition is marred by Wood's naïvety as bibliographer and textual critic; Greg pronounced it 'a slovenly piece of work'. Reference to Wood's volumes is hampered by their lack of line-numbers. There is a full and meticulous edition of *The Poems of John Marston* (Liverpool: Liverpool University Press, 1961) by Arnold Davenport. Among single-play editions that we do not mention elsewhere in this volume, the most important are Gerald A. Smith's *The Fawn* in the Regents series (1965), and those of the collaborate *Eastward Ho* by

C. G. Petter (New Mermaid, 1973) and R. W. Van Fossen (Revels, 1979). The best attempt to determine the authorial shares in this latter play is by David J. Lake, '*Eastward Ho*: linguistic evidence for authorship', *Notes and Queries*, 226 (1981), 158–66; the same issue of *Notes and Queries* contains Lake's valuable articles on the authorship of *Histriomastix* (148–52), the additions to *The Malcontent* (153–8), and *The Insatiate Countess* (166–70). *The Malcontent* and *The Dutch Courtesan* have each appeared in several anthologies.

References and abbreviations

A, B, C	successive Quartos of *The Malcontent* (1604)
Abbott	E. A. Abbott, *A Shakespearian Grammar*, 3rd edn, London: Macmillan, 1883
AM	*Antonio and Mellida*
AR	*Antonio's Revenge*
Beaumont and Fletcher	Francis Beaumont and John Fletcher, *The Works*, ed. A. Glover and A. R. Waller, 10 vols., Cambridge: Cambridge University Press, 1905–12
Brereton	J. Le Gay Brereton, *Elizabethan Drama: Notes and Studies*, Sydney: W. Brooks, 1909
Brooke	*English Drama, 1580–1642*, ed. C. F. T. Brook and N. B. Paradise, Boston: D. C. Heath, 1933
Bullen	*The Works of John Marston*, ed. A. H. Bullen, 3 vols., London: J. C. Nimmo, 1887
(c)	corrected; of a press-variant reading
Caputi	A. Caputi, *John Marston, Satirist*, New York: Cornell University Press, 1961
Colley	J. S. Colley, *John Marston's Theatrical Drama*, Salzburg: Universität Salzburg, 1974
Collier	J. P. Collier, additional notes and corrections to 1825 edn of Dodsley's *Old Plays*
conj.	conjectured by

Crawford	Charles Crawford, *Collectanea: Second Series*, Stratford-upon-Avon: Shakespeare Head Press, 1907
Cunliffe	J. W. Cunliffe, *The Influence of Seneca on Elizabethan Tragedy*, London: Macmillan, 1893
Daniel	P. A. Daniel, conjectures recorded by Bullen, I, lxv–lxviii
Davenport	*The Poems of John Marston* ed. A. Davenport, Liverpool: Liverpool University Press, 1961
Davison	*The Dutch Courtesan* (Fountainwell), ed. P. Davison, Edinburgh: Oliver and Boyd, 1968
DC	*The Dutch Courtesan*
Deighton	K. Deighton, *Marston's Works: Conjectural Readings*, London: G. Bell, 1893
Dilke	*Old English Plays*, ed. C. W. Dilke, 6 vols., London: J. Martin, 1814–16
Dodsley	*A Select Collection of Old Plays*, ed. R. Dodsley, 12 vols., London: R. Dodsley, 1744; 2nd edn 1780
Dyce	*The Works of John Webster* ed. A. Dyce, 4 vols., London: W. Pickering, 1830
ed./edn/eds.	editor/edition/editors
EIC	*Essays in Criticism*
Eidson	J. O. Eidson, 'Senecan elements in Marston's *Antonio and Mellida*', *MLN*, 52 (1937), 196–7
ELH	*ELH: A Journal of Literary History*
ELN	*English Language Notes*
ELR	*English Literary Renaissance*
ES	*English Studies*
Finkelpearl	P. J. Finkelpearl, *John Marston of the Middle Temple*, Cambridge, Mass.: Harvard University Press, 1969
Florio	John Florio, *A World of Words*, London, 1598
Fraser and Rabkin	*Drama of the English Renaissance*, ed. R. A. Fraser and N. Rabkin, 2 vols., New York: Macmillan, 1976

Gair	*Antonio's Revenge* (Revels), ed. W. R. Gair, 1978
Greg, MSR	*Antonio and Mellida* and *Antonio's Revenge*, ed. W. W. Greg, Malone Society Reprint, 1922
Gurr	A. Gurr, *The Shakespearean Stage, 1574–1642*, Cambridge: Cambridge University Press, 2nd edn, 1980
Halliwell	*The Works of John Marston*, ed. J. O. Halliwell, 3 vols., London: J. R. Smith, 1856
Harrier	*An Anthology of Jacobean Drama*, ed. R. C. Harrier, New York: New York University Press, 1963 (also published as The Anchor Anthology)
Harris	*The Malcontent* (New Mermaid) ed. B. Harris, London: Ernest Benn, 1967
Hunter, *AM*	*Antonio and Mellida* (Regents), ed. G. K. Hunter, 1965
Hunter, *AR*	*Antonio's Revenge* (Regents), ed. G. K. Hunter, 1966
Hunter, *Malc.*	*The Malcontent* (Revels), ed. G. K. Hunter, 1975
(i)	inner forme
JEGP	*Journal of English and Germanic Philology*
Jenkins	William Shakespeare, *Hamlet* (Arden), ed. H. Jenkins, London: Methuen, 1982
Jonson	Ben Jonson, *The Works*, ed. C. H. Herford and P. and E. Simpson, 11 vols., Oxford: Oxford University Press, 1925–52
Keltie	*The Works of the British Dramatists*, ed. J. S. Keltie, Edinburgh: W. P. Nimmo, 1870
Kemp	*The Wonder of Women or The Tragedy of Sophonisba*, ed. W. Kemp, New York and London: Garland, 1979
Kyd	Thomas Kyd, *The Spanish Tragedy* (Revels), ed. P. Edwards, 1959
Lake	David J. Lake, 'Webster's additions to *The Malcontent*: linguistic evidence', *Notes and Queries*, 226 (1981), 153–8
Malc.	*The Malcontent*

Marlowe	Christopher Marlowe, *The Plays*, ed. R. Gill, Oxford: Oxford University Press, 1971
MLN	*Modern Language Notes*
MLR	*Modern Language Review*
MP	*Modern Philology*
Montaigne	Michael Eyquem de Montaigne, *Essays*, trans. John Florio, 3 vols., London: Dent, 1965; references are to volume, chapter and page in this Everyman edn
MSR	Malone Society Reprint
Neilson	*The Chief Elizabethan Dramatists*, ed. W. A. Neilson, London: Cassell, 1911
(o)	outer forme
OED	*Oxford English Dictionary*
Orrell	J. Orrell, 'The sources of Marston's *The Wonder of Women or The Tragedie of Sophonisba*', *Notes and Queries*, 208 (1963), 102–3
PBSA	*Papers of the Bibliographical Society of America*
PMLA	*Publications of the Modern Language Association of America*
PQ	*Philological Quarterly*
Q	Quarto
Schoonover	*Antonio and Mellida*, ed. K. L. Schoonover, Ph.D. dissertation, Toronto, 1976
Scott	M. Scott, *John Marston's Plays: Theme, Structure, and Performance*, London: Macmillan, 1978
s.d.	stage direction
SEL	*Studies in English Literature 1500–1900*
s.h.	speech heading (speech prefix)
Shakespeare	William Shakespeare, *The Complete Works*, ed. P. Alexander, London and Glasgow: Collins, 1951
Soph.	*Sophonisba*
SP	*Studies in Philology*
Spencer	*Elizabethan Plays*, ed. H. Spencer, Boston: D. C. Heath, 1933
SQ	*Shakespeare Quarterly*
SV	*The Scourge of Villainy*
Tilley	M. P. Tilley, *A Dictionary of Proverbs*

	in England in the Sixteenth and Seventeenth Centuries, Ann Arbor: University of Michigan Press, 1950
(u)	uncorrected; of a press-variant reading
Walley	*Early Seventeenth Century Plays 1600–1642*, ed. H. R. Walley and J. H. Wilson, New York: Harcourt Brace, 1930
West and Thorssen	M. West and M. Thorssen, 'Observations on the text of Marston's *Sophonisba*', *Anglia*, 98 (1980), 348–56
Wine, *DC*	*The Dutch Courtesan* (Regents), ed. M. L. Wine, 1965
Wine, *Malc.*	*The Malcontent* (Regents), ed. M. L. Wine, 1965
Wood	*The Plays of John Marston*, ed. H. H. Wood, 3 vols., Edinburgh: Oliver and Boyd, 1934–9
WYW	*What You Will*
1633	*The Works of Mr. John Marston*, London: William Sheares, 1633

Seneca, Juvenal, Ovid, Virgil and Cicero are cited from relevant titles in the Loeb Classical Authors series. Marston references are to our own edition, or to Wood's (by volume and page) for plays that we have not included, and to Davenport's for poems. The spelling of all citations has been modernised, unless there is some special reason for preserving the original. The Revels series (formerly Methuen, London) is published by Manchester University Press, Manchester, and The Johns Hopkins University Press, Baltimore, Maryland; the Regents by University of Nebraska Press, Lincoln, Nebraska, and Edward Arnold, London.

Acknowledgements

The title-page of the 1604 Quarto of *The Malcontent* is reproduced by permission of the British Library. The remaining title-pages are reproduced by courtesy of the Bodleian Library. The cover illustration is from a production photograph kindly supplied by the Nottingham Playhouse. We wish to thank Nicole Jackson for invaluable help with typing and proof-reading, and Anne Barton and John Kerrigan for information and ideas about Marston's relationships with Jonson. We are grateful to Sarah Stanton and Kevin Taylor of Cambridge University Press and to the General Editor of this series, Graham Storey, for extracting a typescript from us and bringing our edition to the point of publication, and we especially want to thank Paul Chipchase for his efforts to make our work consistent and accurate and for several excellent suggestions. As joint editors we must resort to blaming each other for the defects that remain.

M.J., M.N.

THE HISTORY OF Antonio and Mellida,

The first part.

As it hath beene sundry times acted, by the children of Paules.

Written by *I. M.*

LONDON

¶Printed for *Mathewe Lownes*, and *Thomas Fisher*, and are to be soulde in Saint Dunstans Church-yarde.

1602.

Title-page of the 1602 Quarto of *Antonio and Mellida* in the Bodleian Library, shelfmark Malone 252 (1)

INTRODUCTORY NOTE

The 'first and second parts' of *Antonio and Mellida* were entered in the Stationers' Register to Matthew Lownes and Thomas Fisher on 24 October 1601. The 'second part' was *Antonio's Revenge*. Both plays were printed by Richard Bradock in the following year, the first for Lownes and Fisher, the second for Fisher alone. The Quartos are in good clear type (of a size approximating to modern English or 14 point), though the punctuation suffers from use of 'badly-cast or otherwise eccentric points' (Greg, MSR, p. x).

W. W. Greg prepared type facsimiles of both plays for a single Malone Society Reprint (1922 for 1921). G. K. Hunter edited each play separately for the Regents series (1965, 1966). There is a useful unpublished edition of *Antonio and Mellida* by Kathryn L. Schoonover (Ph.D. dissertation, Toronto, 1976), and *Antonio's Revenge* has been edited in the Revels series by W. Reavley Gair (1978).

The Quartos' detailed entry directions must be authorial, and the initialled dedication to *Antonio and Mellida* further suggests that Bradock's compositors worked from Marston's holograph. Gair believes that the author's corrected manuscript had been used as a prompt-book. In *Antonio and Mellida* there occurs the stage direction *Enter Andrugio, Lucio, Cole, and Norwod* (IV.i.28). Robert Coles and John Norwood belonged to Paul's Boys around the turn of the century, but it is not clear whether they were to play Andrugio and Lucio or Andrugio's page and another attendant; an annotating book-keeper would be more inclined than the author to specify Cole and Norwood for the name-parts (though it would seem more natural for him to do so on the characters' first entry in III.i), but Marston himself may conceivably have wanted Cole and Norwood to sing the song at 149 s.d. Gair also sees signs of theatrical provenance in the directions in *Antonio's Revenge* for the sounding of midnight chimes at III.i.2 s.d. and for Piero's hypocritical tone at IV.i.112 (where we have amended Q's '*ficto*' to '*Ficte*'), but Marston is likely enough to have been responsible – especially for the Latin. Missing exits and speech prefixes are, respectively, possible and probable pointers to authorial rather than theatrical copy. There is some mislineation in both plays. Identifiable errors in the dialogue are mostly of an easily explicable compositorial kind, but the muddle in *Antonio and Mellida* at IV.i.24–8 (a probable legacy from Marston's own papers – somewhat disorderly at this point) suggests that the Quartos may be more corrupt than their tidy appearance might lead one to suppose. *Antonio's Revenge* is divided into acts and scenes (the latter on neo-classical principles), *Antonio and Mellida* into acts only; modern editors introduce only three scenic divisions into *Antonio and Mellida*, splitting each of the last three acts into two scenes. Schoonover found a mere handful of the most trivial press-variants among a dozen copies of *Antonio and Mellida*, and Gair found none among all extant copies of *Antonio's Revenge* (though Greg had recorded two differences of punctuation, which may not have involved alteration of type). The present text is based on Bodleian copies of the Quartos, Malone 252 (1) and Malone 252 (2).

Antonio and Mellida cannot be earlier than 1599, when the reconstituted Children of Paul's, for whom it was written, began to perform; the portraits shown to Balurdo in V.i, with their inscriptions '*Anno Domini* 1599' and '*Aetatis suae* 24' appear to fix the date in that year. Marston did not reach twenty-four until September/October 1600, but in late 1599 he was strictly in 'the twenty-fourth year of his age'. Given that the Old Style year continued until 25 March, terminal dates of October 1599–March 1600 would be implied. However, not all scholars are prepared to accept the painter's scene as an autobiographical clue. Caputi cannot believe that *Antonio and Mellida* preceded the technically cruder *Jack Drum's Entertainment*, assigned on good evidence to 1600, and Finkelpearl, arguing that *Antonio and Mellida* (as well as *Antonio's Revenge*) reveals Marston's acquaintance with *Hamlet*, regards 'late 1600 as the earliest likely production date' (p. 270). But the proffered resemblances between Shakespeare's play and *Antonio and Mellida* are not especially striking, and may derive from a common indebtedness to the *Ur-Hamlet*.

The plot, like most of Marston's, seems to have been of the playwright's own devising; but *Antonio and Mellida* is dense with the kind of literary allusion – to

Sidney's *Arcadia*, for instance – that seems to have appealed to the coterie audience of the private theatres. Seneca's tragedies are repeatedly quoted and paraphrased, and there are numerous imitations and parodies of plays in the English Senecan tradition, notably Kyd's *Spanish Tragedy*, Marlowe's *Tamburlaine*, and the early tragedies of Shakespeare; so that the play has not unfairly been described as a 'Senecan comedy'. While it would be mistaken to read the whole play as a species of burlesque, it is clear that Marston is capitalising on the artificial effect generated by child actors, to create a kind of dramatised commentary on the dramatic styles favoured by the adult companies. The location of the play in a world of Italianate court corruption, the intrigues, disguisings and revenge-stratagems of its plot, and the passionate extremes of gesture and delivery required by its extravagant rhetoric, all evoke the world of Senecan tragedy.

The two parts of *Antonio and Mellida* were performed by the Children of Paul's in their small indoor theatre in the precincts of St Paul's Cathedral; while they were successful enough to attract Jonson's vitriol in *Poetaster* (1601), there are no records of any revivals in Marston's lifetime, though it may be significant that Marston's fellow Middle Templar, John Ford, appears to have twice imitated the Balurdo–Rossaline tableau in III.ii (123 s.d.) in his *Love's Sacrifice* (?1632) and *The Fancies Chaste and Noble* (1635–6). The only modern revival has been in the condensed version of the two plays prepared by Peter Barnes and directed by Martin Esslin, which the BBC broadcast on 20 February 1977. This radio version was subsequently staged at the Nottingham Playhouse (27 September 1979). In reducing the two plays to the compass of two hours and thirty-five minutes, Barnes made several radical alterations. He smoothed over the differences in tone between the two plays by emphasising the pathos of the first part, and highlighting the burlesque elements of the second. Piero was treated (like his accomplice Strotzo in *Antonio's Revenge*) in a vein of comic extravagance throughout. In order to create a fast-moving plot, Barnes pared away most of Marston's long aria-like speeches, to produce a drama no longer structured around elaborate set-pieces. Such a change was no doubt necessitated by the initial translation to a medium which could find no equivalent for the spectacular tableaux so important to Marston's dramaturgy. More questionable was the decision to excise the induction to *Antonio and Mellida* which, in performance by adult actors, seriously diminished the air of studied artificiality. Full use, on the other hand, was made of musical effects, with a score by Carl Davis. Perhaps the most striking success of the production was in demonstrating the theatrical viability of Marston's violent shifts from parody to pathos, and from tragic rhetoric to farcical burlesque.

[PREFATORY MATERIAL TO THE FIRST EDITION]

[DEDICATION]

To the only rewarder and most just poiser of virtuous merits, the most honourably renowned Nobody, bounteous Maecenas of Poetry and Lord Protector of oppressed innocence, *Do, Dedicoque*.

Since it hath flowed with the current of my humorous blood to affect (a little too much) to be seriously fantastical, here take, most respected patron, the worthless present of my slighter idleness. If you vouchsafe not his protection, then, O thou sweetest perfection, female beauty, shield me from the stopping of vinegar bottles. Which most

---

1 *poiser*: one who weighs or estimates.

2 *Nobody*: 'So Day dedicates *Humour out of Breath* to "Signior Nobody" ' (Bullen); the paradoxical potential of such bogus entities as Nothing and Nobody was a source of unfailing amusement to Renaissance writers. Cf. also the dedications of *Pygmalion's Image* ('To the world's mighty monarch, Good Opinion') and *Scourge of Villainy* ('To his most esteemed and best beloved Self'). *SV* contains poems 'To Detraction' and 'To Everlasting Oblivion', the last of which Marston wittily echoes on his memorial slab in the Temple Church: *Oblivioni Sacrum*.

3 *Maecenas*: the most celebrated literary connoisseur of classical Rome, patron of Virgil and Horace; hence the type of generous and informed patronage.

4 *Do, Dedicoque*: 'I give and dedicate [this work]'; a classical literary formula.

5–20 Marston's style is a fine burlesque of the extravagantly servile manner cultivated in dedications.

6 *humorous*: whimsical, moody.

7 *fantastical*: extravagantly fanciful, capricious.

8–9 *worthless . . . idleness*: parodies the self-deprecating modesty of writers who wish to be taken for gentlemen-amateurs.

9 *his*: its.

11 *stopping*: 'unstoppering' (Hunter); *OED*, however, gives no warrant for this interpretation; perhaps Marston thinks of the Bishop of London's ban on verse satire in 1599 as a 'stopping of vinegar bottles'.

11 *vinegar bottles*: the sour stuff of satire; with a glance at the use of vinegar in treating the pox (Hunter).

wished favour if it fail me, then *Si nequeo flectere superos, Acheronta movebo*. But yet, honour's redeemer, virtue's advancer, religion's shelter, and piety's fosterer, yet, yet, I faint not in despair of thy gracious affection and protection; to which I only shall ever rest most servingman-like, obsequiously making legs and standing, after our freeborn English garb, bareheaded.

Thy only affied slave and admirer,
J.M.

12–13 *Si . . . movebo*: 'if I am unable to bend the gods above to my will, I shall move those of the underworld'; tag adapted from Virgil, *Aeneid*, VII, 312.

18 *making legs*: bowing in a deeply deferential fashion.

19 *bareheaded*: (1) with deferentially doffed hat; (2) without protection.

20 *affied*: assured, bound.

[DRAMATIS PERSONAE

ANDRUGIO, *lately Duke of Genoa*
ANTONIO, *his son*
LUCIO, *counsellor to* ANDRUGIO
PAGE *to* ANDRUGIO
PIERO SFORZA, *Duke of Venice*
FELICHE, BALURDO, ALBERTO, CASTILIO BALTHAZAR, FOROBOSCO — *gentlemen of* PIERO*'s court*
CATZO, *page to* CASTILIO
DILDO, *page to* BALURDO
GALEATZO, *son to the Duke of Florence*
MATZAGENTE, *son to the Duke of Milan*
A PAINTER
MELLIDA, *daughter to* PIERO
FLAVIA, *her gentlewoman*
ROSSALINE, *her cousin*
PAGES
ATTENDANTS
BOY]

Dramatis Personae: this list is based on Hunter.
LUCIO: cf. Italian *luce* = light [of reason].
SFORZA: name of a prominent ducal family who ruled Milan, 1450–1535; hence a type name for an Italianate tyrant; Gair plausibly suggests that Marston was also thinking of Italian *sforzare* = 'force, compel, ravish'.
FELICHE: Italian *felice* = 'happy, fortunate, content'; the Happy Man of Stoic moral philosophy.
BALURDO: 'a fool, a noddy, a dizzard, an idiot, a giddy head' (Florio).
CASTILIO BALTHAZAR: a parodic allusion to Baldassare Castiglione, author of *Il Cortegiano* (1528), the most celebrated of Renaissance courtesy books; here (as in Satire I, lines 27–50, of Marston's *Certain Satires*) a type of sycophantic courtly corruption.
FOROBOSCO: 'a bird called a woodpecker. Also a sneaking, prying, busy fellow' (Florio).
CATZO: 'a man's privy member' (Florio).
DILDO: artificial penis.
MATZAGENTE: 'a killer or queller of people, a man-queller' (Florio).
MELLIDA: intended to suggest sweetness (cf. Italian *melato* = sweet, honeyed).

ANTONIO AND MELLIDA

INDUCTION

Enter GALEATZO, PIERO, ALBERTO, ANTONIO, FOROBOSCO, BALURDO, MATZAGENTE *and* FELICHE, *with parts in their hands, having cloaks cast over their apparel.*

GALEATZO. Come, sirs, come! The music will sound straight for entrance. Are ye ready, are ye perfect?

PIERO. Faith, we can say our parts, but we are ignorant in what mould we must cast our actors.

ALBERTO. Whom do you personate?

PIERO. Piero, Duke of Venice.

ALBERTO. O, ho! Then thus frame your exterior shape
To haughty form of elate majesty,
As if you held the palsy-shaking head
Of reeling chance under your fortune's belt
In strictest vassalage; grow big in thought
As swoll'n with glory of successful arms.

PIERO. If that be all, fear not, I'll suit it right.
Who can not be proud, stroke up the hair, and strut?

Ind. s.d. *parts*: actors were issued not with complete texts of a play, but with individual 'parts', containing only their own lines and cues. The induction mimics a first rehearsal in which the cast place one another's parts in context. Alberto (and later Antonio) acts as a kind of director. The pretence of an unrehearsed play sets the comic tone.

1 *music*: performances in the private theatres were preceded by an hour-long overture, and music was also played between the acts; dramatic 'music for entrance' signalled that the performance was about to begin.

2 *are ye perfect*: have you learnt your lines?

3–4 *Faith . . . actors*: we can speak the lines but are uncertain of the characters we are to play.

8 *elate*: lofty.

13 *suit it right*: fit myself to the conventions of the role.

14 *stroke . . . strut*: conventional gestures; the 'strut' was a stiff-legged, swollen-chested walk cultivated by tragic actors as a sign of pride or heroic dignity; cf. 'stalks' below, line 17.

ALBERTO. Truth, such rank custom is grown popular;
And now the vulgar fashion strides as wide,
And stalks as proud upon the weakest stilts
Of the slight'st fortunes, as if Hercules
Or burly Atlas shouldered up their state.

PIERO. Good. But whom act you?

ALBERTO. The necessity of the play forceth me to act two parts: Andrugio the distressed Duke of Genoa, and Alberto a Venetian gentleman enamoured on the Lady Rossaline, whose fortunes being too weak to sustain the port of her, he proved always disastrous in love, his worth being much underpoised by the uneven scale that currents all things by the outward stamp of opinion.

GALEATZO. Well, and what dost thou play?

BALURDO. The part of all the world.

ALBERTO. The part of all the world? What's that?

BALURDO. The fool. Ay, in good deed la now, I play Balurdo, a wealthy mountebanking Bergamasco's heir of Venice.

15–19 *such . . . state*: with this apparent satire of tragic gesture, compare Hamlet on tragic declamation (*Hamlet*, III.ii.1–34); Finkelpearl, arguing for a late date for *AM*, takes this as a reply to Shakespeare's gibe, hitting particularly at the pretensions of the Admiral's Men in their new theatre, the Fortune. But Alberto's criticism may be as much social as theatrical – directed at ordinary people who put on airs.

19 *state*: stateliness, pomp, splendour.

22 *two parts*: the exigencies of casting frequently led smaller companies into the practice of doubling parts.

25 *port*: grand style of living.

27 *underpoised*: undervalued.

27 *uneven*: unjust.

28–9 *currents . . . opinion*: values all things according to the superficialities of mere sense-impression (the metaphor is from the minting of coinage).

29 *opinion*: in Stoic moral philosophy the false shadow of reason, derived from the senses.

31 *all the world*: cf. the characters of Mankind and Everyman in the Morality drama.

34–5 *mountebanking Bergamasco*: a quack or entertainer from Bergamo, whose citizens were mocked by metropolitan Venetians for their clownish manners.

ALBERTO. Ha, ha! one whose foppish nature might seem create only for wise men's recreation, and like a juiceless bark, to preserve the sap of more strenuous spirits; a servile hound that loves the scent of forerunning fashion; like an empty hollow vault still giving an echo to wit; greedily champing what any other well-valued judgement had beforehand chewed.

FOROBOSCO. Ha, ha, ha! tolerably good; good, faith, sweet wag.

ALBERTO. Umh, why 'tolerably good; good, faith, sweet wag'? Go, go, you flatter me.

FOROBOSCO. Right; I but dispose my speech to the habit of my part.

ALBERTO. (*to* FELICHE) Why, what plays he?

FELICHE. The wolf that eats into the breast of princes, that breeds the lethargy and falling-sickness in honour, makes justice look asquint, and blinks the eye of merited reward from viewing desertful virtue.

ALBERTO. What's all this periphrasis, ha?

FELICHE. The substance of a supple-chapped flatterer.

ALBERTO. O, doth he play Forobosco the parasite? Good i'faith. Sirrah, you must seem now as glib and straight in outward semblance as a lady's

---

39 *strenuous*: vigorous; one of Marston's many coinages, derided by Jonson in *Poetaster*..

40 *forerunning*: running in front (like the fox).

42 *champing*: munching.

44–5 *tolerably good . . . wag*: Forobosco mimics the vapid jargon of the self-styled 'critics' of the pit. Alberto's reply anticipates the echo device frequently employed in the play to draw attention to linguistic folly and vice.

49 *habit*: dress, decorum.

51 *wolf*: the wolf as a type of ravenous appetite; and also *lupus*, an ulcerous skin disease.

52 *lethargy*: 'a disorder characterised by morbid sleepiness' (*OED*).

52–3 *falling-sickness*: epilepsy; bawdily applied to sexual misconduct (esp. in women).

54 *blinks*: closes.

57 *supple-chapped*: glib-mouthed.

60–1 *glib and straight*: i.e. plausible and honest.

busk, though inwardly as cross as a pair of tailor's legs; having a tongue as nimble as his needle, with servile patches of glavering flattery to stitch up the bracks of unworthily honoured –

FOROBOSCO. I warrant you, I warrant you, you shall see me prove the very periwig to cover the bald pate of brainless gentility. Ho, I will so tickle the sense of *bella graziosa madonna* with the titillation of hyperbolical praise that I'll strike it in the nick, in the very nick, chuck.

FELICHE. Thou promisest more than I hope any spectator gives faith of performance. (*To* ANTONIO) But why look you so dusky, ha?

ANTONIO. I was never worse fitted since the nativity of my actorship; I shall be hissed at, on my life now.

FELICHE. Why, what must you play?

ANTONIO. Faith, I know not what – an hermaphrodite, two parts in one: my true person being Antonio, son to the Duke of Genoa, though for the love of Mellida, Piero's daughter, I take this feigned presence of an Amazon, calling myself Florizel and I know not what. I a voice to play a lady! I shall ne'er do it.

ALBERTO. O, an Amazon should have such a voice, virago-like. Not play two parts in one? Away, away; 'tis common fashion. Nay, if you cannot bear two subtle fronts under one hood,

---

62 *busk*: corset-bone.
63 *tailor's legs*: tailors sat cross-legged at their work.
64 *glavering*: deceitful.
65 *bracks*: flaws, tears.
69 *bella graziosa madonna*: 'my lovely and gracious lady'.
71 *in the very nick*: at the very point aimed at; 'tickle' and 'titillation' suggest an obscene *double entendre* on 'nick' = slit.
71 *chuck*: chicken; term of endearment.
74 *dusky*: melancholy.
85 *voice . . . lady*: perhaps the voice of the boy playing Antonio was already breaking; or Marston may simply be playing ingeniously with the convention that allowed these boy actors to play grown men as well as women.
89 *bear . . . hood*: be cunningly two-faced.

idiot go by, go by – off this world's stage! O time's impurity!

ANTONIO. Ay, but when use hath taught me action to hit the right point of a lady's part, I shall grow ignorant, when I must turn young prince again, how but to truss my hose.

FELICHE. Tush, never put them off; for women wear the breeches still.

MATZAGENTE. By the bright honour of a Milanoise,
And the resplendent fulgor of this steel,
I will defend the feminine to death,
And ding his spirit to the verge of hell
That dares divulge a lady's prejudice.

Ex[*eunt* MATZAGENTE, FOROBOSCO, *and* BALURDO].

FELICHE. Rampum scrampum, mount tufty Tamburlaine! What rattling thunderclap breaks from his lips?

ALBERTO. O, 'tis native to his part; for acting a modern braggadoch under the person of Matzagente,

---

90 *go by, go by*: get out of the way, take care; parodic glance at Kyd's *Spanish Tragedy*, III.xii.31.

93 *hit . . . part*: perfect the acting of a woman's role (with obscene *double entendre*).

93 *point*: (1) musical note; (2) lace on stays; (3) place (with bawdy innuendo).

95 *truss my hose*: tie up my breeches.

96–7 *women . . . breeches*: Tilley, B645, M727; 'because 1600 was a leap-year, this may be a possible clue to the dating of the play' (Schoonover).

99 *fulgor*: Latin, brightness.

101 *ding*: beat, thrash.

103 *tufty*: probably a form of 'taffety' (taffeta), which is metaphorically applied to florid, over-decorated language (cf. fustian, bombast); Marlowe's *Tamburlaine* (1587–8) had become a by-word for ranting extravagance by the turn of the century. Schoonover cites 'rufty-tufty' = rumbustious (1606), and suggests also 'proud' and 'bearded'.

106 native: natural.

107 *modern*: (1) of the present day, fashionable; (2) commonplace.

107 *braggadoch*: braggart (from Braggadocchio, the braggart-knight of Spenser's *Faerie Queene*).

the Duke of Milan's son, it may seem to suit with good fashion of coherence.

PIERO. But methinks he speaks with a spruce Attic accent of adulterate Spanish.

ALBERTO. So 'tis resolved; for Milan being half Spanish, half High Dutch and half Italians, the blood of chiefest houses is corrupt and mongrelled; so that you shall see a fellow vainglorious for a Spaniard, gluttonous for a Dutchman, proud for an Italian, and a fantastic idiot for all. Such a one conceit this Matzagente.

FELICHE. But I have a part allotted me which I have neither able apprehension to conceit nor what I conceit gracious ability to utter.

GALEATZO. Whoop! in the old cut? Good, show us a draught of thy spirit.

FELICHE. 'Tis steady, and must seem so impregnably fortressed with his own content that no envious thought could ever invade his spirit; never surveying any man so unmeasuredly happy whom I thought not justly hateful for some true impoverishment; never beholding any favour of Madam Felicity gracing another, which his well-bounded content persuaded not to hang in the front of his own fortune; and therefore as far from envying any man as he valued all men

---

109 *fashion*: form, appearance.

110 *Attic*: pure; derived from the so-called 'Attic style' of rhetoric, with its cultivation of simple elegance; a satiric glance at contemporary arguments about stylistic ideals.

112–15 *Milan . . . mongrelled*: 'Milan was under the German (High Dutch) Spanish rule bequeathed by Charles V' (Hunter).

115–17 *vainglorious . . . proud*: proverbial national vices.

118 *conceit*: take to be.

120 *to conceit*: to understand.

122 *cut*: groove, vein, fashion.

129 *favour*: (1) kindness; (2) lover's gift to be worn as a token of affection.

131–2 *hang . . . fortune*: regard as part of his own good fortune(?); in the emblem books Opportunity is shown as a bald woman with a single lock of hair on her forehead ('front') which a man must seize before she passes.

infinitely distant from accomplished beatitude. These native adjuncts appropriate to me the name of Feliche. [*To* GALEATZO] But last, good, thy humour.

Exit ALBERTO.

ANTONIO. 'Tis to be described by signs and tokens; for unless I were possessed with a legion of spirits 'tis impossible to be made perspicuous by any utterance: for sometimes he must take austere state, as for the person of Galeatzo, the son of the Duke of Florence, and possess his exterior presence with a formal majesty, keep popularity in distance; and on the sudden fling his honour so prodigally into a common arm that he may seem to give up his indiscretion to the mercy of vulgar censure; now as solemn as a traveller and as grave as a puritan's ruff; with the same breath as slight and scattered in his fashion as – as – as a – a – anything; now, as sweet and neat as a barber's casting-bottle; straight, as slovenly as the yeasty breast of an ale-knight; now lamenting, then chafing, straight laughing, then –

FELICHE. What then?

ANTONIO. Faith, I know not what. 'T'ad been a

---

134 *accomplished beatitude*: fully achieved happiness.
135 *native adjuncts*: natural traits.
140–41 *'tis . . . utterance*: no words can express it (spirits might give the gift of tongues, since the Devil is master of languages).
141–58 *for sometimes . . . Proteus*: the bafflingly changeable character described here seems to owe something to Montaigne's characterisation of man; proteans of this sort were to become part of the stock of Fletcher's tragicomedy.
142 *state*: stateliness.
145 *popularity*: the populace.
148 *vulgar censure*: the judgement of the common people.
151 *as . . . anything*: Antonio mimics a 'slight and scattered . . . fashion' of speech; actually this mannerism is particularly associated with Balurdo.
152 *casting-bottle*: bottle for scattering scent.
153–4 *yeasty breast of an ale-knight*: beery breath of a boozer.

right part for Proteus or Gew; ho, blind Gew would ha' done't rarely, rarely.

FELICHE. I fear it is not possible to limn so many persons in so small a tablet as the compass of our plays afford.

ANTONIO. Right. Therefore I have heard that those persons, as he and you, Feliche, that are but slightly drawn in this comedy, should receive more exact accomplishment in a second part; which, if this obtain gracious acceptance, means to try his fortune.

FELICHE. Peace, here comes the Prologue. Clear the stage.

Exeunt.

[*Enter*] *the* PROLOGUE.

The wreath of pleasure and delicious sweets
Begirt the gentle front of this fair troop!
Select and most respected auditors,
For wit's sake do not dream of miracles.
Alas, we shall but falter if you lay
The least sad weight of an unusèd hope
Upon our weakness; only we give up
The worthless present of slight idleness

---

158 *blind Gew*: conjectured to be a blind performing baboon (Hunter); Wood cites several other contemporary allusions to this celebrity.

160 *limn*: paint.

161 *tablet*: panel (of wood etc.) for a painting.

166 *more . . . part*: not fulfilled, though Hunter may be right to suggest that the same actor played Pandulpho Feliche.

1 *wreath*: garland.

1 *delicious sweets*: exquisitely scented flowers.

2 *gentle front*: noble brows (see Additional Note, p. 509 below).

6 *least . . . hope*: the slightest unaccustomed hope.

8 *worthless . . . idleness*: Marston affects the self-deprecating nonchalance proper to the gentleman-amateur.

To your authentic censure. O that our muse
Had those abstruse and sinewy faculties
That with a strain of fresh invention
She might press out the rarity of art,
The pur'st elixèd juice of rich conceit,
In your attentive ears, that with the lip
Of gracious elocution we might drink
A sound carouse unto your health of wit!
But O, the heathy dryness of her brain,
Foil to your fertile spirits, is ashamed
To breathe her blushing numbers to such ears.
Yet, most ingenious, deign to veil our wants;
With sleek acceptance polish these rude scenes;
And if our slightness your large hope beguiles,
Check not with bended brow, but dimpled smiles.

Exit PROLOGUE.

---

9 *authentic*: authoritative.

10 *abstruse and sinewy*: compare the rising fashion for 'strong lines' in poetry; the muscularity and knotty difficulty of style suggested here is exactly Marston's ideal in the *Antonio* plays and *The Malcontent*.

11 *strain*: both 'flow' or 'musical strain, melody', and 'muscular effort'.

13 *elixèd*: distilled.

13 *conceit*: thought, imagination, wit.

15 *gracious elocution*: pleasing eloquence.

17 *heathy*: barren.

18 *Foil*: (1) contrast; (2) rebuff; (3) muck.

19 *numbers*: verses.

20 *veil our wants*: conceal our failings; and perhaps 'vail' = assist.

21 *sleek*: with reference to the 'sleekstone' or polishing stone (Hunter).

23 *Check*: rebuke.

23 *bended*: frowning.

ACT I

SCENE I

The cornets sound a battle within. Enter ANTONIO *disguised like an Amazon.*

ANTONIO. Heart, wilt not break? And thou, abhorrèd life,
Wilt thou still breathe in my enragèd blood?
Veins, sinews, arteries, why crack ye not,
Burst and divulsed with anguish of my grief?
Can man by no means creep out of himself
And leave the slough of viperous grief behind?
Antonio, hast thou seen a fight at sea,
As horrid as the hideous day of doom,
Betwixt thy father, Duke of Genoa,
And proud Piero, the Venetian prince,
In which the sea hath swoll'n with Genoa's blood
And made spring tides with the warm reeking gore
That gushed from out our galley's scupper holes,
In which thy father, poor Andrugio,
Lies sunk or, leapt into the arms of chance,
Choked with the labouring ocean's brackish foam;
Who, even despite Piero's cankered hate,
Would with an armèd hand have seized thy love
And linked thee to the beauteous Mellida.

I.i s.d. *cornets*: wooden instruments preferred to the noisier trumpet in indoor theatres.

I.i s.d. *Amazon*: Amazons were stock figures in courtly masques and entertainments; Antonio's disguise creates a deliberately artificial effect: a gentle burlesque of the usual girl/page disguise may be intended.

1–6 perhaps modelled on *1 Tamburlaine*, V.i.286 ff.

4 *divulsed*: torn apart.

6 *slough*: cast snakeskin.

15 *arms of chance*: Schoonover notes that the sea is a traditional emblem of fortune.

Have I outlived the death of all these hopes?
Have I felt anguish poured into my heart,
Burning like balsamum in tender wounds,
And yet dost live? Could not the fretting sea
Have rolled me up in wrinkles of his brow?
Is death grown coy, or grim confusion nice,
That it will not accompany a wretch,
But I must needs be cast on Venice' shore
And try new fortunes with this strange disguise
To purchase my adorèd Mellida?

The cornets sound a flourish, cease.

Hark how Piero's triumphs beat the air.
O ruggèd mischief, how thou grat'st my heart!
Take spirit, blood; disguise, be confident;
Make a firm stand; here rests the hope of all:
Lower than hell there is no depth to fall.

The cornets sound a sennet. Enter FELICHE *and* ALBERTO, CASTILIO *and* FOROBOSCO, *a Page carrying a shield,* PIERO *in armour,* CATZO *and* DILDO *and* BALURDO. *All these (saving* PIERO*) armed with petronels. Being entered, they make a stand in divided files.*

PIERO. Victorious Fortune, with triumphant hand,
Hurleth my glory 'bout this ball of earth,

---

22 *balsamum*: healing ointment.

23 *fretting*: (1) angry, chafing, turbulent; (2) devouring; (3) wrinkled; the stormy sea perhaps mirrors the rage of Piero (Schoonover).

25 *nice*: choosy.

29 s.d. *flourish*: set of notes to announce the approach of a person of distinction.

30 *triumphs*: triumphal celebrations; the word embraces several kinds of street pageantry, in particular the processions accorded to victorious princes and generals; the elaborate stage directions here require the company to stretch their resources to match this pageant spectacle.

31 *ruggèd*: stormy, harsh, ungentle.

34 proverbial, cf. Tilley, G464.

34 s.d. *sennet*: set of notes used to signal a ceremonial entrance or exit.

34 s.d. *petronels*: large pistols or carbines, normally used by cavalry.

34 s.d. *divided files*: two ranks.

Whilst the Venetian duke is heavèd up
On wings of fair success to overlook
The low-cast ruins of his enemies;
To see myself adored and Genoa quake,
My fate is firmer than mischance can shake.

FELICHE. Stand! The ground trembleth.

PIERO. Ha, an earthquake!

BALURDO. O, I smell a sound.

FELICHE. Piero, stay, for I descry a fume
Creeping from out the bosom of the deep,
The breath of darkness, fatal when 'tis whist
In greatness' stomach. This same smoke, called pride,
Take heed, she'll lift thee to improvidence
And break thy neck from steep security;
She'll make thee grudge to let Jehovah share
In thy successful battles; O, she's ominous,
Enticeth princes to devour heaven,
Swallow omnipotence, outstare dread fate,
Subdue eternity in giant thought,
Heaves up their heart with swelling puffed conceit
Till their souls burst with venomed arrogance.
Beware, Piero, Rome itself hath tried;
Confusion's train blows up this Babel pride.

PIERO. Pish, *Dimitto superos, summa votorum attigi.*

---

42 *earthquake*: traditionally a sign of divine wrath; the slapstick effect after lines 40–1 is deliberate.

46 *whist*: silenced.

47 *stomach*: 'pride, bravery' as well as 'digestion'.

49 *security*: the sin of *securitas*, a culpable indifference to damnation; in this context 'improvidence' probably includes 'neglect of God's Providence'.

57 *Rome . . . tried*: Rome itself has demonstrated the truth of this proposition.

58 *train*: (1) powder-train, fuse; (2) train of events.

58 *Babel*: the type of towering ambition that leads to destruction and confusion; Marston may have in mind the catastrophic Babel-play in which *The Spanish Tragedy* ends.

59 *Dimitto . . . attigi*: 'I renounce the powers above, I have attained the most that prayers can do' (Seneca, *Thyestes*, 888).

Alberto, hast thou yielded up our fixed decree
Unto the Genoan ambassador?
Are they content, if that their duke return,
To send his and his son Antonio's head,
As pledges steeped in blood, to gain their peace?
ALBERTO. With most obsequious, sleek-browed entertain
They all embrace it as most gracious.
PIERO. Are proclamations sent through Italy
That whosoever brings Andrugio's head,
Or young Antonio's, shall be guerdonèd
With twenty thousand double pistolets
And be endearèd to Piero's love?
FOROBOSCO. They are sent every way; sound policy,
Sweet lord.
FELICHE. (*tacite*) Confusion to these limber sycophants!
No sooner mischief's born in regenty
But flattery christens it with 'policy'.
PIERO. Why then, *O me coelitum excelsissimum*!
The intestine malice and inveterate hate
I always bore to that Andrugio
Glories in triumph o'er his misery;
Nor shall that carpet-boy Antonio

---

65 *entertain*: entertainment, welcome.
69 *guerdonèd*: rewarded.
70 *pistolets*: gold coins then worth approximately six shillings. It is difficult to determine precise modern equivalents for Elizabethan currency; it may help the reader to know that an artisan's weekly wage was six shillings and that a gentleman could live in comfort on an income of a hundred pounds per annum.
72 *policy*: contains the sense of 'machiavellian craftiness', as Feliche points out.
74 *tacite*: silently, i.e. 'aside'.
74 *limber*: nimble, pliant.
75 *regenty*: royal government.
77 *O . . . excelsissimum*: 'I am highest of the heavenly powers' (Seneca, *Thyestes*, 911).
78 *intestine*: innate.
81 *carpet-boy*: effeminate stripling (cf. 'carpet-knight').

Match with my daughter, sweet-cheeked Mellida.
No, the public power makes my faction strong.
FELICHE. Ill, when public power strength'neth private wrong.
PIERO. 'Tis horselike not for man to know his force.
FELICHE. 'Tis godlike for a man to feel remorse.
PIERO. Pish, I prosecute my family's revenge,
Which I'll pursue with such a burning chase
Till I have dried up all Andrugio's blood.
Weak rage, that with slight pity is withstood.
The cornets sound a flourish.
What means that fresh triumphal flourish sound?
ALBERTO. The Prince of Milan, and young Florence heir,
Approach to gratulate your victory.
PIERO. We'll girt them with an ample waist of love.
Conduct them to our presence royally.
Let volleys of the great artillery
From off our galleys' banks play prodigal
And sound loud welcome from their bellowing mouths.
Exit PIERO *tantum.*

The cornets sound a sennet. Enter above, MELLIDA, ROSSALINE *and* FLAVIA. *Enter below* GALEATZO *with Attendants;*

---

83 *faction*: either 'course of action', or 'party, unscrupulous supporters'.
84 *Ill, when*: it is bad when.
85 *horselike*: bestial, stupid (paraphrased from Seneca, *Octavia*, 453–4).
92 *Milan*: accent on first syllable.
93 *gratulate*: congratulate.
94 *We'll . . . love*: I'll embrace them with an extravagance of love sufficient to span the largest waist.
97 *banks*: sides (suggested by 'banks of oars').
97 *prodigal*: follows up the subdued pun in 'waist' (line 94).
98 s.d *tantum*: only. Marston now requires a second spectacular procession, accompanied not only by cornets but by the explosions of artillery ordered by Piero.
98 s.d *Enter above . . . enter below*: Gair points out that Marston contrives to present the entire company 'in pageant form', showing the different acting areas available to them; the ladies serve as presenters for the tableau and dumb-shows below.

PIERO [*enters,*] *meeteth him, embraceth; at which the cornets sound a flourish.* PIERO *and* GALEATZO *exeunt. The rest stand still.*

MELLIDA. What prince was that passed through my father's guard?
FLAVIA. 'Twas Galeatzo, the young Florentine.
ROSSALINE. Troth, one that will besiege thy maidenhead,
Enter the walls, i'faith, sweet Mellida,
If that thy flankers be not cannon-proof.
MELLIDA. O Mary Ambree! good thy judgement, wench;
Thy bright elections clear; what will he prove?
ROSSALINE. H'ath a short finger and a naked chin,
A skipping eye; dare lay my judgement, faith,
His love is glibbery: there's no hold on't, wench.
Give me a husband whose aspect is firm,
A full-cheeked gallant with a bouncing thigh:
O, he is the *paradiso delle madonne contente.*
MELLIDA. Even such a one was my Antonio.
The cornets sound a sennet.
ROSSALINE. By my nine-and-thirtieth servant, sweet,
Thou art in love. But stand on tiptoe, fair;
Here comes Sir Tristram Tirlery Whiff, i'faith.

101–3 *besiege . . . cannon-proof*: the metaphor may be suggested by Piero's artillery, and the play of wit is complicated by the conventional use of the upper stage to represent the walls of a city under siege.
103 *flankers*: (1) side-forts; (2) flanks.
104 *Mary Ambree*: ballad heroine, renowned for her exploits at the siege of Ghent (Wood).
105 *Thy . . . clear*: give reasons for your glittering choice; 'clear' is an imperative verb, as 'good' may be in the line above.
108 *glibbery*: slippery, untrustworthy (one of the coinages for which Jonson mocked Marston in *Poetaster*).
111 *paradiso . . . contente*: 'heaven of satisfied women'.
113 *servant*: lover.
115 *Sir . . . Whiff*: 'Tirlery' = flighty, trumpery; 'Whiff' = puff, breath: it is a technical term in the art of tobacco-smoking (Jonson, *Works*, III, 501); Tristram is invoked as a type of courtly adultery (see *Malc.*, I.iii.58).

Enter MATZAGENTE; PIERO [*enters,*] *meets him, embraceth; at which the cornets sound a flourish. They two stand, using seeming compliments, whilst the scene passeth above.*

MELLIDA. Saint Mark, Saint Mark! What kind of thing appears?

ROSSALINE. For fancy's passion, spit upon him. Fie!
His face is varnished. In the name of love,
What country bred that creature?

MELLIDA. What is he, Flavia?

FLAVIA. The heir of Milan, Signor Matzagent.

ROSSALINE. Matzagent? Now, by my pleasure's hope,
He is made like a tilting-staff, and looks
For all the world like an o'er-roasted pig;
A great tobacco-taker too, that's flat;
For his eyes look as if they had been hung
In the smoke of his nose.

MELLIDA. What husband will he prove, sweet Rossaline?

ROSSALINE. Avoid him, for he hath a dwindled leg,
A low forehead, and a thin coal-black beard,
And will be jealous too, believe it, sweet;
For his chin sweats, and h'ath a gander neck,
A thin lip, and a little monkey'sh eye.
Precious! What a slender waist he hath!
He looks like a maypole, or a notchèd stick;
He'll snap in two at every little strain.
Give me a husband that will fill mine arms,

116 *Saint Mark*: the patron saint of Mellida's Venice; perhaps suggested by association with Tristram's uncle, King Mark.

117 *For fancy's passion*: for the love of whimsey; or perhaps 'in pretended rage'.

123–36 *tilting-staff . . . strain*: with these gibes at Matzagente's ridiculous emaciation compare *Malc.*, I.iv.44.

132–3 *chin . . . eye*: marks of licentiousness (Schoonover).

Of steady judgement, quick and nimble sense;
Fools relish not a lady's excellence.

Exeunt all on the lower stage [*except* ANTONIO]*; at which the cornets sound a flourish, and a peal of shot is given.*

MELLIDA. The triumph's ended; but look, Rossaline,
What gloomy soul in strange accoutrements
Walks on the pavement.

ROSSALINE. Good sweet, let's to her, prithee Mellida.

MELLIDA. How covetous thou art of novelties!

ROSSALINE. Pish, 'tis our nature to desire things
That are thought strangers to the common cut.

MELLIDA. I am exceeding willing, but –

ROSSALINE. But what? Prithee go down; let's see her face.
God send that neither wit nor beauty wants,
Those tempting sweets, affection's adamants.

Exeunt [MELLIDA, ROSSALINE, *and* FLAVIA *from the upper stage*].

ANTONIO. Come down; she comes like – O, no simile
Is precious, choice, or elegant enough
To illustrate her descent. Leap heart! she comes,
She comes. Smile heaven, and softest southern wind
Kiss her cheek gently with perfumèd breath;
She comes: creation's purity, admired,
Adored, amazing rarity, she comes.
O now, Antonio, press thy spirit forth
In following passion, knit thy senses close,
Heap up thy powers, double all thy man.

---

146 *common cut*: everyday fashion.

149 *God . . . wants*: God grant she lack neither wisdom nor beauty.

150 *affection's adamants*: the magnets of love.

151–3 *she . . . descent*: Antonio's inability to find a proper simile is meant to seem comically inadequate; the linguistic self-awareness is characteristic of Marston's conscious artifice; cf. below, line 231.

159 *following*: fitting.

160 *man*: manhood.

Enter MELLIDA, ROSSALINE, *and* FLAVIA [*on the main stage*].

She comes.
O how her eyes dart wonder on my heart!
Mount, blood; soul, to my lips; taste Hebe's cup;
Stand firm on deck when beauty's close-fight's up.

MELLIDA. Lady, your strange habit doth beget
Our pregnant thoughts, even great of much desire
To be acquaint with your condition.

ROSSALINE. Good sweet lady, without more ceremonies,
What country claims your birth? and, sweet, your name?

ANTONIO. In hope your bounty will extend itself
In selfsame nature of fair courtesy,
I'll shun all niceness: my name's Florizell,
My country Scythia; I am Amazon,
Cast on this shore by fury of the sea.

ROSSALINE. Nay faith, sweet creature, we'll not veil our names.
It pleased the font to dip me Rossaline;
That lady bears the name of Mellida,
The Duke of Venice' daughter.

ANTONIO. (*To* MELLIDA, *kissing her hand.*)
Madam, I am obliged to kiss your hand
By imposition of a now dead man.

---

163 *Hebe*: cup-bearer to the Olympian gods, the goddess of youth.

164 *close-fight*: according to Smith's *Seaman's Grammar* (1627), 'A ship's close fights are small ledges of wood laid cross one another like the grates of iron in a prison's window, betwixt the mainmast and the foremast, and are called gratings'; used in fighting at close quarters as a protection against boarders.

167 *condition*: identity (including rank and nationality).

170–1 *In hope . . . courtesy*: in the hope that you'll be generous enough to be similarly open with me.

172 *niceness*: modesty, reticence, excessive punctilio.

180 *By imposition of*: at the behest of.

ROSSALINE. Now, by my troth, I long beyond all thought
To know the man; sweet beauty, deign his name.
ANTONIO. Lady, the circumstance is tedious.
ROSSALINE. Troth, not a whit; good fair, let's have it all;
I love not, I, to have a jot left out
If the tale come from a loved orator.
ANTONIO. Vouchsafe me then your hushed observances.
Vehement in pursuit of strange novelties,
After long travel through the Asian main,
I shipped my hopeful thoughts for Brittainy,
Longing to view great nature's miracle,
The glory of our sex, whose fame doth strike
Remotest ears with adoration.
Sailing some two months with inconstant winds,
We viewed the glistering Venetian forts,
To which we made; when lo, some three leagues off,
We might descry a horrid spectacle:
The issue of black fury strewed the sea
With tattered carcasses of splitted ships,
Half-sinking, burning, floating topsy-turvy.
Not far from these sad ruins of fell rage
We might behold a creature press the waves;
Senseless he sprawled, all notched with gaping wounds;
To him we made and, short, we took him up.
The first word that he spake was, 'Mellida',
And then he swooned.
MELLIDA. Ay me!
ANTONIO. Why sigh you, fair?
ROSSALINE. Nothing but little humours; good sweet, on.

---

183 *circumstance*: details.
187 *Vouchsafe . . . observances*: listen quietly and attentively, then.
188 *pursuit*: accented on first syllable.
189 *main*: mainland.
190 *Brittainy*: Britain.
191–2 *great . . . sex*: Queen Elizabeth.
207 *little humours*: a touch of melancholy.

ANTONIO. His wounds being dressed, and life recoverèd,
We 'gan discourse; when lo, the sea grew mad,
His bowels rumbling with windy passion.
Straight swarthy darkness popped out Phoebus' eye,
And blurred the jocund face of bright-cheeked day,
Whilst curdled fogs masked even darkness' brow.
Heaven bade's good night, and the rocks groaned
At the intestine uproar of the main.
Now gusty flaws struck up the very heels
Of our mainmast, whilst the keen lightning shot
Through the black bowels of the quaking air.
Straight chops a wave, and in his sliftered paunch
Down falls our ship, and there he breaks his neck,
Which in an instant up was belched again.
When thus this martyred soul began to sigh:
'Give me your hand', quoth he, 'Now do you grasp
Th'unequal mirror of ragg'd misery;
Is't not a horrid storm? O well-shaped sweet,
Could your quick eye strike through these gashèd wounds
You should behold a heart, a heart, fair creature,
Raging more wild than is this frantic sea.
Wolt do me a favour if thou chance survive?
But visit Venice, kiss the precious white
Of my most – nay, all, all epithets are base
To attribute to gracious Mellida.

209–21 modelled on Seneca, *Agamemnon*, 462–500.

214 *Heaven . . . night*: 'We couldn't see the sky' (Hunter), but with the implication that heaven had cast them off; 'bade's' = bade us.

215 *intestine*: internal; but with the added suggestion of 'intestine strife' = civil war.

216 *flaws*: squalls.

216–17 *struck . . . mainmast*: somersaulted our mast.

219 *sliftered*: cloven.

224 *ragg'd*: rough, harsh; dilapidated; and cf. 'ruggèd', I.i.31.

232 *attribute*: stressed on the first syllable.

Tell her the spirit of Antonio
Wisheth his last gasp breathed upon her breast.'
ROSSALINE. Why weeps soft-hearted Florizell?
ANTONIO. Alas, the flinty rocks groaned at his plaints.
'Tell her', quoth he, 'that her obdurate sire
Hath cracked his bosom'; therewithal he wept
And thus sighed on: 'The sea is merciful;
Look how it gapes to bury all my grief.
Well, thou shalt have it; thou shalt be his tomb.
My faith in my love live; in thee, die woe,
Die unmatched anguish, die Antonio.'
With that he tottered from the reeling deck
And down he sunk.
ROSSALINE. Pleasure's body, what makes my lady weep?
MELLIDA. Nothing, sweet Rossaline, but the air's sharp.
My father's palace, madam, will be proud
To entertain your presence, if you'll deign
To make repose within. Ay me!
ANTONIO. Lady, our fashion is not curious.
ROSSALINE. Faith, all the nobler; 'tis more generous.
MELLIDA. Shall I then know how fortune fell at last,
What succour came, or what strange fate ensued?
ANTONIO. Most willingly; but this same court is vast
And public to the staring multitude.
ROSSALINE. Sweet lady, nay, good sweet; now, by my troth,
We'll be bedfellows; dirt on compliment froth!
Exeunt, ROSSALINE *giving* ANTONIO *the way.*

---

237 *obdurate*: stressed on the second syllable.
238 *cracked his bosom*: broken Antonio's heart.
251 *fashion . . . curious*: Amazons are not fastidious in their manners.
252 *generous*: both 'natural' and 'well-bred'.
255 *vast*: wide (and therefore unsuitable for secrets).
258 *dirt . . . froth*: away with the trivial refinements of courtly manners.
258 s.d. *giving . . . way*: giving the 'Amazon' precedence, ironically a form of 'compliment'.

ACT II

SCENE I

Enter CATZO, *with a capon, eating;* DILDO *following him.*

DILDO. Ha, Catzo, your master wants a clean trencher, do you hear? Balurdo calls for your diminutive attendance.

CATZO. The belly hath no ears, Dildo.

DILDO. Good pug, give me some capon.

CATZO. No capon; no, not a bit, ye smooth bully. Capon's no meat for Dildo; milk, milk, ye glibbery urchin, is food for infants.

DILDO. Upon mine honour –

CATZO. Your honour with a pah! 'Slid, now every jacknapes loads his back with the golden coat of honour; every ass puts on the lion's skin and roars his honour. Upon your honour! By my lady's pantable, I fear I shall live to hear a vintner's boy cry, ''Tis rich neat canary, upon my honour.'

DILDO. My stomach's up.

CATZO. I think thou art hungry.

---

2 *trencher*: a large carving-platter of wood, metal, or earthenware.

4 *belly . . . ears*: proverbial, Tilley, B286.

5 *pug*: a term of endearment (often applied to dolls); also 'harlot, punk', leading into the bawdy play on 'capon'.

6 *capon*: castrated cock, eaten as an aphrodisiac (Schoonover).

6 *bully*: term of affection.

8 *glibbery*: slippery.

12–13 *ass . . . roars*: refers to the fable of the ass and the lion-skin.

14 *pantable*: corruption of 'pantofle', slipper or high-heeled, cork-soled Italian 'chopine'.

17 *My stomach's up*: I'm angry; but Catzo affects to take him literally.

DILDO. The match of fury is lighted, fastened to the linstock of rage, and will presently set fire to the touch-hole of intemperance, discharging the double culverin of my incensement in the face of thy opprobrious speech.

CATZO. I'll stop the barrel thus. [*Gives him food*] Good Dildo, set not fire to the touch-hole.

DILDO. My rage is stopped, and I will eat to the health of the fool thy master Castilio.

CATZO. And I will suck the juice of the capon to the health of the idiot thy master Balurdo.

DILDO. Faith, our masters are like a case of rapiers sheathed in one scabbard of folly.

CATZO. Right Dutch blades. But was't not rare sport at the sea-battle, whilst rounce-robble-hobble roared from the ship sides, to view our masters pluck their plumes and drop their feathers for fear of being men of mark?

DILDO. ''Slud', cried Signor Balurdo, 'O for Don Besicler's armour, in the *Mirror of Knighthood*! What coil's here? O for an armour, cannon-proof! O, more cable, more feather-beds, more

---

19–23 *The . . . speech*: parody of euphuistic fustian.

20 *linstock*: stick to hold a gunner's match.

22 *culverin*: long-barrelled cannon.

25 *Dildo . . . touch-hole*: indecent quibble.

28 *suck . . . capon*: implying that Balurdo is a juiceless eunuch.

30 *case*: matched pair.

32 *Dutch*: 'often with an opprobrious or derisive application' (*OED*).

33–4 *rounce-robble-hobble*: onomatopoeic sobriquet for 'thunder'.

35 *pluck . . . plumes*: (1) hide their plumed officers' helmets; (2) humiliate themselves (cf. 'plume-plucked Richard', *Richard II*, IV.i.108).

36 *men of mark*: (1) men of distinction; (2) targets.

37–8 *Don Besicler*: comic corruption of 'Rosicler', the hero of a Spanish romance translated into English in 1578 as *The Mirror of Princely Deeds and Knighthood* (mocked again in *Malc.*, Insertion i.33–7, V.ii.23).

39 *coil*: noisy disturbance, din (with a pun on the coiled cables used on ships as defence against cannon-fire).

40 *feather-beds*: used, like coiled cables, against cannon-fire until the nineteenth century.

feather-beds, more cable!' till he had as much as my cable hatband to fence him.

Enter FLAVIA *in haste, with a rebato.*

CATZO. Buxom Flavia, can you sing? Song, song!

FLAVIA. My sweet Dildo, I am not for you at this time. Madam Rossaline stays for a fresh ruff to appear in the presence. Sweet, away!

DILDO. 'Twill not be so put off, delicate, delicious, spark-eyed, sleek-skinned, slender-waisted, clean-legged, rarely shaped –

FLAVIA. Who? I'll be at all your service another season. Nay, faith, there's reason in all things.

DILDO. Would I were reason, then, that I might be in all things.

CATZO. The brief and the semiquaver is, we must have the descant you made upon our names, ere you depart.

FLAVIA. Faith, the song will seem to come off hardly.

CATZO. Troth, not a whit, if you seem to come off quickly.

FLAVIA. Pert Catzo! knock it lustily then.

Cantant.

---

42 *cable hatband*: twisted cord of gold, silver or silk, worn round the hat (*OED*).

42 s.d. *rebato*: stiff collar or wire frame used to support a ruff.

46 *presence*: presence-chamber, where the sovereign held court.

53 *in all things*: indecent quibble.

54 *brief . . . semiquaver*: the long and short of it ('brief' = a short note, breve).

55 *descant*: warbled song (*OED*, *sb*. 3); presumably here a part song involving some bawdy play on the names 'Catzo' and 'Dildo'.

57–8 *come off hardly*: turn out badly (with indecent quibble).

59–60 *come off quickly*: finish, retire quickly (with indecent quibble).

61 *knock it*: strike up the music.

61 s.d. *Cantant*: they sing.

Enter FOROBOSCO *with two torches,* CASTILIO *singing fantastically,* ROSSALINE *running a coranto pace, and* BALURDO; FELICHE *following, wondering at them all.*

FOROBOSCO. Make place, gentlemen; pages, hold torches; the prince approacheth the presence.

DILDO. What squeaking cart-wheel have we here, ha? 'Make place, gentlemen; pages, hold torches; the prince approacheth the presence.'

ROSSALINE. Faugh, what a strong scent's here! Somebody useth to wear socks.

BALURDO. By this fair candlelight, 'tis not my feet. I never wore socks since I sucked pap.

ROSSALINE. Savourly put off.

CASTILIO. Ha, her wit stings, blisters, galls off the skin with the tart acrimony of her sharp quickness. By sweetness, she is the very Pallas that flew out of Jupiter's brain-pan. Delicious creature, vouchsafe me your service; by the purity of bounty, I shall be proud of such bondage.

ROSSALINE. I vouchsafe it; be my slave. Signor Balurdo, wilt thou be my servant too?

BALURDO. O God, forsooth, in very good earnest la, you would make me as a man should say, as a man should say –

FELICHE. 'Slud, sweet beauty, will you deign him your service?

ROSSALINE. O, your fool is your only servant. But good Feliche, why art thou so sad? A penny for thy thought, man.

---

61 s.d. *Enter . . . all*: Feliche is used to direct the audience's reaction to this grotesque tableau of courtly affectation.

61 s.d. *coranto*: a lively French dance.

68 *socks*: perhaps with a witty glance at the 'sock' of classical comedy.

71 *Savourly*: (1) sensibly; (2) stinkingly.

72–4 *stings . . . quickness*: parody of pleonastic courtly compliment.

74 *Pallas*: Pallas Athene, the goddess of wisdom, was born from Jupiter's head.

76 *vouchsafe . . . service*: let me be your servant (lover).

77 *bounty*: 'goodness' as well as 'generosity'.

FELICHE. I sell not my thought so cheap; I value my meditation at a higher rate.

BALURDO. In good sober sadness, sweet mistress, you should have had my thought for a penny; by this crimson satin that cost eleven shillings, thirteen pence, threepence halfpenny a yard, that you should, la.

ROSSALINE. What was thy thought, good servant?

BALURDO. Marry, forsooth, how many strike of peas would feed a hog fat against Christ-tide.

ROSSALINE. Paugh! [*She spits*] Servant, rub out my rheum; it soils the presence.

CASTILIO. By my wealthiest thought, you grace my shoe with an unmeasured honour; I will preserve the sole of it as a most sacred relic, for this service.

ROSSALINE. I'll spit in thy mouth, and thou wilt, to grace thee.

FELICHE. [*aside*] O that the stomach of this queasy age
Digests or brooks such raw unseasoned gobs
And vomits not them forth! O slavish sots!
'Servant', quoth you? Faugh! If a dog should crave

---

91 *In . . . sadness*: seriously.

93–4 *crimson . . . yard*: it is not clear whether this is a foolish circumlocution for twelve shillings and fourpence halfpenny, or whether Balurdo is shamed into progressively reducing his claim. Twelve shillings, though a considerable sum, would be modest by the standards of many courtiers, who willingly paid eight times as much for the rich tissues thought proper to their station. Castilio (III.ii.101–4) is billed fourteen and threepence for approximately two yards of taffeta to refurbish his canvas doublet.

97 *strike*: bushels.

98 *against*: for.

98 *Christ-tide*: Christmas.

99 s.d. *She spits*: contemptuous, but not meant to make Rossaline appear as coarse as it might to a modern audience.

108 *brooks*: keeps down.

108 *unseasoned gobs*: unpalatable gobbets; 'unseasoned' also = not mature.

And beg her service, he should have it straight.
She'd give him favours, too, to lick her feet,
Or fetch her fan, or some such drudgery:
A good dog's office, which these amorists
Triumph of. 'Tis rare. Well, give her more ass,
More sot, as long as dropping of her nose
Is sworn rich pearl by such low slaves as those.

ROSSALINE. Flavia, attend me to attire me.

Ex[*eunt*] ROSSALINE *and* FLAVIA.

BALURDO. In sad good earnest, sir, you have touched the very bare of naked truth; my silk stocking hath a good gloss, and, I thank my planets, my leg is not altogether unpropitiously shaped. There's a word: 'unpropitiously'. I think I shall speak 'unpropitiously' as well as any courtier in Italy.

FOROBOSCO. So help me your sweet bounty, you have the most graceful presence, applausive elocuty, amazing volubility, polished adornation, delicious affability –

FELICHE. [*aside*] Whop! Fut, how he tickles yon trout under the gills! You shall see him take him by and by, with groping flattery.

FOROBOSCO. – that ever ravished the ear of wonder. By your sweet self, than whom I know not a more exquisite, illustrate, accomplished, pure, respected, adored, observed, precious, real, magnanimous, bounteous – if you have an idle rich cast jerkin or so, it shall not be cast away, if – Ha, here's a forehead, an eye, a head, a

---

111 *service*: (1) the right to serve as a courtly lover; (2) the servicing of a bitch.

114 *amorists*: an amorist is 'a votary of (sexual) love, a gallant' (*OED*).

122–4 *unpropitiously*: Balurdo, in his clumsy fashion, caricatures Marston's own taste for neologisms.

127–8 *applausive elocuty*: eloquence worthy of applause; Forobosco overwhelms Balurdo with a flood of absurdly periphrastic compliment.

135 *illustrate*: illustrious.

136 *observed*: courted.

136 *real*: regal; in his address to the readers of *SV* Marston ridicules Torquatus (Jonson?) for the use of this word.

137–8 *idle . . . cast*: unused . . . discarded.

hair that would make a – or if you have any spare pair of silver spurs, I'll do you as much right in all kind offices –

FELICHE. [*aside*] – of a kind parasite.

FOROBOSCO. – as any of my mean fortunes shall be able to.

BALURDO. As I am true Christian now, thou hast won the spurs.

FELICHE. [*aside*] – for flattery.
O how I hate that same Egyptian louse,
A rotten maggot, that lives by stinking filth
Of tainted spirits. Vengeance to such dogs
That sprout by gnawing senseless carrion!

Enter ALBERTO.

ALBERTO. Gallants, saw you my mistress, the Lady Rossaline?

FOROBOSCO. My mistress, the Lady Rossaline, left the presence even now.

CASTILIO. My mistress, the Lady Rossaline, withdrew her gracious aspect even now.

BALURDO. My mistress, the Lady Rossaline, withdrew her gracious aspect even now.

FELICHE. [*aside*] Well said, echo.

ALBERTO. My mistress, and his mistress, and your mistress, and the dog's mistress – [*Aside*] precious dear heaven, that Alberto lives to have such rivals!
[*To them*] 'Slid, I have been searching every private room,
Corner, and secret angle of the court,
And yet, and yet, and yet she lives concealed.
Good sweet Feliche, tell me how to find
My bright-faced mistress out.

---

147 *won . . . spurs*: with a pun on 'win your spurs' = win your knighthood for an act of prowess.

149 *Egyptian louse*: cf. Exodus, 8:16 ff.

166–70 apparently parodies *The Spanish Tragedy*, Fourth Addition 17–21 (see below, V.i s.d. and the Additional Note on it, p. 509 below).

FELICHE. Why man, cry out for lantern and candlelight; for 'tis your only way to find your bright-flaming wench, with your light-burning torch; for most commonly these light creatures live in darkness.

ALBERTO. Away, you heretic; you'll be burnt for –

FELICHE. Go, you amorous hound; follow the scent of your mistress' shoe. Away.

[*Exit* ALBERTO.]

FOROBOSCO. Make a fair presence; boys, advance your lights.
The princess makes approach.

BALURDO. And please the gods, now in very good deed, la, you shall see me tickle the measures for the heavens. Do my hangers show?

Enter PIERO, ANTONIO [*disguised as* FLORIZELL], MELLIDA, ROSSALINE, GALEATZO, MATZAGENTE, ALBERTO, *and* FLAVIA. *As they enter,* FELICHE *and* CASTILIO *make a rank for the* DUKE [PIERO] *to pass through.* FOROBOSCO *ushers the* DUKE *to his state; then whilst* PIERO *speaketh his first speech,* MELLIDA *is taken by* GALEATZO *and* MATZAGENTE *to dance, they supporting her;* ROSSALINE *in like manner by* ALBERTO *and* BALURDO; FLAVIA *by* FELICHE *and* CASTILIO.

PIERO. Beauteous Amazon, sit, and seat your thoughts
In the reposure of most soft content.

171–2 *lantern and candlelight*: the bellman's cry, warning householders to hang the legally required lantern at their doors.

182–3 *tickle . . . heavens*: leap high in the dancing.

183 *hangers*: looped straps to carry a rapier.

183 s.d. an elaborately designed tableau, whose ceremonious ordering emblematises the order of court and state.

183 s.d *state*: the throne, canopied with its cloth of state, will be placed centre rear, as in court masques of the period.

183 s.d *supporting*: 'one on either side, like heraldic "supporters" ' (Hunter).

Sound music there! Nay daughter, clear your eyes
From these dull fogs of misty discontent.
Look sprightly, girl. What though Antonio's drowned,
That peevish dotard on thy excellence,
That hated issue of Andrugio,
Yet mayst thou triumph in my victories;
Since, lo, the highborn bloods of Italy
Sue for thy seat of love. Let music sound!
Beauty and youth run descant on love's ground.
[*Music sounds, for dancing.*]

MATZAGENTE. Lady, erect your gracious symmetry;
Shine in the sphere of sweet affection
Your eye, as heavy as the heart of night.

MELLIDA. My thoughts are as black as your beard, my fortunes as ill-proportioned as your legs, and all the powers of my mind as leaden as your wit and as dusty as your face is swarthy.

GALEATZO. Faith, sweet, I'll lay thee on the lips for that jest.

MELLIDA. I prithee intrude not on a dead man's right.

GALEATZO. No; but the living's just possession:
Thy lips and love are mine.

MELLIDA. You ne'er took seisin on them yet. Forbear!
There's not a vacant corner of my heart,
But all is filled with dead Antonio's loss.
Then urge no more; O, leave to love at all;
'Tis less disgraceful not to mount than fall.

---

194 *run . . . ground*: make counterpoint variations on the ground-bass theme of love.

195 *erect . . . symmetry*: courtly periphrasis for 'stand up'.

196–7 *Shine . . . night*: 'Let your eye, which is now as gloomy as night, shine in the area proper to love' (Hunter).

202 *lay thee on the lips*: kiss you.

207 *seisin*: refers to the symbolic act called 'livery of seisin', in which objects are handed over as tokens of possession (*OED*).

MATZAGENTE. Bright and refulgent lady, deign your ear:
You see this blade; had it a courtly lip
It would divulge my valour, plead my love,
Jostle that skipping feeble amorist
Out of your love's seat; I am Matzagent.

GALEATZO. Hark thee, I pray thee taint not thy sweet ear
With that sot's gabble – by thy beauteous cheek,
He is the flagging'st bulrush that e'er drooped
With each slight mist of rain – but with pleased eye
Smile on my courtship.

MELLIDA. What said you, sir? Alas, my thought was fixed
Upon another object. Good, forbear;
I shall but weep. Ay me, what boots a tear!
Come, come, let's dance. O music, thou distill'st
More sweetness in us than this jarring world:
Both time and measure from thy strains do breathe,
Whilst from the channel of this dirt doth flow
Nothing but timeless grief, unmeasured woe.

ANTONIO. [*aside*] O how impatience cramps my crackèd veins,
And curdles thick my blood with boiling rage!
O eyes, why leap you not like thunderbolts
Or cannon-bullets in my rival's face?

---

212 *refulgent*: radiant.

213 *blade . . . lip*: Matzagente's proviso is studiously absurd.

224 *boots*: matters.

225–7 *music . . . breathe*: the Platonic notion that music can restore harmony to a disordered mind; Mellida's speech draws attention to the transcendent symbolism of dancing (cf. *Malc.*, IV.ii.1 ff. and V.v.65 ff.).

226 *jarring*: (1) discordant; (2) racked by quarrels.

227 *time and measure*: musical time and rhythm (as a metaphor of psychological order).

228 *channel of this dirt*: open sewer of this vile earth.

229 *timeless . . . unmeasured*: eternal and infinite (punning on musical sense of 'time and measure').

Ohimè infelice misero, o lamentevol fato.
[*Falls on the ground.*]
ALBERTO. What means the lady fall upon the ground?
ROSSALINE. Belike the falling-sickness.
ANTONIO. [*aside*] I cannot brook this sight; my thoughts grow wild;
Here lies a wretch on whom heaven never smiled.
ROSSALINE. What, servant, ne'er a word, and I here, man?
I would shoot some speech forth to strike the time
With pleasing touch of amorous compliment.
Say, sweet, what keeps thy mind? what think'st thou on?
ALBERTO. Nothing.
ROSSALINE. What's that nothing?
ALBERTO. A woman's constancy.
ROSSALINE. Good, why, wouldst thou have us sluts, and never shift
The vesture of our thoughts? Away, for shame!
ALBERTO. O no, thou'rt too constant to afflict my heart,
Too too firm fixèd in unmovèd scorn.
ROSSALINE. Pish, pish! I fixèd in unmovèd scorn?
Why, I'll love thee tonight.
ALBERTO. But whom tomorrow?
ROSSALINE. Faith, as the toy puts me in the head.

---

234 *Ohimè . . . fato*: 'Alas, unhappy wretch that I am, O lamentable fate'.

235 *What . . . ground*: Alberto draws attention to the emblematic quality of the gesture – perhaps a parody of *The Spanish Tragedy*, I.iii.9, where the Viceroy throws himself to the ground in mimicry of the last turn of Fortune's wheel; cf. also below, IV.i.27, 156, and *AR*, IV.ii.12.

236 *falling-sickness*: epilepsy (punning on female frailty).

243 *nothing . . . constancy*: the usual bawdy play on 'O' (cf. *Hamlet*, III.ii.112–16).

246 *to afflict*: in afflicting.

BALURDO. And pleased the marble heavens, now would I might be the toy, to put you in the head kindly to conceit my – my – my – pray you, give m' an epithet for love.

FELICHE. 'Roaring', 'roaring'.

BALURDO. O love, thou hast murdered me, made me a shadow, and you hear not Balurdo, but Balurdo's ghost.

ROSSALINE. Can a ghost speak?

BALURDO. Scurvily, as I do.

ROSSALINE. And walk?

BALURDO. After their fashion.

ROSSALINE. And eat apples?

BALURDO. In a sort; in their garb.

FELICHE. Prithee, Flavia, be my mistress.

FLAVIA. Your reason, good Feliche?

FELICHE. Faith, I have nineteen mistresses already, and I not much disdain that thou shouldst make up the full score.

FLAVIA. O, I hear you make commonplaces of your mistresses, to perform the office of memory by. Pray you, in ancient times were not those satin hose? In good faith, now they are new dyed, pinked, and scoured, they show as well as if they were new. What, mute, Balurdo?

FELICHE. Ay, in faith, and 'twere not for printing and painting, my breech and your face would be out of reparation.

BALURDO. Ay, in faith, and 'twere not for printing and painting, my breech and your face would be out of reparation.

FELICHE. Good again, echo.

FLAVIA. Thou art, by nature, too foul to be affected.

---

252 *toy*: fancy.
256–64 from Erasmus, *Colloquies* ('Proci et Puellae') (Hunter).
270 *commonplaces*: commonplace-books (with a bawdy *double entendre*).
274 *pinked*: ornamented.
276 *printing*: staining, dyeing.
277 *breech*: arse.
278 *out of reparation*: beyond repair.
283 *be affected*: be loved.

FELICHE. And thou, by art, too fair to be beloved.
By wit's life, most spark spirits but hard chance.
[*Sings*] La ty dine

PIERO. Gallants, the night grows old, and downy sleep
Courts us to entertain his company;
Our tired limbs, bruised in the morning fight,
Entreat soft rest and gentle hushed repose.
Fill out Greek wines; prepare fresh cresset-light:
We'll have a banquet, princes, then good night.

The cornets sound a sennet and the DUKE *goes out in state. As they are going out,* ANTONIO *stays* MELLIDA; *the rest exeunt.*

ANTONIO. What means these scattered looks? Why tremble you?
Why quake your thoughts in your distracted eyes?
Collect your spirits, madam. What do you see?
Dost not behold a ghost?
Look, look where he stalks, wrapped up in clouds of grief,
Darting his soul upon thy wond'ring eyes.
Look, he comes towards thee; see, he stretcheth out
His wretched arms to gird thy lovèd waist
With a most wished embrace. See'st him not yet?
Nor yet? Ha, Mellida; thou well mayst err:
For look, he walks not like Antonio,
Like that Antonio that this morning shone
In glistering habiliments of arms
To seize his love, spite of her father's spite;

---

285 *most . . . chance*: Stoic terseness carried to the point of obscurity: 'most sparkling wits [give their lovers] hard fortune'.

286 *La ty dine*: see Textual Note, p. 486 below.

291 *cresset-light*: oil lamp, usually mounted on a pole.

292 *banquet*: probably here only a light meal of sweetmeats, fruit and wine.

292 s.d. *in state*: calls for a ceremonial exit.

293 *scattered*: distracted.

But like himself, wretched and miserable,
Banished, forlorn, despairing, struck quite through
With sinking grief, rolled up in sevenfold doubles
Of plagues, vanquishable. Hark, he speaks to thee.
MELLIDA. Alas, I cannot hear nor see him.
ANTONIO. Why, all this night about the room he stalked
And groaned and howled with raging passion
To view his love (life-blood of all his hopes,
Crown of his fortunes) clipped by strangers' arms.
Look but behind thee. [*Removes his disguise*]
MELLIDA. O Antonio, my lord, my love, my –
ANTONIO. Leave passion, sweet; for time, place, air, and earth
Are all our foes. Fear and be jealous. Fair,
Let's fly.
MELLIDA. Dear heart, ha, whither?
ANTONIO. O, 'tis no matter whither, but let's fly.
Ha! now I think on't, I have ne'er a home:
No father, friend, no country to embrace
These wretched limbs. The world, the all that is,
Is all my foe; a prince not worth a doit!
Only my head is hoisèd to high rate,
Worth twenty thousand double pistolets
To him that can but strike it from these shoulders.
But come, sweet creature, thou shalt be my home,
My father, country, riches, and my friend:
My all, my soul; and thou and I will live –
Let's think like what – and thou and I will live

309–10 *rolled . . . plagues*: from the idea of a 'double plague' Marston develops the conceit of plague as having a kind of substance like a 'double' (= folded cloth); it really means no more than 'plunged in sevenfold affliction'.
315 *clipped*: embraced.
326 *doit*: small Dutch coin of negligible value.
327 *hoisèd*: raised.
333 *Let's . . . what*: the rhetorical failure comically undercuts the pathos of the speech.

Like unmatched mirrors of calamity.
The jealous ear of night eavesdrops our talk.
Hold thee; there's a jewel; and look thee, there's a note
That will direct thee when, where, how to fly;
Bid me adieu.
MELLIDA. Farewell, bleak misery.
ANTONIO. Stay, sweet, let's kiss before you go.
MELLIDA. Farewell, dear soul.
ANTONIO. Farewell, my life, my heart.
[*Exeunt separately.*]

ACT III

SCENE I

Enter ANDRUGIO *in armour,* LUCIO *with a shepherd gown in his hand, and a Page.*

ANDRUGIO. Is not yon gleam the shuddering morn, that flakes
With silver tincture the east verge of heaven?
LUCIO. I think it is, so please your excellence.
ANDRUGIO. Away, I have no excellence to please.
Prithee observe the custom of the world
That only flatters greatness, states exalts.
'And please my excellence'! O, Lucio,
Thou hast been ever held respected, dear,
Even precious to Andrugio's inmost love;
Good, flatter not. Nay, if thou giv'st not faith
That I am wretched, O read that, read that.

III.i s.d. *armour . . . shepherd gown*: Lucio holds Andrugio's disguise; visually the scene suggests a burlesque inversion of *1 Tamburlaine*, I.ii, where Tamburlaine exchanges his shepherd's garments for 'complete armour'.
1 *flakes*: flecks.
6 *states*: princes.

LUCIO. [*reads*] *Piero Sforza to the Italian princes, fortune: Excellent, the just overthrow Andrugio took in the Venetian Gulf hath so assured the Genoese of the injustice of his cause and the hatefulness of his person, that they have banished him and all his family; and for confirmation of their peace with us have vowed, that if he or his son can be attached, to send us both their heads. We therefore by force of our united league forbid you to harbour him or his blood; but if you apprehend his person, we entreat you to send him or his head to us. For we vow by the honour of our blood to recompense any man that bringeth his head with twenty thousand double pistolets, and the endearing to our choicest love.* *From Venice: Piero Sforza.*

ANDRUGIO. My thoughts are fixed in contemplation
Why this huge earth, this monstrous animal
That eats her children, should not have eyes and ears.
Philosophy maintains that nature's wise
And forms no useless or unperfect thing.
Did nature make the earth, or the earth nature?
For earthly dirt makes all things, makes the man,
Moulds me up honour; and like a cunning Dutchman
Paints me a puppet even with seeming breath
And gives a sot appearance of a soul.
Go to, go to; thou liest, philosophy!
Nature forms things unperfect, useless, vain.
Why made she not the earth with eyes and ears,
That she might see desert and hear men's plaints?
That when a soul is splitted, sunk with grief,

---

13 *fortune*: good fortune to you.

13 *Excellent*: Your Excellencies.

35–6 *Moulds me . . . Paints me*: ethic datives; 'me' (i.e. 'for me') has a purely emphatic function.

35 *cunning Dutchman*: painters from Holland and Germany enjoyed a high reputation in England throughout the sixteenth and seventeenth centuries.

He might fall thus upon the breast of earth
[*Falls on the ground.*]
And in her ear halloo his misery,
Exclaiming thus: 'O thou all-bearing earth
Which men do gape for, till thou cramm'st their mouths
And chok'st their throats with dust, O chawn thy breast
And let me sink into thee! Look who knocks;
[*Beats the ground with his fists.*]
Andrugio calls.' But O, she's deaf and blind;
A wretch but lean relief on earth can find.

LUCIO. Sweet lord, abandon passion, and disarm.
Since by the fortune of the tumbling sea
We are rolled up upon the Venice marsh,
Let's clip all fortune, lest more louring fate –

ANDRUGIO. More louring fate! O Lucio, choke that breath.
Now I defy chance. Fortune's brow hath frowned
Even to the utmost wrinkle it can bend;
Her venom's spit. Alas, what country rests,
What son, what comfort, that she can deprive?
Triumphs not Venice in my overthrow?
Gapes not my native country for my blood?
Lies not my son tombed in the swelling main?
And yet, 'more louring fate'? There's nothing left
Unto Andrugio, but Andrugio;
And that nor mischief, force, distress, nor hell can take.
Fortune my fortunes, not my mind, shall shake.

LUCIO. Spoke like yourself; but give me leave, my lord,

---

43 *fall thus*: cf. above, II.i.235.
46 *gape*: long desperately.
47 *chawn*: cause to gape open.
54 *clip*: embrace, willingly accept.
58 *Her . . . spit*: she has used up all her venom.
66 *Fortune . . . shake*: Hunter compares Seneca, *Medea*, 176: 'Fortune may affect my circumstances but not my resolution.'

To wish your safety. If you are but seen,
Your arms display you; therefore put them off
And take –
ANDRUGIO. Wouldst have me go unarmed among my foes,
Being besieged by passion, ent'ring lists
To combat with despair and mighty grief,
My soul beleaguered with the crushing strength
Of sharp impatience? Ha, Lucio, go unarmed?
Come soul, resume the valour of thy birth;
Myself myself, will dare all opposites.
I'll muster forces, an unvanquished power;
Cornets of horse shall press th'ungrateful earth;
This hollow-wombèd mass shall inly groan
And murmur to sustain the weight of arms;
Ghastly amazement with upstarted hair
Shall hurry on before and usher us,
Whilst trumpets clamour with a sound of death.
LUCIO. Peace, good my lord; your speech is all too light.
Alas, survey your fortunes; look what's left
Of all your forces and your utmost hopes:
A weak old man, a page, and your poor self.
ANDRUGIO. Andrugio lives, and a fair cause of arms;
Why, that's an army all invincible.
He who hath that, hath a battalion royal,
Armour of proof, huge troops of barbèd steeds,
Main squares of pikes, millions of harquebus.
O, a fair cause stands firm and will abide;
Legions of angels fight upon her side.

---

69 *Your arms*: i.e. the heraldry on his armour.
77 *Myself myself*: 'being myself again, I . . .'; cf. *Richard III*, V.iii.182 ff. Wood notes that the following passage is 'full of reminiscences of *Richard III*'. The mood of Andrugio's speeches also seems to be considerably influenced by Richard's language in *Richard II*, III.ii–iii.
77 *dare . . . opposites*: cf. *Richard III*, V.iv.3.
79 *Cornets of horse*: troops of cavalry.
92 *Armour of proof*: impenetrable armour.
92 *barbèd*: armoured.
93 *harquebus*: early musket.
95 *Legions . . . side*: cf. *Richard III*, V.iii.175 ff.; *Richard II*, III.ii.58–62, III.iii.85–90.

LUCIO. Then, noble spirit, slide in strange disguise
Unto some gracious prince and sojourn there,
Till time and fortune give revenge firm means.
ANDRUGIO. No, I'll not trust the honour of a man.
Gold is grown great and makes perfidiousness
A common waiter in most princes' courts.
He's in the checkle-roll. I'll not trust my blood.
I know none breathing but will cog a die
For twenty thousand double pistolets.
How goes the time?
LUCIO. I saw no sun today.
ANDRUGIO. No sun will shine where poor Andrugio breathes.
My soul grows heavy; boy, let's have a song:
We'll sing yet, faith, even despite of fate.
Cantant.
ANDRUGIO. 'Tis a good boy; and by my troth, well sung.
O, and thou felt'st my grief, I warrant thee,
Thou wouldst have struck division to the height,
And made the life of music breathe. Hold, boy.
Why so? [*Boy weeps.*]
For God's sake call me not Andrugio,
That I may soon forget what I have been.
For heaven's name, name not Antonio,
That I may not remember he was mine.
Well, ere yon sun set I'll show myself myself,
Worthy my blood. I was a duke; that's all.
No matter whither but from whence we fall.
Exeunt.

---

101 *waiter*: one who pays court to a superior; servant; spy.
102 *checkle-roll*: i.e. 'checker-roll', the list of those chargeable to the royal exchequer; Hunter suggests a pun on 'shekel'.
102 *my blood*: my own relatives.
103 *cog a die*: cheat at dice.
105 *I . . . today*: cf. *Richard III*, V.iii.277 ff.
111 *struck . . . height*: reached the heights of melodic sublimity.
119 *No . . . fall*: Seneca, *Thyestes*, 925–6: 'magis unde cadas/quam quo refert'; cf. *Malc.*, II.i.26.

SCENE II

Enter FELICHE *walking unbraced.*

FELICHE. Castilio, Alberto, Balurdo! None up?
Forobosco! Flattery, nor thou up yet?
Then there's no courtier stirring; that's firm truth.
I cannot sleep; Feliche seldom rests
In these court lodgings. I have walked all night
To see if the nocturnal court delights
Could force me envy their felicity;
And by plain truth – I will confess plain truth –
I envy nothing but the traverse light.
O, had it eyes and ears and tongues, it might
See sport, hear speech of most strange surquedries.
O, if that candlelight were made a poet,
He would prove a rare firking satirist
And draw the core forth of impostumed sin.
Well, I thank heaven yet that my content
Can envy nothing but poor candlelight.
As for the other glistering copper spangs
That glisten in the tire of the court,
Praise God I either hate or pity them.
Well, here I'll sleep till that the scene of up
Is past at court. [*Lies down*] O calm, hushed, rich content,
Is there a being blessedness without thee?
How soft thou down'st the couch where thou dost rest,

III.ii s.d. *unbraced*: with his clothes unfastened; a visual coding for a night scene (cf. the opening of *AR*).
9 *traverse*: closet.
11 *surquedries*: acts of presumption or excess.
13 *firking*: scourging; perhaps also 'ferreting out'.
14 *impostumed*: ulcerated, pus-filled.
17 *copper spangs*: spangles of imitation gold.
18 *tire*: attire.
20 *scene of up*: levee.
22 *Is . . . blessedness*: does any blest condition exist.

Nectar to life, thou sweet ambrosian feast.

Enter CASTILIO *and his Page* [CATZO]; CASTILIO *with a casting-bottle of sweet water in his hand, sprinkling himself.*

CASTILIO. Am not I a most sweet youth now?
CATZO. Yes, when your throat's perfumed your very words
Do smell of ambergris. O stay, sir, stay!
Sprinkle some sweet water to your shoes' heels,
That your mistress may swear you have a sweet foot.

CASTILIO. Good, very good, very passing passing good.

FELICHE. Fut, what treble minikin squeaks there, ha? 'Good, very good, very very good'!

CASTILIO. I will warble to the delicious concave of my mistress' ear, and strike her thoughts with the pleasing touch of my voice.

Cantant.

CASTILIO. Feliche, health, fortune, mirth and wine –
FELICHE. To thee my love divine.
CASTILIO. I drink to thee, sweeting.
FELICHE. Plague on thee for an ass.

CASTILIO. Now thou hast seen the court, by the perfection of it dost not envy it?

FELICHE. I wonder it doth not envy me.
Why man, I have been borne upon the spirit's wings,
The soul's swift Pegasus, the fantasy;
And from the height of contemplation

---

24 *Nectar . . . ambrosian*: nectar and ambrosia were the drink and food of the Olympian gods.

27 *ambergris*: perfume manufactured from secretion of the sperm-whale.

31 *minikin*: literally, a high lute-string; normally an affectionate term for a woman; here referring to the actor's high voice or small stature; in either case a deliberate deflation of the adult roles played by the child actors.

45 *Pegasus*: winged horse of the Muses, frequently identified with poetic imagination.

Have viewed the feeble joints men totter on.
I envy none, but hate or pity all;
For when I view with an intentive thought
That creature fair, but proud; him rich, but sot;
Th'other witty, but unmeasured arrogant;
Him great, yet boundless in ambition;
Him high-born, but of base life; t'other feared;
Yet feared fears, and fears most to be most loved;
Him wise, but made a fool for public use;
Th'other learned, but self-opinionate –
When I discourse all these, and see myself
Nor fair nor rich nor witty, great, nor feared,
Yet amply suited with all full content,
Lord, how I clap my hands and smooth my brow,
Rubbing my quiet bosom, tossing up
A grateful spirit to omnipotence.

CASTILIO. Ha, ha! But if thou knew'st my happiness
Thou wouldst even grate away thy soul to dust
In envy of my sweet beatitude.
I cannot sleep for kisses; I cannot rest
For ladies' letters that importune me
With such unusèd vehemence of love
Straight to solicit them, that –

FELICHE. Confusion seize me, but I think thou liest.
Why should I not be sought to then as well?
Fut! methinks I am as like a man.
Troth, I have a good head of hair, a cheek
Not as yet waned, a leg, faith, in the full.
I ha' not a red beard, take not tobacco much,
And 'slid, for other parts of manliness –

---

49 *intentive*: intently directed.
54 *Yet . . . fears*: though feared, he is himself afraid; an imitation of Seneca, *Oedipus*, 705–6 (Eidson).
56 *learned*: probably monosyllabic, as often in Marston.
57 *discourse*: go through, consider.
68 *unusèd*: unprecedented.
75 *red beard*: often thought to be self-mockery on Marston's part.

CASTILIO. Pew, waw! you ne'er accourted them in pomp,
Put your good parts in presence graciously.
Ha, and you had, why they would ha' come off,
Sprung to your arms, and sued and prayed and vowed
And opened all their sweetness to your love.
FELICHE. There are a number of such things as thou
Have often urged me to such loose belief;
But 'slid, you all do lie, you all do lie.
I have put on good clothes and smugged my face,
Struck a fair wench with a smart-speaking eye,
Courted in all sorts, blunt and passionate,
Had opportunity, put them to the 'ah',
And by this light, I find them wondrous chaste,
Impregnable – perchance a kiss or so;
But for the rest, O most inexorable.
CASTILIO. Nay then, i'faith, prithee look here.

Shows him the superscription of a seeming letter.

FELICHE. [*reads*] *To her most esteemed, loved, and generous servant, Signor Castilio Balthazar.*
Prithee, from whom comes this? Faith, I must see.
[*Reads*] *From her that is devoted to thee in most private sweets of love, Rossaline.*
Nay, God's my comfort, I must see the rest;
I must, sans ceremony, faith, I must.

FELICHE *takes away the letter by force.*

CASTILIO. O, you spoil my ruff, unset my hair; good, away!
FELICHE. [*reads*] *Item, for strait canvas, thirteen*

78 *parts*: 'accomplishments' as well as 'physical qualities'.
79 *come off*: come on.
85 *smugged*: smoothed, trimmed.
88 *put . . . 'ah'*: made them gasp with admiration.
101 *strait*: narrow, single-width, as opposed to broadcloth.

pence halfpenny; item, for an ell and a half of taffeta to cover your old canvas doublet, fourteen shillings and threepence. 'Slight, this a tailor's bill.

CASTILIO. In sooth, it is the outside of her letter, on which I took the copy of a tailor's bill.

CATZO. But 'tis not crossed, I am sure of that. Lord have mercy on him, his credit hath given up the last gasp. Faith, I'll leave him; for he looks as melancholy as a wench the first night she . . . *Exit.*

FELICHE. Honest musk-cod, 'twill not be so stitched together. Take that, and that [*Hits* CASTILIO] and belie no lady's love. Swear no more by Jesu, this madam, that lady. Hence, go; forswear the presence; travel three years, to bury this bastinado. Avoid, puff-paste, avoid!

CASTILIO. And tell not my lady mother? Well, as I am true gentleman, if she had not willed me on her blessing not to spoil my face, if I could not find in my heart to fight, would I might ne'er eat a potato pie more. [*Exit.*]

Enter BALURDO, *backward;* DILDO *following him with a looking-glass in one hand and a candle in the other hand;* FLAVIA *following him backward with a looking-glass in one hand and a candle in the other;* ROSSALINE *following her.* BALURDO *and* ROSSALINE *stand, setting of faces; and so the scene begins.*

---

102 *ell*: 45 inches; Stone (*Crisis of the Aristocracy*) gives 10–16 shillings a yard as the usual price for taffeta – Castilio has presumably ordered a cheap line; the canvas is also inexpensive.

104 *this*: colloquialism for 'this is'.

108 *crossed*: cancelled, receipted; cf. Day, 1600, 'Here's my bill, I pray see me crossed'; Hall, 1614, 'The debt is paid, the score is crossed' (*OED*).

123 *potato pie*: 'believed to be an aphrodisiac' (Hunter).

123 s.d. the carefully symmetrical arrangement of this tableau underlines its emblematic intention; the mirror is a traditional emblem of vanity. The scene was twice imitated by Ford, in *Love's Sacrifice*, II.i, and *The Fancies Chaste and Noble*, I.ii, an indication of its comic success.

123 s.d *setting of faces*: trying on various expressions.

FELICHE. More fools, more rare fools! O, for time and place long enough and large enough to act these fools! Here might be made a rare scene of folly, if the plot could bear it.

BALURDO. By the sugar-candy sky, hold up the glass higher, that I may see to swear in fashion. O, one loof more would ha' made them shine; God's neaks, they would have shone like my mistress' brow. Even so the duke frowns, for all this Curson world. O, that girn kills, it kills. By my golden – what's the richest thing about me?

DILDO. Your teeth.

BALURDO. By my golden teeth, hold up, that I may put in; hold up, I say, that I may see to put on my gloves.

DILDO. O delicious sweet-cheeked master, if you discharge but one glance from the level of that set face, O, you will strike a wench; you'll make any wench love you.

BALURDO. By Jesu, I think I am as elegant a courtier as – How lik'st thou my suit?

DILDO. All, beyond all, no paregal; you are wondered at [*Aside*] for an ass.

BALURDO. Well, Dildo, no Christian creature shall know hereafter what I will do for thee heretofore.

ROSSALINE. Here wants a little white, Flavia.

DILDO. Ay, but master, you have one little fault: you sleep open-mouthed.

---

127 *plot*: the outline of the action, hung in the tiring-house; Feliche's theatrical metaphors further emphasise the artificiality of the action.

128 *sugar-candy sky*: ridiculous periphrasis for 'sweet heavens'.

130 *loof*: eds. suggest northern dialect = 'hand, palm', hence 'handful' or 'touch'; perhaps an obsolete form of 'loaf' (of cosmetic substance).

133 *Curson*: dialect form of 'Christian'.

133 *girn*: grimace, showing the teeth.

140 *level*: position of taking aim.

141 *set face*: fixed expression; with a pun on 'set' = take aim.

145 *no paregal*: peerless.

BALURDO. Pew, thou jest'st. In good sadness, I'll have a looking-glass nailed to the – the – tester of the bed, that I may see when I sleep whether 'tis so or not; take heed you lie not; go to, take heed you lie not.

FLAVIA. By my troth, you look as like the princess now –

ROSSALINE. Ay, but her lip is, lip – is a little – redder, a very little redder. But by the help of art or nature, ere I change my periwig mine shall be as red.

FLAVIA. O, ay, that face, that eye, that smile, that writhing of your body, that wanton dandling of your fan, becomes prethily, so sweethly; [ROSSALINE *gives her money*] 'tis even the goodest lady that breathes, the most amiable – faith, the fringe of your satin petticoat is ripped. Good faith, madam, they say you are the most bounteous lady to your women that ever – [*Gives more money*] O most delicious beauty! Good madam, let me kith it.

Enter PIERO.

FELICHE. Rare sport, rare sport! A female fool and a female flatterer.

ROSSALINE. Body o' me, the duke! Away the glass!

PIERO. Take up your paper, Rossaline.

ROSSALINE. Not mine, my lord.

PIERO. Not yours, my lady? I'll see what 'tis.

BALURDO. And how does my sweet mistress? O lady dear, even as 'tis an old say, ''Tis an old horse can neither wehee nor wag his tail', even so – [*Aside to* DILDO] do I hold my 'set face' still? – [*To* ROSSALINE] even so, 'tis a bad courtier that can neither discourse nor blow his nose.

---

154 *tester*: canopy.

166–73 *prethily . . . sweethly . . . kith*: Flavia's lisp is a piece of courtly affectation, regarded as alluring; cf. *Hamlet*, III.i.145.

182 *say*: saying (cf. Tilley, H671).

183 *wehee*: whinny.

PIERO. [*reads*] *Meet me at Abraham's, the Jew's, where I bought my Amazon's disguise. A ship lies in the port, ready bound for England. Make haste; come private. Antonio.*
Forobosco, Alberto, Feliche, Castilio, Balurdo!

Enter CASTILIO, FOROBOSCO.

Run, keep the palace, post to the ports, go to my daughter's chamber. Whither now? Scud to the Jew's; stay, run to the gates; stop the gondolets; let none pass the marsh; do all at once. Antonio! His head, his head! Keep you the court; the rest stand still, or run, or go, or shout, or search, or scud, or call, or hang, or do – do – do so–so–so–something. I know not wh–wh–wh–what I do – do – do, nor wh–wh–wh–where I am.

[*Exeunt all save* PIERO, FELICHE.]

O trista traditrice, rea, ribalda fortuna,
Negandomi vendetta mi causa fera morte.

[*Exit.*]

FELICHE. Ha, ha, ha! I could break my spleen at his impatience.

[*Enter* ANTONIO *below and* MELLIDA *above.*]

ANTONIO. *Alma e graziosa fortuna siati favorevole,*
E fortunati siano i voti della mia dolce Mellida, Mellida.

MELLIDA. Alas, Antonio, I have lost thy note.

195–6 *gondolets*: small gondolas.

198–202 *run . . . where*: this comic rant perhaps burlesques *The Spanish Tragedy*, III.ii.22–3.

203–4 *O . . . morte*: 'O you wretched traitress, damned, base Fortune, you cause me a savage death by denying me revenge.'

207–8 *Alma . . . Mellida*: 'Kind and gracious Fortune, be favourable, and may the vows of my sweet Mellida be fortunate.'

209 *note*: the one read by Piero, lines 188–91.

A number mount my stairs; I'll straight return.
[*Exit.*]
[ANTONIO *falls to the ground.*]

FELICHE. Antonio,
Be not affright, sweet prince; appease thy fear;
Buckle thy spirits up; put all thy wits
In wimble action, or thou art surprised.

ANTONIO. I care not.

FELICHE. Art mad or desperate, or –

ANTONIO. Both, both, all, all. I prithee let me lie;
Spite of you all, I can and I will die.

FELICHE. You are distraught; O, this is madness' breath.

ANTONIO. Each man may take hence life, but no man death;
He's a good fellow and keeps open house;
A thousand thousand ways lead to his gate,
To his wide-mouthèd porch; when niggard life
Hath but one little, little wicket through.
We wring ourselves into this wretched world
To pule and weep, exclaim, to curse and rail,
To fret, and ban the fates, to strike the earth
As I do now. Antonio, curse thy birth,
And die.

FELICHE. Nay, heaven's my comfort, now you are perverse;
You know I always loved you; prithee live;
Wilt thou strike dead thy friends, draw mourning tears?

ANTONIO. Alas, Feliche, I ha' ne'er a friend,
No country, father, brother, kinsman left
To weep my fate or sigh my funeral.
I roll but up and down, and fill a seat
In the dark cave of dusky misery.

FELICHE. 'Fore heaven, the duke comes! Hold you; take my key;

---

210 *A number . . . stairs*: she hears people climbing the stairs to her chamber (i.e. to the upper stage) (Hunter).
214 *wimble*: nimble.
220 cf. Seneca, *Phoenissae*, 152.
222 cf. Tilley, D140.
227 *ban*: curse.
227 *strike the earth*: cf. *The Spanish Tragedy*, III.xii.71.

Slink to my chamber; look you, that is it.
There shall you find a suit I wore at sea;
Take it and slip away. Nay, precious,
If you'll be peevish, by this light I'll swear
Thou rail'dst upon thy love before thou died'st
And called her strumpet.

ANTONIO. She'll not credit thee.

FELICHE. Tut, that's all one; I'll defame thy love,
And make thy dead trunk held in vile regard.

ANTONIO. Wilt needs have it so? Why then, Antonio,
Vive speranza in dispetto del fato. [*Exit.*]

Enter PIERO, GALEATZO, MATZAGENTE, FOROBOSCO, BALURDO, *and* CASTILIO, *with weapons.*

PIERO. O my sweet princes, was't not bravely found?
Even there I found the note, even there it lay.
I kiss the place for joy that there it lay.
This way he went; here let us make a stand;
I'll keep this gate myself. O gallant youth!
I'll drink carouse unto your country's health,

Enter ANTONIO [*disguised as a sailor*].

Even in Antonio's skull.

BALURDO. Lord bless us! His breath is more fearful than a sergeant's voice when he cries, 'I arrest.'

ANTONIO. Stop Antonio; keep, keep Antonio!

PIERO. Where, where, man, where?

ANTONIO. Here, here; let me pursue him down the marsh.

PIERO. Hold, there's my signet, take a gondolet.
Bring me his head, his head, and by mine honour,
I'll make thee the wealthiest mariner that breathes.

---

248 *Vive . . . fato*: 'Live hope, in spite of fate.'

254 s.d. Antonio lurks at the entrance before crying out.

257 *sergeant*: arresting officer of a court (cf. Hamlet's 'fell sergeant, Death').

259 *keep*: seek out, catch (apparently an obsolete usage, revived by Marston).

ANTONIO. I'll sweat my blood out till I have him safe. [*Exit.*]
PIERO. Spoke heartily i'faith, good mariner.
O, we will mount in triumph; soon, at night,
I'll set his head up. Let's think where.
BALURDO. Upon his shoulders, that's the fittest place for it. If it be not as fit as if it were made for them, say, 'Balurdo, thou art a sot, an ass.'

Enter MELLIDA *in page's attire, dancing.*

PIERO. Sprightly, i'faith. In truth, he's somewhat like
My daughter Mellida; but alas, poor soul,
Her honour's heels, God knows, are half so light.
MELLIDA. [*aside*] Escaped I am, spite of my father's spite. [*Exit.*]
PIERO. Ho, this will warm my bosom ere I sleep.

Enter FLAVIA *running.*

FLAVIA. O my lord, your daughter!
PIERO. Ay, ay, my daughter's safe enough, I warrant thee.
This vengeance on the boy will lengthen out
My days unmeasuredly.
It shall be chroniclèd, time to come:
Piero Sforza slew Andrugio's son
FLAVIA. Ay, but my lord, your daughter –
PIERO. Ay, ay, my good wench, she is safe enough.
FLAVIA. O then, my lord, you know she's run away.
PIERO. Run away, away; how run away?
FLAVIA. She's vanished in an instant, none knows whither.

---

265 *till . . . safe*: (1) until he's safely caught; (2) until he's safely away; Antonio's impudent humour (cf. 'Here, here', line 261) emphasises the farcical quality of the scene.

271 s.d. *page's attire*: now Mellida takes over Antonio's transvestite disguise, a nicely artificial symmetry.

274–5 *light . . . spite*: the rhyme creates an effect of pert impudence.

278, 284 *safe*: Piero unwittingly echoes Antonio's pun (265).

PIERO. Pursue, pursue, fly, run, post, scud away!

FELICHE *sing*[*s*], *'And was not good King Solomon'.*

Fly, call, run, row, ride, cry, shout, hurry, haste;
Haste, hurry, shout, cry, ride, row, run, call, fly;
Backward and forward, every way about.
Maledetta fortuna che con dura sorte . . .
Che farò, che dirò, per fuggir tanto mal?

[*Exeunt all but* CASTILIO *and* FELICHE.]

CASTILIO. 'Twas you that struck me even now, was it not?

FELICHE. It was I that struck you even now.

CASTILIO. You bastinadoed me, I take it.

FELICHE. I bastinadoed you, and you took it.

CASTILIO. Faith sir, I have the richest tobacco in the court for you; I would be glad to make you satisfaction, if I have wronged you. I would not the sun should set upon your anger; give me your hand.

FELICHE. Content, faith, so thou'lt breed no more such lies.
I hate not man, but man's lewd qualities.

[*Exeunt.*]

289–91 *Fly . . . about*: another burlesque of *The Spanish Tragedy*, III.ii.22–3.

292–3 *Maledetta . . . mal*: 'Accursed Fortune, who with hard luck . . . What shall I do, what shall I say, to escape so great an evil?'

301–2 *I . . . anger*: cf. Ephesians, 4: 26, 'Let not the sun go down upon your wrath.'

305 *lewd*: wicked, base.

ACT IV

SCENE I

Enter ANTONIO *in his sea-gown, running.*

ANTONIO. [*calling aloud*] Stop, stop Antonio; stay Antonio.
[*To himself*] Vain breath, vain breath; Antonio is lost:
He cannot find himself, not seize himself.
Alas, this that you see is not Antonio;
His spirit hovers in Piero's court,
Hurling about his agile faculties
To apprehend the sight of Mellida.
But poor, poor soul, wanting apt instruments
To speak or see, stands dumb and blind, sad spirit
Rolled up in gloomy clouds as black as air
Through which the rusty coach of night is drawn.
'Tis so, I'll give you instance that 'tis so.
Conceit you me: as, having clasped a rose
Within my palm, the rose being ta'en away,
My hand retains a little breath of sweet,
So may man's trunk, his spirit slipped away,
Hold still a faint perfume of his sweet guest.
'Tis so, for when discursive powers fly out
And roam in progress through the bounds of heaven,
The soul itself gallops along with them
As chieftain of this wingèd troop of thought;
Whilst the dull lodge of spirit standeth waste,

1–4 cf. *Romeo and Juliet*, I.i.195–6.
11 *rusty . . . night*: a common classical trope, perhaps adapted from Marlowe: cf. *1 Tamburlaine*, V.i.294, and *Edward II*, IV.iii.46.
13 *Conceit . . . me*: understand me.
18 *discursive*: (1) ratiocinative; (2) running hither and thither.

Until the soul return from – What was't I said?
O, this is naught but speckling melancholy
That morphews tender skins –
I have been – cousin-german – Bear with me
Good – Mellida – Clod upon clod thus fall.
[*Falls to the ground.*]
Hell is beneath, yet heaven is over all.

Enter ANDRUGIO, LUCIO [*and* PAGE].

ANDRUGIO. Come, Lucio, let's go eat. What hast thou got?
Roots, roots? Alas, they are seeded, new cut up.
O, thou hast wrongèd nature, Lucio;
But boots not much; thou but pursu'st the world,
That cuts off virtue 'fore it comes to growth,
Lest it should seed and so o'errun her son,
Dull purblind error. Give me water, boy.
There is no poison in't I hope; they say
That lurks in massy plate; and yet the earth
Is so infected with a general plague
That he's most wise that thinks there's no man fool,
Right prudent that esteems no creature just;
Great policy the least things to mistrust.
Give me assay.
[LUCIO *tastes the roots and water.*]
How we mock greatness now!

LUCIO. A strong conceit is rich, so most men deem;
If not to be, 'tis comfort yet to seem.

24–8 *O . . . all*: see Textual Note, p. 487 below.
24 *speckling*: blemishing.
27 *Clod upon clod*: cf. 'earth to earth'.
30 *they . . . up*: the freshly chopped roots had already begun to sprout.
32 *boots . . . much*: it does not matter much.
32 *thou . . . world*: you only follow the way of the world.
36–7 *they . . . plate*: cf. Seneca, *Thyestes*, 453: 'venenum in auro bibitur' (Wood).
37 *massy plate*: solid silver or gold.
42 *assay*: the act of tasting food before giving it to an exalted personage.

ANDRUGIO. Why, man, I never was a prince till now.
'Tis not the barèd pate, the bended knees,
Gilt tipstaves, Tyrian purple, chairs of state,
Troops of pied butterflies that flutter still
In greatness' summer, that confirm a prince;
'Tis not the unsavoury breath of multitudes,
Shouting and clapping with confusèd din,
That makes a prince. No, Lucio, he's a king,
A true right king, that dares do aught save wrong,
Fears nothing mortal but to be unjust;
Who is not blown up with the flattering puffs
Of spongy sycophants, who stands unmoved
Despite the jostling of opinion,
Who can enjoy himself maugre the throng
That strive to press his quiet out of him,
Who sits upon Jove's footstool, as I do,
Adoring, not affecting, majesty;
Whose brow is wreathèd with the silver crown
Of clear content. This, Lucio, is a king,
And of this empire every man's possessed
That's worth his soul.

LUCIO. My lord, the Genoese had wont to say –

ANDRUGIO. Name not the Genoese; that very word
Unkings me quite, makes me vile passion's slave.

45–65 imitated from Seneca, *Thyestes*, 342 ff. (Hunter); the contrast between the philosophical monarch and the prince enslaved by passion is a Stoic commonplace (cf. Cicero, *Paradoxa Stoicorum*, V), more fully developed in *The Malcontent*.

47 *tipstaves*: ceremonial rods of office.

47 *chairs of state*: canopied thrones.

48 *butterflies*: insubstantial courtiers (cf. *SV*, IV, 84–6).

56 *spongy*: lacking solidity; but cf. also Hamlet's denunciation of Rosencrantz as a 'sponge . . . that soaks up the King's countenance, his rewards, his authorities' (*Hamlet*, IV.ii.12–16).

57 *opinion*: the false shadow of reason created by the senses; here something like 'popular prejudice'.

58 *maugre*: in spite of.

O you that wade upon the glibbery ice
Of vulgar favour, view Andrugio;
Was never prince with more applause confirmed,
With louder shouts of triumph launchèd out
Into the surgy main of government;
Was never prince with more despite cast out,
Left shipwrecked, banished, on more guiltless ground.
O rotten props of the crazed multitude,
How you still double under the lightest chance
That strains your veins! Alas, one battle lost,
Your whorish love, your drunken healths, your houts and shouts,
Your smooth 'God save's', and all your devil's blast
That tempts our quiet to your hell of throngs –
Spit on me, Lucio, for I am turned slave;
Observe how passion domineers o'er me.

LUCIO. No wonder, noble lord, having lost a son,
A country, crown, and –

ANDRUGIO. Ay, Lucio, having lost a son, a son,
A country, house, crown, son. *O lares, miseri lares!*
Which shall I first deplore? My son, my son,
My dear sweet boy, my dear Antonio.

---

69 *wade . . . ice*: proceed across the slippery ice (see Textual Note, p. 488 below).
75 *ground*: cause (punning on 'ground' = shore).
77 *double*: bend (punning on 'double' = use duplicity).
82–3 *slave . . . domineers*: cf. above, 45–65 n.
87 *house*: both 'family' and 'dynasty'.
87 *O . . . lares*: 'O household gods, wretched household gods [i.e. house, family]!' (Seneca, *Hercules Oetaeus*, 756).
88–9 *My . . . Antonio*: cf. *The Spanish Tragedy*, II.v.14–33.

ANTONIO. Antonio?
ANDRUGIO. Ay, echo, ay; I mean Antonio.
ANTONIO. Antonio? Who means Antonio?
ANDRUGIO. Where art? What art? Know'st thou Antonio?
ANTONIO. Yes.
ANDRUGIO. Lives he?
ANTONIO. No.
ANDRUGIO. Where lies he dead?
ANTONIO. Here.
ANDRUGIO. Where?
ANTONIO. Here. [*Raising himself.*]
ANDRUGIO. Art thou Antonio?
ANTONIO. I think I am.
ANDRUGIO. Dost thou but think? What, dost not know thyself?
ANTONIO. He is a fool that thinks he knows himself.
ANDRUGIO. Upon thy faith to heaven, give thy name.
ANTONIO. I were not worthy of Andrugio's blood
If I denied my name's Antonio.
ANDRUGIO. I were not worthy to be called thy father
If I denied my name's Andrugio.
And dost thou live? O, let me kiss thy cheek
And dew thy brow with trickling drops of joy.
Now heaven's will be done, for I have lived
To see my joy, my son Antonio.
Give my thy hand; now fortune do thy worst;
His blood, that lapped thy spirit in the womb,
Thus, in his love, will make his arms thy tomb.
[*They embrace.*]
ANTONIO. Bless not the body with your twining arms
Which is accursed of heaven. O, what black sin
Hath been committed by our ancient house,

90–8 The tone of this passage, built on a witty literalisation of a familiar Stoical *sententia* (line 98), and delicately poised between pathos and parody, is characteristically Marstonian.

109 *lapped*: wrapped, swaddled, shrouded.

112–14 *O . . . heads*: a repeated theme in Senecan tragedy.

Whose scalding vengeance lights upon our heads,
That thus the world and fortune casts us out
As loathèd objects, ruin's branded slaves!

ANDRUGIO. Do not expostulate the heavens' will.
But, O, remember to forget thyself;
Forget remembrance what thou once hast been.
Come, creep with me from out this open air;
Even trees have tongues and will betray our life.
I am a-raising of our house, my boy,
Which fortune will not envy, 'tis so mean,
And like the world, all dirt; there shalt thou rip
The inwards of thy fortunes in mine ears
Whilst I sit weeping, blind with passion's tears;
Then I'll begin, and we'll such order keep,
That one shall still tell griefs, the other weep.

Ex[eunt] ANDRUGIO *[and* LUCIO*],*
leaving ANTONIO *and his* PAGE.

ANTONIO. I'll follow you. Boy, prithee stay a little.
Thou hast had a good voice, if this cold marsh,
Wherein we lurk, have not corrupted it.

Enter MELLIDA, *standing out of sight, in her page's suit.*

I prithee sing, but sirrah, mark you me,
Let each note breathe the heart of passion,
The sad extracture of extremest grief.
Make me a strain; speak groaning like a bell
That tolls departing souls.
Breathe me a point that may enforce me weep,
To wring my hands, to break my cursèd breast,
Rave and exclaim, lie grovelling on the earth,

---

117 *expostulate*: protest about.

122 *house*: by a quibble on 'house', Andrugio suggests the Stoical paradox that his family will be truly 'raised' by their reduction to life in the hovel he is building; its mud walls will constitute a kind of emblematic commentary on the dirt of human existence.

124–5 *rip . . . inwards*: expose the innermost parts.

128 s.d. *his*: Andrugio's.

134 *extracture*: essence.

135 *strain*: melody (punning on 'strain' = flow of impassioned language).

137 *point*: short snatch of melody.

Straight start up frantic, crying, 'Mellida'.
Sing but, 'Antonio hath lost Mellida',
And thou shalt see me, like a man possessed,
Howl out such passion that even this brinish marsh
Will squeeze out tears from out his spongy cheeks,
The rocks even groan, and – prithee, prithee sing,
Or I shall ne'er ha' done; when I am in,
'Tis harder for me end than to begin.

The BOY *runs a note;* ANTONIO *breaks it.*

For look thee, boy, my grief that hath no end
I may begin to plain, but – Prithee sing.

Cantant.

MELLIDA. Heaven keep you, sir.
ANTONIO. Heaven keep you from me, sir.
MELLIDA. I must be acquainted with you, sir.
ANTONIO. Wherefore? Art thou infected with misery?
Seared with the anguish of calamity?
Art thou true sorrow, hearty grief; canst weep?
I am not for thee if thou canst not rave,

ANTONIO *falls on the ground.*

Fall flat on the ground, and thus exclaim on heaven:
'O trifling nature, why inspir'dst thou breath?'
MELLIDA. Stay, sir, I think you namèd Mellida.
ANTONIO. Know'st thou Mellida?
MELLIDA. Yes.

---

146 *when . . . in*: when I've once started.
147 s.d. *runs*: prolongs.
147 s.d. *breaks*: interrupts (symbolic violation of harmony).
149 s.d. *Cantant*: presumably Mellida, also dressed as a page, joins the boy in his song; Antonio's 'Heaven keep you from me' (150) registers shock at this mysterious duplication.
155 s.d. *falls*: cf. above, II.i.235. Marston may also be remembering *Romeo and Juliet*, III.iii.69 ff.
158–80 Mellida's undisguising is balanced against Antonio's at II.i.316 ff., and (within the scene itself) Antonio's dawning recognition of his mistress matches Andrugio's of his son; the careful symmetries create an operatic effect, underlined by the conscious artificiality of the Italian duet that follows.

ANTONIO. Hast thou seen Mellida?
MELLIDA. Yes.
ANTONIO. Then hast thou seen the glory of her sex,
The music of nature, the unequalled lustre
Of unmatched excellence, the united sweet
Of heaven's graces, the most adorèd beauty
That ever struck amazement in the world.
MELLIDA. You seem to love her.
ANTONIO. With my very soul.
MELLIDA. She'll not requite it; all her love is fixed
Upon a gallant, one Antonio,
The Duke of Genoa's son. I was her page,
And often as I waited, she would sigh,
'O dear Antonio', and to strengthen thought
Would clip my neck and kiss, and kiss me thus.
[*Kisses him.*]
Therefore leave loving her; fa, faith, methinks
Her beauty is not half so ravishing
As you discourse of; she hath a freckled face,
A low forehead, and a lumpish eye.
ANTONIO. O heaven, that I should hear such blasphemy!
Boy, rogue, thou liest, and –
[*Recognises* MELLIDA.]
Spavento del mio core, dolce Mellida,
Di grave morte ristoro vero, dolce Mellida,
Celeste salvatrice, sovrana Mellida
Del mio sperar; trofeo vero Mellida.

---

166 *graces*: Marston probably has in mind the Three Graces attendant on Venus.

178 *lumpish*: stupidly dull.

181–98 *Spavento . . . morir*: the opening stanzas of this antiphonal duet recall hymns to the Blessed Virgin and to Christ:

Sweet Mellida, terror of my heart,
Sweet Mellida, true restorative of heavy death,
Heavenly saviour, Mellida, Queen
Of my hope; true trophy of victory, Mellida.
MELLIDA. Antonio, my own beloved and gentle soul,
Delightful beauty, courteous Antonio,
Fair Antonio, my lord and object of my virgin love,
Pleasure of my senses, dear Antonio.

MELLIDA. *Diletta e soave anima mia Antonio,*
Godevole bellezza, cortese Antonio.
Signior mio e virginal amore bell' Antonio,
Gusto dei miei sense, car' Antonio.
ANTONIO. *O smarisce il cor in un soave bacio.*
MELLIDA. *Muoiono i sensi nel desiato desio.*
ANTONIO. *Nel cielo può esser beltà più chiara?*
MELLIDA. *Nel mondo può esser beltà più chiara?*
ANTONIO. *Dammi un bacio da quella bocca beata.*
Lasciami coglier l'aura odorata
Che in sù aleggia, in quelle dolci labbra.
MELLIDA. *Dammi l'impero del tuo gradit' amore,*
Che bea me, con sempiterno onore,
Così così, mi converrà morir.
Good sweet, scout o'er the marsh, for my heart trembles
At every little breath that strikes my ear.
When thou returnest, and I'll discourse
How I deceived the court, then thou shalt tell
How thou escap'dst the watch; we'll point our speech
With amorous kissing, kissing commas, and even suck
The liquid breath from out each other's lips.
ANTONIO. [*to himself, going*] Dull clod, no man but such sweet favour clips.
I go, and yet my panting blood persuades me stay.
Turned coward in her sight? Away, away. [*Exit.*]

ANTONIO. O my heart swoons in a sweet kiss.
MELLIDA. My senses die in longed-for delight.
ANTONIO. Can there be a brighter beauty in heaven?
MELLIDA. Can there be a brighter beauty in the world?
ANTONIO. Give me a kiss from that blessed mouth,
Let me pluck the fragrant breath
That hovers on those sweet lips.
MELLIDA. Give me the empire of your pleasing love,
Which blesses me with eternal honour,
Even so will it befit me to die.

201–2 *When . . . tell*: see Textual Note, p. 489 below.
203 *point*: punctuate.
204 *kissing . . . commas*: see Textual Note, p. 489 below.
206 *Dull . . . clips*: 'Poor-spirited creature (reluctant to leave), don't you know that the delights of love are common to all men' (Hunter).

PAGE. [*aside*] I think confusion of Babel is fallen upon these lovers, that they change their language; but I fear me my master, having but feigned the person of a woman, hath got their unfeigned imperfection and is grown double-tongued. As for Mellida, she were no woman if she could not yield strange language. But howsoever, if I should sit in judgement, 'tis an error easier to be pardoned by the auditors than excused by the authors; and yet some private respect may rebate the edge of the keener censure. [*Exit.*]

Enter PIERO, CASTILIO, MATZAGENTE, FOROBOSCO, FELICHE, GALEATZO [*at one door*]; BALURDO *and his Page* [DILDO], *at another door.*

PIERO. This way she took; search, my sweet gentlemen.
How now, Balurdo, canst thou meet with anybody?

BALURDO. As I am true gentleman, I made my horse sweat, that he hath ne'er a dry thread on him, and I can meet with no living creature but men and beasts. In good sadness, I would have sworn I had seen Mellida even now; for I saw a thing stir under a hedge, and I peeped, and I spied a thing; and I peered and I tweered underneath, and truly a right wise man might have been deceived, for it was –

PIERO. What, in the name of heaven?

---

209 *Babel*: note the impudent explosion of the fiction that these events occur in Italy; Marston glances at Kyd's Babel play, with its 'confusion' of languages, in *The Spanish Tragedy*.

213–14 *double-tongued*: (1) deceitful; (2) bilingual.

216–20 *'tis . . . censure*: it is a fault more easily pardoned by the audience than justified by those responsible for it; but harsher judgement may be qualified by some personal considerations – presumably a reference to Marston's half-Italian birth; 'authors' = originators (the whole company).

230 *tweered*: peered (*OED twire*).

BALURDO. A dun cow.
FELICHE. Sh'ad ne'er a kettle on her head?
PIERO. [*to* MELLIDA] Boy, didst thou see a young lady pass this way?
GALEATZO. [*to* MELLIDA] Why speak you not?
BALURDO. God's neaks, proud elf, give the duke reverence; stand bare, with a – [*Knocks her cap off*] Whogh! Heavens bless me – Mellida, Mellida!
PIERO. Where, man, where?
BALURDO. Turned man, turned man; women wear the breeches; lo here!
PIERO. Light and unduteous! Kneel not, peevish elf;
Speak not, entreat not, shame unto my house,
Curse to my honour. Where's Antonio?
Thou traitress to my hate, what, is he shipped
For England now? Well, whimpering harlot, hence!
MELLIDA. Good father –
PIERO. Good me no goods. Seest thou that sprightly youth?
Ere thou canst term tomorrow morning old
Thou shalt call him thy husband, lord, and love.
MELLIDA. Ay me!
PIERO. Blurt on your 'ay me's'! – Guard her safely hence.
Drag her away – I'll be your guard tonight.
[*To* GALEATZO] Young prince, mount up your spirits and prepare
To solemnise your nuptials' eve with pomp.

234–5 *dun cow . . . kettle*: 'Probably a reference to an inn-sign depicting Guy of Warwick's "Dun Cow" and his kettle' (Wood).

239 *God's neaks*: Marston's favourite nonsense oath.

239 *elf*: imitating Spenser's usage in *The Faerie Queene*, where it is a term for the knights of his fairy kingdom; but also referring to the diminutive stature of the boy playing Mellida.

250 *England*: perhaps a reference to the *Ur-Hamlet*; Finkelpearl analyses the scene as an encounter between an Ophelia-figure and a Claudius-figure who talks a Hamlet-like language.

GALEATZO. The time is scant; now nimble wits appear;
Phoebus begins to gleam; the welkin's clear.
Exeunt all but BALURDO *and his Page* [DILDO].

BALURDO. 'Now nimble wits appear': I'll myself appear;
Balurdo's self, that in quick wit doth surpass,
Will show the substance of a complete –

DILDO. – ass, ass.

BALURDO. I'll mount my courser and most gallantly prick –

DILDO. 'Gallantly prick' is too long, and stands hardly in the verse, sir.

BALURDO. I'll speak pure rhyme and will so bravely prank it
That I'll toss love like a – prank – prank it – a rhyme for 'prank it'?

DILDO. Blanket.

BALURDO. That I'll toss love like a dog in a blanket.
Ha, ha, indeed, la! I think – ha, ha! I think – ha, ha! I think I shall tickle the Muses. And I strike it not dead, say, 'Balurdo, thou art an arrant sot.'

DILDO. Balurdo, thou art an arrant sot.

[*Exeunt.*]

---

261 *welkin*: sky.
264 *complete*: accented on first syllable.
265 *prick*: spur, ride fast.
266–7 *prick . . . too long . . . hardly*: obscene *doubles entendres*; Balurdo's line is hypermetrical by one syllable, but the final anapaest is scarcely a wild variation on the iambic pentameter.
269 *bravely prank it*: show myself off flamboyantly.
274 *tickle*: (1) stir with pleasure; (2) draw music from (as in 'tickle the strings' of an instrument).

SCENE II

Enter ANDRUGIO *and* ANTONIO *wreathed together,* LUCIO [*and* PAGE].

ANDRUGIO. Now come, united force of chapfall'n death;
Come, power of fretting anguish, leave distress.
O, thus enfolded, we have breasts of proof
'Gainst all the venomed stings of misery.
ANTONIO. Father, now I have an antidote
'Gainst all the poison that the world can breathe.
My Mellida, my Mellida doth bless
This bleak waste with her presence. [*To* PAGE] How now, boy,
Why dost thou weep? Alas, where's Mellida?
PAGE. Ay me, my lord.
ANTONIO. A sudden horror doth invade my blood;
My sinews tremble, and my panting heart
Scuds round about my bosom to go out,
Dreading the assailant, horrid passion.
O, be no tyrant, kill me with one blow.
Speak quickly, briefly, boy.
PAGE. Her father found and seized her; she is gone.
ANDRUGIO. Son, heat thy blood; be not froze up with grief.
Courage, sweet boy, sink not beneath the weight
Of crushing mischief. O, where's thy dauntless heart,
Thy father's spirit? I renounce thy blood,
If thou forsake thy valour.

[*Exit* ANTONIO.]

IV.ii s.d. *wreathed together*: father and son form a tableau of United Virtue, to which Andrugio's opening speech supplies the motto.

1 *chapfall'n*: with the jaw hanging open.

2 *fretting*: (1) gnawing, wasting; (2) worrying.

2 *leave distress*: cease tormenting me.

LUCIO. See how his grief speaks in his slow-paced steps;
Alas, 'tis more than he can utter; let him go:
Dumb solitary path best suiteth woe.
ANDRUGIO. Give me my arms, my armour, Lucio.
LUCIO. Dear lord, what means this rage? When lacking use
Scarce saves your life, will you in armour rise?
ANDRUGIO. Fortune fears valour, presseth cowardice.
LUCIO. Then valour gets applause when it hath place
And means to blaze it.
ANDRUGIO. *Numquam potest non esse –*
LUCIO. Patience, my lord, may bring your ills some end.
ANDRUGIO. What patience, friend, can ruined hopes attend?
Come, let me die like old Andrugio,
Worthy my birth. O, blood-true-honoured graves
Are far more blessèd than base life of slaves.
Exeunt.

---

25 Marston's version of the favourite tag, *Curae leves loquuntur, ingentes stupent*, 'Light griefs talk, heavy ones strike dumb' (Seneca, *Hippolytus*, 607).

26 *give . . . armour*: cf. above, III.i s.d.; perhaps Andrugio is here meant to exchange his shepherd gown for armour.

27 *lacking use*: not wearing (armour).

29–32 a mixture of quotation and paraphrase from Seneca, *Medea*, 159–61.

29 *presseth*: oppresses.

30–1 *valour . . . blaze it*: courage is only applauded when displayed by one whose rank and power are sufficient to blazon it abroad.

32 *Numquam . . . esse*: incomplete tag: 'There can never fail to be [a place for courage]'.

36 *blood . . . graves*: the blood-honoured graves of those who have been true to the honour of their family.

ACT V

SCENE I

Enter BALURDO, *a* PAINTER *with two pictures, and* DILDO.

BALURDO. And are you a painter, sir? Can you draw, can you draw?

PAINTER. Yes, sir.

BALURDO. Indeed la! Now so can my father's fore-horse. And are these the workmanship of your hands?

PAINTER. I did limn them.

BALURDO. 'Limn them'? A good word, 'limn them'. Whose picture is this? [*Reads*] '*Anno Domini* 1599.' Believe me, Master Anno Domini was of a good settled age when you limned him; 1599 years old! Let's see the other. [*Reads*] '*Aetatis suae* 24.' By'r Lady, he is somewhat younger. Belike Master Aetatis Suae was Anno Domini's son.

PAINTER. Is not your master a –

DILDO. He hath a little proclivity to him.

PAINTER. 'Proclivity', good youth? I thank you for your courtly 'proclivity'.

BALURDO. Approach, good sir. I did send for you to draw me a device, an *impresa*, by synecdoche, a mot. By Phoebus' crimson taffeta

---

V.i s.d. PAINTER: This scene seems clearly intended to parody the Painter scene from *The Spanish Tragedy*. See Additional Note, p. 509 below.

5 *fore-horse*: lead horse in a team.

17 *proclivity*: tendency (i.e. towards idiocy – understood from the Painter's line).

21 *device . . . impresa*: emblematic design, usually with a motto, carried on a knight's shield at tournaments and triumphs.

21–2 *by synecdoche*: by making a part stand for the whole.

22 *mot*: motto (often spelt, and so pronounced, 'mott').

mantle, I think I speak as melodiously – look you, sir, how think you on't? I would have you paint me for my device a good fat leg of ewe mutton swimming in stewed broth of plums – boy, keel your mouth; it runs over – and the word shall be: *Hold my dish whilst I spill my pottage.* Sure, in my conscience, 'twould be the most sweet device now.

PAINTER. 'Twould scent of kitchen-stuff too much.

BALURDO. God's neaks, now I remember me, I ha' the rarest device in my head that ever breathed. Can you paint me a drivelling, reeling song, and let the word be, *Uh.*

PAINTER. A belch?

BALURDO. O, no, no; 'uh'; paint me 'uh' or nothing.

PAINTER. It cannot be done, sir, but by a seeming kind of drunkenness.

BALURDO. No? Well, let me have a good massy ring with your own posy graven in it, that must sing a small treble, word for word, thus:

And if you will my true lover be
Come follow me to the greenwood.

22–3 *Phoebus' . . . mantle*: a periphrasis for the sun's flames; Balurdo presumably thinks of a costume from some court masque.

25–6 *ewe mutton*: cant term for prostitute.

26 *stewed . . . plums*: for the connection of stewed prunes with brothels ('stews'), see *Measure for Measure*, II.i.86 ff.

27 *keel*: catch the overflow from (cf. 'keel the pot' = skim the pot to prevent it boiling over).

28 *word*: motto.

28–9 *Hold . . . pottage*: obvious bawdy *double entendre*.

31 *kitchen-stuff*: punning on 'household drabs'.

35–9 *Can . . . nothing*: cf. *The Spanish Tragedy*, Fourth Addition 113–29: 'Canst paint me a tear, or a wound, a groan, or a sigh? . . . Canst paint a doleful cry?'

40–1 *seeming*: realistically imitated.

43 *posy*: motto engraved inside a ring.

45–6 *And . . . greenwood*: lines from two popular songs: (1) 'How should I your true love know?'; (2) 'Hey jolly Robin'.

PAINTER. O Lord, sir, I cannot make a picture sing.
BALURDO. Why? 'Slid, I have seen painted things sing as sweet – But I have't will tickle it for a conceit, i'faith.

Enter FELICHE *and* ALBERTO.

ALBERTO. O dear Feliche, give me thy device:
How shall I purchase love of Rossaline?
FELICHE. 'Swill, flatter her soundly.
ALBERTO. Her love is such, I cannot flatter her;
But with my utmost vehemence of speech
I have adored her beauties.
FELICHE. Hast writ good moving unaffected rhymes to her?
ALBERTO. O yes, Feliche, but she scorns my writ.
FELICHE. Hast thou presented her with sumptuous gifts?
ALBERTO. Alas, my fortunes are too weak to offer them.
FELICHE. O, then I have it; I'll tell thee what to do.
ALBERTO. What, good Feliche?
FELICHE. Go and hang thyself, I say, go hang thyself,
If that thou canst not give, go hang thyself.
I'll rhyme thee dead, or verse thee to the rope.
How think'st thou of a poet that sung thus?
Munera sola pacant, sola addunt munera formam;
Munere solicites Pallada, Cypris erit.
Munera, munera.

---

49 *painted things*: women.
50–1 *I . . . conceit*: I have an idea (for the device) which will ensure a satisfactory result.
52 *device*: advice.
54 *'Swill*: God's will.
66 *verse . . . rope*: 'reference to the "neck-verse" of those pleading Benefit of Clergy' (Hunter). Felons convicted of capital offences could plead immunity to hanging by demonstrating their ability to read a verse of Latin scripture – a privilege originally reserved for the clergy.
68–70 *Munera . . . munera*: 'Gifts alone subdue, gifts alone add beauty/ Court Wisdom with a gift, and she will turn to Love/ Gifts, gifts!'

ALBERTO. I'll go and breathe my woes unto the rocks,
And spend my grief upon the deafest seas.
I'll weep my passion to the senseless trees
And load most solitary air with plaints;
For woods, trees, sea, or rocky Apennine
Is not so ruthless as my Rossaline.
Farewell, dear friend, expect no more of me;
Here ends my part in this love's comedy.

Exit ALBERTO [*and*] *exit* PAINTER.

FELICHE. Now, Master Balurdo, whither are you going, ha?

BALURDO. Signor Feliche, how do you, faith, and by my troth, how do you?

FELICHE. Whither art thou going, bully?

BALURDO. And as heaven help me, how do you? How do you i'faith, hee?

FELICHE. Whither art going, man?

BALURDO. O God, to the court; I'll be willing to give you grace and good countenance, if I may but see you in the presence.

FELICHE. O, to court? Farewell.

BALURDO. If you see one in a yellow taffeta doublet cut upon carnation velour, a green hat, a blue pair of velvet hose, a gilt rapier, and an orange-tawny pair of worsted silk stockings, that's I, that's I.

FELICHE. Very good; farewell.

BALURDO. Ho, you shall know me as easily; I ha' bought me a new green feather with a red sprig; you shall see my wrought shirt hang out at my breeches; you shall know me.

71–4 *I'll . . . plaints*: imitates *The Spanish Tragedy*, III.vii.1–8.

75–6 *For . . . Rossaline*: parodic reminiscence of Orlando's doggerel in *As You Like It*, III.ii.78 ff.

77–8 *Farewell . . . comedy*: an epilogue in miniature which impudently draws attention to the actor's last exit as Alberto; he will appear henceforth only as Andrugio (see Induction 21–9).

83 *bully*: term of endearment or familiarity.

88 *grace . . . countenance*: favour and patronage.

91–5 the colours suggest a zany extravagance.

98 *sprig*: spray-shaped ornament.

99 *wrought*: embroidered.

FELICHE. Very good, very good; farewell.

BALURDO. Marry, in the masque 'twill be somewhat hard. But if you hear anybody speak so wittily that he makes all the room laugh, that's I, that's I. Farewell, good signor.

[*Exeunt.*]

SCENE II

Enter FOROBOSCO, CASTILIO, *a* BOY *carrying a gilt harp,* PIERO, MELLIDA *in night apparel*, ROSSALINE, FLAVIA, *two* PAGES.

PIERO. Advance the music's prize; now cap'ring wits
Rise to your highest mount; let choice delight
Garland the brow of this triumphant night.

FOROBOSCO. 'Sfoot, 'a sits like Lucifer himself.

ROSSALINE. Good sweet duke, first let their voices strain
For music's prize. Give me the golden harp;
Faith, with your favour, I'll be umpiress.

PIERO. Sweet niece, content. Boys, clear your voice and sing.

1 *Cantat.*

ROSSALINE. By this gold, I had rather have a servant with a short nose and thin hair than have such a high-stretched minikin voice.

PIERO. Fair niece, your reason?

ROSSALINE. By the sweets of love, I should fear extremely that he were an eunuch.

CASTILIO. Spark spirit, how like you his voice?

---

1 *Advance*: raise up; bring forward.
1 *prize*: i.e. the harp.
3 *triumphant*: the court revels are a continuation of the royal 'triumphs' with which the play begins.
8 s.d. *1 Cantat*: First Boy sings.
10 *short nose . . . thin hair*: supposed to be signs of sexual debility.
11 *minikin*: shrill. See above, p. 51, n. 31.
15 *Spark spirit*: woman of glittering wit, beauty or style.

ROSSALINE. 'Spark spirit, how like you his voice?' So help me, youth, thy voice squeaks like a dry cork shoe. Come, come, let's hear the next.

2 *Cantat.*

PIERO. Trust me, a good strong mean. Well sung, my boy.

Enter BALURDO.

BALURDO. Hold, hold, hold! Are ye blind, could you not see my voice coming for the harp? And I knock not division on the head, take hence the harp, make me a slip and let me go but for ninepence. Saint Mark! Strike up for Master Balurdo.

3 *Cantat.*

Judgement, gentlemen, judgement. Was't not above line? I appeal to your mouths that heard my song.

[*Sings*] Do me right,
And dub me knight,
Balurdo.

ROSSALINE. Kneel down, and I'll dub thee knight of the golden harp.

BALURDO. Indeed la, do, and I'll make you lady of the silver fiddlestick.

ROSSALINE. Come, kneel, kneel.

Enter a Page to BALURDO [*who receives the golden harp*].

BALURDO. My troth, I thank you; it hath never a whistle in't.

---

18 *cork shoe*: the high cork-soled clog known as a chopine.
19 *mean*: one who performs the middle part of a harmonised composition; Hunter suggests counter-tenor, Schoonover tenor or alto.
22 *knock . . . on the head*: triumph in.
22 *division*: the execution of a rapid melodic passage (*OED*).
23 *slip*: counterfeit coin.
27 *above line*: over the net; i.e. successful.
29–31 *Do . . . Balurdo*: a parody of the popular song 'Monsieur Mingo' (cf. *2 Henry IV*, V.iii.72–4).
35 *fiddlestick*: bawdy *double entendre.*
37–8 *it . . . in't*: perhaps 'I can't get a sound from it' (as he tries to blow it?).

ROSSALINE. [*to* MELLIDA] Nay, good sweet coz, raise up your drooping eyes; and I were at the point of 'To have and to hold, from this day forward' I would be ashamed to look thus lumpish. What, my pretty coz, 'tis but the loss of an odd maidenhead. Shall's dance? Thou art so sad, hark in thine ear – I was about to say – but I'll forbear.

BALURDO. [*answering to calls off-stage*] I come, I come. More than most honeysuckle-sweet ladies, pine not for my presence; I'll return in pomp. Well spoke, Sir Jeffrey Balurdo. As I am a true knight, I feel honourable eloquence begin to grope me already. *Exit.*

PIERO. Faith, mad niece, I wonder when thou wilt marry.

ROSSALINE. Faith, kind uncle, when men abandon jealousy, forsake taking of tobacco, and cease to wear their beards so rudely long. O, to have a husband with a mouth continually smoking, with a bush of furze on the ridge of his chin, ready still to slop into his foaming chaps; ah, 'tis more than most intolerable.

PIERO. Nay, faith, sweet niece, I was mighty strong in thought we should have shut up night with an old comedy; the Prince of Florence shall have Mellida, and thou shouldst have –

ROSSALINE. Nobody, good sweet uncle. I tell you, sir, I have thirty-nine servants, and my monkey that makes the fortieth. Now I love all of them lightly for something, but affect none of them seriously for anything. One's a passionate fool and he flatters me above belief; the

---

42–3 *lumpish*: dull, dejected.
52 *grope*: take hold of me (perhaps with a bawdy suggestion).
53–87 compare the dialogue between Beatrice and Leonato in *Much Ado*, II.i.16 ff.
60 *slop*: gobble.
60 *chaps*: jaws.
66 *Nobody*: cf. Dedication, above.
68 *monkey*: monkeys were expensive pets, fashionable in court circles.

second's a testy ape and he rails at me beyond reason; the third's as grave as some censor and he strokes up his mustachios three times and makes six plots of set faces before he speaks one wise word; the fourth's as dry as the bur of an artichoke; the fifth paints and hath always a good colour for what he speaks; the sixth –

PIERO. Stay, stay, sweet niece; what makes you thus suspect young gallants' worth?

ROSSALINE. O, when I see one wear a periwig I dread his hair; another wallow in a great slop, I mistrust the proportion of his thigh; and wears a ruffled boot, I fear the fashion of his leg. Thus something in each thing, one trick in every-thing, makes me mistrust imperfection in all parts; and there's the full point of my addiction.

The cornets sound a sennet. Enter GALEATZO, MATZAGENTE, *and* BALURDO, *in masquery.*

PIERO. The room's too scant; boys, stand in there close.

MELLIDA. [*to* GALEATZO] In faith, fair sir, I am too sad to dance.

PIERO. How's that, how's that? too sad? By heaven, dance,
And grace him too, or – go to, I say no more.

---

76 *bur*: thistly head.
77 *paints*: (1) uses cosmetics; (2) depicts in words; (3) flatters.
78 *good colour*: (1) healthy complexion; (2) plausible argument.
82 *great slop*: wide loose breeches.
84 *ruffled boot*: fashionable loose-topped boot, with turn-over ruffled top, designed to show off coloured stockings.
87 *full point*: conclusion; full account.
87 *addiction*: inclination.
87 s.d. *masquery*: masquing attire.
88 *scant*: small; a reference to the cramped stage at Paul's.
88 *close*: hidden.
91 *grace*: show favour to.

MELLIDA. [*reading the device*] A burning-glass, the word, *Splendente Phoebo*;
'Tis too curious; I conceit it not.
GALEATZO. Faith, I'll tell thee. I'll no longer burn
Than you'll shine and smile upon my love.
For look ye, fairest, by your pure sweets,
I do not dote upon your excellence,
And, faith, unless you shed your brightest beams
Of sunny favour and acceptive grace
Upon my tender love, I do not burn.
Marry, but shine and I'll reflect your beams
With fervent ardour. Faith, I would be loath
To flatter thee, fair soul, because I love,
Not dote, court like thy husband, which thy father
Swears tomorrow morn I must be. This is all,
And now from henceforth, trust me Mellida,
I'll not speak one wise word to thee more.
MELLIDA. I trust ye.
GALEATZO. By my troth, I'll speak pure fool to thee now.
MELLIDA. You will speak the liker yourself.
GALEATZO. Good faith, I'll accept of the coxcomb, so you will not refuse the bauble.
MELLIDA. Nay, good sweet, keep them both; I am enamoured of neither.
GALEATZO. Go to, I must take you down for this. Lend me your ear. [*They walk aside.*]
ROSSALINE. [*reading the device*] A glow-worm, the word, *Splendescit tantum tenebris*.
MATZAGENTE. O lady, the glow-worm figurates

---

92 *Splendente Phoebo*: 'while the sun shines'; the burning-glass and the glow-worm (118) belong to the stock repertory of emblematic devices.
93 *curious*: intricate, obscure.
93 *conceit*: understand.
94–102 a tissue of Petrarchan cliché.
112–13 *coxcomb*: fool's head-dress.
113 *bauble*: fool's sceptre, frequently phallic in appearance (cf. *Romeo and Juliet*, II.iv.86–9).
116 *take . . . down*: humble (with bawdy suggestion?).
119 *Splendescit . . . tenebris*: 'It shines only in darkness.'

my valour, which shineth brightest in most dark, dismal, and horrid achievements.

ROSSALINE. Or rather, your glow-worm represents your wit, which only seems to have fire in it, though indeed 'tis but an *ignis fatuus* and shines only in the dark dead night of fools' admiration.

MATZAGENTE. Lady, my wit hath spurs, if it were disposed to ride you.

ROSSALINE. Faith, sir, your wit's spurs have but walking rowels; dull, blunt, they will not draw blood. The gentlemen-ushers may admit them the presence, for any wrong they can do to ladies.

[*They walk aside.*]

BALURDO. Truly, I have strained a note above E la for a device; look you, 'tis a fair-ruled singing book: the word, *Perfect, if it were pricked.*

FLAVIA. Though you are masked I can guess who you are by your wit. You are not the exquisite Balurdo, the most rarely-shaped Balurdo?

BALURDO. Who, I? No, I am not Sir Jeffrey Balurdo. I am not as well known by my wit as an alehouse by a red lattice. I am not worthy to love and be beloved of Flavia.

FLAVIA. I will not scorn to favour such good parts as are applauded in your rarest self.

BALURDO. Truly, you speak wisely, and like a gentlewoman of fourteen years of age. You know the stone called *lapis*, the nearer it comes to the fire the hotter it is; and the bird which the geometricians call *avis*, the farther it is from the earth the nearer it is to the heaven; and love, the nigher it is to the flame the more remote – there's a word, 'remote' – the more remote it is from the frost. Your wit is quick, a little thing

---

125 *ignis fatuus*: will o' the wisp.
128 *ride*: with bawdy sense.
130 *walking rowels*: i.e. purely ornamental ones.
134–5 *E la*: highest note in the hexachord scale.
136 *Perfect*: (1) complete; (2) faultless.
136 *pricked*: written down (with bawdy quibble).
147–54 *You . . . frost*: euphuistic parody.
154 *thing*: bawdy *double entendre*; cf. Tilley, T189.

pleaseth a young lady, and a small favour contenteth an old courtier; and so, sweet mistress, I truss my codpiece point.

[*Sound a flourish.*] *Enter* FELICHE.

PIERO. What might import this flourish? Bring us word.

FELICHE. Stand away. [*Aside*] Here's such a company of fly-boats hulling about this galliass of greatness that there's no boarding him. [*To* PIERO] Do you hear yon thing called, duke?

PIERO. How now, blunt Feliche, what's the news?

FELICHE. Yonder's a knight hath brought
Andrugio's head,
And craves admittance to your chair of state.

Cornets sound a sennet; enter ANDRUGIO. *in armour.*

PIERO. Conduct him with attendance sumptuous,
Sound all the pleasing instruments of joy,
Make triumph stand on tiptoe whilst we meet;
O sight most gracious, O revenge most sweet!

ANDRUGIO. [*reading the letter*] *We vow by the honour of our birth to recompense any man that bringeth Andrugio's head with twenty thousand double pistolets and the endearing to our choicest love.*

PIERO. We still with most unmoved resolve
confirm
Our large munificence; and here breathe
A sad and solemn protestation:
When I recall this vow, O let our house
Be even commanded, stained and trampled on
As worthless rubbish of nobility.

ANDRUGIO. Then here, Piero, is Andrugio's head,
[*Raising his helmet.*]
Royally casquèd in a helm of steel;

---

157 *truss . . . point*: tie up my codpiece lace; i.e. withdraw from the flyting.
161 *fly-boats*: small, fast sailing-vessels.
161 *hulling*: drifting.
161 *galliass*: large war-vessel with sails and oars.
178 *sad*: serious.

Give me thy love, and take it. My dauntless soul
Hath that unbounded vigour in his spirits
That it can bear more rank indignity
With less impatience than thy cankered hate
Can sting and venom his untainted worth
With the most viperous sound of malice. Strike!
O, let no glimpse of honour light thy thoughts;
If there be any heat of royal breath
Creeping in thy veins, O stifle it.
Be still thyself, bloody and treacherous.
Fame not thy house with an admirèd act
Of princely pity. Piero, I am come
To soil thy house with an eternal blot
Of savage cruelty; strike, or bid me strike.
I pray my death, that thy ne'er-dying shame
Might live immortal to posterity.
Come, be a princely hangman, stop my breath.
O dread thou shame no more than I dread
death.

PIERO. We are amazed, our royal spirits numbed
In stiff astonished wonder at thy prowess,
Most mighty, valiant, and high-tow'ring heart.
We blush, and turn our hate upon ourselves
For hating such an unpeered excellence.
I joy my state, him whom I loathed before
That now I honour, love, nay more, adore.

The still flutes sound a mournful sennet. Enter [LUCIO *and Attendants with*] *a coffin.*

But stay; what tragic spectacle appears?
Whose body bear you in that mournful hearse?

LUCIO. The breathless trunk of young Antonio.

MELLIDA. Antonio, ay me, my lord, my love
my –

---

184 *it*: my head.
190 *glimpse*: flash.
207–8 *I joy . . . adore*: 'It pleases my majesty that he whom I loathed formerly, I now love' (Hunter).
208 s.d *still flutes*: flutes with a soft sound.
209 *tragic spectacle*: tragedies conventionally ended with the pageant spectacle of a funeral procession.
210 *hearse*: bier (usually with ornamented canopy).

ANDRUGIO. Sweet precious issue of most
honoured blood,
Rich hope, ripe virtue, O untimely loss!
[*To* LUCIO] Come hither, friend. Prithee do
not weep.
Why, I am glad he's dead; he shall not see
His father's vanquished by his enemy,
Even in princely honour; nay, prithee speak:
How died the wretched boy?

LUCIO. My lord –

ANDRUGIO. I hope he died yet like my son,
i'faith.

LUCIO. Alas, my lord.

ANDRUGIO. He died unforced, I trust, and
valiantly?

LUCIO. Poor gentleman, being –

ANDRUGIO. Did his hand shake or his eye look
dull,
His thoughts reel, fearful, when he struck the
stroke?
And if they did, I'll rend them out the hearse,
Rip up his cerecloth, mangle his bleak face,
That when he comes to heaven the powers divine
Shall ne'er take notice that he was my son.
I'll quite disclaim his birth; nay, prithee speak;
And 'twere not hooped with steel, my breast
would break.

MELLIDA. O that my spirit in a sigh could mount
Into the sphere where thy sweet soul doth rest!

PIERO. O that my tears, bedewing thy wan cheek,
Could make new spirit sprout in thy cold blood!

BALURDO. Verily, he looks as pitifully as a poor John; as I am true knight, I could weep like a stoned horse.

ANDRUGIO. [*to* PIERO] Villain, 'tis thou hast
murdered my son.
Thy unrelenting spirit – thou black dog,
That took'st no passion of his fatal love –

---

228 *cerecloth*: shroud, winding-sheet.
237–8 *poor John*: dried hake.
239 *stoned*: gelded.
242 *passion*: compassion.

Hath forced him give his life untimely end.
PIERO. O that my life, her love, my dearest blood,
Would but redeem one minute of his breath!
ANTONIO. [*rising from the coffin*] I seize that breath. Stand not amazed, great states:
I rise from death that never lived till now.
Piero, keep thy vow, and I enjoy
More unexpressèd height of happiness
Than power of thought can reach; if not, lo, here
There stands my tomb, and here a pleasing stage,
Most wished spectators of my tragedy;
To this end have I feigned: that her fair eye
For whom I lived, might bless me ere I die.
MELLIDA. Can breath depaint my unconceivèd thoughts?
Can words describe my infinite delight
Of seeing thee, my lord Antonio?
O no, conceit, breath, passion, words, be dumb,
Whilst I instill the dew of my sweet bliss
In the soft pressure of a melting kiss:
Sic, sic, iuvat ire sub umbras.
PIERO. Fair son – now I'll be proud to call thee son –
Enjoy me thus. [*Embraces* ANTONIO] My very breast is thine;
Possess me freely; I am wholly thine.
ANTONIO. Dear father.
ANDRUGIO. Sweet son, sweet son; I can speak no more;
My joy's passion flows above the shore

---

245 *seize*: claim legal possession of.
246 *states*: nobles.
247 *I rise*: Antonio stages a Resurrection by the Power of Love.
247 *never lived*: never knew the full meaning of life.
249 *unexpressèd*: inexpressible.
251–2 *stage . . . tragedy*: Marston toys with the idea of a reversible ending, such as Suckling subsequently supplied for *Aglaura*.
255 *depaint*: depict (an echo of the Painter scene).
261 *Sic . . . umbras*: 'Thus, thus it pleases me to descend into the world of shades' (*Aeneid*, IV, 660).

And chokes the current of my speech.
PIERO. Young Florence prince, to you my lips must beg
For a remittance of your interest.
GALEATZO. In your fair daughter? With all my thought.
So help me, faith, the naked truth I'll unfold;
He that was ne'er hot will soon be cold.
PIERO. No man else makes claim unto her?
MATZAGENTE. The valiant speak truth in brief: no.
BALURDO. Truly, for Sir Jeffrey Balurdo, he disclaims to have had anything in her.
PIERO. Then here I give her to Antonio.
[*To* ANDRUGIO] Royal, valiant, most respected prince,
Let's clip our hands. I'll thus observe my vow:
I promised twenty thousand double pistolets,
With the endearing to my dearest love,
To him that brought thy head; thine be the gold,
To solemnise our houses' unity.
My love be thine, the all I have be thine.
Fill us fresh wine, the form we'll take by this:
We'll drink a health while they two sip a kiss.
Now there remains no discord that can sound
Harsh accents to the ear of our accord,
So please you, niece, to match.
ROSSALINE. Troth, uncle, when my sweet-faced coz hath told me how she likes the thing called wedlock, maybe I'll take a survey of the check-roll of my servants; and he that hath the best parts of – I'll prick him down for my husband.
BALURDO. For passion of love now, remember me to my mistress, Lady Rossaline, when she is pricking down the good parts of her servants. As I am true knight, I grow stiff; I shall carry it.
PIERO. I will.

---

280 *clip*: clasp.
286 *form*: formal ratification.
293–4 *check-roll*: list.
295–9 *parts of . . . stiff*: bawdy *doubles entendres*.

Sound Lydian wires, once make a pleasing note,
On nectar streams of your sweet airs to float.
ANTONIO. Here ends the comic crosses of true love;
O may the passage most successful prove.
[*Exeunt all save* ANDRUGIO.]

Finis.

EPILOGUS

[ANDRUGIO *comes forward for the Epilogue.*]

Gentlemen, though I remain an armed Epilogue, I stand not as a peremptory challenger of desert, either for him that composed the comedy or for us that acted it, but a most submissive suppliant for both. What imperfection you have seen in us, leave with us and we'll amend it; what hath pleased you, take with you and cherish it. You shall not be more ready to embrace anything commendable than we will endeavour to amend all things reprovable. What we are, is by your favour. What we shall be, rests all in your applausive encouragements. *Exit.*

---

302 *Lydian*: the Lydian mode in classical Greek music was thought of as soft and effeminate.

304–5 *comic . . . prove*: perhaps a burlesque reminiscence of *Romeo and Juliet*'s 'star-cross'd lovers'; perhaps intended as an ominously ironic anticipation of *Antonio's Revenge*.

304 *crosses*: (1) afflictions; (2) cross-purposes.

305 *passage*: issue.

1–2 *armed . . . desert*: perhaps an implicit rebuke to Jonson for the belligerence of his armed Prologue in *Poetaster* (1601); if so, this Epilogue must have been a late addition.

11 *applausive encouragements*: encouragement of your applause – the traditional appeal of the classical epilogue.

ANTONIOS
Reuenge.

The second part.

As it hath beene sundry times acted, by the children of Paules.

Written by *I. Marston.*

LONDON
¶ Printed for *Thomas Fisher*, and are to be soulde in Saint Dunstans Church-yarde.
1602.

Title-page of the 1602 Quarto of *Antonio's Revenge* in the Bodleian Library, shelfmark Malone 252 (2)

INTRODUCTORY NOTE

Antonio's Revenge was entered in the Stationers' Register, together with *Antonio and Mellida*, on 24 October 1601. In the following year the two plays (or 'parts') were published in individual Quartos, discussed in the Introductory Note to *Antonio and Mellida* (pp. 3–4 above). The last act of *Antonio's Revenge* is especially well printed.

The two *Antonio* plays seem to have been written at much the same time: from internal evidence *Antonio and Mellida* can most plausibly be dated late 1599 or early 1600; and it is clear that 'a second part' was already in Marston's mind when he wrote the induction to that play (Ind. 163–8). Since *Antonio's Revenge* does not fulfil the promise made there to expand the parts of Galeatzo and Feliche, it can be assumed that a gap of at least some months separated the two plays; but in any event *Antonio's Revenge* must have been completed by late 1600 or early 1601, since the prologue clearly envisages a winter performance.

No true source has been discovered for the plot of Marston's tragedy, but, like many plays written for the knowing audience of the private theatres, it is dense with literary allusion. Striking resemblances in character and situation show that *Antonio's Revenge* has some connection with *Hamlet*; but the absence of close verbal parallels, together with uncertainties surrounding the date of *Hamlet* itself, make it difficult to determine the exact nature of the relationship. While earlier scholars generally supposed that Shakespeare had borrowed from Marston's play, the two most recent editors of *Antonio's Revenge* have argued that both dramatists were drawing on a lost older play, the so-called *Ur-Hamlet*, usually attributed to Thomas Kyd, which seems to have been in existence by 1589. Gair even proposes that the two companies concerned 'may have agreed to co-operate on a play of a similar kind, written, however, from the different viewpoints of boy and adult actor, to form a united challenge to their common rival, the Children of the Chapel' (p. 16). But if both dramatists had been reworking the same original, we might expect a more consistent parallelism between the two plots than actually exists. More persuasive arguments are advanced by the latest *Hamlet* editor,

Harold Jenkins, for believing that it was actually Marston who borrowed from Shakespeare: having shown that a version of Shakespeare's *Hamlet* 'was being acted . . . just possibly even before the end of 1599 and certainly in the course of 1600', he goes on to demonstrate, through a telling series of minor verbal echoes, that Marston must have been familiar with it and that it must have differed little from the published version that we know (Arden edn, 1982, pp. 7–13). The echoes of *Hamlet* that Jenkins finds in *Antonio's Revenge* are indeed precisely the kind we should expect if Marston had seen Shakespeare's play, perhaps more than once, but not yet been able to read it – in this respect they contrast significantly with the more exact recollections of *Hamlet* in *The Malcontent* (1603). The influence of current stage success might well explain why Marston should have rather suddenly departed from his original plan for the second part of his diptych.

Antonio's Revenge was written, like *Antonio and Mellida*, for the Paul's Boys and staged at their small indoor theatre in the precincts of St Paul's Cathedral. As the chief occasion for Jonson's scornful attacks on Marston in *Poetaster* (1601) the play has its place in the so-called Poetomachia, or War of the Theatres, apparently provoked by the extravagant success of a second boy company, the Chapel Children (Hamlet's eyrie of little eyases) in their Blackfriars playhouse. It was to this new company, who already made use of Ben Jonson, that Marston was later to transfer his allegiance. Although *Antonio's Revenge* was successful enough to invite Jonson's special fury, its stage life was brief. Unlike others of Marston's plays, it does not appear to have been performed again in his lifetime; and the only subsequent attempt to revive the play in a professional context has been Peter Barnes's condensed radio version of the two parts (1977), later readapted for the stage in a 1979 Nottingham Playhouse production (see above, pp. 5–6).

[DRAMATIS PERSONAE

THE GHOST OF ANDRUGIO, *lately Duke of Genoa*
ANTONIO, *his son, betrothed to* MELLIDA
PIERO SFORZA, *Duke of Venice*
GASPAR STROTZO, *his accomplice*
JULIO, *son to* PIERO
BALURDO
ALBERTO
CASTILIO BALTHAZAR
FOROBOSCO
PANDULPHO FELICHE
} *gentlemen of* PIERO*'s court*
GALEATZO, *son to the Duke of Florence*
MATZAGENTE, *son to the Duke of Milan*
LUCIO, *servant to* MARIA
TWO SENATORS *of Venice*
MELLIDA, *daughter to* PIERO
MARIA, *mother to* ANTONIO
NUTRICHE, *nurse to* MARIA
A HERALD
TWO MOURNERS
LADIES
PAGES
ATTENDANTS
COURTIERS]

Dramatis Personae: based on Hunter.
SFORZA, BALURDO, CASTILIO BALTHAZAR, FOROBOSCO, MATZAGENTE, MELLIDA: see notes to *Dramatis Personae* of *AM*, p. 8 above.
STROTZO: from Italian *strozzare* = 'strangle' (Q sometimes spells 'Strozzo').
NUTRICHE: Italian, 'a nurse, a foster-mother' (Florio).

THE PROLOGUE

The rawish dank of clumsy winter ramps
The fluent summer's vein, and drizzling sleet
Chilleth the wan bleak cheek of the numbed earth,
Whilst snarling gusts nibble the juiceless leaves
From the nak'd shudd'ring branch, and pills the skin
From off the soft and delicate aspects.
O now, methinks, a sullen tragic scene
Would suit the time with pleasing congruence.
May we be happy in our weak devoir,
And all part pleased in most wished content
– But sweat of Hercules can ne'er beget
So blest an issue. Therefore we proclaim,
If any spirit breathes within this round
Uncapable of weighty passion
(As from his birth being huggèd in the arms
And nuzzled 'twixt the breasts of happiness),
Who winks and shuts his apprehension up
From common sense of what men were, and are,
Who would not know what men must be – let such
Hurry amain from our black-visaged shows;
We shall affright their eyes. But if a breast
Nailed to the earth with grief, if any heart

---

1 *clumsy*: benumbed (*OED*).
1 *ramps*: 'ramp' = either trample in triumph (*OED*, *vb.*[1]3b). or snatch, tear, pluck (*OED*, *vb.*[2]1).
2 *fluent*: flowing (with sap).
5 *pills*: strips.
6 *aspects*: appearances; hence surfaces.
7 *sullen tragic scene*: referring to both the tragic drama itself and the black hangings that customarily draped the stage for tragic performances (see below, line 20).
8 *congruence*: appropriateness, decorum.
9 *May . . . devoir*: may we be fortunate in the weak performance of our duty.
11 *Hercules*: cf. *Malc.*, II.v.8 and IV.v.59–61.
13 *round*: amphitheatre; or perhaps, by extension, any theatre; cf. 'ring' below (23).
14 *Uncapable of*: unable to endure.
17 *winks*: shuts his eyes.

Pierced through with anguish, pant within this
ring,
If there be any blood whose heat is choked
And stifled with true sense of misery,
If aught of these strains fill this consort up,
Th' arrive most welcome. O that our power
Could lackey or keep wing with our desires,
That with unusèd peise of style and sense
We might weigh massy in judicious scale!
Yet here's the prop that doth support our hopes:
When our scenes falter, or invention halts,
Your favour will give crutches to our faults. *Exit.*

---

26 *consort*: a combination of musical instruments.
28 *lackey*: attend closely upon.
29 *unusèd peise*: more than usual weight.
30 *weigh . . . scale*: our play might be considered solid and weighty by discriminating viewers.

ANTONIO'S REVENGE THE SECOND PART OF THE HISTORY OF ANTONIO AND MELLIDA

ACT I

SCENE I

Enter PIERO *unbraced, his arms bare, smeared in blood, a poniard in one hand, bloody, and a torch in the other,* STROTZO *following him with a cord.*

PIERO. Ho, Gaspar Strotzo, bind Feliche's trunk
Unto the panting side of Mellida.
Exit STROTZO.
'Tis yet dead night, yet all the earth is clutched
In the dull leaden hand of snoring sleep;
No breath disturbs the quiet of the air;
No spirit moves upon the breast of earth,
Save howling dogs, nightcrows, and screeching owls,
Save meagre ghosts, Piero, and black thoughts.
[*Clock strikes.*]
One, two. Lord, in two hours what a topless mount
Of unpeered mischief have these hands cast up!
I can scarce coop triumphing vengeance up
From bursting forth in braggart passion.

1.i s.d. *unbraced*: with clothes unfastened.
3 *dead night*: dead of night.
9 *topless mount*: unrivalled heap.
10 *unpeered*: unequalled.
11–12 *I can . . . braggart passion*: 'braggart passion' is exactly what Piero has been indulging; the absurd self-contradiction, combined with the high-pitched ranting of the boy actor may have been intended to give a touch of burlesque to this extravagant opening.

Enter STROTZO.

STROTZO. My lord, 'tis firmly said that –
PIERO. Andrugio sleeps in peace; this brain hath choked
The organ of his breast. Feliche hangs
But as a bait upon the line of death
To 'tice on mischief. I am great in blood,
Unequalled in revenge. You horrid scouts
That sentinel swart night, give loud applause
From your large palms. First know my heart was raised
Unto Andrugio's life upon this ground –
STROTZO. Duke, 'tis reported –
PIERO. We both were rivals in our May of blood
Unto Maria, fair Ferrara's heir.
He won the lady, to my honour's death,
And from her sweets cropped this Antonio;
For which I burnt in inward swelt'ring hate,
And festered rankling malice in my breast,
Till I might belch revenge upon his eyes.
And now (O blessèd now!) 'tis done. Hell, night,
Give loud applause to my hypocrisy.
When his bright valour even dazzled sense
In off'ring his own head, public reproach
Had blurred my name – Speak, Strotzo, had it not –
If then I had –
STROTZO. It had, so please –
PIERO. What had, so please? Unseasoned sycophant,

---

18 *scouts*: spies; 'Piero seems to be referring to the constellations' (Gair).
20–1 *raised . . . ground*: driven to take Andrugio's life by this motive.
36–7 *It had . . . What had*: Strotzo's attempts to interrupt Piero's self-delighting reveries become increasingly comic.
37 *Unseasoned*: impertinent, speaking out of turn.

Piero Sforza is no numbèd lord,
Senseless of all true touch; stroke not the head
Of infant speech till it be fully born.
Go to!

STROTZO. How now? Fut! I'll not smother your speech.

PIERO. Nay, right thine eyes; 'twas but a little spleen.
[*Aside*] Huge plunge!
Sin's grown a slave, and must observe slight evils;
Huge villains are enforced to claw all devils.
[*To* STROTZO] Pish! Sweet thy thoughts, and give me –

STROTZO. 'Stroke not the head of infant speech'! Go to!

PIERO. Nay, calm this storm. I ever held thy breast
More secret and more firm in league of blood
Than to be struck in heat with each slight puff.
Give me thy ears: huge infamy
Press down my honour if even then,
When his fresh act of prowess bloomed out full,
I had ta'en vengeance on his hated head –

STROTZO. Why it had –

PIERO. Could I avoid to give a seeming grant
Unto fruition of Antonio's love?

STROTZO. No.

PIERO. And didst thou ever see a Judas kiss
With a more covert touch of fleering hate?

STROTZO. No.

---

44 *Huge plunge*: vast humiliation; i.e. in having to pay attention to the 'slight evil' (petty villain), Strotzo.
46 *claw*: flatter; 'scratch the backs of'.
51 *struck in heat*: angered.
51 *puff*: boast; quibble on the idea of wind stirring the heat of a fire.
52–61 *huge . . . hate*: refers to the events surrounding Antonio's marriage at the end of *Antonio and Mellida*.
61 *fleering*: sneering.

PIERO. And having clipped them with pretence of love
Have I not crushed them with a cruel wring?
STROTZO. Yes.
PIERO. Say, faith, didst thou e'er hear, or read, or see
Such happy vengeance, unsuspected death?
That I should drop strong poison in the bowl
Which I myself caroused unto his health
And future fortune of our unity;
That it should work even in the hush of night
And strangle him on sudden, that fair show
Of death for the excessive joy of his fate
Might choke the murder! Ha, Strotzo, is't not rare?
Nay, but weigh it – then Feliche stabbed
(Whose sinking thought frighted my conscious heart)
And laid by Mellida, to stop the match,
And hale on mischief; this all in one night!
Is't to be equalled, think'st thou? O, I could eat
Thy fumbling throat for thy lagged censure. Fut!
Is't not rare?
STROTZO. Yes.
PIERO. No! Yes! Nothing but 'no' and 'yes', dull lump?
Canst thou not honey me with fluent speech
And even adore my topless villainy?
Will I not blast my own blood for revenge?
Must not thou straight be perjured for revenge?
And yet no creature dream 'tis my revenge?
Will I not turn a glorious bridal morn

---

63 *clipped*: embraced.
68–74 *That . . . murder*: the wine with which Andrugio was invited to seal the union of their houses (*AM*, V.ii.286–7) was poisoned. Jenkins finds an echo of *Hamlet*, V.ii.264, 281.
74 *choke*: suppress.
76 *sinking*: deep sounding, penetrating.
76 *conscious*: conscience-plagued.
80 *lagged censure*: slowness to express approving judgement.
84 *honey*: flatter.

Unto a Stygian night? Yet naught but 'no' and
'yes'?

STROTZO. I would have told you, if the incubus
That rides your bosom would have patience,
It is reported that in private state
Maria, Genoa's duchess, makes to court,
Longing to see him whom she ne'er shall see,
Her lord, Andrugio. Belike she hath received
The news of reconciliation:
Reconciliation with a death!
Poor lady, shall but find poor comfort in't.

PIERO. O, let me swoon for joy! By heaven, I
think
I ha' said my prayers within this month at least,
I am so boundless happy. Doth she come?
By this warm reeking gore, I'll marry her.
Look I not now like an inamorate?
Poison the father, butcher the son, and marry
the mother, ha!
Strotzo, to bed: snort in securest sleep;
For see, the dapple-grey coursers of the morn
Beat up the light with their bright silver hooves
And chase it through the sky. To bed, to bed!
This morn my vengeance shall be amply fed.

Ex[*eunt.*]

SCENE II

Enter LUCIO, MARIA, *and* NUTRICHE.

MARIA. Stay, gentle Lucio, and vouchsafe thy
hand.

LUCIO. O, madam!

MARIA. Nay, prithee give me leave to say
'vouchsafe'.

---

91 *incubus*: demon of nightmare (i.e. Piero's obsessive passion of revenge).

104 *inamorate*: lover.

105 *Poison . . . ha!*: the extravagant self-delight again invites burlesque.

108 *beat up*: rouse, drive (used of game).

1 *vouchsafe*: condescend to grant (*OED*).

Submiss entreats beseem my humble fate.
Here let us sit. O, Lucio, fortune's gilt
Is rubbed quite off from my slight tinfoiled state,
And poor Maria must appear ungraced
Of the bright fulgor of glossed majesty.
LUCIO. Cheer up your spirits, madam; fairer chance
Than that which courts your presence instantly
Cannot be formed by the quick mould of thought.
MARIA. Art thou assured the dukes are reconciled?
Shall my womb's honour wed fair Mellida?
Will heaven at length grant harbour to my head?
Shall I once more clip my Andrugio,
And wreathe my arms about Antonio's neck?
Or is glib rumour grown a parasite,
Holding a false glass to my sorrow's eyes,
Making the wrinkled front of grief seem fair,
Though 'tis much rivelled with abortive care?
LUCIO. Most virtuous princess, banish straggling fear;
Keep league with comfort, for these eyes beheld
The dukes united; yon faint glimmering light
Ne'er peepèd through the crannies of the east
Since I beheld them drink a sound carouse
In sparkling Bacchus unto each other's health,
Your son assured to beauteous Mellida,
And all clouds cleared of threat'ning discontent.
MARIA. What age is morning of?
LUCIO. I think 'bout five.
MARIA. Nutriche, Nutriche! [*Shaking her.*]

---

4 *Submiss entreats*: submissive entreaties.
8 *fulgor*: Latin, splendour, brightness.
9–11 *fairer . . . thought*: it would be impossible to imagine more fortunate circumstances than those which have brought you here to court.
19 *front*: forehead.
20 *rivelled*: wrinkled.
21 *straggling*: which makes you hang back.
23 *glimmering light*: a connection is ironically implied between the coming dawn and the happy world promised by the ending of *AM*, its 'clouds cleared' (line 28).
26 *Bacchus*: god of wine; hence wine itself.

NUTRICHE. Beshrew your fingers! Marry, you have disturbed the pleasure of the finest dream. O God! I was even coming to it, la. O Jesu! 'twas coming of the sweetest. I'll tell you now, methought I was married, and methought I spent (O lord, why did you wake me?) and methought I spent three spur-royals on the fiddlers for striking up a fresh hornpipe. Saint Ursula, I was even going to bed – and you – methought my husband was even putting out the tapers – when you – Lord, I shall never have such a dream come upon me as long as –

MARIA. Peace, idle creature, peace! When will the court rise?

LUCIO. Madam, 'twere best you took some lodging up
And lay in private till the soil of grief
Were cleared your cheek, and new-burnished lustre
Clothed your presence, 'fore you saw the dukes
And entered 'mong the proud Venetian states.

MARIA. No, Lucio; my dear lord's wise and knows
That tinsel glitter or rich purfled robes,
Curled hairs hung full of sparkling carcanets,
Are not the true adornments of a wife.
So long as wives are faithful, modest, chaste,
Wise lords affect them. Virtue doth not waste
With each slight flame of crackling vanity.

---

31 ff. Nutriche's garrulous style recalls the Nurse in *Romeo and Juliet*; the bawdy reworking of Shakespeare is probably meant to have an ironic effect.

37 *spur-royals*: gold coins then worth fifteen shillings.

38 *hornpipe*: bawdy *double entendre*.

38 *Saint Ursula*: British saint known for her dreams 'in which she foresaw her approaching martyrdom; perhaps also (ironically) because she was the leader of 11,000 virgins' (Hunter).

49 *Venetian states*: nobles of Venice.

51 *purfled*: embroidered.

52 *carcanets*: ornamental chains (usually of gold), set with jewels.

55 *affect*: love.

56 *crackling*: full of empty noise.

A modest eye forceth affection,
Whilst outward gayness light looks but entice.
Fairer than nature's fair is foulest vice.
She that loves art to get her cheek more lovers,
Much outward gauds, slight inward grace, discovers.
I care not to seem fair but to my lord.
Those that strive most to please most strangers' sight,
Folly may judge most fair, wisdom most light.
Music sounds a short strain.
But hark, soft music gently moves the air;
I think the bridegroom's up. Lucio, stand close.
O now, Maria, challenge grief to stay
Thy joy's encounter. Look, Lucio, 'tis clear day.
[*They retire to the rear of the stage.*]

Enter ANTONIO, GALEATZO, MATZAGENTE, BALURDO, PANDULPHO FELICHE, ALBERTO, CASTILIO, *and a Page.*

ANTONIO. Darkness is fled: look, infant morn hath drawn
Bright silver curtains 'bout the couch of night,
And now Aurora's horse trots azure rings,
Breathing fair light about the firmament.
Stand! What's that?
MATZAGENTE. And if a hornèd devil should burst forth
I would pass on him with a mortal stock.
ALBERTO. O, a horned devil would prove ominous
Unto a bridegroom's eyes.
MATZAGENTE. A horned devil! Good, good; ha, ha, ha! Very good!

---

61 *gauds*: showy ornaments, vanities (with connotations of deceit).
64 *light*: immoral (with a quibble on light-coloured, fair).
71 *Aurora's . . . rings*: 'The horse of the dawn [goddess] runs round the azure arena of the sky' (Hunter).
74 *And if*: even if.
75 *pass . . . stock*: strike at him with a deadly thrust.
76 *horned*: alluding to the cuckold's horns.

ALBERTO. Good tanned prince, laugh not. By the joys of love,
When thou dost grin, thy rusty face doth look
Like the head of a roasted rabbit. Fie upon't!

BALURDO. By my troth, methinks his nose is just colour *de roi*.

MATZAGENTE. I tell thee, fool, my nose will abide no jest.

BALURDO. No, in truth, I do not jest; I speak truth. Truth is the touchstone of all things; and if your nose will not abide the truth, your nose will not abide the touch; and if your nose will not abide the touch, your nose is a copper nose and must be nailed up for a slip.

MATZAGENTE. I scorn to retort the obtuse jest of a fool.

BALURDO *draws out his writing tables and writes.*

BALURDO. 'Retort' and 'obtuse'; good words, very good words.

GALEATZO. Young prince, look sprightly; fie, a bridegroom sad!

BALURDO. In truth, if he were retort and obtuse, no question he would be merry; but, and please my genius, I will be most retort and obtuse ere night. I'll tell you what I'll bear soon at night in my shield for my device.

---

81 *rusty*: cf. 'tanned' (79) and 'colour *de roi*' (84); here with suggestion of rottenness and decay; 'perhaps an indication that the boys were using cosmetics for make-up' (Gair).

84 *colour de roi*: according to Cotgrave's *Dictionary* (1611), originally purple, 'though usurped at this day by a kind of bright tawny'.

89 *touch*: test for gold by applying the touchstone.

91 *nailed . . . slip*: nailed to the counter like a counterfeit coin (Wood). The suggestion throughout this speech is that Matzagente may be wearing a false nose because of the ravages of venereal disease.

92 s.d. *writing tables*: notebook carried by aspirant wits (cf. *Malc.*, Ind. 22). Balurdo, like Osric in *Hamlet*, caricatures the Elizabethan appetite for new-coined words, a taste for which Jonson mocked Marston himself in *Poetaster*.

98 *and please*: if it please.

101 *device*: heraldic emblem.

GALEATZO. What, good Balurdo?
BALURDO. O, do me right; *Sir* Jeffrey Balurdo –
Sir, *Sir*, as long as ye live, *Sir*.
GALEATZO. What, good Sir Jeffrey Balurdo?
BALURDO. Marry, forsooth, I'll carry for my device my grandfather's great stone-horse flinging up his head and jerking out his left leg: the word, *Wehee Purt*. As I am a true knight, will't not be most retort and obtuse, ha?
ANTONIO. Blow hence these sapless jests. I tell you, bloods,
My spirit's heavy and the juice of life
Creeps slowly through my stiffened arteries.
Last sleep my sense was steeped in horrid dreams:
Three parts of night were swallowed in the gulf
Of ravenous time when to my slumb'ring powers
Two meagre ghosts made apparition.
The one's breast seemed fresh paunched with bleeding wounds
Whose bubbling gore sprang in frighted eyes.
The other ghost assumed my father's shape.
Both cried, 'Revenge!', at which my trembling joints
(Icèd quite over with a frozed cold sweat)

---

103 *do me right*: recalls the song at his mock-knighting (*AM*, V.II.29–31): 'Do me right,/ And dub me knight,/ Balurdo.'

107 *stone-horse*: stallion (*OED*); the 'great horse' was the charger or war-horse used by knights in tournament and battle.

109 *word* motto

109 *Wehee Purt*: imitating the whinny and snort of a horse.

111 *bloods*: gallants.

114 *dreams*: the persistent dreaming motif in this scene helps to create a phantasmagoric atmosphere for the whole play.

118 *paunched*: stabbed.

119 *gore*: the metre requires a disyllabic pronunciation that relishes the word.

120 *assumed my father's shape*: cf. *Hamlet*, I.ii.243, 'If it assume my noble father's person'.

121–5 *at which . . . stand*: imitates Virgil, *Aeneid*, III, 174–5, and VI, 699–700.

Leapt forth the sheets. Three times I grasped at shades,
And thrice, deluded by erroneous sense,
I forced my thoughts make stand; when, lo, I oped
A large bay window, through which the night
Struck terror to my soul. The verge of heaven
Was ringed with flames and all the upper vault
Thick-laced with flakes of fire; in midst whereof
A blazing comet shot his threat'ning train
Just on my face. Viewing these prodigies
I bowed my naked knee and pierced the star
With an outfacing eye, pronouncing thus:
Deus imperat astris. At which my nose straight bled;
Then doubled I my word, so slunk to bed.

BALURDO. Verily, Sir Jeffrey had a monstrous strange dream the last night; for methought I dreamt I was asleep, and methought the ground yawned and belched up the abominable ghost of a misshapen Simile, with two ugly pages, the one called Master Even-as, going before, and the other Monsieur Even-so, following after, whilst Signor Simile stalked most prodigiously in the midst; at which I bewrayed the fearfulness of my nature, and, being ready to forsake the fortress of my wit, start up, called for a clean shirt, ate a mess of broth, and with that I awaked.

ANTONIO. I prithee, peace. I tell you, gentlemen,
The frightful shades of night yet shake my brain;
My gellied blood's not thawed; the sulphur damps

---

130 *threat'ning*: comets were considered evil portents (cf. *The Revenger's Tragedy*, V.iii.1–27).

134 *Deus . . . astris*: 'God rules the stars.'

134 *nose . . . bled*: another bad omen.

135 *doubled . . . word*: repeated my motto.

144–5 *bewrayed . . . nature*: betrayed my fear (by shitting myself); the burlesque is perhaps intended to pre-empt any audience mockery of Antonio's extravagant rhetoric.

151 *gellied*: both 'jellied' = congealed and 'gelid' (linking 'shake' and 'thawed').

That flow in wingèd lightning 'bout my couch
Yet stick within my sense; my soul is great
In expectation of dire prodigies.
PANDULPHO. Tut, my young prince, let not thy fortunes see
Their lord a coward. He that's nobly born
Abhors to fear; base fear's the brand of slaves.
He that observes, pursues, slinks back for fright,
Was never cast in mould of noble spright.
GALEATZO. Tush, there's a sun will straight exhale these damps
Of chilling fear. Come, shall's salute the bride?
ANTONIO. Castilio, I prithee mix thy breath with his.
Sing one of Signor Renaldo's airs
To rouse the slumb'ring bride from gluttoning
In surfeit of superfluous sleep. Good signor, sing.

Cantant [GALEATZO *and* CASTILIO].

What means this silence and unmovèd calm?
Boy, wind thy cornet; force the leaden gates
Of lazy sleep fly open with thy breath.
My Mellida not up, not stirring yet? Umh!

[LUCIO, MARIA, *and* NUTRICHE *come forward.*]

MARIA. That voice should be my son's, Antonio's.
Antonio!
ANTONIO. Here. Who calls? Here stands Antonio.
MARIA. Sweet son!
ANTONIO. Dear mother!
MARIA. Fair honour of a chaste and loyal bed,
Thy father's beauty, thy sad mother's love,
Were I as powerful as the voice of fate,
Felicity complete should sweet thy state;

---

153 *great*: pregnant.
160 *sun*: i.e. Mellida.
160 *exhale*: evaporate.
163 *Signor Renaldo*: Hunter suggests that this is a direction to perform a song by the Paduan composer Giulio Renaldi (*fl.* 1569).
165 s.d. *Cantant*: they sing.
167 *wind*: blow.
178 *sweet*: sweeten.

But all the blessings that a banished wretch
Can pour upon thy head, take, gentle son;
Live, gracious youth, to close thy mother's eyes,
Loved of thy parents till their latest hour.
How cheers my lord, thy father? O, sweet boy,
Part of him thus I clip, my dear, dear joy.
[*They embrace.*]

ANTONIO. Madam, last night I kissed his princely hand
And took a treasured blessing from his lips.
O mother, you arrive in jubilee
And firm atonement of all boist'rous rage:
Pleasure, united love, protested faith,
Guard my loved father as sworn pensioners;
The dukes are leagued in firmest bond of love
And you arrive even in the solsticy
And highest point of sunshine happiness.
One winds a cornet within.
Hark, madam, how yon cornet jerketh up
His strained shrill accents in the capering air,
As proud to summon up my bright-cheeked love.
Now, mother, ope wide expectation;
Let loose your amplest sense to entertain
Th'impression of an object of such worth
That life's too poor to –

GALEATZO. Nay, leave hyperboles.

ANTONIO. I tell thee, prince, that presence straight appears
Of which thou canst not form hyperboles;
The trophy of triumphing excellence
The heart of beauty, Mellida, appears.
See, look, the curtain stirs; shine, nature's pride,
Love's vital spirit, dear Antonio's bride!

---

188 *atonement*: reconciliation.

190 *pensioners*: guards paid a regular pension or salary (cf. Queen Elizabeth's Gentlemen Pensioners).

192 *solsticy*: solstice, point at which the sun is furthest from the equator.

The curtain's drawn, and the body of FELICHE, *stabbed thick with wounds, appears hung up.*

What villain bloods the window of my love?
What slave hath hung yon gory ensign up,
In flat defiance of humanity?
Awake, thou fair unspotted purity,
Death's at thy window! Awake, bright Mellida!
Antonio calls.

Enter PIERO *as at first, with* FOROBOSCO.

PIERO. Who gives these ill-befitting attributes
Of chaste, unspotted, bright, to Mellida?
He lies as loud as thunder: she's unchaste,
Tainted, impure, black as the soul of hell.

He [ANTONIO] *draws his rapier, offers to run at* PIERO, *but* MARIA *holds his arm and stays him.*

ANTONIO. Dog, I will make thee eat thy vomit up,
Which thou hast belched 'gainst taintless Mellida.
PIERO. Ram't quickly down that it may not rise up
To embraid my thoughts. Behold my stomach's –
Strike me quite through with the relentless edge
Of raging fury. Boy, I'll kill thy love.
Pandulph Feliche, I have stabbed thy son;
Look, yet his life-blood reeks upon this steel.
Albert, yon hangs thy friend. Have none of you
Courage of vengeance? Forget I am your duke.
Think Mellida is not Piero's blood.
Imagine on slight ground I'll blast his honour.
Suppose I saw not that incestuous slave

---

207 s.d. *The curtain's drawn . . . hung up*: Gair (p. 19) suggests that the body is discovered, like Horatio's in *The Spanish Tragedy*, hanging 'in an arbour'; attractive as this suggestion is, lines 206–12 seem to indicate that the body hangs in one of the windows of the tiring-house façade (as indeed Gair's own footnote on this passage assumes); cf. V.iii.49 s.d.

213 s.d. *Enter* PIERO . . . *first*: as in I.i: 'unbraced, his arms bare, smeared in blood', etc.

221 *embraid*: upbraid.

221 *stomach's* –: aposiopesis to suggest incoherent rage.

230 *incestuous*: hyperbole for 'lecherous'.

Clipping the strumpet with luxurious twines.
O, numb my sense of anguish, cast my life
In a dead sleep whilst law cuts off yon maim,
Yon putrid ulcer of my royal blood.

FOROBOSCO. Keep league with reason, gracious sovereign.

PIERO. There glow no sparks of reason in the world;
All are raked up in ashy beastliness.
The bulk of man's as dark as Erebus;
No branch of reason's light hangs in his trunk;
There lives no reason to keep league withal;
I ha' no reason to be reasonable.
Her wedding eve, linked to the noble blood
Of my most firmly reconcilèd friend,
And found even clinged in sensuality!
O heaven! O heaven! Were she as near my heart
As is my liver, I would rend her off.

Enter STROTZO.

STROTZO. Whither, O whither shall I hurl vast grief?

PIERO. Here, into my breast; 'tis a place built wide
By fate to give receipt to boundless woes.

STROTZO. O no; here throb those hearts which I must cleave
With my keen piercing news. Andrugio's dead.

PIERO. Dead?

MARIA. O me most miserable!

PIERO. Dead! alas, how dead?

Give seeming passion.

---

231 *luxurious twines*: lustful embraces.
233 *maim*: blemish.
236 *sparks of reason*: Piero is made to use the neo-Stoical language of Marston's own satires in ironic justification of his villainy; 'spark of reason' recalls the *synteresis*, or spark of divine fire invoked in *SV*, Satire VIII, 211–14.
238 *Erebus*: hell.
239 *branch*: arm of a chandelier.
239 *trunk*: body.
254 s.d. *Give seeming passion*: presumably an exaggeratedly theatrical style is required, as Piero puts on his act; the histrionic partnership of Piero and Strotzo appears to be modelled on that of Richard and Buckingham in *Richard III*.

[*Aside*] Fut! weep, act, feign.
– Dead! alas, how dead?
STROTZO. The vast delights of his large sudden joys
Opened his powers so wide that's native heat
So prodigally flowed t'exterior parts
That th'inner citadel was left unmanned,
And so surprised on sudden by cold death.
MARIA. O, fatal, disastrous, cursèd, dismal!
Choke breath and life. I breathe, I live too long.
Andrugio, my lord, I come, I come. [*Swoons.*]
PIERO. Be cheerful, princess; help, Castilio,
The lady's swoonèd; help to bear her in.
Slow comfort to huge cares is swiftest sin.
BALURDO. Courage, courage, sweet lady; 'tis Sir Jeffrey Balurdo bids you courage. Truly, I am as nimble as an elephant, about a lady.
[*Exeunt* PIERO *and* FOROBOSCO, *with* CASTILIO *and* BALURDO *bearing out* MARIA, *and* LUCIO *and* NUTRICHE *in attendance.*]
PANDULPHO. Dead!
ANTONIO. Dead!
ALBERTO. Dead!
ANTONIO. Why, now the womb of mischief is delivered
Of the prodigious issue of the night.
PANDULPHO. Ha, ha, ha!
ANTONIO. My father dead, my love attaint of lust –
That's a large lie, as vast as spacious hell.
Poor guiltless lady. O, accursèd lie!

258–60 *Opened . . . unmanned*: so released his emotional energies that all the natural heat of his body rushed to its outward parts, leaving the heart fatally cold; by a quibble 'powers' links with the military metaphor in 'citadel'.

267 *Slow . . . sin*: to bring slow comfort to the greatly afflicted is a quick way to sin.

275 *prodigious*: monstrous.

276 *Ha, ha, ha*: recalls the mad laughter of Titus in *Titus Andronicus*, III.i.265.

What, whom, whither, which shall I first lament?
A dead father, a dishonoured wife. Stand!
Methinks I feel the frame of nature shake.
Cracks not the joints of earth to bear my woes?
ALBERTO. Sweet prince, be patient.
ANTONIO. 'Slid, sir, I will not, in despite of thee.
Patience is slave to fools, a chain that's fixed
Only to posts and senseless log-like dolts.
ALBERTO. 'Tis reason's glory to command affects.
ANTONIO. Lies thy cold father dead, his glossèd eyes
New closèd up by thy sad mother's hands?
Hast thou a love, as spotless as the brow
Of clearest heaven, blurred with false defames?
Are thy moist entrails crumpled up with grief
Of parching mischiefs? Tell me, does thy heart
With punching anguish spur thy gallèd ribs?
Then come, let's sit and weep and wreathe our arms;
I'll hear thy counsel.
ALBERTO. Take comfort.
ANTONIO. Confusion to all comfort! I defy it.
Comfort's a parasite, a flatt'ring Jack,
And melts resolved despair. O boundless woe,
If there be any black yet unknown grief,
If there be any horror yet unfelt,
Unthought-of mischief in thy fiendlike power,
Dash it upon my miserable head;
Make me more wretch, more cursèd if thou canst –
O, now my fate is more than I could fear,
My woes more weighty than my soul can bear.
Exit.

---

280 *What, whom, whither, which*: perhaps imitated from *The Spanish Tragedy*, III.ii.22–3.

282 *frame . . . shake*: Antonio feels the earth quake in sympathy with his woes; an implicit s.d.

285 *'Slid*: God's lid (eyelid).

289 *glossèd*: shining; or glazed (*OED*, citing this passage).

292 *blurred*: defiled.

296 *wreathe*: either 'fold' (as a sign of melancholy) or 'intertwine' (as a sign of friendship); see below, IV.ii.110, 110 s.d., 118 s.d.

298–301 *comfort . . . despair*: cf. *Richard II*, II.ii.67–72.

PANDULPHO. Ha, ha, ha!
ALBERTO. Why laugh you, uncle? That's my coz, your son,
Whose breast hangs casèd in his cluttered gore.
PANDULPHO. True, man, true. Why, wherefore should I weep?
Come sit, kind nephew; come on; thou and I
Will talk as chorus to this tragedy.
Entreat the music strain their instruments
With a slight touch whilst we – Say on, fair coz.
ALBERTO. He was the very hope of Italy,
Music sounds softly.
The blooming honour of your drooping age.
PANDULPHO. True, coz, true. They say that men of hope are crushed,
Good are suppressed by base desertless clods,
That stifle gasping virtue. Look, sweet youth,
How provident our quick Venetians are
Lest hooves of jades should trample on my boy;
Look how they lift him up to eminence,
Heave him 'bove reach of flesh. Ha, ha, ha!
ALBERTO. Uncle, this laughter ill becomes your grief.
PANDULPHO. Wouldst have me cry, run raving up and down
For my son's loss? Wouldst have me turn rank mad,
Or wring my face with mimic action,

---

311 *cluttered*: clotted.
313–14 *sit . . . tragedy*: this piece of theatrical self-consciousness recalls *The Spanish Tragedy*, I.i.90–1.
316 *With a slight touch*: gently; the music should continue until the end of the scene (see line 354), emphasising the operatic quality of its laments.
320 *desertless clods*: undeserving oafs (but 'clods' is also metaphoric: hence 'crushed', 'stifled').
323 *jades*: nags.
327–31 *Wouldst . . . player-like*: again the self-conscious reference to the traditional extravagance of tragic acting probably recalls *The Spanish Tragedy* (e.g. III.vii.1 ff.); but an echo of *Hamlet* may also be involved (I.ii.84, II.ii.544–6, III.ii.11–14).
328 *rank*: completely (cf. 'rank folly').
329 *wring*: contort.

Stamp, curse, weep, rage, and then my bosom
    strike?
Away, 'tis apish action, player-like.
If he is guiltless, why should tears be spent?
Thrice-blessèd soul that dieth innocent.
If he is lepered with so foul a guilt,
Why should a sigh be lent, a tear be spilt?
The gripe of chance is weak to wring a tear
From him that knows what fortitude should bear.
Listen, young blood, 'tis not true valour's pride
To swagger, quarrel, swear, stamp, rave, and
    chide,
To stab in fume of blood, to keep loud coil,
To bandy factions in domestic broil,
To dare the act of sins whose filth excels
The blackest customs of blind infidels.
No, my loved youth, he may of valour vaunt
Whom fortune's loudest thunder cannot daunt;
Whom fretful galls of chance, stern fortune's
    siege
Makes not his reason slink, the soul's fair liege;
Whose well-peised action ever rests upon
Not giddy humours, but discretion.
This heart in valour even Jove out-goes:
Jove is without, but this 'bove sense of woes;
And such a one, eternity. Behold!
[*Pointing to* FELICHE.]

---

330 ff. Note the increased stylisation created by the switch to couplets here.
331 *apish*: mindlessly imitative.
336 *gripe*: clutch.
340 *fume*: steam.
340 *keep . . . coil*: make a great row.
341 *bandy factions*: join in factious disputes.
346 *fretful galls*: painful sores caused by rubbing ('fretting').
347 *soul's fair liege*: reason, which should rule the soul.
348 *well-peised*: carefully weighed.
349 *giddy humours*: irrational emotions.
350–1 *Jove . . . woes*: Pandulpho repeats Seneca's argument (*De Providentia*, VI, 6) that the Stoic wise man's exercise of reason makes him superior to the gods: the gods are merely *without* emotions, the wise man raises himself *above* them.
352 *And . . . eternity*: such a man makes himself immortal.

Good morrow, son; thou bidd'st a fig for cold.
Sound louder music; let my breath exact
You strike sad tones unto this dismal act.
[*Exeunt.*]

ACT II

SCENE I

The cornets sound a sennet. Enter two mourners with torches, two with streamers, CASTILIO *and* FOROBOSCO *with torches, a Herald bearing Andrugio's helm and sword, the coffin,* MARIA *supported by* LUCIO *and* ALBERTO, ANTONIO *by himself,* PIERO *and* STROTZO *talking,* GALEATZO *and* MATZAGENTE, BALURDO *and* PANDULPHO; *the coffin set down, helm, sword and streamers hung up, placed by the Herald, whilst* ANTONIO *and* MARIA *wet their handkerchiefs with their tears, kiss them, and lay them on the hearse, kneeling. All go out but* PIERO. *Cornets cease and he speaks.*

PIERO. Rot there, thou cerecloth that enfolds the flesh
Of my loathed foe; moulder to crumbling dust;
Oblivion choke the passage of thy fame!

---

353 *bidd'st a fig*: care nothing.

354 *exact*: require, with authority (*OED*).

355 *act*: action; but the line also marks the end of the first act; the 'act' is also the name for the music played between the acts.

II.i.s.d. See Additional Note, pp. 509–10 below.

1–5 *Rot . . . live*: Piero composes an impudent inversion of traditional epitaphs, mocking the role of monuments as memorials, preservatives of individual prowess and virtue, and emblems of family honour. The effect is one of outrageous blasphemy.

1 *cerecloth*: shroud, winding-sheet,

Trophies of honoured birth drop quickly down;
Let naught of him, but what was vicious, live.
Though thou art dead, think not my hate is dead;
I have but newly twone my arm in the curled locks
Of snaky vengeance. Pale, beetle-browèd hate
But newly bustles up. Sweet wrong, I clap thy thoughts.
O, let me hug my bosom, rub my breast,
In hope of what may hap. Andrugio rots.
Antonio lives; umh; how long? ha, ha, how long?
Antonio packed hence, I'll his mother wed,
Then clear my daughter of supposèd lust,
Wed her to Florence' heir. O, excellent!
Venice, Genoa, Florence at my beck,
At Piero's nod – Balurdo, O, ho! –
O, 'twill be rare, all unsuspected done.
I have been nursed in blood, and still have sucked
The steam of reeking gore. – Balurdo, ho!

Enter BALURDO, *with a beard half off, half on.*

BALURDO. When my beard is on, most noble prince, when my beard is on.

PIERO. Why, what dost thou with a beard?

BALURDO. In truth, one told me that my wit was bald and that a mermaid was half fish and half fish; and therefore, to speak wisely, like one of your council – as indeed it hath pleased you to make me, not only, being a fool, of your council, but also to make me of your council,

---

7 *twone*: twined.

7–8 *curled . . . vengeance*: 'Tisiphone, minister of divine vengeance upon mankind, was represented as having serpents curled round her head' (Hunter).

8 *beetle-browèd*: with dark, prominent eyebrows; hence scowling.

20 s.d. *beard . . . half on*: may recall *The Spanish Tragedy*, IV.iii.18 ff., as eds. suggest. More important is the deliberate disruption of theatrical illusion.

being a fool – if my wit be bald and a mermaid be half fish and half conger, then I must be forced to conclude – the tiring-man hath not glued on my beard half fast enough. God's bores, it will not stick to fall off.

PIERO. Dost thou know what thou hast spoken all this while?

BALURDO. O Lord, duke, I would be sorry of that. Many men can utter that which no man but themselves can conceive; but, I thank a good wit, I have the gift to speak that which neither any man else nor myself understands.

PIERO. Thou art wise. He that speaks he knows not what shall never sin against his own conscience; go to, thou art wise.

BALURDO. Wise? O no; I have a little natural discretion or so; but for wise – I am somewhat prudent; but for wise – O Lord!

PIERO. Hold, take those keys, open the castle vault and put in Mellida.

BALURDO. And put in Mellida? Well, let me alone.

PIERO. Bid Forobosco and Castilio guard;
Endear thyself Piero's intimate.

BALURDO. 'Endear' and 'intimate'! Good, I assure you. I will endear and intimate Mellida into the dungeon presently.

PIERO. Will Pandulpho Feliche wait on me?

BALURDO. I will make him come, most retort and obtuse, to you presently. I think Sir Jeffrey talks like a councillor.
Go to, God's neaks, I think I tickle it. [*Exit.*]

PIERO. I'll seem to wind yon fool with kindest arm.
He that's ambitious-minded, and but man,

---

32 *tiring-man*: the equivalent of wardrobe mistress; abolishes the pretence of an off-stage dramatic world.
33–4 *God's bores*: God's wounds.
61 *God's neaks*: obscure oath.
61 *tickle it*: ensure a satisfactory result (*OED*).
62 *wind*: embrace.

Must have his followers beasts, dubbed slavish sots
Whose service is obedience and whose wit
Reacheth no further than to admire their lord
And stare in adoration of his worth.
I love a slave raked out of common mud
Should seem to sit in counsel with my heart;
High-honoured blood's too squeamish to assent
And lend a hand to an ignoble act;
Poison from roses who could e'er abstract?

Enter PANDULPHO.

How now, Pandulpho, weeping for thy son?

PANDULPHO. No, no, Piero, weeping for my sins;
Had I been a good father he had been
A gracious son.

PIERO. Pollution must be purged.

PANDULPHO. Why taint'st thou then the air with stench of flesh,
And human putrefaction's noisome scent?
I pray his body. Who less boon can crave
Than to bestow upon the dead his grave?

PIERO. Grave? Why, think'st thou he deserves a grave
That hath defiled the temple of –

PANDULPHO. Peace, peace!
Methinks I hear a humming murmur creep
From out his gellied wounds. Look on those lips,
Those now lawn pillows, on whose tender softness
Chaste modest speech, stealing from out his breast,
Had wont to rest itself, as loath to post
From out so fair an inn; look, look, they seem to stir

---

64 *dubbed slavish sots*: servile fools made knights.
72 *abstract*: extract, distil.
76 *gracious*: fortunate, granted heavenly grace.
83–4 *humming . . . wounds*: cf. *Julius Caesar*, III.i.260–2: 'wounds . . . / Which like dumb mouths do ope their ruby lips / To beg the voice and utterance of my tongue'; a victim's wounds reputedly bled afresh in the presence of the murderer.

And breathe defiance to black obloquy.
PIERO. Think'st thou thy son could suffer wrongfully?
PANDULPHO. A wise man wrongfully but never wrong
Can take: his breast's of such well-tempered proof
It may be rased, not pierced by savage tooth
Of foaming malice; showers of darts may dark
Heaven's ample brow, but not strike out a spark,
Much less pierce the sun's cheek. Such songs as these
I often dittied till my boy did sleep;
But now I turn plain fool, alas, I weep.
PIERO. [*aside*] 'Fore heaven, he makes me shrug; would 'a were dead.
He is a virtuous man. What has our court to do
With virtue, in the devil's name! – Pandulpho, hark:
My lustful daughter dies; start not, she dies.
I pursue justice, I love sanctity
And an undefilèd temple of pure thoughts.
Shall I speak freely? Good Andrugio's dead;
And I do fear a fetch; but – umh, would I durst speak –
I do mistrust; but – umh, death! [*Aside*] Is he all, all man,
Hath he no part of mother in him, ha?
No lickerish womanish inquisitiveness?
PANDULPHO. Andrugio's dead!
PIERO. Ay, and I fear his own unnatural blood,
To whom he gave life, hath given death for life.

91–2 *A wise . . . take*: a wise man may be subject to injustice, but can never suffer injury from it.
92 *well-tempered proof*: the idea is of a steel breastplate whose well-tempered strength is impenetrable; but the idea of Stoic 'temperance' is also involved.
93 *rased*: scratched.
95 *strike out*: obliterate.
99 *shrug*: with disdain, irritation.
106 *fetch*: trick.
107 *all man*: made up of nothing but manly qualities.
109 *lickerish*: greedy.

[*Aside*] How coldly he comes on! I see false suspect
Is viced, wrung hardly, in a virtuous heart. –
Well, I could give you reason for my doubts:
You are of honoured birth, my very friend;
You know how godlike 'tis to root out sin.
Antonio is a villain. Will you join
In oath with me against the traitor's life,
And swear you knew he sought his father's death?
I loved him well, yet I love justice more;
Our friends we should affect, justice adore.

PANDULPHO. My lord, the clapper of my mouth's not glibbed
With court oil; 'twill not strike on both sides yet.

PIERO. 'Tis just that subjects act commands of kings.

PANDULPHO. Command then just and honourable things.

PIERO. Even so; myself then will traduce his guilt.

PANDULPHO. Beware, take heed, lest guiltless blood be spilt.

PIERO. Where only honest deeds to kings are free
It is no empire, but a beggary.

PANDULPHO. Where more than noble deeds to kings are free
It is no empire, but a tyranny.

PIERO. Tush, juiceless greybeard, 'tis immunity
Proper to princes that our state exacts,
Our subjects not alone to bear, but praise our acts.

---

114 *viced*: squeezed (but with a quibble to balance 'virtuous').

123–4 *clapper . . . oil*: my tongue is not yet made smooth with courtly flattery.

124 *strike . . . sides*: speak hypocritically.

125–40 the couplets point up the formality and wit of the verbal duel, in which each *sententia* is a thrust or parry.

125 Seneca, *Octavia*, 471 (Cunliffe).

129–30 Seneca, *Thyestes*, 214–15 (Cunliffe); the echoes of *Thyestes* are particularly important in pointing forwards to the hellish banquet of revenge in V.iii.

130 *beggary*: place where beggars live (*OED*).

133–5 *Thyestes*, 205–7 (Cunliffe).

PANDULPHO. O, but that prince that worthful praise aspires,
From hearts, and not from lips, applause desires.
PIERO. Pish!
True praise the brow of common men doth ring,
False only girts the temple of a king.
He that hath strength and's ignorant of power,
He was not made to rule, but to be ruled.
PANDULPHO. 'Tis praise to do not what we can but should.
PIERO. Hence doting stoic! By my hope of bliss,
I'll make thee wretched.
PANDULPHO. Defiance to thy power, thou rifted jawn!
Now, by the loved heaven, sooner thou shalt
Rinse thy foul ribs from the black filth of sin
That soots thy heart than make me wretched. Pish!
Thou canst not coop me up. Hadst thou a gaol
With treble walls like antique Babylon,
Pandulpho can get out. I tell thee, duke,
I have old Fortunatus' wishing-cap,
And can be where I list, even in a trice.
I'll skip from earth into the arms of heaven,
And from triumphal arch of blessedness
Spit on thy frothy breast. Thou canst not slave
Or banish me; I will be free at home
Maugre the beard of greatness. The portholes
Of sheathèd spirit are ne'er corbèd up,

139–40 *Thyestes*, 211–12 (Cunliffe).
140 *girts the temple*: crowns the temples.
143 *Octavia*, 454 (Hunter).
146 *rifted jawn*: yawning abyss; see Textual Note, p. 491 below.
153 *old Fortunatus*: fairy-tale character in Dekker's play of the same name (1599); he travels with a magic cap stolen from the Sultan of Babylon.
157 *frothy*: insubstantial, insignificant, trivial.
157 *slave*: enslave.
159 *Maugre the beard of*: in spite of (cf. 'in the teeth of').
159–62 *The portholes . . . heaven*: i.e. in extreme adversity the resolute Stoic is always prepared to assert his freedom by committing suicide.
159 *portholes*: apertures for ship's cannon.
160 *sheathèd*: closed up in the body.
160 *corbèd*: see Textual Note, p. 491 below.

But still stand open, ready to discharge
Their precious shot into the shrouds of heaven.

PIERO. O torture! Slave, I banish thee the town,
Thy native seat of birth.

PANDULPHO. How proud thou speak'st! I tell thee, duke, the blasts
Of the swoll'n-cheeked winds, nor all the breath of kings,
Can puff me out my native seat of birth.
The earth's my body's, and the heaven's my soul's
Most native place of birth, which they will keep
Despite the menace of mortality.
Why, duke,
That's not my native place where I was rocked:
A wise man's home is wheresoe'er he is wise.
Now, that from man, not from the place, doth rise.

PIERO. Would I were deaf! O plague! Hence, dotard wretch,
Tread not in court. All that thou hast I seize.
[*Aside*] His quiet's firmer than I can disease.

PANDULPHO. Go, boast unto thy flatt'ring sycophants
Pandulpho's slave Piero hath o'erthrown;
Loose fortune's rags are lost; my own's my own.

PIERO*'s going out, looks back.*

'Tis true, Piero; thy vexed heart shall see
Thou hast but tripped my slave, not conquered me.

Exeunt at several doors.

---

161 *still*: always.
162 *precious shot*: i.e. the soul.
162 *shrouds*: rigging.
163–73 Gair cites *De Remediis Fortuitorum*, as translated in Whyttynton's *Seneca*, p. 45, as the model for this passage.
170 *menace of mortality*: threats of death.
174 *that*: i.e. wisdom.
179 *Pandulpho's slave*: i.e. Pandulpho's corporeal self; the idea is that the body is merely the soul's slave.
180 *my own's my own*: assertion of Stoic self-sufficiency.

SCENE II

Enter ANTONIO *with a book*, LUCIO, ALBERTO; ANTONIO *in black.*

ALBERTO. Nay, sweet, be comforted; take counsel and –
ANTONIO. Alberto, peace! that grief is wanton-sick
Whose stomach can digest and brook the diet
Of stale, ill-relished counsel. Pigmy cares
Can shelter under patience' shield, but giant griefs
Will burst all covert.
LUCIO. My lord, 'tis supper time.
ANTONIO. Drink deep, Alberto; eat, good Lucio;
But my pined heart shall eat on naught but woe.
ALBERTO. My lord, we dare not leave you thus alone.
ANTONIO. You cannot leave Antonio alone.
The chamber of my breast is even thronged
With firm attendance that forswears to flinch.
I have a thing sits here; it is not grief,
'Tis not despair, nor the most plague
That the most wretched are infected with;
But the most grief-full, despairing, wretched,
Accursèd, miserable – O, for heaven's sake
Forsake me now; you see how light I am,
And yet you force me to defame my patience.
LUCIO. Fair gentle prince –
ANTONIO. Away, thy voice is hateful; thou dost buzz,
And beat my ears with intimations

II.ii s.d. *with a book . . . in black*: cf. the black-clad Hamlet who enters 'reading on a book' (*Hamlet*, II.ii.166 s.d.); Kyd's Hieronimo also enters 'with a book' (*Spanish Tragedy*, III.xiii s.d.). Gair notes that Hieronimo, like Antonio, is apparently reading Seneca.

2 *wanton-sick*: malingering.

4–6 *Pigmy . . . covert*: version of Seneca, *Medea*, 155–6 (Eidson).

13 cf. *Hamlet*, I.ii.85: 'I have that within . . .'.

14 *most plague*: worst plague.

18 *light*: unstable.

That Mellida, that Mellida is light
And stainèd with adulterous luxury.
I cannot brook't. I tell thee, Lucio,
Sooner will I give faith that virtue's cant
In princes' courts will be adorned with wreath
Of choice respect, and endeared intimate;
Sooner will I believe that friendship's rein
Will curb ambition from utility,
Than Mellida is light. Alas, poor soul,
Didst e'er see her, good heart, hast heard her speak?
Kind, kind soul! Incredulity itself
Would not be so brass-hearted as suspect
So modest cheeks.

LUCIO. My lord –

ANTONIO. Away!
A self-one guilt doth only hatch distrust;
But a chaste thought's as far from doubt as lust.
I entreat you leave me.

ALBERTO. Will you endeavour to forget your grief?

ANTONIO. I'faith I will, good friend, i'faith I will.
I'll come and eat with you. Alberto, see,
I am taking physic; here's philosophy.
[*Shows book.*]
Good honest, leave me; I'll drink wine anon.

ALBERTO. Since you enforce us, fair prince, we are gone.

Exeunt ALBERTO *and* LUCIO.

ANTONIO. (*reads*) *Ferte fortiter: hoc est quo deum antecedatis. Ille enim extra patientiam malorum;*

---

23 *light*: immoral, unfaithful.
24 *luxury*: lechery.
26 *cant*: niche, shrine (with a pun on 'cant' = insincere language).
28 *endeared intimate*: beloved as a close friend.
30 *from utility*: from being used.
38 *A self-one . . . distrust*: 'Only a mind which is guilty about itself suspects other people' (Hunter).
39 *as lust*: as it is from lust.
47–51 *Ferte . . . habet*: Seneca, *De Providentia*, VI, 6: 'Endure bravely; in this you may outdo God; for he is beyond suffering, you above it. Scorn suffering: it is either relieved, or it relieves you. Despise fortune: it has no weapon that can touch your soul.'

vos supra. Contemnite dolorem: aut solvetur, aut solvet. Contemnite fortunam: nullum telum, quo feriret animum habet.
Pish, thy mother was not lately widowed,
Thy dear affièd love lately defamed
With blemish of foul lust when thou wrot'st thus.
Thou, wrapped in furs, beeking thy limbs 'fore fires
Forbid'st the frozen zone to shudder. Ha, ha! 'tis naught
But foamy bubbling of a phlegmy brain,
Naught else but smoke. O, what dank, marish spirit
But would be firèd with impatience
At my –
No more, no more; he that was never blest
With height of birth, fair expectation
Of mounted fortunes, knows not what it is
To be the pitied object of the world.
O poor Antonio, thou mayst sigh!

MELLIDA. [*within*] Ay me!
ANTONIO. And curse –
PANDULPHO. [*within*] Black powers!
ANTONIO. And cry –
MARIA. [*within*] O heaven!
ANTONIO. And close laments with –
ALBERTO. [*within*] O me, most miserable!
PANDULPHO. [*within*] Woe for my dear, dear son!
MARIA. [*within*] Woe for my dear, dear husband!

---

53 *affièd*: betrothed.
55 *beeking*: warming.
56 *Forbid'st . . . shudder*: living in warmth and luxury yourself, you forbid those who live in polar regions to shiver.
57 *foamy . . . brain*: 'the empty and superficial expression of a cold, phlegmatic temperament' (Hunter).
58 *marish*: marsh-like.
66–71 *Ay me . . . in me*: the operatic effect created by the orchestration of voices here is acknowledged in the subdued musical metaphor in 'close' (67, 71) and 'bears his part' (75); and cf. *The Spanish Tragedy*, III.vii.61–3, and *Richard III*, II.ii.71–9.

MELLIDA. [*within*] Woe for my dear, dear love!
ANTONIO. Woe for me all; close all your woes in me,
In me, Antonio! Ha! Where live these sounds?
I can seen nothing; grief's invisible
And lurks in secret angles of the heart.
Come, sigh again, Antonio bears his part.
MELLIDA. [*speaks through the grating*] O, here, here is a vent to pass my sighs.
I have surcharged the dungeon with my plaints.
Prison and heart will burst if void of vent.
Ay, that is Phoebe, empress of the night,
That 'gins to mount. O chastest deity,
If I be false to my Antonio,
If the least soil of lust smears my pure love,
Make me more wretched, make me more accursed
Than infamy, torture, death, hell, and heaven
Can, bound with amplest power of thought; if not,
Purge my poor heart from defamation's blot.
ANTONIO. 'Purge my poor heart from defamation's blot'!
Poor heart, how like her virtuous self she speaks!
Mellida, dear Mellida, it is Antonio;
Slink not away, 'tis thy Antonio.
MELLIDA. How found you out, my lord? Alas, I know
'Tis easy in this age to find out woe.
I have a suit to you.
ANTONIO. What is't, dear soul?
MELLIDA. Kill me; i'faith, I'll wink, not stir a jot.

67, 71 *close*: verb from *close sb.*[2] = musical conclusion or cadence (*OED*); perhaps combined with *sb.*[2] 3 = a closing or uniting together.
75 *bears his part*: sings his part in the harmony.
77 *surcharged*: overloaded.
79 *Phoebe*: the moon.
85 *Can, bound with . . . thought*: 'encompass with the most extreme reach of . . . imagination' (Gair).
94 *wink*: shut my eyes.

For God sake, kill me. In sooth, lovèd youth,
I am much injured; look, see how I creep.
I cannot wreak my wrong, but sigh and weep.
ANTONIO. May I be cursèd, but I credit thee.
MELLIDA. Tomorrow I must die.
ANTONIO. Alas, for what?
MELLIDA. For loving thee. 'Tis true, my sweetest breast;
I must die falsely; so must thou, dear heart.
Nets are a-knitting to entrap thy life.
Thy father's death must make a paradise
To my (I shame to call him) father. Tell me, sweet,
Shall I die thine? Dost love me still, and still?
ANTONIO. I do.
MELLIDA. Then welcome heaven's will.
ANTONIO. Madam,
I will not swell like a tragedian
In forcèd passion of affected strains.
If I had present power of aught but pitying you
I would be as ready to redress your wrongs
As to pursue your love. Throngs of thoughts
Crowd for their passage; somewhat I will do.
Reach me thy hand; think this is honour's bent,
To live unslavèd, to die innocent.
MELLIDA. Let me entreat a favour, gracious love:
Be patient, see me die; good, do not weep;
Go sup, sweet chuck; drink and securely sleep.
ANTONIO. I'faith I cannot, but I'll force my face
To palliate my sickness.
MELLIDA. Give me thy hand. Peace on thy bosom dwell;

---

97 *wreak*: revenge.

107–8 *tragedian . . . strains*: contrasts his manner with the affected and strained tones adopted by the ranting Piero and Strotzo, who, like Richard III and Buckingham, can 'counterfeit the deep tragedian' (see above, I.ii.254 s.d.); cf. also *Hamlet*, II.ii.544–6.

113 *bent*: inclination.

113–27 the love-duet is cast in formalised couplets.

119 *palliate*: alleviate the symptoms of a disease without curing it; also has the sense of 'cloak' or 'disguise' (feelings).

That's all my woe can breathe; kiss; thus, farewell.
ANTONIO. Farewell. My heart is great of thoughts – stay, dove –
And therefore I must speak. But what, O love?
By this white hand, no more! Read in these tears
What crushing anguish thy Antonio bears.

ANTONIO *kisseth* MELLIDA*'s hand; then* MELLIDA *goes from the grate.*

MELLIDA. Good night, good heart.
ANTONIO. Thus heat from blood, thus souls from bodies part.

[*Lies down and weeps.*]

Enter PIERO *and* STROTZO.

PIERO. He grieves; laugh, Strotzo, laugh; he weeps.
Hath he tears? O pleasure! Hath he tears?
Now do I scourge Andrugio with steel whips
Of knotty vengeance. Strotzo, cause me straight
Some plaining ditty to augment despair.

[*Exit* STROTZO.]

Triumph, Piero. Hark, he groans. O rare!
ANTONIO. Behold a prostrate wretch laid on his tomb;
His epitaph thus: *Ne plus ultra*. Ho!

---

122 *great of*: pregnant with.
125 s.d. *the grate*: 'probably a lattice in the stage door' (Hunter).
132 *Some . . . despair*: some song of lament to enhance Antonio's despair.
134 *laid on his tomb*: suggests that Antonio may have stretched himself on Andrugio's 'coffin' (II.i s.d.) so that he resembles a piece of tomb-sculpture.
135 *Ne plus ultra*: 'nothing beyond' – the motto inscribed on the Pillars of Hercules, which, for Mediterranean civilisations, had traditionally marked the limits of the known world. The motto leads his train of thought to 'Herculean woe'.

Let none out-woe me; mine's Herculean woe.
Cantant.
Exit PIERO *at the end of the song.*

Enter MARIA.

May I be more cursèd than heaven can make me
If I am not more wretched than man can conceive me.
Sore forlorn orphan, what omnipotence
Can make thee happy?
MARIA. How now, sweet son; good youth, what dost thou?
ANTONIO. Weep, weep.
MARIA. Dost naught but weep, weep?
ANTONIO. Yes, mother, I do sigh and wring my hands,
Beat my poor breast and wreathe my tender arms.
Hark ye, I'll tell you wondrous strange, strange news.
MARIA. What, my good boy, stark mad?
ANTONIO. I am not.
MARIA. Alas, is that strange news?
ANTONIO. Strange news. Why, mother, is't not wondrous strange
I am not mad, I run not frantic, ha?
Knowing, my father's trunk scarce cold, your love
Is sought by him that doth pursue my life?
Seeing the beauty of creation,
Antonio's bride, pure heart, defamed, and stowed
Under the hatches of obscuring earth?
Heu, quo labor, quo vota ciderunt mea?

---

136 *Herculean woe*: Gair suggests an allusion to the death of Hercules; but the main idea is of an heroic passion of such outsized proportions that none can outgo it. In either case, we are prepared to see Antonio as a Herculean avenger, purging the Augean stables of Piero's court (cf. below, V.iii.129–30).

147 *What . . . mad?*: in this exchange there is another seeming recollection of *Hamlet* (III.iv.105, 137–44).

157 *Heu . . . mea?*: Seneca, *Octavia*, 632: 'Alas! to what purpose are my labour and prayers?'

Enter PIERO.

PIERO. Good evening to the fair Antonio;
Most happy fortune, sweet succeeding time,
Rich hope; think not thy fate a bankrupt though –
ANTONIO. [*aside*] Umh, the devil in his good time and tide forsake thee!
PIERO. How now? Hark ye, prince.
ANTONIO. God be with you.
PIERO. Nay, noble blood, I hope ye not suspect –
ANTONIO. Suspect! I scorn't. Here's cap and leg; good night.
[*Aside*] Thou that wants power, with dissemblance fight.

Exit ANTONIO.

PIERO. Madam. O that you could remember to forget!
MARIA. I had a husband and a happy son.
PIERO. Most powerful beauty, that enchanting grace –
MARIA. Talk not of beauty, nor enchanting grace.
My husband's dead, my son's distraught, accursed.
Come, I must vent my griefs, or heart will burst. *Exit* MARIA.
PIERO. She's gone, and yet she's here; she hath left a print
Of her sweet graces fixed within my heart
As fresh as is her face. I'll marry her.
She's most fair – true! most chaste – most false!
Because most fair, 'tis firm I'll marry her.

Enter STROTZO.

STROTZO. My lord.
PIERO. Ha, Strotzo, my other soul, my life!
Dear, hast thou steeled the point of thy resolve?

---

165 *cap and leg*: i.e. he removes his cap, and bows, 'with the implication of dissemblance' (Hunter).
167 ff. imitated from the wooing of Anne in *Richard III*, I.ii.
176 *false*: because she has earlier preferred Andrugio to Piero.

Will't not turn edge in execution?
STROTZO. No.
PIERO. Do it with rare passion, and present thy guilt
As if 'twere wrung out with thy conscience' gripe.
Swear that my daughter's innocent of lust
And that Antonio bribed thee to defame
Her maiden honour, on inveterate hate
Unto my blood; and that thy hand was fee'd,
By his large bounty, for his father's death.
Swear plainly that thou chok'dst Andrugio
By his son's only egging. Rush me in
Whilst Mellida prepares herself to die,
Halter about thy neck, and with such sighs,
Laments and acclamations lifen it,
As if impulsive power of remorse –
STROTZO. I'll weep.
PIERO. Ay, ay, fall on thy face and cry, 'Why suffer you
So lewd a slave as Strotzo is to breathe?'
STROTZO. I'll beg a strangling, grow importunate –
PIERO. As if thy life were loathsome to thee; then I
Catch straight the cord's end, and, as much incensed
With thy damned mischiefs, offer a rude hand
As ready to gird in thy pipe of breath;
But on the sudden, straight, I'll stand amazed
And fall in exclamations of thy virtues.
STROTZO. Applaud my agonies and penitence.
PIERO. Thy honest stomach that could not digest
The crudities of murder; but, surcharged,

---

181 *turn edge*: become blunt.
183–4 *Do it . . . gripe*: more histrionic instructions.
191 *his son's only egging*: only at his son's behest.
191 *Rush me in*: ethic dative, for emphasis.
194 *lifen*: make lifelike (*OED*).
195 *impulsive*: compelling.
203 *gird . . . breath*: put a cord around your windpipe, strangle you.
208 *crudities*: undigested gobbets of food.
208 *surcharged*: surfeited.

Vomited'st them up in Christian piety.
STROTZO. Then clip me in your arms.
PIERO. And call thee brother, mount thee straight to state,
Make thee of council; tut, tut, what not, what not?
Think on't; be confident; pursue the plot.
STROTZO. Look, here's a trope: a true rogue's lips are mute;
I do not use to speak, but execute.
He lays finger on his mouth, and draws his dagger. [*Exit.*]
PIERO. So, so; run headlong to confusion,
Thou slight-brained mischief; thou art made as dirt
To plaster up the bracks of my defects.
I'll wring what may be squeezed from out his use,
And good night, Strotzo. Swell plump, bold heart,
For now thy tide of vengeance rolleth in.
O now *Tragoedia Cothurnata* mounts;
Piero's thoughts are fixed on dire exploits.
Pell-mell confusion and black murder guides
The organs of my spirit. Shrink not, heart:
Capienda rebus in malis praeceps via est. [*Exit.*]

Finis Actus Secundi.

---

214 *trope*: figurative mode of speaking; here it seems to refer to the rebus Strotzo composes (215 s.d.) and its motto (214–15).

218 *bracks*: cracks.

222 *Tragoedia Cothurnata*: Tragedy clad in buskins (the thick-soled boot of the classical tragic actor); hence formal, stately tragedy. Perhaps, as Foakes suggests, a parodic echo of *The Spanish Tragedy*, IV.i.160.

226 *Capienda . . . est*: Seneca, *Agamemnon*, 154: 'In midst of ills the steep path is the one that should be taken.'

ACT III

SCENE I

A dumb-show. The cornets sounding for the Act. Enter CASTILIO *and* FOROBOSCO, ALBERTO *and* BALURDO *with poleaxes;* STROTZO *talking with* PIERO; [PIERO] *seemeth to send out* STROTZO; *exit* STROTZO. *Enter* STROTZO, MARIA, NUTRICHE *and* LUCIO. PIERO *passeth through his guard and talks with her* [MARIA] *with seeming amorousness; she seemeth to reject his suit, flies to the tomb, kneels and kisseth it.* PIERO *bribes* NUTRICHE *and* LUCIO; *they go to her, seeming to solicit his suit. She riseth, offers to go out;* PIERO *stayeth her, tears open his breast, embraceth and kisseth her, and so they go all out in state.*

Enter two PAGES, *the one with two tapers, the other with a chafing-dish, a perfume in it.* ANTONIO, *in his night-gown and a nightcap, unbraced, following after.*

ANTONIO. The black jades of swart night trot foggy rings
'Bout heaven's brow. [*Clock strikes twelve.*]
'Tis now stark dead night.
Is this Saint Mark's Church?
1 PAGE. It is, my lord.

III.i s.d. Piero's seduction of Maria is blasphemously conducted in a church over her husband's tomb. The dumb-show appears to continue the imitation of the seduction scene in *Richard III*, with Andrugio's hearse–tomb taking the place of Henry's hearse–coffin. But there are also striking resemblances to the players' dumb-show in *Hamlet* (III.ii.130 s.d.).

III.i s.d. *chafing-dish*: here = censer.

1 *swart*: dark-complexioned.

ANTONIO. Where stands my father's hearse?
2 PAGE. Those streamers bear his arms. Ay, that is it.
ANTONIO. Set tapers to the tomb, and lamp the church.
Give me the fire. Now depart and sleep.
Exeunt PAGES.
I purify the air with odorous fume.
[*He swings the chafing-dish.*]
Graves, vaults, and tombs, groan not to bear my weight,
Cold flesh, bleak trunks, wrapped in your half-rot shrouds,
I press you softly with a tender foot.
Most honoured sepulchre, vouchsafe a wretch
Leave to weep o'er thee. Tomb, I'll not be long
Ere I creep in thee, and with bloodless lips
Kiss my cold father's cheek. I prithee, grave,
Provide soft mould to wrap my carcass in.
Thou royal spirit of Andrugio,
Where'er thou hover'st, airy intellect,
I heave up tapers to thee – view thy son! –
In celebration of due obsequies.
Once every night I'll dew thy funeral hearse
With my religious tears.
O, blessèd father of a cursèd son,
Thou died'st most happy since thou lived'st not
To see thy son most wretched and thy wife
Pursued by him that seeks my guiltless blood.
O, in what orb thy mighty spirit soars,
Stoop and beat down this rising fog of shame
That strives to blur thy blood and girt defame
About my innocent and spotless brows.
Non est mori miserum, sed misere mori.

---

6 *lamp*: light up.
18 *intellect*: an intelligence, a spirit (*OED*).
19 *heave up*: raise (in an attitude of religious adoration).
23 *O . . . son*: Hunter compares *The Spanish Tragedy*, IV.iv.84; the dead body of Horatio there, like the tomb here, serves as an embodiment of the violated past, an incarnation of the revenger's obsession.
29 *girt*: gird.
31 *Non . . . mori*: 'It is not dying that is wretched, but dying wretchedly'; a familiar Stoic attitude, but no specific source has been found.

[*Enter Ghost of* ANDRUGIO.]

GHOST OF ANDRUGIO. Thy pangs of anguish rip my cerecloth up;
And lo, the ghost of old Andrugio
Forsakes his coffin. Antonio, revenge!
I was empoisoned by Piero's hand;
Revenge my blood. Take spirit, gentle boy.
Revenge my blood. Thy Mellida is chaste.
Only to frustrate thy pursuit in love
Is blazed unchaste. Thy mother yields consent
To be his wife and give his blood a son,
That made her husbandless and doth complot
To make her sonless; but before I touch
The banks of rest, my ghost shall visit her.
Thou vigour of my youth, juice of my love,
Seize on revenge, grasp the stern-bended front
Of frowning vengeance with unpeisèd clutch.
Alarum Nemesis, rouse up thy blood,
Invent some stratagem of vengeance
Which but to think on may like lightning glide
With horror through thy breast. Remember this:

---

31 s.d. *Enter . . . Andrugio*: Q lacks any s.d. here, but it seems apparent from lines 32–4 that the Ghost is meant to emerge from the tomb. The King's Men certainly possessed a tomb equipped for discoveries of this kind, and used it in *The Second Maiden's Tragedy* (IV.iv) and *The Duchess of Malfi* (V.iii); Paul's Boys presumably had a similar device.

35 *I . . . hand*: Gair compares the Ghost's revelation to Hamlet (*Hamlet*, I.v.38–40).

39 *blazed*: proclaimed (with a suggestion of formal heraldic disgrace).

41 *complot*: join together in a plot.

43 *banks of rest*: i.e. crossed the Styx; in the classical underworld the spirits of the dead remained restless and unsatisfied until Charon ferried them across this river.

45–6 *grasp . . . vengeance*: Marston here conflates the figure of Revenge with the emblem of Opportunity, a woman with a single lock of hair in front, which the resolute man must grasp before she passes (cf. below, V.ii.87).

45 *stern-bended front*: frowning brow.

46 *unpeisèd*: see Textual Note, p. 491 below.

47 *Alarum Nemesis*: awake the goddess of retribution.

Scelera non ulcisceris, nisi vincis.
Exit ANDRUGIO*'s Ghost.*

Enter MARIA, *her hair about her ears,* NUTRICHE *and* LUCIO *with Pages and torches.*

MARIA. Where left you him? Show me, good boys. Away!
[*Exeunt Pages.*]

NUTRICHE. God's me, your hair!

MARIA. Nurse, 'tis not yet proud day;
The neat gay mistress of the light's not up,
Her cheek's not yet slurred over with the paint
Of borrowed crimson; the unprankèd world
Wears yet the night-clothes. Let flare my loosed hair;
I scorn the presence of the night.
Where's my boy? Run! I'll range about the church
Like frantic Bacchanal or Jason's wife
Invoking all the spirits of the graves
To tell me where. Ha! O, my poor wretched blood,
What dost thou up at midnight, my kind boy?
Dear soul, to bed! O, thou hast struck a fright
Unto thy mother's panting –

ANTONIO. *O quisquis nova*
Supplicia functis durus umbrarum arbiter

---

51 *Scelera . . . vincis*: 'The only way to avenge crimes is to conquer [your enemy].'

51 s.d. *her hair about her ears*: a traditional sign of grief or madness.

53 *God's me*: God save me.

53 *proud*: literally 'full', but the other associations of the word lead into the image of dawn as a vain lady of the court (54–6).

54 *neat*: elegantly dressed.

55 *slurred*: smeared.

56 *unprankèd*: cf. 'pranked' = ostentatiously dressed.

58 *presence*: royal presence-chamber.

60 *Bacchanal*: the mad Agave in Euripides' *Bacchae*.

60 *Jason's wife*: the witch, Medea.

66–73 *O . . . Ulciscar*: from Seneca, *Thyestes*, 13–15, 75–81; Antonio adapts the passage by adding the words *Antonii* and *Ulciscar*: 'O whoever you may be, harsh judge of

Disponis, quisquis exeso iaces
Pavidus sub antro, quisquis venturi times
Montis ruinam, quisquis avidorum feros
Rictus leonum, et dira furiarum agmina
Implicitus horres, Antonii vocem excipe
Properantis ad vos: Ulciscar.
MARIA. Alas, my son's distraught. Sweet boy, appease
Thy mutining affections.
ANTONIO. By the astoning terror of swart night,
By the infectious damps of clammy graves,
And by the mould that presseth down
My dead father's skull, I'll be revenged!
MARIA. Wherefore? on whom? for what? Go, go to bed,
Good, duteous son. Ho, but thy idle –
ANTONIO. So I may sleep, tombed in an honoured hearse,
So may my bones rest in that sepulchre.
MARIA. Forget not duty, son; to bed, to bed.
ANTONIO. May I be cursèd by my father's ghost
And blasted with incensèd breath of heaven,
If my heart beat on aught but vengeance!
May I be numbed with horror and my veins
Pucker with singeing torture, if my brain
Digest a thought, but of dire vengeance!
May I be fettered slave to coward chance,
If blood, heart, brain, plot aught save vengeance!

---

ghosts, decreeing fresh punishments for them; whoever you are, lying trembling beneath a hollow rock, fearing the imminent collapse of a mountain; whoever you may be, shuddering at the fierce gaping maws of greedy lions, or at the clutch of fearfully ranked furies – hear Antonio's words, now hastening towards you: "I shall be revenged." '

74–5 *appease . . . affections*: set your disturbed mind at rest (Hunter).
76 *astoning*: stunning, paralysing.
78 *mould*: earth.
81 *idle*: foolish.
87 *beat*: insist (but with a quibble suggested by 'heart').
87, 90, 92, 130 *vengeance*: trisyllabic.

MARIA. Wilt thou to bed? I wonder when thou sleep'st.
I'faith thou look'st sunk-eyed; go couch thy head;
Now, faith, 'tis idle; sweet, sweet son, to bed.

ANTONIO. I have a prayer or two to offer up
For the good, good prince, my most dear, dear lord,
The duke Piero, and your virtuous self;
And then when those prayers have obtained success,
In sooth I'll come – believe it now – and couch
My head in downy mould; but first I'll see
You safely laid. I'll bring ye all to bed:
Piero, Maria, Strotzo, Julio;
I'll see you all laid; I'll bring you all to bed,
And then, i'faith, I'll come and couch my head
And sleep in peace.

MARIA. Look then, we go before.

Exeunt all but ANTONIO.

ANTONIO. Ay, so you must, before we touch the shore
Of wished revenge. O, you departed souls
That lodge in coffined trunks which my feet press –
If Pythagorean axioms be true,
Of spirits' transmigration – fleet no more
To human bodies; rather live in swine,
Inhabit wolves' flesh, scorpions, dogs, and toads
Rather than man. The curse of heaven rains
In plagues unlimited through all his days;
His mature age grows only mature vice,
And ripens only to corrupt and rot

100–6 *couch . . . laid . . . bed . . . sleep*: *doubles entendres* on 'resting' and 'dying'; see below, III.ii.103 s.d.

110 *Pythagorean*: the doctrine of metempsychosis or transmigration of souls, attributed to the Greek philosopher Pythagoras (sixth century B.C.), according to which human souls after death might enter the bodies of animals; here the word's main stress is on the third syllable.

116 *mature*: accent on first syllable.

The budding hopes of infant modesty;
Still striving to be more than man, he proves
More than a devil; devilish suspect,
Devilish cruelty,
All hell-strained juice is pourèd to his veins,
Making him drunk with fuming surquedries,
Contempt of heaven, untamed arrogance,
Lust, state, pride, murder.

ANDRUGIO. Murder!
FELICHE. Murder!
PANDULPHO. Murder!
From above and beneath.

ANTONIO. Ay, I will murder; graves and ghosts
Fright me no more; I'll suck red vengeance
Out of Piero's wounds, Piero's wounds.
[*Retires from forestage.*]

Enter two Boys, with PIERO *in his night-gown and nightcap.*

PIERO. Maria, love, Maria! She took this aisle.
Left you her here? On, lights; away!
I think we shall not warm our beds today.

Enter JULIO, FOROBOSCO *and* CASTILIO.

JULIO. Ho, father, father!
PIERO. How now, Julio, my little pretty son?
[*To* FOROBOSCO] Why suffer you the child to walk so late?
FOROBOSCO. He will not sleep, but calls to follow you,
Crying that bugbears and spirits haunted him.
ANTONIO *offers to come near and stab;* PIERO *presently withdraws.*

---

123 *fuming surquedries*: raging presumption (but 'fuming' also suggests 'clouding the brain' and thus links with 'drunk').

127 s.d. *From . . . beneath*: the parallel with *Hamlet*, I.v.149 ff. is obvious.

132–4 *Maria . . . today*: the spectacle of the frustrated Piero pursuing Maria in his nightclothes seems designed to create a comic anticlimax. This will emphasise the horror and pathos of Julio's murder.

ANTONIO. [*aside*] No, not so.
This shall be sought for; I'll force him feed on life
Till he shall loathe it. This shall be the close
Of vengeance' strain.

PIERO. Away there! Pages, lead on fast with light.
The church is full of damps; 'tis yet dead night.

Ex[*eunt*] *all, saving* JULIO [*and* ANTONIO].

JULIO. Brother Antonio, are you here, i'faith?
Why do you frown? Indeed my sister said
That I should call you brother, that she did,
When you were married to her. Buss me; good truth,
I love you better than my father, 'deed.

ANTONIO. Thy father? Gracious, O bounteous heaven!
I do adore thy justice: *venit in nostras manus*
Tandem vindicta, venit et tota quidem.

[*Holds* JULIO.]

JULIO. Truth, since my mother died I loved you best.
Something hath angered you; pray you, look merrily.

ANTONIO. I will laugh, and dimple my thin cheek
With cap'ring joy; chuck, my heart doth leap
To grasp thy bosom. Time, place, and blood,
How fit you close together! Heaven's tones
Strike not such music to immortal souls
As your accordance sweets my breast withal.

140–3 *No . . . strain*: another close parallel with *Hamlet*: cf. the prayer scene, III.iii.72 ff.

142–3 *close . . . strain*: the closing cadence in the music of revenge.

146 *Brother*: i.e. brother-in-law.

149 *Buss*: kiss.

152–3 *venit . . . quidem*: 'at long last revenge has come into my hands, and come to the full' (Seneca, *Thyestes*, 494–5; Marston substitutes *vindicta* for *Thyestes*).

157 *chuck*: chicken (familiar term of endearment).

159 *How . . . close*: (1) how exactly you harmonise; (2) how fittingly you draw towards a conclusion.

161 *accordance*: musical accord.

Methinks I pace upon the front of Jove,
And kick corruption with a scornful heel,
Griping this flesh, disdain mortality.
O that I knew which joint, which side, which limb,
Were father all, and had no mother in't,
That I might rip it vein by vein and carve revenge
In bleeding rases! But since 'tis mixed together,
Have at adventure, pell-mell, no reverse!
Come hither, boy. This is Andrugio's hearse.
[ANTONIO *draws his dagger.*]

JULIO. O God, you'll hurt me. For my sister's sake,
Pray you do not hurt me. And you kill me, 'deed,
I'll tell my father.

ANTONIO. O, for thy sister's sake I flag revenge.

[*Enter the Ghost of* ANDRUGIO.]

GHOST OF ANDRUGIO. Revenge! [*Exit.*]

ANTONIO. Stay, stay, dear father, fright mine eyes no more.
Revenge as swift as lightning bursteth forth
And cleaves his heart. Come, pretty, tender child,
It is not thee I hate, not thee I kill.
Thy father's blood that flows within thy veins
Is it I loathe, is that revenge must suck.
I love thy soul, and were thy heart lapped up
In any flesh but in Piero's blood
I would thus kiss it; but being his, thus, thus,
And thus I'll punch it. [*Stabs* JULIO.]
Abandon fears;

---

164 *Griping this flesh*: clutching Julio's flesh (so as to cause pain).

165–8 *O . . . rases*: the monstrous extravagance of this conceit is presumably meant to create an effect of grotesque comedy, continued in the pathetic absurdity of Julio's 'And you kill me . . . I'll tell my father', 172–3.

168 *rases*: cuts, slits, scratches (*OED*).

169 *Have at adventure*: take this reckless chance.

174 *flag revenge*: slacken in my revenge.

178–84 *Come . . . kiss it*: see above, lines 165–8.

Whilst thy wounds bleed, my brows shall gush out tears.
JULIO. So you will love me, do even what you will.
ANTONIO. Now barks the wolf against the full-cheeked moon,
Now lions' half-clammed entrails roar for food,
Now croaks the toad, and night-crows screech aloud,
Fluttering 'bout casements of departing souls;
Now gapes the graves, and through their yawns let loose
Imprisoned spirits to revisit earth;
And now, swart night, to swell thy hour out,
Behold I spurt warm blood in thy black eyes.
From under the stage a groan.
Howl not, thou pury mould; groan not ye graves;
Be dumb all breath. Here stands Andrugio's son,
Worthy his father. So; I feel no breath.
His jaws are fall'n, his dislodged soul is fled,
And now there's nothing but Piero left;
He is all Piero, father all; this blood,
This breast, this heart, Piero all,
Whom thus I mangle. Sprite of Julio,
Forget this was thy trunk. I live thy friend.
Mayst thou be twinèd with the soft'st embrace
Of clear eternity; but thy father's blood
I thus make incense of, to Vengeance.
[*Sprinkles the tomb with blood.*]
Ghost of my poisoned sire, suck this fume;
To sweet revenge, perfume thy circling air
With smoke of blood. I sprinkle round his gore,
And dew thy hearse with these fresh-reeking drops.

---

189 *clammed*: stuck together (through emptiness) (Hunter).
196 *pury*: form of obsolete 'putry' = putrid, rotten (*OED*).
201–4 *all Piero . . . thy friend*: the *reductio ad absurdum* of the grotesque conceit developed above (165–8, 178–84).
210–11 *sprinkle . . . drops*: Hunter draws attention to the travesty of Requiem Mass ritual (p. xvii).

Lo, thus I heave my blood-dyed hands to heaven,
Even like insatiate hell, still crying: 'More!
My heart hath thirsting dropsies after gore.'
Sound peace and rest to church, night-ghosts and graves;
Blood cries for blood, and murder murder craves. [*Exit.*]

SCENE II

Enter two Pages with torches, MARIA, *her hair loose, and* NUTRICHE.

NUTRICHE. Fie, fie, tomorrow your wedding day, and weep! God's my comfort, Andrugio could do well, Piero may do better. I have had four husbands myself: the first I called Sweet Duck, the second Dear Heart, the third Pretty Pug; but the fourth, most sweet, dear, pretty, All-in-all; he was the very cockall of a husband. What, lady, your skin is smooth, your blood warm, your cheek fresh, your eye quick; change of pasture makes fat calves, choice of linen clean bodies; and (no question) variety of husbands perfect wives. I would you should know it, as few teeth as I have in my head, I have read Aristotle's *Problems*, which saith that woman receiveth perfection by the man. What then by the *men*? Go to, to bed; lie on your back; dream not on Piero. I say no more; tomorrow is your wedding; do, dream not of Piero.

Enter BALURDO *with a bass viol.*

---

214 *thirsting dropsies*: the heart is swollen with blood (as a dropsical body is swollen with water) but still thirsts for more.

216 *Blood . . . blood*: cf. Tilley, B458: 'Blood will have blood.'

7 *cockall*: one that beats all (*OED*).

14 *Aristotle's Problems*: refers to a 1595 chap-book entitled *The Problems of Aristotle*, sig. E3.

MARIA. What an idle prate thou keep'st! Good nurse, go sleep.
I have a mighty task of tears to weep.

BALURDO. Lady, with a most retort and obtuse leg [*Bows.*] I kiss the curlèd locks of your loose hair. The duke hath sent you the most musical Sir Jeffrey with his not base but most ennobled viol, to rock your baby thoughts in the cradle of sleep.

MARIA. I give the noble duke respective thanks.

BALURDO. 'Respective'; truly, a very pretty word! Indeed, madam, I have the most respective fiddle. [*Plucks it*] Did you ever smell a more sweet sound? My ditty must go thus – very witty, I assure you. I myself in an humorous passion made it, to the tune of my mistress Nutriche's beauty. Indeed, very pretty, very retort and obtuse, I'll assure you. 'Tis thus:

My mistress' eye doth oil my joints
And makes my fingers nimble;
O love, come on, untruss your points –
My fiddlestick wants rosin.
My lady's dugs are all so smooth
That no flesh must them handle;
Her eyes do shine, for to say sooth,
Like a new-snuffèd candle.

MARIA. Truly, very pathetical and unvulgar.

BALURDO. 'Pathetical and unvulgar': words of worth, excellent words! In sooth, madam, I have taken a murr, which makes my nose run most pathetically and unvulgarly. Have you any tobacco?

MARIA. Good signor, your song.

BALURDO. Instantly, most unvulgarly, at your

---

26 *respective*: courteous.
31–2 *humorous passion*: passionate mood.
37 *untruss your points*: unfasten the laces of your clothes.
38 *fiddlestick . . . rosin*: obscene *double entendre*; and see Textual Note, p. 492 below.
39 *dugs*: breasts (more commonly used of animals).
43 *pathetical and unvulgar*: moving and refined.
46 *murr*: severe form of catarrh.
48 *tobacco*: for snuff.

service. Truly, here's the most pathetical rosin. Umh.

Cantant.

MARIA. In sooth, most knightly sung, and like Sir Jeffrey.

BALURDO. Why, look you, lady, I was made a knight only for my voice, and a councillor only for my wit.

MARIA. I believe it. Good night, gentle sir, good night.

BALURDO. You will give me leave to take my leave of my mistress, and I will do it most famously in rhyme:
[*To* NUTRICHE]

Farewell, adieu, saith thy love true,
  As to part loath.
Time bids us part, mine own sweetheart,
  God bless us both. *Exit* BALURDO.

MARIA. Good night, Nutriche. Pages, leave the room.
The life of night grows short; 'tis almost dead.
Exeunt PAGES *and* NUTRICHE.
O thou cold widow-bed, sometime thrice blest
By the warm pressure of my sleeping lord,
Open thy leaves, and whilst on thee I tread
Groan out, 'Alas, my dear Andrugio's dead!'

MARIA *draweth the curtain, and the Ghost of* ANDRUGIO *is displayed sitting on the bed.*

---

51 *rosin*: used figuratively for the sound produced on the viol.

55–7 refers to the mock-knighting in *AM*, V.ii.

68 *dead*: finished.

72 s.d. *Maria . . . bed*: The meaning of this spectacle is complicated by Antonio's earlier *doubles entendres* on rest and death (III.i.100–6); a tomb with a draped hearse above it bears a strong and often deliberate resemblance to a curtained four-poster bed. (Hooker's *Life of Sir P. Carey* records that 'his hearse was set up, being made after the form of a field-bed, covered with black', *OED*.) It is possible that the tomb actually doubles as a bed in this scene; in any case a strikingly ironic emblem is created; see below, lines 103 ff.

Amazing terror, what portent is this?
GHOST OF ANDRUGIO. Disloyal to our hymeneal rites,
What raging heat reigns in thy strumpet blood?
Hast thou so soon forgot Andrugio?
Are our love-bands so quickly cancellèd?
Where lives thy plighted faith unto this breast?
[*She weeps.*]
O weak Maria! Go to, calm thy fears.
I pardon thee, poor soul. O, shed no tears.
Thy sex is weak. That black incarnate fiend
May trip thy faith, that hath o'erthrown my life.
I was empoisoned by Piero's hand.
Join with my son to bend up strained revenge;
Maintain a seeming favour to his suit,
Till time may form our vengeance absolute.

Enter ANTONIO, *his arms bloody,*
[*bearing*] *a torch and a poniard.*

ANTONIO. See, unamazed I will behold thy face,
Outstare the terror of thy grim aspect,
Daring the horrid'st object of the night.
Look how I smoke in blood, reeking the steam
Of foaming vengeance. O, my soul's enthroned
In the triumphant chariot of revenge.
Methinks I am all air and feel no weight
Of human dirt clog. This is Julio's blood.
Rich music, father: this is Julio's blood.
Why lives that mother? [*Pointing to* MARIA.]

---

74 *hymeneal*: marriage.

78 *plighted . . . breast*: faith plighted to this breast (i.e. to me).

84 *bend up strained revenge*: 'i.e. to lift up the head of Vengeance, bent under the weight of the burden of duty' (Gair, connecting the line with III.i.46); or perhaps to draw revenge taut (as it might be, to draw a bow, or wind up an arquebus; *OED, vb.* 3).

86 s.d. Antonio's entry vividly pictures the way in which the revenger becomes the mirror image of his antagonist (cf. Piero at I.i s.d.); the scene which follows corresponds to the closet scene in *Hamlet* (III.iv).

91 *foaming*: frothing at the mouth (cf. II.i.94).

GHOST OF ANDRUGIO. Pardon ignorance.
Fly, dear Antonio.
Once more assume disguise, and dog the court
In feignèd habit till Piero's blood
May even o'erflow the brim of full revenge.
Peace and all blessèd fortunes to you both.
[*To* ANTONIO] Fly thou from court; be peerless in revenge.

Exit ANTONIO.

[*To* MARIA] Sleep thou in rest; lo, here I close thy couch.

Exit MARIA *to her bed,* ANDRUGIO *drawing the curtains.*

And now, ye sooty coursers of the night,
Hurry your chariot into hell's black womb.
Darkness, make flight; graves, eat your dead again;
Let's repossess our shrouds. Why lags delay?
Mount, sparkling brightness; give the world his day. *Exit* ANDRUGIO.

ACT IV

SCENE I

Enter ANTONIO *in a fool's habit with a little toy of a walnut shell and soap to make bubbles;* MARIA *and* ALBERTO.

MARIA. Away with this disguise in any hand!
ALBERTO. Fie, 'tis unsuiting to your elate spirit.
Rather put on some trans-shaped cavalier.

96 *Pardon ignorance*: forgive her for her ignorance of the situation.
103 *Sleep . . . couch*: when combined with the four following lines, this reads as though the Ghost were ushering Maria to a symbolic 'death'.
IV.i s.d. *fool's habit*: this seems like a more literal version of Hamlet's 'antic disposition'.
1 *in any hand*: in any case.
2 *elate*: elevated.
3 *trans-shaped*: transformed (to a condition of poverty).

Some habit of a spitting critic, whose mouth
Voids nothing but gentle and unvulgar
Rheum of censure; rather assume –

ANTONIO. Why then should I put on the very flesh
Of solid folly. No, this coxcomb is a crown
Which I affect, even with unbounded zeal.

ALBERTO. 'Twill thwart your plot, disgrace your high resolve.

ANTONIO. By wisdom's heart, there is no essence mortal
That I can envy, but a plump-cheeked fool.
O, he hath a patent of immunities,
Confirmed by custom, sealed by policy,
As large as spacious thought.

ALBERTO. You cannot press among the courtiers
And have access to –

ANTONIO. What, not a fool? Why, friend, a golden ass,
A baubled fool, are sole canonical,
Whilst pale-cheeked wisdom and lean-ribbèd art
Are kept in distance at the halberd's point,
All held apocrypha, not worth survey.
Why, by the genius of that Florentine,
Deep, deep-observing, sound-brained Machiavel,
He is not wise that strives not to seem fool.

---

4 *spitting critic*: snarling satirist, malcontent.
5 *Voids*: spits out.
5–6 *gentle and unvulgar Rheum*: gentlemanly and courtly spittle.
8 *coxcomb*: fool's cap.
11 *essence mortal*: mortal soul.
13–15 *he hath . . . thought*: both custom and the self-interest of politicians grant fools a freedom of speech as extensive as the reach of human thought itself.
18 *golden ass*: rich fool.
19 *baubled*: equipped with a fool's baton.
19–22 *canonical . . . apocrypha*: the analogy is with the accepted 'canonical' books of the Bible and those which Protestant doctrine considered of doubtful authenticity (the Apocrypha).
20 *art*: learning.
25 *He . . . fool*: Hunter cites Machiavelli, *Discourses*, III, 2: 'It is a very good notion at times to pretend to be a fool.'

When will the duke hold fee'd intelligence,
Keep wary observation in large pay,
To dog a fool's act?

MARIA. Ay, but such feigning, known, disgraceth much.

ANTONIO. Pish!
Most things that morally adhere to souls
Wholly exist in drunk opinion,
Whose reeling censure, if I value not,
It values naught.

MARIA. You are transported with too slight a thought,
If you but meditate of what is past
And what you plot to pass.

ANTONIO. Even in that, note a fool's beatitude:
He is not capable of passion;
Wanting the power of distinction,
He bears an unturned sail with every wind;
Blow east, blow west, he steers his course alike.
I never saw a fool lean; the chub-faced fop
Shines sleek with full-crammed fat of happiness,
Whilst studious contemplation sucks the juice
From wizards' cheeks, who, making curious search

26–7 *hold . . . pay*: maintain paid spies and informers.

31 *morally*: according to the normal human judgement (*OED*).

32 *opinion*: the false shadow of reason, based on mere sense impressions.

33 *reeling censure*: unsteady judgement.

34 *It values naught*: it is worth nothing.

35–7 *You . . . pass*: if you consider what has already happened, and what you hope to bring about, you will see that you have been carried away by too trivial a scheme.

38–59 a mock-encomium upon folly; mock-encomia were popular exercises amongst Inns of Court wits. Erasmus's *Praise of Folly* (*Encomium Moriae*) is the best-known and amongst the most elaborate examples of the genre.

40–2 *Wanting . . . alike*: the sense seems to be that, because the fool feels no passion, he can steer a straight course, whereas other men are blown to and fro as the winds of passion turn their sails.

43 *chub-faced fop*: plump-cheeked fool.

46 *wizards'*: wise men's.

For nature's secrets, the first innating cause
Laughs them to scorn as man doth busy apes
When they will zany men. Had heaven been
kind,
Creating me an honest, senseless dolt,
A good, poor fool, I should want sense to feel
The stings of anguish shoot through every vein;
I should not know what 'twere to lose a father;
I should be dead of sense to view defame
Blur my bright love; I could not thus run mad
As one confounded in a maze of mischief,
Staggered, stark felled with bruising stroke of
chance;
I should not shoot mine eyes into the earth,
Poring for mischief that might counterpoise

Enter LUCIO.

Mischief, murder, and – How now, Lucio?
LUCIO. My lord, the duke with the Venetian states
Approach the great hall to judge Mellida.
ANTONIO. Asked he for Julio yet?
LUCIO. No motion of him. Dare you trust this
habit?
ANTONIO. Alberto, see you straight rumour me
dead.
Leave me, good mother; leave me, Lucio;
Forsake me all.

Exeunt omnes, saving ANTONIO.

Now patience hoop my sides
With steelèd ribs lest I do burst my breast
With struggling passions. Now disguise stand
bold!

---

47 *first innating cause*: the Cause that produces all other causes, God.

48–9 *apes . . . men*: man is traditionally the 'ape of God'.

49 *zany*: 'imitate grotesquely, like the *Zanni* or clown of the *Commedia dell'Arte*' (Hunter).

54–5 *dead . . . love*: too insensitive to be aware of the dishonour that smirches my bright love.

58 *shoot mine eyes*: the figure depends on the notion that sight is produced by beams emanating from the eyes themselves.

64 *No . . . him*: no reference has been made to him.

Poor scornèd habits oft choice souls enfold.
The cornets sound a sennet.

Enter CASTILIO, FOROBOSCO, BALURDO, *and* ALBERTO, *with poleaxes;* LUCIO *bare;* PIERO *and* MARIA *talking together; two* SENATORS, GALEATZO *and* MATZAGENTE, NUTRICHE.

PIERO. [*to* MARIA] Entreat me not. There's not a beauty lives
Hath that imperial predominance
O'er my affects as your enchanting graces;
Yet give me leave to be myself –
ANTONIO. [*aside*] A villain.
PIERO. Just –
ANTONIO. [*aside*] Most just!
PIERO. Most just and upright in our judgement seat.
Were Mellida mine eye, with such a blemish
Of most loathed looseness, I would scratch it out.
Produce the strumpet in her bridal robes,
That she may blush t'appear so white in show
And black in inward substance. Bring her in.
Exeunt FOROBOSCO *and* CASTILIO.
I hold Antonio, for his father's sake,
So very dearly, so entirely choice,
That knew I but a thought of prejudice
Imagined 'gainst his high ennobled blood
I would maintain a mortal feud, undying hate
'Gainst the conceiver's life. And shall justice sleep
In fleshly lethargy for mine own blood's favour,
When the sweet prince hath so apparent scorn

---

70 s.d. *bare*: probably 'unarmed'.

73 *affects*: passions.

76–7 *Most just*: Antonio puns: Piero means he is a just man; Antonio affects to understand Piero's 'Just' as confirming his (Antonio's) assessment, 'A villain'. Piero, in turn, takes up Antonio's sardonic aside, as if it were a superlative correcting Piero's too-modest self-description.

89 *for . . . favour*: out of favouritism to my own family.

By my – I will not call her daughter? Go;
Conduct in the loved youth Antonio.
Exit ALBERTO *to fetch* ANTONIO.
He shall behold me spurn my private good.
Piero loves his honour more than's blood.

ANTONIO. [*aside*] The devil he does, more than both.

BALURDO. Stand back there, fool; I do hate a fool most – most – pathetically. O, these that have no sap of – of – retort and obtuse wit in them – faugh!

ANTONIO. [*blowing bubbles*] Puff! hold, world! Puff! hold, bubble! Puff! hold, world! Puff! break not behind! Puff! thou art full of wind; puff! keep up by wind. Puff! 'tis broke; and now I laugh like a good fool at the breath of mine own lips: he, he, he, he, he!

BALURDO. You fool!

ANTONIO. You fool! Puff!
[*Blows another bubble.*]

BALURDO. I cannot digest the – the – unvulgar fool. Go, fool.

PIERO. Forbear, Balurdo; let the fool alone.
(*Ficte*) [*To* ANTONIO] Come hither. [*To* MARIA] Is he your fool?

MARIA. Yes, my loved lord.

PIERO. [*aside*] Would all the states in Venice
were like thee;
O then I were secured.
He that's a villain or but meanly souled
Must still converse and cling to routs of fools

---

101 ff. Antonio's bubbles are satiric emblems for (*a*) the light and empty Balurdo, so full of wind (vacuous talk) that he is likely to burst ('break behind' – with a coarse *double entendre*); (*b*) as small globes, for the world, seen as puffed up with empty vanities; and (*c*) specifically for Piero's court world – a bubble which the sword of revenge is about to prick. The Restoration 'bubble' = dupe would also be appropriate, though *OED* records no example so early.

112 *Ficte*: Latin, 'feignedly, for a pretence'; here 'in an assumed tone of voice'.

115 *states*: nobles.

That cannot search the leaks of his defects.
O, your unsalted fresh fool is your only man;
These vinegar-tart spirits are too piercing,
Too searching in the unglued joints of shaken
wits.
Find they a chink, they'll wriggle in and in,
And eat like salt sea in his siddow ribs
Till they have opened all his rotten parts
Unto the vaunting surge of base contempt,
And sunk the tossèd galliass in depth
Of whirlpool scorn. Give me an honest fop –
[*To* ANTONIO] Dud-a, dud-a. [*Gives present*]
Why, lo, sir, this takes he
As grateful now as a monopoly.
The still flutes sound softly.

Enter FOROBOSCO *and* CASTILIO, MELLIDA *supported by two Waiting-women.*

MELLIDA. All honour to this royal confluence.
PIERO. Forbear, impure, to blot bright honour's
name
With thy defilèd lips. The flux of sin
Flows from thy tainted body, thou so foul,
So all-dishonoured, canst no honour give,
No wish of good that can have good effect

---

119 *leaks*: weak points; but the word begins a sustained, if somewhat muddled, nautical image, in which Piero identifies himself with the Ship of State.

120 *unsalted fresh*: naïve, innocent, without the sharp tang of wit.

122 *Too . . . wits*: too perceptive about the weak spots of those whose composure they have shaken.

124 *siddow*: soft, tender.

127 *galliass*: type of heavy war-galley, driven by both sails and oars.

129 *Dud-a*: baby-talk suitable to a fool.

129–30 *this . . . monopoly*: he receives this as gratefully as one might a monopoly; referring to the most hated form of royal patronage.

130 s.d. *still flutes*: soft-toned wooden flutes.

131 *confluence*: gathering.

133 *flux*: discharge (probably suggesting menstrual discharge as a sign of female corruptibility – the 'curse').

To this grave senate, and illustrate bloods.
Why stays the doom of death?
1 SENATOR. Who riseth up to manifest her guilt?
2 SENATOR. You must produce apparent proof, my lord.
PIERO. Why, where is Strotzo, he that swore he saw
The very act, and vowed Feliche fled
Upon his sight? on which I brake the breast
Of the adulterous lecher with five stabs.
[*To* CASTILIO] Go fetch in Strotzo.
[*Exit* CASTILIO.]
[*To* MELLIDA] Now, thou impudent,
If thou hast any drop of modest blood
Shrouded within thy cheeks, blush, blush for shame
That rumour yet may say thou felt'st defame.
MELLIDA. Produce the devil; let your Strotzo come;
I can defeat his strongest argument
Which –
PIERO. With what?
MELLIDA. With tears, with blushes, sighs and claspèd hands,
With innocent upreared arms to heaven,
With my unnooked simplicity. These, these
Must, will, can only quit my heart of guilt;
Heaven permits not taintless blood be spilt.
If no remorse live in your savage breast –
PIERO. Then thou must die.
MELLIDA. Yet, dying, I'll be blest.
PIERO. Accurst by me.
MELLIDA. Yet, blest, in that I strove
To live and die –
PIERO. My hate.
MELLIDA. Antonio's love.
ANTONIO. [*aside*] Antonio's love!

---

137 *illustrate*: illustrious.
138 *Why . . . death*: what is holding up the death sentence?
140 *apparent*: obvious, conclusive.
155 *unnooked*: open and straight.

Enter STROTZO, *a cord about his neck*[, *and* CASTILIO].

STROTZO. O what vast ocean of repentant tears
Can cleanse my breast from the polluting filth
Of ulcerous sin? Supreme Efficient,
Why cleav'st thou not my breast with thunderbolts
Of winged revenge?
PIERO. What means this passion?
ANTONIO. [*aside*] What villainy are they decocting now?
Umh!
STROTZO. *In me convertite ferrum, O proceres.*
Nihil iste, nec ista.
PIERO. Lay hold on him. What strange portent is this?
STROTZO. I will not flinch. Death, hell, more grimly stare
Within my heart than in your threat'ning brows.
Record, thou threefold guard of dreadest power,
What I here speak is forcèd from my lips
By the impulsive strain of conscience.
I have a mount of mischief clogs my soul
As weighty as the high-nolled Apennine;
Which I must straight disgorge or breast will burst.
I have defamed this lady wrongfully,
By instigation of Antonio,
Whose reeling love, tossed on each fancy's surge,
Began to loathe before it fully joyed.

---

163 ff. Strotzo's comically self-confident performance here is probably modelled on that of Pedringano in *The Spanish Tragedy*, III.vi.

165 *Supreme Efficient*: First Cause, Prime Mover, God.

170–1 *In me . . . ista*: 'Nobles, turn your swords on me; he has done nothing, nor has she'; cf. Virgil, *Aeneid*, IX, 427–8.

175 *threefold guard*: presumably Cerberus, the three-headed watchdog of the classical underworld.

177 *impulsive strain*: compelling power.

179 *high-nolled*: high-peaked.

184 *joyed*: enjoyed (Mellida).

PIERO. Go, seize Antonio! Guard him strongly in!
Exit FOROBOSCO.
STROTZO. By his ambition being only bribed,
Fee'd by his impious hand, I poisonèd
His agèd father, that his thirsty hopes
Might quench their dropsy of aspiring drought
With full unbounded quaff.
PIERO. Seize me Antonio!
STROTZO. O why permit you now such scum of filth
As Strotzo is to live and taint the air
With his infectious breath?
PIERO. Myself will be thy strangler, unmatched slave.

PIERO *comes from his chair, snatcheth the cord's end, and* CASTILIO *aideth him; both strangle* STROTZO.

STROTZO. Now change your –
PIERO. Ay, pluck, Castilio!
I change my humour. Pluck, Castilio!
Die, with thy death's entreats even in thy jaws!
Now, now, now, now, now. [*Aside*] My plot begins to work.
Why, thus should statesmen do,
That cleave through knots of craggy policies,
Use men like wedges, one strike out another
Till by degrees the tough and knurly trunk
Be rived in sunder. Where's Antonio?

Enter ALBERTO, *running.*

ALBERTO. O, black accursèd fate! Antonio's drowned.
PIERO. Speak, on thy faith, on thy allegiance, speak!
ALBERTO. As I do love Piero, he is drowned.

---

191 *seize me Antonio*: seize Antonio for me (ethic dative).
198 *death's entreats*: entreaties to be killed.
201 *craggy*: rock-like, hard to penetrate.
203 *knurly*: gnarled.
204 *rived*: split.
205 *O . . . drowned*: the black comedy is intensified by having the virtuous Alberto usurp Strotzo's role as ranting tragic actor.

ANTONIO. [*aside*] In an inundation of amazement.
MELLIDA. Ay, is this the close of all my strains in love?
O me, most wretched maid!
PIERO. Antonio drowned? How, how, Antonio drowned?
ALBERTO. Distraught and raving, from a turret's top
He threw his body in the high-swoll'n sea;
And as he headlong topsy-turvy dinged down
He still cried 'Mellida!'
ANTONIO. [*aside*] My love's bright crown!
MELLIDA. He still cried 'Mellida!'
PIERO. Daughter, methinks your eyes should sparkle joy,
Your bosom rise on tiptoe at this news.
MELLIDA. Ay me!
PIERO. How now, 'Ay me!'? Why, art not great of thanks
To gracious heaven for the just revenge
Upon the author of thy obloquies?
MARIA. [*aside*] Sweet beauty, I could sigh as fast as you,
But that I know that which I weep to know:
His fortunes should be such he dare not show
His open presence.
MELLIDA. I know he loved me dearly, dearly, I;
And since I cannot live with him, I die. [*Faints.*]
PIERO. 'Fore heaven, her speech falters; look, she swoons.
Convey her up into her private bed.

MARIA, NUTRICHE, *and the Ladies bear out* MELLIDA, *as being swooned.*

I hope she'll live. If not –
ANTONIO. Antonio's dead!

---

214 *dinged down*: threw himself violently down.
218 *bosom . . . tiptoe*: surely a deliberately ridiculous figure.
222 *obloquies*: disgrace.
225 *should be such*: indeed are such.
227 *dearly, I*: I loved him dearly too; 'dearly' also contains the sense of 'costly': love has brought her death.

The fool will follow too. He, he, he!
[*Aside*] Now works the scene; quick observation scud
To cote the plot, or else the path is lost;
My very self am gone, my way is fled;
Ay, all is lost if Mellida is dead. *Exit* ANTONIO.

PIERO. Alberto, I am kind, Alberto, kind.
I am sorry for thy coz, i'faith I am.
Go, take him down and bear him to his father.
Let him be buried, look ye; I'll pay the priest.

ALBERTO. Please you to admit his father to the court?

PIERO. No.

ALBERTO. Please you to restore his lands and goods again?

PIERO. No.

ALBERTO. Please you vouchsafe him lodging in the city?

PIERO. God's fut, no, thou odd uncivil fellow!
I think you do forget, sir, where you are.

ALBERTO. I know you do forget, sir, where you must be.

FOROBOSCO. You are too malapert, i'faith you are.
Your honour might do well to –

ALBERTO. Peace, parasite! thou bur that only sticks
Unto the nap of greatness.

PIERO. Away with that same yelping cur, away!

ALBERTO. Ay, I am gone; but mark, Piero, this:
There is a thing called scourging Nemesis.
Exit ALBERTO.

233–4 *scene . . . plot*: like other revengers (Hieronimo, Hamlet), Antonio usurps the villain's function as machiavellian 'dramatist'.

233–4 *scud . . . cote*: hasten to keep pace with; dogs are said to 'cote' one another when coursing (*OED*).

248 *where you must be*: i.e. in the grave (and therefore facing the judgement of God).

252 *nap*: the pile or woolly surface of cloth.

255 *There . . . Nemesis*: cf. *The Spanish Tragedy*, 'there is Nemesis and Furies,/And things call'd whips' (Third Addition).

BALURDO. God's neaks! he has wrong, that he has; and, 'sfut, and I were as he, I would bear no coals. La, I – I begin to swell – puff!

PIERO. How now, fool, fop, fool!

BALURDO. Fool, fop, fool! Marry muff! I pray you, how many fools have you seen go in a suit of satin? I hope yet I do not look a fool i'faith. A fool? God's bores, I scorn't with my heel. 'Sneaks, and I were worth but three hundred pound a year more, I could swear richly; nay, but as poor as I am, I will swear the fellow hath wrong.

PIERO. [*aside*] Young Galeatzo! Ay, a proper man;
Florence, a goodly city; it shall be so.
I'll marry her to him instantly.
Then Genoa mine by my Maria's match,
Which I'll solemnise ere next setting sun;
Thus Venice, Florence, Genoa, strongly leagued.
Excellent, excellent! I'll conquer Rome,
Pop out the light of bright religion;
And then, helter-skelter, all cocksure!

BALURDO. Go to, 'tis just; the man hath wrong; go to.

PIERO. Go to, thou shalt have right; go to, Castilio,
Clap him into the palace dungeon;
Lap him in rags and let him feed on slime
That smears the dungeon cheek. Away with him!

BALURDO. In very good truth now, I'll ne'er do so more; this one time and –

PIERO. Away with him; observe it strictly; go!

BALURDO. Why then, O wight,
Alas, poor knight,

257–8 *bear . . . coals*: submit to no such humiliation.
260 *Marry muff*: meaningless expletive.
261–2 *fools . . . satin*: i.e. noblemen (a reference to the Statutes of Apparel, or sumptuary laws).
274–6 *I'll conquer . . . cocksure*: perhaps parodying a well-known speech from Marlowe (*Edward II*, I.iv.97–105, *Massacre at Paris*, xxv.59–66).
285–90 *Why . . . good night*: the song imitates the style of Bottom's passion in *A Midsummer Night's Dream*, V.i.268 ff. (Hunter) to parody two ballads on the death of Essex (Gair).

O welladay, Sir Jeffrey!
Let poets roar,
And all deplore;
For now I bid you good night.
Exit BALURDO *with* CASTILIO.

[*Enter* MARIA.]

MARIA. O piteous end of love! O too too rude hand
Of unrespective death! Alas, sweet maid!
PIERO. Forbear me, heaven! What intend these plaints?
MARIA. The beauty of admired creation,
The life of modest, unmixed purity,
Our sex's glory, Mellida, is –
PIERO. What? O heaven, what?
MARIA. Dead!
PIERO. May it not sad your thoughts, how?
MARIA. Being laid upon her bed, she grasped my hand,
And, kissing it, spake thus: 'Thou very poor,
Why dost not weep? The jewel of thy brow,
The rich adornment that enchased thy breast,
Is lost; thy son, my love is lost, is dead.
And do I live to say Antonio's dead?
And have I lived to see his virtues blurred
With guiltless blots? O world, thou art too subtle
For honest natures to converse withal.
Therefore I'll leave thee; farewell, mart of woe,
I fly to clip my love, Antonio.'
With that her head sunk down upon her breast;
Her cheek changed earth, her senses slept in rest;

---

292 *unrespective*: without respect; therefore 'unselective, arbitrary'.
299 *May . . . how*: provided it will not be too painful to you, tell me how.
303 *enchased*: set with jewels.
307 *guiltless blots*: crimes of which he is innocent.
309 *mart of woe*: place where only sorrow can be obtained.
312 *changed earth*: turned to earth (i.e. died).

Until my fool, that pressed unto the bed,
Screeched out so loud that he brought back her soul,
Called her again, that her bright eyes 'gan ope
And stared upon him; he, audacious fool,
Dared kiss her hand, wished her soft rest, loved bride;
She fumbled out, 'Thanks, good', and so she died.

PIERO. And so she died! I do not use to weep,
But by thy love, out of whose fertile sweet
I hope for as fair fruit, I am deep sad.
I will not stay my marriage for all this.
Castilio, Forobosco, all,
Strain all your wits, wind up invention
Unto his highest bent, to sweet this night;
Make us drink Lethe by your quaint conceits,
That for two days oblivion smother grief;
But when my daughter's exequies approach,
Let's all turn sighers. Come, despite of fate,
Sound loudest music; let's pace out in state.

The cornets sound. Exeunt.

SCENE II

Enter ANTONIO *solus, in fool's habit.*

ANTONIO. Ay, Heaven, thou mayst; thou mayst, Omnipotence.
What vermin bred of putrefacted slime
Shall dare to expostulate with thy decrees?
O Heaven, thou mayst indeed; she was all thine,
All heavenly; I did but humbly beg

---

320 *sweet*: sweetness, blossom.
324–5 *Strain . . . bent*: stretch your powers of invention to their limit (apparently a musical metaphor; but cf. III.ii.84).
325 *sweet*: sweeten, make pleasant.
326 *drink Lethe*: forget our griefs; the waters of the river Lethe, in Hades, brought oblivion.
328 *exequies*: funeral ceremonies.
330 *in state*: in a formal, stately procession.
1 *thou mayst*: i.e. permit such things as Mellida's death.

To borrow her of thee a little time.
Thou gav'st her me, as some weak-breasted dame
Giveth her infant, puts it out to nurse,
And when it once goes high-lone, takes it back.
She was my vital blood; and yet, and yet,
I'll not blaspheme. Look here, behold!

ANTONIO *puts off his cap and lieth just upon his back.*

I turn my prostrate breast upon thy face,
And vent a heaving sigh. O hear but this:
I am a poor, poor orphan; a weak, weak child,
The wrack of splitted fortune, the very ooze,
The quicksand that devours all misery.
Behold the valiant'st creature that doth breathe!
For all this, I dare live, and I will live,
Only to numb some others' cursèd blood
With the dead palsy of like misery.
Then death, like to a stifling incubus,
Lie on my bosom. Lo, sir, I am sped.
My breast is Golgotha, grave for the dead.

Enter PANDULPHO, ALBERTO, *and a Page, carrying* FELICHE*'s trunk in a winding sheet, and lay it thwart* ANTONIO*'s breast.*

PANDULPHO. Antonio, kiss my foot; I honour thee
In laying thwart my blood upon thy breast.
I tell thee, boy, he was Pandolpho's son,
And I do grace thee with supporting him.
Young man,
The domineering monarch of the earth,

---

9 *high-lone*: completely alone.

11 s.d. *lieth . . . back*: the posture again evokes tomb-sculpture; cf. line 23, 'My breast is . . . grave for the dead' and the ritual with Feliche's body (23 s.d.).

15 *wrack . . . fortune*: the wreck left when the ship of fortune has split open (Hunter).

21 *incubus*: nightmare, demonic spirit.

29 *domineering monarch of the earth*: i.e. the Stoic sage; but the line recalls traditional descriptions of King Death, which gives it an ironic resonance.

He who hath naught that fortune's gripe can seize,
He who is all impregnably his own,
He whose great heart heaven cannot force with force,
Vouchsafes his love. *Non servio Deo, sed assentio.*

ANTONIO. I ha' lost a good wife.

PANDULPHO. Didst find her good, or didst thou make her good?
If found, thou mayst re-find, because thou hadst her.
If made, the work is lost; but thou that mad'st her
Liv'st yet as cunning. Hast lost a good wife?
Thrice-blessèd man that lost her whilst she was good,
Fair, young, unblemished, constant, loving, chaste.
I tell thee, youth, age knows young loves seem graced
Which with grey cares' rude jars are oft defaced.

ANTONIO. But she was full of hope.

PANDULPHO. May be, may be; but that which 'may be' stood,
Stands now without all 'may'; she died good;
And dost thou grieve?

ALBERTO. I ha' lost a true friend.

PANDULPHO. I live encompassed with two blessèd souls!
Thou lost a good wife, thou lost a true friend, ha?

---

33 *Non . . . assentio*: 'I am not God's slave, but give my assent to his decrees', Seneca, *De Providentia*, V, 6 (reading *assentior*).

34–8 *I ha' lost . . . cunning*: adapted from the dialogue between Soul and Reason in Whyttynton's version of Seneca's *De Remediis Fortuitorum* (Hunter); Marston continues to paraphrase this dialogue to line 55.

41–2 *age . . . defaced*: an old man knows that young love, which seems so fortunate, is frequently made wretched by the cares and quarrels that come with advancing age.

44–5 *but . . . good*: he means that only death can confirm for all time the merely potential goodness of a life in progress.

Two of the rarest lendings of the heavens;
But lendings, which, at the fixed day of pay
Set down by fate, thou must restore again.
O what unconscionable souls are here!
Are you all like the spokeshaves of the church?
Have you no maw to restitution?
Hast lost a true friend, coz? Then thou hadst
one.
I tell thee, youth, 'tis all as difficult
To find true friend in this apostate age,
That balks all right affiance 'twixt two hearts,
As 'tis to find a fixèd modest heart
Under a painted breast. Lost a true friend!
O happy soul, that lost him whilst he was true!
Believe it, coz, I to my tears have found,
Oft dirt's respect makes firmer friends unsound.

ALBERTO. You have lost a good son.

PANDULPHO. Why, there's the comfort on't, that
he was good.
Alas, poor innocent!

ALBERTO. Why weeps mine uncle?

PANDULPHO. Ha, dost ask me why? ha? ha?
Good coz, look here.

He shows him his son's breast.

Man will break out, despite philosophy.
Why, all this while I ha' but played a part,
Like to some boy that acts a tragedy,
Speaks burly words and raves out passion;
But when he thinks upon his infant weakness,
He droops his eye. I spake more than a god,
Yet am less than a man.

---

52 *unconscionable*: conscienceless.

53 *the spokeshaves of the church*: those who corruptly strip away the wealth of the church for their own use.

54 *maw to restitution*: desire to return what you have devoured.

58 *balks . . . affiance*: hinders any true uniting.

63 *dirt's respect*: the love of gold.

70–4 *Why . . . eye*: the disjunction between the boys' acting style and the play's tragic subject, elsewhere used to create burlesque effects, here becomes a pathetic emblem of man's inadequacy to the heroic aspirations of moral philosophy.

72 *burly*: bombastic.

I am the miserablest soul that breathes.

ANTONIO *starts up.*

ANTONIO. 'Slid, sir, ye lie! by th'heart of grief, thou liest!
I scorn't that any wretched should survive
Outmounting me in that superlative:
Most miserable, most unmatched in woe.
Who dare assume that, but Antonio?

PANDULPHO. Will't still be so? And shall yon bloodhound live?

ANTONIO. Have I an arm, a heart, a sword, a soul?

ALBERTO. Were you but private unto what we know!

PANDULPHO. I'll know it all; first, let's inter the dead;
Let's dig his grave with that shall dig the heart,
Liver and entrails of the murderer.

They strike the stage with their daggers, and the grave openeth.

ANTONIO. [*to Page*] Wilt sing a dirge, boy?

PANDULPHO. No; no song; 'twill be vile out of tune.

ALBERTO. Indeed he's hoarse; the poor boy's voice is cracked.

PANDULPHO. Why, coz, why should it not be hoarse and cracked,
When all the strings of nature's symphony
Are cracked and jar? Why should his voice keep tune,
When there's no music in the breast of man?
I'll say an honest antique rhyme I have –
Help me, good sorrow-mates, to give him grave.

They all help to carry FELICHE *to his grave.*

Death, exile, plaints and woe,

77–81 *'Slid . . . Antonio*: cf. Hamlet's rhetorical competition in grief with Laertes (*Hamlet*, V.i.248–78).

87 s.d. *They . . . daggers*: cf. *The Spanish Tragedy*, III.xii.71.

89 *vile out of tune*: cf. Malevole's 'vilest out-of-tune music', the symbolic discords with which *The Malcontent* opens.

97–106 This dirge again makes use of Seneca's *De Remediis*, probably in Whyttynton's translation: Gair cites parallels to 97–100 on p. 65, and a parallel to 101–2 on p. 33.

Are but man's lackeys, not his foe.
No mortal 'scapes from fortune's war
Without a wound, at least a scar.
Many have led these to the grave,
But all shall follow, none shall save.
Blood of my youth, rot and consume;
Virtue in dirt doth life assume.
With this old saw close up this dust:
Thrice-blessèd man that dieth just.

ANTONIO. The gloomy wing of night begins to stretch
His lazy pinion over all the air;
We must be stiff and steady in resolve.
Let's thus our hands, our hearts, our arms involve.

They wreathe their arms.

PANDULPHO. Now swear we by this Gordian knot of love,
By the fresh turned-up mould that wraps my son,
By the dread brow of triple Hecate,
Ere night shall close the lids of yon bright stars
We'll sit as heavy on Piero's heart
As Etna doth on groaning Pelorus.

ANTONIO. Thanks, good old man. We'll cast at royal chance.
Let's think a plot; then pell-mell vengeance!

Exeunt, their arms wreathed.

The cornets sound for the Act.

---

102 *none shall save*: none shall be saved (exempted).
104 *Virtue . . . assume*: virtue has its true life in death (cf. lines 44–5).
105 *saw*: proverb.
110 *involve*: link together; perhaps the image of three revengers linked in a 'Gordian knot' is meant to suggest the figure of 'triple Hecate' (113).
111 *Gordian*: the Gordian knot, too intricate to be untied, was cut by Alexander the Great.
113 *triple Hecate*: Hecate, the goddess of the underworld and of witchcraft, had three manifestations: as Luna, Diana, and Proserpina = Hecate.
116 *Etna . . . Pelorus*: 'Jupiter crushed Typhoeus beneath Etna; Pelorus, a cape in Sicily, lies "below" (i.e. fifty miles N. of) Etna' (Hunter).
117 *cast . . . chance*: throw dice for high stakes (with a pun on Piero's 'royal' rank).

ACT V

SCENE I

The dumb-show.

Enter at one door CASTILIO *and* FOROBOSCO, *with halberds, four Pages with torches,* LUCIO *bare,* PIERO, MARIA, *and* ALBERTO, *talking.* ALBERTO *draws out his dagger,* MARIA *her knife, aiming to menace the Duke. Then* GALEATZO *betwixt two Senators, reading a paper to them; at which they all make semblance of loathing* PIERO, *and knit their fists at him; two Ladies and* NUTRICHE. *All these go softly over the stage, whilst at the other door enters the Ghost of* ANDRUGIO, *who passeth by them tossing his torch about his head in triumph. All forsake the stage, saving* ANDRUGIO, *who, speaking, begins the Act.*

GHOST OF ANDRUGIO. *Venit dies, tempusque, quo reddat suis*
Animam squallentem sceleribus.
The fist of strenuous vengeance is clutched,
The stern Vindicta tow'reth up aloft
That she may fall with a more weighty peise
And crush life's sap from out Piero's veins.
Now 'gins the leprous cores of ulcered sins

1–2 *Venit . . . sceleribus*: 'The day has come and the very time, when he will pay back the foul spirit for its crimes' (Seneca, *Octavia*, 629–30).

3 *strenuous*: vigorous, energetic, valiant; apparently coined by Marston; the whole line is mocked in Jonson's *Poetaster,* V.iii.291–2, and in the collaborate 'Fletcher' play *The Honest Man's Fortune*, II.i. (Beaumont and Fletcher, X, 233).

4 *Vindicta*: Revenge.

Wheel to a head; now is his fate grown mellow,
Instant to fall into the rotten jaws
Of chap-fall'n death. Now down looks
providence
T'attend the last act of my son's revenge.
Be gracious, observation, to our scene;
For now the plot unites his scattered limbs
Close in contracted bands. The Florence prince,
Drawn by firm notice of the duke's black deeds,
Is made a partner in conspiracy.
The states of Venice are so swoll'n in hate
Against the duke for his accursèd deeds
(Of which they are confirmed by some odd
letters
Found in dead Strotzo's study, which had
passed
Betwixt Piero and the murd'ring slave)
That they can scarce retain from bursting forth
In plain revolt. O, now triumphs my ghost,
Exclaiming 'Heaven's just, for I shall see
The scourge of murder and impiety.' *Exit.*

SCENE II

BALURDO [*speaks*] *from under the stage.*

BALURDO. Ho, who's above there, ho? A murrain on all proverbs! They say hunger breaks through stone walls, but I am as gaunt as lean-ribbed

---

8 *Wheel to a head*: swell to a (round) head.
8–10 *now . . . death*: cf. *Richard III*, IV.iv.1–2.
9 *Instant*: ready.
10 *chap-fall'n*: with the lower jaw gaping open.
10–11 *Now . . . revenge*: again recalls the audience-role of Revenge and Andrea in *The Spanish Tragedy*.
V.ii s.d. *from under the stage*: Balurdo's voice sounds from the same place (the traditional 'hell' of the Elizabethan stage) as the ghosts of Andrugio and Feliche at III.i.126–8; thus Balurdo can see his escape as the rising of a ghost from hell (7–8). The whole passage is an ironic recollection of *AM*, II.i.256–64.
1 *murrain*: plague.
2–3 *hunger . . . walls*: proverbial, Tilley H811.

famine, yet I can burst through no stone walls. O now, Sir Jeffrey, show thy valour; break prison and be hanged.
Nor shall the darkest nook of hell contain
The discontented Sir Balurdo's ghost.

[*He climbs out.*]

Well, I am out well; I have put off the prison to put on the rope. O poor shotten herring, what a pickle art thou in! O hunger, how thou domineerest in my guts! O for a fat leg of ewe mutton in stewed broth, or drunken song to feed on. I could belch rarely, for I am all wind. O cold, cold, cold, cold, cold! O poor knight, O poor Sir Jeffrey! Sing like an unicorn before thou dost dip thy horn in the water of death. O cold, O sing, O cold, O poor Sir Jeffrey, sing, sing!

Cantat.

Enter ANTONIO *and* ALBERTO *at several doors, their rapiers drawn, in their masquing attire.*

ANTONIO. *Vindicta!*
ALBERTO. Mellida!
ANTONIO. Alberto!
ALBERTO. Antonio!
ANTONIO. Hath the duke supped?

9–10 *put . . . rope*: playing on 'be hanged' (6); breaking prison was a hanging matter.

10 *shotten herring*: herring that has spawned: a type of emaciation.

12–14 *fat . . . on*: recalls *AM*, V.i.24–6.

16–17 *Sing . . . death*: Balurdo conflates two pieces of beast lore: the swan was supposed to sing before it died; the unicorn could dip its magically potent horn into water that had been poisoned by serpents and so purify it.

ALBERTO. Yes, and triumphant revels mount aloft;
The duke drinks deep to overflow his grief.
The court is racked to pleasure; each man strains
To feign a jocund eye. The Florentine –
ANTONIO. Young Galeatzo?
ALBERTO. Even he is mighty on our part. The states
Of Venice –

Enter PANDULPHO *running, in masquing attire.*

PANDULPHO. Like high-swoll'n floods, drive down the muddy dams
Of pent allegiance! O, my lusty bloods,
Heaven sits clapping of our enterprise.
I have been labouring general favour firm,
And I do find the citizens grown sick
With swallowing the bloody crudities
Of black Piero's acts; they fain would cast
And vomit him from off their government.
Now is the plot of mischief ripped wide ope:
Letters are found 'twixt Strotzo and the duke
So clear apparent, yet more firmly strong
By suiting circumstance, that as I walked
Muffled, to eavesdrop speech, I might observe
The graver statesmen whispering fearfully.
Here one gives nods and hums what he would speak;

25–8 *triumphant . . . eye*: cf. *Hamlet*, I.iv.8–12; perhaps similar noises off are required here, as at 92–3 below.
27 *racked*: the implication is that the pleasures of court revels are a kind of torture to the reluctant courtiers, 'straining' to appear merry (25–6).
34 *Heaven . . . clapping*: cf. above, V.i.10–11; possibly a dramatised s.d. for thunderclaps (cf. *The Revenger's Tragedy*, IV.ii.200–1).
35 *labouring . . . firm*: trying to consolidate public opinion in our favour.
37 *crudities*: undigested gobbets of food.
38 *cast*: vomit up.
43 *suiting circumstance*: circumstantial confirmation.
46 *hums*: murmurs, mutters inarticulately.

The rumour's got 'mong troop of citizens,
Making loud murmur with confusèd din.
One shakes his head and sighs, 'O ill-used power!'
Another frets and sets his grinding teeth
Foaming with rage, and swears this must not be.
Here one complots and, on a sudden, starts
And cries, 'O monstrous, O deep villainy!'
All knit their nerves and from beneath swoll'n brows
Appears a gloating eye of much mislike;
Whilst swart Piero's lips reek steam of wine,
Swallows lust-thoughts, devours all pleasing hopes
With strong imagination of – what not?
O, now, *Vindicta!* that's the word we have:
A royal vengeance or a royal grave!

ANTONIO. *Vindicta!*

BALURDO. I am a-cold.

PANDULPHO. Who's there? Sir Jeffrey!

BALURDO. A poor knight, God wot; the nose of my knighthood is bitten off with cold. O poor Sir Jeffrey, cold, cold!

PANDULPHO. What chance of fortune hath tripped up his heels
And laid him in the kennel, ha?

ALBERTO. I will discourse it all. Poor honest soul,
Hadst thou a beaver to clasp up thy face
Thou shouldst associate us in masquery
And see revenge.

BALURDO. Nay, and you talk of revenge, my stomach's up, for I am most tyranically hungry. A beaver? I have a head-piece, a skull, a brain of proof, I warrant ye.

---

52 *complots*: sets up a conspiracy.
59 *word*: watchword, slogan.
60 *royal*: punning on Piero's 'royal' status and 'royal' = noble, splendid.
68 *kennel*: gutter.
70 *beaver to clasp up*: helmet to cover.
71 *associate us*: join with us.
74 *stomach*: both 'appetite' and 'indignation'.
75–6 *brain of proof*: impenetrable brain (i.e. thick head).

ALBERTO. Slink to my chamber then and 'tire thee.
BALURDO. Is there a fire?
ALBERTO. Yes.
BALURDO. Is there a fat leg of ewe mutton?
ALBERTO. Yes.
BALURDO. And a clean shirt?
ALBERTO. Yes.
BALURDO. Then am I for you, most pathetically and unvulgarly, la! *Exit.*
ANTONIO. Resolved hearts, time curtails night, opportunity shakes us his foretop. Steel your thoughts, sharp your resolve, embolden your spirit, grasp your swords, alarum mischief, and with an undaunted brow out-scout the grim opposition of most menacing peril.
[*Sounds of revelry off-stage.*]
Hark here! proud pomp shoots mounting triumph up,
Borne in loud accents to the front of Jove.
PANDULPHO. O now, he that wants soul to kill a slave,
Let him die slave and rot in peasant's grave.
ANTONIO. Give me thy hand, and thine, most noble heart;
Thus will we live and, but thus, never part.
Exeunt twined together.

SCENE III

Cornets sound a sennet.

Enter CASTILIO *and* FOROBOSCO, *two Pages with torches,* LUCIO *bare,* PIERO *and* MARIA, GALEATZO, *two* SENATORS, *and* NUTRICHE.

PIERO. (*to* MARIA) Sit close unto my breast, heart of my love;

---

87 *opportunity . . . foretop*: cf. above, III.i.45–6.
90 *out-scout*: out-manoeuvre.
92–3 cf. above, lines 25–8.

Advance thy drooping eyes; thy son is drowned
(Rich happiness that such a son is drowned!),
Thy husband's dead. Life of my joys, most blessed,
In that the sapless log that pressed thy bed
With an unpleasing weight, being lifted hence,
Even I, Piero, live to warm his place.
I tell you, lady, had you viewed us both
With an unpartial eye when first we wooed
Your maiden beauties, I had borne the prize.
'Tis firm I had; for, fair, I ha' done that –

MARIA. [*aside*] Murder!

PIERO. Which he would quake to have adventurèd.
Thou know'st I have –

MARIA. [*aside*] Murdered my husband.

PIERO. Borne out the shock of war, and done, what not,
That valour durst. Dost love me, fairest? Say!

MARIA. As I do hate my son, I love thy soul.

PIERO. Why then, *Io* to Hymen! Mount a lofty note,
Fill red-cheeked Bacchus, let Lyaeus float
In burnished goblets! Force the plump-lipped god
Skip light lavoltas in your full-sapped veins.
'Tis well, brim-full. Even I have glut of blood.
Let quaff carouse; I drink this Bordeaux wine
Unto the health of dead Andrugio,
Feliche, Strotzo, and Antonio's ghosts.
[*Aside*] Would I had some poison to infuse it with,
That, having done this honour to the dead,

---

2 *Advance*: raise.
5 *sapless*: suggests sexual impotence.
5 *log*: cf. Aesop's King Log, 'the type of inertness on the part of rulers' (*OED*).
19 *Io*: a shout of praise given to the wedding-god, Hymen.
19 *Mount*: raise, sound.
20 *Bacchus . . . Lyaeus*: names for the god of wine; hence wine.
22 *lavolta*: lively dance involving high leaps by the male partner.
24 *Let quaff carouse*: let healths go round.

I might send one to give them notice on't. –
I would endear my favour to the full.
Boy, sing aloud, make heaven's vault to ring
With thy breath's strength. I drink. Now loudly
sing.

Cantat.

The song ended, the cornets sound a sennet.

Enter ANTONIO, PANDULPHO, *and* ALBERTO *in masquery,* BALURDO *and a torch-bearer.*

PIERO. Call Julio hither; where's the little soul?
I saw him not today. Here's sport alone
For him, i'faith; for babes and fools, I know,
Relish not substance but applaud the show.

GALEATZO. (*to the conspirators as they stand in rank for the measure*)
(*To* ANTONIO) All blessèd fortune crown your
brave attempt.
(*To* PANDULPHO) I have a troop to second
your attempt.
(*To* ALBERTO) The Venice states join hearts
unto your hands.

PIERO. By the delights in contemplation
Of coming joys, 'tis magnificent.
You grace my marriage eve with sumptuous
pomp.
Sound still, loud music. O, your breath gives
grace
To curious feet that in proud measure pace.

ANTONIO. [*aside*] Mother, is Julio's body –

MARIA. [*aside*] Speak not, doubt not; all is above
all hope.

ANTONIO. [*aside*] Then will I dance and whirl
about the air.
Methinks I am all soul, all heart, all spirit.

---

30 *I . . . full*: (because) I should like to make my favours to the dead as dear as possible.

34 *alone*: especially suited.

36 s.d. *measure*: slow, stately dance.

39 *Venice states*: Venetian nobles; or here, perhaps, the three 'estates' that make up the nation.

44 *curious*: intricately moving.

Now murder shall receive his ample merit.

The Measure.

While the measure is dancing, ANDRUGIO*'s ghost is placed betwixt the music-houses.*

PIERO. Bring hither suckets, candied delicates.
We'll taste some sweetmeats, gallants, ere we sleep.

ANTONIO. [*aside*] We'll cook your sweetmeats, gallants, with tart sour sauce.

GHOST OF ANDRUGIO. [*aside*] Here will I sit, spectator of revenge,
And glad my ghost in anguish of my foe.

The maskers whisper with PIERO.

PIERO. Marry, and shall; i'faith, I were too rude
If I gainsaid so civil fashion. –
The maskers pray you to forbear the room
Till they have banqueted. Let it be so;
No man presume to visit them, on death.

[*Exeunt Courtiers.*]

The maskers whisper again.

Only myself? O, why, with all my heart.
I'll fill your consort; here Piero sits.
Come on, unmask; let's fall to.

The conspirators bind PIERO, *pluck out his tongue, and triumph over him.*

---

49 s.d. *betwixt the music-houses*: at Paul's playhouse 'the design of the "above" created the effect of three house locations; at either side of a central curtained space . . . there was a "*music house*" . . . and in at least one of these houses . . . there was an operating casement window' (Gair, p. 28).

50 *suckets*: sweetmeats of candied fruit (*OED*).

53 *spectator of revenge*: the Ghost's posture as stage audience (the 'above' was often used for additional seating when not required in the play) again recalls the function of Andrea's Ghost in *The Spanish Tragedy* (see above, V.i.10–11); Marston imitates Kyd's ingenious multiplication of stage audiences (and so levels of 'reality') in his final scene.

59 *on death*: on pain of death.

62 s.d. *pluck out his tongue*: cf. *Titus Andronicus*, II.iv, *The Spanish Tragedy*, IV.iv, and *The Revenger's Tragedy*, III.v; in Marston's play the mutilation lacks the clear metaphoric dimension it is given in these other works, however.

ANTONIO. Murder and torture; no prayers, no entreats.
PANDULPHO. We'll spoil your oratory. Out with his tongue!
ANTONIO. I have't, Pandulpho; the veins panting bleed,
Trickling fresh gore about my fist. Bind fast! So, so.
GHOST OF ANDRUGIO. Blest be thy hand. I taste the joys of heaven,
Viewing my son triumph in his black blood.
BALURDO. Down to the dungeon with him; I'll dungeon with him; I'll fool you! Sir Jeffrey will be Sir Jeffrey. I'll tickle you!
ANTONIO. Behold, black dog!
PANDULPHO. Grinn'st thou, thou snarling cur?
ALBERTO. Eat thy black liver!
ANTONIO. To thine anguish see
A fool triumphant in thy misery.
Vex him, Balurdo.
PANDULPHO. He weeps. Now do I glorify my hands;
I had no vengeance if I had no tears.
ANTONIO. [*indicates the banquet*] Fall to, good duke. O these are worthless cates;
You have no stomach to them. Look, look here:
Here lies a dish to feast thy father's gorge.
Here's flesh and blood which I am sure thou lov'st.

[*He uncovers the dish containing Julio's limbs.*] PIERO *seems to condole his son.*

PANDULPHO. Was he thy flesh, thy son, thy dearest son?
ANTONIO. So was Andrugio my dearest father.
PANDULPHO. So was Feliche my dearest son.

Enter MARIA.

76–7 *Now . . . tears*: adapted from Seneca, *Thyestes*, 1096–8. Seneca's following two lines are imitated at 94–6 (Cunliffe); *Thyestes* is, of course, the play from which the cannibal banquet derives.

81 s.d. *Piero . . . son*: note the unexpected pathos of this tableau.

MARIA. So was Andrugio my dearest husband.
ANTONIO. My father found no pity in thy blood.
PANDULPHO. Remorse was banished when thou slew'st my son.
MARIA. When thou empoisonèd'st my loving lord,
Exiled was piety.
ANTONIO. Now, therefore, pity, piety, remorse,
Be aliens to our thoughts: grim fire-eyed rage
Possess us wholly.
[PIERO *again seems to condole his son.*]
PANDULPHO. Thy son? True; and which is my most joy,
I hope no bastard, but thy very blood,
Thy true-begotten, most legitimate
And lovèd issue. There's the comfort on't.
ANTONIO. Scum of the mud of hell!
ALBERTO. Slime of all filth!
MARIA. Thou most detested toad!
BALURDO. Thou most retort and obtuse rascal!
ANTONIO. Thus charge we death at thee. Remember hell,
And let the howling murmurs of black spirits,
The horrid torments of the damnèd ghosts,
Affright thy soul as it descendeth down
Into the entrails of the ugly deep.
PANDULPHO. Sa, sa! No, let him die and die, and still be dying.
They offer to run all at PIERO, *and on a sudden stop.*
And yet not die till he hath died and died
Ten thousand deaths in agony of heart.
ANTONIO. Now, pell-mell! Thus the hand of heaven chokes
The throat of murder. This for my father's blood! *He stabs* PIERO.
PANDULPHO. This for my son! [*Stabs him.*]
ALBERTO. This for them all! [*Stabs him.*]

---

105 *Sa, sa*: shout used when making a thrust in fencing (*OED*).

105 s.d. *They offer . . . stop*: this s.d. and the one at 112 suggest carefully choreographed action, resembling part of the masque dance.

And this, and this! Sink to the heart of hell!
They run all at PIERO *with their rapiers.*
PANDULPHO. Murder for murder, blood for blood doth yell.
GHOST OF ANDRUGIO. 'Tis done, and now my soul shall sleep in rest.
Sons that revenge their father's blood are blest.
The curtains being drawn, exit ANDRUGIO.

Enter GALEATZO, *two* SENATORS, LUCIO, FOROBOSCO, CASTILIO, *and Ladies.*

1 SENATOR. Whose hand presents this gory spectacle?
ANTONIO. Mine.
PANDULPHO. No, mine.
ALBERTO. No, mine.
ANTONIO. I will not lose the glory of the deed
Were all the tortures of the deepest hell
Fixed to my limbs. I pierced the monster's heart
With an undaunted hand.
PANDULPHO. By yon bright-spangled front of heaven, 'twas I;
'Twas I sluiced out his life-blood.
ALBERTO. Tush, to say truth, 'twas all.
2 SENATOR. Blessed be you all; and may your honours live,
Religiously held sacred, even for ever and ever.
GALEATZO. (*to* ANTONIO) Thou art another Hercules to us
In ridding huge pollution from our state.
1 SENATOR. Antonio, belief is fortified
With most invincible approvements, of much wrong
By this Piero to thee. We have found
Beadrolls of mischief, plots of villainy,

---

116 *spectacle*: calls for a tableau arrangement.
128 *for ever and ever*: Gair notes the echo of the liturgical formula 'for ever and ever. Amen.'
129 *Hercules*: the cleansing of the Augean stables is recalled.
132 *approvements*: proofs.
134 *Beadrolls*: catalogues.

Laid 'twixt the duke and Strotzo; which we found
Too firmly acted.
2 SENATOR. Alas, poor orphan!
ANTONIO. Poor?
Standing triumphant over Beelzebub?
Having large interest for blood, and yet deemed poor?
1 SENATOR. What satisfaction outward pomp can yield,
Or chiefest fortunes of the Venice state,
Claim freely. You are well-seasoned props
And will not warp or lean to either part:
Calamity gives man a steady heart.
ANTONIO. We are amazed at your benignity;
But other vows constrain another course.
PANDULPHO. We know the world, and did we know no more
We would not live to know; but since constraint
Of holy bands forceth us keep this lodge
Of dirt's corruption till dread power calls
Our souls' appearance, we will live enclosed
In holy verge of some religious order,
Most constant votaries.
The curtains are drawn; PIERO *departeth.*
ANTONIO. First let's cleanse our hands,
Purge hearts of hatred, and entomb my love;

---

139 *interest*: Piero has had to yield more blood than he originally took.
141 *chiefest fortunes*: greatest rewards, offices.
143 *warp . . . part*: be biased towards either party in a dispute (the metaphor is from mining).
144 *Calamity . . . heart*: proverb, Tilley C15a.
147–8 *and . . . know*: i.e. if we knew of nothing (better) beyond this world, we could not bear to go on living.
148–9 *constraint . . . bands*: i.e. the Christian prohibition of suicide.
149–50 *lodge . . . corruption*: either 'the body' or 'the world'.
150–1 *calls . . . appearance*: i.e. at the Last Trump.
152 *verge*: bounds.
153 s.d. Piero's body is hidden behind the curtains of a discovery space.

Over whose hearse I'll weep away my brain
In true affection's tears.
For her sake here I vow a virgin bed.
She lives in me, with her my love is dead.

2 SENATOR. We will attend her mournful exequies;
Conduct you to your calm sequestered life,
And then –

MARIA. Leave us to meditate on misery,
To sad our thought with contemplation
Of past calamities. If any ask
Where lives the widow of the poisoned lord,
Where lies the orphan of a murdered father,
Where lies the father of a butchered son,
Where lives all woe, conduct him to us three,
The downcast ruins of calamity.

ANTONIO. Sound doleful tunes, a solemn hymn advance,
To close the last act of my vengeance;
And when the subject of your passion's spent,
Sing 'Mellida is dead'; all hearts will relent
In sad condolement, at that heavy sound.
Never more woe in lesser plot was found.
And, O, if ever time create a muse
That to th'immortal fame of virgin faith
Dares once engage his pen to write her death,
Presenting it in some black tragedy,
May it prove gracious, may his style be decked
With freshest blooms of purest elegance;
May it have gentle presence, and the scenes sucked up
By calm attention of choice audience;

154–9 *entomb . . . hearse . . . exequies*: suggest that the action should perhaps conclude with the formal interment of Mellida during the final song (185 s.d.).

170 *advance*: raise (to heaven).

171 *close*: finish; form a cadence to.

175 *plot*: the 'plot' is both Mellida's grave-plot and the 'plot' of the play itself; lines 176–83 develop this idea of the play as monument.

179 *black tragedy*: cf. Prologue 7–20.

182 *gentle presence*: a well-bred and well-behaved audience.

And when the closing Epilogue appears,
Instead of claps may it obtain but tears.
Cantant.
Exeunt omnes.

Antonii Vindictae Finis.

---

184 *Epilogue*: in keeping with the ingenious self-reference of this scene, Antonio has begun to speak as the Epilogue.
Antonii Vindictae Finis: the End of Antonio's Revenge.

THE MALCONTENT.

Augmented by *Marſton.*

With the Additions played by the Kings Maieſties ſeruants.

Written by *Ihon Webſter.*

1604.

AT LONDON
Printed by V.S. for William Aſpley, and are to be ſold at his ſhop in Paules Church-yard.

Title-page of the augmented 1604 Quarto (QC) of *The Malcontent* in the British Library, shelfmark Ashley 3625

INTRODUCTORY NOTE

The Malcontent, entered in the Stationers' Register to William Aspley and Thomas Thorpe on 5 July 1604, presents the most complicated textual puzzle of all these selected plays, and some of our solutions are novel. There is a full discussion, with ample reference to earlier studies, by George K. Hunter in his Revels edition (1975). Other important modern editions include those of Martin Wine (Regents, 1965) and Bernard Harris (New Mermaid, 1967). G. B. Harrison edited the play for the Temple Dramatists series in 1933.

A Quarto of 1604 (printed for Aspley by Valentine Simmes) appeared in three editions, differentiated by Greg in *The Library*, II (1921), 49–57 as A, B and C. QA was evidently set from Marston's manuscript. Extant copies exhibit a score or so press-variants, mainly trifling, in three formes. QB was largely printed from the press-corrected type left standing from QA, but further corrections and insertions were made, some certainly the author's, while the last four sheets were entirely reset, and the prologue and epilogue were added. QB, which is rare, displays only a single press-variant, except that the Pforzheimer exemplar has, for no obvious reason, two sheets, B and G, in unique settings with some three hundred variants (mainly in 'accidentals'). QB served as copy for QC, but more than one exemplar was used: QB's sheet B was in its ordinary state, but whereas pages G2^{v}–H1 of QC are dependent on QB in its Pforzheimer state, pages H1^{v}–H3 of QC are dependent on QB in its original state. Copies of QC exhibit twenty-two press-variants, including five significant ones on C4 and I3^{v}. The type was reset, and the text of QB had apparently been checked against manuscript or perused by somebody capable of remedying an occasional corruption. However, while it seems clear that certain variants between QA and QB (such as the substitution of a new Latin motto at the end of the epistle to the reader, or the change from 'I'll pray' to 'I'll go to church' at I.ii.18) are due to authorial tinkering, there is no sure sign of Marston as reviser in any of the minor verbal variation between QB and QC; indeed, we agree with Hunter that sophistication and modernisation, along with compositorial error, account for the bulk of QC's new readings.

Most editors have, however, used QC as their copy-text because of its substantial expansion of the play. The title-page claimed to publish *The Malcontent* as 'Augmented by *Marston*./With the additions played by the Kings Maiesties servants./Written by *Ihon Webster*.' The new material included eleven interpolations, totalling over 450 lines, and an induction headed 'THE/INDUCTION TO/THE MALECONTENT, AND/the additions acted by the Kings Ma-/iesties servants./Written by *Iohn Webster*.' The induction itself makes it clear that *The Malcontent*, originally performed by a troupe of children at the Blackfriars theatre, had been appropriated by the King's Men, just as an adult-company play featuring 'Jeronimo' – either *The Spanish Tragedy* or the anonymous comedy published in 1605 as *The First Part of Jeronimo* – had been commandeered by the boys.

The first Blackfriars performance must have taken place some time after the publication early in 1602 of Dymock's translation of Guarini's *Il Pastor Fido*, from which Marston borrows extensively. (The borrowings are recorded in the notes to Harris's and Hunter's editions.) Hunter, finding 'a convergence of arguments on 1603' (p. xlvi), suspects that Marston wrote the play in an attempt to reverse the declining fortunes of the children of the Chapel Royal, as the Blackfriars boys were known before regaining prestige as the Children of the Queen's Revels on 4 February 1604; but *The Malcontent* may have been Marston's first piece for the revitalised company – in which he at some stage became a shareholder – after his transfer of allegiance from the rival Paul's Boys. The circumstances in which the King's Men acquired the play remain mysterious. The QC title-page and heading to the induction have been variously interpreted, but most commentators have gratefully accepted E. E. Stoll's theory (in *John Webster*, Boston, 1905) that only the induction is by Webster, all amplification of the basic script being by Marston. Hunter, however, pointed out that the added passages are of two different kinds. Six of them, all in Marston's style at its most distinctive, enlarge on situations set forth in the play as QA and QB present it. Four of the remaining five are dominated by a new character, the fool Passarello, whose role might well have been created (as Hunter suggests) for Robert Armin, the current clown with the King's Men. These passages, all in prose, are constructed, with small regard to established characterisation, as a series of jest-book gags. And the careless insertion of one other passage, structured on the same lines but employing Malevole and Mendoza as the comic duo, has led to a duplicated entry direction and signs of textual disturbance. Hunter tentatively suggested that Webster may have written the five extra passages not obviously in Marston's style. His theory, based on purely literary considerations, has since been confirmed by David J. Lake's patient examination of evidence from linguistic preferences. Lake's objective tests divide the added material into Marston's 'augmentations' and Webster's induction and 'additions' for the King's Men, and thus make perfect sense of QC's title-page. He points out the implication for modern producers of *The Malcontent* who want to act 'the play which Marston wrote, in its best and fullest form': they should use the 'augmented' QC minus the induction and the Websterian additions. 'This cutting of the text will be found desirable, I think, also on artistic grounds, since Passarello is an unnecessary character added by Webster, and the Websterian Additions are in a slow, cumbrous manner very different from Marston's fiery rapidity.'

If the course Lake advocates is correct for a producer, it is also correct for an editor. Drama is a collaborative art, and Marston may have acquiesced in Webster's adaptation of his play for the King's Men. Most commentators have assumed that he himself was an active participant in the transfer. But there is no solid evidence that his augmentations, as distinct from Webster's additions, were made specifically for the King's Men.

Webster's new material, though 'not greatly needful', exploits the scandal of the play's theft, provides a part for a King's Company star, and compensates for the loss of the Blackfriars musical interludes; in artistic terms, it perhaps reinforces the play's self-conscious theatricality in ways other than those naturally afforded by the children's acting style. Two of Webster's additions further adapt the play to the public theatre by intervening between a character's exit at the end of one act and immediate re-entry at the beginning of the next (Acts I and II, and IV and V): at the Globe continuous performance enforced the so-called 'law of re-entry', which the entr'acte music at the private theatres rendered unnecessary. Webster's induction denies the existence of the prologue that Marston had written, and has the King's Men actor William Sly 'extemporise' one. Webster's longest interpolation begins with a redundant entry direction for Bilioso, who is already on stage. The dialogue that follows, in which first Bilioso and Bianca and then Bilioso and Passarello cue each other's jests, implausibly postpones Bilioso's reading of his patent – just received from Piero – as ambassador to Florence: in QAB Piero leaves the stage and the next scenic unit begins as Malevole enters while Bilioso reads – a scene-opening that makes little sense in QC, since Webster has ended his interpolated encounter between Bilioso and Passarello by having Bilioso address to Bianca the obvious exit-line, 'Come, madam, this night thou shalt enjoy me freely, and tomorrow for Florence' (Insertion ii). Webster's incidental satire hits a range of appropriate targets, but his contributions are not well integrated into the basic script.

The Marston augmentations, in contrast, are entirely compatible with the Blackfriars version. Malevole remains at their centre, speaking nearly two-thirds of the new lines. The character of Bilioso is developed as a lively foil to Malevole in a closely linked series of encounters that, since Bilioso is a political weathercock, point up the movements of the plot. The first augmentation in I.iii prolongs and complicates Malevole's psychological torture of Piero, and Malevole's added soliloquy in the same scene aids an audience's grasp of the dramatic situation. Arguably there is some slight loss of pace. The one possible hint in the new Marston material that it may have been written with the King's Men in mind is Malevole's mockery of Bilioso in I.iv.44 as 'father of maypoles', that is, as tall and thin: Bilioso is not so described in the original play, but Webster also imagines him as skinny (Insertion i.66–7), and the King's Company actor John Sinklo, who appears in the induction, is thought to have specialised in thin-man parts. However, Matzagente in *Antonio and Mellida* (with which Sinklo was in no way connected) is reviled as 'like a tilting-staff' and 'like a maypole' (I.i.123, 135); so Bilioso's emaciation may be due to nothing more than a choleric disposition. In whatever circumstances Marston augmented his play, he abided by its concerns and methods.

Marston manifestly conceived *The Malcontent* as a Blackfriars play. 'The cramped, claustrophobic setting of a private theater is absolutely essential to Marston's purposes', in Finkelpearl's view (p. 179). Even if he assisted in the King's Men's rehandling of it, it seems best to put before the reader the private theatre play, with the Marstonian amplifications that do no violence to the original conception, but without the *ad hoc* Websterian accretions. We have, therefore, relegated to an appendix (pp. 513–35 below) the additional material judged to be Webster's: this appendix also summarises Lake's case and speculates about the provenance of QC.

Other editorial decisions involve the attempt to distinguish authoritative improvements and genuine corrections from minor corruptions and unauthoritative regularisations, as the text passed through its various stages of alteration. Our edition is based on a collation of the Bodleian Library copy of QA and the British Library copy of QB with the Scolar Press photo-facsimile (1970) of a British Library copy of QC (Ashley 3625). The Bodleian copies of QC, Malone 252 (4) and Malone 195 (5), have also been consulted, and Hunter's Revels edition has supplied further information about press-variants.

The Malcontent was still part of the King's Men's repertory at the Blackfriars as late as 1635 – which may help to explain Ford's imitation of its dance scenes in *The Broken Heart* (*c.* 1630); but it then vanished from the stage for over two hundred years. It was revived to a mixed critical reception but some commercial success in July–August 1850 at the Olympic Theatre in London. Another century elapsed before it was attempted again in two student productions, by the Southampton University Workshop (6–7 March 1964) and the Oxford University Dramatic Society (14 June 1968). A radio version, adapted and produced by Raymond Raikes, with Maurice Denham, Maxine Audley and John Slater, and music by Guy Halahan, was broadcast in the BBC World Theatre series in 1963. But the play's only revival on the professional stage in this century was that directed by Jonathan Miller at the Nottingham Playhouse (April–May 1973) and subsequently at the Globe Playhouse, London (June 1973). The text was described as 'adapted by John Wells', and the production was widely criticised for introducing an inappropriate element of burlesque into the play; in fact, apart from modernising a few jokes, Wells appears to have presented a text both fairly full and reasonably faithful to the quirky spirit of the original. The induction was omitted, but in other respects (mask-like make-up and dance-like movement, Palladian set, use of brass music by Gabrieli and Marenzio) the production emphasised the mannerist artificiality of Marston's writing.

Although *The Malcontent* is full of literary borrowings, echoes and imitations, the plot seems to have been entirely of Marston's own invention.

[PREFATORY MATERIAL TO THE EARLY EDITIONS]

BENIAMINO IONSONIO
POETAE
ELEGANTISSIMO
GRAVISSIMO
AMICO
SVO CANDIDO ET CORDATO
IOHANNES MARSTON
MVSARVM ALVMNVS

ASPERAM HANC SVAM THALIAM
D. D.

To the Reader

I am an ill orator and, in truth, use to indite more honestly than eloquently, for it is my custom to speak as I think and write as I speak.

In plainness, therefore, understand that in some things I have willingly erred, as in supposing a Duke of Genoa and in taking names different from that city's families – for which some may wittily accuse me, but my defence shall be as honest as many reproofs unto me have been most malicious, since, I heartily protest, it was my care to write so far from reasonable offence that even strangers in whose state I laid my scene should not from thence draw any disgrace to any, dead or living. Yet, in despite of my endeavours, I understand some have been most unadvisedly over-cunning in misinterpreting me,

---

Dedication: 'John Marston, disciple of the muses, gives and dedicates this his harsh comedy to his frank and heartfelt friend, Benjamin Jonson, the weightiest and most finely discerning of poets.' The initials in the last line stand for *dat dedicatque*.

6 *Duke of Genoa*: the city of Genoa had no hereditary dukedom.

14–28 *Yet . . . unity*: Marston makes the Jacobean satirist's standard disclaimer of personal malice; the history of his stormy relations with the authorities suggests that the gesture is largely rhetorical.

and with subtlety as deep as hell have maliciously spread ill rumours, which, springing from themselves, might to themselves have heavily returned. Surely I desire to satisfy every firm spirit, who in all his actions proposeth to himself no more ends than God and virtue do, whose intentions are always simple; to such I protest that, with my free understanding, I have not glanced at disgrace of any but of those whose unquiet studies labour innovation, contempt of holy policy, reverend comely superiority, and established unity. For the rest of my supposed tartness, I fear not but unto every worthy mind it will be approved so general and honest as may modestly pass with the freedom of a satire. I would fain leave the paper; only one thing afflicts me, to think that scenes invented merely to be spoken should be enforcively published to be read, and that the least hurt I can receive is to do myself the wrong. But since others otherwise would do me more, the least inconvenience is to be accepted. I have myself, therefore, set forth this comedy, but so that my enforced absence must much rely upon the printer's discretion; but I shall entreat slight errors in

---

19–20 *heavily returned*: rebounded on them to their cost.

24 *free understanding*: generous intentions.

25–6 *those . . . innovation*: those who restlessly seek overthrow of the established order.

27 *holy policy*: divinely sanctioned institutions and policies (with a witty glance at the play's theme of virtuous machiavellism).

28 *established unity*: the unity of the kingdom under its Established Church.

32–5 *only . . . read*: note Marston's acute consciousness of the missing theatrical dimension in a printed text.

37–8 *least . . . accepted*: Marston implies that others would publish the play in an unauthoritative form.

orthography may be as slightly overpassed and that the unhandsome shape which this trifle in reading presents may be pardoned for the pleasure it once afforded you when it was presented with the soul of lively action.

Sine aliqua dementia nullus Phoebus.

J. M.

---

42 *slightly*: carelessly.

47 *Sine . . . Phoebus*: 'There is no poetic inspiration without some degree of madness' (paraphrased from Seneca, *De Tranquillitate Animi*, XVII, 10).

DRAMATIS PERSONAE

GIOVANNI ALTOFRONTO, *disguised* MALEVOLE, *sometime Duke of Genoa*
PIETRO JACOMO, *Duke of Genoa*
MENDOZA, *a minion to the duchess of* PIETRO JACOMO
CELSO, *a friend to* ALTOFRONT
BILIOSO, *an old choleric marshal*
PREPASSO, *a gentleman-usher*
FERNEZE, *a young courtier, and enamoured on the duchess* [AURELIA]
FERRARDO, *a minion to Duke* PIETRO JACOMO
EQUATO } *two courtiers*
GUERRINO }
AURELIA, *duchess to Duke* PIETRO JACOMO
MARIA, *duchess to Duke* ALTOFRONT
EMILIA } *two ladies attending the duchess* [AURELIA;
BIANCA } BIANCA *married to* BILIOSO]
MAQUERELLE, *an old panderess*
[CAPTAIN, *guarding the citadel*]
[MERCURY, *in the masque*]
[SUITORS]
[PAGES]
[GUARDS]

Dramatis Personae: based on QAB; many of the names are chosen for allegoric effect.
ALTOFRONTO: 'lofty brow'; Finkelpearl notes that in Porta's *De Humana Physiognoma* a high forehead is a sign of bravery and firmness, but that an ironic link with the cuckold Bilioso is also hinted at (cf. I.iv.49–51): the ousted duke has been cuckolded of his dukedom.
MALEVOLE: 'malevolent'.
MENDOZA: the derivation from Italian *mendoso* ('faulty, that may be mended') is supported by the spelling 'Mendozo' in the Dramatis Personae and often within QA.
minion: favourite or lover.
CELSO: 'high, noble, eminent, bright'.
BILIOSO: 'choleric, angry'.
PREPASSO: 'usher'.
FERRARDO: cf. Italian *ferrare* ('to tag points, tie laces'), but with a pun on 'ferret' (see I.iii.27).
EQUATO: perhaps meant to suggest 'equable'.
GUERRINO: 'prisoner of war' (cf. I.iii.76).
BIANCA: 'white, fair'; often spelt 'Beancha' in Q.
MAQUERELLE: French for bawd; also Italian *macarello* ('a bawd, or a pander').

PROLOGUS

An imperfect ode, being but one staff,
spoken by the Prologue

To wrest each hurtless thought to private sense
Is the foul use of ill-bred impudence:
Immodest censure now grows wild,
All overrunning.
Let innocence be ne'er so chaste,
Yet at the last
She is defiled
With too nice-brainèd cunning.
O you of fairer soul,
Control
With an Herculean arm
This harm;
And once teach all old freedom of a pen,
Which still must write of fools whiles't writes of men.

Prologus: from the Induction (152–63) it is clear that this was not used at the Globe.
staff: stanza.
1 *To wrest . . . sense*: to twist harmless thoughts into personal libels.
2 *impudence*: presumptions, but also shamelessness (contrasted with the chastity of innocence).
3 *Immodest*: immoderate, but also unchaste.
13 *old freedom of a pen*: the traditional licence of satire (cf. 'To the Reader', 31).

THE MALCONTENT

Vexat censura columbas.

ACT I

SCENE I

The vilest out-of-tune music being heard, enter BILIOSO *and* PREPASSO.

BILIOSO. Why, how now! Are ye mad, or drunk, or both, or what?

PREPASSO. Are ye building Babylon there?

BILIOSO. Here's a noise in court! You think you are in a tavern, do you not?

PREPASSO. You think you are in a brothel-house, do you not? – This room is ill-scented.

Enter one with a perfume.

So, perfume, perfume; some upon me, I pray thee. – The duke is upon instant entrance; so, make place there!

[*Exit the one with perfume.*]

SCENE II

Enter the Duke PIETRO, FERRARDO, *Count* EQUATO, *Count* CELSO *before, and* GUERRINO.

Vexat censura columbas: 'Our censor punishes the [innocent] doves' (Juvenal, *Satires*, II, 63); another hit at those who have allegedly misconstrued the satiric intentions of his play.

I.i s.d. *The vilest . . . music*: the musical disharmony corresponds to the discordant state of Malevole's mind, but is also meant to comment on the disordered condition of the Genoese court ('Babylon').

3 *Babylon*: Babel, perhaps with a glance at *The Spanish Tragedy*, whose final act makes complex use of Babel/Babylon as a metaphor for social breakdown.

4 *Here's a noise*: incorporates the unruly behaviour of the audience into the play.

PIETRO. Where breathes that music?

BILIOSO. The discord, rather than the music, is heard from the malcontent Malevole's chamber.

FERRARDO. [*calling*] Malevole!

MALEVOLE. (*out of his chamber*) Yaugh,
God o' man, what dost thou there? Duke's
Ganymede, Juno's jealous of thy long stockings.
Shadow of a woman, what wouldst, weasel?
Thou lamb o' court, what dost thou bleat for?
Ah, you smooth-chinned catamite!

PIETRO. Come down, thou ragged cur, and snarl here. I give thy dogged sullenness free liberty; trot about and bespurtle whom thou pleasest.

MALEVOLE. I'll come among you, you goatish-blooded toderers, as gum into taffeta, to fret, to fret. I'll fall like a sponge into water, to suck up, to suck up. Howl again. I'll go to church and come to you.

[*Exit above.*]

PIETRO. This Malevole is one of the most prodigious affections that ever conversed with

---

5 s.d. *chamber*: apparently on an upper stage level.

7 *Ganymede*: Jupiter's cup-bearer, hence effeminate favourite.

8 *Shadow of a woman*: plays with the traditional function of boy actors in women's parts ('shadow' = actor); the joke is that Malevole is also played by a boy, presumably equally 'smooth-chinned' and given to high-pitched 'bleating'.

10 *catamite*: boy kept for sexual purposes (corrupt form of Ganymede).

11–12 *cur . . . dogged*: the play contrasts Malevole as snarling cynic (Greek *kuon* = dog) like the philosopher Diogenes (the so-called 'heavenly dog') with the fawning dogs ('duke's hounds', I.iii.18–19) of the court world. Shakespeare develops a similar pattern in *Timon*.

13 *bespurtle*: bespatter.

16 *toderers*: the sense is probably suggested by the verbs 'totter' and 'dodder'; goats are proverbial for lust – hence 'impotent old lechers'.

16 *gum . . . fret*: cheap taffeta, stiffened with gum, tended to fray ('fret'); 'fret' also has the senses devour, consume, irritate.

20–1 *Malevole . . . affections*: 'Malevole has one of the most unnaturally passionate temperaments.'

nature: a man, or rather a monster, more discontent than Lucifer when he was thrust out of the presence. His appetite is unsatiable as the grave, as far from any content as from heaven. His highest delight is to procure others vexation, and therein he thinks he truly serves heaven; for 'tis his position, whosoever in this earth can be contented is a slave and damned; therefore does he afflict all in that to which they are most affected. Th'elements struggle within him; his own soul is at variance within herself; his speech is halter-worthy at all hours. I like him, faith; he gives good intelligence to my spirit, makes me understand those weaknesses which others' flattery palliates. Hark! they sing.

[*A Song.*]

SCENE III

Enter MALEVOLE *after the song.*

PIETRO. See, he comes. Now shall you hear the extremity of a malcontent: he is as free as air; he blows over every man. – And, sir, whence come you now?

MALEVOLE. From the public place of much dissimulation, the church.

PIETRO. What didst there?

MALEVOLE. Talk with a usurer; take up at interest.

PIETRO. I wonder what religion thou art.

MALEVOLE. Of a soldier's religion.

28–9 *position . . . damned*: Malevole rails against the mortal sin of 'security' ('mortals' chiefest enemy', *Macbeth*, III.v.33).

31 *affected*: inclined.

31 *elements*: i.e. the humours – phlegm, blood, choler, melancholy – whose balance determines the disposition of each individual.

36 s.d. *A Song*: in the context of Malevole's discordant serenade the musical episodes in this play develop a consistent symbolic suggestiveness.

8 *take up*: borrow.

PIETRO. And what dost think makes most infidels now?

MALEVOLE. Sects, sects. I have seen seeming piety change her robe so oft that sure none but some arch-devil can shape her a petticoat.

PIETRO. O, a religious policy.

MALEVOLE. But damnation on a politic religion! I am weary. Would I were one of the duke's hounds now.

PIETRO. But what's the common news abroad, Malevole? Thou dogg'st rumour still.

MALEVOLE. Common news? Why, common words are 'God save ye', 'Fare ye well'; common actions, flattery and cozenage; common things, women and cuckolds. – And how does my little Ferrard? Ah, ye lecherous animal! my little ferret, he goes sucking up and down the palace into every hen's nest, like a weasel. And to what dost thou addict thy time to now more than to those antique painted drabs that are still affected of young courtiers, Flattery, Pride, and Venery?

FERRARDO. I study languages. Who dost think to be the best linguist of our age?

MALEVOLE. Phew, the devil. Let him possess thee, he'll teach thee to speak all languages most readily and strangely; and great reason, marry, he's travelled greatly i' the world and is everywhere.

FERRARDO. Save i'th' court.

MALEVOLE. Ay, save i'th' court. (*To* BILIOSO) And how does my old muckhill, overspread with fresh snow? Thou half a man, half a goat, all a

---

16–17 *religious policy . . . politic religion*: cf. 'holy policy' in 'To the Reader', line 27; Marston is developing his opposition between two kinds of machiavellism, the virtuous and the vicious.

21 *dogg'st*: with a pun on his cynic invective.

24 *cozenage*: cheating.

32 *Venery*: lechery.

35–6 *the devil . . . all languages*: diabolic possession, as the mirror-opposite of inspiration by the Holy Spirit, conferred the gift of tongues.

beast! How does thy young wife, old huddle?

BILIOSO. Out, you improvident rascal!

MALEVOLE. Do, kick, thou hugely-horned old duke's ox, good Master Make-please.

PIETRO. How dost thou live nowadays, Malevole?

MALEVOLE. Why, like the knight Sir Patrick Penlolians, with killing o' spiders for my lady's monkey.

PIETRO. How dost spend the night? I hear thou never sleep'st.

MALEVOLE. O no, but dream the most fantastical . . . O heaven! O fubbery, fubbery!

PIETRO. Dream? What dream'st?

MALEVOLE. Why, methinks I see that signor pawn his footcloth, that *metreza* her plate; this madam takes physic that t'other *monsieur* may minister to her. Here is a pander jewelled; there is a fellow in shift of satin this day that could not shift a shirt t'other night. Here a Paris supports that Helen; there's a Lady Guinevere bears up that Sir Lancelot. Dreams, dreams, visions, fantasies, chimeras, imaginations, tricks, conceits! (*To* PREPASSO) Sir Tristram Trimtram, come aloft Jackanapes with a whim-wham. Here's a knight of the land of Catito shall play at trap with any page in Europe, do the sword-dance with any morris-dancer in Christendom, ride at the ring till the fin of his

---

44 *huddle*: old miser.
47 *Make-please*: toady.
49–50 *Sir Patrick Penlolians*: unknown.
55 *fubbery*: deceit.
58 *footcloth*: rich trappings for a horse.
58 *metreza*: mistress (Italian).
67–8 *come . . . whim-wham*: imitating a trainer's command to his monkey; the monkey's name, Sir Tristram, is presumably arrived at by ironic association with Sir Lancelot, another type of the courtly adulterer.
68–9 *Catito . . . trap*: 'cat' and 'trap' are boys' games, likely to be played by pages; sexual *doubles entendres* are probably intended (in the case of 'Catito' by association with 'catso'), as also with 'ride at the ring', a type of jousting in which the rider has to thrust his spear through a suspended ring.
71 *fin*: lid.

eyes look as blue as the welkin, and run the wild goose chase even with Pompey the Huge.

PIETRO. You run –

MALEVOLE. To the devil. – Now, Signor Guerrino, that thou from a most pitied prisoner shouldst grow a most loathed flatterer! – Alas, poor Celso, thy star's oppressed: thou art an honest lord, 'tis pity.

EQUATO. Is't pity?

MALEVOLE. Ay marry is't, philosophical Equato; and 'tis pity that thou, being so excellent a scholar by art, shouldst be so ridiculous a fool by nature. – I have a thing to tell you, duke; bid 'em avaunt, bid 'em avaunt.

PIETRO. Leave us, leave us.

Exeunt all saving PIETRO *and* MALEVOLE.

Now, sir, what is't?

MALEVOLE. Duke, thou art a *becco*, a *cornuto*.

PIETRO. How?

MALEVOLE. Thou art a cuckold.

PIETRO. Speak; unshale him quick.

MALEVOLE. With most tumbler-like nimbleness.

PIETRO. Who? By whom? I burst with desire.

MALEVOLE. Mendoza is the man makes thee a horned beast; duke, 'tis Mendoza cornutes thee.

PIETRO. What conformance? Relate; short, short!

MALEVOLE. As a lawyer's beard.

There is an old crone in the court,
Her name is Maquerelle;
She is my mistress, sooth to say,
And she doth ever tell me.

Blurt o' rhyme, blurt o' rhyme! Maquerelle is a cunning bawd, I am an honest villain, thy

---

72 *welkin*: sky.

78 *oppressed*: in decline.

88 *becco . . . cornuto*: cuckold (Italian).

91 *unshale*: expose.

96 *conformance*: proof.

102 *Blurt o' rhyme*: a fig for rhyme; it is characteristic of the play's mannerist self-consciousness that a character should be aware of speaking in verse.

103 *honest villain*: Malevole's malcontent role is that of an 'open villain', but the hidden meaning is that his villainy has an honourable purpose (cf. 'holy policy').

wife is a close drab, and thou art a notorious cuckold. Farewell, duke.

PIETRO. Stay, stay.

MALEVOLE. Dull, dull duke, can lazy patience make lame revenge? O God, for a woman to make a man that which God never created, never made!

PIETRO. What did God never make?

MALEVOLE. A cuckold. To be made a thing that's hoodwinked with kindness whilst every rascal fillips his brows; to have a coxcomb with egregious horns pinned to a lord's back, every page sporting himself with delightful laughter, whilst he must be the last must know it. Pistols and poniards, pistols and poniards!

PIETRO. Death and damnation!

MALEVOLE. Lightning and thunder!

PIETRO. Vengeance and torture!

MALEVOLE. Catso!

PIETRO. O, revenge!

MALEVOLE. Nay, to select among ten thousand fairs
A lady far inferior to the most
In fair proportion both of limb and soul;
To take her from austerer check of parents,
To make her his by most devoutful rites,
Make her commandress of a better essence
Than is the gorgeous world, even of a man;
To hug her with as raised an appetite
As usurers do their delved-up treasury,
Thinking none tells it but his private self;
To meet her spirit in a nimble kiss,
Distilling panting ardour to her heart;

---

104 *close drab*: secret whore.

114 *fillips his brows*: makes him a cuckold. Malevole's speech envisages a grotesque version of blind man's buff in which the hoodwinked (blindfold) player has the emblems of cuckoldry pinned on him by the others.

117–23 *Pistols . . . revenge*: this ludicrous antiphon for treble voices is a fine burlesque of revenge-play ranting.

122 *Catso*: prick (Italian *cazzo*); but often a mere interjection.

124–69 *Nay . . . think it*: added in QC.

133 *tells*: counts.

True to her sheets, nay, diets strong his blood,
To give her height of hymeneal sweets –

PIETRO. O God!

MALEVOLE. Whilst she lisps and gives him some court *quelquechose*,
Made only to provoke, not satiate;
And yet, even then the thaw of her delight
Flows from lewd heat of apprehension,
Only from strange imagination's rankness,
That forms the adulterer's presence in her soul
And makes her think she clips the foul knave's loins.

PIETRO. Affliction to my blood's root!

MALEVOLE. Nay, think, but think what may proceed of this:
Adultery is often the mother of incest.

PIETRO. Incest?

MALEVOLE. Yes, incest. Mark! Mendoza of his wife begets perchance a daughter; Mendoza dies; his son marries this daughter. Say you? Nay, 'tis frequent, not only probable, but no question often acted, whilst ignorance, fearless ignorance, clasps his own seed.

PIETRO. Hideous imagination!

MALEVOLE. Adultery? Why, next to the sin of simony, 'tis the most horrid transgression under the cope of salvation.

PIETRO. Next to simony?

MALEVOLE. Ay, next to simony, in which our men in next age shall not sin.

PIETRO. Not sin? why?

MALEVOLE. Because (thanks to some churchmen) our age will leave them nothing to sin with. But adultery – O dullness! – should have exemplary punishment, that intemperate bloods may

---

139 *quelquechose*: insubstantial delicacy (origin of English 'kickshaw').

145 *clips*: embraces.

152 *his son*: i.e. the child produced by his adultery with Pietro's wife, Aurelia.

155 *clasps . . . seed*: embraces his own half-sister.

158 *simony*: corrupt trade in religious offices.

159 *cope of salvation*: cf. 'cope of heaven', the sky.

freeze but to think it. I would damn him and
all his generation; my own hands should do it;
ha, I would not trust heaven with my vengeance
anything.

PIETRO. Anything, anything, Malevole! Thou
shalt see instantly what temper my spirit holds.
Farewell; remember I forget thee not; farewell.

Exit PIETRO.

MALEVOLE. Farewell.
Lean thoughtfulness, a sallow meditation,
Suck thy veins dry! Distemperance rob thy sleep!
The heart's disquiet is revenge most deep.
He that gets blood the life of flesh but spills,
But he that breaks heart's peace the dear soul
kills. –
Well, this disguise doth yet afford me that
Which kings do seldom hear, or great men use –
Free speech; and though my state's usurped,
Yet this affected strain gives me a tongue
As fetterless as is an emperor's.
I may speak foolishly, ay, knavishly,
Always carelessly, yet no one thinks it fashion
To poise my breath; for he that laughs and
strikes
Is lightly felt, or seldom struck again.
Duke, I'll torment thee; now my just revenge
From thee than crown a richer gem shall part.
Beneath God naught's so dear as a calm heart.

SCENE IV

Enter CELSO.

CELSO. My honoured lord –

MALEVOLE. Peace, speak low, peace! O Celso,
constant lord,
Thou to whose faith I only rest discovered,

175–92 added in QC.
177 *Distemperance*: upset of the natural balance, or tempering, of the humours.
188 *poise my breath*: weigh my words.
189 *struck again*: hit back.

Thou, one of full ten millions of men,
That lovest virtue only for itself,
Thou in whose hands old Ops may put her soul,
Behold forever-banished Altofront,
This Genoa's last year's duke. O truly noble!
I wanted those old instruments of state,
Dissemblance and suspect. I could not time it, Celso;
My throne stood like a point in midst of a circle,
To all of equal nearness; bore with none,
Reigned all alike; so slept in fearless virtue,
Suspectless, too suspectless; till the crowd,
Still lickerous of untried novelties,
Impatient with severer government,
Made strong with Florence, banished Altofront.

CELSO. Strong with Florence! Ay, thence your mischief rose,
For when the daughter of the Florentine
Was matched once with this Pietro, now duke,
No stratagem of state untried was left,
Till you of all –

MALEVOLE. Of all was quite bereft.
Alas, Maria too, close prisonèd,
My true-faithed duchess, i'th' citadel!

CELSO. I'll still adhere; let's mutiny and die.

MALEVOLE. O no, climb not a falling tower, Celso;
'Tis well held desperation, no zeal,
Hopeless to strive with fate. Peace! Temporise.
Hope, hope, that never forsak'st the wretched'st man,
Yet bidd'st me live and lurk in this disguise.
What, play I well the free-breathed discontent?
Why, man, we are all philosophical monarchs
Or natural fools. Celso, the court's afire;
The duchess' sheets will smoke for't ere it be long.

---

6 *Ops*: goddess of wealth.
9 *wanted*: lacked.
10 *suspect*: suspicion.
15 *lickerous of*: lusting after.
17 *Made . . . Florence*: supported by the Duke of Florence.

Impure Mendoza, that sharp-nosed lord, that made
The cursèd match linked Genoa with Florence,
Now broad-horns the duke, which he now knows.
Discord to malcontents is very manna;
When the ranks are burst, then scuffle Altofront.

CELSO. Ay, but durst –

MALEVOLE. 'Tis gone; 'tis swallowed like a mineral.
Some way 'twill work. Phewt, I'll not shrink;
He's resolute who can no lower sink.

BILIOSO *entering,* MALEVOLE *shifteth his speech.*

O, the father of maypoles! Did you never see a fellow whose strength consisted in his breath, respect in his office, religion in his lord, and love in himself? Why, then, behold.

BILIOSO. Signor –

MALEVOLE. My right worshipful lord, your court nightcap makes you have a passing high forehead.

BILIOSO. I can tell you strange news, but I am sure you know them already: the duke speaks much good of you.

MALEVOLE. Go to, then; and shall you and I now enter into a strict friendship?

BILIOSO. Second one another?

---

38 *Discord*: cf. I.i and the opening of I.ii.

41 *mineral*: medicine or poison.

43 s.d.–97 s.d. added in QC.

43 s.d. *shifteth his speech*: the part of 'Malevole' is distinguished by a vocal disguise of some sort (cf. Kent in *King Lear* and Vindice in *The Revenger's Tragedy*).

44 *father of maypoles*: lean and lanky person; perhaps alluding to the emaciated figure of the King's Company actor Sinklo.

50–1 *high forehead*: Malevole pretends to think that Bilioso's nightcap makes him appear noble, but covertly alludes to his cuckoldry, while at the same time teasingly invoking his own real name.

MALEVOLE. Yes.
BILIOSO. Do one another good offices?
MALEVOLE. Just. What though I called thee old ox, egregious wittol, broken-bellied coward, rotten mummy? yet since I am in favour –
BILIOSO. Words of course, terms of disport. His grace presents you by me a chain, as his grateful remembrance for – I am ignorant for what; marry, ye may impart. Yet howsoever – come, dear friend. Dost know my son?
MALEVOLE. Your son?
BILIOSO. He shall eat woodcocks, dance jigs, make possets, and play at shuttlecock with any young lord about the court. He has as sweet a lady, too. Dost know her little bitch?
MALEVOLE. 'Tis a dog, man.
BILIOSO. Believe me, a she-bitch. O, 'tis a good creature! Thou shalt be her servant. I'll make thee acquainted with my young wife, too. What, I keep her not at court for nothing. 'Tis grown to supper-time; come to my table: that, anything I have, stands open to thee.
MALEVOLE. (*to* CELSO) How smooth to him that is in state of grace,
How servile, is the rugged'st courtier's face!
What profit, nay, what nature would keep down,
Are heaved to them are minions to a crown.
Envious ambition never sates his thirst,
Till, sucking all, he swells and swells, and bursts.

---

61 *wittol*: willing cuckold.
63 *Words of course*: mere conventional terms.
70 *possets*: hot drinks of curdled and spiced milk.
72–5 *lady . . . bitch . . . servant*: Malevole encourages Bilioso's syntactic confusion of dog and wife.
79 *stands open*: the bawdy *double entendre* confirms that 'servant' and 'acquainted' contain an offer of panderism.
80 *state of grace*: in royal favour; the perversion of religious language is appropriate to 'religious policy' in its corrupt sense.
83 *heaved*: vomited up.

BILIOSO. I shall now leave you with my always-best wishes; only let's hold betwixt us a firm correspondence, a mutual-friendly-reciprocal kind of steady-unanimous-heartily-leagued –

MALEVOLE. Did your signorship ne'er see a pigeon-house that was smooth, round, and white without, and full of holes and stink within? Ha' ye not, old courtier?

BILIOSO. O yes, 'tis the form, the fashion of them all.

MALEVOLE. Adieu, my true court-friend; farewell, my dear Castilio.

Exit BILIOSO.

CELSO. Yonder's Mendoza. *Descries* MENDOZA.

MALEVOLE. True, the privy key.

CELSO. I take my leave, sweet lord. *Exit* CELSO.

MALEVOLE. 'Tis fit; away!

SCENE V

Enter MENDOZA *with three or four Suitors.*

MENDOZA. Leave your suits with me; I can and will. Attend my secretary; leave me.

[*Exeunt Suitors.*]

MALEVOLE. Mendoza, hark ye, hark ye. You are a treacherous villain, God b' wi' ye!

MENDOZA. Out, you base-born rascal!

MALEVOLE. We are all the sons of heaven, though a tripe-wife were our mother. Ah, you

---

88 *correspondence*: agreement.

97 *Castilio*: from Baldassare Castiglione, author of the *The Courtier*, the most famous of Renaissance courtesy books. Malevole feigns to take Bilioso as a model courtier; but Marston always uses the name satirically: cf. the character Castilio Balthazar in the *Antonio* plays.

98 *privy key*: obscene allusion to Mendoza's adultery.

I.v s.d. *with three or four Suitors*: a tableau of fawning court manners is required; see below, lines 26–35.

7 *tripe-wife*: tripe-seller; a type of female coarseness.

whoreson, hot-reined he-marmoset! Aegisthus – didst ever hear of one Aegisthus?

MENDOZA. Gisthus?

MALEVOLE. Ay, Aegisthus; he was a filthy, incontinent fleshmonger, such a one as thou art.

MENDOZA. Out, grumbling rogue!

MALEVOLE. Orestes, beware Orestes!

MENDOZA. Out, beggar!

MALEVOLE. I once shall rise.

MENDOZA. Thou rise?

MALEVOLE. Ay, at the resurrection.
No vulgar seed but once may rise, and shall;
No king so huge but 'fore he die may fall. *Exit.*

MENDOZA. Now, good Elysium, what a delicious heaven is it for a man to be in a prince's favour! O sweet God! O pleasure! O fortune! O all thou best of life! What should I think, what say, what do? To be a favourite, a minion! To have a general timorous respect observe a man, a stateful silence in his presence, solitariness in his absence, a confused hum and busy murmur of obsequious suitors training him, the cloth held up and way proclaimed before him, petitionary vassals licking the pavement with their slavish knees whilst some odd palace-lamprels that

---

8 *hot-reined*: lecherous; the reins (kidneys) were thought to be the seat of the passions.

8–14 *Aegisthus . . . Orestes*: Malevole compares Mendoza to Aegisthus who seduced Agamemnon's wife, Clytemnestra, and helped to contrive the king's death on his return from Troy; he himself claims the role of Agamemnon's avenging son, Orestes.

16–20 *rise . . . fall*: Malevole's play on the different senses of rising and falling (political and theological) is more than a casual turn of wit: it initiates an important pattern of rise–fall imagery, which later comes to include the sexual connotations of the words.

21–59 This mock encomium of princely favour and court women (both proverbial types of shallow inconstancy) is in the tradition of witty paradox cultivated at the Inns of Court.

26 *observe*: to treat with ceremonious respect or reverence (*OED*).

27 *stateful*: stately, suitable to state occasions.

32 *lamprels*: lampreys, blood-sucking parasites.

engender with snakes, and are full of eyes on both sides, with a kind of insinuated humbleness fix all their delights upon his brow! O blessed state! What a ravishing prospect doth the Olympus of favour yield! Death, I cornute the duke! Sweet women, most sweet ladies, nay, angels, by heaven, he is more accursed than a devil that hates you, or is hated by you, and happier than a god that loves you, or is beloved by you. You preservers of mankind, life-blood of society, who would live, nay, who can live without you? O paradise, how majestical is your austerer presence! How imperiously chaste is your more modest face! But O how full of ravishing attraction is your pretty, petulant, languishing, lasciviously-composed countenance, these amorous smiles, those soul-warming sparkling glances, ardent as those flames that singed the world by heedless Phaëthon! In body how delicate, in soul how witty, in discourse how pregnant, in life how wary, in favours how judicious, in day how sociable, and in night how – O pleasure unutterable! Indeed, it is most certain, one man cannot deserve only to enjoy a beauteous woman. But a duchess! In despite of Phoebus, I'll write a sonnet instantly in praise of her. *Exit.*

SCENE VI

Enter FERNEZE *ushering* AURELIA, EMILIA *and* MAQUERELLE *bearing up her train,* BIANCA *attending; all go out but* AURELIA, MAQUERELLE, *and* FERNEZE.

---

51 *Phaëthon*: usurped the chariot of the sun-god and lost control of its horses; a type of destructive and fatal ambition.

51–5 *In body . . . unutterable*: apparently a satiric burlesque of Hamlet's encomium, 'What a piece of work is a man.'

56 *only*: for himself alone.

58 *Phoebus*: Apollo, the god of poetry.

AURELIA. And is't possible? Mendoza slight me! possible?

FERNEZE. Possible.
What can be strange in him that's drunk with favour,
Grows insolent with grace? Speak, Maquerelle, speak.

MAQUERELLE. To speak feelingly, more, more richly in solid sense than worthless words, give me those jewels of your ears to receive my enforced duty. As for my part, 'tis well known I can put up anything (FERNEZE *privately feeds* MAQUERELLE*'s hands with jewels during this speech*), can bear patiently with any man. But when I heard he wronged your precious sweetness, I was enforced to take deep offence. 'Tis most certain he loves Emilia with high appetite; and, as she told me (as you know we women impart our secrets one to another), when she repulsed his suit, in that he was possessed with your endeared grace, Mendoza most ingratefully renounced all faith to you.

FERNEZE. Nay, called you – speak, Maquerelle, speak.

MAQUERELLE. By heaven, 'witch', 'dried biscuit', and contested blushlessly he loved you but for a spurt or so.

FERNEZE. For maintenance.

MAQUERELLE. Advancement and regard.

AURELIA. O villain! O impudent Mendoza!

MAQUERELLE. Nay, he is the rustiest-jawed, the foulest-mouthed knave in railing against our sex; he will rail against women –

AURELIA. How, how?

6–8 *feelingly . . . richly . . . jewels*: Maquerelle contrives to solicit a handsome bribe. The bribing action which continues to line 70 makes a satirical emblematic comment on the stately entry with which the scene opens.

10 *put up*: put up with (with obscene *double entendre*, continued in 'bear . . .').

28 *rustiest-jawed*: most foul-mouthed ('rust' = tooth-decay).

MAQUERELLE. I am ashamed to speak't, I.
AURELIA. I love to hate him; speak.
MAQUERELLE. Why, when Emilia scorned his base unsteadiness, the black-throated rascal scolded and said –
AURELIA. What?
MAQUERELLE. Troth, 'tis too shameless.
AURELIA. What said he?
MAQUERELLE. Why, that at four women were fools, at fourteen drabs, at forty bawds, at four-score witches, and at a hundred cats.
AURELIA. O unlimitable impudency!
FERNEZE. But as for poor Ferneze's fixèd heart,
Was never shadeless meadow drier parched
Under the scorching heat of heaven's dog
Than is my heart with your enforcing eyes.
MAQUERELLE. A hot simile!
FERNEZE. Your smiles have been my heaven, your frowns my hell.
O, pity, then! Grace should with beauty dwell.
MAQUERELLE. Reasonable perfect, by'r Lady.
AURELIA. I will love thee, be it but in despite
Of that Mendoza. 'Witch', Ferneze, 'witch'!
Ferneze, thou art the duchess' favourite;
Be faithful, private; but 'tis dangerous.
FERNEZE. His love is lifeless that for love fears breath;
The worst that's due to sin, O would 'twere death!
AURELIA. Enjoy my favour. I will be sick instantly and take physic; therefore, in depth of night visit –
MAQUERELLE. Visit her chamber, but conditionally you shall not offend her bed; by this diamond!
FERNEZE. By this diamond.
Gives it to MAQUERELLE.

45–7 *Was never. . . enforcing eyes*: a mangled quotation from *Pastor Fido*, like 56–7 (Hunter); in view of the popularity of Guarini's pastoral tragicomedy in avant-garde circles, Ferneze's plagiarism is probably meant to be comically recognisable.

46 *heaven's dog*: the dog-star.

MAQUERELLE. Nor tarry longer than you please; by this ruby!

FERNEZE. By this ruby. *Gives again.*

MAQUERELLE. And that the door shall not creak.

FERNEZE. And that the door shall not creak.

MAQUERELLE. Nay, but swear.

FERNEZE. By this purse. *Gives her his purse.*

MAQUERELLE. Go to, I'll keep your oaths for you. Remember, visit.

Enter MENDOZA, *reading a sonnet.*

AURELIA. 'Dried biscuit'! – Look where the base wretch comes.

MENDOZA. 'Beauty's life, heaven's model, love's
queen' –

MAQUERELLE. [*aside*] That's his Emilia.

MENDOZA. 'Nature's triumph, best on earth' –

MAQUERELLE. [*aside*] Meaning Emilia.

MENDOZA. 'Thou only wonder that the world
hath seen' –

MAQUERELLE. [*aside*] That's Emilia.

AURELIA. [*aside*] Must I then hear her praised? – Mendoza!

MENDOZA. Madam, your excellency is graciously encountered. I have been writing passionate flashes in honour of –

Exit FERNEZE.

AURELIA. Out, villain, villain! O judgement, where have been my eyes? What bewitched election made me dote on thee? What sorcery made me love thee? But begone, bury thy head. O that I could do more than loathe thee!
Hence, worst of ill.
No reason ask; our reason is our will.

Exit with MAQUERELLE.

---

70 *Nay, but swear*: this mock-ritual appears to burlesque the oath-taking in *Hamlet*, I.v.

89 *election*: choice.

MENDOZA. Women! Nay, furies; nay, worse, for they torment only the bad, but women good and bad. Damnation of mankind! Breath, hast thou praised them for this? And is't you, Ferneze, are wriggled into smock-grace? Sit sure. O that I could rail against these monsters in nature, models of hell, curse of the earth, women that dare attempt anything, and what they attempt they care not how they accomplish; without all premeditation or prevention; rash in asking, desperate in working, impatient in suffering, extreme in desiring, slaves unto appetite, mistresses in dissembling, only constant in unconstancy, only perfect in counterfeiting; their words are feigned, their eyes forged, their sighs dissembled, their looks counterfeit, their hair false, their given hopes deceitful, their very breath artificial. Their blood is their only god; bad clothes and old age are only the devils they tremble at. That I could rail now!

SCENE VII

Enter PIETRO, *his sword drawn.*

PIETRO. A mischief fill thy throat, thou foul-jawed slave!
Say thy prayers.
MENDOZA. I ha' forgot 'em.
PIETRO. Thou shalt die!
MENDOZA. So shalt thou. I am heart-mad.
PIETRO. I am horn-mad.
MENDOZA. Extreme mad.
PIETRO. Monstrously mad.

94–113 a comic inversion of Mendoza's encomium on women, above (I.v.21–59); the recurrent rise–fall motif is echoed in the movement from 'heaven . . . blessed . . . state . . . angels . . . paradise' to 'furies . . . damnation of mankind . . . models of hell, curse of the earth . . . devils'. There is a secondary comic contrast with Mendoza's sonnet (76–80).

98 *smock-grace*: intimate favours.

103 *prevention*: precautionary anticipation.

111 *blood*: passion.

3 *horn-mad*: enraged by cuckoldry.

MENDOZA. Why?
PIETRO. Why? Thou, thou hast dishonourèd my bed.
MENDOZA. I? Come, come, sit; here's my bare heart to thee,
As steady as is this centre to the glorious world.
And yet, hark, thou art a *cornuto* – but by me?
PIETRO. Yes, slave, by thee.
MENDOZA. Do not, do not with tart and spleenful breath
Lose him can loose thee. I offend my duke?
Bear record, O ye dumb and raw-aired nights,
How vigilant my sleepless eyes have been
To watch the traitor. Record, thou spirit of truth,
With what debasement I ha' thrown myself
To under-offices, only to learn
The truth, the party, time, the means, the place,
By whom, and when, and where thou wert disgraced.
And am I paid with 'slave'? Hath my intrusion
To places private and prohibited,
Only to observe the closer passages –
Heaven knows with vows of revelation –
Made me suspected, made me deemed a villain?
What rogue hath wronged us?
PIETRO. Mendoza, I may err.
MENDOZA. Err? 'Tis too mild a name; but err and err,
Run giddy with suspect 'fore through me thou know
That which most creatures save thyself do know.
Nay, since my service hath so loathed reject,
'Fore I'll reveal, shalt find them clipped together.

---

4 *Why*: note the farcical anti-climax.
7 *centre*: the centre of the earth, or perhaps the earth as centre of the Ptolemaic universe.
11 *loose thee*: release you from your misery.
21 *closer passages*: the most secret (amorous) actions.
22 *vows of revelation*: vows to tell everything.
28 *hath so loathed reject*: has been so rejected as loathsome.
29 *clipped*: embracing.

PIETRO. Mendoza, thou know'st I am a most plain-breasted man.

MENDOZA. The fitter to make a cuckold. Would your brows were most plain too!

PIETRO. Tell me; indeed, I heard thee rail.

MENDOZA. At women, true. Why, what cold phlegm could choose,
Knowing a lord so honest, virtuous,
So boundless-loving, bounteous, fair-shaped, sweet,
To be contemned, abused, defamed, made cuckold?
Heart! I hate all women for't: sweet sheets, wax lights, antic bedposts, cambric smocks, villainous curtains, arras pictures, oiled hinges, and all the tongue-tied lascivious witnesses of great creatures' wantonness; what salvation can you expect?

PIETRO. Wilt thou tell me?

MENDOZA. Why, you may find it yourself; observe, observe.

PIETRO. I ha' not the patience. Wilt thou deserve me? Tell, give it.

MENDOZA. Take't. Why, Ferneze is the man, Ferneze. I'll prove't. This night you shall take him in your sheets. Will't serve?

PIETRO. It will. My bosom's in some peace. Till night –

MENDOZA. What?

PIETRO. Farewell.

MENDOZA. God, how weak a lord are you!
Why, do you think there is no more but so?

PIETRO. Why?

MENDOZA. Nay, then will I presume to counsel you.
It should be thus:

---

35 *phlegm*: phlegmatic person (phlegm, in Elizabethan physiology, was the humour that produced apathy and indolence).

40 *antic*: grotesque (presumably with carved figures).

41 *arras pictures*: tapestries (presumably erotic).

41 *oiled hinges*: to preserve secrecy.

48–9 *deserve me*: earn my generosity.

You with some guard upon the sudden break
Into the princess' chamber; I stay behind,
Without the door through which he needs must pass.
Ferneze flies – let him. To me he comes; he's killed
By me, observe, by me. You follow; I rail,
And seem to save the body. Duchess comes,
On whom (respecting her advancèd birth
And your fair nature) I know, nay, I do know,
No violence must be used. She comes; I storm,
I praise, excuse Ferneze, and still maintain
The duchess' honour; she for this loves me.
I honour you, shall know her soul, you mine;
Then naught shall she contrive in vengeance
(As women are most thoughtful in revenge)
Of her Ferneze, but you shall sooner know't
Than she can think't. Thus shall his death come sure,
Your duchess brain-caught, so your life secure.

PIETRO. It is too well, my bosom and my heart.
When nothing helps, cut off the rotten part.
Exit.

MENDOZA. Who cannot feign friendship can ne'er produce the effects of hatred. Honest fool duke, subtle lascivious duchess, silly novice Ferneze – I do laugh at ye. My brain is in labour till it produce mischief, and I feel sudden throes, proofs sensible the issue is at hand.
As bears shape young, so I'll form my device,
Which grown proves horrid: vengeance makes men wise. [*Exit.*]

---

65 *advancèd birth*: noble family.
75 *brain-caught*: tricked with cunning.
84 *As bears shape young*: bears were commonly supposed to lick their amorphous offspring into shape.
85 s.d. after this line QC interpolates a scene by Webster; see Appendix, Insertion i, p. 523 below.

ACT II

SCENE I

Enter MENDOZA *with a sconce to observe* FERNEZE*'s entrance, who, whilst the act is playing, enter unbraced, two Pages before him with lights; is met by* MAQUERELLE *and conveyed in. The Pages are sent away.*

MENDOZA. He's caught; the woodcock's head is i'th' noose.
Now treads Ferneze in dangerous path of lust,
Swearing his sense is merely deified.
The fool grasps clouds, and shall beget centaurs;
And now, in strength of panting faint delight,
The goat bids heaven envy him. – Good goose,
I can afford thee nothing but the poor
Comfort of calamity, pity.
Lust's like the plummets hanging on clock-lines,
Will ne'er ha' done till all is quite undone;
Such is the course salt sallow lust doth run,
Which thou shalt try.
I'll be revenged. Duke, thy suspect, duchess, thy disgrace, Ferneze, thy rivalship, shall have swift vengeance. Nothing so holy, no band of nature so strong, no law of friendship so sacred, but I'll profane, burst, violate, 'fore I'll endure

---

II.i s.d. *sconce:* lantern.
II.i s.d. *whilst the act is playing*: the music played between the acts at Blackfriars.
1 *woodcock*: fool, dupe.
3 *merely*: utterly.
4 *The fool . . . centaurs*: Ixion attempted to embrace the goddess Juno, but found in her place only a cloud, which then gave birth to centaurs; ironically predicts the fate of Mendoza's vain ambition as well as Ferneze's.
5 *in strength of*: on the strength of.
9 *plummets . . . clock-lines*: clock-weights.
11 *salt sallow*: lecherous and unhealthy.

disgrace, contempt, and poverty.
Shall I, whose very 'hum' struck all heads bare,
Whose face made silence, creaking of whose shoe
Forced the most private passages fly ope,
Scrape like a servile dog at some latched door?
Learn now to make a leg, and cry, 'Beseech ye,
Pray ye, is such a lord within?', be awed
At some odd usher's scoffed formality?
First sear my brains! *Unde cadis, non quo, refert.*
My heart cries, 'Perish all!' How, how? What fate
Can once avoid revenge, that's desperate?
I'll to the duke. If all should ope – if? tush,
Fortune still dotes on those who cannot blush.
[*Exit.*]

SCENE II

Enter MALEVOLE *at one door;* BIANCA, EMILIA, *and* MAQUERELLE *at the other door.*

MALEVOLE. Bless ye, cast o' ladies! – Ha, Dipsas, how dost thou, old coal?

MAQUERELLE. Old coal?

MALEVOLE. Ay, old coal. Methinks thou liest like a brand under billets of green wood. He that will inflame a young wench's heart, let him lay close to her an old coal that hath first been

---

23 *make a leg*: bow.
26 *Unde cadis, non quo, refert*: 'It is where you fall from, not to, that matters' (Seneca, *Thyestes*, 925–6).
29 *ope*: be exposed.
30 *still*: always.
1 *cast*: pair.
2 *Dipsas*: name of a serpent whose bite caused intolerable thirst; hence the name of a bawd in Ovid, *Amores*, I, viii, and of an enchantress in Lyly's *Endymion*.
2 *coal*: pander.

fired, a panderess, my half-burnt lint, who, though thou canst not flame thyself, yet art able to set a thousand virgins' tapers afire. (*To* BIANCA) And how does Janivere thy husband, my little periwinkle? Is 'a troubled with the cough o' the lungs still? Does he hawk a-nights still? He will not bite.

BIANCA. No, by my troth, I took him with his mouth empty of old teeth.

MALEVOLE. And he took thee with thy belly full of young bones. Marry, he took his maim by the stroke of his enemy.

BIANCA. And I mine by the stroke of my friend.

MALEVOLE. The close stock! O mortal wench! Lady, ha' ye now no restoratives for your decayed Jason? Look ye, crab's guts baked, distilled ox-pith, the pulverised hairs of a lion's upper lip, jelly of cock-sparrows, he-monkey's marrow, or powder of fox-stones? – And whither are all you ambling now?

BIANCA. Why, to bed, to bed.

MALEVOLE. Do your husbands lie with ye?

BIANCA. That were country fashion, i'faith.

MALEVOLE. Ha' ye no foregoers about you? Come, whither in good deed, la now?

MAQUERELLE. In good indeed, la now, to eat the most miraculously, admirably, astonishable-composed posset with three curds, without any drink. Will ye help me with a he-fox? – Here's the duke.

The Ladies go out.

---

8 *lint*: tinder.

11 *Janivere*: cf. January and May, the old husband and young wife of Chaucer's *Merchant's Tale*.

21 *close stock*: secret thrust (fencing term).

23 *Jason*: Jason's wife, the witch Medea, restored the youth of his father Aeson with magic potions.

26 *fox-stones*: fox testicles were, like the other listed substances, a reputed aphrodisiac.

30 *country*: obscene pun.

31 *foregoers*: gentlemen-ushers.

35–6 *posset . . . drink*: thrice-curdled posset without any whey (therefore stronger).

36 *he-fox*: see above, line 26.

MALEVOLE. (*to* BIANCA) Fried frogs are very good, and French-like too.

SCENE III

Enter Duke PIETRO, *Count* CELSO, *Count* EQUATO, BILIOSO, FERRARDO, *and* MENDOZA.

PIETRO. The night grows deep and foul. What hour is't?

CELSO. Upon the stroke of twelve.

MALEVOLE. Save ye, duke!

PIETRO. From thee. Begone, I do not love thee.
Let me see thee no more; we are displeased.

MALEVOLE. Why, God b' wi' thee! Heaven hear my curse:
May thy wife and thee live long together!

PIETRO. Begone, sirrah.

MALEVOLE. [*sings*] 'When Arthur first in court began' –
Agamemnon, Menelaus – was ever any duke a *cornuto*?

PIETRO. Begone, hence.

MALEVOLE. What religion wilt thou be of next?

MENDOZA. Out with him!

MALEVOLE. With most servile patience. Time will come
When wonder of thy error will strike dumb
Thy bezzled sense. –
Slave's i' favour, ay, marry, shall he rise.

---

38 *fried frogs*: another stimulating recipe.

10 *When Arthur . . . began*: first line of a ballad begun by Falstaff in *2 Henry IV* (II.iv.33).

10–11 *Arthur . . . Agamemnon . . . Menelaus*: all cuckolded kings.

18 *bezzled*: fuddled with drink.

19 *Slave's . . . rise*: servility and flattery are the means to prosper.

19–24 *marry . . . fall*: Malevole converts Aesop's fable of the tortoise and the eagle into a parable of courtly rising and falling; the reference to 'subtle hell' suggests that courtly rising is, in moral terms, a kind of Fall.

Good God, how subtle hell doth flatter vice,
Mounts him aloft and makes him seem to fly,
As fowl the tortoise mocked, who to the sky
Th'ambitious shell-fish raised! Th'end of all
Is only that from height he might dead fall.

BILIOSO. Why, when? Out, ye rogue! Begone, ye rascal!

MALEVOLE. 'I shall now leave ye with my best wishes.'

BILIOSO. Out, ye cur!

MALEVOLE. 'Only let's hold together a firm correspondence.'

BILIOSO. Out!

MALEVOLE. 'A mutual-friendly-reciprocal-perpetual kind of steady-unanimous-heartily-leagued –'

BILIOSO. Hence, ye gross-jawed, peasantly – out, go!

MALEVOLE. Adieu, pigeon-house; thou bur, that only stickest to nappy fortunes. The serpigo, the strangury, an eternal uneffectual priapism seize thee!

BILIOSO. Out, rogue!

MALEVOLE. Mayst thou be a notorious wittolly pander to thine own wife, and yet get no office, but live to be the utmost misery of mankind, a beggarly cuckold! *Exit.*

PIETRO. It shall be so.

MENDOZA. It must be so, for where great states
revenge

25–46 added in QC.
27–35 Malevole repeats Bilioso's words from I.iv.86–9.
36 *peasantly*: peasant-like (Bilioso breaks off before finding a suitable noun).
39 *nappy*: rough, shaggy; or perhaps 'richly-piled'.
39 *serpigo*: ringworm.
40 *strangury*: painful bladder disease.
40 *priapism:* persistent erection.
48–50 *states . . . dogged*: a knotty passage made more difficult by textual corruption: 'where a prince seeks revenge it is necessary that those parties whom his own pious demeanour and sense of his high office forbid him to confront directly, be spied on by someone else'.

'Tis requisite the parts which piety
And loft respect forbears be closely dogged.
Lay one into his breast shall sleep with him,
Feed in the same dish, run in self-faction,
Who may discover any shape of danger;
For once disgraced, displayèd in offence,
It makes man blushless, and man is (all confess)
More prone to vengeance than to gratefulness.
Favours are writ in dust, but stripes we feel
Depravèd nature stamps in lasting steel.

PIETRO. You shall be leagued with the duchess.

EQUATO. The plot is very good.

PIETRO. You shall both kill and seem the corpse to save.

FERRARDO. A most fine brain-trick.

CELSO. (*tacite*) Of a most cunning knave.

PIETRO. My lords, the heavy action we intend
Is death and shame, two of the ugliest shapes
That can confound a soul. Think, think of it.
I strike, but yet, like him that 'gainst stone walls
Directs his shafts, rebounds in his own face,
My lady's shame is mine, O God, 'tis mine!
Therefore, I do conjure all secrecy;
Let it be as very little as may be,
Pray ye, as may be.
Make frightless entrance, salute her with soft eyes,
Stain naught with blood; only Ferneze dies,
But not before her brows. O gentlemen,
God knows I love her. Nothing else, but this:
I am not well. If grief, that sucks veins dry,
Rivels the skin, casts ashes in men's faces,
Bedulls the eye, unstrengthens all the blood,
Chance to remove me to another world,

50–2 *dogged . . . dish*: another version of the fawning court dog.
52 *run in self-faction*: appear to join his own faction.
55–6 a stock maxim of policy that can be found in Machiavelli, Guicciardini and Bodin (Hunter).
63, 88 *tacite*: Latin, silently, i.e. aside.
70, 84 *conjure*: accented on second syllable, and meaning 'adjure'.
78 *Rivels*: wrinkles.

As sure I once must die, let him succeed:
I have no child; all that my youth begot
Hath been your loves, which shall inherit me;
Which as it ever shall, I do conjure it,
Mendoza may succeed; he's nobly born,
With me of much desert.

CELSO. (*tacite*) Much!

PIETRO. Your silence answers, 'Ay';
I thank you. Come on now. O, that I might die
Before her shame's displayed. Would I were forced
To burn my father's tomb, unhele his bones,
And dash them in the dirt, rather than this.
This both the living and the dead offends:
Sharp surgery where naught but death amends.

Exit with the others.

SCENE IV

Enter MAQUERELLE, EMILIA, *and* BIANCA *with the posset.*

MAQUERELLE. Even here it is, three curds in three regions individually distinct, most methodically according to art composed, without any drink.

BIANCA. Without any drink?

MAQUERELLE. Upon my honour. Will ye sit and eat?

EMILIA. Good. The composure, the receipt, how is't?

MAQUERELLE. 'Tis a pretty pearl; by this pearl (how does't with me?) thus it is: seven and thirty yolks of Barbary hens' eggs; eighteen spoonfuls and a half of the juice of cock-sparrow bones; one ounce, three drams, four scruples, and one

---

83 *which shall inherit me*: the conceit is that the childless Pietro's only offspring is the love of his courtiers, which must therefore be his heir. This 'heir' is charged with ensuring that Mendoza become the next duke.

91 *unhele*: uncover.

9 *pearl*: Maquerelle is begging a reward, as she did with Ferneze in I.vi.

quarter of the syrup of Ethiopian dates; sweetened with three-quarters of a pound of pure candied Indian eringoes; strewed over with the powder of pearl of America, amber of Cataia, and lamb-stones of Muscovia.

BIANCA. Trust me, the ingredients are very cordial and, no question, good and most powerful in restoration.

MAQUERELLE. I know not what you mean by restoration, but this it doth: it purifieth the blood, smootheth the skin, enliveneth the eye, strengtheneth the veins, mundifieth the teeth, comforteth the stomach, fortifieth the back, and quickeneth the wit; that's all.

EMILIA. By my troth, I have eaten but two spoonfuls, and methinks I could discourse most swiftly and wittily already.

MAQUERELLE. Have you the art to seem honest?

BIANCA. I thank advice and practice.

MAQUERELLE. Why then, eat me o' this posset, quicken your blood, and preserve your beauty. Do you know Doctor Plaster-face? By this curd, he is the most exquisite in forging of veins, sprightening of eyes, dyeing of hair, sleeking of skins, blushing of cheeks, surfling of breasts, blanching and bleaching of teeth, that ever made an old lady gracious by torchlight; by this curd, la.

BIANCA. Well, we are resolved: what God has given us we'll cherish.

MAQUERELLE. Cherish anything saving your husband; keep him not too high, lest he leap the pale. But, for your beauty, let it be your saint;

---

16 *eringoes*: candied sea-holly root; regarded as an aphrodisiac.
17–18 *amber of Cataia*: Chinese ambergris (Cataia = Cathay).
25 *mundifieth*: cleans.
26 *fortifieth the back*: necessary to sexual prowess.
36 *forging of veins*: painting on false veins to conceal the use of cosmetics.
37 *sprightening*: making bright and sprightly.
38 *surfling*: painting or washing with cosmetics.
45–6 *keep . . . pale*: don't feed him too well, lest he jump the fence; the husband is like a horse who needs to be kept under (sexual) control.

bequeath two hours to it every morning in your closet. I ha' been young, and yet, in my conscience, I am not above five and twenty; but, believe me, preserve and use your beauty, for youth and beauty once gone, we are like beehives without honey, out-o'-fashion apparel that no man will wear; therefore, use me your beauty.

EMILIA. Ay, but men say –

MAQUERELLE. Men say! Let men say what the' will. Life o' woman! they are ignorant of your wants. The more in years, the more in perfection the' grow; if they lose youth and beauty, they gain wisdom and discretion. But when our beauty fades, good night with us. There cannot be an uglier thing to see than an old woman, from which, O pruning, pinching, and painting deliver all sweet beauties!

[*Music within.*]

BIANCA. Hark, music!

MAQUERELLE. Peace, 'tis i' the duchess' bedchamber. Good rest, most prosperously-graced ladies.

EMILIA. Good night, sentinel.

BIANCA. 'Night, dear Maquerelle.

Exeunt all but MAQUERELLE.

MAQUERELLE. May my posset's operation send you my wit and honesty, and me your youth and beauty; the pleasing'st rest.

Exit MAQUERELLE.

SCENE V

A Song.

Whilst the song is singing, enter MENDOZA *with his sword drawn, standing ready to*

55–63 imitated from *Pastor Fido*, III, v (Hunter); the *carpe diem* pathos has a distinctly odd effect in the mouth of this ancient grotesque.

II.v s.d. *A Song*: once again note the violent contrast between the harmonies of the song and the discordant violence of the action.

murder FERNEZE *as he flies from the* DUCHESS' *chamber.*

ALL. [*within*] Strike, strike!

(*Tumult within.*)

AURELIA. [*within*] Save my Ferneze! O, save my Ferneze!

Enter FERNEZE *in his shirt, and is received upon* MENDOZA*'s sword.*

ALL. [*within*] Follow, pursue!
AURELIA. [*within*] O, save Ferneze!
MENDOZA. Pierce, pierce!

Thrusts his rapier in FERNEZE.

Thou shallow fool, drop there.
He that attempts a princess' lawless love
Must have broad hands, close heart, with Argus' eyes,
And back of Hercules, or else he dies.

Enter AURELIA, *Duke* PIETRO, FERRARDO, BILIOSO, CELSO, *and* EQUATO.

ALL. Follow, follow!

MENDOZA *bestrides the wounded body of* FERNEZE *and seems to save him.*

MENDOZA. Stand off, forbear, ye most uncivil lords!
PIETRO. Strike!
MENDOZA. Do not. Tempt not a man resolved.
Would you, inhuman murderers, more than death?
AURELIA. O poor Ferneze!
MENDOZA. Alas, now all defence too late!
AURELIA. He's dead.

---

7 *Argus*: in Greek mythology Argus Panoptes had a hundred eyes.

8 *back of Hercules*: Hercules' apocryphal thirteenth labour was to impregnate fifty girls in a single night (see IV.v. 59–61). The true Hercules, Marston implies, is Malevole, cleansing the Augean stable of the court. He was to use the myth even more explicitly in *The Fawn*, whose disguised duke and purger of the corrupt court is named 'Hercules'.

PIETRO. I am sorry for our shame. Go to your bed.
Weep not too much, but leave some tears to shed
When I am dead.
AURELIA. What, weep for thee? My soul no tears shall find.
PIETRO. Alas, alas, that women's souls are blind.
MENDOZA. Betray such beauty!
Murder such youth? Contemn civility!
He loves him not that rails not at him.
PIETRO. Thou canst not move us: we have blood enough. –
And please you, lady, we have quite forgot
All your defects; if not, why then –
AURELIA. Not.
PIETRO. Not.
The best of rest, good night.
Exit PIETRO *with other Courtiers.*
AURELIA. Despite go with thee!
MENDOZA. Madam, you ha' done me foul disgrace. You have wronged him much loves you too much. Go to, your soul knows you have.
AURELIA. I think I have.
MENDOZA. Do you but think so?
AURELIA. Nay, sure I have; my eyes have witnessed thy love. Thou hast stood too firm for me.
MENDOZA. Why, tell me, fair-cheeked lady, who even in tears art powerfully beauteous, what unadvised passion struck ye into such a violent heat against me? Speak, what mischief wronged us? What devil injured us? Speak.
AURELIA. That thing ne'er worthy of the name of man, Ferneze.
Ferneze swore thou lovest Emilia;
Which to advance, with most reproachful breath
Thou both didst blemish and denounce my love.
MENDOZA. Ignoble villain, did I for this bestride
Thy wounded limbs? for this rank opposite
Even to my sovereign? for this, O God, for this

---

29 *loves*: who loves.
46–7 *rank opposite . . . to*: take a stand against.

Sunk all my hopes, and with my hopes my life?
Ripped bare my throat unto the hangman's axe? –
Thou most dishonoured trunk! – Emilia!
[*Kicks* FERNEZE.]
By life, I know her not – Emilia!
Did you believe him?
AURELIA. Pardon me, I did.
MENDOZA. Did you? And thereupon you graced him?
AURELIA. I did.
MENDOZA. Took him to favour, nay, even clasped with him?
AURELIA. Alas, I did.
MENDOZA. This night?
AURELIA. This night.
MENDOZA. And in your lustful twines the duke took you?
AURELIA. A most sad truth.
MENDOZA. O God, O God! How we dull honest souls,
Heavy-brained men, are swallowed in the bogs
Of a deceitful ground, whilst nimble bloods,
Light-jointed spirits, pent, cut good men's throats
And scape! Alas, I am too honest for this age,
Too full of phlegm and heavy steadiness;
Stood still whilst this slave cast a noose about me.
Nay, then, to stand in honour of him and her
Who had even sliced my heart!
AURELIA. Come, I did err,
And am most sorry I did err.
MENDOZA. Why, we are both but dead; the duke hates us;

---

64 *pent*: confined, imprisoned. Mendoza's claim is that dull and heavy spirits when trapped are unable to escape, whereas light and nimble spirits do so ruthlessly and easily. The image of entrapment shifts from bog to prison.

66 *full of phlegm*: cold and unexcitable, as opposed to the hot 'bloods'.

68 *stand in honour of*: defend the honour of.

And those whom princes do once groundly hate,
Let them provide to die, as sure as fate.
Prevention is the heart of policy.
AURELIA. Shall we murder him?
MENDOZA. Instantly?
AURELIA. Instantly, before he casts a plot,
Or further blaze my honour's much-known blot,
Let's murder him.
MENDOZA. I would do much for you; will ye marry me?
AURELIA. I'll make thee duke. We are of Medicis;
Florence our friend; in court my faction
Not meanly strengthful; the duke then dead;
We well prepared for change; the multitude
Irresolutely reeling; we in force;
Our party seconded; the kingdom mazed;
No doubt of swift success: all shall be graced.
MENDOZA. You do confirm me, we are resolute.
Tomorrow look for change; rest confident.
'Tis now about the immodest waist of night;
The mother of moist dew with pallid light
Spreads gloomy shades about the numbèd earth.
Sleep, sleep, whilst we contrive our mischief's birth.
This man I'll get inhumed. Farewell, to bed.
Ay, kiss thy pillow, dream, the duke is dead.
So, so, good night.

Exit AURELIA.

How fortune dotes on impudence! I am in private the adopted son of yon good prince. I must be duke. Why, if I must, I must. Most

---

72 *groundly*: profoundly.
73 *provide*: prepare.
74 *Prevention*: preparation, anticipation.
78 *blaze*: proclaim (metaphor from heraldry).
81 *Medicis*: an assertion of her royal name; but for an English audience who remembered the St Bartholomew's massacre the Medici family were a by-word for murderous machiavellism.
86 *mazed*: in a maze, bewildered.
90 *immodest waist of night*: middle of the night when lechery thrives; for the word-play see *Hamlet*, I.ii.198 and II.ii.231–4.
94 *inhumed*: buried.

silly lord, name me? O heaven! I see God made honest fools to maintain crafty knaves. The duchess is wholly mine, too; must kill her husband to quit her shame. Much! Then marry her! Ay.
O, I grow proud in prosperous treachery!
As wrestlers clip, so I'll embrace you all,
Not to support, but to procure your fall.

Enter MALEVOLE.

MALEVOLE. God arrest thee!

MENDOZA. At whose suit?

MALEVOLE. At the devil's. Ha, you treacherous damnable monster! How dost? How dost, thou treacherous rogue? Ha, ye rascal! I am banished the court, sirrah.

MENDOZA. Prithee, let's be acquainted; I do love thee, faith.

MALEVOLE. At your service, by the Lord, la. Shall's go to supper? Let's be once drunk together, and so unite a most virtuously strengthened friendship. Shall's, Huguenot, shall's?

MENDOZA. Wilt fall upon my chamber tomorrow morn?

MALEVOLE. As a raven to a dunghill. They say there's one dead here, pricked for the pride of the flesh.

MENDOZA. Ferneze. There he is; prithee, bury him.

MALEVOLE. O, most willingly; I mean to turn pure Rochelle churchman, I.

MENDOZA. Thou churchman! Why, why?

MALEVOLE. Because I'll live lazily, rail upon authority, deny king's supremacy in things indifferent, and be pope in mine own parish.

---

108 *God arrest thee*: pun on 'God rest thee.'

119 *Huguenot*: i.e. Puritan, with its frequent connotation of 'hypocrite'.

128 *Rochelle*: Huguenot fortress-town.

131–2 *things indifferent*: Anglican doctrine gave the king power over church matters not directly concerned with salvation. Malevole's Puritan denies even this limited form of supremacy (Hunter).

MENDOZA. Wherefore dost thou think churches were made?

MALEVOLE. To scour ploughshares; I ha' seen oxen plough up altars. *Et nunc seges ubi Sion fuit.*

MENDOZA. Strange.

MALEVOLE. Nay, monstrous! I ha' seen a sumptuous steeple turned to a stinking privy; more beastly, the sacredest place made a dog's kennel; nay, most inhuman, the stoned coffins of long-dead Christians burst up and made hogs' troughs. *Hic finis Priami.* Shall I ha' some sack and cheese at thy chamber? Good night, good mischievous incarnate devil; good night, Mendoza. Ha, ye inhuman villain, good night, 'night, fub!

MENDOZA. Good night; tomorrow morn.

Exit MENDOZA.

MALEVOLE. Ay, I will come, friendly damnation, I will come. I do descry cross-points; honesty and courtship straddle as far asunder as a true Frenchman's legs.

FERNEZE. O!

MALEVOLE. Proclamations, more proclamations!

FERNEZE. O, a surgeon!

MALEVOLE. Hark! lust cries for a surgeon. – What news from limbo? How does the grand cuckold, Lucifer?

FERNEZE. O, help, help! Conceal and save me.

FERNEZE *stirs, and* MALEVOLE *helps him up and conveys him away.*

MALEVOLE. Thy shame more than thy wounds do grieve me far;

136–7 *Et . . . fuit*: 'now there are cornfields where Jerusalem once stood' (adapted from Ovid, *Heroides*, I, 53).

144 *Hic finis Priami*: 'This was Priam's end' (adapted from Virgil, *Aeneid*, II, 554).

148 *fub*: cheat.

151 *cross-points*: steps in the galliard; here 'tricksy deceits'.

152 *courtship*: the courtier's art.

153 *Frenchman's legs*: presumably a symptom of pox, 'the French disease'.

157 *lust cries*: Malevole identifies Ferneze as the morality vice, Lust.

Thy wounds but leave upon thy flesh some scar,
But fame ne'er heals, still rankles worse and
worse;
Such is of uncontrollèd lust the curse.
Think what it is in lawless sheets to lie;
But, O Ferneze, what in lust to die!
Then, thou that shame respects, O, fly converse
With women's eyes and lisping wantonness!
Stick candles 'gainst a virgin wall's white back:
If they not burn, yet at the least they'll black.
Come, I'll convey thee to a private port
Where thou shalt live, O happy man, from
court.
The beauty of the day begins to rise,
From whose bright form night's heavy shadow
flies.
Now 'gins close plots to work; the scene grows
full,
And craves his eyes who hath a solid skull.
Exeunt.

ACT III

SCENE I

Enter PIETRO *the Duke,* MENDOZA, *Count* EQUATO, *and* BILIOSO.

PIETRO. 'Tis grown to youth of day; how shall we
waste this light?

---

167 *converse*: intimacy.
171 *port*: refuge.
172 *O happy man*: invokes the *beatus ille* theme of pastoral poetry (traditionally the other face of satire).
172 *from*: away from.
175 *plots . . . scene grows full*: Malevole sees himself as the dramatist of a play whose *epitasis* or fullest development of plot is about to unfold.
176 *solid skull*: as opposed to empty head.

My heart's more heavy than a tyrant's crown.
Shall we go hunt? Prepare for field.
Exit EQUATO.

MENDOZA. Would ye could be merry.

PIETRO. Would God I could! Mendoza, bid 'em haste.
Exit MENDOZA.
I would fain shift place. O vain relief!
Sad souls may well change place, but not change grief.
As deer, being struck, fly thorough many soils,
Yet still the shaft sticks fast, so –

BILIOSO. A good old simile, my honoured lord.

PIETRO. I am not much unlike to some sick man
That long desirèd hurtful drink; at last
Swills in and drinks his last, ending at once
Both life and thirst. O, would I ne'er had known
My own dishonour! Good God, that men should desire
To search out that which, being found, kills all
Their joy of life! To taste the tree of knowledge,
And then be driven from out paradise!
Canst give me some comfort?

BILIOSO. My lord, I have some books which have been dedicated to my honour, and I ne'er read 'em, and yet they had very fine names: *Physic for Fortune, Lozenges of Sanctified Sincerity*; very pretty works of curates, scriveners, and schoolmasters. Marry, I remember one Seneca,

---

8 *soils*: hunting terminology suggested by the situation; 'soil' = a pool or stretch of water used as a refuge by a hunted deer (*OED*).

15–18 *Good . . . paradise*: Piero finds in his own loss of ignorant happiness another type of the Fall.

22–3 *Physic . . . Sincerity*: the first title may be meant to recall Thomas Twyne's translation of Petrarch, *Physic against Fortune* (1579) as several eds. suggest, but is more likely supposed to seem as typical of neo-Stoical consolation literature as the second is of Puritan pamphlets.

25–9 *Seneca . . . coward*: gibes against the lavish life-style and the suicide of the Stoic philosopher are a commonplace of anti-Stoic writing.

Lucius Annaeus Seneca –
PIETRO. Out upon him! He writ of temperance and fortitude, yet lived like a voluptuous epicure and died like an effeminate coward.
Haste thee to Florence.
Here, take our letters, see 'em sealed; away.
Report in private to the honoured duke
His daughter's forced disgrace; tell him at length
We know too much; due compliments advance.
There's naught that's safe and sweet but
ignorance. *Exit* DUKE.

SCENE II

Enter MALEVOLE *in some frieze gown, whilst* BILIOSO *reads his patent.*

MALEVOLE. I cannot sleep; my eyes' ill-
neighbouring lids
Will hold no fellowship. O thou pale sober
night,
Thou that in sluggish fumes all sense dost steep,
Thou that gives all the world full leave to play,
Unbend'st the feebled veins of sweaty labour.
The galley-slave, that all the toilsome day
Tugs at his oar against the stubborn wave,
Straining his rugged veins, snores fast;
The stooping scythe-man, that doth barb the
field,
Thou mak'st wink sure. In night all creatures
sleep;
Only the malcontent, that 'gainst his fate

---

34 *due compliments advance*: treat him with the ceremonious respect due to his rank.
35 s.d. QC adds over one hundred lines probably by Webster; see Appendix, Insertion ii, p. 525 below.
III.ii s.d. *frieze*: coarse woollen cloth.
III.ii s.d. *patent*: commission as ambassador.
5 *Unbend'st*: relaxes.
9 *barb*: mow.
10 *wink*: close his eyes.

Repines and quarrels, alas, he's goodman tell-
clock!
His sallow jaw-bones sink with wasting moan;
Whilst others' beds are down, his pillow's stone.

BILIOSO. Malevole!

MALEVOLE. (*to* BILIOSO) Elder of Israel, thou honest defect of wicked nature and obstinate ignorance, when did thy wife let thee lie with her?

BILIOSO. I am going ambassador to Florence.

MALEVOLE. Ambassador? Now, for thy country's honour, prithee, do not put up mutton and porridge i' thy cloak-bag. Thy young lady wife goes to Florence with thee too, does she not?

BILIOSO. No, I leave her at the palace.

MALEVOLE. At the palace? Now, discretion shield, man! For God's love, let's ha' no more cuckolds! Hymen begins to put off his saffron robe; keep thy wife i' the state of grace. Heart o' truth, I would sooner have my lady singled in a bordello than in the Genoa palace.
Sin, there appearing in her sluttish shape,
Would soon grow loathsome, even to blushless
sense;
Surfeit would choke intemperate appetite,
Make the soul scent the rotten breath of lust.
When in an Italian lascivious palace,
A lady guardianless,
Left to the push of all allurement,
The strongest incitements to immodesty,
To have her bound, incensed with wanton
sweets,
Her veins filled high with heating delicates,

---

12 *tell-clock*: clock-watcher.
16 *Elder of Israel*: wicked old judge (with a glance at Puritan 'elders').
27 *shield*: forbid.
28–9 *Hymen . . . saffron robe*: the traditional attire of the marriage god.
30 *singled*: alone.
32 *there*: in the brothel. Note the allegorical framework of this speech which converts the court world to that of a morality *psychomachia*.
41 *heating delicates*: delicacies concocted to heat the blood and so inflame lust.

Soft rest, sweet music, amorous maskerers,
Lascivious banquets, sin itself gilt o'er,
Strong fantasy tricking up strange delights,
Presenting it dressed pleasingly to sense,
Sense leading it unto the soul, confirmed
With potent example, impudent custom,
Enticed by that great bawd, Opportunity;
Thus being prepared, clap to her easy ear
Youth in good clothes, well-shaped, rich,
Fair-spoken, promising-noble, ardent, blood-full,
Witty, flattering – Ulysses absent,
O Ithaca, can chastest Penelope hold out?

BILIOSO. Mass, I'll think on't. Farewell.

MALEVOLE. Farewell. Take thy wife with thee.
Farewell.

Exit BILIOSO.

To Florence, um? It may prove good, it may,
And we may once unmask our brows.

SCENE III

Enter Count CELSO.

CELSO. My honoured lord –

MALEVOLE. Celso, peace! How is't? Speak low; pale fears
Suspect that hedges, walls, and trees have ears.
Speak, how runs all?

CELSO. I'faith, my lord, that beast with many heads,
The staggering multitude, recoils apace.
Though thorough great men's envy, most men's malice,
Their much intemperate heat hath banished you,
Yet now they find envy and malice ne'er
Produce faint reformation.
The duke, the too soft duke, lies as a block,

52–3 *Ulysses . . . Penelope*: Ulysses provides an obvious analogue for Malevole as a prince, betrayed by his own followers, who returns in disguise to exact his revenge; Penelope, similarly, corresponds to the resolutely chaste Maria.

For which two tugging factions seem to saw;
But still the iron through the ribs they draw.
MALEVOLE. I tell thee, Celso, I have ever found
Thy breast most far from shifting cowardice
And fearful baseness; therefore, I'll tell thee, Celso,
I find the wind begins to come about;
I'll shift my suit of fortune.
I know the Florentine, whose only force,
By marrying his proud daughter to this prince,
Both banished me and made this weak lord duke,
Will now forsake them all; be sure he will.
I'll lie in ambush for conveniency,
Upon their severance to confirm myself.
CELSO. Is Ferneze interred?
MALEVOLE. Of that at leisure; he lives.
CELSO. But how stands Mendoza? How is't with him?
MALEVOLE. Faith, like a pair of snuffers: snibs filth in other men and retains it in himself.
CELSO. He does fly from public notice, methinks, as a hare does from hounds; the feet whereon he flies betrays him.
MALEVOLE. I can track him, Celso.
O, my disguise fools him most powerfully.
For that I seem a desperate malcontent,
He fain would clasp with me; he is the true slave
That will put on the most affected grace
For some vile second cause.

Enter MENDOZA.

CELSO. He's here.
MALEVOLE. Give place. –
Exit CELSO.

---

19 *whose only force*: whose power alone.
24 *Upon . . . confirm myself*: to build my own strength through the rupture of their alliance.
29 *snuffers*: candle snuffers.
29 *snibs*: snubs (reproves) and removes (snips off, snuffs out).
37 *clasp*: embrace, ally with.
39 *second cause*: ulterior motive (Hunter).

Illo, ho, ho, ho! art there, old truepenny? Where hast thou spent thyself this morning? I see flattery in thine eyes and damnation i' thy soul. Ha, ye huge rascal!

MENDOZA. Thou art very merry.

MALEVOLE. As a scholar, *futuens gratis*. How does the devil go with thee now?

MENDOZA. Malevole, thou art an arrant knave.

MALEVOLE. Who, I? I have been a sergeant, man.

MENDOZA. Thou art very poor.

MALEVOLE. As Job, an alchemist, or a poet.

MENDOZA. The duke hates thee.

MALEVOLE. As Irishmen do bum-cracks.

MENDOZA. Thou hast lost his amity.

MALEVOLE. As pleasing as maids lose their virginity.

MENDOZA. Would thou wert of a lusty spirit! Would thou wert noble.

MALEVOLE. Why, sure my blood gives me I am noble, sure I am of noble kind; for I find myself possessed with all their qualities: love dogs, dice, and drabs, scorn wit in stuff-clothes, have beat my shoemaker, knocked my seamstress, cuckold' my pothecary, and undone my tailor. Noble, why not? Since the stoic said, *Neminem servum non ex regibus, neminem regem non ex*

---

40 *Illo, ho, ho, ho*: falconer's cry to lure the hawk; but clearly meant as part of a pattern of allusions to *Hamlet* (cf. *Hamlet*, I.v.116).

40 *old truepenny*: *Hamlet* again (I.v.150).

45 *futuens gratis*: fornicating for free.

48 *sergeant*: court officer responsible for making arrests.

52 *bum-cracks*: farts, apparently particularly offensive to Irish manners (as Nashe records in *Pierce Penniless*: 'The Irishman will draw his dagger and be ready to kill and slay, if one break wind in his company' – cited by Wood).

58 *gives me*: proves to me.

60 *dogs*: not only lapdogs but fawning courtiers and (ultimately) cynic satirists.

61 *stuff*: coarse material.

62 *knocked*: obscene *double entendre*.

64–6 *Neminem . . . oriundum*: 'There is no slave not descended from kings, no king not descended from slaves' (Seneca, *Epistles*, XLIV, 4, quoting Plato).

servis esse oriundum, only busy Fortune touses, and the provident Chances blends them together. I'll give you a simile: did you e'er see a well with two buckets, whilst one comes up full to be emptied, another goes down empty to be filled? Such is the state of all humanity. Why, look you, I may be the son of some duke, for, believe me, intemperate lascivious bastardy makes nobility doubtful. I have a lusty, daring heart, Mendoza.

MENDOZA. Let's grasp; I do like thee infinitely. Wilt enact one thing for me?

MALEVOLE. Shall I get by it?

[MENDOZA] *gives him his purse.*

Command me; I am thy slave beyond death and hell.

MENDOZA. Murder the duke.

MALEVOLE. My heart's wish, my soul's desire, my fantasy's dream, my blood's longing, the only height of my hopes! How, O God, how? O, how my united spirits throng together! So strengthen my resolve!

MENDOZA. The duke is now a-hunting.

MALEVOLE. Excellent, admirable, as the devil would have it! Lend me, lend me rapier, pistol, cross-bow; so, so, I'll do it.

MENDOZA. Then we agree.

MALEVOLE. As Lent and fishmongers. Come, *cap-à-pie*, how? Inform.

MENDOZA. Know that this weak-brained duke, who only stands
On Florence' stilts, hath out of witless zeal
Made me his heir, and secretly confirmed
The wreath to me after his life's full point.

MALEVOLE. Upon what merit?

MENDOZA. Merit! By heaven, I horn him.
Only Ferneze's death gave me state's life.

---

66 *touses*: ruffles.
76 *grasp*: embrace.
93 *cap-à-pie*: from head to foot; see Textual Note, p. 496 below.
97 *full point*: full stop.
99 *state's life*: political life.

Tut, we are politic; he must not live now.

MALEVOLE. No reason, marry. But how must he die now?

MENDOZA. My utmost project is to murder the duke, that I might have his state, because he makes me his heir; to banish the duchess, that I might be rid of a cunning Lacedaemonian, because I know Florence will forsake her; and then to marry Maria, the banished Duke Altofront's wife, that her friends might strengthen me and my faction; this is all, la.

MALEVOLE. Do you love Maria?

MENDOZA. Faith, no great affection, but as wise men do love great women, to ennoble their blood and augment their revenue. To accomplish this now, thus now: the duke is in the forest next the sea; single him, kill him, hurl him i' the main, and proclaim thou sawest wolves eat him.

MALEVOLE. Um, not so good. Methinks, when he is slain,
To get some hypocrite, some dangerous wretch,
That's muffled o'er with feignèd holiness,
To swear he heard the duke on some steep cliff
Lament his wife's dishonour, and, in an agony
Of his heart's torture, hurled his groaning sides
Into the swollen sea. This circumstance,
Well made, sounds probable; and hereupon
The duchess –

MENDOZA. May well be banished.
O unpeerable invention! Rare!
Thou god of policy! It honeys me.

MALEVOLE. Then fear not for the wife of Altofront;
I'll close to her.

MENDOZA. Thou shalt, thou shalt. Our excellency is pleased.

---

105 *Lacedaemonian*: slang for whore.
123 *circumstance*: circumstantial narrative.
126 *unpeerable*: peerless.
129 *close to*: come to terms with.
130 *Our excellency*: note the comic pomposity; Mendoza already imagines himself duke.

Why wert not thou an emperor? When we
Are duke, I'll make thee some great man, sure.

MALEVOLE. Nay, make me some rich knave, and I'll make myself
Some great man.

MENDOZA. In thee be all my spirit.
Retain ten souls, unite thy virtual powers.
Resolve; ha, remember greatness. Heart, farewell.

Enter CELSO.

The fate of all my hopes in thee doth dwell.

[*Exit* MENDOZA.]

MALEVOLE. Celso, didst hear? O heaven, didst hear
Such devilish mischief? Sufferest thou the world
Carouse damnation even with greedy swallow,
And still dost wink, still does thy vengeance slumber?
If now thy brows are clear, when will they thunder?

Ex[*eunt.*]

SCENE IV

Enter PIETRO, FERRARDO, PREPASSO, *and three* PAGES.

FERRARDO. The dogs are at a fault.

Cornets like horns.

PIETRO. Would God nothing but the dogs were at it! Let the deer pursue safety, the dogs follow the game, and do you follow the dogs. As for me, 'tis unfit one beast should hunt another. I ha' one chaseth me. And't please you, I would be rid of ye a little.

---

135 *virtual*: both 'effective' and 'virtuous'.
1 *a fault*: a break in the line of scent (*OED*).
2–5 *dogs . . . beast*: Pietro, as a cuckold, feels himself a horned beast, pursued like the deer. Court 'dogs', by implication, have become hunting dogs.

FERRARDO. Would your grief would as soon leave you as we to quietness.

PIETRO. I thank you. –

Exeunt [FERRARDO *and* PREPASSO].

Boy, what dost thou dream of now?

1 PAGE. Of a dry summer, my lord; for here's a hot world towards. But, my lord, I had a strange dream last night.

PIETRO. What strange dream?

1 PAGE. Why, methought I pleased you with singing, and then I dreamt you gave me that short sword.

PIETRO. Prettily begged. Hold thee, I'll prove thy dream true; take't.

[*Gives sword.*]

1 PAGE. My duty. But still I dreamt on, my lord, and methought, and't shall please your excellency, you would needs out of your royal bounty give me that jewel in your hat.

PIETRO. O, thou didst but dream, boy; do not believe it. Dreams prove not always true; they may hold in a short sword, but not in a jewel. But now, sir, you dreamt you had pleased me with singing; make that true, as I ha' made the other.

1 PAGE. Faith, my lord, I did but dream, and dreams, you say, prove not always true: they may hold in a good sword, but not in a good song. The truth is I ha' lost my voice.

PIETRO. Lost thy voice, how?

1 PAGE. With dreaming, faith. But here's a couple of sirenical rascals shall enchant ye. What shall they sing, my good lord?

PIETRO. Sing of the nature of women, and then the song shall be surely full of variety, old crotchets, and most sweet closes; it shall be

---

12 *dry summer*: to 'dream of a dry summer' is proverbial (Tilley, S966).

13 *towards*: coming.

37 *sirenical*: like the sirens, whose songs cast enchantment.

41 *crotchets*: both 'quarter notes' and 'perverse whimsies'.

41 *closes*: (1) cadences; (2) embraces.

humorous, grave, fantastic, amorous, melancholy, sprightly, one in all, and all in one.

1 PAGE. All in one?

PIETRO. By'r Lady, too many. Sing, my speech grows culpable of unthrifty idleness; sing.

Song [*by* 2 *and* 3 PAGES].

Ah, so, so, sing. I am heavy. Walk off; I shall talk in my sleep; walk off.

Exeunt PAGES. [PIETRO *sleeps.*]

SCENE V

Enter MALEVOLE, *with cross-bow and pistol.*

MALEVOLE. Brief, brief, who? The duke. Good heaven, that fools should stumble upon greatness! – Do not sleep, duke; give ye good morrow. Must be brief, duke; I am fee'd to murder thee. Start not. Mendoza, Mendoza hired me; here's his gold, his pistol, cross-bow, sword – 'tis all as firm as earth. O fool, fool, choked with the common maze of easy idiots, credulity! Make him thine heir? What, thy sworn murderer?

PIETRO. O, can it be?

MALEVOLE. Can.

PIETRO. Discovered he not Ferneze?

MALEVOLE. Yes, but why, but why? For love to thee? Much, much! To be revenged upon his rival, who had thrust his jaws awry; who being slain, supposed by thine own hands, defended by his sword, made thee most loathsome, him most gracious, with thy loose princess. Thou, closely yielding egress and regress to her, madest

---

43–4 *all in one*: (1) all in one song; (2) all these moods in one woman (Aurelia); the Page's echo suggests a bawdy quibble.

8 *maze*: amazement.

19 *gracious*: in favour.

20 *closely*: secretly.

him heir, whose hot unquiet lust straight toused thy sheets, and now would seize thy state. Politician! Wise man! Death! To be led to the stake like a bull by the horns; to make even kindness cut a gentle throat! Life, why art thou numbed? Thou foggy dullness, speak! Lives not more faith in a home-thrusting tongue than in these fencing tip-tap courtiers?

Enter CELSO, *with a hermit's gown and beard.*

PIETRO. Lord, Malevole, if this be true –

MALEVOLE. If! Come, shade thee with this disguise. If! Thou shalt handle it; he shall thank thee for killing thyself. Come, follow my directions, and thou shalt see strange sleights.

PIETRO. World, whither wilt thou?

MALEVOLE. Why, to the devil. Come, the morn grows late.
A steady quickness is the soul of state.

Exeunt.

ACT IV

SCENE I

Enter MAQUERELLE, *knocking at the Ladies' door.*

MAQUERELLE. Medam, medam, are you stirring, medam? If you be stirring, medam – if I thought I should disturb ye –

[*Enter* PAGE.]

PAGE. My lady is up, forsooth.

28 *tip-tap*: presumably a satirical description of new styles in fencing.
36 *state*: statecraft.
1 *Medam*: affected pronunciation.

MAQUERELLE. A pretty boy, faith. How old art thou?

PAGE. I think fourteen.

MAQUERELLE. Nay, and ye be in the teens – Are ye a gentleman born? Do you know me? My name is Medam Maquerelle; I lie in the old Cunnycourt. – See, here the ladies.

[*Exit* PAGE.]

Enter BIANCA *and* EMILIA.

BIANCA. A fair day to ye, Maquerelle.

EMILIA. Is the duchess up yet, sentinel?

MAQUERELLE. O ladies, the most abominable mischance! O dear ladies, the most piteous disaster! Ferneze was taken last night in the duchess' chamber. Alas, the duke catched him and killed him.

BIANCA. Was he found in bed?

MAQUERELLE. O no, but the villainous certainty is, the door was not bolted, the tongue-tied hatch held his peace. So the naked troth is, he was found in his shirt whilst I, like an arrant beast, lay in the outward chamber, heard nothing; and yet they came by me in the dark, and yet I felt them not, like a senseless creature as I was. O beauties, look to your busk-points, if not chastely, yet charily: be sure the door be bolted. – Is your lord gone to Florence?

BIANCA. Yes, Maquerelle.

MAQUERELLE. I hope you'll find the discretion to purchase a fresh gown 'fore his return. – Now, by my troth, beauties, I would ha' ye once wise. He loves ye, pish! he is witty, bubble! fair-proportioned, mew! nobly-born, wind! Let this be still your fixed position: esteem me every man according to his good gifts, and so ye shall ever remain 'most dear and most worthy to be most dear ladies'.

---

11 *Cunnycourt*: rabbit-warren, i.e. (through a bawdy quibble) the women's quarters.

21–2 *tongue-tied hatch*: carefully oiled half-door.

27 *busk-points*: laces on stays.

38–9 *most dear . . . ladies*: parodies Sidney's dedication of the *Arcadia* to the Countess of Pembroke, 'most dear and worthy to be most dear lady'; here 'dear' = expensive.

EMILIA. Is the duke returned from hunting yet?
MAQUERELLE. They say not yet.
BIANCA. 'Tis now in midst of day.
EMILIA. How bears the duchess with this blemish now?
MAQUERELLE. Faith, boldly; strongly defies defame, as one that has a duke to her father. And there's a note to you: be sure of a stout friend in a corner, that may always awe your husband. Mark the 'haviour of the duchess now: she dares defame; cries, 'Duke, do what thou canst, I'll quit mine honour.' Nay, as one confirmed in her own virtue against ten thousand mouths that mutter her disgrace, she's presently for dances.

Enter FERRARDO.

BIANCA. For dances?
MAQUERELLE. Most true.
EMILIA. Most strange. See, here's my servant, young Ferrard. How many servants think'st thou I have, Maquerelle?
MAQUERELLE. The more, the merrier. 'Twas well said, use your servants as you do your smocks: have many, use one, and change often, for that's most sweet and courtlike.
FERRARDO. Save ye, fair ladies, is the duke returned?
BIANCA. Sweet sir, no voice of him as yet in court.
FERRARDO. 'Tis very strange.
BIANCA. And how like you my servant, Maquerelle?
MAQUERELLE. I think he could hardly draw Ulysses' bow; but, by my fidelity, were his nose

---

47 *note*: useful example.
51 *quit*: acquit.
53 *presently*: immediately.
57 *servant*: lover.
71 *Ulysses' bow*: in the *Odyssey*, XXI, Penelope demands that her suitors string and draw her husband's bow before claiming her hand; the bow is subsequently the instrument of Ulysses' revenge; by implication the allusion continues the heroic parallels between Altofront and Ulysses, Maria and Penelope.

narrower, his eyes broader, his hands thinner, his lips thicker, his legs bigger, his feet lesser, his hair blacker, and his teeth whiter, he were a tolerable sweet youth, i'faith. And he will come to my chamber, I will read him the fortune of his beard.

Cornets sound.

FERRARDO. Not yet returned. I fear – but the duchess approacheth.

SCENE II

Enter MENDOZA *supporting the* DUCHESS [AURELIA], GUERRINO; *the Ladies that are on the stage rise;* FERRARDO *ushers in the* DUCHESS, *and then takes a Lady to tread a measure.* [*Music sounds.*]

AURELIA. We will dance. Music! We will dance.

GUERRINO. '*Les guanto*', lady, '*Pensez bien*', '*Passa regis*', or 'Bianca's brawl'?

AURELIA. We have forgot the brawl.

FERRARDO. So soon? 'Tis wonder.

GUERRINO. Why, 'tis but two singles on the left, two on the right, three doubles forward, a

---

IV.ii s.d. *measure*: slow and stately dance. See Additional Note, p. 510 below.

2 *Les guanto*: a courtly dance; see Textual Note, p. 496 below.

2 *Pensez bien*: probably the name of a dance tune.

3 *Passa regis*: the king's dance; nothing more is known of it; Wood suggests it may be a type of 'King's Jig'.

3 *Bianca's brawl*: possibly the name of an actual dance, or perhaps simply coined by Guerrino as an occasion for bawdy mockery of Bianca (see below, 6–12). A brawl (branle, bransle) was a popular French dance in double time, introduced to England in the mid-sixteenth century; the name is punningly appropriate to a dance scene which undercuts the traditional symbolism of dancing.

6–7 *singles . . . doubles*: dance steps described in Elyot's *The Governor*, I, xxiii.

traverse of six round; do this twice, three singles side, galliard trick-of-twenty, coranto-pace; a figure of eight, three singles broken down, come up, meet, two doubles, fall back, and then honour.

AURELIA. O Daedalus, thy maze! I have quite forgot it.

MAQUERELLE. Trust me, so have I, saving the falling back and then honour.

Enter PREPASSO.

AURELIA. Music, music!

PREPASSO. Who saw the duke? the duke?

Enter EQUATO.

AURELIA. Music!

EQUATO. The duke? Is the duke returned?

AURELIA. Music!

Enter CELSO.

CELSO. The duke is either quite invisible or else is not.

AURELIA. We are not pleased with your intrusion upon our private retirement; we are not pleased; you have forgot yourselves.

Enter a PAGE.

CELSO. Boy, thy master? Where's the duke?

PAGE. Alas, I left him burying the earth with his spread, joyless limbs. He told me he was heavy, would sleep; bade me walk off, for that the

---

8 *traverse of six round*: 'a semi-circular sideways movement bringing the two partners together again so as to begin the repetition' (Hunter).

9 *galliard trick-of-twenty*: probably one of the characteristic leaps performed by the male partner in the galliard (a dance in triple time).

9 *coranto*: a lively dance in double time.

10–11 *broken down*: divided into smaller steps.

11–12 *fall back . . . honour*: step back and curtsy; but Guerrino may well have in mind the bawdy *double entendre* that Maquerelle picks up. With its 'come up' and 'fall back' the dance may also figure the rising and falling movement associated with courtly honour (cf. Malevole's 'bucket' speech at III.iii.69–72).

strength of fantasy oft made him talk in his dreams. I straight obeyed, nor ever saw him since; but, wheresoe'er he is, he's sad.

AURELIA. Music, sound high, as is our heart, sound high!

SCENE III

Enter MALEVOLE, and PIETRO *disguised like an hermit.*

MALEVOLE. The duke – peace! – the duke is dead.

AURELIA. Music!

MALEVOLE. Is't music?

MENDOZA. Give proof.

FERRARDO. How?

CELSO. Where?

PREPASSO. When?

MALEVOLE. Rest in peace, as the duke does; quietly sit. For my own part, I beheld him but dead, that's all. Marry, here's one can give you a more particular account of him.

MENDOZA. Speak, holy father, nor let any brow
Within this presence fright thee from the truth.
Speak confidently and freely.

AURELIA. We attend.

PIETRO. Now had the mounting sun's all-ripening wings
Swept the cold sweat of night from earth's dank breast,
When I, whom men call Hermit of the Rock,
Forsook my cell and clambered up a cliff,
Against whose base the heady Neptune dashed
His high-curled brows; there 'twas I eased my limbs,
When, lo, my entrails melted with the moan
Someone, who far 'bove me was climbed, did make –
I shall offend.

15–52 see Additional Note, p. 510 below.

MENDOZA. Not.
AURELIA. On.
PIETRO. Methinks I hear him yet: 'O female faith!
Go sow the ingrateful sand, and love a woman!
And do I live to be the scoff of men?
To be the wittol-cuckold, even to hug my poison?
Thou knowest, O truth,
Sooner hard steel will melt with southern wind,
A seaman's whistle calm the ocean,
A town on fire be extinct with tears,
Than women, vowed to blushless impudence,
With sweet behaviour and soft minioning,
Will turn from that where appetite is fixed.
O powerful blood, how dost thou slave their soul!
I washed an Ethiop, who, for recompense,
Sullied my name. And must I then be forced
To walk, to live thus black? Must, must! Fie!
He that can bear with "must", he cannot die.'
With that he sighed so passionately deep
That the dull air even groaned. At last he cries,
'Sink shame in seas, sink deep enough!', so dies;
For then I viewed his body fall and souse
Into the foamy main. O then I saw
That which methinks I see: it was the duke,
Whom straight the nicer-stomached sea belched up.
But then –
MALEVOLE. Then came I in; but, 'las, all was too late,
For even straight he sunk.
PIETRO. Such was the duke's sad fate.
CELSO. A better fortune to our Duke Mendoza!
OMNES. Mendoza!

Cornets flourish.

---

30 *wittol-cuckold*: conniving cuckold, acquiescent in his wife's infidelity.

36 *minioning*: caressing.

46 *souse*: may combine the sense of three distinct verbs: (1) to plunge into water; (2) to fall heavily; (3) to descend with force (used of hawks).

MENDOZA. A guard, a guard!

Enter a Guard.

We, full of hearty tears,
For our good father's loss –
For so we well may call him
Who did beseech your loves for our succession –
Cannot so lightly overjump his death
As leave his woes revengeless. (*To* AURELIA)
Woman of shame,
We banish thee forever to the place
From whence this good man comes; nor permit, on death,
Unto the body any ornament;
But base, as was thy life, depart away.

AURELIA. Ungrateful!

MENDOZA. Away!

AURELIA. Villain, hear me!

PREPASSO *and* GUERRINO *lead away the* DUCHESS.

MENDOZA. Begone! – My lords,
Address to public council; 'tis most fit
The train of Fortune is borne up by wit.
Away! Our presence shall be sudden; haste.

All depart saving MENDOZA, MALEVOLE, *and* PIETRO.

MALEVOLE. No, you egregious devil, ha, ye murdering politician, how dost, duke? How dost look now? Brave duke, i'faith!

MENDOZA. How did you kill him?

55–60 *We . . . revengeless*: Mendoza again uses the royal 'we'; the general resemblance to Claudius's opening lines in *Hamlet*, I.ii, will enhance the melodramatic surprise of Aurelia's banishment, but that in turn is undercut by the comic fact that Mendoza has inadvertently returned Aurelia to her husband.

69 *Address to*: prepare for.

70 *The train . . . wit*: note the resemblance of this politic maxim to Malevole's 'steady quickness is the soul of state' (III.v.36) and 'Mature discretion is the life of state' (IV.v.165).

73 *politician*: machiavel.

MALEVOLE. Slatted his brains out, then soused him in the briny sea.
MENDOZA. Brained him, and drowned him too?
MALEVOLE. O, 'twas best, sure work; for he that strikes a great man, let him strike home, or else 'ware he'll prove no man. Shoulder not a huge fellow, unless you may be sure to lay him in the kennel.
MENDOZA. A most sound brain-pan! I'll make you both emperors.
MALEVOLE. Make us Christians, make us Christians.
MENDOZA. I'll hoist ye, ye shall mount.
MALEVOLE. To the gallows, say ye? Come, *Praemium incertum petit certum scelus*. How stands the progress?
MENDOZA. Here, take my ring unto the citadel;
Have entrance to Maria, the grave duchess
Of banished Altofront. Tell her we love her;
Omit no circumstance to grace our person. Do't.
MALEVOLE. I'll make an excellent pander. Duke, farewell; 'dieu, adieu, duke.
MENDOZA. Take Maquerelle with thee, for 'tis found
None cuts a diamond but a diamond.
Exit MALEVOLE.
Hermit, thou art a man for me, my confessor.
O thou selected spirit, born for my good,
Sure thou wouldst make an excellent elder
In a deformed church. – Come,

---

76 *Slatted*: bashed.
76 *soused*: 'briny' suggests a pun on 'soused' = pickled.
83 *kennel*: gutter.
87–8 *hoist . . . mount . . . gallows*: another jocular version of the rising-falling paradox.
89 *Praemium . . . scelus*: 'The reward he seeks is as uncertain as the crime is certain' (Seneca, *Phoenissae*, 632–3).
90 *progress*: development of your plans.
94 *circumstance . . . person*: omit no detail to make me seem more attractive.
96 *'dieu, adieu, duke*: mocking (and threatening) word-play.
100–2 *selected . . . deformed*: Mendoza ridiculously, perhaps deliberately, mangles the religious terms 'elect' and 'reformed'.

We must be inward, thou and I all one.
PIETRO. I am glad I was ordained for ye.
MENDOZA. Go to, then; thou must know that Malevole is a strange villain, dangerous, very dangerous. You see how broad 'a speaks; a gross-jawed rogue. I would have thee poison him; he's like a corn upon my great toe, I cannot go for him; he must be cored out, he must. Wilt do't, ha?
PIETRO. Anything, anything.
MENDOZA. Heart of my life! Thus, then, to the citadel.
Thou shalt consort with this Malevole;
There being at supper, poison him. It shall
Be laid upon Maria, who yields love or dies.
Scud quick.
PIETRO. Like lightning. Good deeds crawl, but mischief flies. *Exit* PIETRO.

Enter MALEVOLE.

MALEVOLE. Your devilship's ring has no virtue. The buff-captain, the sallow Westphalian gammon-faced zaza, cries, 'Stand out'; must have a stiffer warrant, or no pass into the castle of comfort.

---

103 *inward*: intimate.
104 *ordained*: continues Mendoza's vein of mock-piety.
107 *broad*: both 'coarse' and 'outspoken'.
110 *go for him*: walk thanks to him.
110 *cored out*: cut out (like a corn), but with a quibble on 'core' = heart.
119 *buff-captain*: officer in leather jerkin.
119–20 *Westphalian gammon-faced*: pig-faced, or bacon-hued; Westphalia was famous for its hogs.
120 *zaza*: Harris suggests this is a corruption of Hungarian 'huszar' (military freebooter); Brooke and Paradise conjecture 'bully', Spencer 'Saxon'; it may be a mere nonsense coinage.
121 *stiffer*: more compelling.
121–2 *castle of comfort*: the prison is sardonically 'compared to some Court of Love allegory of female favour . . . it seems possible that it was a common euphemism for the mons veneris' (Hunter).

MENDOZA. Command our sudden letter. – Not enter? Sha't! What place is there in Genoa but thou shalt? Into my heart, into my very heart. Come, let's love; we must love, we two, soul and body.
MALEVOLE. How didst like the hermit? A strange hermit, sirrah.
MENDOZA. A dangerous fellow, very perilous. He must die.
MALEVOLE. Ay, he must die.
MENDOZA. Thou'st kill him. We are wise; we
must be wise.
MALEVOLE. And provident.
MENDOZA. Yea, provident. Beware an hypocrite;
A churchman once corrupted, O avoid!
A fellow that makes religion his stalking-horse,
(*Shoots under his belly.*)
He breeds a plague. Thou shalt poison him.
MALEVOLE. Ho, 'tis wondrous necessary. How?
MENDOZA. You both go jointly to the citadel;
There sup, there poison him; and Maria,
Because she is our opposite, shall bear
The sad suspect; on which she dies, or loves us.
MALEVOLE. I run. *Exit* MALEVOLE.
MENDOZA. We that are great, our sole self-good
still moves us.
They shall die both, for their deserts craves more
Than we can recompense; their presence still
Imbraids our fortunes with beholdingness,
Which we abhor; like deed, not doer. Then
conclude,
They live not to cry out ingratitude.
One stick burns t'other, steel cuts steel alone.
'Tis good trust few; but, O, 'tis best trust none.
Exit MENDOZA.

---

123 *Command . . . letter*: you may have our warrant immediately.
137 s.d. miming the manner in which the 'stalking horse' (a trained animal behind which a stalking fowler concealed himself) is used.
142 *opposite*: enemy.
143 *sad suspect*: serious suspicion.
148 *Imbraids*: upbraids.
148 *beholdingness*: obligation.

SCENE IV

Enter MALEVOLE *and* PIETRO *still disguised, at several doors.*

MALEVOLE. How do you? How dost, duke?

PIETRO. O, let the last day fall, drop, drop on our cursed heads!
Let heaven unclasp itself, vomit forth flames!

MALEVOLE. O, do not rant, do not turn player. There's more of them than can well live one by another already. What, art an infidel still?

PIETRO. I am amazed, struck in a swoon with wonder. I am commanded to poison thee.

MALEVOLE. I am commanded to poison thee – at supper.

PIETRO. At supper?

MALEVOLE. In the citadel.

PIETRO. In the citadel?

MALEVOLE. Cross-capers, tricks! Truth o' heaven! He would discharge us as boys do eldern guns, one pellet to strike out another. Of what faith art now?

PIETRO. All is damnation, wickedness extreme. There is no faith in man.

MALEVOLE. In none but usurers and brokers, they deceive no man; men take 'em for blood-suckers, and so they are. Now God deliver me from my friends!

PIETRO. Thy friends?

MALEVOLE. Yes, from my friends, for from mine enemies I'll deliver myself. O, cut-throat friendship is the rankest villainy. Mark this Mendoza, mark him for a villain; but heaven will send a plague upon him for a rogue.

---

4 *rant*: in Restoration theatres a 'rant' had a technical meaning, referring to any high-flown tragic oration – something of this sense may already be present. Pietro, 'still disguised', is of course a 'player' in a double sense.

14 *Cross-capers, tricks*: both dance steps; here 'cross-biting plots, deceits'.

15 *eldern guns*: popguns made of elder-wood.

PIETRO. O world!

MALEVOLE. World! 'Tis the only region of death, the greatest shop of the devil, the cruellest prison of men, out of the which none pass without paying their dearest breath for a fee. There's nothing perfect in it but extreme, extreme calamity, such as comes yonder.

SCENE V

Enter AURELIA, *two Halberds before and two after, supported by* CELSO *and* FERRARDO; AURELIA *in base mourning attire.*

AURELIA. To banishment, lead on to banishment.

PIETRO. Lady, the blessedness of repentance to you!

AURELIA. Why, why? I can desire nothing but death,
Nor deserve anything but hell.
If heaven should give sufficiency of grace
To clear my soul, it would make heaven graceless:
My sins would make the stock of mercy poor.
O, they would tire heaven's goodness to reclaim them.
Judgement is just, yet from that vast villain.
But, sure, he shall not miss sad punishment
'Fore he shall rule. – On to my cell of shame.

PIETRO. My cell 'tis, lady, where, instead of masques,
Music, tilts, tourneys, and such courtlike shows,
The hollow murmur of the checkless winds
Shall groan again, whilst the unquiet sea
Shakes the whole rock with foamy battery.

IV.v s.d. *Halberds*: halberdiers.
9 *yet from*: even though it comes from.
14 *checkless*: unchecked, with the sense of being subject to no controlling authority.
16 *battery*: battering.

There usherless the air comes in and out;
The rheumy vault will force your eyes to weep,
Whilst you behold true desolation.
A rocky barrenness shall pierce your eyes,
Where all at once one reaches where he stands,
With brows the roof, both walls with both his hands.

AURELIA. It is too good. – Blessed spirit of my lord,
O, in what orb soe'er thy soul is throned,
Behold me worthily most miserable.
O, let the anguish of my contrite spirit
Entreat some reconciliation.
If not, O joy triumph in my just grief;
Death is the end of woes, and tears' relief.

PIETRO. Belike your lord not loved you, was unkind.

AURELIA. O heaven!
As the soul loves the body, so loved he.
'Twas death to him to part my presence, heaven
To see me pleased.
Yet I, like to a wretch given o'er to hell,
Brake all the sacred rites of marriage,
To clip a base, ungentle, faithless villain,
O God, a very pagan reprobate –
What should I say? – ungrateful, throws me out,
For whom I lost soul, body, fame, and honour.
But 'tis most fit: why should a better fate
Attend on any who forsake chaste sheets,
Fly the embrace of a devoted heart,
Joined by a solemn vow 'fore God and man,
To taste the brackish blood of beastly lust

---

17 *usherless*: without an usher, unannounced; continues the contrast with the strictly ordered formality of the court world suggested in 'checkless'.

18 *rheumy*: 'rheum' is normally a discharge from the eyes or nose; a sympathetic connection with weeping is suggested.

28 *joy triumph*: enjoy your triumph.

31 ff. Hunter suggests a general parallel between this speech and *Hamlet*, I.ii.140 ff.; perhaps we are also expected to remember the bitter denunciation of the closet scene.

45 *brackish*: salt (and therefore 'lecherous').

In an adulterous touch? O ravenous immodesty,
Insatiate impudence of appetite!
Look, here's your end; for mark, what sap in dust,
What sin in good, even so much love in lust.
Joy to thy ghost, sweet lord, pardon to me!

CELSO. 'Tis the duke's pleasure this night you rest in court.

AURELIA. Soul, lurk in shades; run, shame, from brightsome skies;
In night the blind man misseth not his eyes.
Exit [*with* CELSO, FERRARDO, *and Halberds.*].

MALEVOLE. Do not weep, kind cuckold; take comfort, man; thy betters have been *beccos*; Agamemnon, emperor of all the merry Greeks, that tickled all the true Trojans, was a *cornuto*; Prince Arthur, that cut off twelve kings' beards, was a *cornuto*; Hercules, whose back bore up heaven, and got forty wenches with child in one night –

PIETRO. Nay, 'twas fifty.

MALEVOLE. Faith, forty's enough o' conscience – yet was a *cornuto*. Patience; mischief grows proud; be wise.

PIETRO. Thou pinchest too deep, art too keen upon me.

MALEVOLE. Tut, a pitiful surgeon makes a dangerous sore; I'll tent thee to the ground. Thinkest I'll sustain myself by flattering thee because thou art a prince? I had rather follow a drunkard, and live by licking up his vomit, than by servile flattery.

PIETRO. Yet great men ha' done't.

---

47 *impudence*: shamelessness.
55 *beccos*: cuckolds (Italian *becco* = goat).
59 *Hercules*: his cuckoldry seems to be apocryphal; perhaps Hercules is introduced mainly to point towards Malevole's cleansing of this Augean court.
69 *tent*: probe and clean a wound.

MALEVOLE. Great slaves fear better than love, born naturally for a coal basket, though the common usher of princes' presence, Fortune, ha' blindly given them better place. I am vowed to be thy affliction.

PIETRO. Prithee, be;
I love much misery, and be thou son to me.

Enter BILIOSO.

MALEVOLE. Because you are an usurping duke. (*To* BILIOSO) Your lordship's well returned from Florence.

BILIOSO. Well returned, I praise my horse.

MALEVOLE. What news from the Florentines?

BILIOSO. I will conceal the great duke's pleasure; only this was his charge: his pleasure is that his daughter die, Duke Pietro be banished for banishing his blood's dishonour, and that Duke Altofront be reaccepted. This is all. But I hear Duke Pietro is dead.

MALEVOLE. Ay, and Mendoza is duke. What will you do?

BILIOSO. Is Mendoza strongest?

MALEVOLE. Yes he is.

BILIOSO. Then yet I'll hold with him.

MALEVOLE. But if that Altofront should turn straight again?

BILIOSO. Why, then I would turn straight again.
'Tis good run still with him that has most might:
I had rather stand with wrong than fall with right.

---

75 *Great slaves*: Malevole stresses these two words, as correcting Pietro's 'great men'; whatever their status, flatterers are slaves by nature.

76 *born . . . basket*: born to carry coal baskets (the most menial of tasks).

82 *Because . . . duke*: an ironic comment on Pietro's offer to make him his heir.

89–90 *for banishing*: since Pietro did not in fact banish Aurelia, Wood proposes: 'for [the purpose of] banishing his dishonoured blood'; but a minor inconsistency is possible.

98–9 *turn straight again*: return immediately.

100 *turn straight*: immediately change my allegiance.

MALEVOLE. What religion will you be of now?

BILIOSO. Of the duke's religion, when I know what it is.

MALEVOLE. O Hercules!

BILIOSO. Hercules? Hercules was the son of Jupiter and Alcmena.

MALEVOLE. Your lordship is a very wittol.

BILIOSO. Wittol?

MALEVOLE. Ay, all-wit.

BILIOSO. Amphitryo was a cuckold.

MALEVOLE. Your lordship sweats; your young lady will get you a cloth for your old worship's brows.

Exit BILIOSO.

Here's a fellow to be damned. This is his inviolable maxim: 'Flatter the greatest and oppress the least.' A whoreson flesh-fly, that still gnaws upon the lean, galled backs.

PIETRO. Why dost then salute him?

MALEVOLE. Faith, as bawds go to church, for fashion sake. Come, be not confounded; thou'rt but in danger to lose a dukedom. Think this: this earth is the only grave and Golgotha wherein all things that live must rot; 'tis but the draught wherein the heavenly bodies discharge their corruption; the very muckhill on which the sublunary orbs cast their excrements. Man is the slime of this dung-pit, and princes are the governors of these men; for, for our

---

106 *Hercules*: either an ironic comment on Bilioso's lack of backbone, or an exclamatory appeal to Hercules as Malevole's patron.

108 *Alcmena*: wife of Amphitryon, seduced by Jupiter; the mention of Hercules ridiculously triggers off thoughts of cuckoldry in Bilioso.

110–11 *Wittol . . . all-wit*: the same pun is employed in the character of Allwit in Middleton's *A Chaste Maid in Cheapside*.

117 *flesh-fly*: blow-fly; a type of the parasite, as in Jonson's Mosca.

119 *salute*: greet.

125 *draught*: privy, cesspit.

souls, they are as free as emperors', all of one piece; there goes but a pair of shears betwixt an emperor and the son of a bagpiper; only the dyeing, dressing, pressing, glossing makes the difference. Now what art thou like to lose?
A gaoler's office to keep men in bonds,
Whilst toil and treason all life's good confounds.

PIETRO. I here renounce forever regency.
O Altofront, I wrong thee to supplant thy right,
To trip thy heels up with a devilish sleight;
For which I now from throne am thrown, world-tricks abjure;
For vengeance, though't comes slow, yet it comes sure.
O, I am changed; for here, 'fore the dread power,
In true contrition I do dedicate
My breath to solitary holiness,
My lips to prayer, and my breast's care shall be
Restoring Altofront to regency.

MALEVOLE. Thy vows are heard, and we accept thy faith.

Undisguiseth himself.

Enter FERNEZE *and* CELSO.

Altofront, Ferneze, Celso, Pietro –
Banish amazement. Come, we four must stand
Full shock of fortune. Be not wonder-stricken.

PIETRO. Does Ferneze live?

FERNEZE. For your pardon.

PIETRO. Pardon and love. Give leave to recollect
My thoughts dispersed in wild astonishment.
My vows stand fixed in heaven, and from hence
I crave all love and pardon.

MALEVOLE. Who doubts of providence,

130–1 *of one piece*: all made of the same material; hence only the cutting of a pair of shears marks the difference between an emperor's soul and that of a bagpiper's son (131–2).
133 *dressing . . . glossing*: finishing processes.
136 *confounds*: brings to confusion, destroys.
148 see Textual Note, p. 497 below.
155–65 see Additional Note, p. 510 below.

That sees this change? A hearty faith to all!
He needs must rise who can no lower fall;
For still impetuous vicissitude
Touseth the world; then let no maze intrude
Upon your spirits. Wonder not I rise,
For who can sink that close can temporise?
The time grows ripe for action. I'll detect
My privat'st plot, lest ignorance fear suspect.
Let's close to counsel, leave the rest to fate;
Mature discretion is the life of state.

Exeunt.

ACT V

SCENE I

Enter MALEVOLE *and* MAQUERELLE, *at several doors opposite, singing.*

MALEVOLE. 'The Dutchman for a drunkard,'
MAQUERELLE. 'The Dane for golden locks,'
MALEVOLE. 'The Irishman for usquebaugh,'
MAQUERELLE. 'The Frenchman for the (   ).'

MALEVOLE. O, thou art a blessed creature! Had I a modest woman to conceal, I would put her to thy custody, for no reasonable creature would ever suspect her to be in thy company. Ha, thou art a melodious Maquerelle, thou picture of a woman and substance of a beast.

162 *detect*: expose.

165 s.d. After this line QC adds the Websterian V.i involving Passarello and Bilioso; see Appendix, Insertion iii, p. 530 below.

3 *usquebaugh*: whisky (approximation of Gaelic).

4 (   ): 'pox', but in the theatre the song will come closer to raising a smile if the obvious rhyme-word is suppressed.

10–11 *beast. And*: between these words QC inserts the dialogue of Appendix, Insertion iv, p. 532 below.

And how dost thou think o' this transformation of state now?

MAQUERELLE. Verily, very well; for we women always note the falling of the one is the rising of the other; some must be fat, some must be lean; some must be fools, and some must be lords; some must be knaves, and some must be officers; some must be beggars, some must be knights; some must be cuckolds, and some must be citizens. As for example, I have two court dogs, the most fawning curs, the one called Watch, th'other Catch. Now I, like Lady Fortune, sometimes love this dog, sometimes raise that dog, sometimes favour Watch, most commonly fancy Catch. Now that dog which I favour I feed; and he's so ravenous that what I give he never chaws it, gulps it down whole, without any relish of what he has, but with a greedy expectation of what he shall have. The other dog now –

MALEVOLE. No more dog, sweet Maquerelle, no more dog. And what hope hast thou of the Duchess Maria? Will she stoop to the duke's lure? Will she come, think'st?

MAQUERELLE. Let me see, where's the sign now? Ha' ye e'er a calendar? Where's the sign, trow you?

MALEVOLE. Sign? Why, is there any moment in that?

MAQUERELLE. O, believe me, a most secret power. Look ye, a Chaldean or an Assyrian, I am sure 'twas a most sweet Jew, told me, court any woman in the right sign, you shall not miss.

---

14 *falling . . . rising*: Maquerelle's bawdy *double entendre* equates the rise and fall of political fortunes with sexual rising (erection) and falling (dishonour). The connection is appropriate since at this court the one depends on the other.

20–30 *court dogs . . . other dog now*: Maquerelle's fable is her equivalent of Malevole's bucket simile, linking it with the dog motif.

33–4 *stoop . . . lure*: as a hawk returns to the feathered 'lure' on the falconer's wrist.

35 *sign*: zodiacal sign.

But you must take her in the right vein then, as, when the sign is in Pisces, a fishmonger's wife is very sociable; in Cancer, a precisian's wife is very flexible; in Capricorn, a merchant's wife hardly holds out; in Libra, a lawyer's wife is very tractable, especially if her husband be at the term; only in Scorpio 'tis very dangerous meddling. Has the duke sent any jewel, any rich stones?

Enter CAPTAIN.

MALEVOLE. Ay, I think those are the best signs to take a lady in. – By your favour, signor, I must discourse with the Lady Maria, Altofront's duchess; I must enter for the duke.

CAPTAIN. She here shall give you interview. I received the guardship of this citadel from the good Altofront, and for his use I'll keep't till I am of no use.

MALEVOLE. Wilt thou? O heavens, that a Christian should be found in a buff-jerkin! Captain Conscience, I love thee, captain. We attend.

Exit CAPTAIN.

– And what hope hast thou of this duchess' easiness?

---

46 *precisian*: Puritan; presumably assigned to Cancer because they were of 'crabbed' disposition.

47 *Capricorn*: Hunter suggests the Goat is linked with merchants by a pun on 'corn'; but merchants' wives were considered easy game in aristocratic circles, and the link may be with the lechery of goats.

49–50 *at the term*: at the court sessions; Hunter suggests a pun: 'at the end of his sexual activity'.

50–1 *Scorpio . . . meddling*: the scorpion has a sting in its tail, an allusion to venereal disease.

52 *stones*: jewels (as a bribe); testicles.

54 *take . . . in*: conquer a lady with.

56 *enter for the duke*: a complex quibble: (1) go in on behalf of the duke: (2) go in as though I were the duke (Malevole hints at his real identity); (3) a bawdy pun that follows up the play on 'stones'.

62–3 *Captain Conscience*: recalls Malevole's allegorisation of the citadel as the castle of comfort (IV.iii.121–2).

65 *easiness*: readiness for unchastity.

MAQUERELLE. 'Twill go hard. She was a cold creature ever; she hated monkeys, fools, jesters, and gentlemen-ushers extremely. She had the vile trick on't not only to be truly modestly honourable in her own conscience, but she would avoid the least wanton carriage that might incur suspect, as, God bless me, she had almost brought bed-pressing out of fashion. I could scarce get a fine for the lease of a lady's favour once in a fortnight.

MALEVOLE. Now, in the name of immodesty, how many maidenheads hast thou brought to the block?

MAQUERELLE. Let me see. Heaven forgive us our misdeeds! – Here's the duchess.

SCENE II

Enter MARIA *and* CAPTAIN.

MALEVOLE. God bless thee, lady.

MARIA. Out of thy company.

MALEVOLE. We have brought thee tender of a husband.

MARIA. I hope I have one already.

MAQUERELLE. Nay, by mine honour, madam, as good ha' ne'er a husband as a banished husband; he's in another world now. I'll tell ye, lady, I have heard of a sect that maintained, when the husband was asleep, the wife might lawfully entertain another man, for then her husband was as dead – much more when he is banished.

MARIA. Unhonest creature!

MAQUERELLE. Pish, honesty is but an art to seem so. Pray ye, what's honesty, what's constancy, but fables feigned, odd old fools'

---

71 *carriage*: behaviour.

73 *fine*: fee.

9–12 *sect . . . dead*: a satirical glance at the sect called the Family of Love, or Brownists.

14 *Unhonest*: dishonourable.

chat, devised by jealous fools to wrong our liberty?

MALEVOLE. Mully, he that loves thee is a duke, Mendoza. He will maintain thee royally, love thee ardently, defend thee powerfully, marry thee sumptuously, and keep thee in despite of Rosicler or Donzel del Phoebo. There's jewels. [*Offers jewels*] If thou wilt, so; if not, so.

MARIA. Captain, for God's love, save poor wretchedness
From tyranny of lustful insolence!
Enforce me in the deepest dungeon dwell
Rather than here; here round about is hell. –
O my dear'st Altofront, where'er thou breathe,
Let my soul sink into the shades beneath
Before I stain thine honour; this thou hast,
And long as I can die, I will live chaste.

MALEVOLE. 'Gainst him that can enforce, how vain is strife!

MARIA. She that can be enforced has ne'er a knife.
She that through force her limbs with lust enrolls
Wants Cleopatra's asps and Portia's coals.
God amend you!

Exit with CAPTAIN.

MALEVOLE. Now, the fear of the devil forever go with thee! – Maquerelle, I tell thee, I have found an honest woman. Faith, I perceive, when all is done, there is of women, as of all other things, some good, most bad; some saints, some sinners. For as nowadays no courtier but has his mistress, no captain but has his cockatrice, no cuckold but has his horns, and no fool but has his feather, even so, no woman but has her weakness and feather too, no sex but has his – I can hunt the letter no further. [*Aside*] O God,

---

19 *Mully*: Molly; familiar term of endearment.
23 *Rosicler or Donzel del Phoebo*: heroes of *The Mirror of Knighthood* (cf. Insertion i, 36–7).
36 *Cleopatra . . . Portia*: heroic female suicides (see *Julius Caesar*, IV.ii.150–4; *Antony and Cleopatra*, V.ii).
44 *cockatrice*: slang for whore.
48 *hunt the letter*: continue the alliteration.

how loathsome this toying is to me! That a duke should be forced to fool it! Well, *Stultorum plena sunt omnia*: better play the fool lord than be the fool lord. – Now, where's your sleights, Madam Maquerelle?

MAQUERELLE. Why, are ye ignorant that 'tis said a squeamish, affected niceness is natural to women, and that the excuse of their yielding is only, forsooth, the difficult obtaining? You must put her to't. Women are flax, and will fire in a moment.

MALEVOLE. Why, was the flax put into thy mouth, and yet thou – thou set fire, thou inflame her?

MAQUERELLE. Marry, but I'll tell ye now, you were too hot.

MALEVOLE. The fitter to have inflamed the flax-woman.

MAQUERELLE. You were too boisterous, spleeny, for, indeed –

MALEVOLE. Go, go, thou art a weak pand'ress; now I see,
Sooner earth's fire heaven itself shall waste
Than all with heat can melt a mind that's chaste.
Go thou, the duke's lime-twig. I'll make the duke turn thee out of thine office. What, not get one touch of hope, and had her at such advantage!

MAQUERELLE. Now, o' my conscience, now I think in my discretion, we did not take her in the right sign; the blood was not in the true vein, sure. *Exit.*

Enter BILIOSO.

BILIOSO. Make way there! The duke returns from the enthronement. – Malevole –

MALEVOLE. Out, rogue!

50–1 *Stultorum . . . omnia*: 'The whole world is full of fools' (Cicero, *Epist. Fam.*, IX, xxii, 4).

55 *niceness*: coyness.

72 *lime-twig*: snare (twig covered in bird-lime to entrap small birds).

79 s.d.–116 added in QC.

BILIOSO. Malevole –

MALEVOLE. 'Hence, ye gross-jawed, peasantly – out, go!'

BILIOSO. Nay, sweet Malevole, since my return I hear you are become the thing I always prophesied would be – an advanced virtue, a worthily-employed faithfulness, a man o' grace, dear friend. Come; what? *Si quoties peccant homines* . . . If as often as courtiers play the knaves, honest men should be angry – why, look ye, we must collogue sometimes, forswear sometimes.

MALEVOLE. Be damned sometimes.

BILIOSO. Right. *Nemo omnibus horis sapit*: no man can be honest at all hours; necessity often depraves virtue.

MALEVOLE. I will commend thee to the duke.

BILIOSO. Do; let us be friends, man.

MALEVOLE. And knaves, man.

BILIOSO. Right. Let us prosper and purchase; our lordships shall live, and our knavery be forgotten.

MALEVOLE. He that by any ways gets riches, his means never shames him.

BILIOSO. True.

MALEVOLE. For impudency and faithlessness are the main stays to greatness.

BILIOSO. By the Lord, thou art a profound lad.

MALEVOLE. By the Lord, thou art a perfect knave. Out, ye ancient damnation!

84–5 *Hence . . . go*: quoting Bilioso at II.iii.36–7 where Malevole was also engaged in sarcastic quotation!

88–9 *virtue . . . faithfulness . . . grace*: Bilioso (like his master) systematically degrades the language of Christian virtue to political uses.

90–1 *Si . . . homines*: 'If as often as men sin . . .' (Ovid, *Tristia*, II, 33); Malevole paraphrases the rest of the passage, '. . . Jupiter hurled his thunderbolts, they would soon be pointless'.

93 *collogue*: gloze; deal flatteringly or deceitfully with, feign agreement or belief (*OED*).

96 *Nemo . . . sapit*: Bilioso translates; a popular quotation from Pliny, *Nat. Hist.*, VII, xl, 131.

102 *purchase*: acquire wealth.

BILIOSO. Peace, peace! And thou wilt not be a friend to me as I am a knave, be not a knave to me as I am thy friend, and disclose me. Peace! Cornets!

SCENE III

Enter PREPASSO *and* FERRARDO, *two Pages with lights,* CELSO *and* EQUATO, MENDOZA *in duke's robes, and* GUERRINO.

MENDOZA. On, on; leave us, leave us.

Exeunt all saving MALEVOLE [*and* MENDOZA].

Stay, where is the hermit?

MALEVOLE. With Duke Pietro, with Duke Pietro.

MENDOZA. Is he dead? Is he poisoned?

MALEVOLE. Dead as the duke is.

MALEVOLE. Good, excellent. He will not blab; secureness lives in secrecy. Come hither, come hither.

MALEVOLE. Thou hast a certain strong villainous scent about thee my nature cannot endure.

MENDOZA. Scent, man? What returns Maria, what answer to our suit?

MALEVOLE. Cold, frosty; she is obstinate.

MENDOZA. Then she's but dead; 'tis resolute, she dies.
Black deed only through black deed safely flies.

MALEVOLE. Pew! *Per scelera semper sceleribus tutum est iter.*

MENDOZA. What, art a scholar? Art a politician? Sure, thou art an arrant knave.

MALEVOLE. Who, I? I have been twice an under-sheriff, man.

MENDOZA. Canst thou empoison? Canst thou empoison?

16–17 *Per . . . iter*: 'The safe path to crime is always through crimes'; the most widely quoted and imitated of all Senecan *sententiae (Agamemnon*, 115).

21 After this line QC adds the passage in Appendix, Insertion v, p. 533 below.

MALEVOLE. Excellently; no Jew, pothecary, or politician better. Look ye, here's a box. Whom wouldst thou empoison? Here's a box [*Giving it*] which, opened and the fume ta'en up in conduits through which the brain purges itself, doth instantly for twelve hours' space bind up all show of life in a deep senseless sleep. Here's another [*Giving it*] which, being opened under the sleeper's nose, chokes all the power of life, kills him suddenly.

MENDOZA. I'll try experiments; 'tis good not to be deceived. – So, so; catso!

Seems to poison MALEVOLE [*who falls*].

Who would fear that may destroy?
Death hath no teeth nor tongue;
And he that's great, to him are slaves
Shame, murder, fame, and wrong. –
Celso!

Enter CELSO.

CELSO. My honoured lord?

MENDOZA. The good Malevole, that plain-tongued man,
Alas, is dead on sudden, wondrous strangely.
He held in our esteem good place.
Celso, see him buried, see him buried.

CELSO. I shall observe ye.

MENDOZA. And, Celso, prithee let it be thy care tonight
To have some pretty show, to solemnise
Our high instalment; some music, masquery.
We'll give fair entertain unto Maria,
The duchess to the banished Altofront.
Thou shalt conduct her from the citadel
Unto the palace. Think on some masquery.

CELSO. Of what shape, sweet lord?

MENDOZA. What shape? Why, any quick-done fiction,

---

46 *observe*: obey.

55–62 ironically the 'fiction' that Mendoza disdainfully outlines becomes fact through an extravagantly 'far-fet trick': Mercury (guide of the dead) leads in masquers (dressed as dukes) who include the supposedly dead Genoan dukes Pietro and Malevole/Altofront.

As some brave spirits of the Genoan dukes
To come out of Elysium, forsooth,
Led in by Mercury, to gratulate
Our happy fortune; some such anything,
Some far-fet trick, good for ladies,
Some stale toy or other,
No matter, so't be of our devising.
Do thou prepare't; 'tis but for fashion sake.
Fear not, it shall be graced, man, it shall take.

CELSO. All service.

MENDOZA. All thanks; our hand shall not be close to thee; farewell. –
[*Aside*] Now is my treachery secure, nor can we fall.
Mischief that prospers, men do virtue call.
I'll trust no man; he that by tricks gets wreaths
Keeps them with steel; no man securely breathes
Out of deservèd ranks; the crowd will mutter, 'fool';
Who cannot bear with spite, he cannot rule.
The chiefest secret for a man of state
Is to live senseless of a strengthless hate.

Exit MENDOZA.

MALEVOLE. (*starts up and speaks*) Death of the damned thief! I'll make one i' the masque; thou shalt ha' some brave spirits of the antique dukes!

CELSO. My lord, what strange delusion?

MALEVOLE. Most happy, dear Celso; poisoned with an empty box! I'll give thee all anon. My lady comes to court; there is a whirl of fate comes tumbling on; the castle's captain stands for me, the people pray for me, and the Great Leader of the just stands for me. Then courage, Celso!
For no disastrous chance can ever move him
That leaveth nothing but a God above him.

Exeunt.

---

66 *close*: stingy.
69 *wreaths*: garlands of honour; hence crowns.
71 *deservèd ranks*: those who follow him because of his desert.
74 *senseless of*: untouched by.
75 s.d. Malevole's rising is a kind of resurrection, contrived by 'holy policy'.

SCENE IV

Enter PREPASSO *and* BILIOSO, *two Pages before them;* MAQUERELLE, BIANCA, *and* EMILIA.

BILIOSO. Make room there, room for the ladies. Why, gentlemen, will not ye suffer the ladies to be entered in the great chamber? Why, gallants! And you, sir, to drop your torch where the beauties must sit, too.

PREPASSO. And there's a great fellow plays the knave; why dost not strike him?

BILIOSO. Let him play the knave, o' God's name; think'st thou I have no more wit than to strike a great fellow? – The music! More lights! Revelling-scaffolds! Do you hear? Let there be oaths enough ready at the door; swear out the devil himself. Let's leave the ladies and go see if the lords be ready for them.

All save the LADIES *depart.*

MAQUERELLE. And, by my troth, beauties, why do you not put you into the fashion? This is a stale cut; you must come in fashion. Look ye, you must be all felt, felt and feather, a felt upon your bare hair. Look ye, these tiring-things are justly out of request now. And, do ye hear, you must wear falling-bands, you must come into the falling fashion; there is such a deal o' pinning these ruffs, when the fine clean fall is worth all; and again, if you should chance to take a nap in the afternoon, your falling-

---

4 *drop your torch*: drop pitch from your torch (Hunter).

11 *Revelling-scaffolds*: platforms to accommodate spectators at court revels.

12 *oaths enough*: to drive away interlopers.

18 *felt*: felt hat (with bawdy pun).

19–20 *tiring-things*: head-dresses.

21 *falling-bands*: the turned-down collar which gradually replaced the ruff in the early seventeenth century; it leads to the inevitable puns on 'fall'.

band requires no poting-stick to recover his form. Believe me, no fashion to the falling, I say.

BIANCA. And is not Signor St Andrew Jaques a gallant fellow now?

MAQUERELLE. By my maidenhead, la, honour and he agrees as well together as a satin suit and woollen stockings.

EMILIA. But is not Marshal Make-room, my servant in reversion, a proper gentleman?

MAQUERELLE. Yes, in reversion, as he had his office; as, in truth, he hath all things in reversion: he has his mistress in reversion, his clothes in reversion, his wit in reversion, and, indeed, is a suitor to me for my dog in reversion. But, in good verity, la, he is as proper a gentleman in reversion as – and, indeed, as fine a man as may be, having a red beard and a pair of warped legs.

BIANCA. But, i'faith, I am most monstrously in love with Count Quidlibet-in-Quodlibet. Is he not a pretty, dapper, wimble gallant?

MAQUERELLE. He is even one of the most busy-fingered lords; he will put the beauties to the squeak most hideously.

[*Re-enter* BILIOSO.]

---

26 *poting-stick*: poking-stick; a long, thin iron used to reform pleats; obvious *double entendre*.

29 *Signor St Andrew Jaques*: a gibe at the Scots, and probably a libel on James himself. See Textual Note, p. 498 below.

36 *in reversion*: after the retirement of the present incumbent.

43–4 *red beard . . . warped legs*: sometimes thought to be Marston's mocking self-portrait, but perhaps a gibe at the king with his notorious shambling gait was intended.

46 *Quidlibet-in-Quodlibet*: 'Who you will or What you will'; *What You Will* was the title of the play that Marston wrote probably immediately before *The Malcontent*; a later play, *DC*, refers to a Justice Quodlibet.

47 *wimble*: active, nimble.

48–9 *busy-fingered*: meddlesome; but with a sexual innuendo that helps to explain 'put to the squeak'.

BILIOSO. Room! Make a lane there. The duke is entering. Stand handsomely, for beauty's sake; take up the ladies there. So, cornets, cornets!

SCENE V

Enter PREPASSO, *joins to* BILIOSO; *two Pages with lights,* FERRARDO, MENDOZA; *at the other door, two Pages with lights, and the Captain leading in* MARIA; *the* DUKE *meets* MARIA *and closeth with her; the rest fall back.*

MENDOZA. Madam, with gentle ear receive my suit;
A kingdom's safety should o'erpoise slight rites;
Marriage is merely nature's policy.
Then since, unless our royal beds be joined,
Danger and civil tumult frights the state,
Be wise as you are fair, give way to fate.
MARIA. What wouldst thou, thou affliction to our house?
Thou ever devil, 'twas thou that banishedst
My truly noble lord.
MENDOZA. I?
MARIA. Ay, by thy plots, by thy black stratagems.
Twelve moons have suffered change since I beheld
The lovèd presence of my dearest lord.
O thou far worse than death! He parts but soul
From a weak body, but thou soul from soul
Disseverest, that which God's own hand did knit;
Thou scant of honour, full of devilish wit!
MENDOZA. We'll check your too-intemperate lavishness.
I can and will!

V.v s.d. note the characteristic elaboration of the spectacle; processional scenes of this sort are designed as emblematic statements of regal authority.
2 *o'erpoise*: outweigh.
18 *lavishness*: eloquence.

MARIA. What canst?
MENDOZA. Go to; in banishment thy husband dies.
MARIA. He ever is at home that's ever wise.
MENDOZA. You'st never meet more; reason should love control.
MARIA. Not meet?
She that dear loves, her love's still in her soul.
MENDOZA. You are but a woman, lady; you must yield.
MARIA. O, save me, thou innated bashfulness,
Thou only ornament of woman's modesty!
MENDOZA. Modesty? Death, I'll torment thee.
MARIA. Do, urge all torments, all afflictions try;
I'll die my lord's as long as I can die.
MENDOZA. Thou obstinate, thou shalt die. – Captain, that lady's life
Is forfeited to justice. We have examined her,
And we do find she hath empoisonèd
The reverend hermit; therefore, we command
Severest custody. – Nay, if you'll do's no good,
You'st do's no harm. A tyrant's peace is blood.
MARIA. O, thou art merciful! O gracious devil,
Rather by much let me condemnèd be
For seeming murder than be damned for thee.
I'll mourn no more; come, girt my brows with flowers;
Revel and dance, soul, now thy wish thou hast;
Die like a bride; poor heart, thou shalt die chaste.

Enter AURELIA *in mourning habit.*

AURELIA. 'Life is a frost of cold felicity,
And death the thaw of all our vanity.'
Was't not an honest priest that wrote so?

---

23 *You'st*: you must.
27 *innated*: innate.
44–5 *Life . . . vanity*: from an epigram in Thomas Bastard's *Chrestoleros* (Bullen); Finkelpearl shows that Bastard, prior to his ordination, had been a prominent member of the literary circle which Marston joined at the Middle Temple; hence the personal tribute.

MENDOZA. Who let her in?
BILIOSO. Forbear.
PREPASSO. Forbear.
AURELIA. Alas, calamity is everywhere.
Sad misery, despite your double doors,
Will enter even in court.
BILIOSO. Peace!
AURELIA. I ha' done. One word: take heed! I ha' done.

Enter MERCURY *with loud music.*

MERCURY. Cyllenian Mercury, the god of ghosts,
From gloomy shades that spread the lower coasts,
Calls four high-famèd Genoan dukes to come
And make this presence their Elysium,
To pass away this high triumphal night
With song and dances, court's more soft delight.
AURELIA. Are you god of ghosts? I have a suit depending in hell betwixt me and my conscience; I would fain have thee help me to an advocate.
BILIOSO. Mercury shall be your lawyer, lady.
AURELIA. Nay, faith, Mercury has too good a face to be a right lawyer.
PREPASSO. Peace, forbear! Mercury presents the masque.

Cornets: the song to the cornets, which playing, the masque enters; MALEVOLE, PIETRO, FERNEZE, *and* CELSO, *in white robes, with dukes' crowns upon laurel wreaths, pistolets and short swords under their robes.*

---

53 *Cyllenian*: born on Mount Cyllene.
54 *lower coasts*: Hades.
56 *presence*: presence-chamber.
60 *depending*: pending.
62–4 *Mercury . . . lawyer*: as god of eloquence, Mercury was patron of lawyers.
65 s.d. *pistolets*: pistols. The dance that follows is the symbolic opposite of Aurelia's dance in IV.ii, restoring music to its proper emblematic function with the restoration of Altofront and political harmony.

MENDOZA. Celso, Celso, court Maria for our love.
– Lady, be gracious, yet grace.
MALEVOLE *takes his wife to dance.*
MARIA. With me, sir?
MALEVOLE. Yes, more lovèd than my breath;
With you I'll dance.
MARIA. Why, then, you dance with death.
But come, sir, I was ne'er more apt to mirth.
Death gives eternity a glorious breath;
O, to die honoured, who would fear to die?
MALEVOLE. They die in fear who live in villainy.
MENDOZA. Yes, believe him, lady, and be ruled by him.
PIETRO. Madam, with me?
PIETRO *takes his wife* AURELIA *to dance.*
AURELIA. Wouldst then be miserable?
PIETRO. I need not wish.
AURELIA. O, yet forbear my hand; away, fly, fly!
O, seek not her that only seeks to die.
PIETRO. Poor lovèd soul!
AURELIA. What, wouldst court misery?
PIETRO. Yes.
AURELIA. She'll come too soon. – O my grieved heart!
PIETRO. Lady, ha' done, ha' done.
Come, let's dance; be once from sorrow free.
AURELIA. Art a sad man?
PIETRO. Yes, sweet.
AURELIA. Then we'll agree.

---

70 *dance with death*: the revels led by the 'dead dukes' resemble a traditional Dance of Death in which cadavers 'take out' the great ones of the world in a dance to the grave; Maria's melancholy wit turns the conceit on its head.

71 *apt to*: inclined to.

75 *Yes . . . him*: Mendoza ridiculously supposes Malevole to be Celso, obeying the order to court Maria on his behalf (line 67).

85 *we'll agree*: the moving simplicity of the short dialogue between Pietro and Aurelia is perfectly rounded off by a delicate piece of word-play; 'agree' includes the musical sense of 'come into harmony', so that their emotional agreement seems naturally expressed in the dance into which they move. As with Altofront and Maria, the dancing becomes a sign of marriage harmony restored.

FERNEZE *takes* MAQUERELLE; *and* CELSO, BIANCA; *then the cornets sound the measure, one change and rest.*

FERNEZE. (*to* BIANCA) Believe it, lady; shall I swear? Let me enjoy you in private, and I'll marry you, by my soul.

BIANCA. I had rather you would swear by your body; I think that would prove the more regarded oath with you.

FERNEZE. I'll swear by them both, to please you.

BIANCA. O, damn them not both to please me, for God's sake!

FERNEZE. Faith, sweet creature, let me enjoy you tonight, and I'll marry you tomorrow fortnight, by my troth, la.

MAQUERELLE. On his troth, la! Believe him not; that kind of cony-catching is as stale as Sir Oliver Anchovy's perfumed jerkin. Promise of matrimony by a young gallant, to bring a virgin lady into a fool's paradise, make her a great woman, and then cast her off – 'tis as common, as natural to a courtier, as jealousy to a citizen, gluttony to a puritan, wisdom to an alderman, pride to a tailor, or an empty hand-basket to one of these sixpenny damnations. Of his troth, la! Believe him not; traps to catch polecats!

MALEVOLE. (*to* MARIA) Keep your face constant; let no sudden passion
Speak in your eyes.

MARIA. O my Altofront!

PIETRO. (*to* AURELIA) A tyrant's jealousies
Are very nimble; you receive it all.

AURELIA. (AURELIA *to* PIETRO) My heart, though not my knees, doth humbly fall

---

85 s.d. *change*: set.
87 *Let me enjoy you*: in a nice comic touch, Ferneze shows himself finally irredeemable.
100 *cony-catching*: cheating (with a bawdy quibble).
108 *sixpenny damnations*: cheap whores; the baskets were apparently used as a trade-sign (Hunter).
110 *polecats*: prostitutes.

Low as the earth, to thee.
PIETRO. Peace! Next change.
[To MARIA] No words.
MARIA. Speech to such, ay, O, what will affords!
Cornets sound the measure over again; which danced, they unmask.
MENDOZA. Malevole!
They environ MENDOZA, *bending their pistols on him.*
MALEVOLE. No.
MENDOZA. Altofront, Duke Pietro, Ferneze, ha!
ALL. Duke Altofront! Duke Altofront!
Cornets, a flourish.
MENDOZA. Are we surprised? What strange delusions mock
Our senses? Do I dream, or have I dreamt
This two days' space? Where am I?
They seize upon MENDOZA.
MALEVOLE. Where an arch-villain is.
MENDOZA. O, lend me breath till I am fit to die.
For peace with heaven, for your own souls' sake,
Vouchsafe me life.
PIETRO. Ignoble villain, whom neither heaven nor hell,
Goodness of God or man, could once make good.
MALEVOLE. Base, treacherous wretch, what grace canst thou expect,
That hast grown impudent in gracelessness?
MENDOZA. O, life!
MALEVOLE. Slave, take thy life.
Wert thou defencèd, thorough blood and wounds,

122–3 *delusions . . . have I dreamt*: Mendoza's dukedom dissolves like the 'delusions' or 'dream' of a masque; fiction and fact change places; and as he reassumes the 'I' of the private man, Mendoza feels like Sly in *The Taming of the Shrew*, victim of the Waking Man's Dream. It is perhaps this masque-like dissolution of his wicked power that allows him to be so harmlessly dismissed.

135 *defencèd*: fortified, protected.

The sternest horror of a civil fight,
Would I achieve thee, but prostrate at my feet,
I scorn to hurt thee. 'Tis the heart of slaves
That deigns to triumph over peasants' graves;
For such thou art, since birth doth ne'er enrol
A man 'mong monarchs, but a glorious soul.
O, I have seen strange accidents of state:
The flatterer, like the ivy, clip the oak
And waste it to the heart; lust so confirmed
That the black act of sin itself not shamed
To be termed courtship.
O, they that are as great as be their sins,
Let them remember that th'inconstant people
Love many princes merely for their faces
And outward shows; and they do covet more
To have a sight of these than of their virtues.
Yet thus much let the great ones still conceit:
When they observe not heaven's imposed
conditions,
They are no kings, but forfeit their commissions.

MAQUERELLE. O good my lord, I have lived in the court this twenty year; they that have been old courtiers and come to live in the city, they are spited at and thrust to the walls like apricots, good my lord.

BILIOSO. My lord, I did know your lordship in this disguise; you heard me ever say, if Altofront did return, I would stand for him. Besides, 'twas your lordship's pleasure to call me wittol and cuckold; you must not think, but that I knew you, I would have put it up so patiently.

MALEVOLE. (*to* PIETRO *and* AURELIA) You
o'erjoyed spirits, wipe your long-wet eyes.
Hence with this man. (*Kicks out* MENDOZA) An
eagle takes not flies.

---

137 *achieve*: conquer, destroy.
142–65 lines added in QC.
149, 154 *princes . . . kings*: the press-corrections substituting 'men' for these terms in QC suggest political bowdlerisation.
152 *still conceit*: always keep in mind (see Textual Note, p. 499 below).
158 *thrust . . . apricots*: pushed around; apricots were commonly grown against sunlit walls.
164 *put it up*: put up with it.

(*To* PIETRO *and* AURELIA) You to your vows.
(*To* MAQUERELLE) And thou unto the suburbs.
(*To* BILIOSO) You to my worst friend I would hardly give:
Thou art a perfect old knave. (*To* CELSO *and the* CAPTAIN) All-pleased, live
You two unto my breast; (*To* MARIA) thou to my heart.
The rest of idle actors idly part.
And as for me, I here assume my right,
To which I hope all's pleased. To all, good night.

Cornets, a flourish. Exeunt omnes.

EPILOGUS

Your modest silence, full of heedy stillness,
Makes me thus speak: a voluntary illness
Is merely 'scuseless, but unwilling error,
Such as proceeds from too rash youthful fervour,
May well be called a fault, but not a sin.
Rivers take names from founts where they begin.
Then let not too severe an eye peruse
The slighter breaks of our reformèd Muse,
Who could herself herself of faults detect,
But that she knows 'tis easy to correct,

---

168 *vows*: i.e. of contemplative retirement; but perhaps a renewal of marriage vows is also implied.
168 *suburbs*: i.e. to the brothels.
172–4 *idle actors . . . all's pleased*: a final piece of mannerist self-reference in which Altofront prepares for the final unmasking of the epilogue, with its appeal for applause.
1 *heedy*: heedful.
2–3 *voluntary . . . 'scuseless*: intentional faults are quite inexcusable; see Textual Note, p. 499 below.
8 *breaks*: stylistic disruptions, errors.
9 *detect*: convict.

Though some men's labour. Troth, to err is fit,
As long as wisdom's not professed, but wit.
Then till another's happier Muse appears,
Till his Thalia feast your learnèd ears,
To whose desertful lamps pleased Fates impart
Art above Nature, Judgement above Art,
  Receive this piece, which hope nor fear yet daunteth;
  He that knows most, knows most how much he wanteth.

Finis

---

11 *Though . . . labour*: though some men labour at it.
13 *another's*: usually thought to be Jonson, to whom the play was dedicated.
14 *Thalia*: muse of comedy.
15 *desertful lamps*: well-deserving studies.

THE
Dutch Courtezan.

AS

IT WAS PLAYD IN THE
Blacke-Friars, by the Children
of her Maieſties Reuels.

VVritten
BY IOHN MARSTON.

AT LONDON,
¶ Printed by T. P. for *Iohn Hodgets,*
and are to be ſould at his ſhop in
Paules Church-yard. 1605.

Title-page of the 1605 Quarto of *The Dutch Courtesan* in the Bodleian Library, shelfmark Malone 252 (5)

INTRODUCTORY NOTE

The Dutch Courtesan was printed by Thomas Purfoot for John Hodgets in 1605, having been entered in the Stationers' Register on 26 June of that year. The present text is based upon the Bodleian Library copy of the 1605 Quarto, Malone 252 (5), supplemented by the press-corrections recorded by Martin L. Wine (Regents, 1965) and Peter Davison (Fountainwell, 1968), who each collated all twelve extant copies. Davison notes as many as ninety-six press-variants, affecting every forme (though those in A(i) and H(o) may be fortuitous); most changes are trivial, and some certainly wrong, but others *may* derive from the manuscript rather than good guessing. Davison offers the fullest discussion so far of the Quarto's bibliographical features, which include a clear break between sheets A–E and sheets F–H. He thinks that the text was set from 'a final draft of the play, not prepared fully for the theatre, but lightly prepared by Marston for the printer' (p. 15). Certainly both Davison and Wine (who writes of 'the author's fair copy', rather than his 'draft') seem right in supposing that the manuscript was autograph. The descriptive stage directions, list of dramatis personae, Latin epigraph at the beginning of the play, markings of *sententiae*, occasional errors in the assignment of speeches, confusion over the naming of Burnish/Garnish, and patches of mislineation – all point to Marston's own papers. The Quarto is divided into acts, but notes only 'Scena Prima' of each act, except in Act I, where '*Scena Secunda*' is marked.

The main plot of *The Dutch Courtesan* is borrowed from one of the inset tales in the first book of Nicolas de Montreux's romance, *Les Bergeries de Juliette* (1585). The focus of Montreux's version, however, is upon the friendship of his two central characters, Dellio and the Sieur de la Selve, and the dilemma created for de la Selve when he falls in love with his friend's mistress, the courtesan Cinthye. The dilemma is resolved when Dellio generously decides to give Cinthye to his friend in order to preserve their intimate relationship. Marston, by contrast, uses the story to develop certain ideas on the nature of sexual desire that he encountered in Montaigne's essay 'Upon Some Verses of Virgil' (*Essays*, III, v), which ranks as a second major source for the play; and the focus consequently shifts to the psychological problems created by Malheureux's priggish self-deception. The play explores his progress towards that recognition of the naturalness of one's own desires on which an honest morality must be founded. For the Cocledemoy sub-plot no one clear source exists: apart from a general indebtedness to the extensive Elizabethan literature of roguery, analogues for a number of scenes have been traced in such plays as Edwards's *Damon and Pithias*, Whetstone's *Promos and Cassandra*, Jonson's *Every Man in his Humour*, and Shakespeare's *Much Ado About Nothing* and *Twelfth Night*. The trickery of the goblet scene (III.iii) is derived from Painter's *Palace of Pleasure* (I, 66).

The debt to Florio's translation of Montaigne makes it reasonably certain that the play cannot have been written before the publication of that work in 1603; and it must have been acted before the Quarto's entry in the Stationers' Register. That entry attributes the performance to 'the Children of *her Majesties Revels*', the title granted to the re-formed Children of the Chapel Royal by a royal patent of 4 February 1604, which led Chambers to propose a date of late 1603/1604. However, the anti-Scots satire of II.iii, in which Cocledemoy, in the person of the Scots barber, Andrew Shark, claims to have carried on his shaving (cheating) at court 'this two year', makes late 1604/early 1605 a much more likely date.

The first recorded performance of *The Dutch Courtesan*, however, belongs to 1613, when it was twice staged at court (25 February and 12 December), being amongst the entertainments chosen for the Princess Elizabeth's marriage to the Elector Palatine. Although we know of no other Jacobean or Caroline revivals, it seems to have been among the more successful plays of the period, since the Cocledemoy sub-plot survived, under the name *The Cheater Cheated*, as one of those 'drolls', culled from the most popular pre-war comedies, performed by the underground actors of the Interregnum. After the Restoration it underwent the first of a series of adaptations in the form of Aphra Behn's *The Revenge, or A Match in Newgate* (1680), which in turn provided the basis of *A Woman's*

Revenge, or A Match in Newgate, cobbled together by Christopher Bullock in 1715; and in 1729 it suffered a further degraded metamorphosis in the shape of the ballad-opera, *Love and Revenge, or The Vintner Outwitted*. Finally the low plot once again became detached from the main plot, enjoying an independent and chameleon existence in farce repertory until at least the end of the eighteenth century. Marston's play had to wait until February 1954 for a revival at Joan Littlewood's innovative Theatre Workshop in Stratford East. Although the critics were kinder to the production than to the play itself, Miss Littlewood revived it a second time in April 1959. Five years later *The Dutch Courtesan* formed part of the National Theatre's Chichester Festival season (July 1964), in a production by William Gaskill and Piers Haggard that afterwards transferred to the Old Vic. The damp critical reception accorded this version perhaps accounts for the subsequent neglect of the play by professional companies: since then it has been attempted only in an off-off-Broadway production by the Casa Italiana Renaissance Theatre (June 1966).

PROLOGUE

Slight hasty labours in this easy play
Present not what you would, but what we may;
For this vouchsafe to know, the only end
Of our now study is not to offend.
Yet think not but, like others, rail we could;
Best art presents not what it can but should;
And if our pen in this seem over-slight,
We strive not to instruct but to delight.
As for some few we know of purpose here
To tax and scout, know firm art cannot fear
Vain rage; only the highest grace we pray
Is, you'll not tax until you judge our play.
Think, and then speak: 'tis rashness, and not wit,
To speak what is in passion, and not judgement, fit.
Sit, then, with fair expectance, and survey
Nothing but passionate man in his slight play,
Who hath this only ill, to some deemed worst:
A modest diffidence and self-mistrust.

FABULAE ARGUMENTUM

The difference betwixt the love of a courtesan and a wife is the full scope of the play, which, intermixed with the deceits of a witty city jester, fills up the comedy.

---

1 *easy*: easily written; perhaps also 'lenient, relaxed' (in contrast to the severity of Marston's earlier satires).

3–5 *only . . . could*: 'possibly a backward glance at the Theatre War in which Marston and Jonson were ranged on opposite sides' (Davison).

4 *now*: present.

8 *We delight*: cf. Jonson's Horatian insistence that art must both teach and delight (*et docere et delectare*); a modification of Marston's attitude is suggested at V.ii.81.

10 *tax and scout*: attack and dismiss with scorn.

16–17 *his . . . Who*: i.e. Marston.

Fabulae Argumentum: the Argument of the Play.

FRANCESCHINA, *a Dutch courtesan*
MARY FAUGH, *an old woman*
SIR LIONEL FREEVILL } *two old knights*
SIR HUBERT SUBBOYS }
YOUNG FREEVILL, SIR LIONEL*'s son*
BEATRICE } SIR HUBERT*'s daughters*
CRISPINELLA }
PUTIFER, *their nurse*
TYSEFEW, *a blunt gallant*
CAQUETEUR, *a prattling gull*
MALHEUREUX, YOUNG FREEVILL*'s unhappy friend*
COCLEDEMOY, *a knavishly witty city companion*
MASTER MULLIGRUB, *a vintner*
MISTRESS MULLIGRUB, *his wife*
MASTER BURNISH, *a goldsmith*
LIONEL, *his man*
HOLIFERNES REINSCURE, *a barber's boy*
THREE WATCHMEN
[PAGES]
[GENTLEMEN]
[HALBERDIERS]
[CHRISTIAN]
[SERVANT]
[OFFICERS]

Dramatis Personae: from Q.
FRANCESCHINA: name of the flirtatious serving-maid in the Italian *commedia dell'arte*.
FAUGH: exclamation of disgust.
FREEVILL: free will; perhaps also 'one who freely enjoys the pleasures of the town'.
SUBBOYS: perhaps French *sous bois* = underwood; suggesting pastoral innocence.
BEATRICE: happy, blessed (the name of Dante's ideal mistress; also the heroine of Shakespeare's *Much Ado* who is a model for Crispinella).
CRISPINELLA: pseudo-diminutive from Latin *crispus*: (1) curled, crisped, crimped; (2) in tremulous motion, quivering; the obsolete sense of 'crisp' (bright, shining, clear) may also be relevant.
PUTIFER: from Italian *putiferio* = stench.
TYSEFEW: probably from French *tisonner* + *feu* = poke, fan + fire.
CAQUETEUR: French 'chatterer' (perhaps with a quibble on 'cack').

DRAMATIS PERSONAE

MALHEUREUX: French 'unhappy, luckless'.
COCLEDEMOY: cf. 'cockle-demois' = shells of some sort representing money (*OED*, with a single citation from Chapman's Inns of Court masque); also punning 'cuckold' + *moi*.
MULLIGRUB: 'mulligrubs' = stomach-ache, fit of depression.
REINSCURE: 'reins' = kidneys (traditionally the seat of the affections).

THE DUTCH COURTESAN

Turpe est difficiles habere nugas.

ACT I

SCENE I

Enter three Pages with lights. MULLIGRUB, FREEVILL, MALHEUREUX, TYSEFEW, *and* CAQUETEUR.

FREEVILL. Nay, comfort, my good host Shark, my good Mulligrub.

MALHEUREUX. Advance thy snout; do not suffer thy sorrowful nose to drop on thy Spanish leather jerkin, most hardly-honest Mulligrub.

FREEVILL. What, cogging Cocledemoy is run away with a nest of goblets? True, what then? They will be hammered out well enough, I warrant you.

MULLIGRUB. Sure, some wise man would find them out presently.

Turpe . . . nugas: 'It is shameful to accomplish difficult trifles' (Martial, *Epigrams*, II, lxxxvi, 9): either mocking self-criticism or a reaffirmation of Marston's intention to write an 'easy play'; it may also refer to the fools of the play.

I.i s.d. *lights*: conventional indication of a night scene.

1 *Shark*: swindler.

3 *Advance . . . snout*: mock-heroic locution for 'raise up your head'.

4–5 *Spanish leather*: regarded as the best.

6 *cogging*: cheating.

7 *nest of goblets*: set of goblets made to fit inside one another.

8 *hammered out*: so as to be unrecognisable.

11 *presently*: immediately.

FREEVILL. Yes, sure, if we could find out some wise man presently.

MALHEUREUX. How was the plate lost? How did it vanish?

FREEVILL. In most sincere prose, thus: that man of much money, some wit, but less honesty, cogging Cocledemoy, comes this night late into mine host's Mulligrub's tavern here, calls for a room. The house being full, Cocledemoy, consorted with his movable chattel, his instrument of fornication, the bawd Mistress Mary Faugh, are imparloured next the street. Good poultry was their food: blackbird, lark, woodcock; and mine host here comes in, cries 'God bless you!' and departs. A blind harper enters, craves audience, uncaseth, plays. The drawer, for female privateness' sake, is nodded out, who, knowing that whosoever will hit the mark of profit must, like those that shoot in stone-bows, wink with one eye, grows blind o' the right side and departs.

CAQUETEUR. He shall answer for that winking with one eye at the last day.

MALHEUREUX. Let him have day till then, and he will wink with both his eyes.

FREEVILL. Cocledemoy, perceiving none in the room but the blind harper (whose eyes heaven had shut up from beholding wickedness),

---

13 *wise man*: Freevill points ironically to the impossibility of being a true 'wise man'. (Marston perhaps recalls Diogenes' satiric quest for an honest man, searching Athens with a lantern in broad daylight – one of the Pages' lights could be used to make this connection.)

16–52 Freevill's mock-heroic style identifies him as a burlesque version of the Nuntius of classical tragedy.

21 *consorted with*: accompanied by (as sexual partner).

23 *imparloured*: closeted.

26 *blind harper*: an Homeric figure, comically suitable to the mock-epic context.

27 *uncaseth*: takes his instrument from its case.

27 *drawer*: tapster.

30–1 *stone-bows*: crossbows which used stones as bullets.

35 *have day*: postpone payment.

39 *from beholding*: (1) as a result of beholding; (2) to protect him from beholding.

unclasps a casement to the street very patiently, pockets up three bowls unnaturally, thrusts his wench forth the window, and himself most preposterously, with his heels forward, follows. The unseeing harper plays on, bids the empty dishes and the treacherous candles much good do them. The drawer returns; but, out alas, not only the birds, but also the nest of goblets, were flown away. Laments are raised –

TYSEFEW. Which did not pierce the heavens.

FREEVILL. The drawers moan, mine host doth cry, the bowls are gone.

MULLIGRUB. *Hic finis Priami!*

MALHEUREUX. Nay, be not jaw-fallen, my most sharking Mulligrub.

FREEVILL. 'Tis your just affliction; remember the sins of the cellar, and repent, repent!

MULLIGRUB. I am not jaw-fallen, but I will hang the cony-catching Cocledemoy, and there's an end of't. *Exit.*

CAQUETEUR. [*to* TYSEFEW] Is it a right stone? It shows well by candlelight.

TYSEFEW. So do many things that are counterfeit, but I assure you this is a right diamond.

CAQUETEUR. Might I borrow it of you? It will not a little grace my finger in visitation of my mistress.

TYSEFEW. Why, use it, most sweet Caqueteur, use it.

CAQUETEUR. Thanks, good sir. [*To the others*] 'Tis grown high night. Gentles, rest to you.

Exit [*with a Page*].

---

43 *preposterously*: literally 'rear-end first'.

44–6 *bids . . . them*: the unpaid harper wastes his irony on an empty room.

49 *Which did not*: mock-heroic bathos.

52 *Hic . . . Priami*: 'Such was Priam's end'; the epic burlesque fittingly concludes with a misquotation from Virgil's description of the sack of Troy (*Aeneid*, II, 554).

56 *sins of the cellar*: the sharp practices of Mulligrub's wine cellar, enumerated by Cocledemoy, V.iii.115–28.

58 *cony-catching*: rabbit-catching; cant term for cheating.

60 *right*: genuine.

70 *high night*: deep night.

TYSEFEW. A torch! – Sound wench, soft sleep, and sanguine dreams to you both. – On, boy!

[*Exit with a Page.*]

FREEVILL. Let me bid you good rest.

MALHEUREUX. Not so, trust me, I must bring my friend home: I dare not give you up to your own company; I fear the warmth of wine and youth will draw you to some common house of lascivious entertainment.

FREEVILL. Most necessary buildings, Malheureux. Ever since my intention of marriage, I do pray for their continuance.

MALHEUREUX. Loved sir, your reason?

FREEVILL. Marry, lest my house should be made one. I would have married men love the stews as Englishmen love the Low Countries: wish war should be maintained there lest it should come home to their own doors. What, suffer a man to have a hole to put his head in, though he go to the pillory for it. Youth and appetite are above the club of Hercules.

MALHEUREUX. This lust is a most deadly sin, sure.

FREEVILL. Nay, 'tis a most lively sin, sure.

MALHEUREUX. Well, I am sure, 'tis one of the head sins.

FREEVILL. Nay, I am sure it is one of the middle sins.

MALHEUREUX. Pity, 'tis grown a most daily vice.

FREEVILL. But a more nightly vice, I assure you.

MALHEUREUX. Well, 'tis a sin.

FREEVILL. Ay, or else few men would wish to go to heaven; and, not to disguise with my friend,

---

71 *Sound*: free from disease.

85 *Low Countries*: (1) Netherlands (major theatre of Elizabeth's war against Spain); (2) the 'low' parts of women (with the usual indecent pun on 'country').

88 *hole . . . in*: place to shelter in (with bawdy quibble on 'hole' and 'head'); in a pillory a man literally put his head in a hole.

89–90 *are . . . Hercules*: cannot be restrained by force; 'ironically Hercules symbolised sexual potency as well as strength and virtue' (Davison).

95 *head sins*: (1) chief sins; (2) capital offences; (3) sins commited by the sexual organ.

I am now going the way of all flesh.
MALHEUREUX. Not to a courtesan?
FREEVILL. A courteous one.
MALHEUREUX. What, to a sinner?
FREEVILL. A very publican.
MALHEUREUX. Dear my loved friend, let me be full with you.
Know, sir, the strongest argument that speaks
Against the soul's eternity is lust,
That wise man's folly and the fool's wisdom;
But to grow wild in loose lasciviousness,
Given up to heat and sensual appetite,
Nay, to expose your health and strength and name,
Your precious time, and with that time the hope
Of due preferment, advantageous means
Of any worthy end, to the stale use,
The common bosom, of a money-creature,
One that sells human flesh, a mangonist!
FREEVILL. Alas, good creatures, what would you have them do? Would you have them get their living by the curse of man, the sweat of their brows? So they do. Every man must follow his trade, and every woman her occupation. A poor, decayed mechanical man's wife, her husband is laid up; may not she lawfully be laid down when her husband's only rising is by his wife's falling?

---

103 *way . . . flesh*: normally applied to death, here (via a sardonic recollection of erotic 'death' = intercourse) to sexual vice.
104 *courteous one*: in seventeenth-century pronunciation an easy pun on 'courtesan'.
105 *publican*: uses the gospel formula 'publicans and sinners' to pun on 'public one'.
107–9 cf. Montaigne, III, v, 106.
114 *preferment*: social advancement.
115 *stale*: worn-out (cf. also 'common stale' = prostitute of lowest sort).
117 *mangonist*: one who furbishes up inferior wares for sale (*OED*).
118–61 a formal Defence of Prostitutes in the tradition of paradoxical rhetoric cultivated at the Inns of Court.
120–1 *curse . . . brows*: see Genesis, 3:16–19 (with a sexual innuendo).
123 *mechanical man*: artisan.

A captain's wife wants means, her commander lies in open field abroad; may not she lie in civil arms at home? A waiting-gentlewoman, that had wont to take say to her lady, miscarries or so; the court misfortune throws her down; may not the city courtesy take her up? Do you know no alderman would pity such a woman's case? Why, is charity grown a sin? or relieving the poor and impotent an offence? You will say beasts take no money for their fleshly entertainment. True, because they are beasts, therefore beastly. Only men give to loose, because they are men, therefore manly; and, indeed, wherein should they bestow their money better? In land, the title may be cracked; in houses, they may be burnt; in apparel, 'twill wear; in wine, alas for pity, our throat is but short. But employ your money upon women, and, a thousand to nothing, some one of them will bestow that on you which shall stick by you as long as you live. They are no ingrateful persons; they will give *quid* for *quo*: do ye protest, they'll swear; do you rise, they'll fall; do you fall, they'll rise; do you give them the French crown, they'll give you the French — *O justus justa justum*! They sell their bodies; do not better persons sell their souls? Nay, since

---

128 *civil arms*: (1) the arms of a civilian; (2) the weapons of civil war (insurrection against the husband).

129 *say*: (1) fine serge-like material; (2) test, trial (i.e. of her mistress's lovers).

129 *miscarries*: becomes pregnant.

133 *case*: (1) situation; (2) receptacle (i.e. pudenda).

137 *give to loose*: (1) give money to live loosely; (2) give money to lose all they have, financially and sexually (Davison).

140 *cracked*: faulty.

147 *quid for quo*: *quid pro quo* (tit for tat).

150 *French crown*: (1) coin; (2) baldness, from 'French — [pox]' = syphilis.

151 *justus . . . justum*: Latin 'just'; the nominative case of the adjective declined through its three genders; Freevill's playful iteration merely relishes the ironic aptness of punishment to crime.

151–3 cf. Montaigne, III, v, 111.

all things have been sold – honour, justice, faith, nay, even God Himself –
Ay me, what base ignobleness is it
To sell the pleasure of a wanton bed?
Why do men scrape, why heap to full heaps join?
But for his mistress, who would care for coin?
For this I hold to be denied of no man:
All things are made for man, and man for woman.
Give me my fee!

MALHEUREUX. Of ill you merit well. My heart's good friend,
Leave yet at length, at length; for know this ever:
'Tis no such sin to err, but to persever.

FREEVILL. Beauty is woman's virtue, love the life's music, and woman the dainties or second course of heaven's curious workmanship. Since, then, beauty, love, and woman are good, how can the love of woman's beauty be bad? And *Bonum, quo communius, eo melius*. Wilt, then, go with me?

MALHEUREUX. Whither?

FREEVILL. To a house of salvation.

MALHEUREUX. Salvation?

FREEVILL. Yes, 'twill make thee repent. Wilt go to the Family of Love? I will show thee my creature: a pretty, nimble-eyed Dutch Tanakin; an honest, soft-hearted impropriation; a soft, plump, round-cheeked frow, that has beauty

---

161 *fee*: lawyer's fee for this mock-defence.
163 *Leave . . . length*: give it up now at long last.
164 cf. Montaigne, III, v, 114.
167 *curious*: careful, ingenious.
167–9 *Since . . . bad*: neo-Platonic commonplace.
170 *Bonum . . . melius*: any good thing is better for being shared.
176 *Family of Love*: millenarian Dutch sect widely supposed to practise free love; here = brothel. The Mulligrubs apparently belong to this sect, as Mary Faugh claims to.
177 *Tanakin*: Dutch diminutive of Ann.
178 *impropriation*: property of a religious house.
179 *frow*: Dutchwoman.

enough for her virtue, virtue enough for a woman, and woman enough for any reasonable man in my knowledge. Wilt pass along with me?

MALHEUREUX. What, to a brothel? to behold an impudent prostitution? Fie on't! I shall hate the whole sex to see her. The most odious spectacle the earth can present is an immodest, vulgar woman.

FREEVILL. Good, still; my brain shall keep't. You must go, as you love me.

MALHEUREUX. Well, I'll go to make her loathe the shame she's in.
The sight of vice augments the hate of sin.

FREEVILL. 'The sight of vice augments the hate of sin.'
Very fine, perdy!

Exeunt.

SCENE II

Enter COCLEDEMOY *and* MARY FAUGH.

COCLEDEMOY. Mary, Mary Faugh!

MARY FAUGH. Hem!

COCLEDEMOY. Come, my worshipful, rotten, rough-bellied bawd. Ha, my blue-toothed patroness of natural wickedness, give me the goblets.

MARY FAUGH. By yea and by nay, Master Cocledemoy, I fear you'll play the knave and restore them.

COCLEDEMOY. No, by the Lord, aunt, restitution is Catholic, and thou knowest we love –

---

193 *perdy*: by God.

4 *blue-toothed*: i.e. black-toothed.

10–11 *restitution is Catholic*: according to Catholic doctrine the restoration of stolen property was a necessary prelude to formal absolution; but Protestants believed that the forgiveness of sins could be contingent upon nothing but God's mysterious grace. Cocledemoy ironically contrasts the imputed materialism of Catholic attitudes with the communistic idealism of the Mulligrubs' and Mary Faugh's Familist sect.

MARY FAUGH. What?

COCLEDEMOY. Oracles are ceased; *tempus praeteritum*. Dost hear, my worshipful clyster-pipe, thou ungodly fire that burnt Diana's temple? Dost hear, bawd?

MARY FAUGH. In very good truthness, you are the foulest-mouthed, profane, railing brother, call a woman the most ungodly names. I must confess we all eat of the forbidden fruit; and, for mine own part, though I am one of the Family of Love and, as they say, a bawd that covers the multitude of sins, yet I trust I am none of the wicked that eat fish o' Fridays.

COCLEDEMOY. Hang toasts! I rail at thee, my worshipful organ-bellows that fills the pipes, my fine rattling, phlegmy cough o' the lungs and cold with a pox? I rail at thee? What, my right precious panderess, supportress of barber-surgeons and enhanceress of lotium and diet-drink! I rail at thee, necessary damnation? I'll make an oration, I, in praise of thy most courtly-in-fashion and most pleasurable function, I.

13–14 *tempus praeteritum*: that time has passed; oracles supposedly ceased with the advent of Christ.

14–15 *clyster-pipe*: pipe for administering enemas.

15–16 *fire . . . temple*: the temple of Diana, goddess of chastity, was burnt by Herostratus in 356 B.C.; Mary Faugh embodies the fire of lust (and, no doubt, that of venereal infection).

23 *covers*: (1) conceals; (2) copulates with.

24 *wicked . . . Fridays*: Anglicans as well as Catholics were supposed to abstain from meat on Fridays.

25 *toasts*: small pieces of toast, dipped in wine; Cocledemoy's favourite nonsense oath.

29–31 *supportress . . . drink*: Mary assists the medical profession by spreading diseases.

30 *enhanceress*: one who enhances or raises the price.

30 *lotium*: stale urine, used by barbers as 'lye' for the hair (*OED*), the hair having been rendered sparse by the pox.

30–1 *diet-drink*: medicinal potion (to 'take diet' was to be treated for the pox).

31 *damnation*: both 'damned person' and 'bringer of damnation'.

MARY FAUGH. I prithee do; I love to hear myself praised, as well as any old lady, I.

COCLEDEMOY. List, then. A bawd. First for her profession or vocation: it is most worshipful of all the twelve companies; for as that trade is most honourable that sells the best commodities – as the draper is more worshipful than the pointmaker, the silkman more worshipful than the draper, and the goldsmith more honourable than both, little Mary – so the bawd above all: her shop has the best ware, for where these sell but cloth, satins, and jewels, she sells divine virtues, as virginity, modesty, and such rare gems, and those not like a petty chapman, by retail, but like a great merchant, by wholesale. Wa, ha, ho! And who are her customers? Not base corn-cutters or sow-gelders, but most rare wealthy knights and most rare bountiful lords are her customers. Again, whereas no trade or vocation profiteth but by the loss and displeasure of another – as the merchant thrives not but by the licentiousness of giddy and unsettled youth, the lawyer but by the vexation of his client, the physician but by the maladies of his patient – only my smooth-gummed bawd lives by others' pleasure, and only grows rich by others' rising. O merciful gain! O righteous income! So much for her vocation, trade, and

---

37–69 a formal mock-encomium 'In Praise of Bawds', another Inns of Court exercise in paradox, matching Freevill's Defence of Prostitutes in I.i. Cf. also Mosca's Praise of Parasites in Jonson's *Volpone*, III.i.7–33.

39 *twelve companies*: the twelve chief London livery companies or guilds.

41 *draper*: maker of woollen cloth.

42 *pointmaker*: maker of laces for fastening clothes (like the silkman, not a member of one of the 'twelve companies').

48 *petty chapman*: small trader, pedlar.

49 *wholesale*: bawdy pun.

50 *Wa, ha, ho*: falconer's cry.

51 *corn-cutters*: chiropodists.

53–61 adapted from Montaigne, I, xxi, 104.

61–2 *rising . . . income*: bawdy *doubles entendres*.

life. As for their death, how can it be bad, since their wickedness is always before their eyes, and a death's head most commonly on their middle finger? To conclude, 'tis most certain they must needs both live well and die well, since most commonly they live in Clerkenwell and die in Bridewell. *Dixi*, Mary.

Enter FREEVILL *and* MALHEUREUX, [*preceded by a Page with a light*].

FREEVILL. Come along; yonder's the preface or exordium to my wench, the bawd. – Fetch, fetch!

[*Exit* MARY FAUGH.]

What, Master Cocledemoy! Is your knaveship yet stirring? Look to it, Mulligrub lies for you.

COCLEDEMOY. The more fool he; I can lie for myself, worshipful friend. Hang toasts! I vanish? Ha, my fine boy, thou art a scholar and hast read Tully's *Offices*, my fine knave. Hang toasts!

FREEVILL. The vintner will toast you and he catch you.

COCLEDEMOY. I will draw the vintner to the stoup, and when he runs low, tilt him. Ha, my fine knave, art going to thy recreation?

---

65 *death's head*: bawds commonly wore rings decorated with a skull.

69 *Clerkenwell . . . Bridewell*: respectively a district haunted by prostitutes and a prison; punning on 'well' and playing with 'bride' and 'clerk' (clergyman).

69 *Dixi*: 'I have spoken', classical formula announcing the end of a formal oration.

74 *lies for you*: lies in wait for you.

78 *Tully's Offices*: Cicero's *De Officiis*, one of the most popular textbooks of moral philosophy in the Renaissance; Cocledemoy enjoys parading his learning.

82–3 *I . . . him*: the vintner Mulligrub is likened to a wine-cask from which Cocledemoy will draw liquor by the cupful ('stoup' = tankard), before draining it to the lees (or tilts, as the dregs of a barrel are called); with an elaborate quibble on the language of falconry ('draw' = entice; 'stoop' = a falcon's swoop to the lure; 'tilt' = thrust at).

FREEVILL. Yes, my capricious rascal.

COCLEDEMOY. Thou wilt look like a fool, then, by and by.

FREEVILL. Look like a fool? Why?

COCLEDEMOY. Why, according to the old saying, a beggar when he is lousing of himself looks like a philosopher, a hard-bound philosopher when he is on the stool looks like a tyrant, and a wise man when he is in his belly-act looks like a fool. God give your worship good rest! Grace and mercy keep your syringe straight and your lotium unspilt! [*Exit* COCLEDEMOY.]

Enter FRANCESCHINA.

FREEVILL. See, sir, this is she.

MALHEUREUX. This?

FREEVILL. This.

MALHEUREUX. A courtesan? [*Aside*] Now cold blood defend me! What a proportion afflicts me!

FRANCESCHINA. O mine aderliver love, vat sall me do to requit dis your mush affection?

FREEVILL. Marry, salute my friend, clip his neck, and kiss him welcome.

FRANCESCHINA. O' mine art, sir, you bin very velcome.

FREEVILL. Kiss her, man, with a more familiar affection. So. [FREEVILL *kisses* FRANCESCHINA] – Come, what entertainment? Go to your lute. *Exit* FRANCESCHINA.

---

85 *capricious*: witty, fantastic; 'but also alluding to Latin *capra* or "goat", the animal traditionally denoting lechery' (Wine).

91 *hard-bound*: constipated.

93 *belly-act*: copulation.

95–6 *syringe . . . lotium*: sexual *doubles entendres*.

101 *proportion*: i.e. a disproportion of the four humours making up the human constitution (blood, phlegm, choler and melancholy); an excess of hot blood, caused by lust, overwhelms the cooling effects of phlegm and melancholy.

103 *aderliver*: version of Dutch *alderliefest* = dearest.

105 *clip*: hug.

109 *familiar*: intimate; but an actor might easily suggest a quibble on the Familists.

– And how dost approve my sometimes elected? She's none of your ramping cannibals that devour man's flesh, nor any of your Curtian gulfs that will never be satisfied until the best thing a man has be thrown into them. I loved her with my heart until my soul showed me the imperfection of my body, and placed my affection on a lawful love, my modest Beatrice, which if this short-heels knew, there were no being for me with eyes before her face. But faith, dost thou not somewhat excuse my sometimes incontinency with her enforcive beauties? Speak!

MALHEUREUX. Ha, she is a whore, is she not?

FREEVILL. Whore? Fie, whore! You may call her a courtesan, a cockatrice, or (as that worthy spirit of an eternal happiness said) a suppository. But whore, fie! 'Tis not in fashion to call things by their right names. Is a great merchant a cuckold? You must say he is one of the livery. Is a great lord a fool? You must say he is weak. Is a gallant pocky? You must say he has the court scab. Come, she's your mistress, or so.

[Re-]enter FRANCESCHINA *with her lute.*

– Come, siren, your voice!

113–14 *sometimes elected*: former choice.

114 *ramping*: wild, violent.

115–16 *Curtian gulfs*: the Roman hero, Marcus Curtius, saved his city by leaping into a chasm that had opened in the Forum, by this sacrifice causing it to close again.

121 *short-heels*: wanton.

124 *enforcive*: compelling.

128 *cockatrice*: originally a species of fabulous monster (basilisk) able to kill with a glance; hence cant term for a prostitute.

128–9 *or . . . suppository*: 'The Italian language allows Ariosto to pun obscenely in the prologue to his comedy, *I Suppositi*, on the meaning of the title as not only "the abandoned ones" but also "those who can be had" ' (Wine). Marston is also picking up Cocledemoy's description of Mary Faugh as a 'clyster-pipe'.

132 *one . . . livery*: a member of the guild.

FRANCESCHINA. Vill not you stay in mine bosom tonight, love?

FREEVILL. By no means, sweet breast; this gentleman has vowed to see me chastely laid.

FRANCESCHINA. He shall have a bed, too, if dat it please him.

FREEVILL. Peace! you tender him offence; he is one of a professed abstinence. Siren, your voice, and away!

FRANCESCHINA. (*she sings to her lute*)

THE SONG

The dark is my delight,
So 'tis the nightingale's.
My music's in the night,
So is the nightingale's.
My body is but little,
So is the nightingale's.
I love to sleep 'gainst prickle,
So doth the nightingale.

FREEVILL. Thanks. Buss! So. [*Kisses her*] The night grows old; good rest.

FRANCESCHINA. Rest to mine dear love; rest, and no long absence.

FREEVILL. Believe me, not long.

FRANCESCHINA. Sall ick not believe you long?

Exit FRANCESCHINA.

FREEVILL. O yes. [*To Page*] Come, *via*! Away, boy! On!

Exit, his Page lighting him.

146–53 The setting for Franceschina's song is preserved in British Museum Additional MS. 24665 and is reproduced by Andrew J. Sabol, 'Two unpublished stage songs for the "aery of children" ', *Renaissance News*, 13 (Autumn, 1960), 222–32 (Wine).

152–3 *prickle . . . nightingale*: the nightingale supposedly slept with its breast against a thorn, hence its song; it thus became an emblem for the sufferings of love.

154 *Buss*: kiss me (a buss was more full-blooded than a kiss).

158 *long*: sexual *double entendre*.

160 *via*: away.

[*Re-*]*enter* FREEVILL *and seems to overhear* MALHEUREUX.

MALHEUREUX. Is she unchaste? Can such a one be damned?
O love and beauty, ye two eldest seeds
Of the vast chaos, what strong right you have
Even in things divine, our very souls!
FREEVILL. [*aside*] Wa, ha, ho! Come, bird, come! Stand, peace!
MALHEUREUX. Are strumpets, then, such things so delicate?
Can custom spoil what nature made so good?
Or is their custom bad? Beauty's for use.
I never saw a sweet face vicious;
It might be proud, inconstant, wanton, nice,
But never tainted with unnatural vice.
Their worst is, their best art is love to win.
O that to love should be or shame or sin!
FREEVILL. [*aside*] By the Lord, he's caught! Laughter eternal!
MALHEUREUX. [*aside*] Soul, I must love her. Destiny is weak
To my affection. A common love?
Blush not, faint breast;
That which is ever loved of most is best.
Let colder eld the strong'st objections move;
No love's without some lust, no life without some love.

---

161 s.d. *seems to overhear*: a gesture is required because the normal convention assumes that soliloquies, as interior meditations, are inaudible to others.
163–4 *love . . . chaos*: Malheureux invokes a neo-Platonic creation myth.
166–7 *Wa . . . come*: falconer's cry; in the form used here there may be an echo of *Hamlet*, I.v.116.
169–70 *custom*: (1) social conventions (traditionally opposed to 'nature'); (2) business patronage.
170 *Beauty's for use*: punning on 'use' = (1) usury; (2) employment for sexual purposes.
172–5 the couplets serve to point up the sententious quality of Malheureux's conclusions.
172 *nice*: lascivious.
179 *To*: compared to.
182 *eld*: old age

FREEVILL. [*to* MALHEUREUX] Nay, come on, good sir; what though the most odious spectacle the world can present be an immodest, vulgar woman, yet, sir, for my sake –

MALHEUREUX. Well, sir, for your sake I'll think better of them.

FREEVILL. Do, good sir, and pardon me that
have brought you in.
You know the sight of vice augments the hate of
sin.

MALHEUREUX. Ha, will you go home, sir? 'Tis
high bedtime.

FREEVILL. With all my heart, sir; only do not
chide me.
I must confess –

MALHEUREUX. A wanton lover you have been.

FREEVILL. 'O that to love should be or shame or
sin!'

MALHEUREUX. Say ye?

FREEVILL. 'Let colder eld the strong'st objections
move!'

MALHEUREUX. How's this?

FREEVILL. 'No love's without some lust, no life
without some love!'
Go your ways for an *apostata*! I believe my cast garment must be let out in the seams for you when all is done.
Of all the fools that would all man out-thrust,
He that 'gainst nature would seem wise is worst.

Exeunt.

---

200 *apostata*: apostate.

201 *cast*: cast-off.

201 *let . . . seams*: Freevill's discarded way of life will have to be enlarged to accommodate Malheureux's lust (with an obscene physical innuendo).

203 *all man out-thrust*: excel all mankind (again with sexual *double entendre*).

ACT II

SCENE I

Enter FREEVILL, *Pages with torches, and Gentlemen with music.*

FREEVILL. The morn is yet but young. Here, gentlemen,
This is my Beatrice' window, this the chamber
Of my betrothèd dearest, whose chaste eyes,
Full of loved sweetness and clear cheerfulness,
Have gaged my soul to her enjoyings,
Shredding away all those weak under-branches
Of base affections and unfruitful heats.
Here bestow your music to my voice.
Cantat. [*Exeunt Gentlemen with Pages.*]

Enter BEATRICE *above.*

Always a virtuous name to my chaste love!

BEATRICE. Loved sir,
The honour of your wish return to you.
I cannot with a mistress' compliment,
Forcèd discourses, or nice art of wit
Give entertain to your dear wishèd presence;
But safely thus: what hearty gratefulness,
Unsullen silence, unaffected modesty,
And an unignorant shamefastness can express,
Receive as your protested due. Faith, my heart,
I am your servant.
O let not my secure simplicity
Breed your mislike, as one quite void of skill;

II.i s.d. *with music*: with instruments; music will also have played between the acts at the Blackfriars.
5 *gaged*: engaged, pledged.
5 *enjoyings*: both 'her enjoyment' and 'my enjoying her'.
8 s.d. *Cantat*: he sings.
13 *nice*: sophisticated, refined.
18 *your protested due*: the due which I protest is yours.
20 *secure*: trusting, overconfident.

'Tis grace enough in us not to be ill.
I can some good, and, faith, I mean no hurt;
Do not then, sweet, wrong sober ignorance.
I judge you all of virtue, and our vows
Should kill all fears that base distrust can move.
My soul, what say you – still you love?

FREEVILL. Still.
My vow is up above me and, like time,
Irrevocable. I am sworn all yours.
No beauty shall untwine our arms, no face
In my eyes can or shall seem fair;
And would to God only to me you might
Seem only fair! Let others disesteem
Your matchless graces, so might I safer seem.
Envy I covet not; far, far be all ostent,
Vain boasts of beauties, soft joys, and the rest;
He that is wise pants on a private breast.
So could I live in desert most unknown,
Yourself to me enough were populous.
Your eyes shall be my joys, my wine that still
Shall drown my often cares. Your only voice
Shall cast a slumber on my list'ning sense.
You with soft lip shall only ope mine eyes
And suck their lids asunder. Only you
Shall make me wish to live, and not fear death,
So on your cheeks I might yield latest breath.
O he that thus may live and thus shall die
May well be envied of a deity.

BEATRICE. Dear my loved heart, be not so passionate;
Nothing extreme lives long.

FREEVILL. But not to be extreme!
Nothing in love's extreme. My love receives
No mean.

BEATRICE. I give you faith; and prithee, since,
Poor soul, I am so easy to believe thee,

---

22 *ill*: wicked.
24 *sober*: humble.
33 *only fair*: the fairest of all.
35 *ostent*: ostentation.
38–9 *So . . . populous*: cf. *A Midsummer Night's Dream*, II.i.223–6.
40 *still*: always.
54 *easy*: ready.

Make it much more pity to deceive me.
Wear this slight favour in my remembrance.
Throweth down a ring to him.

FREEVILL. Which when I part from, hope, the best of life,
Ever part from me.

BEATRICE. I take you and your word, which may ever live your servant. See, day is quite broke up – the best of hours.

FREEVILL. Good morrow, graceful mistress. Our nuptial day holds.

BEATRICE. With happy constancy, a wishèd day.
Exit.

FREEVILL. Myself and all content rest with you.

Enter MALHEUREUX.

MALHEUREUX. The studious morn with paler cheek draws on
The day's bold light. Hark how the free-born birds
Carol their unaffected passions.
The nightingales sing.
Now sing they sonnets; thus they cry, 'We love.'
O breath of heaven! Thus they, harmless souls,
Give entertain to mutual affects.
They have no bawds, no mercenary beds,
No politic restraints, no artificial heats,
No faint dissemblings. No custom makes them blush,

57–60 *which . . . servant*: may you always be true to your word.

60–1 *day . . . up*: dawn has fully broken.

66 *studious*: diligent; the morning appears 'studious' both because of its pallor and because it summons men to work.

68 s.d. *The nightingales sing*: either a vocal effect produced by the Children of the Revels choristers, or (as Wine suggests) a sound made by the 'nightingale pipe' of a portable organ.

71 *affects*: passions.

72–91 a standard libertine complaint; the ultimate source is probably, as Wood suggests, Ovid, *Amores*, I, x, 25–36.

73 *politic restraints*: social inhibitions.

No shame afflicts their name. O you happy beasts,
In whom an inborn heat is not held sin,
How far transcend you wretched, wretched man,
Whom national custom, tyrannous respects
Of slavish order, fetters, lames his power,
Calling that sin in us which in all things else
Is nature's highest virtue!
O miseri quorum gaudia crimen habent!
Sure nature against virtue cross doth fall,
Or virtue's self is oft unnatural.
That I should love a strumpet! I, a man of snow!
Now, shame forsake me, whither am I fallen?
A creature of a public use! My friend's love, too!
To live to be a talk to men, a shame
To my professèd virtue! O accursèd reason,
How many eyes hast thou to see thy shame,
And yet how blind once to prevent defame!

FREEVILL. *Diaboli virtus in lumbis est*. Morrow, my friend. Come, I could make a tedious scene of this now, but what, pah! thou art in love with a courtesan? Why, sir, should we loathe all strumpets, some men should hate their own mothers or sisters; a sin against kind, I can tell you.

MALHEUREUX. May it beseem a wise man to be in love?

---

82 *O . . . habent*: quotation from the minor Latin writer Maximianus, culled from Montaigne, where Florio translates: 'O miserable they, whose joys in fault we lay' (*Essays*, III, v, 108).

83 *cross . . . fall*: runs contrary.

85 *man of snow*: cf. Shakespeare's Angelo whose 'blood/Is very snow-broth' (*Measure for Measure*, I.iv.57–8); both plays belong to the period 1603–5 and have an interest in the paradoxical connection between extreme virtue and vice.

92 *Diaboli . . . est*: quotation from St Jerome, culled from Montaigne (III, v, 86) and translated by Florio: 'The devil's master-point lies in our loins.'

97 *kind*: our own nature.

99–102 *May . . . enough*: adapted from Montaigne, III, v, 121.

FREEVILL. Let wise men alone; 'twill beseem thee and me well enough.

MALHEUREUX. Shall I not offend the vow-band of our friendship?

FREEVILL. What, to affect that which thy friend affected? By heaven, I resign her freely! The creature and I must grow off. By this time she has assuredly heard of my resolved marriage, and no question swears, 'God's sacrament, ten tousand divils!' I'll resign, i'faith.

MALHEUREUX. I would but embrace her, hear her speak, and at the most but kiss her.

FREEVILL. O friend, he that could live with the smoke of roast meat might live at a cheap rate.

MALHEUREUX. I shall ne'er prove heartily
received;
A kind of flat ungracious modesty,
An insufficient dullness, stains my 'haviour.

FREEVILL. No matter, sir. Insufficiency and sottishness are much commendable in a most discommendable action. Now could I swallow thee. Thou hadst wont to be so harsh and cold, I'll tell thee:
Hell and the prodigies of angry Jove
Are not so fearful to a thinking mind
As a man without affection. Why, friend,
Philosophy and nature are all one;
Love is the centre in which all lines close,
The common bond of being.

MALHEUREUX. O, but a chaste, reservèd
privateness,
A modest continence.

FREEVILL. I'll tell thee what, take this as firmest
sense:

---

103 *vow-band*: sworn bond.
105 *affect*: desire.
107 *grow off*: part.
113–14 *he . . . rate*: from Montaigne, III, v, 109.
117 *insufficient dullness*: incompetent stupidity, with the added suggestion of sexual inadequacy.
118–20 *Insufficiency . . . action*: quoted from Montaigne, III, v, 121.
127–8 *Love . . . being*; 132–3 *Incontinence . . . light*: adapted from Montaigne, III, v, 82.

Incontinence will force a continence;
Heat wasteth heat, light defaceth light;
Nothing is spoiled but by his proper might.
This is something too weighty for thy floor.

MALHEUREUX. But howsoe'er you shade it, the world's eye
Shines hot and open on't.
Lying, malice, envy are held but slidings,
Errors of rage, when custom and the world
Calls lust a crime spotted with blackest terrors.

FREEVILL. Where errors are held crimes, crimes are but errors.
Along, sir, to her! she is an arrant strumpet;
and a strumpet is a serpigo, venomed
gonorrhoea to man – things actually possessed.
Yet since thou art in love –

Offers to go out, and suddenly draws back.

and again, as good make use of a statue, a body
without a soul, a carcass three months dead –
yet since thou art in love –

MALHEUREUX. Death, man, my destiny I cannot choose.

FREEVILL. Nay, I hope so. Again, they sell but
only flesh, no jot affection; so that even in the
enjoying, *Absentem marmoreamque putes*. Yet
since you needs must love –

MALHEUREUX. Unavoidable, though folly worse
than madness.

FREEVILL. It's true;
But since you needs must love, you must know this:

---

134 *proper*: own.
135 *This . . . floor*: the weight of my argument is too much for you to bear.
136 *shade*: (1) protect; (2) disguise.
138 *slidings*: slight and temporary falls from grace.
141 *Where . . . errors*: adapted from Montaigne, III, v, 118.
143 *serpigo*: skin disease, ringworm; here a symptom of venereal disease.
152 *Absentem . . . putes*: Martial epigram culled from Montaigne, III, v, 112, where Florio translates: 'Of marble you would think she were,/Or that she were not present there.'

He that must love, a fool and he must kiss. –

Enter COCLEDEMOY.

Master Cocledemoy, *ut vales, domine*!

COCLEDEMOY. *Ago tibi gratias*, my worshipful friend. How does your friend?

FREEVILL. Out, you rascal!

COCLEDEMOY. Hang toasts, you are an ass! Much o' your worship's brain lies in your calves. Bread o' God, boy, I was at supper last night with a new-weaned bulchin, bread o' God, drunk, horribly drunk, horribly drunk! There was a wench, one Frank Frailty, a punk, an honest polecat, of a clean instep, sound leg, smooth thigh, and the nimble devil in her buttock. Ah, fist o' grace! When saw you Tysefew, or Master Caqueteur, that prattling gallant of a good draught, common customs, fortunate impudence, and sound fart?

FREEVILL. Away, rogue!

COCLEDEMOY. Hang toasts, my fine boy, my companions are worshipful.

MALHEUREUX. Yes, I hear you are taken up with scholars and churchmen.

Enter HOLIFERNES *the Barber*[*'s boy*].

---

158 *fool . . . kiss*: a quibble implying that both the kisser and the kissed are fools.

159 *ut . . . domine*: welcome, sir.

160 *Ago . . . gratias*: I thank you; the low-life Cocledemoy's ability to respond in Latin is a nice touch of comic surprise.

166 *bulchin*: literally 'bull-calf', but a cant word for 'gallant'.

168 *Frank Frailty*: i.e. Franceschina.

168–9 *punk . . . polecat*: whore.

169 *clean*: well-shaped.

171 *fist*: breaking of wind.

172–3 *of a good draught*: able to swallow a vast amount at a single pull.

173 *common customs*: whoring.

174 *impudence*: 'shamelessness' as well as 'insolence'.

COCLEDEMOY. *Quamquam te Marce fili*, my fine boy. [*To* FREEVILL] Does your worship want a barber-surgeon?

FREEVILL. Farewell, knave. Beware the Mulligrubs.

Exeunt FREEVILL *and* MALHEUREUX.

COCLEDEMOY. Let the Mulligrubs beware the knave. – What, a barber-surgeon, my delicate boy?

HOLIFERNES. Yes, sir, an apprentice to surgery.

COCLEDEMOY. 'Tis my fine boy. To what bawdy house doth your master belong? What's thy name?

HOLIFERNES. Holifernes Reinscure.

COCLEDEMOY. Reinscure? Good Master Holifernes, I desire your further acquaintance – nay, pray ye be covered, my fine boy; kill thy itch and heal thy scabs. Is thy master rotten?

HOLIFERNES. My father, forsooth, is dead –

COCLEDEMOY. And laid in his grave.
Alas, what comfort shall Peggy then have.

HOLIFERNES. None but me, sir, that's my mother's son, I assure you.

COCLEDEMOY. Mother's son? A good witty boy; would live to read an homily well. And to whom are you going now?

HOLIFERNES. Marry, forsooth, to trim Master Mulligrub the vintner.

COCLEDEMOY. Do you know Master Mulligrub?

HOLIFERNES. My godfather, sir.

---

180 *Quamquam . . . fili*: 'Although, Marcus, my son . . .'; Cocledemoy quotes the opening of Cicero's *De Officiis*, evidently a favourite of his (cf. I.ii.78).

182 *barber-surgeon*: surgery and dentistry were formerly the prerogative of the barbering profession; Cocledemoy asks if Freevill needs treatment for venereal disease.

186 *delicate*: charming, pretty.

194 *be covered*: replace your hat (Reinscure is comically deferential to Cocledemoy).

195 *itch . . . scabs*: symptoms of venereal disease.

195 *rotten*: (1) decayed with pox; (2) dead.

197–8 *And . . . have*: on 26 September 1588 a ballad entitled 'Peggy's Complaint for the Death of her Willy' was entered in the Stationers' Register (Bullen).

COCLEDEMOY. Good boy! Hold up thy chops. I pray thee do one thing for me. My name is Gudgeon.

HOLIFERNES. Good Master Gudgeon.

COCLEDEMOY. Lend me thy basin, razor, and apron.

HOLIFERNES. O Lord, sir!

COCLEDEMOY. Well spoken; good English. But what's thy furniture worth?

HOLIFERNES. O Lord, sir, I know not.

COCLEDEMOY. Well spoken; a boy of a good wit. Hold this pawn. Where dost dwell?

HOLIFERNES. At the sign of the Three Razors, sir.

COCLEDEMOY. A sign of good shaving, my catastrophonical fine boy. I have an odd jest to trim Master Mulligrub for a wager – a jest, boy, a humour. I'll return thy things presently. Hold.

HOLIFERNES. What mean you, good Master Gudgeon?

COCLEDEMOY. Nothing, faith, but a jest, boy. Drink that. [*Gives money*] I'll recoil presently.

HOLIFERNES. You'll not stay long?

COCLEDEMOY. As I am an honest man. The Three Razors?

HOLIFERNES. Ay, sir. *Exit* HOLIFERNES.

COCLEDEMOY. Good. And if I shave not Master Mulligrub, my wit has no edge, and I may go cack in my pewter. Let me see – a barber. My scurvy tongue will discover me; must dissemble, must disguise. For my beard, my false hair; for my tongue – Spanish, Dutch, or Welsh;

---

210 *Gudgeon*: (1) small bait-fish; (2) gullible person.
216 *furniture*: professional equipment.
219 *pawn*: pledge.
222 *shaving*: 'fleecing' as well as 'applying the razor'.
222–3 *catastrophonical*: comic fustian formation from 'catastrophe' (jocularly used for buttocks) and Greek *phonos* = sound; the sense is 'farting', as Wood suggests.
223 *trim*: 'cheat' as well as 'barber'.
236 *cack*: shit.

no, a Northern barber; very good. Widow Reinscure's man; well. Newly entertained; right. So. Hang toasts! All cards have white backs, and all knaves would seem to have white breasts. So proceed now, worshipful Cocledemoy.

Exit COCLEDEMOY *in his barber's furniture.*

SCENE II

Enter MARY FAUGH *and* FRANCESCHINA, *with her hair loose, chafing.*

MARY FAUGH. Nay, good sweet daughter, do not swagger so. You hear your love is to be married, true; he does cast you off, right; he will leave you to the world – what then? Though blue and white, black and green leave you, may not red and yellow entertain you? Is there but one colour in the rainbow?

FRANCESCHINA. Grand grincome on your sentences! God's sacrament, ten tousand devils take you! You ha' brought mine love, mine honour, mine body, all to noting.

MARY FAUGH. To nothing? I'll be sworn I have brought them to all the things I could. I ha' made as much o' your maidenhead – and you had been mine own daughter, I could not ha' sold your maidenhead oftener than I ha' done. I ha' sworn for you, God forgive me! I have made you acquainted with the Spaniard, Don Skirtoll; with the Italian, Master Beieroane; with the Irish lord, Sir Patrick; with the Dutch

---

240 *Northern barber*: a piece of thinly veiled anti-Scottish satire – by slyly avoiding 'Scotch' Marston actually makes the point more obvious; Cocledemoy adopts the name 'Andrew Shark' for this role (II.iii.19–20) and presumably a Scots accent with it.

242–3 *All . . . breasts*: as all playing cards look the same from the back, so all knaves try to appear equally innocent.

2 *swagger*: rage, bluster.

8 *grincome*: syphilis.

9 *sentences*: moralistic aphorisms.

merchant, Haunce Herkin Glukin Skellam Flapdragon; and specially with the greatest French; and now lastly with this English – yet, in my conscience, an honest gentleman. And am I now grown one of the accursed with you for my labour? Is this my reward? Am I called bawd? Well, Mary Faugh, go thy ways, Mary Faugh; thy kind heart will bring thee to the hospital.

FRANCESCHINA. Nay, good naunt, you'll help me to anoder love, vill you not?

MARY FAUGH. Out, thou naughty belly! Wouldst thou make me thy bawd? Thou'st best make me thy bawd; I ha' kept counsel for thee. Who paid the apothecary? Was't not honest Mary Faugh? Who redeemed thy petticoat and mantle? Was't not honest Mary Faugh? Who helped thee to thy custom, not of swaggering Ireland captains nor of two-shilling Inns o' Court men, but with honest flat-caps, wealthy flat-caps, that pay for their pleasure the best of any men in Europe, nay, which is more, in London? And dost thou defy me, vile creature?

FRANCESCHINA. Foutra 'pon you, vitch, bawd, polecat! Paugh! did you not praise Freevill to mine love?

MARY FAUGH. I did praise, I confess, I did praise him. I said he was a fool, an unthrift, a true whoremaster, I confess; a constant drab-keeper, I confess. But what, the wind is turned.

FRANCESCHINA. It is, it is, vile woman, reprobate

---

22 *greatest French*: alluding to the 'great pox' or 'French disease'.

28 *hospital*: poor-house.

29 *naunt*: affectionate variant of 'aunt' (cf. 'nuncle').

33 *kept . . . thee*: kept your secrets.

38 *two-shilling*: the fee to be expected from the lawyers and students at the Inns of Court.

39 *flat-caps*: citizens and tradesmen (from their flat woollen caps).

43 *foutra . . . you*: obscene oath (French *foutre*).

48 *drab-keeper*: whoremaster.

50 *reprobate*: damned (a term with specific theological connotations – opposed to 'elect' in Calvinist theology; part of the play's satiric association of sectaries and low-life vice).

woman, naughty woman, it is! Vat sall become of mine poor flesh now? Mine body must turn Turk for twopence. O divila, life o' mine art! Ick sall be revenged. Do ten tousand hell damn me, ick sall have the rogue troat cut; and his love, and his friend, and all his affinity sall smart, sall die, sall hang. Now legion of devil seize him! De gran' pest, St Anthony's fire, and de hot Neapolitan poc rot him!

Enter FREEVILL *and* MALHEUREUX.

FREEVILL. Franceschina!

FRANCESCHINA. O mine seet, dear'st, kindest, mine loving! O mine tousand, ten tousand, delicated, petty seetart! Ah, mine aderlievest affection!

FREEVILL. Why, monkey, no fashion in you? Give entertain to my friend.

FRANCESCHINA. Ick sall make de most of you dat courtesy may. – Aunt Mary! Mettre Faugh! Stools, stools for dese gallants!

Cantat Gallice.

Mine mettre sing non oder song –
Frolic, frolic sir –
But still complain me do her wrong –
Lighten your heart, sir.

52–3 *turn . . . twopence*: to 'turn Turk' is literally to turn infidel; Franceschina means that her situation is so desperate she will have to betray her 'Christian principles' (i.e. sell herself) for any price she can get.

56 *affinity*: kindred.

58 *pest*: plague.

58 *St Anthony's fire*: erysipelas (fever accompanied by violent skin inflammation).

63 *aderlievest*: see I.ii.103.

65 *fashion*: i.e. the custom of welcoming visitors with a kiss.

68 *Mettre*: Mistress.

69 s.d. *Cantat Gallice*: she sings in the French style ('rather fast', Wine).

70–6 a version of lute song XIX from Robert Jones, *First Book of Songs and Airs* (1600); an anonymous setting from a British Library manuscript is reproduced by Andrew J. Sabol, *Renaissance News*, 13 (1960), 222–32.

For me did but kiss her,
For me did but kiss her,
And so let go.
[*To* FREEVILL] Your friend is very heavy.
Ick sall ne'er like such sad company.

FREEVILL. No, thou delightest only in light company.

FRANCESCHINA. By mine trot, he been very sad. – Vat ail you, sir?

MALHEUREUX. A toothache, lady, a paltry rheum.

FRANCESCHINA. De diet is very goot for de rheum.

FREEVILL. How far off dwells the house-surgeon, Mary Faugh?

MARY FAUGH. You are a profane fellow, i'faith. I little thought to hear such ungodly terms come from your lips.

FRANCESCHINA. Pridee now, 'tis but a toy, a very trifle.

FREEVILL. I care not for the value, Frank, but i'faith –

FRANCESCHINA. I'fait, me must needs have it. [*Aside*] Dis is Beatrice' ring; O could I get it! [*To* FREEVILL] Seet, pridee now, as ever you have embraced me with a hearty arm, a warm thought, or a pleasing touch, as ever you will profess to love me, as ever you do wish me life, give me dis ring, dis little ring.

FREEVILL. Prithee be not uncivilly importunate; sha' not ha't. Faith, I care not for thee nor thy jealousy. Sha' not ha't, i'faith.

FRANCESCHINA. You do not love me. I hear of

---

78 *sad*: grave.
79 *light*: (1) merry; (2) wanton.
85 *rheum*: cold; 'particularly appropriate for Malheureux since a rheum was considered a morbid defluxion of *humors*' (Wine); cf. I.ii.100–1.
86 *house-surgeon*: i.e. the surgeon who attends Mary Faugh's brothel-house; Freevill seizes on Franceschina's reference to 'diet' to imply that Malheureux is suffering from a venereal complaint (cf. I.ii.28–31).
91 *toy*: worthless trifle (Beatrice's ring).

Sir Hubert Subboys' daughter, Mistress Beatrice. God's sacrament, ick could scratch out her eyes and suck the holes!

FREEVILL. Go, y'are grown a punk rampant!

FRANCESCHINA. So? Get thee gone! Ne'er more behold min eyes, by thee made wretched!

FREEVILL. Mary Faugh, farewell. – Farewell, Frank.

FRANCESCHINA. Sall I not ha' de ring?

FREEVILL. No, by the Lord!

FRANCESCHINA. By te Lord?

FREEVILL. By the Lord!

FRANCESCHINA. Go to your new blowze, your unproved sluttery, your modest mettre, forsooth.

FREEVILL. Marry, will I, forsooth.

FRANCESCHINA. Will you marry, forsooth?

FREEVILL. Do not turn witch before thy time. [*To* MALHEUREUX] With all my heart, sir, you will stay.

MALHEUREUX. I am no whit myself. *Video meliora proboque*,
But raging lust my fate all strong doth move:
The gods themselves cannot be wise and love.

FREEVILL. Your wishes to you. *Exit* FREEVILL.

MALHEUREUX. Beauty entirely choice –

FRANCESCHINA. Pray ye, prove a man of fashion and neglect the neglected.

MALHEUREUX. Can such a rarity be neglected? Can there be measure or sin in loving such a creature?

FRANCESCHINA. O, min poor forsaken heart!

---

109 *rampant*: violent (with a play on heraldic terminology – 'lion rampant' etc.; punks become another category of rampant beast).

118 *blowze*: a beggar's wench.

119 *unproved sluttery*: untested slut (Franceschina's contemptuous expression for 'virgin').

125–6 *Video . . . proboque*: 'I see and approve the better course', Ovid, *Metamorphoses*, VII, 20; spoken by Medea as she tries to overcome her passion for Jason – in vain, as she continues *deteriora sequor*, 'I follow the worse.'

134 *measure*: restraint.

MALHEUREUX. I cannot contain; he saw thee not that left thee.
If there be wisdom, reason, honour, grace
Of any foolishly esteemèd virtue
In giving o'er possession of such beauty,
Let me be vicious, so I may be loved.
Passion, I am thy slave. Sweet, it shall be my grace
That I account thy love my only virtue.
Shall I swear I am thy most vowed servant?

FRANCESCHINA. Mine vowed? Go, go, go! I can no more of love. No, no, no! You bin all unconstant. O unfaithful men, tyrants, betrayers! De very enjoying us loseth us; and, when you only ha' made us hateful, you only hate us. O mine forsaken heart!

MALHEUREUX. [*aside*] I must not rave. Silence and modesty, two customary virtues. [*To* FRANCESCHINA] Will you be my mistress?

FRANCESCHINA. Mettress? Ha, ha, ha!

MALHEUREUX. Will you lie with me?

FRANCESCHINA. Lie with you? O, no! You men will out-lie any woman. Fait, me no more can love.

MALHEUREUX. No matter; let me enjoy your bed.

FRANCESCHINA. O vile man, vat do you tink on me? Do you take me to be a beast, a creature that for sense only will entertain love, and not only for love, love? O brutish abomination!

MALHEUREUX. Why then, I pray thee love, and with thy love enjoy me.

FRANCESCHINA. Give me reason to affect you. Will you swear you love me?

MALHEUREUX. So seriously that I protest no office so dangerous, no deed so unreasonable, no cost so heavy, but I vow to the utmost tentation of my best being to effect it.

147–9 *O . . . hate us*: cf. Montaigne, III, v, 110.

161–3 *Do . . . love*: Franceschina's feigned indignation gives an ironic twist to Malheureux's own libertine arguments about the naturalness of animal affection (II.i.67 ff.).

171 *tentation*: trial.

FRANCESCHINA. Sall I or can I trust again? O fool,
How natural 'tis for us to be abused!
Sall ick be sure that no satiety,
No enjoying, not time, shall languish your affection?

MALHEUREUX. If there be aught in brain, heart, or hand
Can make you doubtless, I am your vowed servant.

FRANCESCHINA. Will you do one ting for me?

MALHEUREUX. Can I do it?

FRANCESCHINA. Yes, yes; but ick do not love dis same Freevill.

MALHEUREUX. Well?

FRANCESCHINA. Nay, I do hate him.

MALHEUREUX. So?

FRANCESCHINA. By this kiss, I hate him.

MALHEUREUX. I love to feel such oaths; swear again.

FRANCESCHINA. No, no. Did you ever hear of any that loved at the first sight?

MALHEUREUX. A thing most proper.

FRANCESCHINA. Now, fait, I judge it all incredible, until this hour I saw you, pretty fair-eyed yout. Would you enjoy me?

MALHEUREUX. Rather than my breath, even as my being.

FRANCESCHINA. Vell, had ick not made a vow –

MALHEUREUX. What vow?

FRANCESCHINA. O let me forget it; it makes us both despair.

MALHEUREUX. Dear soul, what vow?

FRANCESCHINA. Ha! good morrow, gentle sir; endeavour to forget me as I must be enforced to forget all men. Sweet mind rest in you!

MALHEUREUX. Stay, let not my desire burst me. O my impatient heat endures no resistance, no protraction. There is no being for me but your sudden enjoying.

206–7 *your . . . enjoying*: immediately enjoying you.

FRANCESCHINA. I do not love Freevill.

MALHEUREUX. But what vow, what vow?

FRANCESCHINA. So long as Freevill lives, I must not love.

MALHEUREUX. Then he –

FRANCESCHINA. Must –

MALHEUREUX. Die!

FRANCESCHINA. Ay. – No, there is no such vehemence in your affects. Would I were anything, so he were not!

MALHEUREUX. Will you be mine when he is not?

FRANCESCHINA. Will I? Dear, dear breast, by this most zealous kiss – but I will not persuade you; but if you hate him that I loathe most deadly – yet, as you please, I'll persuade noting.

MALHEUREUX. Will you be only mine?

FRANCESCHINA. Vill I? How hard 'tis for true love to dissemble! I am only yours.

MALHEUREUX. 'Tis as irrevocable as breath: he dies.
Your love.

FRANCESCHINA. My vow, not until he be dead,
Which that I may be sure not to infringe,
Dis token of his death sall satisfy.
He has a ring, as dear as the air to him,
His new love's gift; tat got and brought to me,
I shall assurèd your professèd rest.

MALHEUREUX. To kill a man!

FRANCESCHINA. O, done safely; a quarrel sudden picked, with an advantage strike; then bribe, a little coin, all's safe, dear soul. But I'll not set you on.

MALHEUREUX. Nay, he is gone. The ring. Well, come, little more liberal of thy love.

FRANCESCHINA. Not yet; my vow.

MALHEUREUX. O heaven, there is no hell
But love's prolongings! Dear, farewell.

FRANCESCHINA. Farewell.

208–14 *I . . . Die*: Marston's reworking of the climactic 'Kill Claudio' episode from *Much Ado About Nothing* (IV.i.287).

[*Aside*] Now does my heart swell high, for my revenge
Has birth and form. First, friend sall kill his friend;
He dat survives, I'll hang; besides, de chaste
Beatrice I'll vex. Only de ring –
Dat got, the world sall know the worst of evils;
Woman corrupted is the worst of devils.

Ex[*eunt*] FRANCESCHINA [*and* MARY FAUGH].

MALHEUREUX. To kill my friend! O, tis to kill myself!
Yet man's but man's excrement, man breeding man
As he does worms – or this. *He spits.*
To spoil this, nothing!
The body of a man is of the selfsame soil
As ox or horse; no murder to kill these.
As for that only part which makes us man,
Murder wants power to touch't. – O wit, how vile,
How hellish art thou when thou raisest nature
'Gainst sacred faith! Think more, to kill a friend
To gain a woman, to lose a virtuous self
For appetite and sensual end, whose very having
Loseth all appetite and gives satiety –
That corporal end, remorse and inward blushings
Forcing us loathe the steam of our own heats,
Whilst friendship closed in virtue, being spiritual,
Tastes no such languishings and moment's pleasure
With much repentance, but like rivers flow,

---

249 *Woman . . . devils*: proverbial, Tilley, W641, 648.

251–52 Montaigne, I, xxvii, 197, cites the strictures of the philosopher Aristippus against 'natural conjunction . . . who being urged with the affection he ought his children, as proceeding from his loins, began to spit, saying that also that excrement proceeded from him, and that also we engendered worms and lice'.

256 *wit*: mind, intelligence.

258–67 paraphrased from Montaigne, I, xxvii, 198–9.

And further that they run, they bigger grow.
Lord, how was I misgone! How easy 'tis to err
When passion will not give us leave to think!
A learn'd that is an honest man may fear,
And lust, and rage, and malice, and anything
When he is taken uncollected suddenly:
'Tis sin of cold blood, mischief with waked eyes,
That is the damnèd and the truly vice,
Not he that's passionless but he 'bove passion's
wise.
My friend shall know it all. *Exit.*

SCENE III

Enter MASTER MULLIGRUB *and* MISTRESS MULLIGRUB, *she with bag of money.*

MISTRESS MULLIGRUB. It is right, I assure you, just fifteen pounds.

MULLIGRUB. Well, Cocledemoy, 'tis thou putt'st me to this charge; but, and I catch thee, I'll charge thee with as many irons. Well, is the barber come? I'll be trimmed, and then to Cheapside to buy a fair piece of plate to furnish the loss. Is the barber come?

MISTRESS MULLIGRUB. Truth, husband, surely heaven is not pleased with our vocation. We do

---

268 *misgone*: gone astray.
271 *malice*: a verb (like 'lust' and 'rage') = entertain malice.
272 *uncollected*: off-guard, not in control of his thoughts and feelings.
273 *sin . . . blood*: cf. above, I.ii.100–1.
275 *Not . . . wise*: Malheureux has formerly cultivated the Stoic ideal of extirpating all passion; he now maintains that true wisdom lies in being able to rise above passions without denying their existence.
7 *Cheapside*: market district of London.

wink at the sins of our people, our wines are Protestants, and – I speak it to my grief and to the burden of my conscience – we fry our fish with salt butter.

MULLIGRUB. Go. look to your business; mend the matter, and score false with a vengeance.

Exit [MISTRESS MULLIGRUB].

Enter COCLEDEMOY *like a barber.*

Welcome, friend. Whose man?

COCLEDEMOY. Widow Reinscure's man, and shall please your good worship; my name's Andrew Shark.

MULLIGRUB. How does my godson, good Andrew?

COCLEDEMOY. Very well. He's gone to trim Master Quicquid, our parson. Hold up your head.

MULLIGRUB. How long have you been a barber, Andrew?

COCLEDEMOY. Not long, sir; this two year.

MULLIGRUB. What, and a good workman already! I dare scarce trust my head to thee.

COCLEDEMOY. O, fear not; we ha' polled better

11–12 *wines . . . Protestants*: 'Protestant' here means 'Anglican' as opposed to the 'Reformed' religion of the sectaries; later Cocledemoy will charge that their wines are 'Popish' (V.iii.121); in both cases the implication is that the wines are adulterated, like the religions with which they are associated.

13–14 *fry . . . butter*: presumably to stimulate violent thirst in their customers.

16 *score false*: make up false accounts.

19–20 *Andrew Shark*: i.e. 'a cheating Scotsman' (see above, II.i.240; cf. *Malc.*, V.iv.29).

23 *trim*: (1) cut hair; (2) rob.

24 *Quicquid*: Whoever.

28 *two year*: the clearest internal indication of the date of the play: Andrew Shark claims to have been 'shaving' (cheating) the English for two years; large numbers of Scots courtiers, the object of Marston's satire here, came south with James I at his accession in spring, 1603; the play must therefore belong to 1605.

31 *polled*: (1) cropped; (2) plundered.

men than you. We learn the trade very quickly. Will your good worship be shaven or cut?

MULLIGRUB. As you will. What trade didst live by before thou turnedst barber, Andrew?

COCLEDEMOY. I was a pedlar in Germany, but my countrymen thrive better by this trade.

MULLIGRUB. What's the news, barber? Thou art sometimes at court.

COCLEDEMOY. Sometimes poll a page or so, sir.

MULLIGRUB. And what's the news? How do all my good lords and all my good ladies, and all the rest of my acquaintance?

COCLEDEMOY. [*aside*] What an arrogant knave's this! I'll acquaintance ye! *He spieth the bag.* 'Tis cash. [*To* MULLIGRUB] Say ye, sir?

MULLIGRUB. And what news, what news, good Andrew?

COCLEDEMOY. Marry, sir, you know the conduit at Greenwich and the under-holes that spouts up water?

MULLIGRUB. Very well; I was washed there one day, and so was my wife – you might have wrung her smock, i'faith. But what o' those holes?

COCLEDEMOY. Thus, sir: out of those little holes, in the midst of the night, crawled out twenty-four huge, horrible, monstrous, fearful, devouring –

MULLIGRUB. Bless us!

COCLEDEMOY. Serpents, which no sooner were beheld but they turned to mastiffs, which howled; those mastiffs instantly turned to cocks, which crowed; those cocks in a moment were changed to bears, which roared; which bears are at this hour to be yet seen in Paris Garden,

---

33 *cut*: (1) have your hair cut; (2) have your purse cut; (3) have your throat cut; (4) be castrated.

37 *my countrymen*: the Scots.

40 *poll*: with an additional sexual innuendo: Partridge gives both 'pole' and 'pole-axe' as slang for penis.

66 *Paris Garden*: famous bear-baiting arena in Bankside.

living upon nothing but toasted cheese and green onions.

MULLIGRUB. By the Lord, and this may be! My wife and I will go see them; this portends something.

COCLEDEMOY. [*aside*] Yes, worshipful fist, thou'st feel what portends by and by.

MULLIGRUB. And what more news? You shave the world, especially you barber-surgeons; you know the ground of many things; you are cunning privy searchers; by the mass, you scour all! What more news?

COCLEDEMOY. They say, sir, that twenty-five couple of Spanish jennets are to be seen hand-in-hand dance the old measures, whilst six goodly Flanders mares play to them on a noise of flutes.

MULLIGRUB. O monstrous! This is a lie, o' my word. Nay, and this be not a lie – I am no fool, I warrant – nay, make an ass of me once –

COCLEDEMOY. Shut your eyes close; wink! Sure, sir, this ball will make you smart.

MULLIGRUB. I do wink.

COCLEDEMOY. Your head will take cold. I will put on your good worship's nightcap whilst I shave you.

COCLEDEMOY *puts on a coxcomb on* MULLIGRUB*'s head.*

67–8 *cheese . . . onions*: Cocledemoy's bears are no doubt given to fisting.

72 *fist*: fart or belch.

77 *privy searchers*: (1) spies; (2) sanitary inspectors; (3) probers of the private parts; (4) 'an allusion to the most customary method of diagnosis' (Wood).

77 *scour*: (1) wash, cleanse; (2) flush out.

81 *old measures*: stately dance.

82 *noise*: consort (cf. line 108 below).

88 *wink*: close the eyes.

89 *ball*: of soap.

93 s.d. *coxcomb*: fool's cap; here, because presented as a 'nightcap', probably meant to imply cuckoldry, and including a witty emblematic pun on Cocledemoy's own name.

[*Aside*] So, mum! Hang toasts! Faugh! *Via*! Sparrows must pick and Cocledemoy munch.

[*Exit* COCLEDEMOY.]

MULLIGRUB. Ha, ha, ha! Twenty-five couple of Spanish jennets to dance the old measures! Andrew makes my worship laugh, i'faith. Dost take me for an ass, Andrew? Dost know one Cocledemoy in town? He made me an ass last night, but I'll ass him. Art thou free, Andrew? Shave me well; I shall be one of the Common Council shortly; and, then, Andrew – why Andrew, Andrew, dost leave me in the suds?

Cantat.

Why, Andrew, I shall be blind with winking. Ha, Andrew! Wife! Andrew! What means this? Wife! My money! Wife!

Enter MISTRESS MULLIGRUB.

MISTRESS MULLIGRUB. What's the noise with you? What ail you?

MULLIGRUB. Where's the barber?

MISTRESS MULLIGRUB. Gone. I saw him depart long since. Why, are not you trimmed?

MULLIGRUB. Trimmed! O, wife, I am shaved! Did you take hence the money?

MISTRESS MULLIGRUB. I touched it not, as I am religious.

MULLIGRUB. O Lord, I have winked fair!

Enter HOLIFERNES.

HOLIFERNES. I pray, godfather, give me your blessing.

MULLIGRUB. O Holifernes! O, where's thy mother's Andrew?

HOLIFERNES. Blessing, godfather!

102–3 *one . . . Council*: i.e. an alderman of the city of London.

104 s.d. *Cantat*: he sings (? 'Andrew, dost leave me').

105 *blind . . . winking*: Wine notes a parallel with Malheureux's 'mischief with waked eyes' (II.ii.273).

MULLIGRUB. The devil choke thee! Where's Andrew, thy mother's man.

HOLIFERNES. My mother hath none such, forsooth.

MULLIGRUB. My money – fifteen pounds! Plague of all Andrews! Who was't trimmed me?

HOLIFERNES. I know not, godfather; only one met me, as I was coming to you, and borrowed my furniture, as he said, for a jest' sake.

MULLIGRUB. What kind of fellow?

HOLIFERNES. A thick, elderly, stub-bearded fellow.

MULLIGRUB. Cocledemoy, Cocledemoy! Raise all the wise men in the street! I'll hang him with mine own hands! O wife, some *rosa solis*!

MISTRESS MULLIGRUB. Good husband, take comfort in the Lord, I'll play the devil, but I'll recover it; have a good conscience; 'tis but a week's cutting in the term.

MULLIGRUB. O wife, O wife! O Jack, how does thy mother? – Is there any fiddlers in the house?

MISTRESS MULLIGRUB. Yes, Master Creak's noise.

MULLIGRUB. Bid 'em play, laugh, make merry. Cast up my accounts, for I'll go hang myself presently. I will not curse, but a pox on Cocledemoy! He has polled and shaved me; he has trimmed me!

Exeunt.

---

133 *thick*: burly.

137 *rosa solis*: 'a cordial or liqueur originally made from . . . the plant sundew, but subsequently composed of spirits (esp. brandy) with various essences or spices, sugar etc.' (*OED*).

141 *cutting*: cheating.

141 *term*: period when the courts were in session, and London therefore at its most crowded.

145 *Master Creak*: presumably punning on the noise made by the fiddlers rather than the actual name of the music master in charge of the Blackfriars consort; signals the beginning of the entr'acte music.

148 *Cast up*: reckon up.

ACT III

SCENE I

Enter BEATRICE, CRISPINELLA, *and* NURSE PUTIFER.

PUTIFER. Nay, good child o' love, once more Master Freevill's sonnet o' the kiss you gave him!

BEATRICE. Sh'a't, good nurse. [*Reads*]

Purest lips, soft banks of blisses,
Self alone, deserving kisses,
O, give me leave to, etc.

CRISPINELLA. Pish! sister Beatrice, prithee read no more; my stomach o' late stands against kissing extremely.

BEATRICE. Why, good Crispinella?

CRISPINELLA. By the faith and trust I bear to my face, 'tis grown one of the most unsavoury ceremonies. Body o' beauty! 'tis one of the most unpleasing, injurious customs to ladies. Any fellow that has but one nose on his face, and standing collar and skirts also lined with taffeta sarcenet, must salute us on the lips as familiarly – Soft skins save us! There was a stub-bearded John-a-Stile with a ployden's face saluted me last day and struck his bristles through my lips. I ha' spent ten shillings in pomatum since to

---

2 *sonnet*: term for any love-lyric.
4 *Sh'a't*: (thou) shalt have it.
14–18 *'tis one . . . lips*: adapted from Montaigne, III, v, 110–11.
17 *standing collar*: fashionable high, starched, embroidered collar.
17 *skirts*: lower part of gown or coat.
17–18 *taffeta sarcenet*: fine silk.
20 *John-a-Stile*: fictitious name for one of the parties in a legal exemplum (cf. John A. Citizen).
20 *ployden*: from Edmund Plowden (1518–85); i.e. 'a lawyer's face'.
22 *pomatum*: pomade.

skin them again. Marry, if a nobleman or a knight with one lock visit us, though his unclean goose-turd-green teeth ha' the palsy, his nostrils smell worse than a putrefied marrowbone, and his loose beard drops into our bosom, yet we must kiss him with a cur'sy. A curse! For my part, I had as lief they would break wind in my lips.

BEATRICE. Fie, Crispinella, you speak too broad.

CRISPINELLA. No jot, sister. Let's ne'er be ashamed to speak what we be not ashamed to think. I dare as boldly speak venery as think venery.

BEATRICE. Faith, sister, I'll be gone if you speak so broad.

CRISPINELLA. Will you so? Now bashfulness seize you! We pronounce boldly robbery, murder, treason, which deeds must needs be far more loathsome than an act which is so natural, just, and necessary as that of procreation. You shall have an hypocritical vestal virgin speak that with close teeth publicly which she will receive with open mouth privately. For my own part, I consider nature without apparel; without disguising of custom or compliment, I give thoughts words, and words truth, and truth boldness. She whose honest freeness makes it her virtue to speak what she thinks will make it her necessity to think what is good. I love no prohibited things, and yet I would have nothing prohibited by policy but by virtue; for, as in the fashion of the time, those books that are called in are most in sale and request, so in

---

28 *with a cur'sy*: politely; 'cur'sy' (Q spelling retained for the sake of the word-play with 'curse') covers modern 'curtsy' and 'courtesy'.

32 *No jot*: not in the least.

32–4 *Let's . . . think*: from Montaigne, III, v, 67.

34 *venery*: sex.

38–57 extensive paraphrase of three passages from Montaigne, III, v, 70, 67, 70.

55 *called in*: withdrawn from circulation, banned.

nature those actions that are most prohibited are most desired.

BEATRICE. Good quick sister, stay your pace. We are private, but the world would censure you; for truly, severe modesty is women's virtue.

CRISPINELLA. Fie, fie! Virtue is a free, pleasant, buxom quality. I love a constant countenance well; but this froward, ignorant coyness, sour, austere, lumpish, uncivil privateness, that promises nothing but rough skins and hard stools – ha, fie on't! good for nothing but for nothing. – Well, nurse, and what do you conceive of all this?

PUTIFER. Nay, faith, my conceiving days be done. Marry, for kissing, I'll defend that; that's within my compass. But for my own part, here's Mistress Beatrice is to be married, with the grace of God; a fine gentleman he is shall have her, and I warrant a strong: he has a leg like a post, a nose like a lion, a brow like a bull, and a beard of most fair expectation. This week you must marry him, and I now will read a lecture to you both, how you shall behave yourselves to your husbands the first month of your nuptial. I ha' broke my skull about it, I can tell you, and there is much brain in it.

CRISPINELLA. Read it to my sister, good nurse, for I assure you I'll ne'er marry.

PUTIFER. Marry, God forfend! What will you do then?

CRISPINELLA. Faith, strive against the flesh. Marry? No, faith; husbands are like lots in the

---

58 *stay . . . pace*: restrain yourself.

61–7 *virtue . . . nothing*: adapted from Montaigne, III, v, 67.

67 *nothing*: the same pun that Shakespeare elaborates at such length in *Much Ado*; 'nothing' was pronounced 'noting' = (1) observing; (2) branding with disgrace; the obscene sense of 'nothing' (female pudenda) is also relevant.

69 ff. Wood notes that Putifer is closely modelled on the Nurse in *Romeo and Juliet*.

80 *broke my skull*: racked my brains.

lottery: you may draw forty blanks before you find one that has any prize in him. A husband generally is a careless, domineering thing that grows like coral, which as long as it is under water is soft and tender, but as soon as it has got his branch above the waves is presently hard, stiff, not to be bowed but burst; so when your husband is a suitor and under your choice, Lord, how supple he is, how obsequious, how at your service, sweet lady! Once married, got up his head above, a stiff, crooked, knobby, inflexible, tyrannous creature he grows; then they turn like water: more you would embrace, the less you hold. I'll live my own woman, and if the worst come to the worst, I had rather prove a wag than a fool.

BEATRICE. O, but a virtuous marriage –

CRISPINELLA. Virtuous marriage! There is no more affinity betwixt virtue and marriage than betwixt a man and his horse. Indeed, virtue gets up upon marriage sometimes and manageth it in the right way, but marriage is of another piece; for as a horse may be without a man, and a man without a horse, so marriage, you know, is often without virtue, and virtue, I am sure, more oft without marriage. But thy match, sister, by my troth, I think 'twill do well. He's a well-shaped, clean-lipped gentleman, of a handsome but not affected fineness, a good faithful eye, and a well-humoured cheek. Would he did not stoop in the shoulders, for thy sake! See, here he is.

88–9 *blanks . . . prize*: sexual *double entendre*.

90–101 *thing . . . hold*: more bawdy: the husband becomes a kind of penis incarnate.

105–13 *Virtuous . . . without marriage*: adapted from Montaigne, III, v, 73, but given a bawdy twist by the *doubles entendres* that flow from the 'horse'/'whores' pun.

117 *well-humoured*: not merely 'good-humoured' but also 'showing a healthy balance of the humours' (cf. I.ii.101).

117–18 *stoop in the shoulders*: 'Make love to other women' (Davison); but it may be quite literal.

Enter FREEVILL *and* TYSEFEW.

FREEVILL. Good day, sweet.

CRISPINELLA. Good morrow, brother. Nay, you shall have my lip. – Good morrow, servant.

TYSEFEW. Good morrow, sweet life.

CRISPINELLA. Life? Dost call thy mistress life?

TYSEFEW. Life, yes, why not life?

CRISPINELLA. How many mistresses hast thou?

TYSEFEW. Some nine.

CRISPINELLA. Why, then, thou hast nine lives, like a cat.

TYSEFEW. Mew! You would be taken up for that.

CRISPINELLA. Nay, good, let me still sit; we low statures love still to sit, lest when we stand we may be supposed to sit.

TYSEFEW. Dost not wear high cork shoes – chopines?

CRISPINELLA. Monstrous ones. I am, as many other are, pieced above and pieced beneath.

TYSEFEW. Still the best part in the –

CRISPINELLA. And yet all will scarce make me so high as one of the giant's stilts that stalks before my Lord Mayor's pageant.

TYSEFEW. By the Lord, so; I thought 'twas for something Mistress Joyce jested at thy high insteps.

CRISPINELLA. She might well enough, and long enough, before I would be ashamed of my short-

---

130 *taken up*: interrupted, checked, rebuked.

134–5 *high . . . chopines*: a current fashion from Italy.

137 *pieced*: 'added to; apparently referring to the high hair-do above and the chopines below' (Wine); but also with a play on 'pieced' = patched up (as in 'pieced beauty').

138 *part in the –*: Tysefew is presumably about to say 'middle' (obscene play on 'piece' = part); cf. below, III.iii.29.

140–1 *giant's . . . pageant*: referring to the Lord Mayor's Show, a processional pageant that wound through the streets of London each 29 October to celebrate the inauguration of the new mayor; customarily featured in London civic pageantry were the giants Gog and Magog (or 'Gotmagot' and 'Corineus'), mythic guardians of the city whose figures had adorned the Guildhall from the time of Henry V.

ness. What I made or can mend myself I may blush at; but what nature put upon me, let her be ashamed for me; I ha' nothing to do with it. I forget my beauty.

TYSEFEW. Faith, Joyce is a foolish, bitter creature.

CRISPINELLA. A pretty, mildewed wench she is.

TYSEFEW. And fair –

CRISPINELLA. As myself.

TYSEFEW. O, you forget your beauty now.

CRISPINELLA. Troth, I never remember my beauty but as some men do religion – for controversy's sake.

BEATRICE. A motion, sister –

CRISPINELLA. *Nineveh*, *Julius Caesar*, *Jonas*, or *The Destruction of Jerusalem*?

BEATRICE. My love here –

CRISPINELLA. Prithee, call him not love: 'tis the drab's phrase; nor sweet honey, nor my cony, nor dear duckling: 'tis the citizen terms; but call me him –

BEATRICE. What?

CRISPINELLA. Anything. What's the motion?

BEATRICE. You know this night our parents have intended solemnly to contract us; and my love, to grace the feast, hath promised a masque.

FREEVILL. You'll make one, Tysefew, and Caqueteur shall fill up a room.

TYSEFEW. 'Fore heaven, well remembered! He borrowed a diamond of me last night to grace his finger in your visitation. The lying creature will swear some strange thing on it now.

157–9 *I . . . sake*: a gibe at the Puritan taste for theological controversy.

160–2 *motion . . . Jerusalem*: Beatrice intends to put a motion (proposal); Crispinella affects to understand 'motion' = puppet-play, and names some popular titles.

165 *drab*: whore.

166 *cony*: rabbit (here a term of affection).

174 *fill . . . room*: make up the rest of the party.

177 *in . . . visitation*: when visiting you; cf. the business with Beatrice's ring in the main plot.

Enter CAQUETEUR.

CRISPINELLA. Peace, he's here. Stand close, lurk.

CAQUETEUR. Good morrow, most dear and worthy to be most wise. How does my mistress?

CRISPINELLA. Morrow, sweet servant; you glister; prithee, let's see that stone.

CAQUETEUR. A toy, lady, I bought to please my finger.

CRISPINELLA. Why, I am more precious to you than your finger.

CAQUETEUR. Yes, or than all my body, I swear.

CRISPINELLA. Why, then, let it be bought to please me. Come, I am no professed beggar.
[*She tries to snatch the ring.*]

CAQUETEUR. Troth, mistress! Zoons! Forsooth, I protest!

CRISPINELLA. Nay, if you turn Protestant for such a toy –

CAQUETEUR. In good deed la! Another time I'll give you a –

CRISPINELLA. Is this yours to give?

CAQUETEUR. O God! Forsooth, mine, quoth you? Nay, as for that –

CRISPINELLA. Now I remember, I ha' seen this on my servant Tysefew's finger.

CAQUETEUR. Such another.

CRISPINELLA. Nay, I am sure this is it.

CAQUETEUR. Troth, 'tis, forsooth. The poor fellow wanted money to pay for supper last night, and so pawned it to me. 'Tis a pawn, i'faith, or else you should have it.

TYSEFEW. [*aside to* CAQUETEUR] Hark ye, thou base lying – How dares thy impudence hope to prosper? Were't not for the privilege of this respected company, I would so bang thee!

CRISPINELLA. Come hither, servant. What's the matter betwixt you two?

CAQUETEUR. Nothing. [*Aside to* CRISPINELLA] But, hark you, he did me some uncivil discourtesies last night, for which, because I should

---

191 *Zoons*: oath = 'by God's wounds'.
212 *servant*: suitor.

not call him to account, he desires to make me any satisfaction. The coward trembles at my very presence, but I ha' him on the hip; I'll take the forfeit on his ring.

TYSEFEW. What's that you whisper to her?

CAQUETEUR. Nothing, sir, but satisfy her that the ring was not pawned, but only lent by you to grace my finger; and so told her I craved your pardon for being too familiar or, indeed, over-bold with your reputation.

CRISPINELLA. Yes, indeed, he did. He said you desired to make him any satisfaction for an uncivil discourtesy you did him last night, but he said he had you o' the hip and would take the forfeit of your ring.

TYSEFEW. How now, ye base poltroon!

CAQUETEUR. Hold, hold! My mistress speaks by contraries.

TYSEFEW. Contraries?

CAQUETEUR. She jests, faith, only jests.

CRISPINELLA. Sir, I'll no more o' your service. You are a child; I'll give you to my nurse.

PUTIFER. And he come to me, I can tell you, as old as I am, what to do with him.

CAQUETEUR. I offer my service, forsooth,

TYSEFEW. Why, so; now every dog has his bone to gnaw on.

FREEVILL. The masque holds, Master Caqueteur.

CAQUETEUR. I am ready, sir. [*To* PUTIFER] Mistress, I'll dance with you, ne'er fear, I'll grace you.

PUTIFER. I tell you, I can my singles and my doubles and my trick o' twenty, my coranto pace, my traverse forward, and my falling back yet, i'faith.

---

219 *I . . . hip*: I have him at a disadvantage (wrestling term).
219–20 *take . . . ring*: take his ring as a forfeit.
232 *poltroon*: spiritless coward.
242 *every . . . bone*: Tilley, D464, D470.
248–50 *singles . . . falling back*: dance steps, with usual *double entendre* on 'falling back'.

BEATRICE. Mine, the provision for the night is ours.
Much must be our care; till night we leave you.
I am your servant; be not tyrannous.
Your virtue won me; faith, my love's not lust.
Good, wrong me not; my most fault is much trust.

FREEVILL. Until night only. My heart be with you! –
Farewell, sister.

CRISPINELLA. Adieu, brother. – Come on, sister, for these sweetmeats.

FREEVILL. Let's meet and practise presently.

TYSEFEW. Content; we'll but fit our pumps. –
Come, ye pernicious vermin!

Exeunt [*all but* FREEVILL].

Enter MALHEUREUX.

FREEVILL. My friend, wished hours! What news from Babylon?
How does the woman of sin and natural concupiscence?

MALHEUREUX. The eldest child of nature ne'er beheld
So damned a creature.

FREEVILL. What! *In nova fert animus mutatas dicere formas.* Which way bears the tide?

MALHEUREUX. Dear loved sir, I find a mind courageously vicious may put on a desperate security, but can never be blessed with a firm

---

252 *provision . . . ours*: we are responsible for the night's arrangements.

265 *Babylon*: Freevill jocularly identifies Franceschina with the Biblical Whore of Babylon.

267 *eldest . . . nature*: presumably Adam.

269–70 *In . . . formas*: 'My spirit prompts me to tell of forms changed anew' (opening line of Ovid's *Metamorphoses*).

271–4 close paraphrase of Montaigne, III, ii, 25.

272–3 *desperate security*: security founded on despair; 'despair' and 'security' are specific theological sins, the one deriving from the conviction that one is incapable of salvation, the other from disbelief in the possibility of damnation.

enjoying and self-satisfaction.

FREEVILL. What passion is this, my dear Lindabrides?

MALHEUREUX. 'Tis well, we both may jest. I ha' been tempted to your death.

FREEVILL. What, is the rampant cockatrice grown mad for the loss of her man?

MALHEUREUX. Devilishly mad.

FREEVILL. As most assured of my second love?

MALHEUREUX. Right.

FREEVILL. She would have had this ring.

MALHEUREUX. Ay, and this heart; and in true proof you were slain, I should bring her this ring, from which she was assured you would not part until from life you parted. For which deed, and only for which deed, I should possess her sweetness.

FREEVILL. O bloody villainess! Nothing is defamed but by his proper self. Physicians abuse remedies, lawyers spoil the law, and women only shame women. You ha' vowed my death?

MALHEUREUX. My lust, not I, before my reason would; yet I must use her. That I, a man of sense, should conceive endless pleasure in a body whose soul I know to be so hideously black!

FREEVILL. That a man at twenty-three should cry, 'O sweet pleasure!' and at forty-three should sigh, 'O sharp pox!' But consider man furnished with omnipotency, and you overthrow him; thou must cool thy impatient appetite. 'Tis fate, 'tis fate.

MALHEUREUX. I do malign my creation that I am subject to passion. I must enjoy her.

FREEVILL. I have it; mark: I give a masque tonight
To my love's kindred. In that thou shalt go;
In that we two make show of falling out,
Give seeming challenge, instantly depart

274–5 *Lindabrides*: character from sixteenth-century Spanish romance, *The Mirror of Princely Deeds and Knighthood* (trans. 1578), frequently mocked by Marston.

300–2 close paraphrase of Montaigne, III, vii, 155.

With some suspicion to present fight.
We will be seen as going to our swords;
And after meeting, this ring only lent,
I'll lurk in some obscure place till rumour,
The common bawd to loose suspicions,
Have feigned me slain, which – in respect myself
Will not be found, and our late seeming quarrel –
Will quickly sound to all as earnest truth.
Then to thy wench; protest me surely dead,
Show her this ring, enjoy her, and, blood cold,
We'll laugh at folly.

MALHEUREUX. O, but think of it.

FREEVILL. Think of it! Come, away! Virtue, let sleep thy passions;
What old times held as crimes are now but fashions.

Exeunt.

SCENE II

Enter MASTER BURNISH *and* LIONEL; MASTER MULLIGRUB, *with a standing cup in his hand, and an obligation in the other.* COCLEDEMOY *stands at the other door, disguised like a French pedlar, and overhears them.*

MULLIGRUB. I am not at this time furnished, but there's my bond for your plate.

---

310 *present*: immediate.
322 *What . . . fashions*: Seneca, *Epistles*, xxxix, 6; quoted in Montaigne, III, ii, 26.
III.ii s.d. *standing cup*: chalice with stem and base.
III.ii s.d. *obligation*: bond.
III.ii s.d. *other door*: the Blackfriars stage evidently had a door on each side (as well as a central opening).
1 *furnished*: i.e. with money.

BURNISH. Your bill had been sufficient; you're a good man. A standing cup parcel-gilt, of thirty-two ounces, eleven pound, seven shillings, the first of July. Good plate, good man, good day, good all!

MULLIGRUB. 'Tis my hard fortune; I will hang the knave. No, first he shall half rot in fetters in the dungeon, his conscience made despairful. I'll hire a knave o' purpose shall assure him he is damned, and after see him with mine own eyes hanged without singing any psalm. Lord, that he has but one neck!

BURNISH. You are too tyrannous. You'll use me no further?

MULLIGRUB. No, sir; lend me your servant, only to carry the plate home. I have occasion of an hour's absence.

BURNISH. With easy consent, sir. [*To* LIONEL] Haste, and be careful. *Exit* BURNISH.

MULLIGRUB. Be very careful, I pray thee; to my wife's own hands.

LIONEL. Secure yourself, sir.

MULLIGRUB. To her own hand.

LIONEL. Fear not; I have delivered greater things than this to a woman's own hand.

[*Exit* LIONEL.]

COCLEDEMOY. Monsieur, please you to buy a fine delicate ball, sweet ball, a camphor ball?

MULLIGRUB. Prithee, away!

COCLEDEMOY. Or a ball to scour, a scouring ball, a ball to be shaved?

MULLIGRUB. For the love of God, talk not of shaving! I have been shaved. Mischief and a

---

3–7 *sufficient . . . good all*: this passage with its play on different senses of 'good' seems to echo *The Merchant of Venice*, I.iii, where Shylock reflects on Antonio's 'bond': 'my meaning in saying he is a good man is to have you understand me that he is sufficient' (13–15).

4 *parcel-gilt*: partly gilded (usually on inner surface).

24 *Secure yourself*: rest easy.

26 *greater things*: bawdy innuendo.

31–2 *ball . . . shaved*: Cocledemoy is peddling soap (*OED ball sb.*[1] 10b), but his verbal juggling suggests that quibbles are involved, perhaps on laxative pills or cannonballs.

thousand devils seize him! I have been shaved.

Exit MULLIGRUB.

COCLEDEMOY. The fox grows fat when he is cursed. I'll shave ye smoother yet. Turd on a tile-stone! my lips have a kind of rheum at this bowl; I'll have't. I'll gargalise my throat with this vintner, and when I have done with him, spit him out. I'll shark. Conscience does not repine. Were I to bite an honest gentleman, a poor grogram poet, or a penurious parson that had but ten pigs' tails in a twelvemonth, and for want of learning had but one good stool in a fortnight, I were damned beyond the works of supererogation; but to wring the withers of my gouty, barmed, spigot-frigging jumbler of elements, Mulligrub, I hold it as lawful as sheep-shearing, taking eggs from hens, caudles from asses, or buttered shrimps from horses – they make no use of them, were not provided for them. And therefore, worshipful Cocledemoy,

---

35 *thousand . . . him*: Wine notes that Mulligrub's passion drives him to a comic echo of Franceschina's favourite oath (cf. II.ii.9–10, 54–5).

36–7 *fox . . . cursed*: Tilley, F632.

38 *my . . . rheum*: my mouth waters.

39 *gargalise*: gargle.

43 *grogram*: a coarse fabric made of silk, mohair, and wool (*OED*).

43–6 *penurious . . . fortnight*: the ill-educated parson is relegated to a living so poor that it renders only pigs' tails in place of tithe pigs and so starves him into constipation.

46–7 *works of supererogation*: good deeds of the pious superfluous to their salvation; in Catholic doctrine they might be transferred to the benefit of sinners; Cocledemoy envisages crimes beyond the reach of such vicarious rescue.

48 *barmed*: fermented.

48 *spigot-frigging jumbler*: one who adulterates his barrels of wine by tampering with the spigot.

50 *caudles*: hot medicinal drinks made from thin gruel laced with wine and spices.

hang toasts, on, in grace and virtue to proceed! Only beware, beware degrees. There be rounds in a ladder and knots in a halter; 'ware carts. Hang toasts! the Common Council has decreed it. I must draw a lot for the great goblet. *Exit.*

SCENE III

Enter MISTRESS MULLIGRUB *and* LIONEL, *with a goblet.*

MISTRESS MULLIGRUB. Nay, I pray you, stay and drink. And how does your mistress? I know her very well; I have been inward with her, and so has many more. She was ever a good, patient creature, i'faith. With all my heart, I'll remember your master, an honest man; he knew me before I was married. An honest man he is, and a crafty. He comes forward in the world well, I warrant him; and his wife is a proper woman, that she is. Well, she has been as proper a woman as any in Cheap; she paints now, and yet she keeps her husband's old customers to him still. In troth, a fine-faced wife in a wainscot carved seat is a worthy ornament to a tradesman's shop, and an attractive, I warrant; her husband shall find it in the

---

54–7 *proceed . . . decreed*: punning on the idea of 'proceeding' to an academic degree, but the 'degrees' Cocledemoy has in mind are the 'rounds' (rungs) of the ladder to the scaffold; there is a further pun on 'degrees' and 'decreed'.

56 *carts*: used to take criminals to execution.

3 *inward*: intimate.

6–7 *knew me*: sexual innuendo.

8 *comes forward*: bawdy *double entendre*.

9, 11 *proper*: (1) decent, respectable; (2) typical (i.e. given to sin); (3) sexually well equipped.

11 *Cheap*: Cheapside (hardly known for its proprieties: cf. Middleton's ironically titled *A Chaste Maid in Cheapside*).

11 *paints*: uses cosmetics.

custom of his ware, I'll assure him. God be with you, good youth. I acknowledge the receipt.

Exit LIONEL.

I acknowledge all the receipt. Sure, 'tis very well spoken! 'I acknowledge the receipt!' Thus 'tis to have good education and to be brought up in a tavern. I do keep as gallant and as good company, though I say it, as any she in London. Squires, gentlemen, and knights diet at my table, and I do lend some of them money; and full many fine men go upon my score, as simple as I stand here, and I trust them; and truly they very knightly and courtly promise fair, give me very good words, and a piece of flesh when time of year serves. Nay, though my husband be a citizen and's cap's made of wool, yet I ha' wit and can see my good as soon as another; for I have all the thanks. My silly husband, alas, he knows nothing of it; 'tis I that bear, 'tis I that must bear a brain for all.

[*Enter* COCLEDEMOY.]

COCLEDEMOY. Fair hour to you, mistress!

MISTRESS MULLIGRUB. [*aside*] 'Fair hour'! Fine term; faith, I'll score it up anon. [*To* COCLEDEMOY] A beautiful thought to you, sir.

COCLEDEMOY. Your husband, and my master, Master Burnish, has sent you a jowl of fresh salmon; and they both will come to dinner to season your new cup with the best wine; which cup your husband entreats you to send back by me that his arms may be graved o' the side, which he forgot before it was sent.

---

17 *ware*: both his goods and his wife.
26 *go . . . score*: keep an account with me; also bawdily suggestive ('go' = 'come').
29–30 *piece . . . serves*: (1) game in season; (2) sexual *double entendre*.
33 *silly*: simple-minded, innocent.
34 *bear*: sexual *double entendre*.
41 *jowl*: head and shoulders.

MISTRESS MULLIGRUB. By what token are you sent? By no token? Nay, I have wit.

COCLEDEMOY. He sent me by the same token that he was dry-shaved this morning.

MISTRESS MULLIGRUB. A sad token, but true. Here, sir. [*Gives the cup*] I pray you commend me to your master, but especially to your mistress. Tell them they shall be most sincerely welcome. *Exit.*

COCLEDEMOY. 'Shall be most sincerely welcome'! Worshipful Cocledemoy, lurk close. Hang toasts, be not ashamed of thy quality! Every man's turd smells well in's own nose. Vanish, foist! *Exit.*

[*Re-*]*enter* MISTRESS MULLIGRUB, *with Servants and furniture for the table.*

MISTRESS MULLIGRUB. Come, spread these table diaper napkins and – do you hear? – perfume! This parlour does so smell of profane tobacco. I could never endure this ungodly tobacco since one of our elders assured me, upon his knowledge, tobacco was not used in the congregation of the Family of Love. – Spread, spread handsomely! – Lord, these boys do things arsy-varsy! – You show your bringing up. I was a gentlewoman by my sister's side, I can tell ye so methodically. 'Methodically' – I wonder where I got that word. O, Sir Aminadab Ruth bade me kiss him methodically.

---

50 *dry-shaved*: cheated, stripped clean.

58–9 *Every . . . nose*: Montaigne, III, viii, 166 (quoting Erasmus).

60 *foist*: (1) rogue, roguery; (2) stench (cf. Cocledemoy's favourite 'fist').

62 *diaper*: patterned linen.

68 *arsy-varsy*: topsy-turvy.

71–4 *methodically . . . it*: characteristically wry self-mockery at Marston's own taste for neologisms; as Crawford suggested, an in-joke may be involved since the word was perhaps culled from Montaigne (III, viii, 165).

72–3 *Sir Aminadab Ruth*: the Biblical names (both from the Book of Ruth) are meant to evoke a Puritan.

I had it somewhere, and I had it indeed.

Enter MASTER MULLIGRUB.

MULLIGRUB. Mind, be not desperate; I'll recover all.
All things with me shall seem honest that can be profitable.
He must ne'er wince, that would or thrive or save,
To be called niggard, cuckold, cut-throat, knave.

MISTRESS MULLIGRUB. Are they come, husband?

MULLIGRUB. Who? What? How now, what feast towards in my private parlour?

MISTRESS MULLIGRUB. Pray leave your foolery. What, are they come?

MULLIGRUB. Come? who come?

MISTRESS MULLIGRUB. You need not make't so strange.

MULLIGRUB. Strange?

MISTRESS MULLIGRUB. Ay, strange. You know no man that sent me word that he and his wife would come to dinner to me, and sent this jowl of fresh salmon beforehand?

MULLIGRUB. Peace, not I, peace! The messenger hath mistaken the house; let's eat it up quickly before it be inquired for. Sit to it. Some vinegar, quick! Some good luck yet. Faith, I never tasted salmon relished better. O, when a man feeds at other men's cost!

MISTRESS MULLIGRUB. Other men's cost! Why, did not you send this jowl of salmon?

MULLIGRUB. No.

MISTRESS MULLIGRUB. By Master Burnish' man?

MULLIGRUB. No.

MISTRESS MULLIGRUB. Sending me word that he and his wife would come to dinner to me?

MULLIGRUB. No, no.

MISTRESS MULLIGRUB. To season my new bowl?

---

74 *had it*: bawdy innuendo.

78–9 *He . . . knave*: mock-*sententia*, no doubt to be delivered in a posture of heroic seriousness.

82 *towards*: in preparation.

MULLIGRUB. Bowl?

MISTRESS MULLIGRUB. And withal willed me to send the bowl back?

MULLIGRUB. Back?

MISTRESS MULLIGRUB. That you might have your arms graved on the side?

MULLIGRUB. Ha?

MISTRESS MULLIGRUB. By the same token you were dry-shaven this morning before you went forth?

MULLIGRUB. Pah, how this salmon stinks!

MISTRESS MULLIGRUB. And thereupon sent the bowl back, prepared dinner – nay, and I bear not a brain!

MULLIGRUB. Wife, do not vex me. Is the bowl gone? Is it delivered?

MISTRESS MULLIGRUB. Delivered? Yes, sure, 'tis delivered.

MULLIGRUB. I will never more say my prayers! Do not make me mad. 'Tis common. Let me not cry like a woman! Is it gone?

MISTRESS MULLIGRUB. Gone! God is my witness, I delivered it with no more intention to be cozened on't than the child new born; and yet –

MULLIGRUB. Look to my house. I am haunted with evil spirits. Hear me, do, hear me! If I have not my goblet again, heaven, I'll to the devil; I'll to a conjuror. Look to my house. I'll raise all the wise men i' the street.

[*Exit.*]

MISTRESS MULLIGRUB. Deliver us! What words are these? I trust in God he is but drunk, sure.

[*Re-*]*enter* COCLEDEMOY.

COCLEDEMOY. [*aside*] I must have the salmon, too. Worshipful Cocledemoy, now for the masterpiece. God bless thy neck-piece, and foutra! [*To* MISTRESS MULLIGRUB] Fair mistress, my master –

---

131 *cozened on't*: cheated out of it.
141 *neck-piece*: neck.

MISTRESS MULLIGRUB. Have I caught you? – What, Roger!

COCLEDEMOY. Peace, good mistress, I'll tell you all. A jest, a very mere jest! Your husband only took sport to fright you. The bowl's at my master's; and there is your husband, who sent me in all haste, lest you should be over-frighted with his feigning, to come to dinner to him –

MISTRESS MULLIGRUB. Praise heaven it is no worse!

COCLEDEMOY. And desired me to desire you to send the jowl of salmon before, and yourself to come after to them; my mistress would be right glad to see you.

MISTRESS MULLIGRUB. I pray carry it. Now thank them entirely. Bless me, I was never so out of my skin in my life! Pray thank your mistress most entirely.

COCLEDEMOY. [*aside*] So now, figo! worshipful Moll Faugh and I will munch. Cheaters and bawds go together like washing and wringing. *Exit.*

MISTRESS MULLIGRUB. Beshrew his heart for his labour! How everything about me quivers! [*To Servant*] What, Christian, my hat and apron. Here, take my sleeves. – And how I tremble! So, I'll gossip it now for't, that's certain. Here has been revolutions and false fires indeed.

[*Re-*]*enter* MULLIGRUB.

MULLIGRUB. Whither now? What's the matter with you now? Whither are you a-gadding?

MISTRESS MULLIGRUB. Come, come, play the fool no more; will you go?

147–8 *only . . . you*: played a trick only to frighten you.
162 *figo*: contemptuous gesture made with the thumb between the first two fingers (deriving from an indecent pun on Italian *fica* = fig; cf. also 'a Spanish fig for . . . !').
168 *apron*: decorative garment.
168 *sleeves*: frequently detachable at this time.
169 *gossip it*: join in.
170 *revolutions*: changes, turnabouts.

MULLIGRUB. Whither, in the rank name of madness, whither?

MISTRESS MULLIGRUB. Whither? Why, to Master Burnish, to eat the jowl of salmon. Lord, how strange you make it!

MULLIGRUB. Why so? why so?

MISTRESS MULLIGRUB. Why so? Why, did not you send the selfsame fellow for the jowl of salmon that had the cup?

MULLIGRUB. 'Tis well, 'tis very well.

MISTRESS MULLIGRUB. And willed me to come and eat it with you at the goldsmith's?

MULLIGRUB. O, ay, ay, ay. Art in thy right wits?

MISTRESS MULLIGRUB. Do you hear? Make a fool of somebody else. And you make an ass of me, I'll make an ox of ye – do you see?

MULLIGRUB. Nay, wife, be patient; for, look you, I may be mad, or drunk, or so; for my own part, though you can bear more than I, yet I can do well: I will not curse nor cry, but heaven knows what I think. Come, let's go hear some music; I will never more say my prayers. Let's go hear some doleful music. Nay, if heaven forget to prosper knaves, I'll go no more to the synagogue. Now I am discontented. I'll turn sectary; that is fashion.

Exeunt.

---

191 *make an ox of you*: horn you, make you a cuckold.

197 *music*: to calm the passions; signal for the entr'acte to begin.

200 *synagogue*: Puritan chapel.

200–1 *Now . . . fashion*: implying that sectarianism is simply a mask for social and political discontent.

ACT IV

SCENE I

Enter SIR HUBERT SUBBOYS, SIR LIONEL FREEVILL, CRISPINELLA [*Ladies and Gentlemen*], *Servants with lights.*

SIR HUBERT. More lights! Welcome, Sir Lionel Freevill, brother Freevill shortly. – Look to your lights!

SERVANT. The maskers are at hand.

SIR HUBERT. Call down our daughter. Hark, they are at hand. Rank handsomely.

Enter the Maskers, [*including among them* FREEVILL, TYSEFEW, *and* CAQUETEUR; *as*] *they dance,* [BEATRICE *enters. The formal dancing over, the Maskers choose partners among the guests for ordinary dancing,* FREEVILL *choosing* BEATRICE.] *Enter* MALHEUREUX *and take* BEATRICE *from* FREEVILL. *They draw.*

FREEVILL. Know, sir, I have the advantage of the place;
You are not safe. I would deal even with you.

MALHEUREUX. So.

They exchange gloves as pledges.

FREEVILL. So.

BEATRICE. I do beesech you, sweet, do not for me
Provoke your fortune.

SIR LIONEL. What sudden flaw is risen?

SIR HUBERT. From whence comes this?

FREEVILL. An ulcer long time lurking now is burst.

---

6 *Rank handsomely*: draw yourselves up in your proper places (for the dance).

8 *even*: honestly, fairly.

SIR HUBERT. Good sir, the time and your designs are soft.

BEATRICE. Ay, dear sir, counsel him, advise him; 'twill relish well from your carving. – Good, my sweet, rest safe.

FREEVILL. All's well, all's well. This shall be ended straight.

SIR HUBERT. The banquet stays; there we'll discourse more large.

FREEVILL. Marriage must not make men cowards.

SIR LIONEL. Nor rage fools.

SIR HUBERT. 'Tis valour not where heat but reason rules.

Ex[*eunt.*] *Only* TYSEFEW *and* CRISPINELLA *stay.*

TYSEFEW. But do you hear, lady, you proud ape, you,
What was the jest you brake of me even now?

CRISPINELLA. Nothing. I only said you were all mettle – that you had a brazen face, a leaden brain, and a copper beard.

TYSEFEW. Quicksilver! thou little more than a dwarf, and something less than a woman.

CRISPINELLA. A wisp, a wisp, a wisp! Will you go to the banquet?

TYSEFEW. By the Lord, I think thou wilt marry shortly, too; thou growest somewhat foolish already.

---

15 *soft*: peaceful.
20 *stays*: is waiting.
22 *'Tis . . . rules*: Stoic commonplace.
26 *mettle*: spirit (punning on 'metal').
27 *copper*: (1) red; (2) showy, worthless; Marston himself is said to have had a red beard.
28 *Quicksilver*: witty one.
28–9 *thou . . . woman*: wittily self-conscious reference to the fact that all parts at Blackfriars were played by boys, female roles presumably by the smallest ones.
30 *wisp*: perhaps only 'insubstantial thing' (cf. will-o'-the-wisp); Fraser and Rabkin suggest 'figure of straw for a scold to rail at' (*OED*); Wine cites the proverb 'As wise as a wisp' (Tilley, W540), where 'wisp' = woodcock (ironic).

CRISPINELLA. O, i'faith, 'tis a fair thing to be married, and a necessary. To hear this word 'must'! If our husband be proud, we must bear his contempt, if noisome, we must bear with the goat under his armholes, if a fool, we must bear his babble, and, which is worse, if a loose liver, we must live upon unwholesome reversions; where, on the contrary side, our husbands – because they may, and we must – care not for us. Things hoped with fear and got with strugglings are men's high pleasures when duty pales and flats their appetite.

TYSEFEW. What a tart monkey is this! By heaven, if thou hadst not so much wit I could find in my heart to marry thee. Faith, bear with me for all this.

CRISPINELLA. Bear with thee? I wonder how thy mother could bear thee ten months in her belly when I cannot endure thee two hours in mine eye.

TYSEFEW. Alas for you, sweet soul! By the Lord, you are grown a proud, scurvy, apish, idle, disdainful, scoffing – God's foot! because you have read *Euphues and his England*, *Palmerin de Oliva*, and the *Legend of Lies*!

CRISPINELLA. Why, i'faith, yet, servant, you of all others should bear with my known unmalicious humours. I have always in my heart given you your due respect, and, heaven may be

---

40 *babble*: punning on 'bauble' = (1) fool's sceptre; (2) penis.

41 *unwholesome reversions*: venereal disease inherited after the husband's death.

46 *pales and flats*: weakens and dulls.

58 *Euphues and his England*: John Lyly's 1580 sequel to his famous romance, *Euphues: The Anatomy of Wit* (1578), a by-word for its ornate style.

58–9 *Palmerin de Oliva*: a romance in the series translated by Munday under the title of *The Mirror of Knighthood*, available from 1588.

59 *Legend of Lies*: Tysefew's epitome of romance fictions; Davison suggests a satiric glance at Chaucer's *Legend of Good Women*.

sworn, I have privately given fair speech of you, and protested –

TYSEFEW. Nay, look you, for my own part, if I have not as religiously vowed my heart to you, been drunk to your health, swallowed flap-dragons, ate glasses, drunk urine, stabbed arms, and done all the offices of protested gallantry for your sake; and yet you tell me I have a brazen face, a leaden brain, and a copper beard! Come, yet, and it please you.

CRISPINELLA. No, no, you do not love me.

TYSEFEW. By ——, but I do now; and whosoever dares say that I do not love you, nay, honour you, and if you would vouchsafe to marry –

CRISPINELLA. Nay, as for that, think on't as you will, but God's my record – and my sister knows I have taken drink and slept upon't – that if ever I marry it shall be you; and I will marry, and yet I hope I do not say it shall be you neither.

TYSEFEW. By heaven, I shall be as soon weary of health as of your enjoying! Will you cast a smooth cheek upon me?

CRISPINELLA. I cannot tell. I have no crumped shoulders, my back needs no mantle; and yet marriage is honourable. Do you think ye shall prove a cuckold?

TYSEFEW. No, by the Lord, not I!

CRISPINELLA. Why, I thank you, i'faith. Heigh-ho! I slept on my back this morning and dreamt the strangest dreams. Good Lord, how things

---

68–9 *swallowed flapdragons*: 'a game . . . in which raisins, or even candle-ends, were set aflame in brandy and then swallowed still burning' (Wine).

69 *stabbed arms*: and dripped blood into a glass of wine before drinking it.

75 *By* —: see Textual Note, p. 501 below.

80 *taken drink*: pledged with a drink.

85–6 *cast a smooth cheek*: look favourably.

87 *crumped*: hunched.

88 *back . . . mantle*: to cover a hump; and cf. III.i.117–18 (Davison).

93–4 *I slept . . . dreams*: cf. Cocledemoy's song at IV.v.76–89.

will come to pass! Will you go to the banquet?

TYSEFEW. If you will be mine, you shall be your own. My purse, my body, my heart, is yours; only be silent in my house, modest at my table, and wanton in my bed, and the Empress of Europe cannot content, and shall not be contented, better.

CRISPINELLA. Can any kind heart speak more discreetly affectionately! My father's consent, and as for mine –

TYSEFEW. Then thus, and thus, so Hymen should begin;
[He kisses her.]
Sometimes a falling out proves falling in.
Ex[eunt.]

SCENE II

Enter FREEVILL, *speaking to some within;* MALHEUREUX *at the other door.*

FREEVILL. As you respect my virtue, give me leave
To satisfy my reason, though not blood. –
So, all runs right: our feignèd rage hath ta'en
To fullest life; they are much possessed
Of force must most all quarrel. Now, my right friend,
Resolve me with open breast, free and true heart,
Cannot thy virtue, having space to think
And fortify her weakened powers with reason,
Discourses, meditations, discipline,

---

105 *Hymen*: the rites of Hymen, marriage.
106 *falling in*: reconciliation (with bawdy quibble).
3–4 *ta'en . . . life*: been accepted as the real thing.
4–5 *they . . . quarrel*: see Textual Note, p. 501 below.
9 *meditations*: intellectual and spiritual exercises.

Divine ejaculatories, and all those aids against
devils –
Cannot all these curb thy low appetite
And sensual fury?
MALHEUREUX. There is no God in blood, no
reason in desire.
Shall I but live? Shall I not be forced to act
Some deeds whose very name is hideous?
FREEVILL. No.
MALHEUREUX. Then I must enjoy Franceschina.
FREEVILL. You shall:
I'll lend this ring; show it to that fair devil.
It will resolve me dead;
Which rumour, with my artificial absence,
Will make most firm. Enjoy her suddenly.
MALHEUREUX. But if report go strong that you
are slain,
And that by me, whereon I may be seized,
Where shall I find your being?
FREEVILL. At Master Shatewe's the jeweller's, to
whose breast
I'll trust our secret purpose.
MALHEUREUX. Ay, rest yourself;
Each man hath follies.
FREEVILL. But those worst of all,
Who with a willing eye do, seeing, fall.
MALHEUREUX. 'Tis true, but truth seems folly in
madness' spectacles.
I am not now myself – no man. Farewell.
FREEVILL. Farewell.
MALHEUREUX. When woman's in the heart, in
the soul hell.
Exit MALHEUREUX.
FREEVILL. Now repentance, the fool's whip, seize
thee!
Nay, if there be no means I'll be thy friend,
But not thy vice's; and with greatest sense
I'll force thee feel thy errors to the worst.

---

10 *ejculatories*: short prayers.
13 *blood*: passion, lust.
19 *artificial*: feigned.
27 *with . . . eye*: cf. II.ii.273.

The vilest of dangers thou shalt sink into.
No jeweller shall see me; I will lurk
Where none shall know or think; close I'll
withdraw
And leave thee with two friends – a knave and
whore.
But is this virtue in me? No, not pure;
Nothing extremely best with us endures.
No use in simple purities; the elements
Are mixed for use. Silver without alloy
Is all too eager to be wrought for use:
Nor precise virtues ever purely good
Holds useful size with temper of weak blood.
Then let my course be borne, though with side
wind;
The end being good, the means are well
assigned. *Exit.*

SCENE III

Enter FRANCESCHINA *melancholy,*
COCLEDEMOY *leading her.*

COCLEDEMOY. Come, cacafuego, Frank o' Frank Hall! Who, who, ho! Excellent! Ha, here's a plump-rumped wench, with a breast softer than a courtier's tongue, an old lady's gums, or an

---

37 *close*: secretly.
38 *knave*: himself in disguise, or Cocledemoy.
39–45 *But . . . blood*: based on Montaigne, II, xx, 399 (opening of the essay entitled 'We taste nothing purely').
43 *eager*: brittle.
44 *precise*: rigorous, over-nice; cf. 'precisian' = Puritan.
44–5 *Nor . . . blood*: nor do strict virtues which are always unalloyed have any sensible proportion to a temperament weakened by passion.
46 *side wind*: indirect means.
IV.iii s.d. *melancholy*: implies the use of conventional gestures, such as the 'folded arms' associated with love-melancholy.
1 *cacafuego*: Spanish for spitfire; from Latin *cacare*, to discharge excrement, and Spanish *fuego*, fire (*OED*).
1–2 *Frank . . . Hall*: i.e. Mistress Libertine of Liberty Hall.

old man's *mentula*. My fine rogue –

FRANCESCHINA. Pah, you poltroon!

COCLEDEMOY. Goody fist, flumpum pumpum! Ah, my fine wagtail, thou art as false, as prostituted, and adulterate, as some translated manuscript. Buss, fair whore, buss!

FRANCESCHINA. God's sacrament, pox!

COCLEDEMOY. *Hadamoy key*, dost thou frown, *medianthon teukey*? Nay, look here. *Numeron key*, silver *blithefor cany*, *os cany* goblet: *us key ne moy blegefoy oteeston* pox on you, gosling!

FRANCESCHINA. By me fait, dis bin very fine langage. Ick sall bush ye now. Ha, be garzon, vare had you dat plate?

COCLEDEMOY. *Hedemoy key*, get you gone, punk rampant, *key*, common up-tail!

Enter MARY FAUGH *in haste.*

MARY FAUGH. O, daughter, cousin, niece, servant, mistress!

COCLEDEMOY. Humpum plumpum squat, I am gone. *Exit* COCLEDEMOY.

MARY FAUGH. There is one Master Malheureux at the door desires to see you. He says he must not be denied, for he hath sent you this ring, and withal says 'tis done.

FRANCESCHINA. Vat sall me do now, God's sacrament! Tell him two hours hence he sall be most affectionately velcome. Tell him (vat sall me do?) – tell him ick am bin in my bate, and ick sall perfume my seets, mak-a mine body so

---

5 *mentula*: Latin, penis.

8 *wagtail*: cant for 'courtesan' (cf. 'up-tail', line 20).

12–20 perhaps it is the thought of the 'translated manuscript' (line 9–10) that sets off Cocledemoy's flow of bogus Greek. It is of course fully in accord with his sense of himself as a scholar, and is meant, like the stolen plate, to dazzle Franceschina into bed with him.

15 *gosling*: little fool.

17 *be garzon*: by God's son.

32 *bate*: bath.

33 *seets*: sweets or (more likely) sheets; see Textual Note, pp. 501–2 below.

delicate for his arm, two hours hence.

MARY FAUGH. I shall satisfy him; two hours hence; well.

Exit MARY [FAUGH].

FRANCESCHINA. Now ick sall revange. Hay, begar, me sall tartar de whole generation! Mine brain vork it. Freevill is dead; Malheureux sall hang; and mine rival, Beatrice, ick sall make run mad.

[*Re-*]*enter* MARY FAUGH.

MARY FAUGH. He's gone, forsooth, to eat a caudle of cock-stones, and will return within this two hours.

FRANCESCHINA. Very vell. Give monies to some fellow to squire me; ick sall go abroad.

MARY FAUGH. There's a lusty bravo beneath, a stranger, but a good stale rascal. He swears valiantly, kicks a bawd right virtuously, and protests with an empty pocket right desperately. He'll squire you.

FRANCESCHINA. Very velcome. Mine fan! Ick sall retorn presantly.

[*Exit* MARY FAUGH.]

Now sall me be revange. Ten tousant devla! Dere sall be no Got in me but passion, no tought but rage, no mercy but blood, no spirit but divla in me. Dere sall noting tought good for me, but dat is mischievous for others. *Exit.*

---

34 *delicate*: delicious.
38 *begar*: by God.
38 *tartar*: torture.
43 *cock-stones*: kidney-beans (an aphrodisiac).
47 *bravo*: daring villain.
48 *stranger*: foreigner.
48 *stale*: 'possibly meaning something like "an old hand at this", "inured" ' (Wine); this would be a slight extension of *OED stale a*[1] 4, 'past the fitting season for marriage'.

SCENE IV

Enter SIR HUBERT, SIR LIONEL, BEATRICE, CRISPINELLA, *and* NURSE; TYSEFEW *following*.

SIR LIONEL. Did no one see him since? Pray God – nay, all is well. A little heat, what? He is but withdrawn. And yet I would to God – but fear you nothing.

BEATRICE. Pray God that all be well, or would I were not!

TYSEFEW. He's not to be found, sir, anywhere.

SIR LIONEL. You must not make a heavy face presage an ill event. I like your sister well; she's quick and lively. Would she would marry, faith!

CRISPINELLA. Marry? Nay, and I would marry, methinks an old man's a quiet thing.

SIR LIONEL. Ha, mass, and so he is!

CRISPINELLA. You are a widower?

SIR LIONEL. That I am, i'faith, fair Crispinella; and I can tell you, would you affect me, I have it in me yet, i'faith.

CRISPINELLA. Troth, I am in love. Let me see your hand. Would you cast yourself away upon me willingly?

SIR LIONEL. Will I? Ay, by the –

CRISPINELLA. Would you be a cuckold willingly? By my troth, 'tis a comely, fine, and handsome sight for one of my years to marry an old man; truth, 'tis restorative. What a comfortable thing it is to think of her husband, to hear his venerable cough o' the everlastings, to feel his rough skin, his summer hands and winter legs, his almost no eyes, and assuredly no teeth! And then to think what she must dream of when she considers others' happiness and her own want – 'tis a worthy and notorious comfortable match!

SIR LIONEL. Pish, pish! will you have me?

CRISPINELLA. Will you assure me –

---

27 *cough . . . everlastings*: (1) eternal coughing; (2) fatal cough.

SIR LIONEL. Five-hundred pound jointure?

CRISPINELLA. That you will die within this fortnight?

SIR LIONEL. No, by my faith, Crispinella.

CRISPINELLA. Then Crispinella, by her faith, assures you she'll have none of you.

Enter FREEVILL, *disguised like a pander, and* FRANCESCHINA.

FREEVILL. By'r leave, gentles and men of nightcaps, I would speak, but that here stands one is able to express her own tale best.

FRANCESCHINA. Sir, mine speech is to you. You had a son, Matre Freevill?

SIR LIONEL. Had, ha, and have!

FRANCESCHINA. No point; me am come to assure you dat one Mestre Malheureux hath killed him.

BEATRICE. O me, wretched, wretched!

SIR HUBERT. Look to our daughter.

SIR LIONEL. How art thou informed?

FRANCESCHINA. If dat it please you to go vid me, ick sall bring you where you sall hear Malheureux vid his own lips confess it; and dere ye may apprehend him, and revenge your and mine love's blood.

SIR HUBERT. Your love's blood, mistress! Was he your love?

FRANCESCHINA. He was so, sir; let your daughter hear it. – Do not veep, lady. De yong man dat be slain did not love you, for he still lovit me ten tousant tousant times more dearly.

BEATRICE. O my heart! I will love you the better; I cannot hate what he affected. O passion! O my grief! which way wilt break, think, and consume?

---

40 s.d. *disguised*: Freevill takes over Cocledemoy's protean role.

41–2 *men of nightcaps*: 'probably "men of law" . . . rather than the more usual meaning of "nocturnal bullies" (see *OED*)' (Wine).

45, 48 *Matre . . . Mestre*: Master.

47 *No point*: French *point* = not at all.

CRISPINELLA. Peace!

BEATRICE. Dear woes cannot speak.

FRANCESCHINA. For look you, lady, dis your ring he gave me, vid most bitter jests at your scorned kindness.

BEATRICE. He did not ill not to love me, but sure he did not well to mock me: gentle minds will pity though they cannot love. Yet peace and my love sleep with him! – Unlace, good nurse. – Alas, I was not so ambitious of so supreme an happiness that he should only love me; 'twas joy enough for me, poor soul, that I only might only love him.

FRANCESCHINA. O, but to be abused, scorned, scoffed at! O, ten tousand divla, by such a one, and unto such a one!

BEATRICE. I think you say not true. – Sister, shall we know one another in the other world?

CRISPINELLA. What means my sister?

BEATRICE. I would fain see him again. O my tortured mind!
Freevill is more than dead; he is unkind.

Ex[*eunt*] BEATRICE *and* CRISPINELLA *and* NURSE.

SIR HUBERT. Convey her in, and so, sir, as you said,
Set a strong watch.

SIR LIONEL. Ay, sir, and so pass along
With this same common woman.
[*To* FRANCESCHINA]
You must make it good.

FRANCESCHINA. Ick sall, or let me pay for his, mine blood.

SIR HUBERT. Come, then, along all, with quiet speed.

SIR LIONEL. O fate!

---

69 *Dear . . . speak*: a version of the favourite Senecan tag, *Curae leves loquuntur, ingentes stupent* ('Light woes speak, the heavy ones strike dumb', *Hippolytus*, 607); cf. *AM*, IV.ii.25.

76 *Unlace*: Beatrice asks the Nurse to untie the laces of her stays to relieve the pressure of emotion (cf. *Antony and Cleopatra*, I.iii.71).

TYSEFEW. O, sir, be wisely sorry, but not passionate.

Ex[eunt;] manet FREEVILL.

FREEVILL. I will go and reveal myself. Stay! No, no!
Grief endears love. Heaven! to have such a wife
Is happiness to breed pale envy in the saints.
Thou worthy, dove-like virgin without gall,
Cannot that woman's evil, jealousy,
Despite disgrace, nay, which is worst, contempt,
Once stir thy faith? O truth, how few sisters hast thou!
Dear memory!
With what a suff'ring sweetness, quiet modesty,
Yet deep affection, she received my death!
And then with what a patient, yet oppressèd kindness
She took my lewdly intimated wrongs!
O, the dearest of heaven!
Were there but three such women in the world,
Two might be saved. Well, I am great
With expectation to what devilish end
This woman of foul soul will drive her plots;
But Providence all wicked art o'ertops,
And impudence must know, though stiff as ice,
That fortune doth not alway dote on vice. *Exit.*

SCENE V

Enter SIR HUBERT, SIR LIONEL, TYSEFEW, FRANCESCHINA, *and three* [CONSTABLES] *with halberds.*

---

98 *dove-like . . . gall*: the pigeon or dove was popularly supposed to have no gall, the source within the liver of bitterness and rancour; cf. *Hamlet*, II.ii.572.

109 *Two . . . saved*: hyperbolically implies that Beatrice of all women in the world is saved; in the unlikely event that there could be two others like her, then they too might win salvation.

113 *impudence*: shamelessness.

113 *stiff*: inflexible, obstinate, proud.

SIR HUBERT. Plant a watch there. Be very careful, sirs.
The rest with us.

TYSEFEW. The heavy night grows to her depth of quiet;
'Tis about mid-darkness.

FRANCESCHINA. Mine shambre is hard by; ick sall bring you to it presantment.

SIR LIONEL. Deep silence! On!

Exeunt. [CONSTABLES *remain.*]

COCLEDEMOY. (*within*) Wa, ha, ho!

Enter MULLIGRUB.

MULLIGRUB. It was his voice; 'tis he. He sups with his cupping-glasses. 'Tis late; he must pass this way. I'll ha' him; I'll ha' my fine boy, my worshipful Cocledemoy. I'll moy him. He shall be hanged in lousy linen. I'll hire some sectary to make him an heretic before he die, and when he is dead, I'll piss on his grave.

Enter COCLEDEMOY.

COCLEDEMOY. Ah, my fine punks, good night, Frank Frailty, Frail o' Frail Hall! *Bonus noches*, my *ubiquitari*!

MULLIGRUB. 'Ware polling and shaving, sir!

COCLEDEMOY. A wolf, a wolf, a wolf!

Exit COCLEDEMOY, *leaving his cloak behind him.*

MULLIGRUB. Here's something yet: a cloak, a cloak! Yet I'll after. He cannot 'scape the watch.

---

6 *presantment*: presently (i.e. 'at once').

10 *cupping-glasses*: (1) glasses used in cupping blood (appropriate to Cocledemoy's leech-like trade); (2) glasses for 'cupping' = drinking deep.

12 *moy*: nonsense verb formed from last syllable of Cocledemoy's name.

17 *Bonus noches*: Cocledemoy's corruption of Spanish *buenos noches* = good night; another piece of characteristic polyglot swagger.

18 *ubiquitari*: people who can be everywhere (Latin).

I'll hang him if I have any mercy. I'll slice him. *Exit.*

[*Re-*]*enter* COCLEDEMOY. [*The* CONSTABLES *step forward.*]

1 CONSTABLE. Who goes there? Come before the constable.

COCLEDEMOY. Bread o' God, constable, you are a watch for the devil! Honest men are robbed under your nose. There's a false knave in the habit of a vintner set upon me. He would have had my purse, but I took me to my heels. Yet he got my cloak: a plain stuff cloak, poor, yet 'twill serve to hang him. 'Tis my loss, poor man that I am. [*Exit.*]

2 CONSTABLE. Masters, we must watch better. Is't not strange that knaves, drunkards, and thieves should be abroad, and yet we of the watch, scriveners, smiths, and tailors, never stir?

[*Re-*]*enter* MULLIGRUB *running with* COCLEDEMOY'*s cloak.*

1 CONSTABLE. Hark! who goes there?

MULLIGRUB. An honest man and a citizen.

2 CONSTABLE. Appear, appear! What are you?

MULLIGRUB. A simple vintner.

1 CONSTABLE. A vintner, ha? and simple? Draw nearer, nearer. Here's the cloak!

2 CONSTABLE. Ay, Master Vintner, we know you. A plain stuff cloak: 'tis it.

1 CONSTABLE. Right, come! O, thou varlet, dost not thou know that the wicked cannot 'scape the eyes of the constable?

MULLIGRUB. What means this violence? As I am an honest man, I took the cloak –

1 CONSTABLE. As you are a knave, you took the cloak; we are your witnesses for that.

---

23 *if . . . mercy*: 'if God gives me the slightest chance'; or perhaps 'hanging is the most merciful thing I'll do to him'.

31 *stuff*: woollen material.

MULLIGRUB. But hear me, hear me! I'll tell you what I am.

2 CONSTABLE. A thief you are.

MULLIGRUB. I tell you my name is Mulligrub.

1 CONSTABLE. I will grub you! In with him to the stocks! There let him sit till tomorrow morning, that Justice Quodlibet may examine him.

MULLIGRUB. Why, but I tell thee –

2 CONSTABLE. Why, but I tell thee! We'll tell thee now.

[CONSTABLES *put* MULLIGRUB *in the stocks.*]

MULLIGRUB. Am I not mad? Am I not an ass? Why, scabs – God's foot, let me out!

2 CONSTABLE. Ay, ay, let him prate; he shall find matter in us scabs, I warrant. God's-so, what good members of the commonwealth do we prove!

1 CONSTABLE. Prithee, peace! Let's remember our duties, and let's go sleep in the fear of God.

Exeunt, having left MULLIGRUB *in the stocks.*

MULLIGRUB. Who goes there? Illo, ho, ho! Zounds, shall I run mad, lose my wits! Shall I be hanged? – Hark, who goes there? Do not fear to be poor, Mulligrub; thou hast a sure stock now.

[*Re-*]*enter* COCLEDEMOY *like a bellman.*

COCLEDEMOY. The night grows old,
And many a cuckold
Is now – Wha, ha, ha, ho!

---

57 *grub*: root out.

59 *Quodlibet*: Latin 'What you please'; in English 'a scholastic debate or thesis'.

66 *matter . . . scabs*: (1) sense in us rascals; (2) pus in us sores.

70 *let's go sleep*: the Constable has a sound Dogberry-like grasp of 'duties'.

71–2 *Illo . . . mad*: another recollection of *Hamlet*, where the onset of the Prince's 'madness' is signalled by this falconer's cry; cf. I.ii.50, 106 above.

75 *stock*: (1) tradesman's stock; (2) stocks.

75 s.d. *bellman*: town crier or night watchman.

Maids on their backs
Dream of sweet smacks
And warm – Wo, ho, ho, ho!

I must go comfort my venerable Mulligrub; I must fiddle him till he fist. Fough! –

Maids in your night-rails,
Look well to your light ——.
Keep close your locks,
And down your smocks;
Keep a broad eye,
And a close thigh –

Excellent, excellent! – Who's there? Now, Lord, Lord, Master Mulligrub! Deliver us! What does your worship in the stocks? I pray come out, sir.

MULLIGRUB. Zounds, man, I tell thee I am locked!

COCLEDEMOY. Locked! O world, O men, O time, O night! that canst not discern virtue and wisdom and one of the Common Council! What is your worship in for?

MULLIGRUB. For (a plague on't!) suspicion of felony.

COCLEDEMOY. Nay, and it be such a trifle, Lord, I could weep to see your good worship in this taking. Your worship has been a good friend to

---

82 *comfort*: one of the duties of the common bellman was to visit condemned men in prison (see Webster's *The Duchess of Malfi*, IV.ii.173–5).

83 *fiddle*: cheat.

85 *light* —: J.A.B. Somerset (*The Comic Turn in English Drama, 1470–1616*, Ph.D. dissertation, University of Birmingham, 1966, p. 471) suggests that the blank may be an instruction to the actor to solicit the obvious rhyme from the audience.

90 ff. This episode evidently owes something to the exchange between Feste and Malvolio in *Twelfth Night*, V.ii.

95–6 *O world . . . O night!*: burlesques a favourite passage of Marston's from Kyd's *Spanish Tragedy* (III.ii.22).

97 *one . . . Council*: mocking allusion to Mulligrub's boast at II.iii.102–3.

103 *taking*: (1) state of arrest; (2) plight; (3) emotional condition.

me; and, though you have forgot me, yet I knew your wife before she was married; and, since, I have found your worship's door open, and I have knocked, and God knows what I have saved. And do I live to see your worship stocked?

MULLIGRUB. Honest bellman, I perceive thou know'st me;
I prithee call the watch.
Inform the constable of my reputation,
That I may no longer abide in this shameful habitation;
And hold thee all I have about me.

Gives him his purse.

COCLEDEMOY. 'Tis more than I deserve, sir. Let me alone for your delivery.

MULLIGRUB. Do, and then let me alone with Cocledemoy: I'll moy him!

COCLEDEMOY. Maids in your –

[*Re-enter the* CONSTABLES.]

Master Constable, who's that i'th' stocks?

1 CONSTABLE. One for a robbery; one Mulligrub he calls himself.

COCLEDEMOY. Mulligrub?

1 CONSTABLE. Bellman, know'st thou him?

COCLEDEMOY. Know him? O, Master Constable, what good service have you done. Know him? He's a strong thief; his house has been suspected for a bawdy tavern a great while, and a receipt for cutpurses, 'tis most certain. He has been long in the black book, and is he ta'en now?

2 CONSTABLE. By'r Lady, my masters, we'll not

104–7 *knew . . . door open . . . knocked:* sexual *doubles entendres*, but alluding also to his thefts.

108 *saved*: i.e. by knocking on the open door, as a bellman should, and so warning the household to lock up. Cocledemoy, however, thinks of the money he has saved through the allegedly generous freedoms of Mrs Mulligrub, and through his thefts.

127 *strong*: flagrant, formidable.

128 *receipt*: fence.

130 *black book*: register of criminals.

trust the stocks with him; we'll have him to the justice's, get a *mittimus* to Newgate presently. – Come, sir, come on, sir!

MULLIGRUB. Ha, does your rascalship yet know my worship in the end?

1 CONSTABLE. Ay, the end of your worship we know.

MULLIGRUB. Ha, goodman constable, here's an honest fellow can tell you what I am.

2 CONSTABLE. 'Tis true, sir; you're a strong thief, he says, on his own knowledge. Bind fast, bind fast! We know you: we'll trust no stocks with you. Away with him to the gaol instantly!

MULLIGRUB. Why, but dost hear – bellman! rogue! rascal! God's – why, but –

The CONSTABLE *drags away* MULLIGRUB.

COCLEDEMOY. Why, but! Wha, ha, ha! Excellent, excellent! Ha, my fine Cocledemoy, my vintner fists! I'll make him fart crackers before I ha' done with him. Tomorrow is the day of judgement. Afore the Lord God, my knavery grows unparegal! 'Tis time to take a nap, until half an hour hence. God give your worship music, content, and rest!

Exeunt [COCLEDEMOY *and the other* CONSTABLES].

---

133 *mittimus*: warrant for imprisonment.

133 *Newgate*: London prison.

137 *end of your worship*: (1) limits of your worth, status; (2) the end you're coming to; 'your worship' is a term of respect proper only to members of the gentry; by addressing the constable as 'goodman', a term of civility proper to those just below the gentry, Mulligrub is being at once condescending and ingratiating (cf. the modern 'officer').

149 *crackers*: squibs.

152 *unparegal*: unequalled (mock-heroic bombast).

153 *music*: signal for the entr'acte music.

ACT V

SCENE I

Enter FRANCESCHINA, SIR LIONEL, TYSEFEW, [FREEVILL *disguised as before*], *with Officers.*

FRANCESCHINA. You bin very velcome to mine shambra.

SIR LIONEL. But how know ye, how are ye assured,
Both of the deed and of his sure return?

FRANCESCHINA. O, mynheer, ick sall tell you. Mettre Malheureux came all breatless running a my shambra, his sword all bloody: he tell-a me he had kill Freevill, and prayed-a me to conceal him. Ick flatter him, bid bring monies, he should live and lie vid me. He went, whilst ick (me hope vidout sins) out of mine mush love to Freevill betray him.

SIR LIONEL. Fear not, 'tis well: good works get grace for sin.

She conceals them behind the curtain.

FRANCESCHINA. Dere, peace, rest dere; so, softly, all go in.
[*Aside*] De net is lay; now sall ick be revenge.
If dat me knew a dog dat Freevill love,
Me would puisson him; for know de deepest hell
As a revenging woman's naught so fell.

Enter MARY FAUGH.

---

13 *good . . . sin:* Sir Lionel's adherence to the doctrine of justification by works distinguishes him from the Puritans of the play who would, of course, accept justification by faith alone.

13 s.d. *curtain*: hanging across the rear wall of the Blackfriars stage.

15–18 burlesque of revenge-play rhetoric.

MARY FAUGH. Ho, Cousin Frank, the party you wot of,
Master Malheureux.
FRANCESCHINA. Bid him come up, I pridee.
Cantat saltatque cum cithera.

Enter MALHEUREUX.

FRANCESCHINA. O mynheer man, aderliver love,
Mine ten tousant times velcome love!
Ha, by mine trat, you bin de just – vat sall me say?
Vat seet honey name sall I call you?
MALHEUREUX. Any from you
Is pleasure. Come, my loving prettiness,
Where's thy chamber? I long to touch your sheets.
FRANCESCHINA. No, no, not yet, mine seetest, soft-lipped love:
You sall not gulp down all delights at once.
Be min trat, dis all-fles-lovers, dis ravenous wenches
Dat sallow all down whole, vill have all at one bit!
Fie, fie, fie!
Be min fait, dey do eat comfits vid spoons.
No, no, I'll make you chew your pleasure vit love:
De more degrees and steps, de more delight,
De more endearèd is de pleasure height.
MALHEUREUX. What, you're a learned wanton, and proceed by art!
FRANCESCHINA. Go, little vag! Pleasure should have a crane's long neck,
To relish de ambrosia of delight.
And ick pridee tell me,

---

20 s.d. *Cantat . . . cithera*: she sings and dances to the cittern (lute-like instrument).
23 *trat*: troth.
29 *wenches*: i.e. wenchers.
30 *sallow*: swallow.
32 *comfits*: sugarplums (or similarly preserved fruits).
34–5 paraphrased from Montaigne, III, v, 110.
37–8 adapted from Montaigne, III, v. 109.

For me loves to hear of manhood very mush,
I'fait, ick pridee – vat vas me a-saying? –
O, ick pridee tell-a me,
How did you kill-a Mettre Freevill?

MALHEUREUX. Why, quarrelled o' set purpose, drew him out,
Singled him, and having the advantage
Of my sword and might, ran him through and through.

FRANCESCHINA. Vat did you vid him van he was sticken?

MALHEUREUX. I dragged him by the heels to the next wharf
And spurned him in the river.

Those in ambush rusheth forth and take him.

SIR LIONEL. Seize, seize him! O monstrous! O ruthless villain!

MALHEUREUX. What mean you, gentlemen? By heaven –

TYSEFEW. Speak not of anything that's good.

MALHEUREUX. Your errors gives you passion; Freevill lives.

SIR LIONEL. Thy own lips say thou liest.

MALHEUREUX. Let me die
If at Shatewe's the jeweller he lives not safe untouched.

TYSEFEW. Meantime to strictest guard, to sharpest prison.

MALHEUREUX. No rudeness, gentlemen: I'll go undragged.
O wicked, wicked devil!

Exit [*with Officers*].

SIR LIONEL. Sir, the day
Of trial is this morn. Let's prosecute
The sharpest rigour and severest end:
Good men are cruel when they're vice's friend.

---

45 *Singled him*: separated him from the others (hunting term).

49 *spurned*: kicked.

SIR HUBERT. Woman, we thank thee with no empty hand;
[*Gives money.*]
Strumpets are fit, fit for something. Farewell.
All save FREEVILL *depart.*

FREEVILL. Ay, for hell!
O thou unreprievable, beyond all
Measure of grace damned immediately!
That things of beauty created for sweet use,
Soft comfort, and as the very music of life,
Custom should make so unutterably hellish!
O heaven,
What difference is in women and their life!
What man, but worthy name of man, would leave
The modest pleasures of a lawful bed,
The holy union of two equal hearts,
Mutually holding either dear as health,
The undoubted issues, joys of chaste sheets,
The unfeigned embrace of sober ignorance,
To twine the unhealthful loins of common loves,
The prostituted impudence of things
Senseless like those by cataracts of Nile,
Their use so vile takes away sense! How vile
To love a creature made of blood and hell,
Whose use makes weak, whose company doth shame,
Whose bed doth beggar, issue doth defame!

[*Re-*]*enter* FRANCESCHINA.

FRANCESCHINA. Mettre Freevill live! Ha, ha! Live at Mestre Shatewe's! Mush at Mettre Shatewe's! Freevill is dead; Malheureux sall hang; and, sweet divil! dat Beatrice would but run mad, dat she would but run mad, den me would dance and sing. [*To* FREEVILL] Mettre Don Dubon, me pray ye now go to Mestress

---

64–84 Freevill's position is now surprisingly close to that of Malheureux in their first exchange (I.i. 106–17).

90–1 *Mettre . . . Dubon*: Freevill's name as a 'stranger' (cf. IV.iii.48); the name chosen (French *du bon*) ironically points to his virtuous identity.

Beatrice; tell her Freevill is sure dead, and dat he curse herself especially, for dat he was sticked in her quarrel, swearing in his last gasp dat if it had bin in mine quarrels 'twould never have grieved him.

FREEVILL. I will.

FRANCESCHINA. Pridee do, and say anyting dat vill vex her.

FREEVILL. Let me alone to vex her.

FRANCESCHINA. Vill you ? Vill you mak-a her run mad? Here, take dis ring; say me scorn to wear anyting dat was hers or his. I pridee torment her. Ick cannot love her; she honest and virtuous, forsooth!

FREEVILL. Is she so? O vile creature! Then let me alone with her.

FRANCESCHINA. Vat, vill you mak-a her mad? Seet, by min trat, be pretta servan! Bush! Ick sall go to bet now. [*Exit.*]

FREEVILL. Mischief, whither wilt thou? O thou tearless woman!
How monstrous is thy devil! the end of hell as thee!
How miserable were it to be virtuous,
If thou couldst prosper!
I'll to my love, the faithful Beatrice;
She has wept enough, and, faith, dear soul, too much.
But yet how sweet it is to think how dear
One's life was to his love: how mourned his death!
'Tis joy not to be expressed with breath.
But, O, let him that would such passion drink
Be quiet of his speech, and only think. *Exit.*

SCENE II

Enter BEATRICE *and* CRISPINELLA.

---

109 *Bush*: buss.
112 *as thee:* is as thee.

BEATRICE. Sister, cannot a woman kill herself?
Is it not lawful to die when we should not live?
CRISPINELLA. O sister, 'tis a question not for us; we must do what God will.
BEATRICE. What God will! Alas, can torment be
His glory, or our grief His pleasure? Does not the nurse's nipple, juiced over with wormwood, bid the child it should not suck? And does not heaven, when it hath made our breath bitter unto us, say we should not live? O my best sister,
To suffer wounds when one may 'scape this rod
Is against nature, that is, against God.
CRISPINELLA. Good sister, do not make me weep. Sure Freevill was not false:
I'll gage my life that strumpet, out of craft
And some close second end, hath maliced him.
BEATRICE. O sister, if he were not false, whom have I lost!
If he were, what grief to such unkindness!
From head to foot I am all misery;
Only in this, some justice I have found:
My grief is like my love, beyond all bound.

Enter NURSE [PUTIFER].

PUTIFER. My servant, Master Caqueteur, desires to visit you.
CRISPINELLA. For grief's sake, keep him out! His discourse is like the long word *Honorificabilitudinitatibus*: a great deal of sound and no sense. His company is like a parenthesis to a discourse: you may admit it, or leave it out, it makes no matter.
[*Exit* NURSE.]

Enter FREEVILL *in his* [*disguise*].

FREEVILL. By your leave, sweet creatures.

---

26 *Honorificabilitudinitatibus*: Medieval Latin ablative/dative plural and famous as the longest word known. It was used by Nashe in *Lenten Stuff* and Shakespeare in *Love's Labour's Lost*, V.i.38–9, to mock the ridiculously inflated jargon of some professions.

CRISPINELLA. Sir, all I can yet say of you is you are uncivil.

FREEVILL. You must deny it. [*To* BEATRICE]
By your sorrow's leave,
I bring some music to make sweet your grief.

BEATRICE. Whate'er you please. O, break my heart!
Canst thou yet pant? O, dost thou yet survive?
Thou didst not love him if thou now canst live.

FREEVILL. (*sings*)

O Love, how strangely sweet
Are thy weak passions,
That love and joy should meet
In selfsame fashions!
O, who can tell
The cause why this should move?
But only this,
No reason ask of love!

[BEATRICE] *swoons.*

CRISPINELLA. Hold, peace! The greatest soul is swooned. – O my best sister!

FREEVILL. Ha! get you gone, close the doors. – My Beatrice!

Discovers himself.

Cursed be my indiscreet trials! O my immeasurably loving!

CRISPINELLA. She stirs; give air! she breathes.

BEATRICE. Where am I, ha? How have I slipped off life?
Am I in heaven? O my lord, though not loving,
By our eternal being, yet give me leave
To rest by thy dear side. Am I not in heaven?

FREEVILL. O eternally much loved, recollect your spirits!

BEATRICE. Ha, you do speak! I do see you; I do live!
I would not die now. Let me not burst with wonder!

FREEVILL. Call up your blood; I live to honour you

---

40 *weak*: causing weakness.

50 s.d. *Discovers himself*: removes his disguise.

As the admirèd glory of your sex.
Nor ever hath my love been false to you;
Only I presumed to try your faith too much,
For which I most am grieved.

CRISPINELLA. Brother, I must be plain with you: you have wronged us.

FREEVILL. I am not so covetous to deny it;
But yet, when my discourse hath stayed your quaking,
You will be smoother-lipped; and the delight
And satisfaction which we all have got
Under these strange disguisings, when you know,
You will be mild and quiet, forget at last.
It is much joy to think on sorrows past.

BEATRICE. Do you, then, live? and are you not untrue?
Let me not die with joy! Pleasure's more extreme
Than grief; there's nothing sweet to man but mean.

FREEVILL. Heaven cannot be too gracious to such goodness.
I shall discourse to you the several chances;
But, hark, I must yet rest disguised.
[*Reassumes disguise.*]
The sudden close of many drifts now meet;
Where pleasure hath some profit, art is sweet.

Enter TYSEFEW.

TYSEFEW. News, news, news, news!

CRISPINELLA. Oysters, oysters, oysters, oysters!

TYSEFEW. Why, is not this well now? Is not this

---

69 *smoother-lipped*: more polite.
76 *mean*: i.e. the 'golden mean' of Aristotelian moral philosophy.
78 *discourse . . . chances*: explain how everything fell out.
80 *drifts*: plots.
81 *Where . . . sweet*: suggests a mean between the extremes of instruction and delight which the Prologue (line 8) seemingly opposes.
83 *Oysters*: Crispinella mockingly treats Tysefew's interruption as though it were a London street cry.
84–95 rough paraphrase of Montaigne, II, xxxv, 474.

better than louring and pouting and puling, which is hateful to the living and vain to the dead? Come, come, you must live by the quick, when all is done; and for my own part, let my wife laugh at me when I am dead, so she'll smile upon me whilst I live. But to see a woman whine, and yet keep her eyes dry; mourn, and yet keep her cheeks fat; nay, to see a woman claw her husband by the feet when he is dead, that would have scratched him by the face when he was living – this now is somewhat ridiculous.

CRISPINELLA. Lord, how you prate!

TYSEFEW. And yet I was afraid, i'faith, that I should ha' seen a garland on this beauty's hearse; but time, truth, experience, and variety are great doers with women.

CRISPINELLA. But what's the news? The news, I pray you.

TYSEFEW. I pray you! Ne'er pray me, for by your leave you may command me. This 'tis:
The public sessions, which this day is past,
Hath doomed to death ill-fortuned Malheureux.

CRISPINELLA. But, sir, we heard he offered to make good
That Freevill lived at Shatewe's the jeweller's –

BEATRICE. And that 'twas but a plot betwixt them two.

TYSEFEW. O, ay, ay, he gaged his life with it; but know,
When all approached the test, Shatewe denied
He saw or heard of any such complot,
Or of Freevill; so that his own defence
Appeared so false that, like a madman's sword,
He struck his own heart. He hath the course of law
And instantly must suffer. But the jest
(If hanging be a jest, as many make it)
Is to take notice of one Mulligrub,
A sharking vintner.

---

97 *quick*: living.

106 *ill-fortuned*: play on the literal translation of the name of 'Malheureux'.

112 *complot*: conspiracy.

FREEVILL. What of him, sir?
TYSEFEW. Nothing but hanging. The whoreson slave is mad before he hath lost his senses.
FREEVILL. Was his fact clear and made apparent, sir?
TYSEFEW. No, faith, suspicious; for 'twas thus protested:
A cloak was stol'n; that cloak he had; he had it,
Himself confessed, by force. The rest of his defence
The choler of a justice wronged in wine,
Joined with malignance of some hasty jurors,
Whose wit was lighted by the justice' nose;
The knave was cast.
But, Lord, to hear his moan, his prayers, his wishes,
His zeal ill-timed, and his words unpitièd,
Would make a dead man rise and smile,
Whilst he observed how fear can make men vile.
CRISPINELLA. Shall we go meet the execution?
BEATRICE. I shall be ruled by you.
TYSEFEW. By my troth, a rare motion. You must haste,
For malefactors goes like the world, upon wheels.
BEATRICE. Will you man us? [*To* FREEVILL]
You shall be our guide.
FREEVILL. I am your servant.
TYSEFEW. Ha, servant! Zounds, I am no companion for panders! You're best make him your love.
BEATRICE. So will I, sir; we must live by the quick, you say.

---

123 *fact*: guilt, crime.
129 *Whose . . . nose*: the choleric appearance of the wine-soaked judge's nose inflamed the jurymen to return a guilty verdict.
130 *cast*: condemned.
137 *motion*: (1) proposal; (2) movement ('Shall we go . . .?', line 135); (3) puppet-play (alluding to their dialogue in III.i.160 ff.).
138 *wheels*: i.e. those of the execution cart; 'to go upon wheels' is to hurry.
139 *man us*: squire us.

TYSEFEW. 'Sdeath o' virtue! What a damned thing's this!
Who'll trust fair faces, tears, and vows? 'Sdeath, not I!
She is a woman – that is, she can lie.

CRISPINELLA. Come, come, turn not a man o' the time, to make all ill
Whose goodness you conceive not, since the worst of chance
Is to crave grace for heedless ignorance.

Exeunt.

SCENE III

Enter COCLEDEMOY *like a Sergeant.*

COCLEDEMOY. So, I ha' lost my sergeant in an ecliptic mist. Drunk, horrible drunk! He is fine! So now will I fit myself. I hope this habit will do me no harm. I am an honest man already. Fit, fit, fit as a punk's tail, that serves everybody. By this time my vintner thinks of nothing but hell and sulphur; he farts fire and brimstone already. Hang toasts! the execution approacheth.

Enter SIR LIONEL, SIR HUBERT, MALHEUREUX *pinioned,* TYSEFEW, BEATRICE, FREEVILL, CRISPINELLA, FRANCESCHINA, *and* [*Officers with*] *halberds.*

MALHEUREUX. I do not blush, although condemned by laws.
No kind of death is shameful but the cause,
Which I do know is none; and yet my lust

---

149 *lie*: bawdy pun.
150 *turn . . . ill*: don't follow the cynical fashion of libelling everyone.
V.iii s.d. *Sergeant*: officer charged with carrying out court summonses.
2 *ecliptic mist*: i.e. a mist of alcohol which has eclipsed his reason.
5 *Fit*: it fits as well as.

Hath made the one (although not cause) most just.
May I not be reprieved? Freevill is but mislodged;
Some lethargy hath seized him – no, much malice.
Do not lay blood upon your souls with good intents;
Men may do ill, and law sometime repents.

COCLEDEMOY *picks* MALHEUREUX' *pocket of his purse.*

SIR LIONEL. Sir, sir, prepare; vain is all lewd defence.

MALHEUREUX. Conscience was law, but now law's conscience.
My endless peace is made, and to the poor –
My purse, my purse!

COCLEDEMOY. Ay, sir, and it shall please you, the poor has your purse already.

MALHEUREUX. You are a wily man.
[*To* FRANCESCHINA] But now, thou source of devils, O, how I loathe
The very memory of that I adored!
He that's of fair blood, well-miened, of good breeding,
Best famed, of sweet acquaintance and true friends,
And would with desperate impudence lose all these,
And hazard landing at this fatal shore,
Let him ne'er kill nor steal, but love a whore!

FRANCESCHINA. De man does rave. Tink o' Got, tink o' Got, and bid de flesh, de world, and the dibil farewell.

MALHEUREUX. Farewell.

FREEVILL. Farewell.

FRANCESCHINA. Vat is't you say? Ha!

FREEVILL *discovers himself.*

FREEVILL. Sir, your pardon; with my this defence,

---

13 *mislodged*: misplaced.
17 *lewd*: poor, sorry.

Do not forget protested violence
Of your low affections; no requests,
No arguments of reason, no known danger,
No assurèd wicked bloodiness,
Could draw your heart from this damnation.
MALHEUREUX. Why, stay!
FRANCESCHINA. Unprosperous divil! vat sall me do now?
FREEVILL. Therefore, to force you from the truer danger,
I wrought the feignèd, suffering this fair devil
In shape of woman to make good her plot;
And, knowing that the hook was deeply fast,
I gave her line at will, till with her own vain strivings
See here she's tired. O thou comely damnation,
Dost think that vice is not to be withstood?
O, what is woman merely made of blood!
SIR LIONEL. You 'maze us all; let us not be lost in darkness.
FREEVILL. All shall be lighted, but this time and place
Forbids longer speech; only what you can think
Has been extremely ill is only hers.
SIR LIONEL. To severest prison with her –
With what heart canst live? what eyes behold a face?
FRANCESCHINA. Ick vill not speak; torture, torture your fill,
For me am worse than hanged: me ha' lost my will.
Exit FRANCESCHINA *with the guard.*
SIR LIONEL. To the extremest whip and gaol!
FREEVILL. Frolic, how is it, sir?
MALHEUREUX. I am myself. How long was't ere I could
Persuade my passion to grow calm to you!

---

38 *protested*: declared, confessed.
41 *assurèd . . . bloodiness*: i.e. the clearly revealed bloodthirstiness of Franceschina.
50 *tired*: (1) pulled in; (2) exhausted (like a played-out fish).
52 *merely . . . blood*: composed only of passion.
60 *will*: obscene pun on 'will' = penis.

Rich sense makes good bad language, and a friend
Should weigh no action, but the action's end.
I am now worthy yours, when, before,
The beast of man, loose blood, distempered us.
He that lust rules cannot be virtuous.

Enter MULLIGRUB, MISTRESS MULLIGRUB, *and* OFFICERS.

OFFICER. On afore there! Room for the prisoners!

MULLIGRUB. I pray you, do not lead me to execution through Cheapside. I owe Master Burnish, the goldsmith, money, and I fear he'll set a sergeant on my back for it.

COCLEDEMOY. Trouble not your sconce, my Christian brother, but have an eye unto the main chance. I will warrant your shoulders; as for your neck, Plinius Secundus, or Marcus Tullius Cicero, or somebody it is, says that a threefold cord is hardly broken.

MULLIGRUB. Well, I am not the first honest man that hath been cast away, and I hope shall not be the last.

COCLEDEMOY. O sir, have a good stomach and maws; you shall have a joyful supper.

MULLIGRUB. In troth, I have no stomach to it; and it please you, take my trencher; I use to fast at nights.

MISTRESS MULLIGRUB. O husband, I little thought you should have come to think on God

---

68 *distempered*: 'deranged', or perhaps here 'destroyed our temperamental affinity'.

72–4 *I . . . it*: Mulligrub's pathetic concern for proprieties derives from a story in Montaigne, I, xl, 270; the exchange with Cocledemoy (84–88) is drawn from the same passage.

75 *sconce*: pate.

78–80 *Plinius . . . broken*: Cocledemoy's parade of erudition is characteristically inaccurate: the proverb is from Ecclesiastes, 4:12, as Marston's audience would have known.

85 *maws*: jaws.

87 *trencher*: platter of wood or metal.

thus soon. Nay, and you had been hanged deservedly, it would never have grieved me; I have known of many honest, innocent men have been hanged deservedly – but to be cast away for nothing!

COCLEDEMOY. Good woman, hold your peace, your prittles and your prattles, your bibbles and your babbles; for I pray you hear me in private. I am a widower, and you are almost a widow; shall I be welcome to your houses, to your tables, and your other things?

MISTRESS MULLIGRUB. I have a piece of mutton and a feather-bed for you at all times. [*To* MULLIGRUB] I pray, make haste.

MULLIGRUB. I do here make my confession: if I owe any man anything, I do heartily forgive him; if any man owe me anything, let him pay my wife.

COCLEDEMOY. I will look to your wife's payment, I warrant you.

MULLIGRUB. And now, good yoke-fellow, leave thy poor Mulligrub.

MISTRESS MULLIGRUB. Nay, then I were unkind, i'faith; I will not leave you until I have seen you hang.

COCLEDEMOY. But brother, brother, you must think of your sins and iniquities. You have been a broacher of profane vessels; you have made us drink of the juice of the whore of Babylon; for whereas good ale, perries, braggets, ciders, and

---

91–5 *Nay . . . nothing*: Mrs Mulligrub's comic indignation recalls that of Socrates' wife, as recorded by Montaigne, II, xii, 300.

102 *piece of mutton*: cf. 'piece of flesh' (III.iii.29); 'mutton' is cant for whore.

112 *unkind*: unnatural.

115 ff. Cocledemoy performs a mock-sermon in Puritan style.

117 *broacher . . . vessels*: obscene *double entendre*; 'vessels' = (1) wine casks; (2) (women's) bodies.

118 *juice . . . Babylon*: (1) Italian (and therefore Popish) wine; (2) obscene innuendo.

119 *perries*: plural of 'perry', a drink made from fermented pear-juice.

119 *braggets*: ales fermented with honey.

metheglins was the true ancient British and Trojan drinks, you ha' brought in Popish wines, Spanish wines, French wines, *tam Marti quam Mercurio*, both muscadine and malmsey, to the subversion, staggering, and sometimes overthrow of many a good Christian. You ha' been a great jumbler. O, remember the sins of your nights, for your night works ha' been unsavoury in the taste of your customers.

MULLIGRUB. I confess, I confess, and I forgive as I would be forgiven. Do you know one Cocledemoy?

COCLEDEMOY. O, very well. Know him! An honest man he is, and a comely, an upright dealer with his neighbours, and their wives speak good things of him.

MULLIGRUB. Well, wheresoe'er he is, or whatsoe'er he is, I'll take it on my death he's the cause of my hanging. I heartily forgive him; and if he would come forth he might save me, for he only knows the why and the wherefore.

COCLEDEMOY. You do, from your hearts and midriffs and entrails, forgive him, then? You will not let him rot in rusty irons, procure him to be hanged in lousy linen without a song, and, after he is dead, piss on his grave?

MULLIGRUB. That hard heart of mine has procured all this, but I forgive as I would be forgiven.

COCLEDEMOY. Hang toasts, my worshipful Mulligrub! Behold thy Cocledemoy, my fine vintner, my catastrophonical fine boy, behold and see! [*Discovers himself.*]

---

120 *metheglins*: strong meads.
121 *Trojan*: referring to the myth that Britain was founded by the Trojan exile, Brutus, as a new Troy.
122–3 *tam . . . Mercurio*: as much for war (Mars) as for trade (Mercury); motto of the poet George Gascoigne.
123 *muscadine and malmsey*: sweet, fortified wines.
126 *jumbler*: adulterator of wine; but 'to jumble' is also 'to have intercourse'; Cocledemoy continues his bawdy quibbling through 'overthrow . . . jumbler . . . sins of your nights . . . night works . . . customers'.

TYSEFEW. Bliss o' the blessed, who would but look for two knaves here!

COCLEDEMOY. No knave, worshipful friend, no knave; for, observe, honest Cocledemoy restores whatsoever he has got, to make you know that whatsoe'er he has done has been only *euphoniae gratia* – for wit's sake: I acquit this vintner as he has acquitted me. All has been done for emphasis of wit, my fine boy, my worshipful friends.

TYSEFEW. Go, you are a flattering knave.

COCLEDEMOY. I am so; 'tis a good thriving trade. It comes forward better than the seven liberal sciences or the nine cardinal virtues; which may well appear in this: you shall never have flattering knave turn courtier, and yet I have read of many courtiers that have turned flattering knaves.

SIR HUBERT. Was't even but so? Why, then, all's well.

MULLIGRUB. I could even weep for joy!

MISTRESS MULLIGRUB. I could weep, too, but God knows for what!

TYSEFEW. Here's another tack to be given – your son and daughter.

SIR HUBERT. Is't possible? Heart, ay, all my heart, will you be joined here?

TYSEFEW. Yes, faith, father; marriage and hanging are spun both in one hour.

158–9 *euphoniae gratia*: for the sake of euphony; Cocledemoy (perhaps through a confused association with *Euphues: The Anatomy of Wit*) mistranslates.

165 *comes forward*: flourishes.

165–6 *seven . . . sciences*: the seven subjects of the medieval university curriculum: grammar, logic and rhetoric (the *trivium*); arithmetic, geometry, music, astronomy (the *quadrivium*).

166 *nine . . . virtues*: properly seven: justice, prudence, temperance, fortitude ('the natural virtues'); faith, hope and charity ('the theological virtues').

176 *tack*: joining, match.

180–1 *marriage . . . hour*: proverbial, Tilley, W232.

COCLEDEMOY. Why, then my worshipful good friends, I bid myself most heartily welcome to your merry nuptials and wanton jigga-joggies.
[*Coming forward and addressing the audience.*]
And now, my very fine Heliconian gallants, and, you, my worshipful friends in the middle region:
If with content our hurtless mirth hath been,
Let your pleased minds at our much care be seen;
For he shall find, that slights such trivial wit,
'Tis easier to reprove than better it.
We scorn to fear, and yet we fear to swell;
We do not hope 'tis best: 'tis all, if well.
Exeunt.

Finis.

185 *Heliconian*: Mount Helicon was the home of the Muses; the actor playing Cocledemoy steps out of his part to deliver a formal epilogue.

186 *middle region*: there is no general agreement as to whether this refers to the pit (Walley), the galleries (Wine), the middle gallery of three (Gurr), or the audience in general (Davison); in any case it offers a last opportunity for indecent suggestiveness.

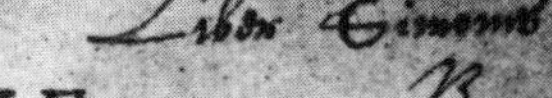

THE

VVONDER

of VVomen

Or

The Tragedie of Sophonisba

as it hath beene sundry times Acted at the *Blacke Friers.*

Written by IOHN MARSTON

LONDON.

Printed by *Iohn Windet* and are to be sold neere *Ludgate.*

1606.

Title-page of the 1606 Quarto of *Sophonisba* in the Bodleian Library, shelfmark Malone 186 (1)

INTRODUCTORY NOTE

Eleazer Edgar entered *The Wonder of Women, or The Tragedy of Sophonisba* in the Stationers' Register on 17 March 1606, and in the same year a Quarto was printed by John Windet. The composition, press-work and proof-reading of this Quarto have been analysed by William Kemp in the introduction to his accurate old-spelling edition (New York: Garland, 1979). Kemp, collating fifteen of the eighteen known copies, found some sixty press-variants in formes C (i), D (o), E (i), E (o), F (o), and G (o), with E (o) existing in four states and F (o) in no fewer than five. One copy, in the National Library of Scotland, has a cancel title-page, omitting the first title, *The Wonder of Women*, and the reference to performance at the Blackfriars. None of the press-corrections that can be accepted without hesitation (straightforward emendations of typographical mistakes) would have required re-examination of the manuscript, and since the corrector made some demonstrably bad guesses, his most interesting substitutions must be viewed with distrust (see the Textual Notes on IV.i.128, 130, V.ii.81). Kemp shows that the text was probably set by three compositors, one at work on every sheet and solely responsible for sheet D, a second helping out with sheets B and C, and a third playing a similar subsidiary role in sheets E–G. The first few sheets seem to have been the most carefully set (or the most diligently corrected before press-work began).

Sophonisba is entirely in verse, and Marston has for this tragedy adopted the neo-classical and Jonsonian practice of placing speech prefixes within the line when a new speech continues a pentameter. So, except for a few patches of minor disorder near stage directions, the verse yields few problems of lineation. The elaborate stage directions evince an author's solicitude over the theatrical presentation of his play, and the prefatory matter (including the signed note 'To the General Reader') likewise points to the Quarto's having been set from specially prepared holograph. It is divided into acts and scenes, though there is no scene-heading for V.iv; the end of each act is indicated by the formula 'Actus Primi./FINIS.', and so on.

The present text has been prepared from one of the two Bodleian Library copies, Malone 186 (1); but the other, Malone 252 (7), has also been consulted, and Kemp's collation of all available copies of Q has provided further information about press-variants. Ours is the only modern-spelling edition of *Sophonisba* except Bullen's, which is eclectic in adopting readings from Q or 1633, as though they were of equal authority. In fact, even 1633's emendation at II.iii.108, which Kemp praises as 'a brilliant improvement over a garbled quarto reading' (p. 39), is just a guess, and in our view an erroneous one.

The chief sources of the action and characters in Marston's tragedy were the accounts of the Second Punic War in Livy's *History of Rome* and Appian's *Roman History*. Livy had been translated into English by Philemon Holland in 1600, and Appian by 'W.B.' in 1578. The witch Erictho is developed from an unrelated classical text, Book VI of Lucan's *Pharsalia*. For the verbal encapsulation of pertinent ideas and attitudes Marston is heavily indebted to Florio's Montaigne, and Kemp examines the influence of Seneca and Machiavelli. Kemp seems right in asserting that no known sixteenth-century dramatisation of Sophonisba's story had any significant effect on Marston, but that he probably read the *Sophonisbe* of Nicolas de Montreux, whose romance *Les Bergeries de Juliette* (1585) is a major source for *The Dutch Courtesan*; Montreux's *Sophonisbe* (1601) affords in Gelosses a counterpart to Marston's unhistorical Gelosso.

In the general outline of his plot Marston adheres fairly closely to Appian, but the ending of the play – in particular Massinissa's vow to protect Sophonisba and his distraction on receiving the command to surrender her to Scipio – seems to be modified by Livy. In Livy's account, however, Massinissa does not fall in love with Sophonisba until after the capture of Syphax; he marries her, but Scipio's hostility drives him to offer her poison before the marriage is consummated. Neither source affords any precedent for Marston's idealising of Sophonisba as a Stoic martyr; Appian calls her 'a worthless woman', and it is only in her death that Livy finds anything to admire, speaking of her 'high spirit' and the 'fearless way in which, without the slightest trepidation, she drank the poison'. John Orrell has speculated that Marston was influenced by the more forthright praise of a marginal note to the 1578 English translation of Appian – 'she dieth like a noble-hearted lady' – to present Sophonisba as the blameless heroine of an essentially 'Roman' tragedy. Indeed, for all the play's exotic African setting, it would appear (from Marston's address to the reader) to have been written in deliberate competition with Jonson's *Sejanus* (performed 1603, printed 1605); and in the character of its heroine it looks back to the Portia of Shakespeare's *Julius Caesar*, and beyond that to his *Lucrece*, though its general effect is perhaps closer to the emotional heroics of Caroline tragedy. Marston's other major alterations to his sources – the blackening of Syphax, who actually died of grief in Rome, the elaboration of Hasdrubal's attempted poisoning of the hero, and the climactic single combat of Massinissa and Syphax – are all designed to reinforce the heroic impression proper to a tragedy of stoical resistance in the 'Roman' style.

Caputi argues that 'despite the Stationers' entry, *Sophonisba* was neither produced nor published until the spring or summer [of 1606]', having been composed during the second half of 1605 and early in 1606 (p. 269). Since the title-page does not refer to the Blackfriars actors as 'The Children of the Queen's Revels', he concludes that the play was acted after the queen's patronage had been withdrawn from the Blackfriars children early in 1606. Marston pre-announced *Sophonisba* in a prefatory note to the second edition of *The Fawn*, which had first been entered in the Stationers' Register on 12 March 1606.

The play's first performance season may well have been its last: though the evidence of such plays as Ford's *The Broken Heart* and Massinger's *The Emperor of the East* would suggest that the Caroline dramatists were familiar with *Sophonisba*, there is no record of any revival before 1642; and though Wood and others have seen it as a forerunner of Restoration tragedy, it evidently excited no particular interest after 1660, Nathaniel Lee's tragedy of the same name (1676) being apparently quite independent of it. There is no sign that this neglect is about to be remedied. While several critics have concurred in Eliot's opinion that *Sophonisba* is Marston's best play, the theatre has remained sceptical.

Yet the success of recent revivals of *The Broken Heart* and *Perkin Warbeck* suggests that the austerely monumental character of this Jacobean precursor need prove no bar to its theatrical resurrection.

[PREFATORY MATERIAL TO THE FIRST EDITION]

TO THE GENERAL READER

Know that I have not laboured in this poem to tie myself to relate anything as an historian, but to enlarge everything as a poet. To transcribe authors, quote authorities, and translate Latin prose orations into English blank verse, hath, in this subject, been the least aim of my studies. Then, equal reader, peruse me with no prepared dislike, and if aught shall displease thee, thank thyself, if aught shall please thee, thank not me, for I confess in this it was not my only end. Jo[hn] Marston.

ARGUMENTUM

A grateful heart's just height; ingratitude
And vow's base breach with worthy shame
pursued;
A woman's constant love, as firm as fate;
A blameless counsellor well born for state;
The folly to enforce free love: these, know,
This subject with full light doth amply show.

3–5 *To . . . verse*: a glance at Jonson's *Sejanus*, for whose publication in 1605 Marston had contributed encomiastic verses.

7 *studies*: the dignified term indicates the seriousness with which Marston, despite his repudiation of Jonson's scholarly method, intends his own version of classical tragedy to be taken.

7 *equal*: just, unprejudiced.

9–11 *please . . . end*: Marston implies that here, in contrast to his comedies, his principal aim has been to instruct rather than to please; cf. *DC*, Prol. 8.

Argumentum: the 'argument' or subject-matter of the play.

1 *just height*: probably both 'proper loftiness' and 'high pitch of justified emotion'.

2 *vow's . . . pursued*: the base violation of a vow punished with well-deserved shame.

4 *well . . . state*: naturally fitted to the management of state affairs.

5 *free love*: love that is an expression of free will.

[DRAMATIS PERSONAE]

INTERLOCUTORES

MASSINISSA } *kings in Libya, rivals for* SOPHONISBA
SYPHAX
ASDRUBAL, *father to* SOPHONISBA
GELOSSO, *a senator of Carthage*
BYTHEAS, *a senator of Carthage*
HANNO MAGNUS, *captain for Carthage*
JUGURTH, MASSINISSA*'s nephew*
SCIPIO } *generals of Rome*
LAELIUS
VANGUE, *an Ethiopian slave*
CARTHALON, *a senator of Carthage*
GISCO, *a surgeon of Carthage*
NUNTIUS
SOPHONISBA, *daughter to* ASDRUBAL *of Carthage*
ZANTHIA, *her maid*
ERICTHO, *an enchantress*
ARCATHIA } *waiting-women to* SOPHONISBA.
NYCEA
[PAGES]
[BOYS]
[USHERS]
[ATTENDANTS]
[GUARD]

Dramatis Personae: from Q.
Massinissa: *c*. 240–148 B.C., king of the Eastern Numidian Massyles tribe; brought up at Carthage, he fought the Romans (212–206) until won over to the Roman side by Scipio.
Syphax: king of the Numidian Masaesyles people; hostile to Massinissa, he tried to maintain friendship with both Rome and Carthage, until converted to the Carthaginian cause by Sophonisba. After his defeat by Massinissa and Laelius he was imprisoned in Italy, where he died.
Asdrubal: Hasdrubal, third of four Carthaginian generals with this name. Led a Carthaginian army in Spain (214–206 B.C.), where, with Mago, he destroyed the forces of Publius Scipio in 211. After his defeat by Scipio Africanus he retreated to Africa where he was held responsible for the catastrophe of Campi Magni and committed suicide following charges of treason.
Hanno Magnus: leader of the anti-Hannibal peace party in Carthage.

Scipio: Publius Cornelius Scipio Africanus Major (236–183/4 B.C.), brilliant and innovative Roman general who, having established Roman power in Spain, carried the war into Africa, inflicting a series of defeats on the Carthaginians, culminating in the destruction of Hannibal's armies at Zama (202).
Laelius: Gaius Laelius, plebeian military commander who owed his advancement to his close friend, Scipio Africanus.
Nuntius: Messenger; the use of a Nuntius to narrate important off-stage actions is one of the devices by which Marston seeks to establish the classical credentials of his tragedy; compare Webster's apology for his omission of 'the passionate and weighty Nuntius' in his address 'To the Reader' of *The White Devil*.
Sophonisba: Livy's Sophoniba (properly Saphanba'al), daughter of Hasdrubal. Married to Syphax whom she won to Carthage; after her husband's defeat she committed suicide, reputedly with poison supplied by the enamoured Massinissa, in order to escape being taken to Italy for Scipio's triumph. 'Details of her story (e.g. that before her marriage to Syphax, she had been betrothed to Massinissa) may be false, but the outline need not be questioned' (*Oxford Classical Dictionary*).
Erictho: borrowed from Lucan's *Pharsalia*, Book VI, she has no equivalent in Marston's main sources.

PROLOGUS

Cornets sound a march.

Enter at one door the PROLOGUE, *two Pages with torches,* ASDRUBAL *and* JUGURTH, *two Pages with lights,* MASSINISSA *leading* SOPHONISBA, ZANTHIA *bearing* SOPHONISBA'*s train,* ARCATHIA *and* NYCEA, HANNO *and* BYTHEAS; *at the other door two Pages with targets and javelins, two Pages with lights,* SYPHAX *armed from top to toe;* VANGUE *follows.*

These, thus entered, stand still, whilst the PROLOGUE, *resting between both troops, speaks.*

The scene is Libya, and the subject thus:
Whilst Carthage stood the only awe of Rome,
As most imperial seat of Libya,
Governed by statesmen, each as great as kings
(For seventeen kings were Carthage' feodars);
Whilst thus she flourished, whilst her Hannibal
Made Rome to tremble, and the walls yet pale:
Then in this Carthage Sophonisba lived,
The far-famed daughter of Great Asdrubal;
For whom, 'mongst others, potent Syphax sues,
And well-graced Massinissa rivals him,
Both princes of proud sceptres; but the lot
Of doubtful favour Massinissa graced;
At which Syphax grows black; for now the night

---

s.d. *Cornets*: wooden instruments preferred in the indoor theatres to the more raucous trumpet.

s.d. *Enter . . . follows*: the dumb-show, opposing the wedding procession of Massinissa and Sophonisba to the martial entry of Syphax, prefigures the central conflict of the tragedy.

s.d. *lights*: presumably, in this case, candles, as opposed to the 'torches' carried by the first two pages.

s.d. *targets*: shields.

2 *only . . . Rome*: the only power feared by Rome.

5 *feodars*: vassals.

14 *black*: i.e. with melancholy rage.

Yields loud resoundings of the nuptial pomp:
Apollo strikes his harp, Hymen his torch,
Whilst louring Juno, with ill-boding eye,
Sits envious at too forward Venus. Lo,
The instant night; and now ye worthier minds,
To whom we shall present a female glory
(The wonder of a constancy so fixed,
That fate itself might well grow envious),
Be pleased to sit, such as may merit oil
And holy dew stilled from diviner heat;
For rest thus knowing: what of this you hear,
The author lowly hopes, but must not fear;
For just worth never rests on popular frown,
To have done well is fair deeds' only crown.
Nec se quaesiverit extra.

Cornets sound a march; the PROLOGUE *leads* MASSINISSA'*s troops over the stage, and departs;* SYPHAX' *troops only stay.*

---

16 *Apollo*: god of music and poetry.
16 *Hymen*: god of weddings.
17 *Juno*: Juno Pronuba, the goddess of married love.
18 *Venus*: goddess of erotic love.
19 *instant*: pressing, urgent, importunate.
20–1 *female . . . fixed*: carries through the emphasis of the title (*The Wonder of Women*) on the miracle of Sophonisba's virtue; the female sex was supposedly frail and inconstant by nature.
23–4 *oil . . . dew*: oil (the chrism, used in ritual anointing) and dew are traditional signs of divine blessing; here they stand for expressions of the poet's divine inspiration ('diviner heat').
24 *stilled*: distilled.
25 *rest . . . knowing*: rest in this knowledge.
25–6 *what . . .fear*: the author has small hopes that you will understand much of his play, but this causes him no distress.
29 *Nec . . . extra*: adapted from Persius, *Satires*, I, 7, where the context implies: 'nor will he have looked [for praise] to anyone outside himself'.

THE TRAGEDY OF SOPHONISBA

ACT I

SCENE I

SYPHAX *and* VANGUE.

SYPHAX. Syphax, Syphax, why wast thou cursed a king?
What angry god made thee so great, so vile
Contemned, disgracèd? Think, wert thou a slave,
Though Sophonisba did reject thy love,
Thy low neglected head unpointed at,
Thy shame unrumoured and thy suit unscoffed,
Might yet rest quiet. Reputation,
Thou awe of fools and great men, thou that chok'st
Freest addictions and mak'st mortals sweat
Blood and cold drops in fear to lose or hope
To gain thy never-certain seldom-worthy gracings,
Reputation,
Were't not for thee Syphax could bear this scorn,
Not spouting up his gall among his blood
In black vexations; Massinissa might
Enjoy the sweets of his preferrèd graces
Without my dangerous envy or revenge.
Were't not for thy affliction all might sleep

---

3 *Contemned*: scorned.

8–9 *chok'st . . . addictions*: overwhelms the noblest and most generous inclinations.

11 *seldom-worthy gracings*: i.e. reputation frequently adorns those who are least worthy of it.

14–15 *gall . . . vexations*: refers to the physiological doctrine of the four humours (blood, phlegm, choler and melancholy); the ideal balance of these substances is upset and the black bile of melancholy ('gall') pollutes the blood of Syphax's otherwise 'sanguine' temperament.

16 *preferrèd graces*: the benefits of social advancement.

18 *thy affliction*: the curse of reputation.

In sweet oblivion; but (O greatness' scourge!)
We cannot without envy keep high name,
Nor yet disgraced can have a quiet shame.
VANGUE. Scipio –
SYPHAX. Some light in depth of hell. Vangue, what hope?
VANGUE. I have received assured intelligence,
That Scipio, Rome's sole hope, hath raised up men,
Drawn troops together for invasion –
SYPHAX. Of this same Carthage?
VANGUE. With this policy:
To force wild Hannibal from Italy –
SYPHAX. And draw the war to Afric?
VANGUE. Right.
SYPHAX. And strike
This secure country with unthought-of arms.
VANGUE. My letters bear he is departed Rome,
Directly setting course and sailing up –
SYPHAX. To Carthage, Carthage! O thou eternal youth,
Man of large fame, great and abounding glory,
Renownful Scipio, spread thy two-necked eagles,
Fill full thy sails with a revenging wind,
Strike through obedient Neptune, till thy prows
Dash up our Libyan ooze, and thy just arms
Shine with amazeful terror on these walls!
O now record thy father's honoured blood

---

28 *Hannibal*: 247–183/2 B.C., great Carthaginian general who led his forces over the Alps (218 B.C.) to a series of stunning victories over the Romans on their own soil. Recalled to Africa in 203 and defeated by Scipio Africanus at Zama (202). Committed suicide to avoid falling into Roman hands in 183/2.

30 *unthought-of arms*: unexpected military attack.

31 *bear*: report.

35 *two-necked*: apparently an anachronistic reference to the double-headed eagle of the Holy Roman Empire.

39 *amazeful*: bewildering, stunning.

40 *record*: remember, think on.

40 *father's*: Cneius Cornelius Scipio, consul 222 B.C.; killed fighting Hasdrubal's army at Ilorci in Spain, 211 B.C.

Which Carthage drunk, thy uncle Publius' blood
Which Carthage drunk, thirty thousand souls
Of choice Italians Carthage set on wing.
Remember Hannibal, yet Hannibal,
The consul-queller. O then enlarge thy heart,
Be thousand souls in one! Let all the breath,
The spirit of thy name and nation, be mixed
    strong
In thy great heart! O fall like thunder-shaft,
The wingèd vengeance of incensèd Jove,
Upon this Carthage! for Syphax here flies off
From all allegiance, from all love or service,
His now free'd sceptre once did yield this city.
Ye universal gods, light, heat, and air,
Prove all unblessing Syphax, if his hands
Once rear themselves for Carthage but to curse
    it!
It had been better they had changed their faith,
Denied their gods, than slighted Syphax' love,
So fearfully will I take vengeance.
I'll interleague with Scipio. – Vangue,
Dear Ethiopian Negro, go wing a vessel,
And fly to Scipio: say his confederate,
Vowed and confirmed, is Syphax; bid him haste
To mix our palms and arms; will him make up,
Whilst we are in the strength of discontent,
Our unsuspected forces well in arms,
For Sophonisba, Carthage, Asdrubal,
Shall feel their weakness in preferring weakness,

---

41 *uncle Publius*: Publius Cornelius Scipio, younger brother of Cneius; consul 218 B.C. when he was defeated by Hannibal at the Trebia; led the Roman forces in Spain until his defeat and death on the upper Baetius in 211.

45 *queller*: killer, conqueror.

54 *Prove . . . unblessing*: deny all blessing to.

60 *wing*: set swift sails on (poetic usage).

63 *palms*: the palms of victory accorded to triumphant commanders.

63 *will*: request.

63 *make up*: either intrans. ('draw together his forces') or trans. ('add his number to our unsuspected forces').

67 *preferring*: both 'choosing' and 'giving preferment to'.

And one less great than we. To our dear wishes,
Haste, gentle Negro, that this heap may know
Me and their wrong.

VANGUE. Wrong?

SYPHAX. Ay, though 'twere not, yet know, while kings are strong,
What they'll but think, and not what is, is wrong.
I am disgraced in and by that which hath
No reason: love, and woman; my revenge
Shall therefore bear no argument of right;
Passion is reason when it speaks from might.
I tell thee, man, nor kings nor gods exempt,
But they grow pale if once they find contempt.
Haste!

Exeunt.

SCENE II

Enter ARCATHIA, NYCEA *with tapers,* SOPHONISBA *in her night attire, followed by* ZANTHIA.

SOPHONISBA. Watch at the doors; and till we be reposed
Let no one enter. Zanthia, undo me.

ZANTHIA. With this motto under your girdle:
You had been undone if you had not been undone.
Humblest service!

SOPHONISBA. I wonder, Zanthia, why the custom is

---

69 *heap*: rabble (perhaps anticipating the heaps of the slain).

70 *their wrong*: the wrong they have done me.

71–2 *while . . . wrong*: i.e. might makes right (a stock 'machiavellian' *sententia*).

75 *bear. . . right*: be subjected to no demonstrations of its rightness.

77–8 *I tell . . . contempt*: Syphax's attitude resembles that of Atreus in Seneca's *Thyestes* (Kemp).

4 *You . . . undone*: punning elaborately on four senses of 'undone': (1) ruined; (2) unbuttoned, unlaced; (3) deflowered; (4) 'un-done' = not copulated with.

To use such ceremony, such strict shape,
About us women. Forsooth the bride must steal
Before her lord to bed; and then delays,
Long expectations, all against known wishes.
I hate these figures in locution,
These about-phrases forced by ceremony.
We must still seem to fly what we most seek,
And hide ourselves from that we fain would
find us.
Let those that think and speak and do just acts,
Know form can give no virtue to their acts,
Nor detract vice.
ZANTHIA. 'Las, fair princess, those that are
strongly formed
And truly shaped, may naked walk, but we,
We things called women, only made for show
And pleasure, created to bear children
And play at shuttlecock, we imperfect mixtures,
Without respective ceremony used,
And ever compliment, alas, what are we?
Take from us formal custom and the courtesies
Which civil fashion hath still used to us,
We fall to all contempt. O women, how much,
How much are you beholding to ceremony!
SOPHONISBA. You are familiar. Zanthia, my shoe,
ZANTHIA. 'Tis wonder, madam, you tread not
awry.

---

7 *ceremony*: the elaborate customs of the bridal bedding, some of which are described in Puttenham, *The Art of English Poesy*, I, xxvi, included the pretence of barring the door against the bridegroom acted out below, lines 34 ff.

11 *figures in locution*: ceremonious figures of speech, courtly turns of phrase.

12 *about-phrases*: periphrasis, elegant circumlocution.

16–17 *form . . . vice*: ceremony can make their actions neither more virtuous nor more vicious than they naturally are.

22 *imperfect mixtures*: the idea is presumably that the proverbially unstable temperament of women reveals a less perfect mixture of the four humours than in the male constitution.

23–4 *Without . . . we*: what are we without the display of respectful ceremony and constant compliments?

26 *civil fashion*: the manners of polite society.

27 *We . . . contempt*: we become completely contemptible.

SOPHONISBA. Your reason. Zanthia.
ZANTHIA. You go very high.
SOPHONISBA. Hark, music, music!

The LADIES *lay the* PRINCESS *in a fair bed and close the curtains whilst* MASSINISSA *enters.*

NYCEA. The bridegroom!
ARCATHIA. The bridegroom!
SOPHONISBA. Haste, good Zanthia, help, keep yet the doors!
ZANTHIA. Fair fall you, lady; so, admit, admit.

Enter four Boys, anticly attired, with bows and quivers, dancing to the cornets a fantastic measure; MASSINISSA *in his night-gown, led by* ASDRUBAL *and* HANNO, *followed by* BYTHEAS *and* JUGURTH. *The Boys draw the curtains, discovering* SOPHONISBA, *to whom* MASSINISSA *speaks.*

MASSINISSA. You powers of joy, gods of a happy bed,
Show you are pleased; sister and wife of Jove,
High-fronted Juno, and thou Carthage' patron,
Smooth-chinned Apollo, both give modest heat
And temperate graces!

MASSINISSA *draws a white ribbon forth of the bed, as from the waist of* SOPHONISBA.

---

31 *go . . . high*: *double-entendre*: (1) walk on very high soles; (2) give yourself lofty airs.

32 s.d. *curtains*: either those of a four-poster placed on the stage, or those in front of the 'discovery space' in the façade of the tiring-house.

34 *keep . . . doors*: defend the doors (see above, note to line 7).

35 s.d. *Boys . . . quivers*: as befits a wedding masquerade, the boys are dressed as Cupids.

38 *High-fronted*: high-browed, noble (cf. Altofronto in *The Malcontent*).

39 *smooth-chinned*: Apollo, the god of reason, was traditionally represented as beardless, in contrast to his wild rival Dionysus.

40 s.d. *white ribbon*: the maiden-girdle worn by unmarried women, removed by the groom on the wedding night.

Lo, I unloose thy waist.
She that is just in love is godlike chaste.
Io to Hymen!

Chorus with cornets, organ, and voices: Io to Hymen!

SOPHONISBA. A modest silence, though't be thought
A virgin's beauty and her highest honour,
Though bashful feignings nicely wrought
Grace her that virtue takes not in, but on her,
What I dare think I boldly speak:
After my word my well-bold action rusheth.
In open flame then passion break!
Where virtue prompts, thought, word, act never blusheth.
Revenging gods, whose marble hands
Crush faithless men with a confounding terror,
Give me no mercy if these bands
I covet not with an unfeignèd fervour;
Which zealous vow when aught can force me t'lame,
Load with that plague Atlas would groan at, shame.
Io to Hymen!

Chorus: Io to Hymen!

ASDRUBAL. Live both high parents of so happy birth,
Your stems may touch the skies and shadow earth;

---

42 *Io:* Greek and Latin shout of triumph.
42 s.d. *Chorus*: songs 'sung very sweetly by musicians at the chamber door of the bridegroom and bride . . . were called *Epithalamies*' (Puttenham, *Art of English Poesy*).
42 s.d. *organ*: small portable instrument or 'portative organ'.
46 *virtue . . . her*: whose virtue is an outward show rather than inner reality.
47 *What . . . speak*: cf. Montaigne, III, v, 67.
48 *well-bold*: healthily frank and forward.
53 *these bands*: the bonds of matrimony.

Most great in fame, more great in virtue shining.
Prosper, O powers, a just, a strong divining.
Io to Hymen!

Chorus: Io to Hymen!

Enter CARTHALON, *his sword drawn, his body wounded, his shield struck full of darts;* MASSINISSA *being ready for bed.*

CARTHALON. To bold hearts, fortune! Be not you amazed,
Carthage, O Carthage, be not you amazed.
MASSINISSA. Jove made us not to fear; resolve, speak out;
The highest misery of man is doubt.
Speak, Carthalon.
CARTHALON. The stooping sun, like to some weaker prince,
Let his shades spread to an unnatural hugeness,
When we, the camp that lay at Utica,
From Carthage distant but five easy leagues,
Descried from off the watch three hundred sail,
Upon whose tops the Roman eagles stretched
Their large-spread wings, which fanned the evening air,
To us cold breath, for well we might discern
Rome swam to Carthage.
ASDRUBAL. Hannibal, our anchor is come back; thy sleight,
Thy stratagem, to lead war unto Rome,
To quit ourselves, hath taught now-desperate Rome
T'assail our Carthage: now the war is here.
MASSINISSA. He is nor blest nor honest that can fear.

---

63 ff. Carthalon fulfils the part of the Nuntius, the self-conscious classical imitation being deliberately emphasised by the Latinate periodic syntax of his speeches, the studied deployment of heroic simile (117–23), and the lofty style of his rhetoric.

77 *our . . . back*: the strategy designed to give us security has recoiled upon us (see Textual Note, p. 503 below).

79 *quit*: free, deliver.

HANNO. Ay, but to cast the worst of our distress –
MASSINISSA. To doubt of what shall be is
wretchedness.
Desire, fear, and hope receive no bond,
By whom we in ourselves are never but beyond.
On!
CARTHALON. Th'alarum beats necessity of fight.
Th'unsober evening draws out reeling forces,
Soldiers, half men, who to their colours troop
With fury, not with valour; whilst our ships
Unrigged, unused, fitter for fire than water,
We save in our barred haven from surprise.
By this our army marcheth toward the shore,
Undisciplined young men, most bold to do,
If they knew how, or what; when we descry
A mighty dust, beat up with horses' hooves;
Straight Roman ensigns glitter; Scipio –
ASDRUBAL. Scipio!
CARTHALON. Scipio, advancèd like the god of
blood,
Leads up grim war, that father of foul wounds,
Whose sinewy feet are steeped in gore, whose
hideous voice
Makes turrets tremble and whole cities shake;
Before whose brows flight and disorder hurry;
With whom march burnings, murder, wrong,
waste, rapes;
Behind whom a sad train is seen, woe, fears,
Tortures, lean need, famine, and helpless tears.
Now make we equal stand in mutual view.
We judged the Romans eighteen thousand foot,
Five thousand horse; we almost doubled them

---

82 *cast*: calculate.

83–5 *To . . . beyond*: paraphrased from Montaigne, I, iii, 25; the sense is 'it is a wretched state to be anxious about the future: there are no assurances to be had for desire, fear, or hope – emotions which prevent us from resting in ourselves by constantly projecting us into the future'.

87 *beats . . . of*: signals the need to.

88 *unsober*: drunken, intemperate, confused.

99–106 *Scipio . . . tears*: Scipio's advance is imaged as an allegorical pageant procession, a Triumph of Rapine.

In number, not in virtue; yet in heat
Of youth and wine, jolly and full of blood,
We gave the sign of battle: shouts are raised
That shook the heavens; pell-mell our armies join;
Horse, targets, pikes, all against each opposed,
They give fierce shock, arms thundered as they closed.
Men cover earth, which straight are coverèd
With men and earth; yet doubtful stood the fight,
More fair to Carthage, when lo, as oft you see
In mines of gold, when labouring slaves delve out
The richest ore, being in sudden hope
With some unlooked-for vein to fill their buckets,
And send huge treasure up, a sudden damp
Stifles them all, their hands yet stuffed with gold,
So fell our fortunes, for look as we stood proud
As hopeful victors, thinking to return
With spoils worth triumph, wrathful Syphax lands
With full ten thousand strong Numidian horse,
And joins to Scipio. Then lo, we all were damped;
We fall in clusters, and our wearied troops
Quit all. Slaughter ran through us straight; we fly,
Romans pursue, but Scipio sounds retreat,
As fearing trains and night. We make amain
For Carthage most, and some for Utica,
All for our lives. – New force, fresh arms with speed!
You have sad truth of all; no more: I bleed.

---

110 *virtue*: courage (Latin *virtus*), manly prowess (Italian: *virtù*).
115 *closed*: engaged in hand-to-hand combat.
124 *look as*: just as.
128 *damped*: discouraged, stupefied.
132 *trains*: tricks, stratagems, ambushes.

BYTHEAS. O wretched fortune! [*Tears his hair.*]
MASSINISSA. Old lord, spare thy hairs.
What, dost thou think baldness will cure thy grief?
What decree the Senate?

Enter GELOSSO *with commissions in his hand, sealed.*

GELOSSO. Ask old Gelosso, who returns from them,
Informed with fullest charge. Strong Asdrubal,
Great Massinissa, Carthage' general,
So speaks the Senate: counsel for this war
In Hanno Magnus, Bytheas, Carthalon,
And us Gelosso, rests. Embrace this charge,
You never yet dishonoured Asdrubal,
High Massinissa, by your vows to Carthage,
By god of great men, glory, fight for Carthage.
Ten thousand strong Massulians, ready trooped,
Expect their king; double that number waits
The leading of loved Asdrubal. Beat loud
Our Afric drums, and whilst our o'er-toiled foe
Snores on his unlaced casque, all faint, though proud
Through his successful fight, strike fresh alarms.
Gods are not, if they grace not bold, just arms.
MASSINISSA. Carthage, thou straight shalt know
Thy favours have been done unto a king.
Exit with ASDRUBAL *and the Page.*
SOPHONISBA. My lords, 'tis most unusual such sad haps
Of sudden horror should intrude 'mong beds
Of soft and private loves; but strange events
Excuse strange forms. O you that know our blood,
Revenge if I do feign: I here protest,
Though my lord leave his wife a very maid,
Even this night, instead of my soft arms
Clasping his well-strung limbs with glossful steel,
What's safe to Carthage shall be sweet to me.
I must not, nor I am once ignorant

---

137 *What . . . grief*: cf. Montaigne, I, iv, 34.

My choice of love hath given this sudden danger
To yet strong Carthage: 'twas I lost the fight;
My choice vexed Syphax, enraged Syphax struck
Arms' fate; yet Sophonisba not repents:
O we were gods if that we knew events.
But let my lord leave Carthage, quit his virtue,
I will not love him, yet must honour him,
As still good subjects must bad princes. Lords,
From the most ill-graced hymeneal bed
That ever Juno frowned at, I entreat
That you'll collect from our loose-formed speech
This firm resolve: that no low appetite
Of my sex' weakness can or shall o'ercome
Due grateful service unto you or virtue.
Witness, ye gods, I never until now
Repined at my creation; now I wish
I were no woman, that my arms might speak
My heart to Carthage. But in vain, my tongue
Swears I am woman still: I talk too long.

Cornets, a march. Enter two Pages with targets and javelins, two Pages with torches; MASSINISSA *armed cap-à-pie;* ASDRUBAL *armed.*

MASSINISSA. Ye Carthage lords, know Massinissa knows
Not only terms of honour, but his actions;
Nor must I now enlarge how much my cause
Hath dangered Carthage, but how I may show
Myself most prest to satisfaction.
The loathsome stain of kings, ingratitude,
From me O much be far! And since this torrent,

169–70 *struck Arms' fate*: determined the fate of battle.
177 *collect*: conclude, infer.
177 In this line, since Q prints 'formed' as 'form'd, 'our' may be disyllabic.
185 s.d. *Enter . . . torches*: visual echo of the prologue-tableau.
185 s.d. *cap-à-pie*: from head to foot (Old French).
187 *Not . . . actions*: not only the rhetoric of honour, but honourable action too.
188 *enlarge*: expatiate upon.
190 *prest to satisfaction*: ready to give satisfaction (for the danger I have caused).

War's rage, admits no anchor, since the billow
Is risen so high we may not hull, but yield
This ample state to stroke of speedy swords,
What you with sober haste have well decreed
We'll put to sudden arms; no, not this night,
These dainties, this first-fruits of nuptials,
That well might give excuse for feeble ling'rings,
Shall hinder Massinissa. Appetite,
Kisses, loves, dalliance, and what softer joys
The Venus of the pleasing'st ease can minister,
I quit you all. Virtue perforce is vice;
But he that may, yet holds, is manly wise.
Lo then, ye lords of Carthage, to your trust
I leave all Massinissa's treasure. By the oath
Of right good men stand to my fortune just.
Most hard it is for great hearts to mistrust.
CARTHALON. We vow by all high powers.
MASSINISSA. No, do not swear;
I was not born so small to doubt or fear.
SOPHONISBA. Worthy, my lord –
MASSINISSA. Peace, my ears are steel;
I must not hear thy much-enticing voice.
SOPHONISBA. By Massinissa, Sophonisba speaks
Worthy his wife: go with as high a hand
As worth can rear; I will not stay my lord.
Fight for our country; vent thy youthful heat
In fields, not beds; the fruit of honour, fame,
Be rather gotten than the oft disgrace
Of hapless parents, children. Go, best man,
And make me proud to be a soldier's wife,
That values his renown above faint pleasures.
Think every honour that doth grace thy sword
Trebles my love. By thee I have no lust
But of thy glory. Best lights of heaven with thee!

---

194 *hull*: drift to the wind with sails furled.
195 *ample state*: comfortable condition.
203–4 *Virtue . . . wise*: enforced virtue is no better than vice; the man who is in a position to indulge himself, and yet holds back, shows true manly wisdom.
207 *stand . . . just*: be just custodians of my fortune.
215 *stay*: stop.

Like wonder, stand or fall, so though thou die
My fortunes may be wretched, but not I.
MASSINISSA. Wondrous creature, even fit for gods, not men,
Nature made all the rest of thy fair sex
As weak essays, to make thee a pattern
Of what can be in woman! Long farewell.
He's sure unconquered in whom thou dost dwell,
Carthage' Palladium. See that glorious lamp,
Whose lifeful presence giveth sudden flight
To fancies, fogs, fears, sleep, and slothful night,
Spreads day upon the world: march swift amain;
Fame got with loss of breath is god-like gain!

The Ladies draw the curtains about SOPHONISBA; *the rest accompany* MASSINISSA *forth; the cornets and organs playing loud full music for the Act.*

225–7 *wonder . . . Wondrous*: again alluding to the title of the play; 'wonder' is one of the emotions which, according to Aristotelian critics, should be evoked by tragedy.

229 *essays*: (rough or preliminary) attempts.

232 *Carthage' Palladium*: the guardian of Carthage, like the 'palladium' or image of Pallas on which the safety of Troy depended.

236 s.d. *organs*: used interchangeably with the singular form; need not imply more than one instrument.

236 s.d. *music for the Act*: entr'acte music and lengthy overtures were regular features of performances at the indoor 'private' theatres, like the Blackfriars.

ACT II

SCENE I

Whilst the music for the first Act sounds, HANNO, CARTHALON, BYTHEAS, GELOSSO, *enter: they place themselves to counsel,* GISCO, *th'empoisoner, waiting on them;* HANNO, CARTHALON, *and* BYTHEAS *setting their hands to a writing, which being offered to* GELOSSO, *he denies his hand, and, as much offended, impatiently starts up and speaks.*

GELOSSO, HANNO, BYTHEAS, CARTHALON.

GELOSSO. My hand, my hand? Rot first; wither in agèd shame.
HANNO. Will you be so unseasonably wood?
BYTHEAS. Hold such preposterous zeal as stand against
The full decree of Senate? All think fit.
CARTHALON. Nay, most unevitable necessary
For Carthage' safety, and the now sole good
Of present state, that we must break all faith
With Massinissa. Whilst he fights abroad,
Let's gain back Syphax, making him our own
By giving Sophonisba to his bed.
HANNO. Syphax is Massinissa's greater, and his force
Shall give more side to Carthage: as for's queen

II.i s.d. Marston opens this act, like the first, with a solemn tableau.
II.i s.d. *empoisoner*: poisoner, 'an Italianate intrusion into the story' (Wood).
2 *wood*: mad.
6–7 *the . . . state*: the immediate requirements of statecraft which must now be reckoned the only good.
12 *give . . . Carthage*: more greatly enlarge the Carthaginian side.

And her wise father, they love Carthage' fate;
Profit and honesty are one in state.
GELOSSO. And what decrees our very virtuous
Senate
Of worthy Massinissa, that now fights
And, leaving wife and bed, bleeds in good arms
For right old Carthage?
CARTHALON. Thus 'tis thought fit:
Her father Asdrubal on sudden shall take in
Revolted Syphax; so with doubled strength,
Before that Massinissa shall suspect,
Slaughter both Massinissa and his troops,
And likewise strike with his deep stratagem
A sudden weakness into Scipio's arms,
By drawing such a limb from the main body
Of his yet powerful army; which being done,
Dead Massinissa's kingdom we decree
To Sophonisba and great Asdrubal
For their consent; so this swift plot shall bring
Two crowns to her, make Asdrubal a king.
GELOSSO. So, first faith's breach, adultery,
murder, theft!
CARTHALON. What else?
GELOSSO. Nay, all is done, no mischief left.
CARTHALON. Pish, prosperous success gives
blackest actions glory;
The means are unremembered in most story.
GELOSSO. Let me not say gods are not.
CARTHALON. This is fit:
Conquest by blood is not so sweet as wit;
For howsoe'er nice virtue censures of it,
He hath the grace of war that hath war's profit.
But Carthage, well advised that states comes on
With slow advice, quick execution,

---

14 *state*: statecraft, machiavellian 'policy'.
24 *arms*: (1) Scipio's own limbs (as synecdoche for his martial vigour); (2) limbs of the army, considered as a 'body' of men; (3) armaments.
33 *prosperous . . . glory*: success makes the wickedest actions become glorious (since history is written by its winners).
36 *as wit*: as conquest by cunning.
37 *nice*: over-scrupulous.
37 *censures of it*: judges the matter.

Have here an engineer long bred for plots,
Called an empoisoner, who knows this sound
excuse:
The only dew that makes men sprout in courts
is use.
Be't well or ill, his thrift is to be mute;
Such slaves must act commands, and not
dispute,
Knowing foul deeds with danger do begin,
But with rewards do end; sin is no sin,
But in respects –

GELOSSO. Politic lord, speak low; though heaven
bears
A face far from us, gods have most long ears;
Jove has a hundred marble marble hands.

CARTHALON. O ay, in poetry or tragic scene!

GELOSSO. I fear gods only know what poets mean.

CARTHALON. Yet hear me, I will speak close
truth and cease:
Nothing in nature is unserviceable,
No, not even inutility itself.
Is then for naught dishonesty in being?
And if it be sometimes of forcèd use,
Wherein more urgent than in saving nations?
State shapes are soldered up with base, nay
faulty,
Yet necessary functions; some must lie,
Some must betray, some murder, and some all;
Each hath strong use, as poison in all purges;

---

41 *engineer*: plotter, layer of snares.

43 *The . . . use*: only by making himself useful can a man hope to rise in the court world; 'use' may also convey the sense of becoming accustomed to crime.

44 *Be't . . . mute*: Whether he's ordered to do something good or bad, the sensible and profitable thing for him to do is to keep quiet.

49 *Politic*: machiavellian, unscrupulous.

52 *poetry . . . scene*: Carthalon scoffs at the notion of poetic justice; Marston's conscious self-reference places his sarcasm in a highly ironic light, as Gelosso's riposte emphasises.

54 *close*: strict, secret, confidential.

55–6 *Nothing . . . itself*: from Montaigne, III, i. 8.

60–1 *State . . . functions*: adapted from Montaigne, III, i. 8.

Yet when some violent chance shall force a state
To break given faith, or plot some stratagems,
Princes ascribe that vile necessity
Unto heaven's wrath; and sure, though't be no vice,
Yet 'tis bad chance: states must not stick too nice.
For Massinissa's death sense bids forgive:
Beware to offend great men and let them live;
For 'tis of empire's body the main arm,
He that will do no good shall do no harm.
You have my mind.

GELOSSO. Although a stage-like passion and weak heat
Full of an empty wording might suit age,
Know I'll speak strongly truth. Lords, ne'er mistrust
That he who'll not betray a private man
For his country, will ne'er betray his country
For private men; then give Gelosso faith.
If treachery in state be serviceable,
Let hangmen do it. I am bound to lose
My life, but not my honour, for my country.

64–7 *Yet . . . wrath*: cf. Machiavelli, *The Prince*, Ch. XVIII: 'a prudent ruler cannot, and should not, honour his word when it places him at a disadvantage . . . And a prince will never lack good excuses to colour his bad faith.'

68 *stick too nice*: stand upon over-scrupulous points of principle.

69–70 *For . . . live*: it is only common sense to accept Massinissa's death, because it is a mistake to leave great men alive after you've betrayed them; cf. Machiavelli, *The Prince*, Ch. III: 'any injury a prince does a man should be of such a kind that there is no fear of revenge'.

71–2 *For . . . harm*: it is the principal maxim of statecraft that only the man who lacks the will to do good will be spared the necessity of harming others; cf. Machiavelli, *The Prince,* Ch. XV: 'a man who neglects what is actually done for what should be done learns the way to self-destruction . . . The fact is that a man who wants to act virtuously in every way necessarily comes to grief among so many who are not virtuous.'

77–9 *he . . . men*: Montaigne, III, i. 8–9.

Our vow, our faith, our oath, why they're ourselves,
And he that's faithless to his proper self
May be excused if he break faith with princes.
The gods assist just hearts, and states that trust
Plots before Providence are tossed like dust.
For Massinissa (O, let me slack a little
Austere discourse, and feel humanity!)
Methinks I hear him cry, 'O fight for Carthage!
Charge home! wounds smart not for that so just, so great,
So good a city.' Methinks I see him yet
Leave his fair bride even on his nuptial night
To buckle on his arms for Carthage. Hark!
Yet, yet, I hear him cry, 'Ingratitude,
Vile stain of man, O ever be most far
From Massinissa's breast! Up, march amain!
Fame got with loss of breath is god-like gain.'
And see, by this he bleeds in doubtful fight,
And cries 'For Carthage!' whilst Carthage – Memory,
Forsake Gelosso! Would I could not think,
Nor hear, nor be, when Carthage is
So infinitely vile! See, see, look here!

Cornets. Enter two Ushers, SOPHONISBA, ZANTHIA, ARCATHIA; HANNO, BYTHEAS, *and* CARTHALON *present* SOPHONISBA *with a paper, which she having perused, after a short silence, speaks.*

SOPHONISBA. Who speaks? What, mute? Fair plot! What? blush to break it?
How lewd to act when so shamed but to speak it.
Is this the Senate's firm decree?
CARTHALON. It is.
SOPHONISBA. Hath Syphax entertained the stratagem?
CARTHALON. No doubt he hath, or will.

---

103 s.d. Note the powerful dramatic effect created by the silent tableau which Marston creates here.

SOPHONISBA. My answer's thus,
What's safe to Carthage shall be sweet to me.
CARTHALON. Right worthy.
HANNO. Royalest.
GELOSSO. O very woman!
SOPHONISBA. But 'tis not safe for Carthage to destroy.
Be most unjust, cunningly politic,
Your head's still under heaven. O trust to fate:
Gods prosper more a just than crafty state.
'Tis less disgrace to have a pitied loss,
Than shameful victory.
GELOSSO. O very angel!
SOPHONISBA. We all have sworn good Massinissa faith;
Speech makes us men, and there's no other bond
'Twixt man and man but words. O equal gods,
Make us once know the consequence of vows –
GELOSSO. And we shall hate faith-breakers worse than man-eaters.
SOPHONISBA. Ha, good Gelosso, is thy breath not here?
GELOSSO. You do me wrong. As long as I can die,
Doubt you that old Gelosso can be vile?
States may afflict, tax, torture, but our minds
Are only sworn to Jove. I grieve, and yet am proud
That I alone am honest: high powers, you know
Virtue is seldom seen with troops to go.
SOPHONISBA. Excellent man, Carthage and Rome shall fall
Before thy fame. – Our lords, know I the worst?
CARTHALON. The gods foresaw, 'tis fate we thus are forced.

118–19 *Speech . . . words*: stock Aristotelian doctrine (see *Politics*, I, ii); cf. also Tilley, S735.
124 *Doubt you*: do you suspect that.
125 *tax*: impose burdens, oppress.

SOPHONISBA. Gods naught foresee, but see, for to their eyes
Naught is to come or past; nor are you vile
Because the gods foresee; for gods and we
See as things are; things are not for we see.
But since affected wisdom in us women
Is our sex' highest folly, I am silent;
I cannot speak less well, unless I were
More void of goodness. Lords of Carthage, thus:
The air and earth of Carthage owes my body;
It is their servant; what decree they of it?

CARTHALON. That you remove to Cirta, to the palace
Of well-formed Syphax, who with longing eyes
Meets you; he that gives way to fate is wise.

SOPHONISBA. I go. What power can make me wretched? What evil
Is there in life to him that knows life's loss
To be no evil? Show, show thy ugliest brow,
O most black chance; make me a wretched story;
Without misfortune virtue hath no glory.
Opposèd trees makes tempests show their power,
And waves forced back by rocks makes Neptune tower.
Tearless O see a miracle of life,
A maid, a widow, yet a hapless wife.

Cornets. SOPHONISBA, *accompanied with the Senators, depart; only* GELOSSO *stays.*

GELOSSO. A prodigy! let nature run cross-legged,
Ops go upon thy head, let Neptune burn,

132–3 *Gods . . . past*: the doctrine that all time is perpetually present to the gods.

134–5 *for . . . see*: both gods and men see things as they are; things are not as they are because ['for' in the text] the gods and we see them so (Wood).

140 *owes*: owns (air and earth considered as parts of a single entity).

152–7 *miracle . . . woman*: again picking up the 'wonder' of the title.

155 *Ops*: Roman goddess of fertility and plenty, here simply the earth.

155 *Neptune*: god of the sea, here simply the sea.

Cold Saturn crack with heat, for now the world
Hath seen a woman!
Leap nimble lightning from Jove's ample shield,
And make at length an end! The proud hot breath
Of thee-contemning greatness, the huge drought
Of sole self-loving vast ambition,
Th'unnatural scorching heat of all those lamps
Thou rear'dst to yield a temperate fruitful heat,
Relentless rage, whose heart hath no one drop
Of human pity – all, all loudly cry,
'Thy brand, O Jove, for know the world is dry!'
O let a general end save Carthage' fame!
When worlds do burn, unseen's a city's flame.
Phoebus in me is great; Carthage must fall;
Jove hates all vice, but vows' breach worst of
all. *Exit.*

SCENE II

Cornets sound a charge. Enter MASSINISSA *in his gorget and shirt, shield, sword; his arm transfixed with a dart.* JUGURTH *follows, with his cuirass and casque.*

MASSINISSA. Mount us again; give us another horse.

JUGURTH. Uncle, your blood flows fast; pray ye withdraw.

---

156 *Saturn*: god and planet of melancholy, a cold, moist humour.

160 *thee-contemning greatness*: greatness that despises your power (i.e. Jove's); Gelosso catalogues a series of human vices whose unnaturally passionate heat has rendered the world as dry as tinder for Jove's lightning to burn.

162–3 *lamps . . . heat*: referring literally to the heavenly bodies, here standing for tyrannic princes.

169 *Phoebus . . . great*: Gelosso sees himself as inspired by Apollo, the god of prophecy.

169 *Carthage must fall*: echoing the elder Cato's celebrated slogan, *Delenda est Carthago* ('Carthage must be destroyed').

II.ii s.d. *gorget*: armour for the throat.

II.ii s.d. *cuirass and casque*: chest-piece and helmet.

MASSINISSA. O Jugurth, I cannot bleed too fast, too much,
For that so great, so just, so royal Carthage.
My wound smarts not, blood's loss makes me not faint,
For that loved city. O nephew, let me tell thee,
How good that Carthage is: it nourished me,
And when full time gave me fit strength for love,
The most adorèd creature of the city
To us before great Syphax did they yield,
Fair, noble, modest, and 'bove all, my own,
My Sophonisba. O Jugurth, my strength doubles;
I know not how to turn a coward; drop
In feeble baseness I cannot. Give me horse;
Know I am Carthage' very creature, and I am graced
That I may bleed for them. Give me fresh horse.
JUGURTH. He that doth public good for multitude
Finds few are truly grateful.
MASSINISSA. O Jugurth, fie, you must not say so, Jugurth.
Some commonwealths may let a noble heart,
Too forward, bleed abroad and bleed bemoaned
But not revenged at home; but Carthage, fie,
It cannot be ungrate, faithless through fear,
It cannot, Jugurth: Sophonisba's there.
Beat a fresh charge.

Enter ASDRUBAL, *his sword drawn, reading a letter;* GISCO *follows him.*

ASDRUBAL. Sound the retreat; respect your health, brave prince;
The waste of blood throws paleness on your face.
MASSINISSA. By light, my heart's not pale: O my loved father,

---

10 *To . . . yield*: 'One of the vital points of difference between Livy's account and Appian's. Asdrubal's important part in the attempted assassination of Massinissa is another' (Wood).

23 *ungrate*: ungrateful.

We bleed for Carthage; balsam to my wounds,
We bleed for Carthage; shall's restore the fight?
My squadron of Massulians yet stands firm.
ASDRUBAL. The day looks off from Carthage; cease alarms;
A modest temperance is the life of arms.
Take our best surgeon Gisco; he is sent
From Carthage to attend your chance of war.
GISCO. We promise sudden ease.
MASSINISSA. Thy comfort's good.
ASDRUBAL. [*aside*] That nothing can secure us but thy blood!
[*To* GISCO] Infuse it in his wound, 'twill work amain.
GISCO. O Jove!
ASDRUBAL. What Jove? Thy god must be thy gain;
And as for me – Apollo Pythian!
Thou know'st a statist must not be a man.
Exit ASDRUBAL.

Enter GELOSSO *disguised like an old soldier, delivering to* MASSINISSA (*as he* [*is*] *preparing to be dressed by* GISCO) *a letter, which* MASSINISSA *reading, starts, and speaks to* GISCO.

MASSINISSA. Forbear; how art thou called?
GISCO. Gisco, my lord.
MASSINISSA. Um, Gisco. Ha! touch not mine arm. (*To* GELOSSO) Most only man!
[*To* GISCO] Sirra, sirra, art poor?
GISCO. Not poor.
MASSINISSA. Nephew, command
MASSINISSA *begins to draw.*
Our troops of horse make indisgraced retreat;

---

32 *looks off from*: does not regard favourably.
40 *Apollo Pythian*: Apollo in his aspect as deity of the oracle at Delphi.
41 *statist*: machiavellian politician.
43 *only*: peerless.
43–4 *Um . . . poor?*: see Textual Note, p. 504 below.
45 *make . . . retreat*: retreat without disgrace, in good order.

Trot easy off. – Not poor. – Jugurth, give charge
My soldiers stand in square battalia,
Exit JUGURTH.
Entirely of themselves. – Gisco, thou'rt old;
'Tis time to leave off murder; thy faint breath
Scarce heaves thy ribs, thy gummy blood-shot eyes
Are sunk a great way in thee, thy lank skin
Slides from thy fleshless veins; be good to men.
Judge him, ye gods, I had not life to kill
So base a creature. [*Sheathes his sword*] Hold, Gisco, live;
The god-like part of kings is to forgive.

GISCO. Command astonished Gisco.

MASSINISSA. No, return,
Haste unto Carthage; quit thy abject fears;
Massinissa knows no use of murderers.
[*Exit* GISCO.]

Enter JUGURTH, *amazed, his sword drawn.*

Speak, speak! let terror strike slaves mute;
Much danger makes great hearts most resolute.

JUGURTH. Uncle, I fear foul arms; myself beheld
Syphax on high speed run his well-breathed horse
Direct to Cirta, that most beauteous city
Of all his kingdom; whilst his troops of horse
With careless trot pace gently toward our camp,
As friends to Carthage. Stand on guard, dear uncle,
For Asdrubal, with yet his well-ranked army,
Bends a deep threat'ning brow to us, as if
He waited but to join with Syphax' horse,
And hew us all to pieces. O my king,

---

47 *stand . . . battalia*: draw themselves up in a square.
48 *Entirely of themselves*: as an entire and integrated unit.
48 ff. Wood suggests that this episode is modelled on one in Montaigne (I, xxiii, 123–5) where a French prince argues a would-be assassin out of his intentions and employment.
55 *The . . . forgive*: Tilley, E179.

My uncle, father, captain over all,
Stand like thyself, or like thyself now fall.
Thy troops yet hold good ground. Unworthy wounds,
Betray not Massinissa!

MASSINISSA. Jugurth, pluck,
Pluck. So, good coz.

[JUGURTH *pulls out the dart from* MASSINISSA'*s arm.*]

JUGURTH. O God! Do you not feel?

MASSINISSA. No, Jugurth, no; now all my flesh is steel.

GELOSSO. Off base disguise! High lights scorn not to view
A true old man. Up, Massinissa, throw
The lot of battle upon Syphax' troops,
Before he join with Carthage; then amain
Make through to Scipio; he yields safe abodes.
Spare treachery, and strike the very gods.

MASSINISSA. Why wast thou born at Carthage? O my fate!
Divinest Sophonisba! I am full
Of much complaint, and many passions,
The least of which expressed would sad the gods
And strike compassion in most ruthless hell.
Up, unmaimed heart, spend all thy grief and rage
Upon thy foe; the field's a soldier's stage,
On which his action shows. If you are just,
And hate those that contemn you, O you gods,
Revenge worthy your anger, your anger. O,
Down man, up heart! Stoop, Jove, and bend thy chin

---

77 *lights*: luminaries, illustrious ones.

82 *Spare . . . gods*: to spare treachery is to offend the gods themselves.

90 *action*: both 'deeds' and 'performance'.

92 *Revenge . . . anger*: Revenge yourselves, in a manner worthy of the anger of gods, on those who have provoked your anger.

93 *Down . . . heart*: Let my heart (the seat of courage), triumph over my mere human weakness.

93–4 *bend . . . breast*: dignified epic periphrasis for 'nod'.

To thy large breast; give sign thou'rt pleased,
and just;
Swear good men's foreheads must not print the
dust.

Exeunt.

SCENE III

Enter ASDRUBAL, HANNO, BYTHEAS.

ASDRUBAL. What Carthage hath decreed, Hanno,
is done;
Advanced and born was Asdrubal for state;
Only with it his faith, his love, his hate
Are of one piece. Were it my daughter's life
That fate hath sung to Carthage safety brings,
What deed so red but hath been done by kings?
Iphigenia! He that's a man for men,
Ambitious as a god, must like a god
Live clear from passions; his full aimed-at end,
Immense to others, sole self to comprehend,

---

95 *good . . . dust*: either 'good men must not be made to grovel', or 'good men must not be killed and left face-down in the dust'.

2 *Advanced*: raised.

3–4 *Only . . . piece*: only in the arts of statesmanship do my various emotions find a common cause.

4–5 *Were . . . brings*: if fate had decreed that only the sacrifice of my daughter's life could secure the safety of Carthage.

6 *red*: bloody.

7 *Iphigenia*: Marston expects his audience to remember the story of Iphigenia, sacrificed by her father, Agamemnon, in order to secure favourable winds for the Greek expedition to Troy.

7–14 A perverted application of the Stoic doctrine that the wise man can make himself equal to the gods by cultivation of reason and systematic extirpation of the passions (which render him vulnerable to the vicissitudes of the exterior world).

10 *Immense . . . others*: a task too great for others (but playing on the literal Latin sense of *immensus* = without boundaries).

10 *sole . . . comprehend*: (1) fully understand himself; (2) entirely contain himself (within the limits of his own head, 'round in's own globe').

Round in's own globe; not to be clasped, but holds
Within him all; his heart being of more folds
Than shield of Telamon, not to be pierced though struck.
The god of wise men is themselves, not luck.

Enter GISCO.

See him by whom now Massinissa is not.
Gisco, is't done?
GISCO. Your pardon, worthy lord,
It is not done; my heart sunk in my breast,
His virtue mazed me, faintness seized me all.
Some god's in kings that will not let them fall.
ASDRUBAL. His virtue mazed thee. Um. Why now I see
Thou'rt that just man that hath true touch of blood,
Of pity, and soft piety. Forgive?
Yes, honour thee; we did it but to try
What sense thou hadst of blood. Go, Bytheas,
Take him into our private treasury
[*Aside to* BYTHEAS] And cut his throat; the slave hath all betrayed.
BYTHEAS. Are you assured?
ASDRUBAL. Afeared, for this I know:
Who thinketh to buy villainy with gold,
Shall ever find such faith so bought so sold. –
Reward him thoroughly.
A shout, the cornets giving a flourish.
HANNO. What means this shout?
ASDRUBAL. Hanno, 'tis done; Syphax' revolt by this

---

11 *globe*: literally 'skull', but also alluding to the doctrine that man is a microcosm, or little world (cf. *Hamlet*, I.v.97, 'this distracted globe').

11–12 *not . . . all*: being so entirely self-contained, the wise man will remain beyond the grasp of others.

13 *shield of Telamon*: borne by Ajax, son of Telamon; a huge man-covering shield.

14 *god . . . luck*: the Stoic doctrine that the wise man is indifferent to fortune, given a characteristically egotistic twist.

18 *mazed*: confused and astonished.

Hath secured Carthage; and now his force come in
And joined with us give Massinissa charge
And assured slaughter. O ye powers, forgive!
Through rotten'st dung best plants both sprout and live;
By blood vines grow.

HANNO. But yet think, Asdrubal,
'Tis fit at least you bear grief's outward show;
It is your kinsman bleeds. What need men know
Your hand is in his wounds? 'Tis well in state
To do close ill, but 'void a public hate.

ASDRUBAL. Tush, Hanno, let me prosper, let routs prate;
My power shall force their silence or my hate
Shall scorn their idle malice; men of weight
Know, he that fears envy let him cease to reign;
The people's hate to some hath been their gain.
For howsoe'er a monarch feigns his parts,
Steal anything from kings but subjects' hearts.

Enter CARTHALON *leading in bound* GELOSSO.

CARTHALON. Guard, guard the camp. Make to the trench. – Stand firm.

ASDRUBAL. The gods of boldness with us! How runs chance?

CARTHALON. Think, think how wretched thou canst be, thou art;

35–6 *Through . . . grow*: a piece of folk wisdom; cf. Webster, *The White Devil*, III.ii.193–4; *Richard II*, V.vi.45–6. (See F. L. Lucas's note in Webster, *Works*, I, 232–3.)

39 *Your hand is in*: you are among those responsible for.

40 *close*: secret.

40 *'void*: avoid.

41 *routs*: the rabble.

44–7 *he . . . hearts*: cf. Machiavelli, *The Prince*, Ch. XVII: 'a prince should not worry if he incurs reproach for his cruelty so long as he keeps his subjects united and loyal . . . it is far better to be feared than loved if you cannot be both'.

50 ff. Carthalon again plays the role of Nuntius, the classical imitation once more emphasised by the epic simile at lines 69–74, and the Latinate syntax of his narration.

Short words shall speak long woes.
GELOSSO. Mark, Asdrubal.
CARTHALON. Our bloody plot to Massinissa's ear
Untimely by this lord was all betrayed.
GELOSSO. By me it was, by me, vile Asdrubal;
I joy to speak't.
ASDRUBAL. Down, slave!
GELOSSO. I cannot fall.
CARTHALON. Our trains disclosed, straight to his well-used arms
He took himself, rose up with all his force
On Syphax' careless troops, Syphax being hurried
Before to Cirta, fearless of success,
Impatient Sophonisba to enjoy;
Gelosso rides to head of all our squadrons,
Commands make stand in thy name, Asdrubal,
In mine, in his, in all. Dull rest our men,
Whilst Massinissa, now with more than fury,
Chargeth the loose and much-amazèd ranks
Of absent Syphax, who with broken shout,
In vain expecting Carthage secondings,
Give faint repulse. A second charge is given:
Then look as when a falcon towers aloft
Whole shoals of fowl and flocks of lesser birds
Crouch fearfully, and dive, some among sedge,
Some creep in brakes, so Massinissa's sword,
Brandished aloft, tossed 'bout his shining casque,

---

51 *Short . . . woes*: a version of Marston's favourite Senecan tag, *Curae leves loquuntur, ingentes stupent*, 'Light woes speak, heavy ones strike dumb' (*Hippolytus*, 607).

56 *Our trains disclosed*: our plots having been disclosed.

59 *fearless of*: not doubting.

62 *Commands . . . stand*: orders them to halt.

67 *Carthage secondings*: support from the Carthaginian troops.

69 *look as*: just as.

72 *brakes*: thickets.

Made stoop whole squadrons; quick as thought he strikes,
Here hurls he darts, and there his rage-strong arm
Fights foot to foot; here cries he 'Strike, they sink!'
And then grim slaughter follows; for by this,
As men betrayed they curse us, die, or fly, or both.
Of ten, six thousand fell. Now was I come,
And straight perceived all bled by his vile plot.

GELOSSO. Vile? Good plot, my good plot, Asdrubal!

CARTHALON. I forced our army beat a running march,
But Massinissa stuck his spurs apace
Upon his speedy horse, leaves slaughtering;
All fly to Scipio, who with open ranks
In view receives them; all I could effect
Was but to gain him.

ASDRUBAL. Die.

GELOSSO. Do what thou can,
Thou canst but kill a weak old honest man.

GELOSSO *departs, guarded.*

CARTHALON. Scipio and Massinissa by this strike
Their claspèd palms, then vow an endless love;
Straight a joint shout they raise, then turn they breasts
Direct on us, march strongly toward our camp,
As if they dared us fight. O Asdrubal,
I fear they'll force our camp.

ASDRUBAL. Break up and fly.
This was your plot.

HANNO. But 'twas thy shame to choose it.

---

74 *Made stoop*: caused to submit; but 'stoop' as a familiar term in falconry has at least an associative link with the epic simile; a hawk stoops or swoops down upon its prey; here the squadrons are 'stooped on' by Massinissa's sword; cf. Chapman's *The Gentleman Usher*, I.i: 'A cast of falcons on their merry wings,/Daring the stooped prey that shifting flies' (*OED, stooped*).

87 *gain*: capture.

89–90 *strike . . . palms*: shake hands.

CARTHALON. He that forbids not an offence, he does it.
ASDRUBAL. The curse of women's words go with you. – Fly! –
You are no villains! – Gods and men, which way? –
Advise vile things!
HANNO. Vile?
ASDRUBAL. Ay.
CARTHALON. Not.
BYTHEAS. You did all.
ASDRUBAL. Did you not plot?
CARTHALON. Yielded not Asdrubal?
ASDRUBAL. But you enticed me.
HANNO. How?
ASDRUBAL. With hope of place.
CARTHALON. He that for wealth leaves faith is abject.
HANNO. Base.
ASDRUBAL. Do not provoke my sword; I live.
CARTHALON. More shame,
T'outlive thy virtue and thy once great name.
ASDRUBAL. Upbraid ye me?
HANNO. Hold!
CARTHALON. Know that only thou
Art treacherous: thou shouldst have had a crown.
HANNO. Thou didst all, all; he for whom mischief's done,
He does it.
ASDRUBAL. Broad scorn upon feigned powers! –
Make good the camp – no, fly – yes – what? – wild rage!

---

96 Cunliffe cites Seneca, *Troades*, 291: 'he who, when he may, forbids not sin, commands it'.
101 *place*: political advancement.
107–8 Cunliffe cites Seneca, *Medea*, 500–1: 'Who profits by a sin has done the sin.'
108–13 see Textual Note on 108, pp. 504–5 below.

To be a prosperous villain, yet some heat, some hold;
But to burn temples and yet freeze, O cold!
Give me some health; now your blood sinks; thus deeds
Ill-nourished rot; without Jove naught succeeds.
Exeunt.

Organ mixed with recorders for this Act.

ACT III

SCENE I

SYPHAX, *his dagger twon about her hair, drags in* SOPHONISBA *in her nightgown petticoat; and* ZANTHIA *and* VANGUE *following.*

SYPHAX. Must we entreat, sue to such squeamish ears?
Know, Syphax has no knees, his eyes no tears;
Enragèd love is senseless of remorse.
Thou shalt, thou must: kings' glory is their force.
Thou art in Cirta, in my palace, fool.
Dost think he pitieth tears that knows to rule?
For all thy scornful eyes, thy proud disdain,
And late contempt of us, now we'll revenge.
Break stubborn silence. Look, I'll tack thy head
To the low earth, whilst strength of two black knaves
Thy limbs all wide shall strain. Prayer fitteth slaves;

110–11 *To . . . cold*: 'Being a successful villain at least permits a certain warm glow of satisfaction, some believe, but to outrage the gods and not profit by it is intolerable' (West and Thorssen).

III.i s.d. *twon*: twined, wound.

2 *has no knees*: will never kneel.

3 *senseless of*: incapable of feeling.

Our courtship be our force. Rest calm as sleep,
Else at this quake; hark, hark, we cannot weep.
SOPHONISBA. Can Sophonisba be enforced?
SYPHAX. Can? See.
SOPHONISBA. Thou mayst enforce my body, but not me.
SYPHAX. Not?
SOPHONISBA. No.
SYPHAX. No?
SOPHONISBA. No. Off with thy loathèd arms,
That lie more heavy on me than the chains
That wear deep wrinkles in the captive's limbs.
I do beseech thee.
SYPHAX. What?
SOPHONISBA. Be but a beast,
Be but a beast.
SYPHAX. Do not offend a power
Can make thee more than wretched: yield to him
To whom fate yields. Know, Massinissa's dead.
SOPHONISBA. Dead?
SYPHAX. Dead.
SOPHONISBA. To gods' of good men shame.
SYPHAX. Help, Vangue, my strong blood boils.
SOPHONISBA. O save thine own yet fame.
SYPHAX. All appetite is deaf; I will, I must.
Achilles' armour could not bear out lust.
SOPHONISBA. Hold thy strong arm, and hear, my Syphax; know
I am thy servant now: I needs must love thee,
For (O, my sex, forgive!) I must confess
We not affect protesting feebleness,

12–13 *Rest . . . quake*: if you yield you may rest as calm as sleep, if not, then tremble at this force.

24 *thine own yet fame*: the reputation which you still possess (but are in danger of losing).

26 *Achilles' armour*: the forging of Achilles' arms by the god Hephaistos forms one of the more splendid episodes of epic ornament in the *Iliad* (Book XVIII); the impenetrability of the armour may be further suggested by the legend that Achilles' mother Thetis made his body proof against all wounds by dipping him in a magical spring in infancy, leaving only his heel unprotected.

26 *bear out*: withstand.

30 *We not affect*: we do not love.

Entreats, faint blushings, timorous modesty;
We think our lover is but little man
Who is so full of woman. Know, fair prince,
Love's strongest arm's not rude; for we still
prove
Without some fury there's no ardent love.
We love our love's impatience of delay;
Our noble sex was only born t'obey
To him that dares command.

SYPHAX. Why, this is well.
Th'excuse is good. Wipe thy fair eyes, our
queen,
Make proud thy head. Now feel more friendly
strength
Of thy lord's arm; come, touch my rougher skin
With thy soft lip. Zanthia, dress our bed.
Forget old loves, and clip him that through
blood
And hell acquires his wish; think not, but kiss;
The flourish 'fore love's fight is Venus' bliss.

SOPHONISBA. Great dreadful lord, by thy
affection,
Grant me one boon. Know I have made a vow –

SYPHAX. Vow? What vow? Speak.

SOPHONISBA. Nay, if you take offence,
Let my soul suffer first, and yet –

SYPHAX. Offence?
Not, Sophonisba; hold, thy vow is free
As – come, thy lips.

SOPHONISBA. Alas, cross misery!
As I do wish to live, I long to enjoy
Your warm embrace, but, O my vow, 'tis thus:
If ever my lord died, I vowed to him
A most, most private sacrifice, before
I touched a second spouse. All I implore,
Is but this liberty.

SYPHAX. This? Go, obtain.
What time?

SOPHONISBA. One hour.

---

34 *Love's . . . rude*: not even the most violent expressions of love are barbaric.

43 *clip*: embrace.

SYPHAX. Sweet, good speed, speed, adieu! –
Yet, Syphax, trust no more than thou mayst view. –
Vangue shall stay.
SOPHONISBA. He stays.

Enter a Page, delivering a letter to SOPHONISBA *which she privately reads.*

SYPHAX. Zanthia, Zanthia!
Thou art not foul, go to; some lords are oft
So much in love with their known ladies' bodies,
That they oft love their – Vails: hold, hold, thou'st find
To faithful care kings' bounty hath no shore.
ZANTHIA. You may do much.
SYPHAX. But let my gold do more.
ZANTHIA. I am your creature.
SYPHAX. Be, get, 'tis no stain;
The god of service is however gain. *Exit.*
SOPHONISBA. Zanthia, where are we now? Speak worth my service;
Ha' we done well?
ZANTHIA. Nay, in height of best.
I feared a superstitious virtue would spoil all,
But now I find you above women rare.
She that can time her goodness hath true care
Of her best good. Nature at home begins;
She whose integrity herself hurts, sins.
For Massinissa, he was good, and so;
But he is dead, or worse, distressed, or more
Than dead, or much distressed. O sad, poor –
Who ever held such friends? No, let him go;

---

58 *good speed, speed*: good fortune, hurry.
63 *Vails*: wages, tips, bribes; as Bullen notes, the line is intelligible on the twin assumptions that Marston here employs the figure aposiopesis and that Syphax is feeing the waiting-woman.
64 *shore*: limit.
71 *But . . . rare*: ironic inversion of the 'wonder' theme, announced by the title.
76–7 *But . . . distressed*: 'the authentic tones of Juliet's Nurse' (Wood); cf. Nutriche in *AR*.

Such faith is praised, then laughed at, for still know
Those are the living women that reduce
All that they touch unto their ease and use,
Knowing that wedlock, virtue, or good names,
Are courses and varieties of reason,
To use or leave as they advantage them,
And absolute within themselves reposed,
Only to greatness ope, to all else closed.
Weak sanguine fools are to their own good nice;
Before I held you virtuous, but now wise.

SOPHONISBA. Zanthia, victorious Massinissa lives,
My Massinissa lives. O steady powers,
Keep him as safe as heaven keeps the earth,
Which looks upon it with a thousand eyes,
That honest valiant man! and Zanthia,
Do but record the justice of his love,
And my for ever vows, for ever vows.

ZANTHIA. Ay, true madam; nay, think of his great mind,
His most just heart, his all of excellence,
And such a virtue as the gods might envy.
Against this, Syphax is but – and you know,
Fame lost, what can be got that's good for –

SOPHONISBA. Hence!
Take, nay, with one hand.

ZANTHIA. My service.

SOPHONISBA. Prepare
Our sacrifice.

ZANTHIA. But yield you, ay or no?

---

79 *still*: merely intensifies 'know'.

80 *living*: truly alive (perhaps also 'immortal'; cf. 'living fame').

82–6 argument corruptly derived from Montaigne, III, v, 93–5.

83 *courses . . . reason*: merely modes of action and attributes constructed by human reason (and therefore subject to rational manipulation).

85 *And . . . reposed*: 'and such women, being centred entirely in and on themselves, are'; a comic version of Asdrubal's pseudo-Stoic morality (II.iii.7–14).

86 *ope*: open.

87 *to . . . nice*: over-scrupulous about pursuing their own advantage.

SOPHONISBA. When thou dost know –
ZANTHIA. What then?
SOPHONISBA. Then thou wilt know.
Exit ZANTHIA.
Let him that would have counsel 'void th'advice
Of friends made his with weighty benefits,
Whose much dependence only strives to fit
Humour, not reason, and so still devise
In any thought to make their friend seem wise.
But above all, O fear a servant's tongue,
Like such as only for their gain to serve.
Within the vast capacity of place
I know no vileness so most truly base.
Their lord's their gain; and he that most will give,
With him they will not die but they will live.
Traitors and these are one; such slaves once trust,
Whet swords to make thine own blood lick the dust.

Cornets and organs playing full music, enters [under the conduct of ZANTHIA *and* VANGUE,] *the solemnity of a sacrifice; which being entered, whilst the attendants furnish the altar,* SOPHONISBA [*sings a*] *song; which done, she speaks.*

Withdraw, withdraw.
All but ZANTHIA *and* VANGUE *depart.*

106–7 *Whose . . . reason*: whose heavily dependent position makes them seek to flatter our impulses rather than minister to our reason.
111 *place*: employment (especially public or court position).
116 s.d. *organs*: interchangeable with the singular form; need not imply more than one instrument.
116 s.d. *full*: full-toned, loud.
116 s.d. *solemnity*: ceremonial procession; the careful s.d. suggests the importance of the spectacular element.
116 s.d. *altar*: a stock theatrical property, presumably carried on to the stage by members of the procession.
116 s.d. *song*: the ceremony provides an occasion for one of those musical interludes so popular in the private theatres.

I not invoke thy arm, thou god of sound,
Nor thine, nor thine, although in all abound
High powers immense. But jovial Mercury,
And thou, O brightest female of the sky,
Thrice-modest Phoebe, you that jointly fit
A worthy chastity and a most chaste wit,
To you corruptless honey and pure dew
Upbreathes our holy fire. Words just and few
O deign to hear! If in poor wretches' cries
You glory not, if drops of withered eyes
Be not your sport, be just; all that I crave
Is but chaste life or an untainted grave.
I can no more; yet hath my constant tongue
Let fall no weakness, though my heart were
wrung
With pangs worth hell; whilst great thoughts
stop our tears,
Sorrow unseen, unpitied, inward wears.
You see now where I rest, come is my end.
Cannot heaven virtue 'gainst weak chance defend?
When weakness hath outborne what weakness
can –
What should I say? – 'tis Jove's, not sin of
man.
– Some stratagem now, let wit's god be shown;
Celestial powers by miracles are known.
I have't; 'tis done. – Zanthia, prepare our bed.
Vangue!

VANGUE. Your servant.

SOPHONISBA. Vangue, we have performed

118–19 *thy . . . thine*: seems to suggest that the altar is adorned with images of the classical gods.

118 *god of sound*: Apollo, god of music.

120–2 *Mercury . . . Phoebe*: gods of wit and chastity (Phoebe = Diana, the moon goddess).

124–5 *To . . . fire*: implicit s.d.; on the altar a flame burns, into which Sophonisba throws some sweet incense.

124 *corruptless*: incorruptible.

132–3 *whilst . . . wears*: another version of the favourite *curae leves* theme (see above, II.iii.51).

133 *inward wears*: gnaws away at our inner selves.

135 *Cannot . . . defend*: cannot heaven defend virtue against the weak powers of mere chance or fortune?

137 *'tis . . . man*: the fault is Jove's, not man's.

Due rites unto the dead.
SOPHONISBA *presents a carouse to* VANGUE.
Now to thy lord,
Great Syphax, healthful cups, which done, the king
Is right much welcome.
VANGUE. Were it as deep as thought,
Off it should thus. *He drinks.*
SOPHONISBA. My safety with that draught.
VANGUE. Close the vault's mouth lest we do slip in drink.
SOPHONISBA. To what use, gentle Negro, serves this cave,
Whose mouth thus opens so familiarly,
Even in the king's bedchamber?
VANGUE. O my queen,
This vault with hideous darkness and much length
Stretcheth beneath the earth into a grove,
One league from Cirta – I am very sleepy –
Through this, when Cirta hath been strong begirt
With hostile siege, the king hath safely 'scaped
To, to –
SOPHONISBA. The wine is strong.
VANGUE. Strong?
SOPHONISBA. Zanthia!
ZANTHIA. What means my princess?
SOPHONISBA. Zanthia, rest firm
And silent; help us; nay, do not dare refuse.
ZANTHIA. The Negro's dead.
SOPHONISBA. No, drunk.
ZANTHIA. Alas!
SOPHONISBA. Too late,
Her hand is fearful whose mind's desperate.
It is but sleepy opium he hath drunk.

147 *cave*: trap-door on the stage.

Help, Zanthia.

They lay VANGUE *in* SYPHAX' *bed and draw the curtains.*

There lie Syphax' bride; a naked man
Is soon undressed; there bide dishonoured passion.

They knock within, forthwith SYPHAX *comes.*

SYPHAX. Way for the king!
SOPHONISBA. Straight for the king. I fly
Where misery shall see naught but itself.
Dear Zanthia, close the vault when I am sunk,
And whilst he slips to bed, escape; be true;
I can no more; come to me. Hark, gods, my breath
Scorns to crave life, grant but a well-famed death.

She descends.

Enter SYPHAX, *ready for bed,* [*with attendants.*]

SYPHAX. Each man withdraw; let not a creature stay
Within large distance.
ZANTHIA. Sir.
SYPHAX. Hence, Zanthia;
Not thou shalt hear; all stand without ear-reach
Of the soft cries nice shrinking brides do yield,
When –
ZANTHIA. But, sir –
SYPHAX. Hence! – Stay, take thy delight by steps,
Think of thy joys, and make long thy pleasures.
O silence, thou dost swallow pleasure right;
Words take away some sense from our delight.
Music!
Be proud, my Venus; Mercury, thy tongue,

---

161 s.d. *They . . . curtains*: a grotesque version of the bed-trick motif found in *Measure for Measure*, *All's Well that Ends Well*, and other plays. For the location, see above (I.ii.32 s.d.).

168 *I . . . more*: I can say no more.

Cupid, thy flame; 'bove all, O Hercules,
Let not thy back be wanting; for now I leap
To catch the fruit none but the gods should reap.

Offering to leap into bed, he discovers VANGUE.

Ha! can any woman turn to such a devil?
Or – or – Vangue, Vangue –

VANGUE. Yes, yes.

SYPHAX. Speak, slave,
How cam'st thou here?

VANGUE. Here?

SYPHAX. Zanthia, Zanthia,
Where's Sophonisba? Speak at full, at full.
Give me particular faith, or know thou art not.

ZANTHIA. Your pardon, just-moved prince, and private ear.

SYPHAX. Ill actions have some grace, that they can fear.

VANGUE. How came I laid? Which way was I made drunk?
Where am I? Think. Or is my state advanced?
O Jove, how pleasant is it but to sleep
In a king's bed!

SYPHAX. Sleep there thy lasting sleep,
Improvident, base, o'er-thirsty slave.

SYPHAX *kills* VANGUE.

Die pleased, a king's couch is thy too-proud grave. –
Through this vault say'st thou?

ZANTHIA. As you give me grace
To live, 'tis true.

SYPHAX. We will be good to Zanthia;

180–1 *Hercules . . . back*: a strong back is synonymous with sexual prowess; for Hercules as sexual athlete, see *Malc.*, II.v.8, IV.v.59–62.

182 s.d. The s.d. emphasises that what follows is a second travesty wedding night (cf. above, I.ii.32 ff.), in which the bridegroom is once again bilked of his pleasure.

188 *just-moved*: justly angry.

191 *state*: rank.

195 *couch . . . grave*: Syphax's sardonic joke depends partly on the resemblence of many of the grander Renaissance tombs to four-poster beds.

Go, cheer thy lady, and be private to us.
ZANTHIA. As to my life.
She descends after SOPHONISBA.
SYPHAX. I'll use this Zanthia,
And trust her as our dogs drink dangerous Nile,
Only for thirst, then fly the crocodile.
Wise Sophonisba knows love's tricks of art;
Without much hindrance pleasure hath no heart.
Despite all virtue or weak plots I must:
Seven-wallèd Babel cannot bear out lust.
Descends through the vault.

SCENE II

Cornets sound marches. Enter SCIPIO *and* LAELIUS, *with the complements of a Roman general before them. At the other door,* MASSINISSA *and* JUGURTH.

MASSINISSA. Let not the virtue of the world suspect
Sad Massinissa's faith, nor once condemn
Our just revolt. Carthage first gave me life;
Her ground gave food, her air first lent me breath.
The earth was made for men, not men for earth.
Scipio, I do not thank the gods for life,
Much less vile men, or earth; know, best of lords,
It is a happy being breathes well-famed,
For which Jove fees these thus. Men, be not fooled
With piety to place, tradition's fear;

---

198 *be private to us*: keep my secrets.
200 *dogs . . . Nile*: 'Dogs on the banks of the Nile were supposed to drink by snatches, running, from fear of the crocodiles' (Bullen, citing Aelian's *Varia Historia*, I, 4).
III.ii s.d. *complements . . . general*: heraldic accoutrements proper to Roman generals.
5 *The . . . earth*: the world was made for men to enjoy, men were not made to serve their native earth (punning on 'earth' = grave).
8–9 *It . . . thus*: see Textual Note, pp. 505–6 below.
10 *piety to place*: patriotism.

A just man's country Jove makes everywhere.
SCIPIO. Well urgeth Massinissa, but to leave
A city so ingrate, so faithless, so more vile
Than civil speech may name, fear not; such vice
To scourge is heaven's most grateful sacrifice.
Thus all confess, first they have broke a faith
To thee most due, so just to be observed
That barbarousness itself may well blush at them.
Where is thy passion? They have shared thy crown,
The proper right of birth, contrived thy death.
Where is thy passion? Given thy beauteous spouse
To thy most hated rival. Statue, not man!
And last, thy friend Gelosso, man worth gods,
With tortures have they rent to death.
MASSINISSA. O Gelosso,
For thee full eyes.
SCIPIO. No passion for the rest?
MASSINISSA. O Scipio,
My grief for him may be expressed by tears,
But for the rest, silence, and secret anguish
Shall waste, shall waste. Scipio, he that can weep
Grieves not, like me, private deep inward drops
Of blood. My heart, for gods' rights give me leave
To be a short time man.

13–14 *vile . . . civil*: speech is properly and literally 'civil' because it enables men to form societies and live in cities (see above, II.i.118–19); the opposition of 'civil' and 'vile' is helped by a quibbling recollection of the Latin *civilis* and *vilis*.

18 *barbarousness*: the barbarians in classical thought are those who live outside cities (civil society) and lack the use of civil speech (Latin or Greek).

25 *full eyes*: my eyes are full of tears.

27–31 *My grief . . . blood*: yet another version of the *curae leves* theme (see above, II.iii.51; cf. also *Hamlet*, I.ii.76–86).

31–2 *for . . . man*: for God's sake allow me to exhibit human weakness for a little while.

SCIPIO. Stay, prince.
MASSINISSA. I cease;
Forgive if I forget thy presence. Scipio,
Thy face makes Massinissa more than man,
And here before your steady power a vow
As firm as fate I make: when I desist
To be commanded by thy virtue, Scipio,
Or fall from friend of Rome's, revenging gods
Afflict me with your torture. I have given
Of passion and of faith my heart.
SCIPIO. To counsel then;
Grief fits weak hearts, revenging virtue men.
Thus I think fit: before that Syphax know
How deeply Carthage sinks, let's beat swift march
Up even to Cirta, and whilst Syphax snores
With his, late thine –
MASSINISSA. With mine? No, Scipio;
Libya hath poison, asps, knives, and too much earth
To make one grave. With mine? Not; she can die.
Scipio, with mine? Jove say it, thou dost lie.
SCIPIO. Temperance be Scipio's honour.
LAELIUS. Cease your strife;
She is a woman.
MASSINISSA. But she is my wife.
LAELIUS. And yet she is no god.
MASSINISSA. And yet she's more:
I do not praise gods' goodness, but adore;
Gods cannot fall, and for their constant goodness,
Which is necessited, they have a crown
Of never-ending pleasures; but faint man,
Framed to have his weakness made the heavens' glory,
If he with steady virtue holds all siege
That power, that speech, that pleasure, that full sweets,
A world of greatness can assail him with,

---

49 *Temperance . . . honour*: may I show my honour by remaining calm in the face of your insult.
54 *necessited*: necessitated.
57 *holds*: resists.

Having no pay but self-wept misery,
And beggar's treasure heaped, – that man I'll praise
Above the gods.
SCIPIO. The Libyan speaks bold sense.
MASSINISSA. By that by which all is, proportion,
I speak with thought.
SCIPIO. No more.
MASSINISSA. Forgive my admiration:
You touched a string to which my sense was quick.
Can you but think? Do, do; my grief, my grief
Would make a saint blaspheme. Give some relief;
As thou art Scipio, forgive that I forget
I am a soldier; such woes Jove's ribs would burst;
Few speak less ill that feel so much of worst.
My ear attends.
SCIPIO. Before, then, Syphax join
With new-strengthed Carthage, or can once unwind
His tangled sense from out so wild amaze,
Fall we like sudden lightning 'fore his eyes;
Boldness and speed are all of victories.
MASSINISSA. Scipio, let Massinissa clip thy knees;
May once these eyes view Syphax? Shall this arm
Once make him feel his sinew? O ye gods,
My cause, my cause! Justice is so huge odds,
That he who with it fears, heaven must renounce
In his creation.
SCIPIO. Beat then a close quick march.

---

62 *bold*: audacious, presumptuous.
63 *proportion*: the harmony by which the universe was supposedly ordered.
64 *admiration*: display of extravagant wonder.
70 *Few . . . worst*: few men who feel such pain speak with such restraint.
73 *amaze*: panic, but also 'a maze'.
79–81 *Justice . . . creation*: justice puts such odds on your side that heaven must repudiate the creation of anyone who fears despite the justice of his cause.

Before the morn shall shake cold dews through skies,
Syphax shall tremble at Rome's thick alarms.
MASSINISSA. Ye powers, I challenge conquest to just arms.
With a full flourish of cornets, they depart.

Organs, viols, and voices play for this Act.

ACT IV

SCENE I

Enter SOPHONISBA *and* ZANTHIA, *as out of a cave's mouth.*

SOPHONISBA. Where are we, Zanthia?
ZANTHIA. Vangue said the cave
Opened in Belos' forest.
SOPHONISBA. Lord, how sweet
I scent the air! The huge long vault's close vein,
What damps it breathed! In Belos' forest, say'st?
Be valiant, Zanthia; how far's Utica
From these most heavy shades?
ZANTHIA. Ten easy leagues.
SOPHONISBA. There's Massinissa: my true Zanthia,
Shall's venture nobly to escape, and touch
My lord's just arms? Love's wings so justly heave
The body up, that as our toes shall trip
Over the tender and obedient grass
Scarce any drop of dew is dashed to ground.

---

84 *I . . . arms*: I demand that just arms be allowed to conquer.
6 *heavy*: both 'dark' and 'melancholy'.

And see the willing shade of friendly night
Makes safe our instant haste. Boldness and speed
Make actions most impossible succeed.
ZANTHIA. But, madam, know the forest hath no way
But one to pass, the which holds strictest guard.
SOPHONISBA. Do not betray me, Zanthia.
ZANTHIA. I, madam?
SOPHONISBA. No,
I not mistrust thee, yet, but –
ZANTHIA. Here you may
Delay your time.
SOPHONISBA. Ay, Zanthia, delay,
By which we may yet hope, yet hope – alas,
How all benumbed's my sense! Chance hath so often struck
I scarce can feel. I should now curse the gods,
Call on the furies, stamp the patient earth.
Cleave my stretched cheeks with sound, speak from all sense,
But loud and full of players' eloquence. –
No, no; what shall we eat?
ZANTHIA. Madam, I'll search
For some ripe nuts which autumn hath shook down
From the unleaved hazel; then some cooler air
Shall lead me to a spring. Or I will try
The courteous pale of some poor foresters
For milk. *Exit* ZANTHIA.
SOPHONISBA. Do, Zanthia, O happiness
Of those that know not pride or lust of city!
There's no man blessed but those that most men pity.
O fortunate poor maids, that are not forced
To wed for state, nor are for state divorced!

---

14 *instant*: pressing.
14 *Boldness and speed*: perhaps a deliberate echo of III.ii.75.
31 *pale*: enclosure.
36 *state*: reasons of state.

Whom policy of kingdoms doth not marry,
But pure affection makes to love or vary;
You feel no love which you dare not to show,
Nor show a love which doth not truly grow.
O you are surely blessèd of the sky;
You live, that know not death before you die.

Through the vault's mouth, in his night-gown, torch in his hand, SYPHAX *enters just behind* SOPHONISBA; [ZANTHIA *follows*].

You are –
SYPHAX. In Syphax' arms; thing of false lip,
What god shall now release thee?
SOPHONISBA. Art a man?
SYPHAX. Thy limbs shall feel. Despite thy virtue, know
I'll thread thy richest pearl. This forest's deaf
As is my lust. Night and the god of silence
Swells my full pleasures; no more shalt thou delude
My easy credence. Virgin of fair brow,
Well-featured creature, and our utmost wonder,
Queen of our youthful bed, be proud.

SYPHAX *setteth away his light, and prepareth to embrace* SOPHONISBA.

I'll use thee –

SOPHONISBA *snatcheth out her knife.*

SOPHONISBA. Look thee, view this. Show but one strain of force,
Bow but to seize this arm, and by myself,
Or more, by Massinissa, this good steel
Shall set my soul on wing. Thus, formed gods, see,
And, men with gods' worth, envy naught but me!
SYPHAX. Do, strike thy breast; know, being dead, I'll use

---

50 *utmost wonder*: Syphax exhibits his moral ignorance by travestying the 'wonder' of the title; cf. also lines 69, 74, 81–2.

51 *proud*: with a pun on the sense 'sexually excited'.

With highest lust of sense thy senseless flesh,
And even then thy vexèd soul shall see,
Without resistance, thy trunk prostitute
Unto our appetite.

SOPHONISBA. I shame to make thee know
How vile thou speakest; corruption then as much
As thou shalt do; but frame unto thy lusts
Imagination's utmost sin. Syphax,
I speak all frightless, know I live or die
To Massinissa, nor the force of fate
Shall make me leave his love, or slake thy hate.
I will speak no more.

SYPHAX. Thou hast amazed us. Woman's forcèd use,
Like unripe fruit's no sooner got but waste;
They have proportion, colour, but no taste.
[*Aside*] Think, Syphax. – Sophonisba, rest thine own.
Our guard!

Enter a Guard.

Creature of most astonishing virtue,
If with fair usage, love, and passionate courtings,
We may obtain the heaven of thy bed,
We cease no suit; from other force be free.
We dote not on thy body, but love thee.

SOPHONISBA. Wilt thou keep faith?

SYPHAX. By thee, and by that power
By which thou art thus glorious, trust my vow.
Our guard convey the royalest excellence
That ever was called woman to our palace;
Observe her with strict care.

SOPHONISBA. Dread Syphax, speak,
As thou art worthy, is not Zanthia false?

SYPHAX. To thee she is.

SOPHONISBA. As thou art then thyself,
Let her not be.

SYPHAX. She is not.

The Guard seizeth ZANTHIA.

ZANTHIA. Thus most speed.
When two foes are grown friends, partakers bleed.

SYPHAX. When plants must flourish, their manure
must rot.
SOPHONISBA. Syphax, be recompensed, I hate
thee not.
Ex[eunt] SOPHONISBA,
[ZANTHIA, *and Guard.*]
SYPHAX. A wasting flame feeds on my amorous
blood,
Which we must cool, or die. What way all
power,
All speech, full opportunity, can make,
We have made fruitless trial. Infernal Jove,
You resolute angels that delight in flames,
To you, all-wonder-working spirits, I fly.
Since heaven helps not, deepest hell we'll try.
Here in this desert the great soul of charms,
Dreadful Erictho lives, whose dismal brow
Contemns all roofs or civil coverture.
Forsaken graves and tombs, the ghosts forced
out,
She joys to inhabit.

Infernal music plays softly whilst ERICTHO *enters, and when she speaks ceaseth.*

A loathsome yellow leanness spreads her face,
A heavy hell-like paleness loads her cheeks,
Unknown to a clear heaven; but if dark winds
Or thick black clouds drive back the blinded
stars,
When her deep magic makes forced heaven
quake

---

97 *charms*: spells.
99 *Contemns*: despises.
99 *civil coverture*: civilised shelter.
101 s.d. *Infernal music*: presumably indicates eerie or discordant music appropriate to hell; but may also mean that the musicians are to be placed under the stage; cf. *Antony and Cleopatra*, IV.iii.
102 ff. the description of Erictho is closely based on Lucan, *Pharsalia*, VI, 507 ff., and Marston draws on Lucan's account of the Thessalian witches generally (lines 434 ff.).

And thunder spite of Jove, Erictho then
From naked graves stalks out, heaves proud her head
With long unkempt hair loaden, and strives to snatch
The night's quick sulphur; then she bursts up tombs;
From half-rot cerecloths then she scrapes dry gums
For her black rites; but when she finds a corpse
New graved, whose entrails yet not turn
To slimy filth, with greedy havoc then
She makes fierce spoil, and swells with wicked triumph
To bury her lean knuckles in his eyes;
Then doth she gnaw the pale and o'ergrown nails
From his dry hand; but if she find some life
Yet lurking close, she bites his gelid lips,
And, sticking her black tongue in his dry throat,
She breathes dire murmurs, which enforce him bear
Her baneful secrets to the spirits of horror.
To her first sound the gods yield any harm,
As trembling once to hear a second charm.
She is –

ERICTHO. Here, Syphax, here; quake not, for know
I know thy thoughts: thou wouldst entreat our power
Nice Sophonisba's passion to enforce
To thy affection, be all full of love.
'Tis done, 'tis done; to us heaven, earth, sea, air,
And Fate itself obeys; the beasts of death,
And all the terrors angry gods invented,
T'afflict the ignorance of patient man,

---

110 *night's quick sulphur*: lightning ('quick' = both 'rapid' and 'living').
111 *cerecloths*: winding-sheets, shrouds.
119 *gelid*: frigid (but probably with the usual Marston pun on 'jellied' = jelly-like, soft).

Tremble at us; the rolled-up snake uncurls
His twisted knots at our affrighting voice.
Are we incensed? the king of flames grows pale,
Lest he be choked with black and earthy fumes,
Which our charms raise. Be joyed, make proud thy lust.
I do not pray you, gods; my breath's, 'You must.'

SYPHAX. Deep-knowing spirit, mother of all high
Mysterious science, what may Syphax yield
Worthy thy art, by which my soul's thus eased?
The gods first made me live, but thou live pleased.

ERICTHO. Know then, our love, hard by the reverend ruins
Of a once glorious temple reared to Jove,
Whose very rubbish (like the pitied fall
Of virtue much unfortunate) yet bears
A deathless majesty, though now quite rased,
Hurled down by wrath and lust of impious kings,
So that, where holy flamens wont to sing
Sweet hymns to heaven, there the daw and crow,
The ill-voiced raven, and still-chattering pie,
Send out ungrateful sound and loathsome filth;
Where statues and Jove's acts were vively limned
Boys with black coals draw the veiled parts of nature,
And lecherous actions of imagined lust;
Where tombs and beauteous urns of well-dead men

---

135 *king of flames*: the sun.
138 *breath*: word; Erictho commands, rather than entreats, the gods.
142 *thou live*: you first made me live.
143 ff. imitating Montaigne, III, ix, 245–6; but the wealth of concrete detail here draws on Marston's own experience of England's ruined monastic churches.
149 *flamens*: priests.
150 *daw*: jackdaw.
151 *pie*: magpie.
153 *vively limned*: painted to the life.
156 *well-dead*: who died well.

Stood in assurèd rest, the shepherd now
Unloads his belly, corruption most abhorred
Mingling itself with their renownèd ashes:
Ourself quakes at it.
There once a charnel-house, now a vast cave,
Over whose brow a pale and untrod grove
Throws out her heavy shade, the mouth thick arms
Of darksome yew, sun-proof, for ever choke;
Within rests barren darkness; fruitless drought
Pines in eternal night; the steam of hell
Yields not so lazy air: there, that's my cell;
From thence a charm, which Jove dare not hear twice,
Shall force her to thy bed. But, Syphax, know,
Love is the highest rebel to our art.
Therefore I charge thee, by the fear of all
Which thou know'st dreadful, or more, by ourself,
As with swift haste she passeth to thy bed,
And easy to thy wishes yields, speak not one word,
Nor dare, as thou dost fear thy loss of joys,
T'admit one light, one light.

SYPHAX. As to my fate
I yield my guidance.

ERICTHO. Then, when I shall force
The air to music, and the shades of night
To form sweet sounds, make proud thy raised delight:
Meantime, behold, I go a charm to rear,
Whose potent sound will force ourself to fear.

[*Exit* ERICTHO.]

---

167 *lazy*: sluggish.

170 *highest*: proudest, most powerful.

176 *As to my fate*: heavily ironic, since Syphax, like Faustus before him, is about to fall victim to the mortal sin of demoniality (copulation with an evil spirit).

179 *proud*: vigorous, sexually excited, swelling (as well as 'exalted').

179 *raised delight*: extreme pleasure (but with an obvious sexual innuendo).

SYPHAX. Whither is Syphax heaved? At length shall's joy
Hopes more desired than heaven? Sweet labouring earth,
Let heaven be unformed with mighty charms;
Let Sophonisba only fill these arms,
Jove we'll not envy thee. Blood's appetite
Is Syphax' god; my wisdom is my sense;
Without a man I hold no excellence.
Give me long breath, young beds, and sickless ease;
For we hold firm, that's lawful which doth please.

Infernal music, softly.

Hark, hark, now rise infernal tones,
The deep-fetched groans
Of labouring spirits that attend
Erictho.

ERICTHO. (*within*) Erictho!

SYPHAX. Now crack the trembling earth, and send
Shrieks that portend
Affrightment to the gods which hear
Erictho.

ERICTHO. (*within*) Erictho!

A treble viol and a bass lute play softly within the canopy.

SYPHAX. Hark, hark, now softer melody strikes mute
Disquiet Nature. O thou power of sound,

---

182 *heaved*: raised up (punning on 'heaven', line 183).
182 *shall's joy*: shall we enjoy.
183 *labouring*: i.e. about to give birth to Syphax's hopes.
186 *Blood*: passion, lust.
187 *sense*: sensuality.
188 *Without a man*: outside man's own body.
189 *young beds*: the beds of young women.
189 *sickless*: free from ill-health.
195 *within*: Erictho's voice comes from inside the tiring-house, as opposed to the 'infernal tones' which 'rise' from beneath the state (cf. above, line 101 s.d.).
200 s.d. *within the canopy*: presumably the curtained 'discovery' space in the centre of the tiring-house façade.

How thou dost melt me! Hark, now even heaven
Gives up his soul amongst us. Now's the time
When greedy expectation strains mine eyes
For their loved object; now Erictho willed
Prepare my appetite for love's strict gripes.
O you dear founts of pleasure, blood and beauty,
Raise active Venus worth fruition
Of such provoking sweetness. Hark, she comes!

A short song to soft music above.

Now nuptial hymns enforcèd spirits sing.
Hark, Syphax, hark!

Cantant.

Now hell and heaven rings
With music spite of Phoebus. Peace, she comes.

Enter ERICTHO *in the shape of* SOPHONISBA, *her face veiled, and hasteth in the bed of* SYPHAX.

Fury of blood's impatient. Erictho,
'Bove thunder sit: to thee, egregious soul,
Let all flesh bend. Sophonisba, thy flame

---

203 *melt*: dissolve in sensuous ecstasy.
203–4 *heaven . . . soul*: Syphax ironically takes this infernal music as an expression of the divine soul of creation.
207 *strict gripes*: (1) close, tight embrace; (2) severe pains (the *double entendre* is heavily ironic and no doubt unwitting).
208–9 *O . . . Venus*: again the metaphors barely conceal the gross sexual suggestiveness.
209–10 *worth . . . Of*: worthy consummation with.
210 s.d. *music above*: Marston strains the resources of his theatre, calling for music from three separate locations, to enhance the supernatural effect of the scene.
213 *spite of Phoebus*: in spite of the assumed hostility of Apollo (god of reason, as well as patron of music).
215 *'Bove thunder*: i.e. in a position to control Jove's thunderbolts of divine punishment.
215 *egregious*: great, renowned, excellent (perhaps with ironic play on the opposite, hostile sense of gross, flagrant, outrageous).
216 *Let . . . bend*: may all mankind do homage (with

But equal mine, and we'll joy such delight,
That gods shall not admire, but even spite.

SYPHAX hasteneth within the canopy, as to SOPHONISBA's bed.

A bass lute and a treble viol play for the Act.

ACT V

SCENE I

SYPHAX draws the curtains and discovers ERICTHO lying with him.

ERICTHO. Ha, ha, ha!
SYPHAX. Light, light!
ERICTHO. Ha, ha!
SYPHAX. Thou rotten scum of hell –
O my abhorrèd heat! O loathed delusion!

They leap out of the bed; SYPHAX takes him to his sword.

ERICTHO. Why, fool of kings, could thy weak soul imagine
That 'tis within the grasp of heaven or hell
To enforce love? Why, know love dotes the Fates,
Jove groans beneath his weight: mere ignorant thing,
Know we, Erictho, with a thirsty womb,
Have coveted full threescore suns for blood of kings.

---

ironically unwitting indecent innuendo).
218 *but . . . spite*: but even feel spiteful envy.
3 *heat*: lust.
4 *fool of kings*: of all kings the most foolish.
6 *dotes*: makes fools of.
7 *his*: love's.

We that can make enragèd Neptune toss
His huge curled locks without one breath of wind;
We that can make heaven slide from Atlas' shoulder;
We, in the pride and height of covetous lust,
Have wished with woman's greediness to fill
Our longing arms with Syphax' well-strung limbs:
And dost thou think, if philtres or hell's charms
Could have enforced thy use, we would have deigned
Brain-sleights? No, no. Now are we full
Of our dear wishes. Thy proud heat, well wasted,
Hath made our limbs grow young. Our love, farewell.
Know he that would force love, thus seeks his hell.

ERICTHO *slips into the ground as* SYPHAX *offers his sword to her.*

SYPHAX. Can we yet breathe? Is any plagued like me?
Are we? Let's think: O now contempt, my hate
To thee, thy thunder, sulphur, and scorned name!
He whose life's loathed, and he who breathes to curse
His very being, let him thus with me

SYPHAX *kneels at the altar.*

Fall 'fore an altar sacred to black powers,
And thus dare heavens: O thou whose blasting flames
Hurl barren droughts upon the patient earth,

---

12 *We . . . shoulder*: exaggerated epic periphrasis for 'raise a storm'.
15 *well-strung*: well-sinewed.
17 *thy use*: my use of you.
19 *proud . . . wasted*: (1) swollen lust thoroughly spent; (2) warmth and pride of life utterly consumed.
26 *thus*: do thus.
28–9 *thou . . . earth*: the sun-god, Helios.

And thou, gay god of riddles and strange tales,
Hot-brainèd Phoebus, all add if you can
Something unto my misery;
If aught of plagues lurk in your deep-trenched
brows
Which yet I know not, let them fall like bolts
Which wrathful Jove drives strong into my
bosom!
If any chance of war, or news ill-voiced,
Mischief unthought of lurk, come, gift us all,
Heap curse on curse, we can no lower fall.

Out of the altar the ghost of ASDRUBAL *ariseth.*

ASDRUBAL. Lower, lower.
SYPHAX. What damned air is formed
Into that shape? Speak, speak, we cannot quake;
Our flesh knows not ignoble tremblings; speak,
We dare thy terror. Methinks hell and fate
Should dread a soul with woes made desperate.
ASDRUBAL. Know me the spirit of great Asdrubal,
Father to Sophonisba, whose bad heart
Made justly most unfortunate; for know,
I turned unfaithful, after which the field
Chanced to our loss, when of thy men there fell
Six thousand souls, next fight of Libyans ten.
After which loss we unto Carthage flying,
Th'enragèd people cried their army fell
Through my base treason. Straight my
revengeful Fury
Makes them pursue me; I with resolute haste

---

30 *gay . . . tales*: Phoebus Apollo, patron of the enigmatic oracle at Delphi, whose prophecies were issued in riddles, and whose delight in ambiguities won him the name of Apollo Loxias ('crooked').

31 *Hot-brainèd*: Phoebus Apollo is also a sun-god.

34 *bolts*: thunderbolts.

43 *desperate*: in a condition of theological despair, convinced of one's own inevitable damnation.

44 ff. The ghost adopts the rhetorical manner associated with the Nuntius figures of the play.

49 *next . . . ten*: alongside a force of ten thousand Libyans.

52 *Fury*: see Textual Note, p. 507 below.

Made to the grave of all our ancestors,
Where poisoned, hoped my bones should have long rest;
But see, the violent multitude arrives,
Tear down our monument, and me now dead
Deny a grave; hurl us among the rocks
To stanch beasts' hunger; therefore thus ungraved
I seek slow rest. Now dost thou know more woes,
And more must feel. Mortals, O fear to slight
Your gods and vows. Jove's arm is of dread might.
SYPHAX. Yet speak: shall I o'ercome approaching foes?
ASDRUBAL. Spirits of wrath know nothing but their woes. *Exit.*

Enter NUNTIUS.

NUNTIUS. My liege, my liege,
The scouts of Cirta bring intelligence
Of sudden danger; full ten thousand horse,
Fresh and well-rid, strong Massinissa leads,
As wings to Roman legions that march swift,
Led by that man of conquest, Scipio.
SYPHAX. Scipio?
NUNTIUS. Direct to Cirta. *A march far off is heard.*
Hark, their march is heard
Even to the city.
SYPHAX. Help, our guard, my arms!
Bid all our leaders march. Beat thick alarms.
I have seen things which thou wouldst quake to hear.
Boldness and strength! the shame of slaves be fear.
Up, heart, hold sword! though waves roll thee on shelf,

---

57 *me . . . dead*: conscious Latinism (*mihi iam mortuo*).
59–60 *thus . . . rest*: in classical myth the ghosts of those denied proper burial are doomed to wander the earth.
76 *roll . . . shelf*: drive you on to the rocks.

Though fortune leave thee, leave not thou
thyself.
Ex[*eunt,* SYPHAX] *arming.*

SCENE II

Enter two Pages, with targets and javelins; LAELIUS *and* JUGURTH, *with halberds;* SCIPIO *and* MASSINISSA *armed; cornets sounding a march.*

SCIPIO. Stand!
MASSINISSA. Give the word. Stand!
SCIPIO. Part the file.
MASSINISSA. Give way.
Scipio, by thy great name, but greater virtue,
By our eternal love, give me the chance
Of this day's battle. Let not thy envied fame
Vouchsafe t'oppose the Roman legions
Against one weakened prince of Libya.
This quarrel's mine: mine be the stroke of fight.
Let us and Syphax hurl our well-forced darts
Each unto other's breast. O, what should I say?
Thou beyond epithet, thou whom proud lords of
fortune
May even envy – alas, my joy's so vast
Makes me seem lost – let us thunder and
lightning
Strike from our brave arms! Look, look, seize
that hill!
Hark, he comes near. From thence discern us
strike
Fire worth Jove; mount up, and not repute
Me very proud, though wondrous resolute.

---

v.ii s.d. The presence of pages *with targets and javelins* (echoing the play's opening tableau) is a symbolic representation of the battle fought off-stage.

1 *Part . . . file*: having halted, the troops are ordered to form 'divided files'.

12 *lost*: i.e. in my speech.

15 *worth*: worthy of.

15–16 *mount . . . proud*: climb that hill and do not suppose me proud.

My cause, my cause is my bold heart'ning odds,
That sevenfold shield; just arms should fright the gods
SCIPIO. Thy words are full of honour; take thy fate.
MASSINISSA. Which we do scorn to fear. To Scipio state
Worthy his heart. Now let the forcèd brass
Sound on!
Cornets sound a march. SCIPIO *leads his train up to the mount.*
Jugurth, clasp sure our casque,
Arm us with care; and Jugurth, if I fall
Through this day's malice or our fathers' sins,
If it in thy sword lie, break up my breast,
And save my heart that never fell nor's due
To aught but Jove and Sophonisba. Sound,
Stern heart'ners unto wounds and blood, sound loud,
For we have namèd Sophonisba.
Cornets, a flourish.
So!
Cornets, a march far off.
Hark, hark, he comes. Stand blood! Now multiply
Force more than fury. Sound high, sound high, we strike
For Sophonisba!

---

17 *My . . . odds*: it is my just cause which creates the overwhelming odds that so embolden my heart (cf. above, II.ii.79–81).

20–1 *To . . . heart*: may Scipio's renown match his magnanimity.

21 *forcèd*: strongly blown.

22 s.d. Though a 'mount' might be presented by a property on the large public stages, at the Blackfriars the upper-stage balcony must have served instead.

26 *nor's due*: nor is owed; nor belongs (see Textual Note p. 507 below).

Enter SYPHAX, *armed, his Pages with shields and darts before; cornets sounding marches.*

SYPHAX. For Sophonisba!
MASSINISSA. Syphax!
SYPHAX. Massinissa!
MASSINISSA. Betwixt us two,
Let single fight try all.
SYPHAX. Well urged.
MASSINISSA. Well granted.
Of you, my stars, as I am worthy you,
I implore aid; and O, if angels wait
Upon good hearts, my genius be as strong
As I am just.
SYPHAX. Kings' glory is their wrong.
He that may only do just act's a slave.
My god's my arm, my life my heaven, my grave
To me all end.
MASSINISSA. Give day, gods, life and death,
To him that only fears blaspheming breath.
For Sophonisba!
SYPHAX. For Sophonisba!

Cornets sound a charge. MASSINISSA *and* SYPHAX *combat.* SYPHAX *falls.* MASSINISSA *unclasps* SYPHAX' *casque, and, as ready to kill him, speaks* SYPHAX.

SYPHAX. Unto thy fortune, not to thee, we yield.
MASSINISSA. Lives Sophonisba yet unstained –
speak just –
Yet ours unforced?
SYPHAX. Let my heart fall more low
Than is my body, if only to thy glory
She lives not yet all thine.
MASSINISSA. Rise, rise, cease strife.

---

32 s.d. *Pages . . . darts*: a spectacular symmetrical confrontation of the two champions with their attendant weapon-bearers is envisaged; the use of martial music helps to compensate for the small scale of such epic scenes on the Blackfriars stage.

38 *Kings' . . . wrong*: the glory of kings is in their ability freely to do wrong.

40 *My . . . arm*: 'So Mezentius in the *Aeneid*, X.772: – "Dextra mihi deus" ' (Bullen).

41 *life and death*: see Textual Note, p. 508 below.

Hear a most deep revenge; from us take life.

Cornets sounded a march, SCIPIO *and* LAELIUS *enter.* SCIPIO *passeth to his throne.* MASSINISSA *presents* SYPHAX *to* SCIPIO*'s feet, cornets sounding a flourish.*

To you all power of strength; and next to thee,
Thou spirit of triumph, born for victory,
I heave these hands. March we to Cirta straight,
My Sophonisba with swift haste to win,
In honour and in love all mean is sin.

Ex[eunt] MASSINISSA *and* JUGURTH.

SCIPIO. As we are Rome's great general, thus we press
Thy captive neck, but as still Scipio,
And sensible of just humanity,
We weep thy bondage. Speak, thou ill-chanced man,
What spirit took thee when thou wert our friend
(Thy right hand given both to gods and us
With such most passionate vows and solemn faith)
Thou fled'st with such most foul disloyalty
To now weak Carthage, strength'ning their bad arms,
Who lately scorned thee with all loathed abuse,
Who never entertain for love but use?

SYPHAX. Scipio, my fortune is captived, not I,
Therefore I'll speak bold truth; nor once mistrust
What I shall say, for now, being wholly yours,

---

49 s.d. *sounded*: having sounded.
54 *mean*: moderation.
55–6 *thus . . . neck*: the gesture is perhaps borrowed from *1 Tamburlaine*, IV.ii, where it blasphemously parodies an image in Foxe's *Book of Martyrs*, showing Henry VIII triumphing over the Pope; the ultimate source is the Biblical 'The Lord said unto my Lord, Sit thou at my right hand, until I make thine enemies thy footstool', Psalms, 110:1.
66 ff. closely modelled on Holland's Livy.

I must not feign. Sophonisba, 'twas she,
'Twas Sophonisba that solicited
My forced revolt; 'twas her resistless suit,
Her love to her dear Carthage, 'ticed me break
All faith with men; 'twas she made Syphax false,
She that loves Carthage with such violence
And hath such moving graces to allure
That she will turn a man that once hath sworn
Himself on's father's bones her Carthage' foe,
To be that city's champion and high friend.
Her hymeneal torch burnt down my house;
Then was I captived, when her wanton arms
Threw moving clasps about my neck. O charms,
Able to turn even Fate! But this in my true grief
Is some just joy, that my love-sotted foe
Shall seize that plague, that Massinissa's breast
Her hands shall arm, and that ere long you'll try
She can force him your foe as well as I.
SCIPIO. Laelius, Laelius, take a choice troop of horse,
And spur to Cirta. To Massinissa thus:
Syphax' palace, crown, spoil, city's sack,
Be free to him; but if our new-leagued friend
Possess that woman of so moving art,
Charge him with no less weight than his dear vow,
Our love, all faith, that he resign her thee;
As he shall answer Rome, will him give up
A Roman prisoner to the Senate's doom:

---

71 *resistless*: irresistible.
79 *hymeneal torch*: torch carried in wedding procession (here standing for the fire of Sophonisba's love, and the heat of resentment it inspired in Syphax).
84–5 *breast . . . arm*: his soldier's breast (the seat of his passion) will (1) arm, protect, and (2) put arms in her hands; a rather precious piece of quibbling built around the pun on 'arms'.
85 *try*: determine.
90 *free*: allowed.
94 *will him*: order him to.

She is a Carthaginian, now our law's.
Wise men prevent not actions, but ever cause.
SYPHAX. [*aside*] Good malice, so, as liberty so dear,
Prove my revenge. What I cannot possess
Another shall not – that's some happiness.
Exeunt, the cornets flourishing.

SCENE III

The cornets afar off sounding a charge. A SOLDIER *wounded at one door. Enters at the other* SOPHONISBA, *two Pages before her with lights, two women bearing up her train.*

SOLDIER. Princess, O fly! Syphax hath lost the day,
And captived lies. The Roman legions
Have seized the town, and with inveterate hate
Make slaves or murder all. Fire and steel,
Fury and night, hold all. Fair Queen, O fly!
We bleed for Carthage, all of Carthage die. *Exit.*

The cornets sounding a march. Enter Pages with javelins and targets, MASSINISSA *and* JUGURTH, MASSINISSA*'s beaver shut.*

MASSINISSA. March to the palace.
SOPHONISBA. Whate'er man thou art,
Of Libya thy fair arms speak; give heart
To amazed weakness; hear her, that for long time

96 *now our law's*: now subject to Roman law.
97 *Wise . . . cause*: wise men do not simply anticipate actions but always seek to determine them.
v.iii s.d., 6 s.d. *Pages . . . with lights . . . with javelins and targets*: another reminiscence of the opening tableau.
6 s.d. *beaver shut*: with the visor on his helmet closed.

Hath seen no wishèd light. Sophonisba,
A name for misery much known, 'tis she
Entreats of thy graced sword this only boon:
Let me not kneel to Rome, for though no cause
Of mine deserves their hate, though Massinissa
Be ours to heart, yet Roman generals
Make proud their triumphs with whatever captives.
O 'tis a nation which from soul I fear,
As one well knowing the much-grounded hate
They bear to Asdrubal and Carthage' blood;
Therefore with tears that wash thy feet, with hands
Unused to beg, I clasp thy manly knees;
O save me from their fetters and contempt,
Their proud insults and more than insolence.
Or, if it rest not in thy grace of breath
To grant such freedom, give me long-wished death;
For 'tis not much-loathed life that now we crave,
Only an unshamed death and silent grave
We will now deign to bend for.

MASSINISSA. Rarity,

MASSINISSA disarms his head.

By thee and this right hand thou shalt live free.

SOPHONISBA. We cannot now be wretched.

MASSINISSA. Stay the sword.
Let slaughter cease; sounds soft as Leda's breast

Soft music.

Slide through all ears. This night be love's high feast.

SOPHONISBA. O'erwhelm me not with sweets; let me not drink
Till my breast burst, O Jove, thy nectar, think –

She sinks into MASSINISSA's arms.

---

10 *wishèd*: longed for.
15 *ours to heart*: bound to us in love.
31 *Leda's breast*: perhaps thought of as especially soft by association with the swan, in whose shape Jove raped her.
34 *O . . . think*: see Textual Note, p. 508 below.

MASSINISSA. She is o'ercome with joy.
SOPHONISBA. Help – help to bear
Some happiness, ye powers! I have joy to spare,
Enough to make a god. O Massinissa!
MASSINISSA. Peace!
A silent thinking makes full joys increase.

Enter LAELIUS.

LAELIUS. Massinissa!
MASSINISSA. Laelius!
LAELIUS. Thine ear.
MASSINISSA. Stand off.
LAELIUS. From Scipio thus: by thy late vow of faith,
And mutual league of endless amity,
As thou respects his virtue or Rome's force,
Deliver Sophonisba to our hand.
MASSINISSA. Sophonisba?
LAELIUS. Sophonisba.
SOPHONISBA. My lord
Looks pale, and from his half-burst eyes a flame
Of deep disquiet breaks. The gods turn false
My sad presage!
MASSINISSA. Sophonisba?
LAELIUS. Even she.
MASSINISSA. She killed not Scipio's father, nor his uncle,
Great Cneius.
LAELIUS. Carthage did.
MASSINISSA. To her what's Carthage?
LAELIUS. Know 'twas her father Asdrubal struck off
His father's head. Give place to faith and fate.
MASSINISSA. 'Tis cross to honour.
LAELIUS. But 'tis just to state.
So speaketh Scipio. Do not thou detain
A Roman prisoner, due to this great triumph,

46–7 *The . . . presage*: may the gods turn my grim presentiment false.
52 *cross to*: contrary to.
52 *just to state*: (1) just to the rights of the state; (2) just according to the politic demands of statecraft.

As thou shalt answer Rome and him.
MASSINISSA. Laelius,
We now are in Rome's power. Laelius,
View Massinissa do a loathèd act,
Most sinking from that state his heart did keep.
Look, Laelius, look, see Massinissa weep.
Know I have made a vow, more dear to me
Than my soul's endless being, she shall rest
Free from Rome's bondage.
LAELIUS. But dost thou forget
Thy vow, yet fresh, thus breathed: 'When I desist
To be commanded by thy virtue, Scipio,
Or fall from friend of Rome, revenging gods
Afflict me with your torture.'
MASSINISSA. Laelius, enough.
Salute the Roman, tell him we will act
What shall amaze him.
LAELIUS. Wilt thou yield her then?
MASSINISSA. She shall arrive there straight.
LAELIUS. Best fate of men
To thee.
MASSINISSA. And Scipio.
[*Exit* LAELIUS *with Pages.*]
– Have I lived, O heavens,
To be enforcedly perfidious?
SOPHONISBA. What unjust grief afflicts my worthy lord?
MASSINISSA. Thank me, ye gods, with much beholdingness,
For mark, I do not curse you.
SOPHONISBA. Tell me, sweet,
The cause of thy much anguish.
MASSINISSA. Ha, the cause?
Let's see: wreathe back thine arms, bend down thy neck,

---

58 *Most . . . keep*: utterly fallen away from that exalted condition of courage he once maintained.
69–70 *Best . . . thee*: I wish you the best of fortune.
70 *And Scipio*: I wish the same to Scipio.
76 *wreathe . . . arms*: clasp your arms behind your back.

Practise base prayers, make fit thyself for bondage

SOPHONISBA. Bondage!

MASSINISSA. Bondage, Roman bondage.

SOPHONISBA. No, no!

MASSINISSA. How then have I vowed well to Scipio?

SOPHONISBA. How then to Sophonisba?

MASSINISSA. Right, which way?
Run mad! – impossible! – distraction!

SOPHONISBA. Dear lord, thy patience; let it maze all power,
And list to her in whose sole heart it rests
To keep thy faith upright.

MASSINISSA. Wilt thou be slaved?

SOPHONISBA. No, free.

MASSINISSA. How then keep I my faith?

SOPHONISBA. My death
Gives help to all. From Rome so rest we free;
So brought to Scipio, faith is kept in thee.

MASSINISSA. Thou darest not die – some wine! – thou darest not die!

Enter a Page with a bowl of wine.

SOPHONISBA. How near was I unto the curse of man, joy!
How like was I yet once to have been glad!
He that ne'er laughed may with a constant face
Contemn Jove's frown: happiness makes us base.

She takes a bowl, into which MASSINISSA *puts poison.*

Behold me, Massinissa, like thyself,
A king and soldier; and I prithee keep
My last command.

MASSINISSA. Speak, sweet.

SOPHONISBA. Dear, do not weep.
And now with undismayed resolve behold,
To save you – you (for honour and just faith
Are most true gods, which we should much adore),

---

82 *maze*: confound.

With even disdainful vigour I give up
An abhorred life.
She drinks.
You have been good to me,
And I do thank thee, heaven. O my stars,
I bless your goodness, that with breast unstained,
Faith pure, a virgin wife, tried to my glory,
I die, of female faith the long-lived story;
Secure from bondage and all servile harms,
But more – most happy in my husband's arms.
She sinks [into MASSINISSA*'s arms.]*

JUGURTH. Massinissa, Massinissa!

MASSINISSA. Covetous,
Fame-greedy lady, could no scope of glory,
No reasonable proportion of goodness,
Fill thy great breast, but thou must prove
immense,
Incomprehense in virtue? What, wouldst thou
Not only be admired, but even adored?
O glory ripe for heaven! Sirs, help, help, help!
Let us to Scipio with what speed you can;
For piety make haste, whilst yet we are man.
Exeunt, bearing SOPHONISBA *in a chair.*

---

103 *tried*: tested, afflicted.

103 *to my glory*: (1) to the point where I won glory; (2) for the benefit of my fame.

104 *I . . . story*: the line provides a motto for Sophonisba's heroic tableau of death, picking up once again the 'wonder' of the title, and reminding the audience of Marston's contribution to her 'long-lived story'; like so many tragedies of the period, *Sophonisba* asks to be read as a kind of monument to its dead heroine.

108 *scope*: delimited ambition.

109 *proportion*: the idea of 'proportion' and moderation is an important one in the play (cf. above, III.ii.63, 'that by which all is, proportion'); Massinissa's tribute hovers on the verge of a rebuke to Sophonisba's more-than-human excess of virtue.

110 *immense*: used in the Latin sense of *immensus* = immeasurable, as well as with the suggestion of superhuman hugeness.

111 *Incomprehense*: conscious Latinism, coined from *incomprehensus* = boundless, beyond comprehension.

115 *piety*: Latin *pietas* = dutiful and affectionate loyalty; as well as 'pity'.

SCENE IV

Cornets a march. Enter SCIPIO *in full state, triumphal ornaments carried before him, and* SYPHAX *bound; at the other door,* LAELIUS.

SCIPIO. What answers Massinissa? Will he send
That Sophonisba of so moving tongue?
LAELIUS. Full of dismayed unsteadiness he stood,
His right hand locked in hers, which hand he gave
As pledge from Rome she ever should live free.
But when I entered and well urged his vow
And thy command, his great heart sunk with shame,
His eyes lost spirit, and his heat of life
Sank from his face, as one that stood benumbed,
All mazed, t'effect impossibilities;
For either unto her or Scipio
He must break vow. Long time he tossed his thoughts,
And as you see a snowball being rolled,
At first a handful, yet, long bowled about,
Insensibly acquires a mighty globe,
So his cold grief through agitation grows,
And more he thinks, the more of grief he knows.

V.iv s.d. Marston calls for the nearest that the Blackfriars can provide to a full Roman 'triumph'; the 'full state' probably suggests that Scipio should enter beneath a royal canopy, held by a retinue of splendidly dressed attendants, and the effect is enhanced by martial music accompanying the parade of 'triumphal ornaments' (bundles of captured weapons, etc.) and captives (Syphax).

3 ff. Laelius here plays the role of Nuntius, using the full-blown heroic rhetoric appropriate to the part (see esp. lines 13–17).

10 *mazed*: stunned.

10 *t'effect*: as though he were asked to perform.

15 *Insensibly*: imperceptibly.

At last he seemed to yield her.
SYPHAX. Mark, Scipio!
Trust him that breaks a vow?
SCIPIO. How then trust thee?
SYPHAX. O, misdoubt him not when he's thy slave like me.

Enter MASSINISSA, *all in black.*

MASSINISSA. Scipio!
SCIPIO. Massinissa!
MASSINISSA. General!
SCIPIO. King!
MASSINISSA. Lives there no mercy for one soul of Carthage,
But must see baseness?
SCIPIO. Wouldst thou joy thy peace,
Deliver Sophonisba straight and cease;
Do not grasp that which is too hot to hold.
We grace thy grief, and hold it with soft sense;
Enjoy good courage, but 'void insolence.
I tell thee Rome and Scipio deign to bear
So low a breast as for her say, 'We fear.'
MASSINISSA. Do not, do not; let not the fright of nations
Know so vile terms. She rests at thy dispose.
SYPHAX. To my soul joy. Shall Sophonisba then
With me go bound, and wait on Scipio's wheel?
When th' whole world's giddy, one man cannot reel.
MASSINISSA. Starve thy lean hopes; and, Romans, now behold
A sight would sad the gods, make Phoebus cold.

---

23 *see baseness*: see himself made base.
27 *'void*: avoid.
30–1 *let . . . terms*: the men whom all nations fear should never use so base a word.
31 *She . . . dispose*: (1) she is in your power, waiting for you to determine her fate; (2) the body waits for you to dispose of it.
33 *wheel*: the chariot wheel of a triumphing general.
36 *sad*: sadden.

Organ and recorders play to a single voice. Enter in the meantime the mournful solemnity of MASSINISSA'*s presenting* SOPHONISBA'*s body.*

Look, Scipio, see what hard shift we make
To keep our vows. Here, take, I yield her thee;
And Sophonisba, I keep vow, thou art still free.
SYPHAX. Burst, my vexed heart; the torture that most racks
An enemy is his foe's royal acts.
SCIPIO. The glory of thy virtue live for ever;
Brave hearts may be obscured, but extinct never.
SCIPIO *adorns* MASSINISSA.
Take from the general of Rome this crown,
This robe of triumph, and this conquest's wreath,
This sceptre, and this hand; for ever breathe
Rome's very minion. Live worth thy fame,
As far from faintings as from now base name.
MASSINISSA. Thou whom, like sparkling steel, the strokes of chance
Made hard and firm, and, like wild-fire turned,
The more cold fate, more bright thy virtue burned,
And in whole seas of miseries didst flame;
On thee, loved creature of a deathless fame,
MASSINISSA *adorns* SOPHONISBA.
Rest all my honour! O thou for whom I drink

---

36 s.d. the triumphal procession with which the scene began is now balanced by the equally formal ritual ('mournful solemnity') of a funeral procession.

36 s.d. *to . . . voice*: either they accompany a single voice in a song; or they play a single melody without harmonies or ornament.

42 ff. in these concluding rituals the honour of the triumph is formally transferred from Scipio to Massinissa, and from Massinissa to Sophonisba: triumph and funeral become one, linking the 'wonder' and 'tragedy' of Marston's double title.

42–3 *The . . . never*: note the latent metaphors of light in 'glory' (as effulgence), 'obscured' (in the Latin sense of darkened), and 'extinct' (put out).

47 *very minion*: true favourite.

So deep of grief, that he must only think,
Not dare to speak, that would express my woe –
Small rivers murmur, deep gulfs silent flow.
My grief is here, not here. – Heave gently then;
Women's right wonder, and just shame of men.
Cornets a short flourish. Exeuntque,
manet MASSINISSA.

Finis.

EPILOGUS

MASSINISSA. And now
With lighter passion, though with most just fear,
I change my person, and do hither bear
Another's voice, who with a phrase as weak
As his deserts, now willed me (thus formed)
speak:
If words well sensed, best suiting subject grave,
Noble true story, may once boldly crave
Acceptance gracious; if he whose fires
Envy not others, nor himself admires;
If scenes exempt from ribaldry or rage
Of taxings indiscreet, may please the stage –
If such may hope applause, he not commands
Yet craves as due the justice of your hands.

55–6 *that . . . woe*: anticipates the silence in which the play itself ends.
57 *Small . . . flow*: a last variation on the *curae leves* theme (cf. II.iii.51).
58 *here, not here*: in my heart, not in my mouth (or eyes).
58 *Heave*: raise up (the body).
6 *well sensed*: full of matter (sense as opposed to bombastic sound).
7 *true*: tragedy was conventionally supposed to deal with the truth.
7 *once*: for once.
8 *he*: the author.
8 *fires*: creative powers, heat of the imagination.
11 *taxings indiscreet*: personal satire.

But freely he protests, howe'er it is –
Or well, or ill, or much, not much amiss –
With constant modesty he doth submit
To all, save those that have more tongue than
wit.

17 Q appends: 'After all, let me entreat my reader not to tax me for the fashion of the entrances and music of this tragedy, for know, it is printed only as it was presented by youths, and after the fashion of the private stage; nor let some easily amended errors in the printing afflict thee, since thy own discourse will easily set upright any such unevenness.' Marston was too sanguine in that second sentence. In the first, he appears to regard the spectacular and musical effects as compromising the classical elegance of his tragedy.

NOTES

TEXTUAL NOTES

The purpose of these notes is to record substantive departures from the foundation text and a selection of readings from later editions, and to justify our choice of variants. The lemma is always italicised, unless it is a speech heading in capitals; variants to the right of the lemma and not enclosed in quotation marks are printed in roman, regardless of the style of type in the edition from which they are drawn. For abbreviations used see 'References and abbreviations', pp. xxx–xxxiv above. In notes for *The Malcontent* the symbols A, B and C are used to denote the three consecutive Quartos of 1604; Q refers to reading in which all three concur. Unattributed emendations are our own.

Antonio and Mellida

Ind. 1 s.h.: 1633; not in Q.

Ind. 37 *create*: Hunter, conj. Daniel; great Q.

Ind. 43 *chewed*: Bullen; shew'd Q.

Ind. 76 *shall*: 1633; shalt Q.

Ind. 102 s.d.: Bullen; Exit Ant. & Al. Q.

Ind. 138 s.h.: A. Q; Schoonover gives this speech and that at lines 157–8 ('*Anto.*' in Q) to Galeatzo, on the grounds that he alone has not discussed his characterisation. But it seems clear that Antonio butts in to describe Galeatzo's role for him; it is a common, and effective, trick of Marston's to have one character pre-empt another's reply.

I.i.55 *heart*: Bullen; hurt Q.

I.i.71 *endearèd*: 1633; indeened Q.

I.i.75 *regenty*: Q; a possible Marston nonce form unrecorded by *OED*, which has 'regentry' (two sixteenth-century examples only) and 'regency' (common from the fifteenth century on), either of which *may* have been intended here.

I.i.105 *elections*: 1633; electious Q; election's Keltie, which would leave 'clear' adjectival.

I.i.111 *delle . . . contente*: Hunter; dell . . . contento Q.

I.i.114 *tiptoe*: Dilke; tiptoed Q; tiptoes Hunter; the singular is Marston's preferred form, as at *AM*, V.ii.169; *WYW*, Wood, II, 291.

I.i.115 *Sir*: Saint Q; the emendation, which seems more pointedly satirical, assumes that Marston's customary 'S.' (used for both 'Saint' and 'Sir') was incorrectly expanded.

I.i.133 *monkey'sh*: Hunter; monkish Q. *OED* cites Q under *monkish* 2, common in the sixteenth century, 'resembling a monk or what pertains to a monk'. Although *OED*'s first citation of *monkeyish* is for 1621, monkeys and apes belong to the Elizabethan–Jacobean satirist's vocabulary of abuse (as in Marston's Satire IX), and the 'low forehead' of Rossaline's description (line 130) provides an associative link with monkeys; cf. *The Tempest*, IV.i.247–8, 'apes/ With foreheads villainous low'; and cf. a mistress with 'little ferret eyes' in *Fawn*, Wood, II, 177.

I.i.210 *windy*: Schoonover, conj. Brereton; winde Q.

II.i.38 *Besicler's*: Bessiclers Q; though eds. assume that this is Balurdo's malapropism for 'Rosicler's', '*Ro*' may easily have been misread as '*Be*'.

II.i.93–4 *eleven . . . yard*: Q. Balurdo is given to nonsense, but Marston may have intended to cross our either 'thirteen pence' or 'three pence'.
II.i.193 *Let . . . sound*: Bullen; printed as s.d. in Q.
II.i.233 *rival's*: Dilke; riuals Q; rivals' Hunter.
II.i.234 *Ohimè*: spelt 'Oy me' in Q.
II.i.254 *m' an*: Hunter; in an Q.
II.i.256 s.h.: Dilke; speech continued to Feliche in Q.
II.i.280 *painting*: 1633; pointing Q. Schoonover argues that, as Q's reading does make sense (tying, lacing, fastening), it may 'evince Balurdo's proclivity for *lapsus linguae*'. Perhaps Balurdo misunderstands the joke, supposing that it has something to do with tying up one's breeches.
II.i.285 *spirits*: Q; spirit's Hunter; spirit conj. Brereton. See commentary to this line. 'Spark spirit' is an appellation (= person of sparkling wit) at V.ii.15–16.
II.i.286 *La ty dine*: Q italicises this cryptic phrase. Schoonover's s.d., incorporated here, suggests its probable purpose. Cf. the nonsense syllables 'la la ly ro' three times in *What You Will*, once italicised (Wood, II, 249), and '*ta ly re, ly re, ro*' and '*fa, la, ly, re, lo, la*' (each time italicised) in Marston's contribution to *Eastward Ho* (Wood, III, 92, 94), and also the refrains in Thomas Heywood's *The Rape of Lucrece*, especially '*ha fa derry dino*' (ed. Allan Holaday, Urbana, Illinois: University of Illinois Press, 1950, line 2304).
II.i.293–310: Dilke assigned lines 293–4 to Mellida, and Brereton would give Mellida 'What do you see?' in 295 and 'to thee' in 310, so as further to suggest a resemblance to the closet scene (III.iv) in *Hamlet*. Finkelpearl finds the emendations 'persuasive' (p. 270). But the situations in *Hamlet* and here are entirely different, since the 'ghost' to which Antonio draws Mellida's attention is himself. His speech is simply a histrionic means of eliciting anagnorisis – the moment of recognition.
II.i.310 *vanquishable*: Q; unvanquishable Dilke and eds. The emendation, though it slightly improves the metre, seems particularly pointless in Hunter's edn, since he retains Q's comma after the immediately preceding 'plagues'. Either Antonio is vanquishable or the plagues are not.
III.i.12 s.h.: Bullen; not in Q.
III.i.15 *injustice*: Dilke; justice Q; perhaps the compositor misread 'th'injustice'.
III.i.67 *Spoke*: Dilke; Speake Q.
III.i.71 *Wouldst*: Would'st thou Q; the omission is idiomatic and improves the metre.
III.i.101 *waiter*: 1633; water Q (a possible spelling of 'waiter').
III.ii.9 *traverse*: Keltie; Trauense Q.
III.ii.82 *thou*: Dilke; then Q.
III.ii.104 *this*: Q; this is 1633, Hunter. 'This' for 'this is' is a common colloquialism in the period (Abbott 461).
III.ii.108 s.h.: Dilke; Dil. Q.
III.ii.124 *More fools*: Hunter; More foole Q, which Schoonover defends as a neologism ('foolery') not listed in *OED*.
III.ii.145 s.h.: Brereton conj., and eds.; Catz. Q.
III.ii.154 *the – the– tester*: the the testarn Q; eds. follow 1633 in

omitting one 'the', and may well be right to do so; it is often impossible to know whether a duplication in the text is Marston's deliberate attempt to suggest a mannerism or convey feeling, or a case of inadvertent dittography by author, scribe or compositor. Balurdo stammers in search of novel words in *AR*, IV.i. 97–100, 110, and perhaps has trouble here in imagining where to nail the looking-glass ('tester' is *OED*'s spelling).

III.ii.160 s.h.: Dilke; speech continued to Flavia in Q.

III.ii.182–7 *O . . . nose*: So Schoonover, for the punctuation and stage directions of this speech.

III.ii.191 *Antonio*: Dilke; printed at beginning of 192 in Q.

III.ii.192 s.d.: So Hunter for the positioning; printed after 'priuate' in 191 in Q. Hunter adds Alberto to the characters who enter, but we need not suppose that amid the confusion everyone has time to respond.

III.ii.200–2: We have modernised to convey the pronunciation probably intended. Piero is stuttering. Q spells 'su' and 'who' where we spell 'so–' and 'wh–'.

III.ii.207–8 *siati . . . E . . . i voti della mia dolce*: Dilke; siate . . . Et . . . vuoti del mia dulce Q.

III.ii.220 *may take*: take Q; takes Dilke and eds.; the present emendation improves the metre as well as the sense, and renders more exact the Senecan parallel: 'anyone can rob a man of life, but no one of death' (*Phoenissae*, 152).

III.ii.248 *speranza*: Hunter; esperanza Q (the Spanish form).

III.ii.261 *me*: 1633; me me Q; Hunter and Schoonover follow Q and punctuate to suggest stuttering, but the repetition damages the metre, and in this instance a printer's error seems more likely.

III.ii.266 *Spoke*: Dilke; Speake Q.

III.ii.274 *honour's*: honours 1633; honour Q.

III.ii.292–3 *che con dura sorte . . . per fuggir*: Dilke (substantially); chy condura sorta . . . pur fugir Q.

IV.i.2 *Antonio is*: Antonio's Q.

IV.i.17 *Hold*: 1633, Holds Q. This edn reinterprets the syntax of lines 13–17. Eds. who follow Q have been misled by Q's too-heavy punctuation: a colon after 'sweete' in line 15 and a semi-colon after 'trunke' in line 16.

IV.i.24–8 *O . . . all*: The lines appear as follows in Q:

O, this is naught, but speckling melancholie.
I haue beene
That Morpheus tender skinp   Cosen germane
Beare with me good
Mellida: clod vpon clod thus fall.
Hell is beneath; yet heauen is ouer all.

This passage has been cited (Hunter, p. xix; Scott, p. 14; Colley, p. 184) in illustration of Marston's fondness for aposiopesis, as a means of rendering the breakdown of language under the pressure of extreme passion. However, Antonio does, after all, manage a formal closing couplet, and the immediately preceding incoherence begins to disappear once it is appreciated that Q's 'Morpheus' is not the god of dreams and son of sleep but a scurfy eruption. *OED* gives 'morphue' as a fifteenth–seventeenth century spelling (with a 1610 example from Bishop Hall), and Elyot's *Dictionary* (1559 edn), under 'Alphos', even has 'morpheu'. The 1607 Quarto of *What You Will* prints 'perseu' for pursue, 'sineus' for sinews, and 'valieus' for values. So 'morpheus' is a possible Marstonian spelling of a verb formed from the noun. The transitive verb occurs, in the past participial form, in Hall's *Satires*, IV, 5, 26, and Webster's *Duchess of Malfi*, II.i. It was evidently a satirist's word. Timothy Bright's *A Treatise of Melancholy* (1586), Ch. XXX, sig. M1, p. 177, refers to 'that morphewe, which ofte staineth melancholicke bodies, and bespeckleth their skinne here and there with blacke staines of this humour' (old spelling retained). The collocation of both Bright and Q of speckling, melancholy and morphew renders inescapable our interpretation (a modernisation, not an emendation) of Q's 'Morpheus' as 'morphews'. This, in turn, necessitates the transposition of 'I . . . beene' and 'That . . . skinp'. And now, if we simply take the words as they come, we are left with three iambic pentameters, which fall into complete sentences. Perhaps the dashes that we have introduced could be dispensed with, and full stops inserted after 'skins', 'cousin-german' and 'Mellida'. The shifts in thought are, however, somewhat abrupt, and it is far from clear who or what are referred to as cousins-german. So we have chosen to indicate Q's disruptions, and thus suggest a certain disconnectedness in Antonio's train of thought. If accepted, Q's 'skinp' would be a case of most violent truncation of sense. Except for a few hyphenated compounds, no English word begins thus, and 'skinp' is unpronounceable, but one might suppose a separate, truncated epithet: '. . . skin p– '. We prefer to assume a misreading of the Secretary sign for terminal 's' or 'es', which can closely resemble a rather small Secretary 'p'.

IV.i.28 s.d.: Bullen; Enter Andrugio, Lucio, Cole, and Norwod. Q. Paul's Boys actors Robert Coles and John Norwood must have played either Andrugio and Lucio or two Pages.

IV.i.69 *wade upon*: Schoonover, conj. Wood; made open Q; make upon Deighton conj.; slide upon Bullen. Metrical considerations support the change to 'upon', and 'oppen' is probably a mistake for 'upon' in *Soph.*, II.iii.108. As Wood points out, the primary meaning of 'wade', current in Marston's time, is go, proceed, move forward through or upon something, often with an implication of difficulty or danger. The press-variant 'wade'/'made' occurs in *Soph.*, V.ii.73, and the misprint 'wade' for 'made' in *AM*, III.ii.48. Hunter explained Q 'made open' as 'broke the ice for others to follow'.

IV.i.77 *double*: double, falter Q. We accept Deighton's suggestion that 'double' and 'falter' were originally alternatives, one of which, probably 'falter', Marston forgot to erase.

IV.i.79 *houts and shouts*: Q; this duplication, though in a twelve-syllable line, is less suspect. Eds. modernise to 'hoots', but it seems worth preserving the formulaic jingle.

IV.i.80 *devil's blast*: conj. Brereton; diuelslast Q; devils' lust conj. Deighton; devil's last Keltie; devils lost Bullen; devils, last Hunter; devils' last Schoonover. The loss of a letter is among the most frequent accidents in Q; and a reference to noise seems to be required.

IV.i.87 *miseri*: Bullen; misereri Q.

IV.i.103 *name's*: name Q; the emendation makes the parallelism exact.

IV.i.152 *infected*: Q; the common Elizabethan form 'infect' would tighten the line metrically.
IV.i.157 *inspir'dst*: enspiredst Q; our spelling indicates the pronunciation required by the metre.
IV.i.170 *one*: 1633; on Q. Q's spelling is ambiguous.
IV.i.181 *Spavento*: Q; Speranza conj. Daniel.
IV.i.189–97 *smarisce . . . Muoiono . . . esser . . . più . . . può esser . . . Lasciami . . . in sù aleggia . . . l'impero . . . con sempiterno onore*: suamisce . . . Murono . . . lesser . . . pia . . . pol esser . . . Bassiammi . . . in sua neggia . . . pimpero . . . cosempiterno . . . honore Q. Dilke made most of the corrections; '*in sù aleggia*' is from Schoonover: Dilke read '*in seco reggia*', Bullen '*ha sua seggia*', Hunter '*in sù anneggia*'; '*l'impero*' is from Hunter: Dilke read '*per impero*'.
IV.i.200–2: Q prints (our ellipses): 'eare, . . . returnest: . . . Court:'; Hunter and Schoonover assume an omission after line 200. Other eds. omit 'and' or replace it with 'then'. But repunctuated the passage makes sense: in line 201 Mellida shifts from modern English to Romance usage in contemplating future events. See Abbot 348, and cf. 'when they shall know', *Richard II*, I.iv.49. We have altered Q's 'thou shall' in line 202 to 'thou shalt'.
IV.i.204 *kissing, kissing*: Q; kissing Bullen. The line is a tolerable alexandrine if 'amorous' is slurred into a disyllable and 'even' into a monosyllable, and the repetition is deliberate, clinching the conceit begun in 'point'; 'kissing' is first a noun, then a verb. They will punctuate their speech with kisses, these acting as commas.
IV.i.209 s.h.: Bullen; speech continued to Antonio in Q.
IV.i.217–18 *auditors . . . authors*: Q; auditors' . . . author's Hunter (i.e. the judgement of the auditors . . . of the author). But 'authors' is presumably used in the broad sense to include all those responsible.
IV.i.261 *to*: 1633; not in Q.
IV.ii.10 s.h.: Bullen; Ant. Q.
IV.ii.11 s.h.: Dilke; And. Q.
V.ii.4 s.h.: Hunter; speech continued to Piero in Q; assigned to a Page by Dilke.
V.ii.10 *thin*: a thin Q; presumably the compositor picked up the inappropriate article from the context.
V.ii.13 *sweets*: Hunter; sweete Q.
V.ii.24 *Saint Mark!*: Sir Marke Q; Schoonover suggests that Sir Mark was the name of the music master at St Paul's, but this is probably another case of confusion over Marston's ambiguous 'S.'; at I.i.116 Mellida's exclamation appears as 'S. *Marke*, S. *Marke*' in Q, and the expletive occurs eight times in *WYW*.
V.ii.45 *thine*: Dilke; mine Q.
V.ii.64 *Florence*: Bullen; Milan Q; the error must have been Marston's, but he would not have let it stand had his attention been drawn to it, and he would surely have approved had his printer made the correction.
V.ii.94–6, 102–7: These opening and closing lines of Galeatzo's speech are printed as prose in Q. Either one of the two instances of 'I'll' in line 94, as well as 'you'll' in 95, must be disyllabic to fit the metre; they can be so pronounced without expansion to 'shall' or

'will'; 'pure' in line 96 is also disyllabic; and disyllabic 'I'll' or 'word' would again improve the metre of line 107.

V.ii.176 *resolve*: Dilke; resolu'd Q.

V.ii.217 *father's*: fathers Q; father 1633.

V.ii.273 *ne'er*: Q; 'never' would regularise the line, but since Andrugio's disclaimer in line 266 only Piero's two lines have been unaffected by metrical stumble.

V.ii.290 *you*: Dilke; your Q.

V.ii.305 s.d., EPILOGUS s.d.: Hunter adds these, since Q had Andrugio enter in armour at line 166 s.d.

Antonio's Revenge

We have adhered to the traditional modern scene divisions, based on complete clearance of the stage, in order to keep this sequel consistent with *AM*. The *AR* Quarto, reflecting the neo-classical notions of a scenic unit that Marston evidently adopted for *Antonio's Revenge* and for *The Malcontent*, indicates further divisions (in the form 'SCENA SECVNDA', etc.) after I.ii.68, I.ii.213, I.ii.246, II.i.72 (with Pandulpho's entry following), II.ii.136 *Exit* s.d., II.ii.177, III.i.51 *Exit* s.d., III.i.145 s.d., IV.i.70 s.d. for sennet, IV.i.130, IV.ii.23, V.ii.19 *Cantat* s.d., V.iii.32 s.d. for sennet, V.iii.115 *Exit* s.d.

PROLOGUE 10 *pleased*: pleas'd Q; 'pleasèd' or substitution of 'in a' for 'in' would fill the metrical gap.

I.ii.58 *gayness*: gainesse Q; gayness' Hunter, but we assume inversion of object and verb, with 'entice' an aberrant singular enforced by the rhyme: 'outward gayness entices light looks'.

I.ii.68 s.d.: Q includes Forobosco in the entry.

I.ii.109 *Wehee*: *OED* spelling; Wighy Q, as in *AM*, III.ii.183; 'wyhee' in *Fawn* (Wood, II, 198).

I.ii.123 *grasped*: Bullen; gasp't Q.

I.ii.126 *through*: Q; perhaps Marston intended the disyllabic 'thorough'.

I.ii.147 *ate*: eate Q; eat eds.; Q's spelling is a common Elizabethan and Jacobean form of the past tense, as well as of the present, and elimination of the first, rather than the second, 'e' provides a more helpful modernisation.

I.ii.179 *a banished*: a poore banisht Q; the hypermetrical 'poore' clumsily anticipates 'pour' ('powre' in Q) in the next line.

I.ii.220 s.h.: 1633; not in Q.

I.ii.221 *stomach's* – : stomack's: Q; eds. assume aposiopesis, but loss of a plural monosyllabic noun from the end of Q's line is possible.

I.ii.233 *maim*: 1633; maine Q.

I.ii.260 *th'inner*: Bullen; thinner Q.

I.ii.280 *whither, which*: Q; transposition of these two words would regularise the metre; cf. the nouns and adjectives in line 281.

I.ii.296 *let's*: and let's Q; omitting the first of Q's three instances of 'and' regularises the metre and makes for a crisper line.

I.ii.341 *broil*: broyles Q; the probabilities are in favour of Marston's having written an exact rhyme, and Q's singular 'coyle' is idiomatic, as in *The Spanish Tragedy*, III.xiii.45, 'What coil is that you keep?'; the '-s' ending of the following couplet in Q may have contributed to the compositor's slip.

II.i.25–6 *and half fish*: Q; and half flesh Halliwell, Keltie, Wood; but 'half fish and half conger' below (31) supports Q's nonsense.

II.i.104 *And*: Q; metrically the line would be better without the conjunction, which may have been picked up from the line below.

II.i.113 *How coldly he comes on!*: Daniel conj.; How could he come on, Q; Now could he come on! Hunter.

II.i.146 *jawn*: Iawne Q; Marstonian variant of 'chawn' or 'chine', a cleft or fissure; Marston's spelling helps convey the sense of a *yawning* abyss.

II.i.160 *corbèd*: corb'd Q; curb'd Keltie, Hunter; Gair (following Huyshe) takes the Q word to be a coinage from 'corbel' or 'corbeil'; the former (a stone or timber projection from a wall to support something) is irrelevant, but the latter, though unrecorded by *OED* before the eighteenth century, fits the nautical metaphor: *OED*'s first example, from Kersey's 1706 edition of Edward Philipps's dictionary, reads: 'In fortification, *corbeils* are little buckets . . . which being filled with earth are often set one against another on breastworks or elsewhere, leaving certain portholes, from whence to fire upon the enemy under covert.' There is no doubt a quibbling suggestion of 'curbed' as well.

II.i.180 s.d. PIERO'*s* Q; Piero Bullen and eds.

II.ii.14 *most plague*: Q; an adjective of two syllables, stressed on the first, may have been accidentally omitted from between these two words; the repetition of 'most' in lines 14–16 seems clumsy, rather than rhetorically justified.

II.ii.26 *cant*: Bullen; scant Q.

II.ii.38 *self-one*: Q; self-sown Bullen; *OED* glosses this nonce use of 'self-one' as 'alone with itself'.

II.ii.84 *infamy, torture*: Q; transposition of these words would make for a metrically more regular line.

II.ii.86 *from*: 1633; with Q.

II.ii.137–40: Q lines end '. . . me/. . . wretched/. . .forlorne/. . . happie'. Accepting the present edition's lineation, omission of 'I am' would regularise line 138, and line 137 would be improved by the replacement of 'cursèd' with 'accursed' (as at 171 below). But the irregularities may be authorial.

II.ii.194 *lifen*: lyfen Q; liven Keltie and most eds., but this first appears (with the modern, inappropriate sense) in the late nineteenth century. *OED* cites only the present instance of 'lifen', but it reappears in Webster's *The White Devil*, 'To the Reader', line 19.

II.ii.224 *Pell-mell confusion*: Pell mell: confusion Q; eds. take 'Pell mell' as an exclamation and print 'Pell-mell! Confusion . . . ', but the adjectival use is more idiomatic here, as in *1 Henry IV*, V.i.82, 'a time/Of pell-mell havoc and confusion'.

III.i.2 s.d.; Bullen; (12) Q.

III.i.46 *unpeisèd*: Gair; vnpaized Q; impeised Hunter. Gair's is a straightforward normalisation of Q's spelling. Marston is very fond of 'peise' (meaning gravity or weight) and its derivatives, preferring the spelling 'paise' or 'paize' (though the related 'poise' also occurs). Gair's defence of the Q reading, though somewhat strained ('so resolute that it is not weighed down by the severity of the task'), provides sufficient justification for retaining it; and cf. III.ii.84 and III.ii.90–4; 'clutch', 'peise' and 'vengeance' are again linked at V.i.3–5.

III.i.54 *mistress*: Wood, conj. Daniel; mistes Q.
III.i.66 s.h.: Bullen, not in Q.
III.i.67 *durus*: Hunter; dirus Q.
III.i.69 *antro*: 1633; antri Q.
III.i.70 *feros*: Bullen; feres Q.
III.i.75 *mutining*: Q; mutinous some eds.
III.i.103 *Julio*: Hunter, conj. Wood; Luceo Q.
III.i.114 *rains*: raines Q; raignes 1633; reigns Hunter.
III.i.120–5: Q prints 120–1 ('More . . . cruelty') as one line; Hunter and Gair divide ' . . . proves/. . . suspect/. . . juice/. . . drunk/ . . . heaven/. . . murder'. Once 121 has been treated as a short line, Q's lineation gives better verse; 126–8 would complete 125's pentameter, but we have preserved Q's choral arrangement, retaining its brace.
III.i.122 *strained*: Bullen; straid Q.
III.i.178 *cleaves*: Bullen, Wood, Hunter; clears Q, which Gair explains as 'relieves Andrugio's spirit of its discontent at the delay in the execution of the revenge'; but the emendation is strongly supported by IV.i.166–7.
III.ii.15 *then by*: Hunter, then be Q.
III.ii.38: Q prints the line as part of the song, and it does fit metrically, but the joke is better if Balurdo's words have a specific innocent reference as well.
III.ii.52 s.d. *Cantant*: Q; Cantat Hunter; but perhaps the Pages join in.
III.ii.108 s.d.: After this Q adds '*Explicit Actus tertius*'.
IV.i.19 *baubled*: Hunter; babl'd Q.
IV.i.20 *ribbèd*: ribd Q.
IV.i.104 *keep up by*: Q; kept up by Hunter, conj. Wood; keep up thy Bullen; Q offers quite a satisfactory imperative.
IV.i.109 *the – the –*: thee, the Q; thee, thou Hunter. Balurdo was stuttering in 97–100, and is again searching for a newly acquired word, 'unvulgar' (III.ii.44); 'the' was a common spelling of 'thee', and the compositor evidently misunderstood.
IV.i.112 *Ficte*: ficto Q; cf. '*tacite*' in *AM*, I.i.74, and *Malc.*, II.iii.63, 87.
IV.i.142 *vowed*: vowed that Q; the omission improves the metre; the compositor appears to have picked up 'that' from the previous line.
IV.i.145 s.d., 162 s.d.: Someone has to respond to Piero's command. The s.d. at 145 is Gair's; and as a consequence he has Castilio enter with Strotzo at 162.
IV.i.177 *impulsive*: Bullen; pulsiue Q, which Gair retains, but metre requires the emendation; 'impulsive' appears at II.ii.195; 'compulsive' (first *OED* citation from *Hamlet*) is a possible alternative.
IV.i.188 *hopes*: Bullen; hope Q.
IV.i.199 *Now . . . now. My*: Now . . . now, my Q. Other eds. make the fifth 'now' start a sentence, 'Now, my plots . . .', but the present punctuation better suits the rhythm of the line. Omission of one 'now' would improve it further, but perhaps the five 'nows' should have a line to themselves and 'My . . . do' (199–200) form an alexandrine.
IV.i.260 s.h.: 1633; not in Q.

IV.i.285–90: Hunter's arrangement; Q lineates '. . . knight/. . . roare/. . . night'.
IV.i.322 *I will*: 1633; will Q ('I' printed as catchword).
IV.ii.113 *dread*: dead Q; although the *difficilior lectio* principle would favour Q, and Hecate is goddess of the underworld, particularisation of her 'brow' as dead seems unnatural and pointless.
V.ii.65 *my*: 1633; thy Q; Balurdo has referred to himself in the second person when he is alone at lines 5, 11, 17; the mannerism seems less apt when he is answering Pandulpho, but he may still be mumbling to himself as much as addressing his questioner.
V.ii.92 *Hark, here! proud*: Harke here, proud Q; Hark! here proud Bullen (followed by Gair, substantially); Hark, hear! Proud Hunter.
V.iii.170 s.h.: Bullen; And. Q.

The Malcontent

For a full collation, including all press-variants, see Hunter's Revels edn. These notes record departures from QC and significant QA and QB dialogue variants.
TO THE READER 47 *Sine . . . Phoebus*: B, C; Me mea sequentur fata A ('let my destiny pursue me').
PROLOGUS 1–14: B, C (but placed at the end of the play); not in A; our heading conflates B and C.
SCENE II: Q divisions have been retained; they are based on neo-classical notions of units of movement initiated by the entries of main characters.
I.ii.11 *ragged*: C; rugged A, B.
I.ii.18 *go to church*: B, C; pray A.
I.ii.32 *within herself*: C; not in A, B; though the more succinct version is attractive, the chances are that the expansion is Marston's
I.iii.6 *the church*: A, C, but deleted from many copies; not in B.
I.iii.9 *art*: A, B; art of C.
I.iii.11 *dost*: C; dost thou A, B.
I.iii.15 *petticoat*: C; new Peticote A, B.
I.iii.18–19 *I am . . . now*: B, C; not in A.
I.iii.39 *i'the*: ithe A, B; in the C.
I.iii.47 *Make-please*: the most pointed modernisation of Q 'Make-pleece'.
I.iii.50 *Penlolians*: B, C; Penlohans A (c); Penlobrans A (u).
I.iii.60–1 *there is*: C; there A, B.
I.iii.76 *Guerrino*: Dodsley; Guerchino Q.
I.iii.124–69 *Nay . . . think it*: C; not in A, B.
I.iii.167 *should have*: shue, should C; should show Dyce and eds.; our emendation assumes a typographical accident, perhaps with some miscorrection.
I.iii.176–93: C; not in A, B.
I.iv.20 *this*: A, B; his C.
I.iv.26 *no*: B, C; not in A.
I.iv.43 s.d.–97 s.d.: C; not in A, B.
I.iv.46 *religion in*: Dyce; religion on Q.

I.iv.85: Dodsley altered the rhyme-word to 'burst'; Collier changed also to 'swell . . . swell'.
I.v.34 *insinuated*: B, C; insinuating A.
I.v.35 *delights*: B, C; lights A.
I.vi.10 *up*: A; not in B, C.
I.vi.28 *jawed*: iawde A, B; jade C.
I.vi.30 *against*: C; agen A, B; agin' Hunter.
I.vi.42 *at a*: Dodsley; a Q.
I.vi.67 s.d., 71 s.d.: B, C; not in A.
I.vi.70 s.h.: Dodsley; assigned to Malevole in Q.
I.vi.78 *on*: B, C; of A.
I.vi.93 *ask*: C; else A, B.
I.vi.93 *our . . . our*: B, C; my . . . my A.
I.vi.108 *sighs*: sights Q; a spelling variant.
I.vii.6 *sit*: Q; sir Dyce conj.
I.vii.7 *the*: B, C; this A.
I.vii.26 *'fore*: A, B; for C.
I.vii.32 *cuckold*: B, C; Cornuto A.
I.vii.40 *antic*: the better modernisation of Q 'antique'.
I.vii.41 *the*: C; ye A, B.
I.vii.85 s.d.: after this line QC adds a scene; see Appendix, Insertion i, p. 523 below.
II.i s.d. *Pages*: B, C; Dutches Pages A.
II.i.10 *quite undone*: C; quite is vndone A, B.
II.ii.5 *billets*: C; these billets A, B.
II.ii.10–11 s.d.: B; not in A, C.
II.ii.11 *does*: do's A, B; doth C.
II.ii.12 *'a*: A, B; hee C.
II.ii.23 *Jason*: A; Jasons B, C.
II.ii.27 *all you*: A, B; you C.
II.ii.33 s.h.: A, B; C assigns to Bianca.
II.ii.38–9: C; not in A, B. QC's addition of Malevole's parting advice, with the instruction that it be addressed to Bianca, and the reassignment to Bianca of the previous speech, given in QAB to Maquerelle, are seen by Wine (p. xv) as evidence of authorial revision; Wine assumes that Marston altered the prefix and added lines 38–9 'to make the transfer intelligible'. But Maquerelle is the expert on restoratives, and the information that she in QAB, or Bianca in QC, conveys to Malevole about a three-curd posset 'without any drink' elicits a surprised, sceptical or admiring exclamation from Bianca when Maquerelle conveys it to her at II.iv.4. We have followed Hunter in retaining QAB's ascription of 38–9 to Maquerelle, assuming that she butts in. Hunter also adds a s.d. to indicate that Malevole addresses Maquerelle in lines 22–6. This would mean that QB's 'Jasons' in line 23 is a genuine correction (kept in QC) – and has the virtue of maintaining the implication that Maquerelle is a witch (Dipsas . . . Medea). But in lines 22–6 Malevole's concern is with an aphrodisiac for Bilioso, and if those lines are addressed to Maquerelle Malevole's added parting-shot to Bianca makes little sense. The ladies' posset and the aphrodisiac for Bilioso are separate issues. QC's new line sounds like the work of Marston, who must surely have supplied it. If he also changed the s.h. in 33, he had probably forgotten his original intentions, and had he been reminded of them, would have endorsed QAB.

II.iii.7 *b' wi'*: buy A, B; be with C.
II.iii.19 *Slave's . . . rise*: slaues I fauour, I mary shall he, rise, Q (A lacks the comma before 'rise'). Our reading is essentially Wine's improvement on Dyce's, but Wine ends with a question mark.
II.iii.21 *Mounts*: C; Mount A, B.
II.iii.25–46: C; not in A, B.
II.iii.49 *which*: Spencer; with Q.
II.iii.50 *loft*: B, C; soft A.
II.iii.53 *discover*: B, C; disseuer A.
II.iii.54 *displayèd*: B, C; discouered A.
II.iii.61 s.h.: Dyce; assigned to Mendoza in Q, but, as Hunter points out, the stratagem is Mendoza's (I.vii.59–61), and he carries it out (II.v.1–15); so Pietro must be the speaker.
II.iii.63 s.d., 87 s.d.: B, C; not in A.
II.iii.85 *nobly*: A; noble B, C.
II.iii.91 *unhele*: vnheale C; vnhill A, B.
II.iii.94 s.d. *the*: C; not in A, B.
II.iv s.d. *the*: C; a A, B.
II.iv.2 *methodically*: A, B; methodicall C.
II.iv.5 *ye*: yee A, B; you C.
II.iv.21 *restoration*: restauration B, C; operation A.
II.iv.33 *o'*: a' A, B; of C.
II.iv.42 *Well*: A, B; We C.
II.iv.55, 58 *the'*: the A, B; they C.
II.iv.65 *i' the*: ithe A, B; in the C.
II.iv.69 s.d.: B, C; Exeunt at seuerall dores A.
II.iv.72 s.d.; B, C; Exit A.
II.v.1 s.d. (*Tumult within*): A, B; not in C.
II.v.5 s.d.: B, C; not in A.
II.v.6 *princess'*: Dyce; Princes Q; prince's Hunter, since the word may be 'used for both sexes in this period'.
II.v.9 s.d.: A, B; not in C.
II.v.46–7 *for . . . sovereign?*: A, B; not in C.
II.v.64 *pent*: A, B; spent C; the word is unpunctuated in Q; Hunter defends C, but 'pent' is a Marstonian word (as in *AR*, V.ii.33), and makes much better sense (see commentary).
II.v.95 *thy*: A, B; the C.
II.v.110 *Ha*: A, B; ah C.
II.v.112 *Ha*: A, B; Ah C.
II.v.135 *ha'*: A, B, haue C.
II.v.147 *Ha, ye*: A, B (yee); ah you C.
II.v.158 *does*: A, B; dooth C.
III.i.9 *sticks*: C; stick A, B.
III.i.10 s.h.: C; assigned to Mendoza in B; continued to Pietro in A.
III.i.10 *honoured*: Hunter; honest Q, but 'honest' almost always carries overtones of condescension towards a social inferior, and 'honoured lord' is used at III.iii.1.
III.i.34 *compliments*: C; complaints A, B.
III.i.35 s.d.: after this line C adds over 100 lines; see Appendix, Insertion ii, p. 525 below.
III.ii.16 s.d.: B, C; not in A.
III.ii.23 *i'*: A, B; in C.
III.ii.33 *blushless*: Hunter; blushes Q. Hunter's emendation gives the

required sense, and an easy, and unnoticed, omission of 'l' from 'blushles' is all that need be postulated; cf. 'blushless impudence' at IV.iii.35.

III.ii.34 *choke*: Dodsley; cloake A, B; cloke C.

III.ii.42–53: Dodsley; prose in Q. Lines 50–1 might perhaps end '. . . fair-spoken/. . . witty'; and transposition of 'rich' and 'fair-spoken' would further improve the metre.

III.ii.53 *Ithaca, can*: A, B; Ithacan C.

III.iii.9 *find*: B, C; faind A.

III.iii.30 *himself*: A, B; itself C.

III.iii.43 *i'*: A, B; in C.

III.iii.44 *ye*: A, B; thou C.

III.iii.47 *does*: doz A, B; dooth C.

III.iii.86 *So*: Q; to Dodsley.

III.iii.93–4 *Come . . . Inform*: Dodsley; come *a cape a pe*, how in forme Q. Hunter reads 'Come 'a [= 'Will he come'] *cap-a-pe*? How in form?', and glosses, 'How is he [the Duke] accoutred, in armour ('head-to-foot') or otherwise?' However, 'a' must be attached to the succeeding phrase, since '*a cape a pe*' is a Marstonian form found in *Soph.*, I.ii.185 s.d. We have regularised to *OED*'s spelling of the 'Old French' expression (which is consistently associated with arming and accoutring). Malevole repeats, in elliptical form, his request of lines 90–1; the sense is 'Come, I want to be armed from head to foot. How can I get the equipment? Tell me.'

III.iii.116 *i'*: A, B; in C.

III.iv.3 *safety*: Dyce; safely Q. 'The emendation restores the pattern of the triple pursuit' (Hunter); a simple l/t confusion.

III.iv.6 *And't*: C; and A, B.

III.iv.7 *ye*: yee A, B; you C.

III.iv.9 *leave . . . we*: C; as wee, leaue you A, B.

III.iv.22 *and't*: C; and A, B.

III.iv.29 *ha'*: A, B; haue C.

III.v.4 *Must*: A, B; you must C.

III.v.7 *sword*: A, B; and sword C.

III.v.29 s.h.: Dyce; assigned to Celso in Q.

III.v.29 *Lord, Malevole*: Hunter; Lord Maleuole Q. Pietro does not think of Malevole as a lord.

IV.i.32 *'fore*: A, B; for C. As Hunter explains, 'The point is not that she should look good when Bilioso returns, but that she use his departure for her own advantage.'

IV.i.57–9 *See . . . Maquerelle*: Spencer, acting on Neilson's conjecture, gave this section of the speech to Bianca – with good reason; but perhaps both ladies lay claim to Ferrardo, who is clearly a wimble youth, 'into every hen's nest, like a weasel' (I.iii.28); alternatively, line 69 could be assigned to Emilia (though it is Bianca whom Ferrardo courts in V.v).

IV.ii.2 *Les guanto*: les quanto B, C; Lesquanto A. Dyce notes that a Bodleian Library manuscript contains a list of dances including 'Quarto dispayne' (according to Collier), 'Quanto-dispaine' (according to Halliwell); and Dyce himself points to mention of a 'courtly dance' called '*Les Guanto*' in Munday's *Banquet of Dainty Conceits* (1588); these references suggest a Spanish dance that would presumably have been '*Los guantes*', as Dyce conjectures. The corruption in *The Malcontent* is perhaps more likely to be linguistic than textual, but Munday gives sufficient warrant for at least the emendation of 'q' to 'g' (if only as a regularisation of the spelling).

IV.ii.7 *doubles*: B, C; double A.

IV.ii.19 s.h.: A; no s.h. in B; C assigns to Prepasso.

IV.ii.29 *bade*: A, B; bid C.

IV.ii.30 *talk*: B, C; talking A.

IV.ii.31 *ever*: B, C; neuer A.

IV.iii.30 *the*: C; their A, B; this whole line would be improved metrically by omission of the redundant 'cuckold'; the attributive use of 'wittol' creates a Marstonian enough expression, but the duplication may have been unintentional.

IV.iii.43 *so*: A; too B, C.

IV.iii.51–2: This arrangement of the verse rhymes two alexandrines.

IV.iii.54 s.h.: B, C; Cry all A.

IV.iii.60 s.d.: B, C; To Emilia A.

IV.iii.87 *I'll*: Ile C; Iste A, B.

IV.iii.88 *Come*: B, C; O ô me A.

IV.iii.96 *'dieu, adieu*: due, adue Q, which Hunter interprets as 'due adieu' (meaning 'a suitably ceremonious farewell').

IV.iii.115–17: This arrangement of the verse rhymes two alexandrines.

IV.iii.117: assigned as in A; B continues to Mendoza; C continues 'like lightning' to Mendoza, but gives Pietro the rest of line 117.

IV.iii.137 s.d.: B, C; not in A. Harris, acting on Wood's conjecture, incorporates it into the text.

IV.iv.2 *on*: C; in A, B.

IV.iv.4 *rant*: rand B, C; raue A.

IV.iv.7 *amazed*: amazde B, C; mazde A.

IV.iv.15 *He*: B, C; not in A.

IV.iv.15 *eldern*: B, C; elder A.

IV.iv.20 s.h.: Dyce; assigned to Mendoza in Q.

IV.v.1 *lead*: Dyce; led A, B; ledde C. Dyce's spelling is simply an interpretation of Q's, and the imperative has the more point. As Hunter says, 'Aurelia demands to be led to her punishment; she does not merely comment on her situation.'

IV.v.8 *tire*: B, C; try A.

IV.v.11 *'Fore*: B, C; for A.

IV.v.20 *pierce*: B, C; paine A.

IV.v.32 *loves*: Dyce; lou'd Q.

IV.v.78 *ha'*: A, B; hath C.

IV.v.84 *from*: B, C; for A.

IV.v.90 *banishing*: Q; publishing Neilson, conj. Deighton.

IV.v.103–12: B, C; not in A.

IV.v.120 *Faith*: A, B; Yfaith C.

IV.v.122 *thou'rt*: th'art A, B; thou arte C.

IV.v.129 *for, for*: Q; but the first 'for' has no obvious logical force ('but' would be more natural), and the duplication may be accidental.

IV.v.130 *emperors'*: Hunter; Emperour(e)s Q.

IV.v.141 *though't*: C; tho't B; that A.

IV.v.142 *here, 'fore*: Dodsley; heerefore Q.

IV.v.148: Q centres these names (in italics, like most names) under the immediately preceding entry. Eds. delete the line as a superfluous s.d. Hunter incorporates it into the dialogue, supposing that Malevole refers to 'the tableau of restoration now assembled on the stage'. The names do form a decasyllable. The conjuror has just turned himself into Altofront and produced Ferneze from his hat, and the line is perhaps the equivalent of 'hey presto'. But the names may be relics of a Jonsonian listing of the participants in what Marston once treated as a new scenic unit; cf. *Soph.*, II.i.s.d.

IV.v.157 *who*: A, B; not in C.

IV.v.159 *Touseth*: Towzeth B, C; Looseth A.

IV.v.165 s.d.: After this line C adds a scene, 'ACTVS V. SCENA I.' See Appendix, Insertion iii, p. 530 below.

V.i.10–11 *beast. And*: Between these words C adds the dialogue of Appendix, Insertion iv, p. 532 below.

V.i.13 *Verily, very*: B, C; Verie verie A.

V.i.21 *the most*: B, C; most A.

V.i.24 *raise*: B, C; rouse A.

V.i.34 *come*: A, B; cowe C.

V.i.61 *heavens*: B, C; heauen A.

V.ii.25 *love*: A, B; sake C.

V.ii.31 *this*: C; tis A; t'is B.

V.ii.79 s.d. – 116: C; not in A, B.

V.iii s.d. *and* GUERRINO: Dyce; Bilioso and Guerrino Q.

V.iii.15 *deed safely*: deede, safely C; deedes safely A, B.

V.iii.21: After this line C adds Appendix, Insertion v, p. 533 below.

V.iii.27 *ta'en*: tane A, B; taken C.

V.iii.32 *power*: B, C; pores A.

V.iii.37 *nor*: A, B; or C.

V.iii.38 *are*: B, C; one A.

V.iii.40 s.d.: C prints twice, after line 33 and after line 39.

V.iii.55 *What*: Dodsley; Why Q.

V.iii.63 *fashion*: A; a fashion B, C.

V.iii.70 *with*: A, C; both B.

V.iii.71 *deservèd*: B, C; distuned A.

V.iii.74 s.d.: A, B; not in C.

V.iii.87 s.d.: A; not in B, C.

V.iv SCENE IV: no new scene marked in Q.

V.iv.19 *bare hair*: B, C; head A.

V.iv.27 *falling*: B, C; falling band A.

V.iv.29 *St Andrew Jacques*: S. Andrew Iaques A; S. Andrew B, C. The omission of 'Jaques', hinting at King James, must be due to censorship.

V.iv.36 *had*: A, C; did B.

V.iv.44 *warped*: warpt A, B; wrapt C.

V.iv.47 *wimble*: Bullen conj.; vn-ydle B, C; windle A; *OED*'s only other citation of 'unidle' is from *Astrophil and Stella*, Sonnet 26, where the word is much more natural; here it seems a weak miscorrection; 'wimble' = active, nimble, occurs in *AM*, III.ii.216.

V.v. s.d. *with lights*, FERRARDO: A, B; and lights, Ferrard C.

V.v.18 *We'll*: Dodsley; Weele Q; Well Hunter.

V.v.33 *forfeited*: A, B; forteified C.

V.v.32–7: Q lineation; Harris and Hunter follow Wood's conjectural arrangement: '. . . Captain/. . . justice/. . . find/. . . hermit/. . . custody/. . . harm/. . . blood'; but this buries the final couplet.

V.v.44 s.h.: B, C; A puts s.h. before line 45.

V.v.50: A adds the s.d. '*Vnto Maria*'; perhaps it was intended for line 68.
V.v.55 *Genoan*: B, C; Genoa A.
V.v.67 *court*: B, C; count A.
V.v.71 *to*: C; for A, B.
V.v.84 *Come*: B, C; Come down A, which fits the metre, but Aurelia seems not to be up anywhere; 'downe' might be a misreading of 'dance', or some other monosyllable.
V.v.107–8 *handbasket*: B, C; not in A.
V.v.113 s.d.: A; not in B, C.
V.v.115 s.d.: B, C; not in A.
V.v.116 s.h.: Q; Dyce, followed by Hunter, assigned 'Peace . . . words' in line 116 to Malevole.
V.v.120 *Pietro*: B, C; Lorenzo A.
V.v.126 *breath till*: breath, til B, C; breath to liue til A.
V.v.135 *thorough*: through Q, but the metre requires the disyllabic spelling.
V.v.142–64: C; not in A, B.
V.v.149 *princes*: C (?u); men C (?c); here and in line 154 the more specific words were politically rash.
V.v.152 *conceit*: Hunter; conceale C; conceive Dyce and most eds.; Hunter's emendation restores sense and is graphically plausible, supposing the manuscript read 'conceate'; for 'conceit' = conceive, see *AM*, Ind. 120, V.i.51, V.ii.93.
V.v.154 *kings*: C (?u); men C (?c).
V.v.166 s.h.: Dodsley; not in C.
V.v.166 *o'erjoyed*: ore-ioy'd B, C; are ioyd A.
V.v.170–1 *All . . . breast*: A has a comma after 'liue', B and C a full stop; so Wood supposes that all 170 is addressed to Bilioso, with 'all-pleased live' meaning 'nevertheless, I am willing to let you live'.
V.v.172: B, C; not in A.
EPILOGUS 1–18: B, C; not in A.
EPILOGUS 3 *'scuseless*: scusles B; sensles C; most eds. read 'senseless', but Hunter seems right to regard C's word as a misreading or sophistication of B's more pointed one, meaning that intentionally committed error is totally inexcusable, unintentional error is less culpable.

The Dutch Courtesan

I.i.19 *host's*: Wine; hostes Q; hoste 1633; hostess Bullen.
I.i.20–3 *The . . . street*: Q punctuation, with a comma added after 'Cocledemoy'. Wine takes 'consorted with' to mean 'had (sexual) commerce with' and reads 'Cocledemoy consorted with . . . Mary Faugh; are imparlor'd', with the subject of 'are imparlor'd' understood; but *OED* cites contemporary instances of 'consorted with' meaning 'in the company of', and there are Shakespearean examples (*LLL*, I.i.245, *R3*, III.iv.73).
I.i.56 *cellar*: Bullen, sellar Q; seller Halliwell; both modernisations make sense, and there is doubtless a pun.
I.i.62, 67 s.h.: Walley, conj. Brereton; Free. Q.
I.i.84 *love*: 1633; lou'd Q; Wine accepts Q and glosses, 'past tense used with force of *loved and love*'.

I.i.147 *quid*: Bullen; quite Q; quit 1633.
I.i.164 *persever*: Q spelling retained for metre and rhyme.
I.i.166 *dainties*: 1633; daintines Q.
I.ii.30 *enhanceress*: Bullen, inhauncres Q (u); inhauntres Q (c), 1633; here the reading of Q (u) (= one who 'enhances' or raises the price), which must have bewildered the press-corrector, is more pointed and provides a better parallel to 'supportress', though Davison follows Q (c) and glosses 'associate'; *OED inhaunt* and *haunt* might give him some support: an 'inhauntress' would be 'one who haunts, a devotee'.
I.ii.30 *lotium*: Q (c); lotinw Q (u).
I.ii.32 *thy*: Q (c); the Q (u).
I.ii.34 *function*: Q (c); functis Q (u).
I.ii.35 *hear*: Q (c); haue Q (u).
I.ii.36 *lady*: Ladie Q (c); Iade Q (u).
I.ii.56–7 *giddy . . . youth*: Q (c); giddie youth, and vnsetled Q (u).
I.ii.74–5: Q (c) adds the superfluous s.d. '*Enter Cocledemoy*' between these two lines.
I.ii.83 *stoup*: stoope Q (c); sloope Q (u); Wood conjectures 'stroup', used in a Northern dialectal sense of 'spout', 'spigot', and paraphrases: 'I will drain the vintner dry: draw off his substance till the level falls below the spigot, and then tilt the barrel to run off the rest.'
I.ii.146 s.h.: Walley; not in Q, which consequently omits the next s.h. for Freevill.
I.ii.182 *eld*: Q (c); field Q (u).
I.ii.182 *strongs't*: Q (c); straight Q (u).
II.i.18 *protested*: Q (c); pretested Q (u).
II.i.37 *pants*: Q (c); pant Q (u).
II.i.47 *he that thus*: Q (c); that he thus Q (u).
II.i.50–5: prose in Q; our division of the first three lines differs slightly from other editorial arrangements as verse. Bullen suggests 'a pity' (for Q's 'pity') in line 55, but 'more' can be pronounced as a disyllable.
II.i.91 *once*: Q; one's Davison.
II.i.103 *vow-band*: Wine; vowe band Q; vowe[d] band Bullen.
II.i.108 *assuredly*: Bullen; assurely Q; surely conj. Brereton.
II.i.171 *fist*: fiest Q; feast Bullen.
II.i.177 *companions are*: Q (c); companion as Q (u). Wine follows Q (u), wrongly designating it the corrected reading in his collation notes, but Malheureux's reply vindicates Q (c).
II.i.181–2 *Does . . . barber-surgeon*: Q; Bullen and Wood give the line to Holifernes.
II.i.189 s.h.: 1633; not in Q.
II.ii.20 *Sir*: Walley; S. Q.
II.ii.39 *flat-caps*: Halliwell; atte-cappes Q (with letters missing or failing to print).
II.ii.63 *aderlievest*: Wine; a deere leevest Q.
II.ii.119 *unproved*: Bullen; vnproude Q, which Wood interprets as 'unproud'.
II.ii.123–4 *With . . . stay*: Q; Davison allocates to Franceschina.
II.ii.139 *Of*: Q; Or 1633, which Wine and Davison adopt; but cf. the construction in II.i.78–9.
II.ii.234 *professèd*: 1633; pofessed Q; possessed Wood.

II.ii.253 *soil*: Walley; soule Q; mould Bullen.
II.ii.270 *learn'd*: Q's apostrophe is here retained to indicate the unmodern monosyllabic pronunciation.
II.iii s.d. *bag*: Q (c); a bag Q (u).
II.iii.11 *wines*: Q (c); wiues Q (u).
II.iii.86 *make*: Q (c); masle Q (u).
III.i.25 *turd*: 1633; turnd Q.
III.i.54 *of the*: of Q; cf. V.ii.150.
III.i.279 *man*: Wood; men Q.
III.i.290 *villainess*: Wine; villaines Q; villains Bullen.
III.ii s.d. BURNISH: Bullen; Garnish Q, but Burnish in *Dramatis Personae* Q. The normalisation affects subsequent speech headings and directions in this scene and the text at III.iii.41, 102, 179.
III.ii.31 *Or*: Wood; One Q; Wun' Bullen; Wan' Davison. Misreading (of 'or' as 'on' = one) seems more likely than the aural error implied by the emendations of Bullen and Davison.
III.iii.1 s.h. MISTRESS: Mrs. 1633; not in Q.
III.iii.47 s.h. MISTRESS: Mrs. 1633; Mr. Q.
III.iii.129 *God*: 1633; Good Q.
III.iii.140 *too. Worshipful Cocledemoy*: Davison; to worship; Cocledemoy Q (u); to, worship: Cocledemoy Q (c). Q's mistake arises from misinterpretation of the abbreviation 'Worsh.' (as on G2[v], IV.v.106, and four times on H4, V.iii.149, 155, 182, 186).
III.iii.195 *cry*: Bullen, cary Q.
IV.i.5 s.h.: Walley, conj. Brereton; Lyo. Q.
IV.i.6 s.d.: The additions are Wine's.
IV.i.37 *husband*: husbands Q. Q's grammar is not impossible, but an easy misprint seems slightly more probable.
IV.i.46 *pales*: Q; palles 1633; palls Bullen.
IV.i.49 *to marry*: 1633; to my marry Q.
IV.i.58 *Euphues*: Ephues Q (c); Ephius Q (u).
IV.i.69 *ate*: eate Q; this common past participial form is usually spelt 'eat' by modernising eds., but 'ate', phonetically [ɛt], is less ambiguous for the modern reader.
IV.i.75 *By* ——: By ( ) Q; since Q exhibits a good range of offensive oaths, perhaps the brackets indicate stage business (Davison).
IV.ii.4–5 *they . . . quarrel*: they are much possest/Of force most, most all quarrell Q, which Wine glosses: 'They who are most possessed of force ("weight", faculty of reason) nearly all quarrel', and Davison's paraphrase is similar. This makes sense of a kind, but the awkward redundancy of 'much possessed . . . most' is bothersome, and can it be fortuitous that 'of force' means 'necessarily' when, and only when, preceded or followed by 'must', which 'most' so closely resembles? Q's punctuation is unreliable, and may be misleading here. Somewhat doubtfully, we have amended, and interpret: 'they whom the devil drives must perforce nearly all quarrel'; cf. 'devils . . . sensual fury' at the end of the speech (10–12) and Franceschina's outburst in IV.iii.54–8. In line 4 the relative pronoun 'who' must be understood; its actual presence would fill a metrical gap, and it may have been accidentally omitted, but Marston's penchant for ellipses perhaps tilts the balance in favour of Q.
IV.iii.1 *cacafuego*: *OED* spelling; catafugo Q; Q's 'u' for 'ue' is a spelling variant, its 't' for 'c' probably (in view of Cocledemoy's

scatological turns of phrase) a misreading, as in line 9 below.

IV.iii.9 *adulterate*: 1633; adulcerate Q.

IV.iii.33 *seets*: Q; feets Wine; 'seets' could be 'sweets' (as at II.ii.61–3, V.i.24, 27, 108) or, more likely, 'sheets' (since Franceschina regularly says 'sall' for 'shall'); if 'sweets' is intended, Franceschina presumably just means that she will apply the scent bottle, perhaps concentrating on the erogenous zones; Lavateur talks of wearing 'perfumed sweets' (a pomander?) in *WYW*, but Wood (II, 249) conjectures 'sheets'; 'sheets fumed with violets' turn up later in *WYW* (p. 264), and 'sweet sheets' in *Malc.*, I.vii.39.

IV.iii.38 *a knave and whore*: a whore and knave Q; the transposition recovers an effective rhyme.

IV.iii.48 *stale*: Q; Bullen conjectured 'tall'.

IV.iv.15, 39 *Crispinella*: Crisp. Q, which Wine retains, as he retains 'Cris' at IV.iv.38, but this is the printer's abbreviation, as in the speech prefixes and stage directions, not a colloquial foreshortening; cf. 'Const.' for Constable on G2v, IV.v.125, and the note above on III.iii.140.

IV.iv.66 *wilt*: 1633; will Q.

IV.v.38 s.h. 1 CONSTABLE: CONSTABLE 1 1633; 2. Q.

IV.v.70 *let's*: 1633; let Q.

IV.v.123 s.h., 124 s.h.: Davison assigned 'Mulligrub?' to Cocledemoy. Q includes it within a single speech ('One . . . him?') by 1 Constable.

IV.v.128 *and*: Q (c); But Q (u).

IV.v.153 *worship*: Q; Worships Davison, but the 'worshipful Cocledemoy' is presumably addressing himself.

V.i.5 *mynheer*: Myn-here Q (c); Man-here Q (u).

V.i.21 *aderliver*: Wine; a dere liuer Q.

V.i.36 *learned*: lerned Q; metrically the word might be either monosyllabic or disyllabic here.

V.i.37–40: Q divides after '. . . haue a/. . . Delight/. . . manhood'.

V.i.45 *the*: th' Q, but Halliwell's lineation, which, like Wine and other eds., we have adopted, requires the article to be syllabic.

V.i.49 s.d. *take*: 1633; takes Q.

V.i.63 s.d. *depart*: 1633; departs Q.

V.i.66 *damned*: dambd Q (c); doombd Q (u).

V.i.78 *twine*: Q (c); twaine Q (u).

V.i.102 *say*: Wood; sea Q; see Bullen.

V.i.108 *Vat*: Q (c); I dat Q (u).

V.ii.29 s.d. *disguise*: 1633; discourse Q.

V.ii.38 s.d., 46 s.d.: Q has the single s.d. at line 38, '*He sings, she sounds.*'

V.ii.58 *loved*: 1633; laued Q.

V.ii.67 s.h.: 1633; not in Q.

V.ii.111 *Shatewe*: 1633; Shatews Q.

V.ii.121 *whoreson*: Whoresone Q (c); Whoresome Q (u).

V.ii.124 *suspicious*: 1633; suspitions Q.

V.ii.132: the syllabification of verb-endings is as in Q; the line is metrical if 'and his' is slurred into a single syllable.

V.ii.143 *You're*: Bullen; your Q; you Davison.

V.ii.150–2: these lines come at the foot of a page in Q; perhaps they should be lined '. . . time/. . . not/. . . chance/. . . ignorance', though this would rhyme a five-syllable line with a pentameter.

V.ii.150 *o' the*: of Q; idiom requires the article; cf. *The Revenger's Tragedy* Q 1607/8, Sig. A3, where Vendice says that he will become 'a man a'th Time', cynically adjusting to a corrupt age, and *Antony and Cleopatra*, II.vii.98, 'Be a child o'th' time'; the contraction 'o' the', which occurs several times in *DC*, is here metrically desirable.

V.iii.23 *wily man*: Bullen; Welyman Q; wely-man 1633.

V.iii.36 *say*: sea Q; see Bullen, Wine; but cf. V.i.102.

V.iii.47 *shape*: Halliwell; shaps Q; shapes 1633.

V.iii.62 *sir*: Walley; sirs Q.

V.iii.76 *brother*: Wine, conj. Brereton; brothers Q.

V.iii.115 *brother, brother*: Bullen; brothers, brothers Q.

V.iii.119 *braggets, ciders*: Bragets, Syders Q (c); Bragoes, Syder Q (u).

V.iii.151 *catastrophonical*: Wood; catastrophomicall Q, but cf. II.i.222–3.

V.iii.158 *euphoniae*: Q (c); Euphomae Q (u).

V.iii.168 *courtier*: courtyer Q (c); courtyers Q (u).

V.iii.188 *at . . . seen*: Bullen; as our much care hath bin Q; as our much care be seene 1633; Q's 'hath bin' has been accidentally repeated from the end of the preceding line; 1633's conjecture is a good one, which Bullen improves.

The Tragedy of Sophonisba

TO THE GENERAL READER 5 *blank*: 1633; black Q.

ARGUMENTUM 1 *height*: 1633; haight Q, which Kemp interprets as 'hate', following Q's punctuation ('haight: Ingratitude.'). This makes good sense, but Q's 'haight' = 'height' at III.i.69 and V.i.13 (Kemp is obviously wrong to interpret this latter instance as 'hate' also), and Q otherwise spells 'hate' in the normal way.

I.ii.77 *anchor*: Q; Bullen regarded this as 'an obvious misprint' and emended to 'rancour', but Deighton cited *The Winter's Tale*, I.ii.213–14, in support of Q; there 'his anchor . . . still came home' means that it repeatedly failed to hold.

I.ii.121 *fill*: 1633; full Q; *OED* cites 'full', somewhat dubiously, as a separate form, but it seems better to modernise.

I.ii.124 *we*: 1633; yee Q.

I.ii.135 *sad*: Kemp, conj. Wood; said Q; 1633, Halliwell, and Bullen gave line 135 and Bytheas's exclamation (line 136) to Hanno; Wood gave 135 to Bytheas.

I.ii.147 *god*: Q; th' God 1633.

I.ii.172 *my*: 1633; me Q.

I.ii.185 s.d. *cap-à-pie*: *OED* spells thus; Q's, and probably Marston's spelling is 'a cape a pee' (cf. *Malc.*, III.iii.94).

I.ii.198 *this*: Q; these 1633.

I.ii.201 *loves, dalliance*: Q; but perhaps this should be 'love's dalliance'.

I.ii.217 *fields*: Kemp; field Q.

I.ii.229 *thee*: Q; of thee Deighton conj.

II.i.4 *Senate? All think fit.*: Q punctuation; Bullen prints 'Senate, all think fit?' with 'which' understood after the comma.

II.i.39 *comes*: Q; come Halliwell, Bullen, Kemp; the third person plural in '-s' is so common in Shakespeare and his contemporaries

(Abbott 333) that emendation, even on grounds of euphony, is best avoided.

II.i.51 *a hundred marble marble*: Q; a hundred hundred marble Wood conj., but as West and Thorssen note, epizeuxis is a marked stylistic mannerism of Marston's in this play.

II.i.89 *feel*: Q (c); cell Q (u).

II.i.96 *ever*: 1633; ouer Q.

II.i.106 *Is this . . . It is*: Through compositor error this line appears twice in Q, at the bottom of C2 and at the top of C2v. It begins in Q with the speech prefix (absent from line 104) '*So.*' on C2, '*Sopho.*' on C2v, and reads 'decrees' on C2, 'decree' on C2v.

II.i.134–5 *and we . . . we see*: and We/See as thinges are things are not, for we see Q; not We,/See as things are things, are not, as we see 1633; not we,/See as things are; things are not as we see Bullen.

II.i.164 *no*: Q; not Kemp; Q is idiomatic if 'no one drop' = 'no single drop'.

II.ii.11 *own*: Bullen; not in Q; metre and sense require the addition.

II.ii.20 *may let*: Q (c); melt at Q (u).

II.ii.21 *bleed abroad*: Wood; bleeds abrode Q (u); bleeds abroad Q (c).

II.ii.41 s.d. *a letter*: Q (c); letter Q (u).

II.ii.43–4 *Um . . . poor?*: Bullen; Q places the s.d. '*To Gelosso*' at the right of an otherwise blank line between 43 and 44; all eds. save Bullen take it as introducing 'Sirra . . . poor?'; but Gisco answers, and from the ensuing dialogue it is clear that, the letter borne by that 'most only man' Gelosso having alerted Massinissa to Gisco's murderous intentions, Massinissa is implicitly asking whether Gisco's motives are mercenary.

II.ii.44 s.d. *draw*: drawe Q (c); drane Q (u).

II.ii.50 *blood-shot*: bloud-shut Q.

II.ii.54 *creature . . . live*: Creature, hold Gisco ( ) liue Q. Kemp deduces that Q's empty parentheses were written in the manuscript to accommodate a s.d. to be inserted later. Between 'Creature' and 'Hold' he adds 'Gisco attempts to drink his own poison.' This gives point to 'Hold', which suggests that Gisco is dissuaded from some action, but he may simply be about to flee or kneel, and any attempt by Gisco at suicide would take the focus from Massinissa's own refusal to kill him. West and Thorssen argue that if a s.d. is required it should be 'Puts up', to create an *Iliad*-derived tableau of Stoic forbearance in which Massinissa spares his would-be assassin while ostentatiously sheathing his weapon. However, they would prefer to fill the parentheses with 'yet' – on analogy with III.i.24, where Q reads '(yet)'; but they misunderstand the purpose of these later parentheses. Though II.ii.54 is a syllable short, the insertion of 'yet' would not, as they suppose, improve it metrically.

II.ii.71 *over*: O ouer Q; the omission improves sense and metre, and the compositor could easily have picked up the exclamation from the previous line or from 'ouer'.

II.ii.76 *No, Jugurth*: Kemp; Not Jugurth Q. Marston sometimes uses 'Not' where we might expect 'No', but a standard instance of the rhetorical figure ploce at its simplest ('No, Jugurth, no') seems marginally more probable.

II.ii.81 *abodes*: Q; abode Kemp.

II.iii.9 *aimed-at end*: aimedat end Q (c); aimdeattend Q (u) (with a slight space between 'e' and 'a').

II.iii.96 *an*: not in Q.

II.iii.108 *Broad . . . powers*: Brode skorne oppen faind powers Q; Brooke open scorne, faint powers 1633. Though Bullen and Kemp follow 1633, it represents nothing more than a desperate guess, unconvincing both in itself and as an original from which Q's reading could have derived. Wood's conjecture, 'upon', gains support from the same confusion in *AM*, IV.i.69, and a word stressed on the second syllable is metrically preferable to 'open'. An alternative emendation might be 'oppone' = 'oppose' (see *OED*). West and Thorssen accept Q's reading as the verb 'open' in the sense 'reveal, make manifest'. Asdrubal, who is probably being restrained (cf. 'Hold!' in line 105), 'oscillates between wild rage and panic depression'. In view of the curious punctuation within Q's version of line 108 ('dos it.*Asd*.: – Brode') it is possible that Hanno should utter the good alexandrine, 'He does it, Asdrubal. Broad scorn upon feigned powers!', before Asdrubal speaks.

III.i.23–4 *Dead . . . fame*: Lineated as in Q (though it is forced to break line 24). The lines constitute two pentameters which would divide '. . . Vangue/My . . .'; but rearrangement would obscure the rhyme, and Marston is partial to alexandrines.

III.i.26, 205 *bear*: Q; bar Bullen.

III.i.27 *my Syphax*: Q; me; Syphax 1633 and eds.; but 'my' is acceptable as registering Sophonisba's new strategy of pretended affection.

III.i.50 *Not*: Q; No Kemp.

III.i.58 *good speed, speed*: Q; Kemp sees compositorial duplication here and prints 'speed' only once; metrically a disyllabic pronunciation of 'hour' would fit Kemp's line, while a monosyllabic pronunciation (along with stress on 'good') fits Q's.

III.i.63 *their . . . hold*: Bullen; their vails, hold Q.

III.i.110 *to*: Q; do Bullen, which may be right, but the intensive, connective or metrically imposed use of 'to' was possible at the time, and 1633 made no change.

III.i.142–5 *Due . . . draught*: This new arrangement restores regular verse. Q divides '. . . dead/. . . don/. . . welcome/. . . thus/. . . draught'.

III.i.142 s.d. Q adds '&&&'; Marston's intention may have been to note Sophonisba's surreptitious doctoring of the drink. The directions at 142, 145, 161, 163 and 169 (all on D4^{v}) are printed in roman in Q, and so are typographically indistinguishable from the dialogue; Kemp includes s.d. 163 as part of Sophonisba's speech, but it disturbs otherwise good verse (taking 'Zanthia' in 161 as disyllabic, to form an alexandrine).

III.i.191 *Think*: Q; think I 1633.

III.i.201 *then*: Kemp; the Q; that Bullen.

III.ii.8–9 *It . . . thus*: Kemp; It is a happy being breath well fam'd,/ For which *Ioue* sees these thus Q; 1633 first changed 'sees' to 'fees', a word to which Marston is partial. Kemp explains: 'Massinissa says that Jove pays (''fees'') the wicked Carthaginians (''these'') by allowing him to preserve his honourable reputation through joining the Romans'; i.e 'these' = the 'vile men' of line

7. Bullen regarded the text as corrupt, but rejected his own proposals ('sees me thus', 'sees this use'). Deighton defended Q, interpreting 'these' as 'being' and 'breath', and 'thus' as 'happy' and 'well famed': in other words, the divine perspective offers the only measure of a creature's happiness or a life's moral worth. West and Thorssen, retaining 'breath' but reading 'fees' and taking it to mean 'employs', interpret: 'the only end for which Jove employs men and countries is to nurture a human being content with integrity, a life renowned for its quality' (p. 356). Kemp's version, though less compelling than he imagines, has the virtues of linking 'these' with its most natural antecedent, and of giving some point to 'For', but the jingle 'fees these' is harsh; altering 'these' to 'those' would not only make it less so but slightly sharpen the sense. Emendation of 'these' to 'thee' would yield a further set of possibilities.

III.ii.38 *Rome's*: Romes Q; Rome Bullen, to match V.iii.65, where Laelius quotes this vow back at Massinissa; but there is no way of telling which of the versions is right; Marston may well have written both.

III.ii.39 *with*: Bullen; worth Q. Though Q is defensible as meaning 'worthy of', in this case we can probably assume that the correct reading is given at V.iii.66. The compositor has picked up 'or' from the following two words.

III.ii.73 *wild*: wilde Q (c); vilde Q (u).

III.ii.78 *sinew*: sinue Q; sinne 1633 and eds.; Wood defends Q as metrically preferable but follows 1633; Kemp retains the Q reading. If Q is right, 'his' = 'its' with 'this arm' as antecedent.

IV.i.4 *damps*: Bullen; dumps Q. The words may be related (see *OED dumps sb.*[1]), but dumps (fits of melancholy) are exclusively psychological, while damps, according to *OED*, may be both psychological and physical, and actual vapours are obviously required here (cf. *AR*, III.i.77, 145).

IV.i.9 *justly*: Q (u); nimbly Q (c). This is the most problematical of all the press-variants. Either (a) the compositor made a 'memorial error' influenced by 'just' earlier in the line, and the corrector restored the manuscript reading; or (b) the corrector made an unauthoritative attempt to improve the line, while normalising the spelling of 'leagues' – Q (u) has 'leages' – three lines above. As there is no clear evidence elsewhere that the press-corrector consulted copy, but some indication of bad guessing at IV.i.128, 130, and V.ii.81, it seems safest to accept the *difficilior lectio*; 'just' and 'justly' are favourite Marston words, which he is quite capable of using in rather odd ways.

IV.i.42 s.d.: Q neglects to bring back Zanthia between her exit at line 32 and her arrest and speech at lines 86–7.

IV.i.70 *fruit's*: fruites Q.

IV.i.81 *royalest*: roialst Q; royal'st Bullen; the full modernisation can be similarly disyllabic, and is less of a tongue-twister in combination with 'excellence'.

IV.i.101 s.d.: so placed in Q; Bullen transfers to immediately before line 125.

IV.i.110–12 *then . . . rites*: Q has no punctuation within this passage. Bullen places a comma, here strengthened to a semi-colon, after 'tombs', to imply that Erictho scrapes gum from cerecloths – no doubt rightly, as a cerecloth is a winding-sheet impregnated with glutinous matter. Kemp changes 'From' to 'For' and punctuates after 'searcloaths', not after 'tombes', so turning 'then . . . rites' into two parallel constructions, and improving the rhetorical flow. The lines compress and modify several scattered sentences in Lucan's account, where his concern is mainly with funeral pyres, so *Pharsalia* cannot be cited in support of either Bullen or Kemp.

IV.i.128 *love*: 1633; Ioue Q. This confusion is very common in sixteenth- and seventeenth-century texts. Syphax wants something more from Sophonisba than the 'jovial disposition' to which Bullen detects an allusion. The Q press-corrector's feeble attempt to give the line meaning consisted in inserting a comma after 'be' in 'be alfull' (as Q printed these words).

IV.i.130 *beasts*: Q (u); heastes Q (c). Extant copies of Q preserve E (o) in four states, 'heastes' first appearing in the third state, along with two obvious corrections of simple typographical errors. Kemp accepts the new reading as 'much more likely than the old to represent the author's meaning' (p. 61), presumably taking 'heastes' as 'hests' or commands. But the passage in which the line occurs is indebted to Book VI of Lucan's *Pharsalia* and the parallels prove that Q (u)'s 'beasts' was what Marston wrote: 'Every creature that has power to kill and was born to do mischief dreads the Thessalian witches and provides their skill with the means of death. The fierce tiger and the angry lion, king of beasts, lick their hands and fawn upon them; for them the snake unfolds his chilly coils and stretches at full length on the frosty ground; knotted vipers split apart and unite again' (Loeb edn, lines 485–90). So 'heastes' probably represents a meddlesome guess which the press-corrector made without reference to the manuscript (for a Secretary 'b' would not easily be misread as 'h') but under the influence of 'obayes', wrongly diagnosing a literal misprint, 'b' for 'h', due to foul case. This must make us suspicious of the few other press-corrections that are not certain emendations of trivial mechanical errors.

IV.i.132 *the ignorance*: 1633; th'ignorance Q.

IV.i.133 *uncurls*: 1633; vncurlde Q, which ends the line in a comma, to suggest (impossibly) that 'vncurlde' is a participial adjective, like 'roulde'. The past tense would be possible, but scarcely apt: Erictho is not referring to a single past occasion.

IV.i.172 *know'st*: 1633; knowest Q.

IV.i.189 *sickless*: Q; sickness' Bullen; West misreads Q as 'ficklesse'. *OED* cites three other examples of 'sickless'.

V.i.7 *mere*: Bullen; more Q, which seems impossibly feeble.

V.i.17 *deigned*: Bullen; dam'd Q, an easy misreading if the manuscript spelling was 'dain'd' (cf. 'daine' in Q at V.iii.28, V.iv.28).

V.i.32–3: Q divides after 'aught', which would leave line 33 unmetrical, unless 'trenched' (Q 'trench'd') were made disyllabic and 'plagues' pronounced like 'agues', as it may be in *AM*, II.i.310.

V.i.47 *after which*: Q; after that Bullen, so as to reverse the sequence and put the loss in battle before the treachery; but Asdrubal had first 'turned unfaithful' to Sophonisba and Massinissa.

V.i.52 *Fury*: fury Q; Furies Bullen, who is obviously right in assuming that the reference is to avenging goddesses, not Asdrubal's vindictive wrath; but there is no reason why one of the Erinyes (perhaps Tisiphone, the avenger) should not interest herself in Asdrubal's case.

V.ii.11 *joy's*: Bullen; joyes Q.

V.ii.26 *nor's due*: nor's adue Q; nor sued 1633 and eds., a shrewd guess, which, however, implies a rather complex typographical muddle in Q. Our alternative emendation requires only the deletion of one letter; 'nor's' = 'nor is' or 'nor was'.

V.ii.39 *act's*: Q; acts 's Bullen.

V.ii.41 *life and death*: Q; life, not death 1633 and eds.; but Massinissa's prayer is that the gods grant him life and the conquest of his opponent.

V.ii.76 *once* Q (c); one Q (u).

V.ii.81 *Threw moving clasps*: Bullen; Threw mouing claspt Q (u); There mouing claspt Q (c). None of the press-reader's corrections that are certainly right need have resulted from inspection of the manuscript, and 'There' is probably just a plausible guess, Bullen's being a better one. With 'moving clasps' cf. 'moving graces' in line 75 and 'moving art' in line 91.

V.ii.90 *new-leagued*: Bullen; new laughed Q.

V.iii.34 *nectar, think* –: Kemp; Nectar, thinke Q; Nectar, skinke 1633; nectar-skink Bullen, which he glosses 'draught of nectar'. However, 'skink' as liquor is Scots, contemptuous, and unrecorded by *OED* before 1824. 1633, which retains the comma after 'Nectar', was evidently offering the word as the verb meaning to pour out; several *OED* citations involve nectar or the gods. But this yields a sense opposite to that which is required, since Sophonisba is rhetorically refusing an excess of joys. West and Thorssen (p. 356) argue that there is really no crux: 'Sophonisba's lines are dramatically intelligible as the ecstatic utterance of a fainting woman, imagining herself surfeiting in celestial nectar.' She is telling Jove to have a care for his nectar – not to pour it all out upon her.

V.iv.2 *tongue*: tong Q (u); tongs Q (c): we agree with Kemp that this is a miscorrection made (while the s.h. in line 1 was being changed from '*Sy.*' to '*Sc.*') without recourse to the manuscript, but are sceptical about Kemp's suggestion that the press-corrector thought 'tongs' = forceps.

V.iv.6 *his*: this Q, but the pertinent vow (to Rome) has not been mentioned in the immediate context; cf. 'Know . . . breathed', V.iii.60–3.

ADDITIONAL NOTES

Antonio and Mellida

PROLOGUE 2 *gentle*: Marston appeals to the self-conscious gentility of the 'select and most respected auditors' at Paul's. The flattering tone of the prologue is so extravagant that it is tempting (especially in the light of Marston's Dedication) to find a degree of playful irony. Certainly the Epilogue, while remaining respectful, strikes a sturdier and more independent note.

V.i s.d PAINTER: V.i evidently parodies the Painter scene from *The Spanish Tragedy* (Fourth Addition), but there are dating problems. The second Quarto of Kyd's play, in which the additions first appeared, was published in the same year as *Antonio and Mellida* (1602), and the Painter scene is sometimes thought to be amongst those additions for which Jonson was paid by Henslowe in 1601/2. Though Caputi and Finkelpearl assign *AM* to the second half of 1600, it is usually dated 1599, partly on the basis of lines 8–15 of V.i. itself; and even if the Stationers' Register entry of 24 October 1601 is taken as the only certain limit of Marston's play, the time scheme remains unrealistically tight. John Kerrigan has privately suggested that Marston may have revised the scene for publication as late as 1602, by way of a riposte to Jonson's attacks on him in *Poetaster* (1601). Certainly the armed Epilogue to *AM* seems (like the armed Prologue to the Folio *Troilus and Cressida*) to glance at the armed Prologue of *Poetaster* (unless Jonson is mocking Marston, and Marston reflecting on the Epilogue to *Cynthia's Revels*), and is likely enough to be a late addition. But on the whole it is perhaps easier to suppose that the Painter scene of *The Spanish Tragedy* pre-dates Jonson's contributions to the play (cf. also II.i.166–70).

Antonio's Revenge

II.i s.d.: This processional dumb-show needs attention; the stage directions in Q are almost certainly Marston's own and can reveal a great deal about the theatrical dimension of the play. The action here includes the setting up of Antonio's tomb, a semi-permanent structure which is the symbolic focus of this scene and of III.i. It may indeed be intended to remain on the stage, providing a kind of unspoken commentary on the action until the end of the play. The 'hearse' referred to here is the framework decorated with banners, heraldic devices, candles, epitaphs and other tokens of mourning, set up over the coffins of noblemen when they were placed in a church (*OED*, *sb.* 2a and 2c). Some hearses were portable and carried in the funeral procession: this one may either be carried on with the coffin, or placed on the stage in the act-interval. Many tombs were canopied with a permanent 'hearse', supporting rich coverings (*OED*, *sb.* 2b), and Marston apparently intends an imperceptible conflation of the two, just as his 'coffin' becomes the tomb-chest of Act III. The chief mourners are led by a Herald who carries the emblems of Andrugio's knighthood – helmet and sword – and who directs the placing of his armorial achievements, the 'streamers', or heraldic pennons. The Herald's presence emphasises the important social function of such monuments for a traditional and hierarchical society (see, for instance, John Weever, *Ancient Funeral Monuments*, 1631). Piero's iconoclastic contempt for symbolic ordering is immediately indicated by the directions that have Piero and Strotzo 'talking'.

The Malcontent

IV.ii.s.d.: Another scene in which Marston makes striking emblematic use of the private theatre musical conventions. The intricate patterning of seventeenth-century dance and the harmonies of its music (whose ideal cosmic and political symbolism had been elaborated by Marston's fellow member of the Middle Temple, Sir John Davies, in his poem *Orchestra*) provide an intensely ironic counterpoint to the real subject of the scene – adultery, murder and social breakdown. Its dramatic power is suggested by Ford's imitation of the scene nearly thirty years later in *The Broken Heart*.

IV.iii.16–52: The tone of this long oration is characteristically difficult to fix. It has the solemnity fitting to Pietro's religious disguise, and the lofty rhetorical style considered appropriate to his role as Nuntius (cf. Gertrude's account of Ophelia's end, *Hamlet*, IV.vii.166–84). On the other hand, the fact that Pietro is describing his own death gives the situation a comic unreality, though the emotions of bitter jealousy and despair that he attributes to the dying duke are real enough. A theatrical disguise becomes (as in the case of Malevole/Altofront) the vehicle for venting his actual feelings upon those who have betrayed him. As always, the artificiality of the occasion is emphasised by the piping voice behind the beard. Marston is probably aiming for a complex audience reaction of the kind in which Beaumont and Fletcher were later to specialise, where intense emotionalism is made to coexist with a wry recognition of the dramatist's witty artifice.

IV.v.155–65: A speech knit up of curious contradictions. For practical purposes it is difficult to distinguish between Altofront's divine Providence and the machiavellian 'providence' (foresightedness) espoused by Mendoza (IV.iii.135–6), especially in a world seemingly governed by the arbitrary 'rise' and 'fall' of fortune. In fact Malevole effectually equates the two by accounting for his rise with the machiavellian maxim 'who can sink that close can temporise?' (161). Perhaps 'holy policy' is best defined, in Marston's view, by a kind of sublime punning.

APPENDIX: INTRODUCTION AND TEXT OF WEBSTER'S ADDITIONS TO *THE MALCONTENT*

WEBSTER'S ADDITIONS TO *THE MALCONTENT*

This appendix prints those additions to the third Quarto (QC) of *The Malcontent* that are judged to be by John Webster. As explained in our introduction to the play, Webster's authorship of the induction is generally accepted. Hunter pointed out that QC's insertions within the body of the play fall, in their style and structure, into two groups, one of which is unmistakably Marstonian, the other possibly Websterian. David J. Lake, in 'Webster's additions to *The Malcontent*: linguistic evidence', *Notes and Queries*, 226 (1981), 153–8, confirms Hunter's tentative division, and we have found that each of the putatively Websterian interpolations seems clearly related to the adaptation of Marston's script for the King's Men. Marston's own augmentations bear no such signs of their occasion. His preface to the first Quarto (QA) states that he himself had 'set forth this comedy' – by which he evidently meant that he had provided the publisher with a manuscript – but asks the reader to excuse printing-errors because his 'enforced absence' had prevented his seeing the play through the press. The publication of QB gave him the chance to make corrections and minor revisions. The printing history of *The Fawn* (1606) is much the same (a second Quarto, corrected and lightly revised, having been printed largely from standing type), and similar statements were made about the author's provision of good copy (he had been his 'own setter-out'), his absence at the time of the initial printing, and his partial amendment of the text for the second Quarto. (See David A. Blostein's Revels edn., pp. 42–52.) There is no evidence that Marston oversaw the proofing and printing of *The Malcontent* QC. A possible explanation of the mixture of the Marstonian and non-Marstonian in QC's alterations, large and small, might be that the King's Men really did get hold of the Blackfriars 'book' of the play; that this contained not only trivial variants, authoritative and unauthoritative, but also Marston's expansion (whether made for the Blackfriars or for a proposed transfer to the Globe); that Webster then added his contributions; and that this was the manuscript collated with exemplars of QB to serve as printer's copy for QC.

Aspley may well have obtained the manuscript from the King's Men, without Marston's being involved. Aspley would have been eager to capitalise on the King's Men's take-over of the play, and his relations with the company seem to have been close: in 1600 he had published good quartos of Shakespeare's *2 Henry IV* and *Much Ado About Nothing*.

Lake's case in support of Hunter's postulated division of QC's extra passages begins with a search for contrasting linguistic preferences between Marston's and Webster's undoubted plays. As Webster's three unaided plays were written in the decade 1610–20, Lake also examines Webster's early collaborations with Dekker, *Westward Ho* and *Northward Ho*, which belong to 1604–5. Fortunately Webster's shares in these two comedies can be distinguished with almost complete confidence; all objective evidence, some of it bibliographical, indicates the same clear-cut divisions: to the studies cited by Lake one might add Frederick E. Pierce, *The Collaboration of Webster and Dekker* (New Haven, 1909), and Tony Halsall, 'The collaboration of Dekker and Webster in *Westward Ho* and *Northward Ho*', *PBSA*, 72 (1978), 65–8. Lake shows that after the *Antonio* plays Marston made fairly liberal use of *has* and *does*, preferring them to *hath* and *doth* in *The Dutch Courtesan*, *The Fawn* and the basic *Malcontent* as represented in QAB. (In the Stoic tragedy, *Sophonisba*, he reverted, for the sake of decorum, to an almost exclusive use of the formal *hath* and *doth*.) The overall figures for *The Dutch Courtesan*, *The Fawn*, and *The Malcontent* QAB are *has* 93, *hath* 68; *does* 51, *doth* 26. Webster scarcely employed the modern forms at all, except in the tragicomedy *The Devil's Law Case* – the last of his plays, written as late as 1617. The overall figures, excluding *The Devil's Law Case*, are *has* 11, *hath* 159; *does* 3, *doth* 58. The Marstonian augmentations of *The Malcontent* use *has* once, *doth* once: this barely constitutes evidence, but, so far as it goes, it is consistent with his authorship. For the induction the figures are *hath* 6, *doth* 1, with no instances of the alternative forms, and for the 'Websterian' additions *hath* 10, *doth* 2, again with no instances of *has* or *does*. There is thus a remarkable discrepancy between the putatively Websterian additions to *The Malcontent*, which are consistent with Webster's practices, and the rest of the play. Confining the contrast to that between the unaugmented play and Webster's additions to the body of the text, we get *hath/doth*: *has/does* figures of 28:20 and 0:12. This difference is statistically significant: the probability is less than one in 1000 that it is fortuitous. The Passarello scenes are as colloquial as anything in the play, so there is no reason why Marston should there deviate from his normal practices. Moreover, whereas Marston's augmentations use his connectives, *among*, *betwixt* and *whilst*, along with his colloquialisms *ye* (10 times) and *ha'*, Webster's additions use his preferred *amongst*, *between* (in the induction), and *while*, and avoid *ha'* and all but a single example of *ye*; while the indefinite use of *your*, of which the young Webster was fond, is restricted to, and remarkably common in, his putative contributions to the play. Lake shows also that significant parallels with Webster's plays are concentrated within the Websterian additions. Texts of the induction and the Websterian insertions follow.

THE INDUCTION TO *THE MALCONTENT*, AND THE ADDITIONS ACTED BY THE KING'S MAJESTY'S SERVANTS.

WRITTEN BY JOHN WEBSTER

Enter WILL SLY, *a* TIRE-MAN *following him with a stool.*

TIRE-MAN. Sir, the gentlemen will be angry if you sit here.

SLY. Why? We may sit upon the stage at the private house. Thou dost not take me for a country gentleman, dost? Dost think I fear hissing? I'll hold my life thou took'st me for one of the players.

TIRE-MAN. No, sir.

SLY. By God's slid, if you had, I would have given you but sixpence for your stool. Let them that have stale suits sit in the galleries. Hiss at me! He that will be laughed out of a tavern or an ordinary shall seldom feed well or be drunk in good company. – Where's Harry Condell,

---

INDUCTION s.d. SLY: member of the Chamberlain's/King's Men 1594–1608.

INDUCTION s.d. TIRE-MAN: in charge of properties and wardrobe.

4 *the private house*: the Blackfriars, where the play was originally performed, was a small indoor theatre of the type fictively called 'private' playhouses, to distinguish them from the large and less exclusive open theatres like the Globe, for which the induction was written. Sly presents himself as a Blackfriars wit, loftily indifferent to the coarse manners of the 'public' theatres.

9 *God's slid*: God's eyelid.

10 *sixpence*: ironically the standard price for a stool on the stage.

11 *stale*: unfashionable.

13 *ordinary*: eating-house.

14 *Condell*: member of King's Men 1590–1627; helped to assemble the First Folio of Shakespeare's plays (1623).

Dick Burbage, and Will Sly? Let me speak with some of them.

TIRE-MAN. An't please you to go in, sir, you may.

SLY. I tell you, no. I am one that hath seen this play often, and can give them intelligence for their action. I have most of the jests here in my table-book.

Enter SINKLO.

SINKLO. Save you, coz.

SLY. O cousin, come, you shall sit between my legs here.

SINKLO. No indeed, cousin; the audience then will take me for a viol da gamba and think that you play upon me.

SLY. Nay, rather that I work upon you, coz.

SINKLO. We stayed for you at supper last night at my cousin Honeymoon's, the woollen-draper. After supper we drew cuts for a score of apricocks, the longest cut still to draw an apricock. By this light, 'twas Mistress Frank Honeymoon's fortune still to have the longest

---

15 *Burbage*: the principal tragic actor in the King's Men; his roles included Richard III, Hamlet, Othello and Macbeth, as well as Altofront/Malevole in this play.

15 *Sly*, earlier anxious that he might be mistaken 'for one of the players', now calls for himself – one of many wittily self-conscious devices by which the induction seeks to recreate the artificial quality of performance by a child company.

20–1 *give . . . action*: instruct them in the proper performance of their roles.

22 *table-book*: a notebook or commonplace-book for recording favourite passages, standard equipment for the young connoisseurs of theatre apparently (cf. Hamlet's 'tables').

22 s.d. SINKLO: minor actor with the company, known for his emaciated frame.

23 *coz*: cousin, familiar term of affection.

27 *viol da gamba*: bass viol, ancestor of the cello.

28–9 *play upon . . . work upon*: obscene *doubles entendres*.

32 *cuts*: straws, lots (with indecent quibble).

33 *apricocks*: apricots; the old spelling is here retained as fitting the bawdy context.

cut; I did measure for the women. – What be these, coz?

Enter DICK BURBAGE, HARRY CONDELL, JOHN LOWIN.

SLY. The players. – God save you.

BURBAGE. You are very welcome.

SLY. I pray you, know this gentleman, my cousin: 'tis Master Doomsday's son, the usurer.

CONDELL. I beseech you, sir, be covered.

SLY. No, in good faith, for mine ease. Look you, my hat's the handle to this fan. God's so, what a beast was I, I did not leave my feather at home! Well, but I'll take an order with you.

Puts his feather in his pocket.

BURBAGE. Why do you conceal your feather, sir?

SLY. Why, do you think I'll have jests broken upon me in the play, to be laughed at? This play hath beaten all your gallants out of the feathers: Blackfriars hath almost spoiled Blackfriars for feathers.

SINKLO. God's so, I thought 'twas for somewhat our gentlewomen at home counselled me to wear my feather to the play; yet I am loath to spoil it.

SLY. Why, coz?

SINKLO. Because I got it in the tilt-yard. There was a herald broke my pate for taking it up; but I have worn it up and down the Strand, and

---

37 s.d. LOWIN: recently hired member of the company who enjoyed a long and distinguished career.

42 *be covered*: Sly has obsequiously doffed his hat, as though to a superior; the episode recalls *Hamlet*, V.ii, perhaps because Sly had played Osric.

44 *handle to this fan*: Sly's hat is adorned with such an extravagantly large feather that it resembles the handle of a fan.

44 *God's so*: corruption of Italian *cazzo* ('prick')?

46 *take . . . you*: make an arrangement with you.

49–51 *This play . . . feathers*: cf. the mockery of the fashion for feathers at V.ii.45–6. Sly appears to claim that Marston's play has damaged the feather-trade centred on Blackfriars.

57 *tilt-yard*: Sly's feather originally adorned the helmet of one of the combatants at a Whitehall tilt.

met him forty times since, and yet he dares not challenge it.

SLY. Do you hear, sir, this play is a bitter play?

CONDELL. Why, sir, 'tis neither satire nor moral, but the mean passage of a history; yet there are a sort of discontented creatures that bear a stingless envy to great ones, and these will wrest the doings of any man to their base, malicious applyment. But should their interpretation come to the test, like your marmoset they presently turn their teeth to their tail and eat it.

SLY. I will not go so far with you, but I say any man that hath wit may censure if he sit in the twelvepenny room, and I say again the play is bitter.

BURBAGE. Sir, you are like a patron that, presenting a poor scholar to a benefice, enjoins him not to rail against anything that stands within compass of his patron's folly. Why should not we enjoy the ancient freedom of poesy? Shall we protest to the ladies that their painting makes them angels, or to my young gallant that his expense in the brothel shall gain him reputation? No sir, such vices as stand not accountable to law should be cured as men heal tetters, by casting ink upon them. Would you be satisfied in anything else, sir?

SLY. Ay, marry, would I: I would know how you came by this play.

CONDELL. Faith, sir, the book was lost, and because 'twas pity so good a play should be lost, we found it and play it.

SLY. I wonder you would play it, another company having interest in it.

---

63 *moral*: morality play.
64 *mean*: ordinary.
68 *applyment*: personal application of a 'general' satire.
69 *marmoset*: monkey; once introduced to meat, monkeys (according to the natural historian Gesner) were prone to eat their own flesh.
73 *twelvepenny room*: expensive box beside the stage.
85 *tetters*: skin eruptions.

CONDELL. Why not Malevole in folio with us, as Jeronimo in decimo-sexto with them? They taught us a name for our play: we call it *One for Another.*

SLY. What are your additions?

BURBAGE. Sooth, not greatly needful; only as your salad to your great feast, to entertain a little more time, and to abridge the not-received custom of music in our theatre. I must leave you, sir. *Exit* BURBAGE.

SINKLO. Doth he play the malcontent?

CONDELL. Yes, sir.

SINKLO. I durst lay four of mine ears the play is not so well acted as it hath been.

CONDELL. O no, sir, nothing *ad Parmenonis suem.*

LOWIN. Have you lost your ears, sir, that you are so prodigal of laying them?

SINKLO. Why did you ask that, friend?

LOWIN. Marry sir, because I have heard of a fellow would offer to lay a hundred-pound wager, that was not worth five baubees; and in

---

94 *in folio*: i.e. with full-size actors, as opposed to the 'decimo-sexto' miniatures of the boy-companies.

95 *Jeronimo*: the hero of Kyd's *The Spanish Tragedy* and of the so-called *First Part of Hieronimo* (which may actually have been written for a boy-company to exploit the popularity of Kyd's play).

101–2 *not-received custom of music*: musical interludes, in the form of overtures and entr'actes, were a striking feature of private house performances, which also made more elaborate use of songs, dances and consort music in the action of the play than did the public playhouses (though music within the body of *The Malcontent* would be normal enough for a King's Men play).

108–9 *ad Parmenonis suem*: 'compared to Parmeno's pig'. Plutarch (*Symposiaca Problemata*, V, i, 674) writes of Parmeno, whose imitation of pig-noises was so accomplished that his admirers were convinced that the grunting of a real pig paled by comparison. Condell makes Sinklo's admiration of the boy-Malevole appear similarly pig-headed.

115 *baubees*: Scottish halfpennies (a familiar glance at James's penurious Scots followers).

this kind you might venture four of your elbows. Yet God defend your coat should have so many!

SINKLO. Nay, truly, I am no great censurer, and yet I might have been one of the college of critics once. My cousin here hath an excellent memory, indeed, sir.

SLY. Who, I? I'll tell you a strange thing of myself; and I can tell you, for one that never studied the art of memory, 'tis very strange too.

CONDELL. What's that, sir?

SLY. Why, I'll lay a hundred pound I'll walk but once down by the Goldsmiths' Row in Cheap, take notice of the signs, and tell you them with a breath instantly.

LOWIN. 'Tis very strange.

SLY. They begin as the world did, with Adam and Eve. There's in all just five and fifty. I do use to meditate much when I come to plays, too. What do you think might come into a man's head now, seeing all this company?

CONDELL. I know not, sir.

SLY. I have an excellent thought: if some fifty of the Grecians that were crammed in the horse-belly had eaten garlic, do you not think the Trojans might have smelt out their knavery?

CONDELL. Very likely.

SLY. By God, I would they had, for I love Hector horribly.

SINKLO. O, but coz, coz:

116–17 *four of your elbows*: fools' coats were frequently made ridiculous with four elbows.

120–1 *college of critics*: the self-appointed élite of playhouse wits. The noisy interventions of their partisan claques were a particular peril for private theatre dramatists.

128 *Cheap*: Cheapside contained a row of goldsmiths' shops and houses.

138 *excellent thought*: induced by the reek of garlic from the pit; an occasion for some by-play with the audience.

143 *Hector*: 'loved' by Sly for patriotic reasons: the British were said to be descended from the Trojans.

'Great Alexander, when he came to the tomb of Achilles,
Spake with a big loud voice, "O thou thrice blessèd and happy!" '

SLY. Alexander was an ass to speak so well of a filthy cullion.

LOWIN. Good sir, will you leave the stage? I'll help you to a private room.

SLY. Come, coz, let's take some tobacco. – Have you never a prologue?

LOWIN. Not any, sir.

SLY. Let me see, I will make one extempore. Come to them and, fencing of a congee with arms and legs, be round with them:
'Gentlemen, I could wish for the women's sakes you had all soft cushions; and gentlewomen, I could wish that for the men's sakes you had all more easy standings.'
What would they wish more but the play now?
And that they shall have instantly.

[*Exeunt*].

146–7 *Great . . . happy*: Sinklo responds to Sly with lines that remember Hector's destroyer, Achilles, in a comically mangled misquotation from John Harvey's already clumsy hexameter translation of Petrarch's Sonnet CLIII (printed in Gabriel Harvey's *Three Proper . . . Letters*, 1580).

149 *cullion*: knave.

151 *private room*: box.

152 *tobacco*: another piece of swagger on Sly's part; smoking was a conspicuous feature of gallant exhibitionism in the theatre.

156 *fencing of a congee*: making an extravagant French bow.

159–61 *soft cushions . . . easy standings*: obscene *doubles entendres*. This mock-prologue burlesques the epilogue to *As You Like It*.

INSERTIONS

(i) After I.vii.85 s.d.

Enter MALEVOLE *and* PASSARELLO.

MALEVOLE. Fool, most happily encountered. Canst sing, fool?

PASSARELLO. Yes, I can sing fool, if you'll bear the burden; and I can play upon instruments, scurvily, as gentlemen do. O that I had been gelded! I should then have been a fat fool for a chamber, a squeaking fool for a tavern, and a private fool for all the ladies.

MALEVOLE. You are in good case since you came to court, fool. What, guarded, guarded!

PASSARELLO. Yes, faith, even as footmen and bawds wear velvet, not for an ornament of honour, but for a badge of drudgery; for, now the duke is discontented, I am fain to fool him asleep every night.

MALEVOLE. What are his griefs?

PASSARELLO. He hath sore eyes.

MALEVOLE. I never observed so much.

PASSARELLO. Horrible sore eyes; and so hath every cuckold, for the roots of the horns spring in the eyeballs, and that's the reason the horn

INSERTION i s.d. PASSARELLO: cf. Italian *passerelle* (according to Florio, a 'little plaice or flounder . . . dried fish called Poor John').

3–4 *bear the burden*: (1) sing the chorus; (2) pay the cost.

4 *play upon instruments*: with an indecent quibble.

9 *case*: condition, clothes.

10 *guarded*: trimmed with elaborate facings.

12 *velvet*: the Elizabethan Statutes of Apparel forbade the wearing of velvet to anyone below knightly rank unless ambassadors, gentlemen of the queen's household, or gentlemen of a disposable income of over one hundred pounds a year.

of a cuckold is as tender as his eye, or as that growing in the woman's forehead twelve years since, that could not endure to be touched. The duke hangs down his head like a columbine.

MALEVOLE. Passarello, why do great men beg fools?

PASSARELLO. As the Welshman stole rushes when there was nothing else to filch: only to keep begging in fashion.

MALEVOLE. Pue, thou givest no good reason; thou speakest like a fool.

PASSARELLO. Faith, I utter small fragments, as your knight courts your city widow with jingling of his gilt spurs, advancing his bush-coloured beard, and taking tobacco. This is all the mirror of their knightly compliments. Nay, I shall talk when my tongue is a-going once; 'tis like a citizen on horseback, evermore in a false gallop.

MALEVOLE. And how doth Maquerelle fare nowadays?

PASSARELLO. Faith, I was wont to salute her as our Englishwomen are at their first landing in Flushing: I would call her whore. But now that antiquity leaves her as an old piece of plastic t' work by, I only ask her how her rotten teeth fare every morning, and so leave her. She was the first that ever invented perfumed smocks for the gentlewomen, and woollen shoes, for fear of

---

22–4 A pamphlet of 1588 records the monstrous deformity of Margaret Griffith who had 'a crooked horn of four inches long . . . in the midst of [her] forehead'.

25 *columbine*: drooping flower whose form suggested the cuckold's horns.

26–7 *beg fools*: one of the grosser forms of patronage, by which the king granted custody of idiots (and use of their estates) to petitioners.

35 *bush-coloured*: Hunter suggests 'bush' = fox's tail.

36–7 *mirror . . . compliments*: gibe at the Spanish romance, *The Mirror of Knighthood*; 'compliments' = style of courtship.

43–4 *Englishwomen . . . in Flushing*: camp-followers arriving to serve the garrison.

45 *plastic*: any malleable substance.

creaking, for the visitant. She were an excellent lady, but that her face peeleth like Muscovy glass.

MALEVOLE. And how doth thy old lord that hath wit enough to be a flatterer and conscience enough to be a knave?

PASSARELLO. O, excellent; he keeps beside me fifteen jesters to instruct him in the art of fooling, and utters their jests in private to the duke and duchess. He'll lie like to your Switzer or lawyer; he'll be of any side for most money.

MALEVOLE. I am in haste; be brief.

PASSARELLO. As your fiddler when he is paid. He'll thrive, I warrant you, while your young courtier stands like Good Friday in Lent: men long to see it because more fatting days come after it; else he's the leanest and pitifull'st actor in the whole pageant. Adieu, Malevole.

MALEVOLE. [*aside*] O world most vile, when thy
loose vanities,
Taught by this fool, do make the fool seem
wise!

PASSARELLO. You'll know me again, Malevole?

MALEVOLE. O ay, by that velvet.

PASSARELLO. Ay, as a pettifogger by his buckram bag. I am as common in the court as an hostess's lips in the country; knights and clowns and knaves and all share me; the court cannot possibly be without me. Adieu, Malevole.

[*Exeunt.*]

(ii) After III.i.35 s.d.

Enter BILIOSO *and* BIANCA.

BILIOSO. Madam, I am going ambassador for

51–2 *Muscovy glass*: talc or mica.
59 *Switzer*: Swiss mercenary soldier.
66–7 *leanest . . . pageant*: another joke at the expense of Sinklo (?); the self-reference again emphasises for the Globe audience the artificial quality of the action.
72 *pettifogger*: inferior lawyer.
72–6 Passarello speaks as the incarnation of Folly.

Florence; 'twill be great charges to me.

BIANCA. No matter, my lord, you have the lease of two manors come out next Christmas; you may lay your tenants on the greater rack for it; and, when you come home again, I'll teach you how you shall get two hundred pounds a year by your teeth.

BILIOSO. How, madam?

BIANCA. Cut off so much from housekeeping; that which is saved by the teeth, you know, is got by the teeth.

BILIOSO. 'Fore God, and so I may; I am in wondrous credit, lady.

BIANCA. See the use of flattery; I did ever counsel you to flatter greatness, and you have profited well. Any man that will do so shall be sure to be like your Scotch barnacle, now a block, instantly a worm, and presently a great goose; this it is to rot and putrefy in the bosom of greatness.

BILIOSO. Thou art ever my politician. O, how happy is that old lord that hath a politician to his young lady! I'll have fifty gentlemen shall attend upon me; marry, the most of them shall be farmers' sons, because they shall bear their own charges; and they shall go apparelled thus: in sea-water green suits, ash-colour cloaks, watchet stockings, and popinjay-green feathers.

4–5 *manors . . . rack*: when the leases on his manors expire Bilioso will be able to rackrent his tenantry. The squeezing of tenants and looting of the countryside to support the extravagant life-style of courtiers is often attacked in early-seventeenth-century writing.

10 *housekeeping*: the feudal practice of hospitality in a great house; the decay of this custom is another standard subject of Jacobean satire and lament.

18 *Scotch barnacle*: the lore surrounding the barnacle goose, supposedly hatched from a type of barnacle found in northern Scotland, may be gleaned from Gerard's *Herbal* (1597), Ch. 188; a standard comparison (like the mushroom) for the rapidly rising courtier; 'block' (= shell or tree-stump), 'worm' and 'goose' are also terms of insult.

28 *watchet*: pale blue.

28 *popinjay*: blue-green.

Will not the colours do excellent?

BIANCA. Out upon't! They'll look like citizens riding to their friends at Whitsuntide, their apparel just so many several parishes.

BILIOSO. I'll have it so; and Passarello, my fool, shall go along with me; marry, he shall be in velvet.

BIANCA. A fool in velvet?

BILIOSO. Ay, 'tis common for your fool to wear satin; I'll have mine in velvet.

BIANCA. What will you wear, then, my lord?

BILIOSO. Velvet, too; marry, it shall be embroidered, because I'll differ from the fool somewhat. I am horribly troubled with the gout. Nothing grieves me but that my doctor hath forbidden me wine, and you know your ambassador must drink. Didst thou ask thy doctor what was good for the gout?

BIANCA. Yes; he said ease, wine, and women were good for it.

BILIOSO. Nay, thou hast such a wit. What was good to cure it, said he?

BIANCA. Why, the rack. All your empirics could never do the like cure upon the gout the rack did in England, or your Scotch boot. The French harlequin will instruct you.

BILIOSO. Surely, I do wonder how thou, having for the most part of thy lifetime been a country body, shouldst have so good a wit.

BIANCA. Who, I? Why, I have been a courtier thrice two months.

BILIOSO. So have I this twenty year, and yet there was a gentleman-usher called me coxcomb t'other day, and to my face too. Was't not a backbiting

---

32 *apparel . . . parishes*: i.e. totally mismatched.

35–8 *velvet . . . satin*: see above, Insertion i.12, note.

48 *good for it*: she means, of course, 'tend to induce it'.

51 *empirics*: empirical physicians; frequently equivalent to 'quack'.

53 *Scotch boot*: iron boot into which wedges were driven, progressively crushing the foot.

54 *French harlequin*: perhaps alluding to the mountebank quack as a *commedia dell'arte* figure (cf. *Volpone*).

rascal? I would I were better travelled, that I might have been better acquainted with the fashions of several countrymen; but my secretary, I think, he hath sufficiently instructed me.

BIANCA. How, my lord?

BILIOSO. 'Marry, my good lord', quoth he, 'your lordship shall ever find amongst a hundred Frenchmen forty hot-shots; amongst a hundred Spaniards, threescore braggarts; amongst a hundred Dutchmen, fourscore drunkards; amongst a hundred Englishmen, fourscore and ten madmen; and amongst an hundred Welshmen –'

BIANCA. What, my lord?

BILIOSO. 'Fourscore and nineteen gentlemen.'

BIANCA. But since you go about a sad embassy, I would have you go in black, my lord.

BILIOSO. Why, dost think I cannot mourn unless I wear my hat in cypress, like an alderman's heir? That's vile, very old, in faith.

BIANCA. I'll learn of you shortly. O, we should have a fine gallant of you, should not I instruct you! How will you bear yourself when you come into the Duke of Florence' court?

BILIOSO. Proud enough, and 'twill do well enough. As I walk up and down the chamber I'll spit frowns about me, have a strong perfume in my jerkin, let my beard grow to make me look terrible, salute no man beneath the fourth button; and 'twill do excellent.

BIANCA. But there is a very beautiful lady there; how will you entertain her?

BILIOSO. I'll tell you that when the lady hath entertained me. But to satisfy thee, here comes the fool.

Enter PASSARELLO.

---

65 *several countrymen*: men of different nations.

70 *hot-shots*: reckless or hot-headed fellows (*OED*); with sexual *double entendre*?

77 *gentlemen*: a stock gibe at Welsh pride.

81 *cypress*: black veiling.

92–3 *salute . . . button*: never bow low.

Fool, thou shalt stand for the fair lady.

PASSARELLO. Your fool will stand for your lady most willingly and most uprightly.

BILIOSO. I'll salute her in Latin.

PASSARELLO. O, your fool can understand no Latin.

BILIOSO. Ay, but your lady can.

PASSARELLO. Why then, if your lady take down your fool, your fool will stand no longer for your lady.

BILIOSO. A pestilent fool! 'Fore God, I think the world be turned upside down too.

PASSARELLO. O no, sir; for then your lady and all the ladies in the palace should go with their heels upward, and that were a strange sight you know.

BILIOSO. There be many will repine at my preferment.

PASSARELLO. O ay, like the envy of an elder sister that hath her younger made a lady before her.

BILIOSO. The duke is wondrous discontented.

PASSARELLO. Ay, and more melancholic than a usurer having all his money out at the death of a prince.

BILIOSO. Didst thou see Madam Floria today?

PASSARELLO. Yes, I found her repairing her face today. The red upon the white showed as if her cheeks should have been served in for two dishes of barberries in stewed broth, and the flesh to them a woodcock.

BILIOSO. A bitter fowl! Come, madam, this night thou shalt enjoy me freely, and tomorrow for Florence.

100–1 *stand . . . uprightly*: sexual *double entendre*.

106 *take down*: reduce, bring low, humiliate (both intellectually and sexually).

110 *world . . . upside down*: as at the feast of All Fools, for instance.

128–9 *flesh . . . woodcock*: perhaps the sense is that the flesh surrounding her unnaturally red cheeks looks like that of a stewed woodcock served with barberries.

130 *fowl*: pun on 'fool' (see Textual Note, p. 534 below).

Ex[*eunt* BILIOSO *and* BIANCA.]

PASSARELLO. What a natural fool is he that would be a pair of bodice to a woman's petticoat, to be trussed and pointed to them! Well, I'll dog my lord; and the word is proper, for when I fawn upon him he feeds me; when I snap him by the fingers he spits in my mouth. If a dog's death were not strangling, I had rather be one than a serving-man; for the corruption of coin is either the generation of a usurer or a lousy beggar. [*Exit.*]

(iii) After IV.v.165 s.d.

Enter BILIOSO *and* PASSARELLO.

BILIOSO. Fool, how dost thou like my calf in a long stocking?

PASSARELLO. An excellent calf, my lord.

BILIOSO. This calf hath been a reveller this twenty year. When Monsieur Gundi lay here ambassador, I could have carried a lady up and down at arm's end in a platter; and I can tell you, there were those at that time who, to try the strength of a man's back and his arm, would be coistered. I have measured calves with most of the palace, and they come nothing near me; besides, I think there be not many armours in the arsenal will fit me, especially for the headpiece. I'll tell thee –

PASSARELLO. What, my lord?

BILIOSO. I can eat stewed broth as it comes

---

134 *pair of bodice*: this was the usual expression, as with 'pair of stays'. QC spells 'bodies'.

135 *trussed and pointed*: tied with laces ('points') but carrying through the 'fowl' word-play.

136 *dog*: Passarello adopts the tone of a snarling cynic 'dog' while picturing himself as a fawning court 'dog'.

12 *coistered*: 'coiled up into a small compass . . . inconvenienced' (*OED*, citing no other instance); Harris suggests 'probably nonce word, and bawdy'.

16 *headpiece*: Bilioso's head is enlarged by his cuckold's horns.

seething off the fire, or a custard as it comes reeking out of the oven; and I think there are not many lords can do it. [*Sniffs his pomander*] A good pomander, a little decayed in the scent, but six grains of musk, ground with rose-water and tempered with a little civet, shall fetch her again presently.

PASSARELLO. O ay, as a bawd with aqua-vitae.

BILIOSO. And, what, dost thou rail upon the ladies as thou wert wont?

PASSARELLO. I were better roast a live cat, and might do it with more safety. I am as secret as thieves to their painting. There's Maquerelle, oldest bawd and a perpetual beggar. Did you never hear of her trick to be known in the city?

BILIOSO. Never.

PASSARELLO. Why, she gets all the picture-makers to draw her picture; when they have done, she most courtly finds fault with them one after another, and never fetcheth them. They, in revenge of this, execute her in pictures as they do in Germany, and hang her in their shops. By this means is she better known to the stinkards than if she had been five times carted.

BILIOSO. 'Fore God, an excellent policy.

PASSARELLO. Are there any revels tonight, my lord?

BILIOSO. Yes.

PASSARELLO. Good my lord, give me leave to break a fellow's pate that hath abused me.

BILIOSO. Who's pate?

PASSARELLO. Young Ferrard, my lord.

BILIOSO. Take heed, he's very valiant. I have known him fight eight quarrels in five days, believe it.

---

24 *civet*: perfume obtained from anal glands of the civet cat.

24 *fetch*: restore.

31 *as thieves to*: see Textual Note, p. 534 below

41 *stinkards*: stinking fellows, *hoi polloi*.

42 *carted*: convicted bawds were taken by cart through the London streets to be exposed to public odium, before being whipped at Bridewell.

PASSARELLO. O, is he so great a quarreller? Why then, he's an arrant coward.

BILIOSO. How prove you that?

PASSARELLO. Why, thus: he that quarrels seeks to fight; and he that seeks to fight seeks to die; and he that seeks to die seeks never to fight more; and he that will quarrel and seeks means never to answer a man more, I think he's a coward.

BILIOSO. Thou canst prove anything.

PASSARELLO. Anything but a rich knave, for I can flatter no man.

BILIOSO. Well, be not drunk, good fool. I shall see you anon in the presence.

Ex[*eunt.*]

(iv) After V.i.10, 'beast.'

Enter PASSARELLO.

MAQUERELLE. O fool, will ye be ready anon to go with me to the revels? The hall will be so pestered anon.

PASSARELLO. Ay, as the country is with attorneys.

MALEVOLE. What hast thou there, fool?

PASSARELLO. Wine. I have learned to drink since I went with my lord ambassador. I'll drink to the health of Madam Maquerelle.

MALEVOLE. Why, thou wast wont to rail upon her.

PASSARELLO. Ay, but since I borrowed money of her. I'll drink to her health now, as gentlemen visit brokers, or as knights send venison to the city, either to take up more money or to procure longer forbearance.

MALEVOLE. Give me the bowl. I drink a health to Altofront, our deposed duke. [*Drinks.*]

54–5 *Why . . . coward*: another paradoxical exercise in mock-logic of the kind popular at the Inns of Court.

3 *pestered*: crowded.

11 *since*: since that time.

14 *take up*: borrow.

PASSARELLO. I'll take it. [*Drinks*] So. Now I'll begin a health to Madam Maquerelle. [*Drinks.*]
MALEVOLE. Pew! I will not pledge her.
PASSARELLO. Why, I pledged your lord.
MALEVOLE. I care not.
PASSARELLO. Not pledge Madam Maquerelle! Why, then, will I spew up your lord again with this fool's finger.
MALEVOLE. Hold; I'll take it. [*Drinks.*]
MAQUERELLE. Now thou hast drunk my health, fool, I am friends with thee.
PASSARELLO. Art? art?
When Griffon saw the reconcilèd quean
Offering about his neck her arms to cast,
He threw off sword and heart's malignant stream,
And lovely her below the loins embraced.
Adieu, Madam Maquerelle. *Exit* PASSARELLO.

(v) After V.iii.21

Enter MALEVOLE *and* MENDOZA.

MENDOZA. Hast been with Maria?
MALEVOLE. As your scrivener to your usurer, I have dealt about taking of this commodity; but she's cold, frosty. Well, I will go rail upon some great man, that I may purchase the bastinado, or else go marry some rich Genoan lady and instantly go travel.
MENDOZA. Travel when thou art married?
MALEVOLE. Ay, 'tis your young lord's fashion to do so, though he was so lazy, being a bachelor, that he would never travel so far as the university; yet, when he married her, tails off, and catso for England!
MENDOZA. And why for England?

30–3 *When Griffon . . . embraced*: parodies a 1598 translation from Ariosto's *Orlando Furioso* by Richard Haydocke (Hunter, drawing on Richard Madelaine).
6 *bastinado*: beating.
12 *tails off*: turns tail.

MALEVOLE. Because there is no brothel-houses there.

MENDOZA. Nor courtesans?

MALEVOLE. Neither; your whore went down with the stews, and your punk came up with your Puritan.

Textual Notes to Appendix

Ind.45 *feather*: Dodsley; father C.

Ind.143 *they*: Dyce; he C.

Ins.i.34–5 *jingling . . . bush-coloured*: jingling of his guilt spurres, aduancing his bush colored C (c); something of his guilt: some aduancing his high colored C (u).

Ins.ii.130 *fowl*: fowle C; Hunter follows Dodsley in altering to 'fool', and cites *King Lear*, I.iv.135, 'A bitter fool'. We have preferred to retain QC's spelling as a signal to Webster's punning, continued in 'trussed and pointed' (135).

Ins.ii.132 s.d.: C has a premature '*Exit*' after 'woodcock' in line 129.

Ins.iii.31 *as thieves to*: to thieues as C; to the thieves as Bullen; to ladies as Dodsley; to them as Dyce; to th'se'ves as Harrier. Hunter suggests 'th'Eves', and is tempted by Dyce's emendation, but follows QC. As Hunter says, Bullen's emendation assumes that 'the thieves' refers to the ladies 'in a rather eighteenth century mode' (the ladies are deceivers and rob men of virility). Etymology, as well as the nature of their trade, ensures that thieves are furtive, and a simple transposition seems the best means of restoring sense to the passage; the ladies' painting is a clandestine activity, and Passarello will keep as 'secret as thieves' about it; there are insinuations of dishonesty all round.

Ins.iv.12 *her.*: C; most eds. lighten the stop to a comma, and give Passarello a single sentence in which 'since' means 'because'.

Ins.v: C's addition begins with a superfluous s.d. (Malevole and Mendoza are on stage and talking to each other) and a virtual duplication of lines V.iii.11–13. Eds. have suggested that Marston, for reasons of dramatic economy, intended to replace lines V.iii.1–21 with a simpler beginning to the scene. However, QC's insertion is inadequately integrated. It breaks the natural run of the dialogue whereby in QAB Mendoza's 'Canst thou empoison?' (V.iii.22) stems directly from his apparent desire to have Maria killed and the subsequent exchange in V.iii.16–21. If Marston at some stage wanted to begin the scene with QC's version of Mendoza's query about Maria he must surely have meant to keep

---

19 *stews*: brothels; the Southwark stews were closed by royal proclamation in 1546; Marston connects their demise with the rise of Puritanism, but suggests that the change was merely cosmetic – 'whores' have become 'punks' (the new word).

lines 14–19. Moreover, the cornets called for or announced by Bilioso at the end of V.ii presumably herald Q's large formal entry, which Bilioso had foreshadowed as early as V.ii.80–1. Even if lines V.iii.1–21 were omitted, QC's entry for Malevole would still be as redundant as the listing of Bilioso in the initial Q entry to V.iii, with its elaborate procession which is immediately dismissed. Linguistic evidence points to Webster's authorship of Insertion v, and hence to his responsibility for the anomalies. However, once QC's addition has been excised, there nevertheless remains a slight inconsistency in Mendoza's asking Malevole if he can empoison (V.iii.22–3), when he has just given Mendoza to understand, through an equivocal answer, that he has poisoned the hermit (V.iii.4–5).